Debrett's

ILLUSTRATED GUIDE

The Canadian Establishment

Debrett's

ILLUSTRATED GUIDE TO

The
Canadian Establishment

PETER C. NEWMAN
GENERAL EDITOR

METHUEN

Published in Great Britain, 1984 by
Debrett's Peerage Limited, 73-77 Britannia Road,
London SW6, England.

Printed and bound in the United States
by R.R. Donnelley & Sons Ltd.

1 2 3 4   83   87   86   85   84

CANADIAN CATALOGUING IN PUBLICATION DATA
Main entry under title:
Debrett's illustrated guide to the Canadian establishment

Includes index.
ISBN 0-458-96790-4

1. Elite (Social sciences)–Canada–Biography.
2. Capitalists and financiers–Canada–Biography.
3. Canada–Biography. I. Newman, Peter C., 1929-

HN110.Z9E45 1983   305.5'2'0971   C83-099004-6

ENDPAPERS: St. Andrew's Society Ball, Montreal, 1878, in honour of Princess Louise and the Marquis of Lorne. (Notman Photographic Archives, McCord Museum, Montreal)

HALF-TITLE: A platter at Rideau Hall in Ottawa. (John Reeves)

TITLE PAGE: Fancy dress skating carnival Victoria Rink, Montreal in honour of Prince Arthur (Duke of Connaught), 1870 a composite photograph composed and hand-painted by Notman of Montreal. (Notman Photographic Archives, McCord Museum, Montreal)

FACING: Mementoes at the house of Rear-Admiral Gordon L. Edwards, Victoria. (John Reeves)

OVERLEAF: The sailpast of the Royal Vancouver Yacht Club, 1983. (John Reeves)

Acknowledgements

GENERAL EDITOR
Peter C. Newman

MANAGING EDITOR AND RESEARCH DIRECTOR
Robin Brass

PRINCIPAL PHOTOGRAPHER
John Reeves

EDITOR
Greg Cable

EDITORIAL ASSISTANT
Rosemary Phelan

PHOTO ASSISTANT
Nancy Halpin

EDITORIAL, RESEARCH, AND WRITING STAFF
Doris Cowan, Gary Michael Dault, Freya Godard, Monica Hanula, Herb Hilderley, Doug Hunter, Janet Inksetter, Dan Liebman, David Marshall, Kim Matheson, Peter Milroy, Catherine Munro, Geralyn Poynter, Paul Russell, Robert Stonehouse, Des Walsh.

DESIGN
Brant Cowie/Artplus Ltd.

INSIGNIA PAINTINGS
Peter Mossman

PRODUCTION
Steve Eby, Gaynor Fitzpatrick

PUBLISHER
Frederick D. Wardle

FOR DEBRETT
Sir Iain Moncrieffe of that Ilk
Robert Jarman

The publishers wish to thank the generous assistance provided by the many individuals and associations in compiling lists, validating references, and in allowing the editors access to archives. Particular thanks are due to:

Allan Arlett of the Canadian Centre for Philanthropy, Deryk Bodington, Alice Brass, Paul Burkhart, Michael Burns, J.H. Crang, Jill Cuthbertson of the Royal Canadian Yacht Club, Chris Dahl, Jim Dudley of the Royal Vancouver Yacht Club, Andrew Duncanson, Peter Edwards of the Royal Canadian Yacht Club, Perle Garcia, Dr. Philippe Garigue, the Glassco family, the staff of the Glenbow Museum, John Gould, Marion Hanly, Colonel Ralph Harper of St. Andrews Society of Montreal, Marion Henderson of the Royal Agricultural Winter Fair, Fred W. Hotson, Heather Lang-Runtz, Carl Lochnan for the article "Marks of Honour," Kim McArthur, Larry Milberry, Roger Nantel of the Chancellery of Canadian Orders and Decorations, the staff of the National Photography Collection of the Public Archives of Canada, the Notman Photographic Archives of the McCord Museum, A. de L. Panet, Martha Rankine of Parkwood, Malcolm Richardson, J. Donald Ross, the Royal Military College in Kingston, Carol Rule, Henri Soucie, Tom Suddon. Thanks, too, to the hundreds of people who responded to our questionnaire, to the many photographers and other sources whose credit lines accompany the pictures, and to the many sources of information who prefer to remain anonymous.

"*Every nation needs an 'Establishment,' an elite, of some kind—or we are stuck with eternal mediocrity as a national fate. Every effort to construe such an Establishment is invidious, extrusive, hurtful, challenging, delicious and... necessary!*"

SCOTT SYMONS

Contents

A skating party at Rideau Hall, the centre of Establishment life in Ottawa. The artist was Robert William Rutherford (active 1877-88).

Preface

An AUTHORITY CONSULTED world-wide, Debrett's Peerage has been a prime reference source on the British aristocracy since its first edition was issued during the 18th century. Late in the 1970s, the publishing house was purchased by an imaginative group of young men who wanted to broaden Debrett's appeal and expand its operations. Sir Iain Moncreiffe, patron of Debrett's, commented at the time that he "realized our old-established work on chronicling the British peerage was becoming truly international."

His own links with Canada go a long way back: "My great-grandfather's grandmother, Lady Elisabeth Moncreiffe, was a sister of the ninth Earl of Dalhousie, who governed Canada between 1819 and 1828; it was he after whom Dalhousie University in Halifax is named." Moncreiffe deems Canada a country "worthy of much closer examination than has hitherto been afforded it" and adds a personal note. It is a reminiscence of the sort that catches the familial links paralleling the political and economic ties which have bound, and in many ways still bind, Canada and Britain: Lady Elisabeth Moncreiffe "was a keen botanist who died in 1848 when her night-cap took fire from a candle: her brother Dalhousie had sent her many interesting Canadian trees and shrubs across the Atlantic, many of which are still growing at Moncreiffe. And my late wife's energetic great-aunt, 'Bee,' Marchioness of Willingdon, was one of the most remarkable characters I've ever known; she governed her dedicated husband and his harassed staff when he was Governor General of Canada from 1926 to 1931."

The chronicling of family history, such a well-polished tradition in Britain and other parts of the world but a relatively undiscovered art in Canada, hinges on gathering and weaving such snippets.

Robert Jarman, chief animator among the new owners of Debrett's, approached me early last year with the notion that I should act as general editor of an illustrated volume based on the decade's worth of research I had done into the Establishment families of Canada. This book, which draws on my previous writings, is the result.

I am greatly indebted to Robert Jarman for originating the concept; to Fred Wardle, publisher of Methuen, and Robin Brass, managing editor and research director for this project, who between them pulled it all together; and to John Reeves, a magician with a camera, who took most of the original shots. Camilla Newman has acted as my creative conscience and in-house editor.

The greatest debt, however, is to the many writers, editors, "listees," and organizations who directly or indirectly have contributed fact and opinion to the pages which follow.

My own writing in this book is limited to "The Power Network." As general editor I have assisted the team of editors, writers, and photographers in capturing the nature of our Establishment. Completeness is not assured: the chronicling of our national equivalent of the aristocracies elsewhere in the world will continue. I do believe, however, that many readers will find the photographs and descriptions contained in this volume both useful and entertaining.

PETER C. NEWMAN August 1983

I

The Power Network

ABOVE: The Rolex Challenge Cup, awarded annually to the winning team in the International Polo Series, Gormley, Ontario. FACING PAGE: Bank towers in the Toronto financial district, the heart of the business Establishment.

Patrolling the Perfumed Stockades of Canada's Establishment

PETER C. NEWMAN

FROM VICTORIA TO ST. JOHN's and back again, the Canadian Establishment radiates across the country in a thin and shifting network of instant alliances and longstanding allegiances. Whether it's business, politics, the professions, or culture—it's all the same. The leaders of these cliques constitute a surprisingly compact, self-effacing but powerful confederacy that holds the keys to the Canadian Kingdom.

The members of each power network greet, accept, and protect one another on a wide spectrum of intimacy—the degree of warmth depending on the commonality of their individual objectives at any given moment. But no matter how much their immediate goals may temporarily conflict (during Argus takeovers, Governor General's Awards nominations, or Tory leadership conventions), they always manage to take the others' concerns into account. Though some still anoint their own successors, it is a kinship bound more by merit and necessity than by bloodline and legacy: when a nation's elite is less than three generations removed from steerage, it cannot afford too many pretensions.

Economic power has shifted according to the way money is made. Now well beyond the era of fur, railway, and banking barons and just recently evolved from the mining and oil fortunes, new wealth is flowing into very different lifestyles. There are many more decision makers; breeding and manners have become deflated currencies. At the same time, Canada's monetary centre of gravity has shifted from Montreal to Toronto and is pushing, through an ebb-and-flow cycle, ever westward. But the action that counts still accrues to the centre, whether it's setting up a tax shelter in Curaçao or funding a festival in Dawson City. Most of the authority clearly remains anchored in Toronto, where much of the business and cultural Establishment lives, loves, and deals.

What makes the Canadian Establishment very different from any other national elite is that, unlike Britain's, for example, it is not reinforced by a resident aristocracy. Titles, with or without money, are not the Canadian way. Because of the tension between private and public sectors, the Establishment in Canada does not constitute the country's ruling class. There are subtle but essential divergences in this country among those who rule, those who exercise economic authority, and those who control the various strata of national decision making.

Wealth is no dependable hallmark of power. Canada's richest man—Kenneth Thomson, the newspaper proprietor whose father struck it rich in North Sea oil—is an unassuming introvert who ducks the slightest show of power outside his own empire. His only hobby has been collecting the acres of Krieghoff paintings that hang in his downtown Toronto office. Other less-cultured millionaires in the *nouveau riche* pastures of the New West tend to behave like sunstruck sybarites—especially during those delicious periods between economic busts when loose cash itches to be spent.

Overall, the Canadian Establishment's dominant ethic rejects both the unbridled hype of American capitalists and the outdated affectations of the British upper class. It is instead stolidly based on a system of beliefs that counts the rule of

JACK CLEMENT

John Porter (LEFT) and Wallace Clement have analyzed the economic and class structure of Canadian society. Porter's Vertical Mosaic *surprised Canadians with its revelations of dramatic inequalities along ethnic, regional, and economic lines.*

the worthy and the responsible as the highest virtue. Whether or not Canadian society actually operates on such a meritocratic ideology is less important than the apparent national consensus that it *should*.

The existence of an Establishment—a cabal of power brokers bent on what Lord Russell called "the production of intended effects"—still offends the Canadian sensibility. It negates the popular notion of Canada as a land of freely accessible opportunities symbolized by wide-open spaces and Cinemascope horizons. This egalitarian ideal is reinforced by the fact that even the most outspoken of the power wielders strenuously disavow any mutual benefits from their Establishment credentials. Innocence is always relative, but theirs is an almost unconscious link: they think the same way *naturally*. They don't *need* to conspire, because their ideas mesh without their having to consult one another to weigh motives. They recognize so few conflicts of interest, in short, because their interests so seldom conflict.

Most Canadians tend to view the class system—if they think of it at all—as referring mainly to lifestyle or level of sophistication. It's as though nearly everyone belonged to what George Orwell called "the lower-upper-middle class"—a class that can give its offspring the advantages of education but not much in the way of inherited wealth or social position.

It was not until 1965 that the power structure of this country was examined in detail. That was the year the late John Porter, a Carleton University sociologist, published his monumental *Vertical Mosaic* and banished forever the comfortable notion of Canada as a classless society. In 600 well-documented pages, Porter tabulated the country's dramatic inequalities of income and opportunity, demonstrating that only about 10 per cent of Canadian families could actually afford the "middle-class" lifestyle then considered average. He argued that the corporate elite was rooted in 183 dominant corporations controlling the majority of economic activity and found that only 6.6 per cent of its members were French-Canadian. He concluded that effective power resided in a predominantly Anglo-Saxon economic elite of only a few hundred: ethnic origin was as significant for access to the elite in 1951 as it had been in 1885 and 1910.

"In my book," he told *Maclean's*, at the time of publication, "I showed that the majority of the political leaders in Canada have been drawn from the middle class. The upper class doesn't seem attracted to the turbulence of politics and, in any case, the privileges they enjoy are not threatened by the holders of political power. Nor is there any tradition of working-class participation in politics." Porter also postulated the theory that there is in this country a continuous circulation of elites: "Although it has a class structure peculiar to its own history and geography, Canada is probably not unlike other western industrial nations in relying heavily on its elite groups to make major decisions and to determine the shape and direction of its development. . . . Power arises because of the general social need for order."

Porter's original thesis was expanded and brought up to date a decade later by Wallace Clement, who concluded that "Canada has been and remains a society controlled by elites. With increasing economic concentration over the past twenty years, the structure has become increasingly closed, thus making it more difficult for those outside the inner circles of power to break through."

BECAUSE THEY HAVE DELIBERATELY set themselves apart from the politicians, the Canadian Establishment's adherents exercise a mandate often bereft of public accountability. Their reluctant annual payment of income taxes (after every available shelter has been exhausted) is all too often the outside limit of their citizenship. Few of the paladins of real wealth in this country —with exceptions, such as the Koerners in British Columbia, the Harvies in Calgary, the Richardsons in Winnipeg, Floyd Chalmers and Arthur Gelber in Toronto, and (in his time) Sam Bronfman in Montreal—are saluted as genuine philanthropists. Collectively, "the givers" endow universities, preserve landmarks, donate art works, and raise money for appropriate charities, but the impulse toward creative generosity is hardly overwhelming.

Instead of a single, monolithic Establishment, they form overlapping rings of power shaped like the Olympic symbol. There is no social compact, yet the confederacy of regional Establishment groupings—loosely knit yet interlocking—forms a psychological entity. Its members share habits of thought and action, similar beliefs, values, and enemies. Common patterns of forbearance and indulgence, a cultivated shabbiness of dress and decor—these and other subtleties identify the core group to the initiated. Automatic accreditation is gained through gentle signals that bespeak shared experience: those musty portraits crated off from grandfather's Westmount mansion before he sold it; the nickname of that fusty Latin teacher at Upper Canada who caned boys for conjugating the verb "to be" improperly; a summer together once at St. Andrews-by-the-Sea; the way the garden at the country place glowed that season of Andrea's coming out; a friend in common who retired in disgust to Bermuda after Edgar Benson came out with that White Paper on Taxation.

Historically, much of the Canadian business community moved from primitive to decadent without ever becoming particularly civilized in the process. But there has always existed a thin upper crust of moneyed Old Families whose presumption of entitlement needed no external sanction. Their self-appointed mission in life (apart from making themselves even more comfortable) has been to spend the currency of their lives acting out preordained destinies.

This attitude applies even within family situations. Nobody ever seems to bear-hug anybody. There is a strong suggestion that even in their most intimate moments they regard love, like the accidents of birth and death, as an awkward intrusion. They assume that once they have become adult, rich, and powerful, not much more is

Palm Beach is an international mecca for the well-to-do. Shown are the houses of Conrad Black (ABOVE LEFT), Paul Desmarais (ABOVE RIGHT), and Bud McDougald; the latter house is now owned by the Fennell family. The aerial view shows the Bath and Tennis Club at left and the huge estate of Marjorie Merriweather Post. The photograph below shows an interior view of the Everglades Club, of which Bud McDougald was a governor.

John A. (Bud) McDougald (1908-1978) in one of his 35 classic cars. One of the founders of Argus Corp., he took over its direction in 1969 from E.P. Taylor.

expected of them—and that the tumble of psychic catastrophes and raw emotions which agitate ordinary lives will always be visited on people to whom one has not been properly introduced.

Their wives and daughters, if they choose the relaxed route through life, bronze themselves ever so carefully, balancing the effects of poolside and links, and rarely bother with Canadian Novembers or Februaries; they flee the cold or familial angst by heading for Palm Beach, Palm Springs, or Papeete. They recruit the best support staff in the city for clothes, accessories, and grooming, and apply their Lancôme palette with fingers as steady as those of elephant hunters. Their self-possession can be a bit much.

Cradled in an Indian summer of extended adolescence, the sons and daughters of the rich live in taken-for-granted but rarely ostentatious luxury. Established family wealth (with its palace guard of legal retainers, chartered accountants, and investment counsellors) is not so much for spending on private fripperies as for influencing positions and events. That much is learned early.

The hereditary pews of the Establishment—formerly taken up by the ossified hierar-chies of another age—now seat a new breed of ambitious, bucking, crown princes and princesses.

It was the death of John Angus "Bud" McDougald in 1978 and the capture of his Argus empire by Conrad Black that proclaimed the arrival of this new order. Unlike most dominant elites, which drive themselves into oblivion through the congenital profligacy or unfettered feyness of their offspring, Canada's Establishment has managed to spawn an impressive clutch of sons and daughters, much more in touch with life's realities than their patrician predecessors ever were. "Canada is widely assumed to be an egalitarian society, but the extent to which rich men's sons dominated the financial news in the 1970s was absolutely astonishing," Alexander Ross noted in *Canadian Business*. "It was almost as though control of major portions of the Canadian economy were being *passed on*, like family memberships in the Granite Club. Sometimes the succession was polite and gentlemanly, as with the genteel struggle for control of The Bay. Sometimes it was vicious, as with the Bronfman take-over of Brascan. But nearly always the struggles involved younger editions of familiar names: Eaton, Thomson, Weston, Bronfman and the Black boys. Few interlopers were involved. In Canada, we like to keep it in the family."

Aside from the initial rush that comes from taking over their fathers' or uncles' fiscal fiefdoms, these young bucks quickly discover that living on inherited money is a secondary thrill at best. While unearned fortunes do not necessarily bring uneasiness, neither do they accord their owners much distinction.

These sons of the gentry—whatever their chronological age—can be spotted easily enough. Their manner, their toned bodies, the way they step into a room, displays their expectation of success. An elegantly rumpled appearance gets them waved through airport security inspections without body checks; their keys never seem to

The United Church of Canada's co-educational Albert College in Belleville, Ontario, was founded in 1857 by Methodist Episcopalian adherents in eastern Ontario. The college once held degree-granting status as an affiliate of Victoria University and currently enjoys a strong international reputation, with 200 students enrolled from many countries. The school moved to its present campus (ABOVE) in 1923.

beep, and they carry no change. In their roster of untouchables, digital watches and fake-leather anything rank very high; half-moon reading glasses, vintage vehicles, and private art galleries with northern exposures remain in premium demand.

They appear to be constantly in motion and know the best ways of dealing with any of several world financial capitals. Unlike their fathers, they are convinced that the Connaught in London is superior to Claridge's, even if reservations have to be made personally. ("Have a dog barking in the background when phoning the Connaught," comes the advice, "to minimize fears that some fool travel agent might be involved.")

To acquire this rarefied sense of style and destiny, the children of the gentry follow well-trodden paths through the portals of the private schools where they learn their manners, then on to the exclusive clubs where they eventually lunch.

THERE WAS A TIME WHEN no headmaster of a Canadian private school was acceptable unless he had studied at Oxford or Cambridge. Anglophilia permeated the institutions, with new boys having to serve as "fags" to seniors (the equivalent of being a batman in the army), canings being inflicted for the slightest offence, and boys expressing creativity through pranks dear to the Tom Brown tradition. The main legacy of the British influence remains the prefect system. A headmaster of Ridley College at St. Catharines, Ontario, once described the advantages of becoming a prefect as "promoting a dawning understanding of the need for order in the community, of the burdens of leadership, and the place of proud humility in a man's life."

In recent years, the schools have been modernized, with the accent as much on scholarship as on tradition, but the British links persist. In the autumn of 1979, for example, the thorny problem facing the poohbahs who run Upper Canada College in Toronto was how to celebrate their 150th anniversary. After considerable brow furrowing, the answer seemed obvious: why not invite the Duke over? Edinburgh is, after all, the school's patron, having enjoyed a long association with Toronto's—and, arguably, Canada's—most prestigious private school. The ensuing festivities were mobbed by so many graduates that the Auto-

Upper Canada College as it appeared on King Street West in Toronto before it moved in 1891 to its present location on Avenue Road north of St. Clair Avenue. The school was founded in 1829 under a royal charter granted by George IV.

Bishop Strachan School, the oldest independent school for girls in Canada, is located a short walk away from UCC. It was founded in 1867 by Anglican clergy and laymen. Boys are admitted until the end of grade two.

St. Andrew's College, founded in 1899, occupies a pleasant campus in Aurora, Ontario. Like many private schools, it is located in a peaceful small town within reach of the big city.

The art studio at BSS has changed little since this photograph was taken.

The present Upper Canada College building dates only from 1956. It replaced an earlier building, which also had a clock tower.

The view from Neuchâtel Junior College in Switzerland. This co-educational school, administered jointly by a Canadian board and the Swiss public-school system, offers the Ontario grade 13 curriculum to a select group of students.

motive Building at the Canadian National Exhibition had to be rented to accommodate their black-tie dinner. A grand time was had by all, and afterward everyone thought it only proper that genuine royalty should have taken time out to salute one of Canada's most regal institutions.

It is not the oldest of the country's 70-odd private schools (King's College School in Windsor, Nova Scotia, was founded 40 years earlier, in 1788), but UCC commands the respect of generations of Canadian *prominenti* in business, culture, and public service. The school is a family affair. One out of five of the approximately 200 day boys and 800 boarders is the son of an Old Boy. (That, of course, is how the "old boys' network" got its name.)

The school worships its enduring traditions, such as the events surrounding the Fenian Raids of 1866, when a company of lightly armed UCC boys provided Toronto's only military garrison. During the Second World War, 74 per cent of the 1,580 UCC Old Boys won commissions; 26 of them attained flag or general rank. Roughly one-third of Canada's most influential corporate directors are private-school grads — half of them from UCC.

But Upper Canada is only the largest and richest of such institutions. Other Ontario private schools for boys favoured by Establishment parents include Trinity College School at Port Hope, St. Andrew's in Aurora, Ridley in St. Catharines, Lakefield in Lakefield, Hillfield in Hamilton, and Ashbury in Ottawa. Their influence spreads across the country. St. Andrew's, for example, has educated Newfoundland's two Crosbie brothers, ex–Premier Frank Moores, and ex–Liberal leader Ed Roberts.

Outside Ontario, many private schools are in a similiar league, with Selwyn House and Lower

Canada College in Montreal; Bishop's College School in Lennoxville, Quebec; St. George's in Vancouver; Shawnigan Lake and Brentwood on Vancouver Island; and St. John's Ravenscourt in Winnipeg. The Maritimes have a long roster of equivalent institutions, including the Halifax Grammar School, King's and Edgehill at Windsor, and Netherwood at Rothesay, New Brunswick.

The most prestigious girls' school is probably Bishop Strachan, on seven valuable acres just half-a-dozen manicured blocks from UCC. It fashions the kind of wily maidens who can turn a curtsy into an effortless bob at debutante balls, then marry promptly and well. Describing Bishop Strachan and its former principal, etiquette arbiter Eve Drobot once noted: "Saying that Bishop Strachan is a school is like saying the Taj Mahal is a building. And saying that Miss Katherine Wicks runs the place is like saying Elizabeth II has a job as a monarch." Other desirable Ontario girls' schools include Branksome Hall, Havergal, St. Clement's, and Loretto Abbey in Toronto, Strathallan in Hamilton, and Alma in St. Thomas.

The fastest-growing and most interesting private school outside Toronto is the co-educational Strathcona-Tweedsmuir at Okotoks, where the sons and daughters of Calgary's recently rich flock to learn how to tone down and speak up. Nine Canadian private schools are now co-educational, but the best of them is not in Canada at all but in Switzerland—Neuchâtel Junior College.

The private schools are essential to instilling Establishment values. Youthful impressions, absorbed through willing pores, set lifetime priorities, presumptions, and even partnerships. Even though private schools in Canada are only slightly tainted by the snobbishness characteristic of their British equivalents, they still manage to instill the idea that privilege exists on this side of the Atlantic and that rebellion, however fleeting a temptation, is ultimately self-defeating.

The major shortcoming of the private school is that its boys and girls emerge from puberty somewhat removed from life's realities—and from one another. They are polished to perfection for a world that no longer exists. This can be only a temporary obstacle to some, curable by a couple of years in a job or at university. But for a surprising number of the alumni, their time in residence turns out to be the emotional high of a circumscribed adult life.

It is a tidy, taut world—and there is that problem of meeting head-on afterward the sloppiness of life on the outside—but the men and women who have attended private school are probably the better for it. Perhaps that sums up the ultimate justification of these avuncular institutions: they test and stretch potential at an early age and push young men and women to discover that the hardest limits to overcome are those which are self-imposed.

FREQUENTING THE PRIVATE LUNCHING club, to which most private-school pupils graduate, has become more than slightly outdated, but being a member in good standing is as important as ever. It's as though the point of joining is not so much to use a club as to see whether you can get in. When a country's economic elite is rich in cash and poor in ancestry, it can be more important to know how to count than to read or write well, and a club membership as often as not is a diploma attesting to one's fluency in that most international of languages: money.

The club game has thus been reduced to a process of social certification. By joining the most exclusive of these institutions, the Establishment's adherents can pretend to themselves that they are part of a select assemblage who *are*, instead of those who merely *do*. "My club," an overly self-conscious club member once explained, "is an oasis of civilization in a desert of democracy."

The York Club took over the George H. Gooderham House on Toronto's St. George Street in 1909. The interior view shows the magnificent entrance hall with its detailed wood carving and impressive staircase.

The National Club on Bay Street in Toronto's financial district is a favourite lunching spot with the investment community.

The new-breed wheelers are dealing in the smart places where they can sniff out the fast money, looking past their luncheon companions' shoulders to see who's breaking bread with their competitors. The quick-buck artists are elsewhere, but venerability, prestige, and the really big money still reside in the clubs. Apart from the fact that just belonging continues to be a requirement for assimilation into senior Establishment ranks, the clubs provide a rare opportunity for their members to sit around the great unlit fireplaces, like tribal elders, and rage against the panting parvenus and politicians trying to usurp their rightful influence. There is something very comforting in the pleasure of the expected: walking up the same staircase grandfather used to climb in the processional glide from street to club level; easing back in one's favourite ox-blood leather chair, knowing the waiter's name, and trusting the food absolutely.

Each club worth joining has its own internal geography, with the maitre d' adept at "dressing" the dining room, spreading out the big hitters, knowing who is trying to take over whose company, diluting the grey clumps of has-beens, ostracizing the resident lout. The members themselves, straining to the very limits of their condescension, revel in the ritual but even the least perceptive of them realize that the jig is nearly up: club life isn't what it used to be.

The decline dates back to the 1971 federal budget, which eliminated club dues as a valid tax deduction. At one time Royal Trust, for example, wrote off club dues for 78 of its top executives. And no longer do the sons of the rich automatically follow in their fathers' footsteps. The pattern of, say, Conrad Black's being given a life membership in the Toronto Club for his 21st birthday is rarely being repeated.

Montreal's once-hallowed Mount Stephen Club, incidentally the locale Brian Mulroney once upon a time chose for his wedding reception, declined fastest (though there is no known cause-effect relationship). It now offers discounts for diplomatic receptions, hosts corporate seminars, and lent itself out as the main set for the CBC-TV series *Empire Inc.* The St. James's lost considerable status when it gave up its old clubhouse, and the University Club on Mansfield is no longer worth joining. In Montreal, only the Mount Royal (for anglophones) and the Saint-Denis (for francophones) can still boast undiminished prestige.

The place that *really* picks its members is the 158-year-old Montreal Racket Club on Concorde Street; membership is limited to 100. The club's early activities included the sport of rat killing. The club professional would obtain a sackful of the rodents from the harbour and release them in the main court. Members wagered whose pet fox terrier would kill the most rats as they watched from the galleries. Its proudest moment seems to have been the time Major Erle (later General Erle of Majuba Hill) lost an eye during a rackets game. As his eyeball plopped to the floor, according to club records, the good major clapped his hand to the empty socket and announced to the gallery: "The Ladies won't look at me now..." To

The Mount Stephen Club on Montreal's Drummond Street occupies the house built by George Stephen. Completed in 1883, the Italian Renaissance–style mansion cost about $600,000 to build.

which the club chronicler added the approving footnote: "A fine instance of pluck!"

One-eyed majors aside, the Montreal club scene took a significant step forward in 1979, when the St. James's not only allowed women to join but actually permitted them to use the same dining room as "regular" members. Margaret Birch, then Ontario's provincial secretary, had broken the barrier at Toronto's Albany Club the year before. Most clubs still practise sex discrimination with such discreet differences as asking "the ladies" to use separate entrance doors.

Other forms of discrimination persist, however. The Toronto Club did budge a bit toward change by admitting René Lévesque (for dinner) just 23 days after Bud McDougald, its patron saint and monitor of proprieties, died in 1978, but it has yet to sign up its first Jew. The York Club's first (and for many years *only*) Jewish member was Sigmund Samuel, a steel merchant who became a well-known philanthropist and art collector and held formal levées in his Forest Hill house (now occupied by Fred Eaton) on New Year's Day. Lazarus Phillips, the Montreal lawyer, was one of those who broke the barrier at the Mount Royal Club, but Sam Bronfman never did make it. The Manitoba Club allowed the first Jew to join in 1972 and the Vancouver Club relented only when the ice-breaking candidate happened to be an outstanding judge of the provincial supreme court.

The rich do not have to be Jewish to suffer this kind of nonsense. Stephen Roman, the mining magnate, has been kept out of the Toronto clubs on the silly pretext that he is a Slovak who, before he rose to become a multimillionaire, worked as a guard on the Welland Canal. Club admission policies are vague enough to justify the exclusion of almost anyone. In Calgary, for example, Ed Lakusta, the president of Petro-Canada, was recently denied a seat on the board of directors at the Petroleum Club because he works for a state-owned agency.

Toronto club life continues to be dominated by the York and the Toronto but equally meaningful contacts are now made in the Cambridge Club's locker rooms as more and more of the younger set get into fitness. The Badminton and Racquet, Rosedale Golf, Toronto Golf, Granite, and Royal Canadian Yacht Club as well as the Calgary Golf and Country and the Earl Grey, Edmonton's May-fair, Winnipeg's St. Charles, Halifax's Oakfield, Vancouver's Capilano and Royal Vancouver Yacht Club, and the Royal Montreal Golf and Country Club remain vital organizations. The main sports clubs (Osler Bluff and Craigleith in Collingwood, Ontario; the Long Point Company, whose hunting preserves jut into Lake Erie; the Ristigouche in New Brunswick; the Madawaska, the Tadenac, and Griffith Island in Georgian Bay) are still favourite haunts.

Outside the country, the association many crave is membership in Lyford Cay, the Nassau refuge pioneered by E.P. Taylor in the 1950s. Owned by its members (limited to 950), the Bahamas hideout gives the Canadian contingent a chance to internationalize contacts with such jet-setters as the Cadburys, Clitheroes, Marton-meres, and Astors of England; the Bismarcks of Germany; the Colytons of Monaco; the Saint-Phalles of France; the Annenbergs, Firestones, Forstmanns, Heinzes, Houghtons, Kaisers, Loebs, Mellons, Paleys, Pews, Revsons, Rockefellers, Strauses, Whitneys, and Wyckoffs of the U.S.; the Archduke Charles of Austria; the Goulandris, Kulunkundis, and Livanos shipping families of Greece; Crown Prince Hassan of Jordan; the Hoeghs of Norway; the Guireys of Eire; the Guinles of Brazil; and the Bacardis, formerly of Cuba.

The club's roster is an international who's who, taking advantage of the perfect climate for

---

The Mount Stephen Club (LEFT) is noted for its fine interior woodwork in a variety of woods; the door hinges are gold plated. The building was saved from destruction when the Club, founded in 1926, took it over as its headquarters.

meteorology and taxes. So many Canadians belong (more than a hundred) that some of the club's annual meetings have been held in Toronto.

Among the Canadian members are the Judd Whittalls, Donald McGiverin, Ted and Loretta Rogers, the John Carmichaels, R. Fraser Elliotts, Rowland Frazees, Signy Eaton and the Fred Eatons, the Leighton McCarthys, J. David Molsons, Paul and Jacqueline Desmarais, the H. Heward Stikemans, expatriates from the Alberta Oil Patch like Frank McMahon, Harold Siebens and Ronald Banister, the Peter Holdroyds, Helen Stephens (the former Mrs. F. Ronald Graham of Vancouver), the Art Stollerys, Robert and Galena Schmon and the Arthur A. Schmons, the J.W. Sharps, a brace of Timminses, the Bassett clan, Bruce and Lynne Verchere, a contingent of Dunns from Quebec, a raft of Thomsons of the old Nesbitt Thomson connection, and Arthur and Sheila Hailey, the authors. They all call it paradise.

THE PALADINS OF CANADA'S Establishment disavow the possession of power, even if they value its exercise. They are accustomed to running things, promoting those men (plus the occasional woman) recognized as reliable. Much of this process operates through negative sanctions; the overly ambitious or unsuitable interloper is blocked by invisible but unbreachable barriers.

Like the exclusive clubs and private schools that have supplied so many of their past members, the various Establishments close and open their doors according to sets of unspoken values that can be called Canadian mainly because they can't properly be described as anything else. There are certain people—the Belzberg brothers in Vancouver and Calgary, for example—who, no matter how many deals they make with Establishment firms, no matter how often they best their competitors, may never be part of its world. They and many others are the victims of the Establishments' most potent weapon: the power to exclude.

The most recent illustration of this unanimity in exercising their power involved the machinations of Leonard Rosenberg of Toronto, an ungainly Jewish financier with curious connections who was well on his way to creating an $8 billion financial empire of trust companies and banks—until he was stopped dead in his tracks by the federal and Ontario governments. The prohibitive legislation to confiscate his companies was harsh enough to rank as the economic equivalent of the War Measures Act of October 1970 but, up to the time this book went to press, he had yet to be charged with any offence. Not only did the Establishment fail to protest against the confiscation of private property, but Rosenberg was ostracized to the extent of not being able to open a bank account anywhere in Canada.

Less dramatic but equally vicious treatment was meted out to Robert Campeau, an Ottawa construction tycoon daring enough to bid, in September 1980, more than $532 million for control of the upper-crusty Royal Trustco, a plum repository of WASP fortunes and defiance. Almost unanimously (Andy Sarlos, the Toronto financier, and Gus Van Wielingen, the Calgary oilman, were two notable exceptions), the money managers swung in behind Royal Trust's chairman, Ken White, in his dogged determination to block the attempted takeover. At considerable cost to their own shareholders, a consortium of Canadian banks, financial houses, and industrial corporations rejected Campeau's generous offer; the thinly veiled conspiracy culminated in an Ontario Securities Commission ruling that suspended White's trading rights. The rush to stall Campeau's $24-per-share bid left many a corporate and bank treasury holding Royal Trust shares worth half as much. Campeau, who had also made unsuccessful runs at Markborough Properties (which was acquired instead by the Hudson's Bay Company) and at Bushnell Communications in Ottawa, moved on and now does most of his business in the United States. It was never clear just what was held against Campeau, except perhaps that he was Pierre Trudeau's frequent skiing companion.

As these two cases show, the ability to withhold favours is most frequently exercised through Canada's ultimate veto-endowed institutions: the Big Five chartered banks—the Royal, the Commerce, the Bank of Montreal, the Toronto-Dominion, and the Bank of Nova Scotia.

The bankers decide who will succeed and who will fail. Even during the depth of the Great Recession of the early 1980s, when their own balance sheets looked shaky, the bankers exercised papal control over the economy.

The executive board meetings of the five largest banks represent the greatest source of non-governmental power in the country. During these deliberations are formed, strengthened, and multiplied the personal relationships through which the Canadian Establishment consolidates its existence and swells its authority.

The banks encounter little opposition to their fiscal hegemony. Canadians *believe* in banking; there are nearly as many bank branches as taverns in this country. The Big Five bank chairmen who set the tone and policies for their lower-ranked colleagues regard themselves as chief custodians of Canada's free-enterprise system. With the exception of Bill Mulholland, the Yankee trader who runs the Bank of Montreal like an enlightened warrior of the Crusades, most senior bankers discharge their powers with the sanctimonious air of Presbyterian elders. They are seldom pushy and never impatient, always careful, gracious, proper, and, above all, serene in their faith. They view banking as a beneficial discipline, foreordained to reward the worthy and the able.

Responsibility—that highest of Canadian virtues—is a concept that bankers live and breathe. Despite their exalted place in the country's fiscal firmament, they are middle-class men and mighty proud of it. Fitted more by temperament than by birth for their high station, no matter how high they rise most bankers retain a kind of green-eyeshade, good-boy-who-got-terrific-marks mien. They are dutiful soldiers, dutiful sons, dutiful husbands—steadfast ecclesiasts in a heretical and disorderly world.

Unlike the brasher corporate men, who relish the knowledge that anywhere they go people will move for them, give way, run errands, *obey*, bankers lead muted lives. Graham Towers, when he was governor of the Bank of Canada, once found himself at a hotel in the Maritimes without enough cash to pay his bill. When a suspicious cashier demanded identification before he would honour his cheque, Towers tried (with considerable embarrassment) to avoid revealing who he was. He finally pulled out a dollar bill and reluctantly showed the startled cashier his signature, then decorating all of Canada's paper currency.

The chairmen of the Big Five operate from offices furnished like *Forsyte Saga* drawing rooms, designed to convey the impression that instead of being men of power they are merely guardians at the gates. They seldom step outside their head offices, even for lunch, preferring to entertain clients in the banks' own executive dining rooms, which serve low-voltage cocktails followed by meticulously prepared meals. (Quiche Lorraine is the specialty at Commerce headquarters, which also features a bracing drink of apple juice and ginger ale with a touch of Angostura bitters; the Royal's chef roasts the best salted almonds in the country.) Over silver platters and escutcheoned china, away from the noise and confusion of everyday commerce, dollar power in this country find its ultimate expression.

Canadian businessmen aspire to bank boards the way politicians sigh for the Senate and, once appointed, seldom surrender the honour. The late Colonel R.S. McLaughlin, for instance, was a director of the Dominion Bank and of its successor, the Toronto-Dominion, from 1917 to 1959. Whether the banks make greater use of their directors than vice versa is a moot point. The ground rules are well understood by everyone

Sam McLaughlin persuaded his doubting father, carriage-maker Robert McLaughlin, that cars were more than a passing fancy and in 1908 the McLaughlin Motor Company produced its first McLaughlin-Buicks. In 1918 they merged with GM to form General Motors of Canada, with "Mr. Sam" as president and his brother George as vice-president. Sam retired as president in 1945, remaining as chairman until his death in 1972. The photo at top left shows the McLaughlin brothers with their father. Standing, left, is John James McLaughlin, who started a soft-drink company that became Canada Dry. Standing, right, is Colonel R. Samuel McLaughlin. Seated at left is Robert, the father, and at right is George William McLaughlin. The top right photo shows Sam McLaughlin with three of his five daughters in 1928. To his left is his youngest, Eleanor. Beside her is Mary Eileen, the eldest, who was married first to Eric Phillips, one of the Argus Corp. founders, and second to the father of Frank McEachren. At the right is Isabel McLaughlin.

Parkwood, Sam McLaughlin's beautiful house in Oshawa, was designed by Darling and Pearson, the firm that designed the Parliament Buildings in Ottawa. Built in 1917, it was altered and extended in the 1930s to the designs of John M. Lyle, who also did the Royal Alexandra Theatre in Toronto. Every one of the 55 rooms reflects the owner's love of beauty and eye for detail, as these views show. The house and grounds are now open to the public.

Parkwood, seen from the garden.

Robert McLaughlin (BELOW) was a keen amateur painter and his grand-daughter Isabel, shown above painting at Parkwood, is a respected professional artist.

The main stairway, with domed ceiling light and 1930s steel railing.

A corner of the Grand Room.

The billiard room, panelled in oak with murals by F.S. Challener.

involved; a bank gets any given piece of business because it knows the potential borrower—one of the "right" people—a little more intimately than do its rivals. The men who supply these contacts are the board members—who know exactly what's happening within their own industries, which firms are poor risks, what the prospects are for new ventures. In return, the directors gain business intelligence—from their fellow directors, from briefings by bank economists, and from the chairmen, who report on the innermost concerns of the Bank of Canada governor.

The federal Bank Act decrees that whenever loans to any director's companies are being discussed, that director must leave the room or risk a $5,000 fine. Board members *do* walk out—to a chorus of chuckles and self-disparaging remarks—but those loans are seldom turned down.

CANADA IS HELD TOGETHER through the influence of a relatively tiny coterie of power wielders, but the country's genesis as an egalitarian, liberal democracy cuts deep. Power is a difficult commodity to isolate in such a free-form society. Its dictionary definition, "ability to compel obedience," is not broad enough to describe how it is actually exercised; neither is Max Weber's view of power as "the chance of a man or a group or a number of men to realize their own will in a communal action, even against the resistance of others who are participating in it." C. Wright Mills's "power elite" theory is not really relevant, because Canada has no military complex worth complaining about—no group of centurions sliding in and out of a Pentagon, state department, White House, or the equivalent of a Ford Foundation or Council on Foreign Relations. There is no centre point comparable to the Pittsburgh Mellons strong enough to control any region, though the McCains and Irvings approach that stature in the closed duchy of New Brunswick. Power in Canada is like mercury: contained, yet able to flow with the temperature of the times.

One of the distorting factors in any serious study of this phenomenon is that so much of the decision making that counts is exercised by surrogates. Two-thirds of Canada's hundred largest corporations are owned outside the country. Even when local managers—like Lorne Lodge at IBM or Bob Hurlbut at General Foods—have plenty of autonomy, their authority is not final; they answer to outside boards of directors. The chief executive officers who run these companies must act, when the chips are counted, as colonial administrators responsible to distant men in a foreign land.

There are exceptions. Bill Twaits, who served as president, then chairman, of Imperial Oil for 14 years, became one of the Canadian business community's most respected spokesmen. When he retired in 1974, he was offered 40 directorships—but Imperial still insisted that he give up Box 39B at the Royal Agricultural Winter Fair, which he had proudly held since 1960.

Most, though not all, American companies treat Canada as a slightly backward acreage of their northern sales territories, reflecting the comment by Jacques Maisonrouge, head of the IBM World Trade Corporation, that "for business purposes, the boundaries that separate one nation from another are no more real than the equator."

For years, few members of Canada's Establishment resisted the Americanization of Canadian business; it was one of the only national elites in world history that cheerfully encouraged its own co-optation. The attitude of E.P. Taylor, a most successful Canadian entrepreneur in his day, was typical: "If it weren't for the racial issue in the U.S. and the political problems they have, I would think that the two countries could come together....I'm against this trend of trying to reduce American ownership in Canadian companies. I think nature has to take its course."

This let's-surrender-with-profit syndrome until recently prevented Canada's capitalist class from attaining any clear perspective of itself and its long-term role. The powerful in Canada have always lived with a colonial mentality. Northrop Frye once interpreted that attitude as frostbite on the roots of the Canadian imagination. "Colonialism," he wrote, "produces a disease for which I think the best name is prudery. By this I do not mean reticence in sexual matters. I mean the instinct to seek a conventional or commonplace expression of an idea."

Frye's description of the prudery of spirit, the snobbish modesty, and the reticence to take risks until recently characterized Canada's current Establishment. Part of this phenomenon is that the wealth and authority once organized around families (as it still is in the Maritimes) have been replaced by the national power networks of the huge corporations. Many of the most influential men in Canadian cities and towns no longer belong to local power clusters; they are instead the smooth ambassadors of large multinational and transnational entities. Careers are no longer made in communities, but strictly within corporate hierarchies.

At the same time, a wide gulf separates those individuals who have *real* power that moves with them no matter what their job or location, and those with *mandated* power which is inherent in their position and is not portable. The enduring stereotype of the Really Big Businessman is the flinty-eyed tycoon, the dollar-cigar empire builder who practises a Darwinian ethic that allows only the cagiest to survive. Yet these domineering old titans, epitomized by Sir Herbert Holt and Sir James Dunn, have long since been replaced by smooth managerial types who feed the furnaces of their ambitions by meshing group effort instead of pioneering economic exploitation.

This new corporate breed seldom emerges into public light. The chief executive officers of most large corporations are men in flight, harried individuals driven by the necessity of coming down to their bottom lines with ever-better results. Their careers become an endless sequence of moving sales-and-profit targets. The essence of this approach is that life can be lived according to situation ethics and calculable rules, that results are more important than process, that what really matters most is the implacable momentum toward a common goal.

Surprisingly, most Canadian CEOs survived the Great Recession of 1980-82—unlike their counterparts in Japan, where the heads of 80 publicly listed companies resigned because they had failed to meet their profit targets. Even so, the tenure of the Canadian managers is relatively short and, once out of office, they remain trusted advisors to their former companies, fund raisers, and freelance directors—but, in reality, they are ghosts.

BECAUSE THEY BELIEVE SO implicitly in themselves, most members of this uppity crew are seldom able to distinguish between the public interest and their own, calling down curses on bureaucrats and politicians who refuse to acknowledge the two as one and the same.

This is where the twin sources of power in this country diverge. For an elite to flex its muscles freely requires the kind of compliant political authority that Canada has seldom elected. What the private sector's leaders demand from their Parliamentary representatives is a vaguely defined nirvana known as "maintaining investor confidence." Translated, that means laws enacted and enforced for the business community's direct benefit. What makes the stock market move up, in truth, has about as much effect on employment as who wins the annual running of the Queen's Plate, but the movers and shakers genuinely believe that the only good government is a hang-loose administration willing to grant their money-making efforts unbridled rein.

Occasionally—very occasionally—this does in fact happen. A business-government axis was forged during the Second World War by C.D. Howe. Under his administration, defence output grew so fast that by 1943 war-related industries

C.D. Howe, seen here with his wife Alice, was the most powerful man in Canada during the Second World War. His dollar-a-year men formed the core of the Canadian business establishment in the immediate post-war years.

employed 1,100,000 Canadians (compared with a peak enrolment of 1,086,000 in the armed forces) and the gross national product leaped from $5 billion in 1939 to $12 billion by 1945.

The dollar-a-year men who spent the war working mainly for Howe in Ottawa considered themselves grossly underpaid and overworked, but what came out of their experience was a great sense of comradeship: a knotting together of people making common cause. Eating lunch and often dinner with the same group for five years produced, for the first time in the experience of most participants, a consensus about the kind of country they wanted after the war, the sort of business practices they believed in and early glimmerings that Toronto and Montreal were not the only commercial centres in Canada that mattered. They began to exchange confidences, to sponsor one another for club memberships, to share perceptions and ambitions. It was an enduring trust and, even though the Establishment has had many roots, no badge of honour ever carried more prestige than the phrase, "I put in time under C.D."

The men and one woman (John Turner's mother, Phyllis, who was chief of the Oil and Fats Administration branch in the wartime Prices and Trade Board) who ran Ottawa's civilian war machine formed the post-war Establishment that lasted for the next two decades.

After Howe's passing, the private and public sectors grew ever further apart, at first forming an uneasy alliance and, more recently, struggling against each other for supremacy. Businessmen, if powerful enough, learned first hand that no government would allow them either to go bankrupt or to shut plants and increase unemployment. So they raised prices and profits with impunity and governments protected them with subsidies and by increasing the total money supply. In return, they were charged higher taxes and their freedom of action was drastically reduced through Ottawa's regulatory agencies.

By the 1980s, both sides were bitter and confused. The business community reacted to the escalating initiatives of the Trudeau government with self-righteous rage; and, determined to find policy initiatives that might maintain them in their accustomed perch of power, the federal Liberals jettisoned their traditional approach of sedate populism, which in the past had allowed them to strike the most marketable balance between elitism and egalitarianism. Trudeau and his mandarin court of advisors decided to unfold their universe a bit, to become a movement of pragmatic interventionists. They lashed out in one new direction after another, epitomized by the National Energy Program. The policy was aimed at accomplishing the desirable goal of Canadianization of the country's most vital industry. Business reacted with a mixture of barely suppressed sputterings and outraged threats of exodus. But as the more sensitive among the Establishment's adherents began to read the situation more closely, they realized that the issue hit at a basic contradiction inherent in any democratic capitalist society.

Capitalism, by definition, allocates top priority to economic efficiency, using Adam Smith's "invisible hand" to obtain the most productive output from labour, capital, and resources. Social democracies, on the other hand, emphasize entirely different objectives, such as compassion and equality, which run counter to the functional dictates of the bottom-line ethic. With governments less willing to field policies that foster individual enterprise and businessmen becoming increasingly opposed to satisfying the voracious demands for the expansion of social services, the two value systems drifted apart.

Despite all of this, free enterprise still lives and the profit motive continues to flourish. As the economy becomes entrenched on the downside of Canada's greatest period of sustained growth, the ages-old concept of commercial proprietorships is being reasserted in high-yield, beat-inflation investments. Fresh wealth is being created by the service industries; by the fast-food dispensaries, the syndicators, franchisers, and microchip merchandisers—lords of new technology who have learned to lease time, compress space, and invent their own languages. Information is money, they boast as they leap aboard the high-tech bandwagon.

Despite such success, many serious investors project a gloomy mindset about Canada's future, complaining that the economy does not work any more. They have begun pumping more of their available investment funds south of the border and wish they could somehow cast their ballots for Maggie Thatcher or Ronnie Reagan, instead of for all those free-spending auctioneers the Canadian political system keeps spawning. Their gaze is directed in supplication toward Brian Mulroney, the new Conservative leader, with prayers that he won't turn out to be a populist in a three-piece suit.

With Mulroney shepherding the Tories (and John Turner in the wings as the putative Liberal chieftain) it looked, in mid-1983, as if the breach between business and government might be healed. Turner, after all, is regarded as the darling of the Toronto business and legal communities, while Mulroney (a Bank of Commerce director, close friend of Power Corp.'s Paul Desmarais and Argus Corp.'s Conrad Black) has operated at the core of the Establishment since taking over the presidency of the Iron Ore Company of Canada in 1977. But both men are well aware that the roots of power in this country lie close to the ground. Like their predecessors, they are likely to dissociate themselves from their business connections.

Sir Charles Tupper and Sir Robert Borden (who both served as Conservative prime ministers) founded the Crown Life Insurance Company; Arthur Meighen became one of Bay Street's outstanding financiers; Mackenzie King had been a personal advisor to John D. Rockefeller, Jr.; R.B. Bennett was president of Calgary Power and owner of the E.B. Eddy Co.; Louis St. Laurent held many corporate directorships both before and after serving as Canada's 12th prime minister. But none of these or Canada's other prime ministers succumbed to the business ethic once in office.

Like it or not, the Establishment may find that, if either is installed in power, neither Mulroney nor Turner will become their champions. A new configuration of forces is taking shape in this country that stand in direct opposition to the traditional aspirations of the economic elite, and no political leader who counts on survival beyond one term can afford to ignore them.

That may be why the Establishment's more thoughtful adherents feel themselves besieged —nervous about the present and terrified of the future. Suffering from a loss of deference, a vanishing political base, and fear of a world they never made, they are retreating behind their private battlements. Instead of indulging in outward trappings of wealth and power (thus making targets of themselves), they are escaping into self-imposed anonymity, mainly by trying to become "regular guys": funny but sensitive, bright but unpretentious, endearingly neurotic.

This is very different from the American way, in which wealth is flaunted and extroverts rule the roost. Writing in *New York* magazine, Nicholas Pileggi once characterized those who really wield, retain, and covet power in his city as "the kind of men who answer bedside telephones while making love." It is highly doubtful if a similar survey could be attempted in Canada—and, if it were, results would show that all previous activity was suspended for six rings while a compromise solution was debated; by then, neither option would be viable.

Capitalism in this country continues to be nourished by the same Calvinist impulses that initially forced it to bloom in these cold-frame latitudes. Money making, so runs the Protestant ethic, is next to Godliness because it is the inevitable result of hard work, and prosperity is a sure sign of salvation because it means that God is smiling down on its recipient. It is unforgivably sinful to admit to one's wealth—and the devil will get those who do so in public. The ideal is to be *careful*, plainly dressed and plain spoken, close with one's money and emotions. All pleasure and

splendour must be made to look accidental rather than planned. It is a view of life that stresses the sombre virtues—the dutiful feeling of a hard day's work well done, the idea that the good man always more than earns his keep, a kind of fierce pragmatism that stresses the hard-and-fast, here-and-now aspect of life. "The aggressive egalitarianism that has always been a secular religion for Americans has no counterpart in this country," Dennis Braithwaite once observed in the *Toronto Sun*. "Reverence for the Establishment—which prompted the United Empire Loyalists to forsake the Revolution and settle here in the first place—is the most easily identifiable characteristic of Canadians."

CANADA'S CLASS AND POWER structure was initially shaped by the cultural traditions of the French and British colonial empires, fed by cornering indigenous products for export; there was little attempt to develop domestic processing. The founding economic class in Canada, as McGill University historian R.T. Naylor has pointed out, had *mercantile* roots, accumulating its wealth through "circulation" rather than through manufacturing or other, more creative activities.

Before the Conquest of 1759, the French had overextended themselves in the interior fur trade; to protect their routes, commercial and political interests merged to demand military protection from France. The young colony prospered, but it was a passive development—a response to external demand for fish, fur, timber, and, eventually, wheat, minerals, pulp and paper. One of the major consequences of this staple theory of growth was the evolution of a "metropolis-hinterland" economy, which still accounts for current regional disparities and conflicts. What developed was a smug urban mercantile class ensconced in the cities—with no prosperous heartland to share their wealth and authority.

The gold Beaver Club medal. Begun in Montreal in 1785 by the founders of the North West Company, the club was restricted to fur traders who had spent a winter in the pays d'en haut. *Members included James McGill, who left a legacy to found McGill University; Alexander Mackenzie, the first to reach the Pacific overland; and William McGillivray, who headed the Nor'Westers in 1821 when, after a bitter struggle, they were absorbed by the Hudson's Bay Company. Shown are the obverse of the medal presented to Hippolyte Trottier Des Rivières (the date shows that he first wintered on the frontier in 1743) and the reverse of James McGill's medal. Meetings were riotous frontier-style feasts of pemmican and venison, followed by toasts and voyageur songs. The club's name has been adopted for the restaurant of the Queen Elizabeth Hotel, where dining is a tamer affair*

Sir George Simpson (1787-1860) became governor of the Hudson's Bay Company in 1826, soon after it absorbed the North West Company. He ruled more than a quarter of North America and travelled briskly, usually with a piper, all over his empire from his headquarters at Lachine.

The earliest Canadian fortunes had grown out of the fur trade and landholdings along with the early shipping lines and the merchant adventurers who supplied the young colony. Then the railway barons, who chartered 1,300 railroads that in many instances became wellheads of family empires, emerged during the second half of the 19th century.

These old-style tycoons regarded themselves as contemporary inheritors of that mantle of esteem once borne by gladiators, nobles, and bishops—walking proof to an invidiously competitive society that ability and application could be spectacularly repaid. They owned private railway cars that carried pianos, bathtubs with gold-plated taps, wine "cellars" (cushioned to protect the vintages from the thump of railbeds), fireplaces, and Tiffany lamps. They lived in capricious castles filled with the icy nuances of their class.

THIS LIFESTYLE FLOURISHED NOWHERE more conspicuously than in Montreal's Square Mile. Between the late 1860s and the mid-1920s, in the

The earliest fortunes in the Ottawa-Hull area were made in lumbering. Ezra Butler Eddy (1827-1906), shown here with his first wife Zaida, arrived in Ottawa from the United States in 1854 and began by selling matches door to door. He expanded into other wood products and paper making. He was elected mayor of Hull several times and represented the city in the Quebec legislature. The E.B. Eddy Company is now part of the Weston empire. The early photograph below shows E.B. Eddy's sawmills at Ottawa.

36

John Rudolphus Booth (1826-1925) arrived in 1858 and rented a shingle mill from the Wrights, who had pioneered logging in the area a half-century earlier and developed the system of transporting square timber in huge rafts down the Ottawa and St. Lawrence rivers to Quebec, for loading onto ships to England. Shown below are J.R. Booth's mills at Ottawa. Booth developed a 4250 square-mile timber empire that was one of the continent's largest and built a railway, the Canada Atlantic, to transport his products to the United States.

area bounded by Guy Street and Côte des Neiges Road to the west, University Street to the east, Cedar and Pine Avenues to the north, and Dorchester Street to the south, there was created a non-Canadian enclave that would forever be England. Rich Montrealers looked to the late Victorian and Edwardian eras for inspiration to define their narrow universe—a convoluted, self-contained world with its own itinerant muffin-man. A host was judged on such niceties as how he disposed of his cherry pits.

Murray Ballantyne, the son of a rich Montrealer who was a member of Sir Robert Borden's wartime cabinet, lived inside the Square Mile and recalled its ambience: "The style of houses in the Square Mile varied greatly, as taste changed. The Harrison Stephens house was coolly formal outside, a Salem magnate's house translated from wood to stone. But then, Stephens was born in New England. Sir Hugh Allan was born in Scotland, as anyone may see by glancing at his 'crag.' In some ways the most elegant of all, though not a mansion in size, is the house built by Sir Mortimer Davis about 1910 at Pine and Peel. It is said to have been designed by Stanford White. After he built it, Sir Mortimer said: 'Now when I beat my dinner gong, all Montreal will come.' So they did, and at least once to meet the Prince of Wales. All these houses had large conservatories, often supported by large greenhouses. Not only were flowers grown in abundance, but sometimes fruits such as grapes, peaches, and nectarines as well. In the largest mansions, gardeners would don felt slippers in the early morning to renew and refresh the many plants and bouquets arranged throughout the rooms.

"Some households had more than nine servants," Ballantyne continued. "A few had many more. One magnificent establishment had 32. This was considered by everybody to be excessive, but the house in question was very large; it was filled with great paintings, beautiful furniture, and *objets d'art*, and all was done in great style and without any vulgarity. Our staff comprised coachman, groom, chauffeur, butler, cook, kitchen maid, permanent char, housemaid, and tablemaid. Like any house of our time, there were three dining rooms: the main dining room, the children's, and the servants' hall. As a child, I took all my meals in the children's dining room. Early on I was permitted to join the family at eight o'clock breakfast in the main dining room. Still later when we were all grown up and father semi-retired, we came down to breakfast when we pleased and ordered what we pleased. By the time I went to school, I had lunch with mother if she was not entertaining. I was allowed to come to dinner when I was 11. Unlike some other houses, we did not dress for dinner when alone. But when we gave dinner parties, black tie was informal. Any large dinner or concert called for white tie and opera hat."

The most prestigious receptions were held at Ravenscrag, the baronial cloister built by Sir Hugh Allan (shipping) on the slopes of Mount Royal in 1861. When the ruling family of Luxembourg was offered refuge in Montreal during the Second World War, they turned down the offer of Ravenscrag because they "didn't wish to live in such a palace." The streets were filled with the residences of these self-made barons: Mount Stephen (CPR), Strathcona (CPR), Shaughnessy (CPR), and Atholstan (*Montreal Star*); of baronets and knights: Abbott (prime minister), Allan (shipping), Meredith (law and banking), Tait (law), Gordon (textiles), Drummond (sugar and banking), Beatty (CPR), Holt (everything), Hingston (medicine and banking), Macdonald (tobacco), Van Horne (CPR), and Forget (stockbroking); and of mere millionaires: Angus (CPR), Caverhill (hardware), Linton (shoes), McIntyre (CPR), Greenshields (wholesale drygoods, law, and stock

A meet at the kennels of the Montreal Hunt in 1898. This building was on Côte St. Catherine Road near Côte des Neiges and survived until 1936, when it was demolished and some decorative parts were moved to the club's present location at St. Augustin.

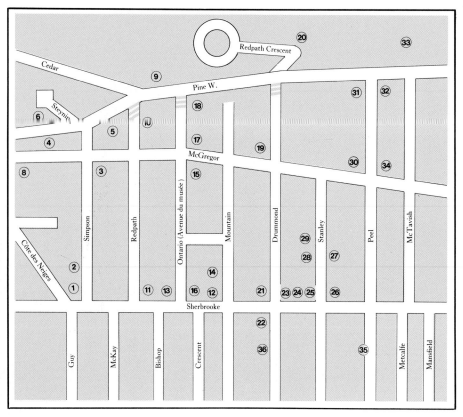

Some Square Mile Landmarks

1. *Linton Apartments, 1509 Sherbrooke St.W.*
2. *James Linton, 3424 Simpson St.*
3. *Trafalgar School for Girls*
4. *J.N. Greenshields, 1517 McGregor St.*
5. *Percy Walters Park, site of Sir George Simpson house*
6. *J. Henry Birks, 1547 Pine Ave. W.*
8. *J.B. Learmont, 1564 McGregor St.*
9. *Sir Henry Thornton*
10. *Ogilvie, 3655 Redpath Ave.*
11. *Church of St. Andrew and St. Paul*
12. *The Château Apartments*
13. *Montreal Museum of Fine Arts, 3410 Ave. du musée (formerly Ontario)*
14. *C.C. Ballantyne, 3484 Mountain St.*
15. *Sen. J.M. Wilson, 3501 Ave. du musée*
16. *Thomas Tait, 3415 Ave. du musée*
17. *Herbert Molson, 3617 Ave. du musée*
18. *Sir Rodolphe Forget (later Sen. Donat Raymond), 3685 Ave. du musée*
19. *Charles R. Hosmer, 3630 Drummond St.*
20. *W.R.G. Holt, 1295 Redpath Cres.*
21. *Huntley R. Drummond, 3418 Drummond St.*
22. *Ritz-Carlton Hotel, 1228 Sherbrooke St.W.*
23. *James Baxter (now Corby's)*
24. *Sen. Louis Forget (now United Services Club)*
25. *Mount Royal Club, 1175 Sherbrooke St. W.*
26. *Sir William Van Horne (demolished 1972)*
27. *Andrew Allan, 3433 Stanley St.*
28. *W.M. Birks, 3448 Stanley St.*
29. *Sen. Lorne MacDougall, 3454 Stanley St.*
30. *James Ross, 3644 Peel St.*
31. *Sir Charles Meredith, 1110 Pine Ave. W.*
32. *Sir Mortimer Davis, 1020 Pine Ave. W.*
33. *Sir Hugh Allan, Ravenscrag*
34. *E.B. Greenshields, 3529 Peel St.*
35. *Montreal Amateur Athletic Association, 2070 Peel St.*
36. *Lord Mount Stephen (now Mount Stephen Club)*

Sir George Drummond (1829-1910) (INSET) came to Montreal as director of Redpath Sugar and became a prominent industrialist. His bilingual Montreal-born wife, Grace Julia Parker, was described by Edgar Andrew Collard as being "less concerned with social position than with what could be done with it." Lady Drummond was one of the founders of the Montreal branch of the Victoria Order of Nurses and the Women's Canadian Club of Montreal. The first woman in Montreal to address a public banquet, she was considered mildly eccentric for preferring walking to riding and for having no partition in her limousine.

This view along Sherbrooke Street in the 1890s is dominated by the red sandstone house that Sir George Drummond built in the 1880s at the southeast corner of Sherbrooke and Metcalfe. It was demolished in 1926.

Scottish-born George Stephen (1829-1921), who became Lord Mount Stephen in 1889, was one of the financiers who backed the Canadian Pacific Railway. He was president of the Bank of Montreal from 1870 to 1881 and president of the CPR from 1881 to 1888. Six years after building his extraordinary house (RIGHT) he returned to Britain.

Sir Mortimer Barnett Davis (1864-1928) built his father's cigar business into the giant Imperial Tobacco Co., now part of Imasco. The remarkable Davis was president of the Baron de Hirsch Institute, the philanthropic and cultural centre of Montreal's Jewish community, as well as a director of the Royal Montreal Golf Club. His house at the corner of Pine Avenue and Peel Street in Montreal (RIGHT) was given to McGill University by Arthur Blaikie Purvis of C-I-L.

Mr. and Mrs. Gault, 1899. Mathew Gault, M.P., originally from Strabane, Ireland, founded Sun Life, now one of the biggest life insurance companies in the world, and his brothers, A.F. and R.L. Gault, ran the dry-goods firm of Gault Brothers and Company.

Sir William Macdonald (1831-1917) left the giant Macdonald Tobacco empire to his bookkeeper, Walter Stewart. Stewart placed ownership of the firm in a foundation that, under his son David, sold it in 1974 to Reynolds Industries. The Macdonald-Stewart Foundation occupies the Louis Forget house on Sherbrooke Street and funds various heritage projects, including the Montreal Military and Marine Museum.

R.B. Angus in 1874. He was another of the CPR financiers and was later president of the Bank of Montreal. His daughter Mary Isabella married B.T. Rogers, founder of B.C. Sugar.

43

Donald Alexander Smith (1820-1914), who became Lord Strathcona and Mount Royal, is well known as one of the CPR backers, but his profits from American railways were even greater. A major shareholder in the Bank of Montreal, he became its president in 1887. He and his cousin George Stephen gave Montreal the Royal Victoria Hospital to commemorate Queen Victoria's Golden Jubilee. Strathcona's Montreal mansion at Dorchester and Fort housed his collection of Oriental art and paintings by Raphael, Titian, Gainsborough, Reynolds, Romney, and Constable. The current Lord Strathcona, his great-grandson, lives in London.

Lord Shaughnessy aboard a Canadian Pacific steamship. Thomas George Shaughnessy, born in Milwaukee in 1853, went into railroading in the United States. He joined the CPR as general purchasing agent in 1882, becoming president in 1899. His mansion on Dorchester Boulevard (ABOVE RIGHT) has been purchased by the Canadian Centre for Architecture, headed by Phyllis Lambert, and renovated as its headquarters.

Peter Redpath (1812-1894) (RIGHT) built his father's sugar refinery into a huge enterprise and was an important Montreal philanthropist. Among his gifts to McGill University were the Redpath Library and the Redpath Museum.

The house and garden of Hugh Paton at L'Abord à Plouffe in the 1920s. Paton was Sir Herbert Holt's brother-in-law.

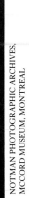

The ships of the Allan Line were a familiar sight along the Montreal waterfront for a century. Alexander Allan ("Captain Sandy") of Ayrshire founded the business in 1819 and five of his sons fanned out to open offices on both sides of the Atlantic. Hugh Allan (1810-1882) (ABOVE LEFT) came to Montreal in 1826, built up the business, and ushered the line into the age of steam. Sir Hugh (knighted in 1871) had ambitions to finance the Canadian Pacific Railway, but revelations of his "political contributions" and the involvement of American backers exploded in the Pacific Scandal of 1873, which brought down John A. Macdonald's government and ended Allan's dream of building a transportation empire. After Sir Hugh died, his brother Andrew ("Old Andrew") succeeded him as senior partner. In the early 1900s the company found it difficult to match the financial strength of the CPR in building new ships and in 1909 it was purchased by the CPR, headed by Sir Thomas Shaughnessy. The Allan Line was absorbed into Canadian Pacific in 1915-17. Sir Hugh Montagu Allan (1860-1951) (ABOVE RIGHT) second son of Sir Hugh Allan, was born Hugh Andrew but changed his name to avoid confusion with his cousin. He went to Bishop's College School and entered the family business at 21. A financier and president of the Merchant's Bank, he and his wife were leaders of Montreal Society. He was master of the foxhounds at the Montreal Hunt for many years and in 1910 gave the Allan Cup for competition among amateur hockey teams.

Sir Hugh Montagu Allan outlived all his children, shown in this photograph at Cacouna. His son Hugh was killed in the First World War and his younger daughters Gwendolyn and Anna were lost in the sinking of the Lusitania. *His eldest daugher, Marguerite Martha Allan (1895-1942), was an actress, playwright, founder of the Montreal Repertory Theatre, and ardent supporter of the Dominion Drama Festival.*

Sir Montagu Allan's summer house at Cacouna on the Lower St. Lawrence is now a religious retreat. This pleasant village a few miles downstream from Rivière du Loup was also a favourite summer retreat of R.S. McLaughlin.

broking), Ross (CPR and streetcars), Beardmore (leather), Workman (hardware and railways), Workman (steel and coal), Reford (shipping), Drummond (steel), Timmins (mining), MacDougall (stockbroking), Mackay (wholesale dry goods), Learmont (hardware), Pillow (CPR connection), Hosmer (CPR connection), Molson (brewing), Dawes (brewing), Paton (cartage), Mackenzie (stockbroking), Killam (finance), Ogilvie (flour), Birks (jewellery), and Morgan (department stores).

Perhaps the most colourful Montrealer of his day was Donald Alexander Smith, who rose from junior fur trader in the Hudson's Bay Company to become its governor, being at the same time president of the Bank of Montreal—as well as chief financial agent of (and chief profiteer from) construction of the Canadian Pacific Railway. Along the way, he also settled the initial Riel rebellion, toppled Sir John A. Macdonald's first administration, established the police force preceding the RCMP, was tossed out of Parliament for bribing voters to re-elect him, and came close to being jailed on more than one occasion. Invitations to the largest of his four houses—a baronial red stone castle in Montreal at 1157 Dorchester Street— were sought by every social climber in town.

Smith slavishly followed the official order of precedence and kept a private guest tally that classified his visitors according to rank. The impressive roll call included George V and Queen Mary (who came to Canada in 1901 as the Duke and Duchess of Cornwall and York), a prince and princess, eight dukes, seven marquesses, 21 earls, six viscounts, six governors general, 26 lieutenant-governors, seven prime ministers, 27 provin-

Ravenscrag, the most magnificent of the Montreal mansions, was built by Sir Hugh Allan in the 1860s and inherited by Sir Hugh Montagu Allan. With its palatial rooms, large stables, and view from the slopes of Mount Royal, it was used as an unofficial Government House when the Governor General came to Montreal. Sir Montagu and Lady Allan gave it to the Royal Victoria Hospital in 1943 and today it houses the Allan Memorial Institute. The photo at top right shows a stone horse's head over the stable door.

cial premiers, four archbishops, 17 bishops, 14 chief justices, 29 Supreme Court judges, 31 mayors, and 58 generals. Smith's list even tidily separated this latter group into 47 generals of the Imperial Army and 11 colonial commanders. The dining room opened into a garden for summer teas, occasionally attended by more than 2,000 guests.

The most powerful of the Montreal set was, without doubt, Sir Herbert Holt, who controlled 300 companies on three continents, worth nearly $4 billion. Originally the engineer in charge of punching the CPR through the sliding-earth passes of the Rockies and the Selkirks, he designed in 1914 the railway transportation network that supplied the ammunition to halt the Kaiser's initial thrust across France. During the sombre beginnings of the Second World War, he quietly gave Britain a full squadron of Spitfires. His mills turned out 10 per cent of the world's newsprint. Just before the 1929 crash, he was on the verge of putting together a utilities combine that would have become the world's richest corporation. His Montreal Light, Heat and Power was the largest privately owned utility then in existence; he established Famous Players Corporation, Consolidated Paper, and Dominion Textile, spent 26 years as head of the Royal Bank (multiplying its assets fifteenfold), and became such a dominant influence that the mention of his name could affect a whole stock market.

The Renaissance man among the Square Milers was Sir William Van Horne, hero of the CPR's construction, who turned the debt-ridden pioneer line into one of the world's great transportation systems. He also invented a grasshopper killer, an avalanche deflector, a submarine detector, and became an outstanding amateur botanist, palaeontologist, and landscape painter.

Van Horne loved to deflate the stuffier members of his set with elaborate practical jokes. One favourite was his cigar prank. A firm of cut-rate tobacconists had capitalized on his fame by calling a five-cent brand the "Van Horne." He ordered hundreds of the leafy horrors, removed their bands, mixed them in his humidor with expensive Perfectos, then palmed them off on his guests. His visitors, wishing to acknowledge his reputation as a connoisseur, would inhale the tarry fumes and exclaim: "Ah, Sir William, what a delightful aroma!" They could only smile icily at Van Horne's crude guffaw, after which followed his explanation. He once hired a man simply because he had butted one of the dud cigars and asked, "How much does the stable boy charge you for these things?"

Van Horne's 52-room mansion housed one of the largest collections of Japanese porcelain in North America and 200 paintings, valued at $30 million. Velvet wall hangings provided the mellow backdrop for his works by Rubens, Titian, Murillo, Velasquez, El Greco, Renoir, Reynolds, Goya, Hogarth, Turner, and Courbet. He had four Rembrandts, two Goyas, a Leonardo da Vinci study of a woman's head, and four paintings by Franz Hals. (The Van Horne mansion, amid great lamentation and political taking of stances, was torn down in 1972 to make way for a high-rise.)

The prime exhibit of the idle rich who populated the Square Mile in its heyday was not a house but Elwood Hosmer himself. He spent much of his life drinking gin and smoking $1.25 Coronas in one of the lobby lounge chairs at the Ritz-Carlton Hotel, often answering nature's calls in the pot of a nearby palm tree. The Ritz had been originally financed in 1912 by a group that included Elwood's father (Charles Hosmer, who founded CP Telegraphs and became president of Ogilvie Flour Mills) and soon became the gathering place for the Montreal elite. They lunched in the Oak Room, took tea in the Palm Court, dined in the Oval Room, held debut parties in the Grand Ballroom, and moved in—if they had had a row at home—to dine on caviar Astrakhan and Grande

Noah Timmins (1867-1936), seen at right, made his fortune from the Hollinger Mine, richest gold mine in the Porcupine, and other subsequent mining ventures. Bud McDougald, nephew of Timmins' fellow backer John McMartin, eventually drew the company into the Argus net. One of the many Timmins family interests was Timmins Aviation, which became Innotech, the company that builds the interiors of Challengers (including Conrad Black's) and other corporate jets.

When the Noah Timmins house (BELOW) on Belvedere Place at the top of Westmount was sold in the 1960s, a large slice was taken out to produce two still-sizable buildings.

Pouring gold at the Hollinger Mine.

Louis Forget (1853-1911) and his nephew Sir Rodolphe Forget (1861-1919) (TOP LEFT) were a formidable francophone team in the English-dominated financial community. Louis Forget was the first French Canadian to join the Montreal Stock Exchange, the first to be its chairman, and a founding member of the Mount Royal Club. Sir Rodolphe, besides his many business ventures, was an MP from 1904 to 1917 and in 1911 actually won two seats, Charlevoix and Montmorency. Blanche McDonald (CENTRE), daughter of Quebec stock broker Alexandre Rodrigue McDonald, married Sir Rodolphe Forget in 1894, after the death of his first wife, Alexandra Tourville. Their sons, Gilles, Maurice, and Jacques, became stock brokers; their daughter, Thérèse (RIGHT), led the fight for women's rights in Quebec, winning the right to vote in the provincial elections in 1940. She married Pierre Casgrain (1886-1950) of the Quebec family of lawyers, politicians, and men of letters. Among his relations were Philippe Baby Casgrain, responsible for securing the Plains of Abraham as a national inheritance, and H.R. Casgrain, priest, historian, and a founder of the Royal Society of Canada. Pierre himself was Speaker of the House of Commons (1936-40), secretary of state, and a justice of the Quebec Superior Court. Thérèse Casgrain (1896-1981) entered politics with the CCF but never won an election and was appointed to the Senate in 1970.

Elaine Casgrain in her Packard, circa 1911.

The J.K.L. Ross house on Peel Street.

Fine Champagne de Napoleon 1800.

Elwood's days reached a peak in the evening when he would pass out, half-covered by the funny papers (his favourite reading) and surrounded by cigar ash from his day's sojourn. Bellboys would matter-of-factly carry him outside, where a chauffeur helped transfer him to his limousine for the two-block drive home. He owned four of the finest Canalettos in any private collection. This routine was seriously disrupted only once. In 1927, Elwood suddenly decided to fly the Atlantic. The attempt ended when his aircraft, the *Flying Whale*, crashed after takeoff from the Azores. He and three companions spent twelve hours drifting in the ocean until they were picked up by the liner *Minnewaska*. Elwood returned to the more stable Ritz-Carlton armchair.

Prime candidate for the title of most-extravagant Montrealer was J.K.L. Ross, son of the James Ross who had amassed a fortune as leader of the "Big Four" contracting team that pushed the CPR through the mountains. (The others were Sir Herbert Holt, Sir William Mackenzie, and Sir Donald Mann.) Between 1913, when his father died, and 1928, when he was declared bankrupt, Ross exhausted a fortune estimated at $16 million. His extravagances included travel by private train (not just private *car*) and indiscriminate wagers of

PUBLIC ARCHIVES CANADA/PA 131992

Sir Herbert Holt (1856–1941) with his sons Andrew (left) and Robert and Robert's daughter Pam aboard a Canadian Pacific liner. His other son was Herbert Jr.

THE ROYAL BANK OF CANADA ARCHIVES

A rare photograph of Sir Herbert Holt smiling, as he turns a valve to unload the first shipment of oil from Colombia to the Port of Montreal in 1926.

FRED. W. HOTSON

One of Robert Holt's more lasting investments was his support of Bob Noorduyn's Norseman aircraft at the start of the Second World War. Examples of this Canadian-designed bushplane are still at work in the North. The Holts continued their interest in aviation after the war. When personal and corporate aviation was still a costly novelty they had not one but three aircraft, which are shown here in 1948. Left to right: a Grumman Mallard formerly owned by J.P. Bickell of McIntyre Porcupine Mines and bought by Andrew Holt in 1948, who sold it in 1950 to the Ontario Paper Company of Thorold, where it is still in service; another Mallard, first owned by Lord Beaverbrook, who sold it to Herbert Holt, Jr.—it was hangared in Canada during the summer months and used in winter between Nassau and Grenada, where Holt had a nutmeg farm; nearest the camera is Robert Holt's ex-RCAF Grumman Goose.

PUBLIC ARCHIVES CANADA/C 8549

NOTMAN PHOTOGRAPHIC ARCHIVES, MCCORD MUSEUM, MONTREAL

The American-born Sir William Cornelius Van Horne (1843-1915) began his career as a telegraph operator on the Illinois Central. In 1882 he was made general manager of the Canadian Pacific Railway and in 1888 he became president. He was probably the most knowledgeable art collector among the magnates of his day and was also an accomplished amateur painter. The two views show the hallway and living room of his Montreal house, which was demolished in 1972.

NOTMAN PHOTOGRAPHIC ARCHIVES, MCCORD MUSEUM, MONTREAL

Van Horne built an architecturally striking summer house on Ministers Island, St. Andrews, New Brunswick. On the mainland nearby was his private railway station. Van Horne himself painted the frieze in the child's bedroom shown above right.

The Ritz-Carlton on Sherbrooke Street in Montreal was financed by a group of Square Milers who believed that Montreal should have a luxury hotel on a par with New York's finest. Opened in 1912, it has managed to retain its air of elegance in a less formal age, as these views show, and remains a favourite haunt of the English-speaking Establishment.

John Wilson McConnell (1877-1963), shown here as a young man and, later in life, in his Pine Avenue house, was a major Montreal financier who controlled St. Lawrence Sugar and many other companies. He took over the Montreal Star in 1938 on the death of Lord Atholstan. The foundation which administers his estate is the largest in the country. He was an important benefactor to McGill University and used his influence to keep the parvenu Sam Bronfman off the board of governors. He presented $1 million to McGill in 1951 for the extension of Dr. Wilder Penfield's Montreal Neurological Institute.

Lily May, Mrs. McConnell, third from right, at the Bal de tête, *Museum of Fine Arts, Montreal.*

An early photo of the Royal St. Lawrence Yacht Club.
FACING: *Travelling in style. The Mayfair Lounge on the Canadian Pacific steamship* Empress of Britain, *in service from 1931 until it was sunk in 1940. The most luxurious vessel in the CP fleet, it was a popular boat on the Montreal-Liverpool route.*

$5,000 or $10,000. He once bet $50,000 on a single horse race—and won. He had up to eight Rolls-Royces at any one time; his 40-room house on Peel Street was staffed by 30 servants. The *Gloria*, one of his seven yachts, was a 122-foot sloop—same class as King George V's *Britannia*—and he raced it out of Cowes as a member of the exclusive Royal Yacht Squadron. Ross maintained two big racing stables and one of his horses, Sir Barton, became the first Triple Crown champion when he won the Kentucky Derby, the

Belmont Stakes, and the Preakness in 1919. Although he was officially declared bankrupt on November 1, 1928, and was left with only $300 in cash, a codicil to his father's will set him up with a relatively modest income that allowed him to spend the last two decades of his life (he died in 1951) in Montego Bay, Jamaica, on an estate eventually sold to Lord Beaverbrook.

Another extravagant though much more private spender was Izaak Walton Killam, president of Royal Securities, who was wont to carry a fresh

ABOVE: The 1878 St. Andrew's Society Ball at the Windsor Hotel in Montreal in honour of Princess Louise and the Marquis of Lorne. The annual ball attracts 700 kilted and gowned revellers. The guest of honour is a prominent Scot, debutantes are presented, the haggis is piped in, and dancing continues till dawn. The first St. Andrew's Ball in Montreal took place in 1816. The society itself was formed in 1835 to care for needy immigrant Scots and the rules still require that members be of Scottish descent.

LEFT: The receiving line at a recent ball. Left to right: Clifford and Heather Maclean, Colonel J. Ralph Harper, the Countess and Earl of Strathmore and Kinghorne (guests of honour), Natalie and Reford MacDougall. RIGHT: David Macdonald Stewart, president of the Macdonald Stewart Foundation, and his wife Liliane.

Debutantes at the 1981 ball.

Col. J. Ralph Harper, honorary life ball chairman, dances with Margery Rhea.

The family of Senator Lorne Webster in 1925. The children are, from left to right, R. Howard, Eric, Marian, Colin W., Richard C., and Lorne Stuart.

Of the six children, R.H. Webster (RIGHT) has become the most prominent. His diverse business holdings include a controlling interest in Burns Foods. At one time he owned the Toronto Globe and Mail, of which he is still honorary chairman and his nephew, Norman Webster, is editor-in-chief. Another nephew, Lorne, heads the Prenor Group, a financial services empire that includes Trust Général.

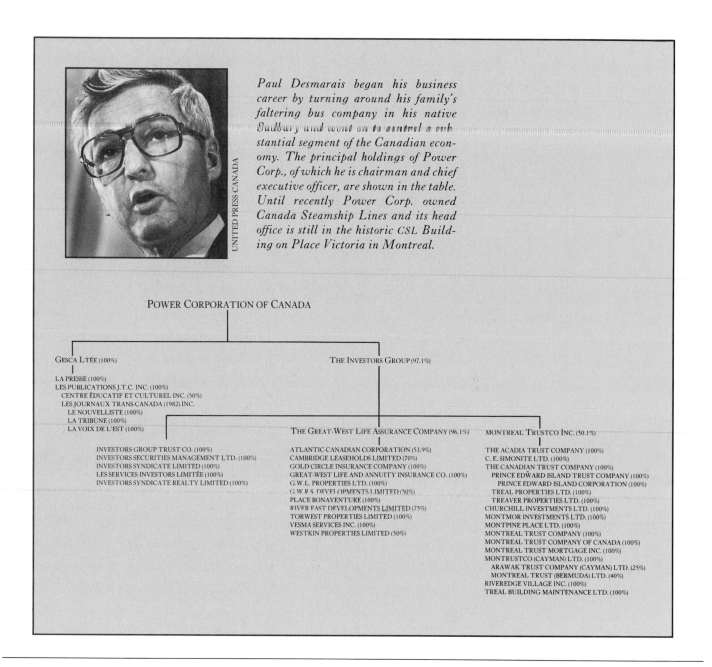

Paul Desmarais began his business career by turning around his family's faltering bus company in his native Sudbury and went on to control a substantial segment of the Canadian economy. The principal holdings of Power Corp., of which he is chairman and chief executive officer, are shown in the table. Until recently Power Corp. owned Canada Steamship Lines and its head office is still in the historic CSL Building on Place Victoria in Montreal.

UNITED PRESS CANADA

POWER CORPORATION OF CANADA

GESCA LTÉE (100%)

LA PRESSE (100%)
LES PUBLICATIONS J.T.C. INC. (100%)
CENTRE ÉDUCATIF ET CULTUREL INC. (50%)
LES JOURNAUX TRANS-CANADA (1982) INC.
LE NOUVELLISTE (100%)
LA TRIBUNE (100%)
LA VOIX DE L'EST (100%)

THE INVESTORS GROUP (97.1%)

INVESTORS GROUP TRUST CO. (100%)
INVESTORS SECURITIES MANAGEMENT LTD. (100%)
INVESTORS SYNDICATE LIMITED (100%)
LES SERVICES INVESTORS LIMITÉE (100%)
INVESTORS SYNDICATE REALTY LIMITED (100%)

THE GREAT-WEST LIFE ASSURANCE COMPANY (96.1%)

ATLANTIC-CANADIAN CORPORATION (53.9%)
CAMBRIDGE LEASEHOLDS LIMITED (70%)
GOLD CIRCLE INSURANCE COMPANY (100%)
GREAT-WEST LIFE AND ANNUITY INSURANCE CO. (100%)
G.W.L. PROPERTIES LTD. (100%)
G.W.R.S. DEVELOPMENTS LIMITED (50%)
PLACE BONAVENTURE (100%)
RIVER EAST DEVELOPMENTS LIMITED (75%)
TORWEST PROPERTIES LIMITED (100%)
VESMA SERVICES INC. (100%)
WESTKIN PROPERTIES LIMITED (50%)

MONTREAL TRUSTCO INC. (50.1%)

THE ACADIA TRUST COMPANY (100%)
C. E. SIMONITE LTD. (100%)
THE CANADIAN TRUST COMPANY (100%)
PRINCE EDWARD ISLAND TRUST COMPANY (100%)
PRINCE EDWARD ISLAND CORPORATION (100%)
TREAL PROPERTIES LTD. (100%)
TREAVER PROPERTIES LTD. (100%)
CHURCHILL INVESTMENTS LTD. (100%)
MONTMOR INVESTMENTS LTD. (100%)
MONTPINE PLACE LTD. (100%)
MONTREAL TRUST COMPANY (100%)
MONTREAL TRUST COMPANY OF CANADA (100%)
MONTREAL TRUST MORTGAGE INC. (100%)
MONTRUSTCO (CAYMAN) LTD. (100%)
ARAWAK TRUST COMPANY (CAYMAN) LTD. (25%)
MONTREAL TRUST (BERMUDA) LTD. (40%)
RIVEREDGE VILLAGE INC. (100%)
TREAL BUILDING MAINTENANCE LTD. (100%)

egg down the street to the Mount Royal Hotel barbershop for special shampoo treatments. His wife, Dorothy, once instructed a senior vice-president of Royal Securities to engage a suite on a train to take her dog down to New York, carefully specifying that the animal was to sleep only on a lower berth.

The Square Milers continued to intermarry, ride to hounds, arrange balls, have tea at the Ritz, and blackball each other at the Mount Royal Club, but their dominance declined rapidly after the First World War. Nearly every one of the great houses lost at least one son in the "right" regiments, recruited so that the Square Milers could go into battle surrounded by their own. By 1926, when Frank McKenna opened a florist shop in the Paton house, the mansions began to be subdivided and the Square Mile was never the same.

Nearly all of Montreal's great old fortunes vanished (except the Molsons')—though the Hosmer and Davis estates still rate a mention in the local telephone book. The CPR fortunes moved to the

The Mount Royal Club, the most exclusive in Montreal. The building at Stanley and Sherbrooke was designed for the club in 1906 by Stanford White

third-generation, who ceased taking major investment initiatives. Money that once shouted now only whispers. The Cassilses, Redpaths, Gaults, McCalls, and many other once-great families disappeared from contention.

BUSINESS FIRST BEGAN ITS exodus from Montreal when Sir Henry Thornton formed the CNR in 1922 out of the bankrupt shells of the Canadian Northern, the Grand Trunk, and the Grand Trunk Pacific, allowing the Bank of Commerce in Toronto to become a fiscal force in national railways. The Ontario government had been financing railway construction into its own northland as early as 1902, and that triggered the Cobalt, Porcupine, and Kirkland Lake mining booms which brought the riches of the Canadian Shield under Toronto's dominance. While Montrealers continued to regard the mining market as "a bit undignified," speculative wealth poured into Toronto. The 1934 amalgamation of the Toronto Stock Exchange and the Standard Stock and Mining Exchange contrasted with the Montreal Stock Exchange's insistence on relegating mining stocks to trading on the floor of the lesser Montreal Curb Market.

None of this had much visible effect on the English Montrealers of the '30s, '40s, or '50s; they lived out their lives with an imperviousness that Charles Dickens would have found entirely contemporary. But by the 1960s, St. James Street, once the chief metaphor for Canadian capitalism, had suffered an ignominious decline. The floor of the Montreal Stock Exchange was redone as a theatre; what was left of the investment industry moved up the hill around Place Ville Marie.

As the WASPs and Jews moved out, fleeing after their children and their money (sent on ahead to Toronto schools and bank vaults, respectively), a vacuum was created. Although some English-speaking leadership remains—David Culver at Alcan, Charles Bronfman at Seagrams and Leo Kolber at Cemp, Fred Burbidge at CPR, Drummond Birks, Rowlie Frazee at the Royal Bank, Paul Paré at Imasco, Jim Burns at Power, lawyers Heward Stikeman and Philip Vineberg, Howard and Lorne Webster, Stephen Jarislowsky, a handful of Molsons, and some others—more and more

63

TRUTH · DUTY · VALOUR

J.R.

J.R.

Founded in 1876 as a school for naval officers, the Royal Military College at Kingston is the senior military college. (The others are Royal Roads in Victoria and Collège militaire royal de Saint-Jean.) Here budding officers are trained in the substance and customs of military life, receiving at the same time a university education. On the facing page, the top photo shows the view from the Parade Square of the Currie Building, the adjoining Mackenzie Building and, to the right, the "Stone Frigate," built in 1819-20 as part of the Old Naval Dockyard that formerly occupied this site. The lower photos opposite show a window of the beautiful Chapel and Yeo Hall. Shown below are the Chapel in Currie Hall, the Officers' Mess (BOTTOM LEFT), and the Cadets' Dining Hall.

French Canadians are moving into positions of influence that are *national* in reach.

Apart from Paul Desmarais, who is still the most dynamic business presence in the province, and Brian Mulroney, whose Conservative Party leadership win is significant for the positive signal it sent Quebec citizens about their future in Confederation, current power wielders include: Pierre Arbour (Laduboro Oil), Philippe de Gaspé Beaubien (head of Télémedia), Laurent Beaudoin (president of Bombardier), Roger Beaulieu (lawyer and corporate director), Marcel Bélanger (accountant and director), Michel Bélanger (CEO, National Bank of Canada), Jean Béliveau (hockey hero and corporate director), André Bisson (Quebec chief of the Bank of Nova Scotia), Jean Boulanger and Guy Coulombe (Hydro-Québec), Jean Campeau (Caisse de Dépôt), Marcel Caron (the senior Montreal partner of Clarkson, Gordon), Guy Charbonneau (insurance agency executive and Mulroney confidant), André Charron (president of Levesque, Beaubien), Claude Castonguay (life insurance), Michel Cogger (Mulroney advisor), Jacques Courtois (lawyer, bank vice-president, and Tory fund raiser), Etienne Crevier (insurance executive), Jean de Grandpré (Bell Canada), Philippe de Grandpré (lawyer), Charles Demers (corporate director), Robert Demers (lawyer, ex-treasurer of the Quebec Liberal party), Robert De Coster (Sidbec), Pierre Des Marais (printer), Claude Ducharme (law), Jacques Francoeur (newspaper publisher), Raymond Garneau (Montreal City & District Savings Bank), Jean-Paul Gourdeau (engineering), Jean-Paul Goyer (troubleshooter), Claude Hébert (war hero and independently wealthy corporate executive), Bernard Lamarre (consulting engineer), Bernard Landry (director), Roger Létourneau (Quebec City lawyer and corporate director), J. Louis Lévesque (horses), Pierre Macdonald (Bank of Montreal), Andre Monast (Quebec City lawyer and corporate director), Pierre Nadeau (director), Jean Ostiguy (Richardson Greenshields), Jean-Michel Paris (Caisse de Dépôt), Gérard Parizeau (the insurance man), Pierre Peladeau (newspaper publisher), Laurent Picard (former CBC president, now Royal Commissioner and commerce professor), Marcel Piché (lawyer and corporate director), Gérard Plourde (CEO of UAP), Jean-Marie Poitras (CEO of Laurentian Mutual Assurance, Quebec City), Maurice Riel (lawyer and Liberal fund-raiser), Alfred Rouleau of Lévis (who heads the Caisses Populaires), and Antoine Turmel (of Provigo).

IF THERE IS ONE MAN who symbolizes the dramatic shift of economic, cultural, and professional power away from Montreal, he is Roy Fraser Elliott. The son of one of Ottawa's original mandarins (C.F. Elliott was Canada's first deputy minister of national revenue), in short order he studied law, got a Harvard M.B.A., married a Westmount girl and joined the Quebec Bar, becoming enough of an authority to write the *Quebec Corporation Manual*. By the mid-1970s he had made a private fortune (based on getting into CAE Industries at its start and remaining its largest shareholder) and sat on 21 corporate boards representing assets of $11.6 billion. He was the Liberal Party's chief Quebec fund raiser and spent both the 1972 and 1974 election nights at Pierre Trudeau's elbow. He belonged to nine clubs (including the ultra-exclusive Honourable Company of Edinburgh Golfers) and, until the election of the Parti Québécois in 1976, was at the very centre of Quebec's Anglo Establishment.

Then he purchased a mansion on Dunvegan Road in Toronto's posh Forest Hill district—and switched worlds. He set out to make himself the linchpin of his adopted city by trying to win its cultural triple crown. He has become head of the board of trustees of the Art Gallery of Ontario, is on the boards of the Canadian Opera Company and the Toronto General Hospital—and he is a senior vice-president of the Toronto Symphony, chairman of the Canadian Cultural Property

Roy Fraser Elliott in the lower lobby of his Toronto office in Commerce Court.

Export Review Board, and director of the Opera-Ballet House Corporation, which is seeking permanent homes for Toronto's ballet and opera companies.

Elliott is only the most visible (and to all appearances most successful) of the Montreal transplants. The migration of money and talent to Toronto following the electoral triumphs of René Lévesque's separatists has been one of the more significant yet little-noted migrations of a way of life in recorded history. Ian Sinclair, the former CP chairman who once ran English Montreal, and

W.A. Arbuckle, who presided over Montreal's most discreet investment portfolios, now both live in Oakville. Peter and Edward Bronfman keep Toronto apartments. Bluma and Bram Appel set out to conquer Toronto Society—and succeeded. Even those institutions that for political reasons must retain their nominal head offices in Montreal have long ago transferred their computers to Toronto, so that what remains in French Canada is largely rented office furniture.

Among the most distinguished exiles are members of the dynasty founded by Henry Mor-

Former chairman and chief executive officer of Canadian Pacific, Ian Sinclair is still chairman of Canadian Pacific Enterprises. Under his management the historic transportation company was transformed into a multinational conglomerate with interests in such areas as steel, gas, oil, forest products, real estate, and insurance.

gan, who opened his department store in Montreal in 1845. The family moved into financial services with Morgan Trust in 1916 and eventually sold the retail side of the business to the Hudson's Bay Company. Bartlett Morgan, a fixture of the Montreal Establishment at mid-century, is now honorary chairman of Morgan Financial Services, the family holding company that still operates out of Montreal with family member Cleveland Patterson as chairman. But David Morgan, chairman of the $200 million Morgan Trust of Canada whose major holdings are trust companies in Switzerland and the Cayman Islands, now lives outside Toronto. And John D. Morgan, chairman of Morgan Bancorp with oil and gas, credit, investment counselling, and real-estate interests, joined the exodus in 1983.

Montreal remains the country's most charming metropolis, the only large town other than Quebec City where the visitor is aware of a strong sense of history. This tingle of past glories emanates from the mountain, the St. Lawrence River, the archbishop's palace, the restored buildings around Bonsecours Market, and, of course, the overwhelming French presence.

Yet there prevails the air of a place that's lost something. And what Montrealers have lost (at least what the English-Canadian Establishment has lost) is the feeling that they live in the centre of the action. The ultimate blow came in the spring of 1983, when Bill Mulholland, chairman of the Bank of Montreal, once Westmount's unofficial finishing school, moved to Georgetown, Ontario, so that he could be closer to his decision-making staff in downtown Toronto.

WITH THIS SHIFT, Toronto reconfirmed its supremacy within Canada's economic firmament.

While most Canadians who don't live there mistrust the city's influence over their lives, Torontonians themselves do not comprehend why the rest of the country cannot be just like them—or, in many instances, could not bear to. Torontonians see themselves, if not precisely as the custodians of Canada's colonies beyond the Humber, at least as guardians of the ideal that life's main purpose is to turn as many dollars as one can by being smarter than the next fellow, fast on both feet, and proficient at selling the idea of motion as progress.

By the mid-1980s, this bottom-line philosophy was not quite as fashionable as it had been, perhaps because of the Montreal influence. Quebeckers had made introspection their "national" characteristic; Torontonians turned it into an industry. The trauma of having become a major world capital, the obligation of having to set the economic and cultural priorities for a huge and uncaring hinterland, began to sap Toronto's self-confidence. Local psychiatrists scanned their crammed appointment books, leaned back in their couches, and complained of psychic jet lag.

Toronto's power brokers work no harder than their compadres in other city states, but most of them expend so much energy contemplating their private affairs and analyzing others' reactions to their quips and foibles that the time left over for business is necessarily rushed. Emotional tangles and guilt trips begin to count more than block trades, bills of lading, torts, and debt-equity ratios.

What allows Toronto to maintain its financial pre-eminence is an infrastructure that can be reproduced in miniature but not fully duplicated in any other Canadian city. Here is the fountainhead of bank and investment funds that finance everything from pipelines across the Rockies to motels in Halifax. Toronto has the prestigious auditing firms: Clarkson Gordon and Thorne Riddell both have 2,000 accountants and other professionals on their payrolls. Legal factories such as Blake Cassels (with 131 lawyers) and McCarthy & McCarthy (with 125) can in one shirt-sleeved weekend put together a shopping-centre project in Moose Jaw or set up an offshore bank in the Caymans. Anything seems possible—and that's what gives the city its national clout. That and the grand scale of its financial transactions.

Gordon Gray, chairman of A.E. LePage (the Toronto-based company has become the world's second-largest real-estate firm) once calculated that with its 70 million square feet of office space, Toronto is twice as dominant in relation to its economic hinterland as is New York, which has only 15 per cent of the available American office accommodation. Manhattan is the home address of about one-tenth of *Fortune*'s 500, while Toronto houses nearly half the corporate head offices in similar Canadian listings.

ABOVE AND BEYOND the mundane circles of the city's fiscal power, there exists the rarefied world of Toronto Society, whose tendrils stretch, however gingerly, back to the Family Compact of the 19th century. At first, the Upper Class Anglicans who formed that governing elite (through connections with the British colonial tie) rejected the "lesser" Methodists and Presbyterians, who were "in trade." The Baldwins, Boultons, and Ridouts ruled the roost over the Eatons, the Burtons, and the Masseys.

Both groups vied in the fierceness of their loyalty to all things British. When the Duke and Duchess of Cornwall and York visited Toronto in 1901, a local newspaper described the city as "loyal Toronto—the heart of English-speaking Canada, the great centre of Imperial impulse, and first among cities of Great Britain in devotion to the British flag and the British Crown."

This habit of humbling themselves before the British lion was turned into dogma by Vincent Massey during the years he spent as Canada's High Commissioner in London. Lord Cranborne, who served as Lord Privy Seal in Churchill's government and later inherited the title Marquess of Salisbury, caught that eccentricity perfectly in his offhand remark: "Fine fellow, Vincent—but he does make one feel a bit of a savage."

The Leading Financial Men of Toronto, published in 1912, purporting to list the city's financial and social elite, included the familiar "Old Toronto" names—Mulock, Jarvis, Robinson, Cawthra, Osler, Strathy, and Robertson, among

"Toronto has no social classes/only the Masseys and the masses" was B.K. Sandwell's comment on the opening of another Massey benefaction to Toronto, on this occasion the Fred Victor Mission. No other family has had such an influence on the life of the city; the Massey name is commemorated in such institutions as Massey Hall, Hart House, and Massey College. Their great wealth came from the farm-equipment company started by Daniel Massey and his son Hart in 1846. The company's growth kept pace with the development of Canada itself, and the opening of the West and the spread of railways brought huge new markets. Hart took charge when his father died in 1852 and Charles, Hart's son, took over in 1872. The family's direct involvement ended in 1925 when Vincent Massey resigned the presidency of Massey-Harris (now Massey-Ferguson) to pursue his career in public life.

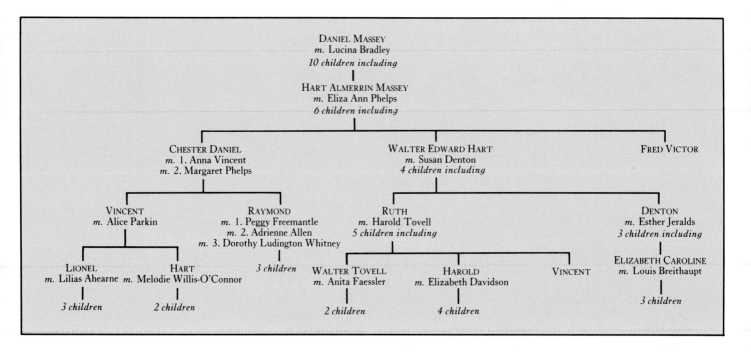

DANIEL MASSEY
m. Lucina Bradley
10 children including

HART ALMERRIN MASSEY
m. Eliza Ann Phelps
6 children including

CHESTER DANIEL
m. 1. Anna Vincent
m. 2. Margaret Phelps

WALTER EDWARD HART
m. Susan Denton
4 children including

FRED VICTOR

VINCENT
m. Alice Parkin

RAYMOND
m. 1. Peggy Freemantle
m. 2. Adrienne Allen
m. 3. Dorothy Ludington Whitney

RUTH
m. Harold Tovell
5 children including

DENTON
m. Esther Jeralds
3 children including

LIONEL
m. Lilias Ahearne

HART
m. Melodie Willis-O'Connor

3 children

WALTER TOVELL
m. Anita Faessler

HAROLD
m. Elizabeth Davidson

VINCENT

ELIZABETH CAROLINE
m. Louis Breithaupt

3 children

2 children

2 children

4 children

3 children

Batterwood at Port Hope was Vincent Massey's home and remains in the family. This group of family and friends was photographed there at Christmas 1929. Left to right, back row: J.M. Macdonnell, Burgon Bickersteth (warden of Hart House), W.L. Grant, Anne Macdonnell, Margaret Grant, Ruth Grierson, George Smith. Middle row: Maude Grant, Louise Parkin holding daughter Elizabeth, Charity Grant, Marjorie Macdonnell, Lady Parkin (mother of Vincent Massey's wife, Alice), Alice Massey, Lionel Massey. Front row: Alison Grant, Katherine Macdonnell, George Grant (the professor and philosopher), Hart Massey, Peter Macdonnell (the Edmonton lawyer).

Vincent Massey and his wife, Alice, at Batterwood. Massey was instrumental in developing the Canadian system of official honours. The Queen wanted to confer a knighthood on him, but John Diefenbaker would not hear of it.

Raymond Massey (1896-1983), Vincent's younger brother (RIGHT), had a long career as an actor, best known for his roles in London's West End, his portrayal of Abraham Lincoln, and his television role as Dr. Gillespie in the Dr. Kildare *series.*

J.R.

Opened in 1919, Hart House was built as a social and cultural centre for male students at the University of Toronto. It was conceived by Vincent Massey and named for his grandfather Hart Almerrin Massey.

Karsh portrait of Vincent Massey, the first Canadian-born governor general. He served from 1952 to 1959, when he was succeeded by Georges Vanier. Earlier Massey had been high commissioner for Canada in the United Kingdom (1935-46).

others. Sociologist Merrijoy Kelner noted that almost half the men listed were Protestants born in rural Ontario. Most of the others were born in Toronto, other parts of Canada, or in Scotland, England, or Ireland: "Only three of the one hundred men selected were of European origin. These three men (two of whom were brothers) came from cultivated German-Jewish families and upon arrival in Toronto entered the business of manufacturing and selling pianos. Although there were more than 18,000 Jews in Toronto by 1911, the vast majority of them were from eastern Europe. The urban German Jews—Abraham and Samuel Nordheimer and Gerhard Heintzman—had very little in common with the relatively unsophisticated East European Jews. Culturally, they were closer to the Anglo-Saxons with whom they subsequently intermarried. Eventually these early German-Jewish families lost both their German and their Jewish identities and became part of the Anglo-Saxon Establishment. All three of these men belonged to the most exclusive clubs in Toronto and appear to have been fully accepted by the society of the day."

The postwar influx of Czechs, Poles, Italians, Germans, and other central Europeans changed the character of the city. The collapse of the temperance movement dealt a severe blow to the encrusted old ethic, as did the lifting of Sabbath restrictions on sports, films, and concerts. Genuine Old Torontonians were becoming so difficult to find that Pierre Berton wrote in *Toronto: The New City*: "Occasionally a rare specimen is encountered in the panelled confines of the Toronto Club, or perhaps at the Hunt Ball. I understand that one or two are being mounted and stuffed for posterity at the Royal Ontario Museum. But the typical Torontonians today are the New Torontonians."

Still, occasionally, something is heard from these old ties, such as an open house at the J.S. McLean mansion (no longer owned by the McLeans) on Bayview Avenue; the fact that Mrs.

Aemilius Jarvis attended a Hunt Ball with Norman Elder; that Grace Gooderham has moved into the Palace Pier; or that Sir William Mulock's great-great-granddaughter is marrying fashionable stock broker Edward R. Barbour.

In these circles, the "family" is thought of as a sacred institution, not as the result of any heightened filial feelings but because it is the instrument through which money is passed on. Most of the families that might have become great financial dynasties petered out because they failed to establish systems of succession that would maintain and expand family investments. When George Gooderham, a sixth-generation descendant of what was once a dominant Canadian family, was married, Lady Gooderham, his great-aunt, gave a shower for his bride. The more than a hundred women relatives who turned up had to be identified with name cards.

The one remaining legacy of the Old Toronto is New Toronto's preoccupation with British royalty. In pre-war days, presentation at a Buckingham Palace reception was the ultimate accolade. That's no longer true—but Toronto hostesses still jockey for seats near whatever royal couple comes to town. That, in surrogate fashion, is one reason for the popularity of Ontario's lieutenant-governor, whose presence at social occasions lends a touch of class, a hint of representative royalty. This has been particularly true under the office's two most recent occupants, Pauline McGibbon and John Aird. The fact that Murray and Marvelle Koffler regularly and discreetly entertain British royalty at their Jokers Hill farm has been carefully noted.

The biggest fuss over royalty was made by the partners of Argus under the regimes of E.P. Taylor and John A. "Bud" McDougald. Whenever the Queen, Prince Philip, or any other member of the royal family would visit Toronto, he or she would quietly be put up at Bud's. In 1974, when Princess Anne and her husband, Captain Mark Phillips, officiated at the opening of the Royal Agricultural

The Cawthra family came to Upper Canada from Yorkshire in 1803. Joseph Cawthra settled in York (Toronto) and made his fortune supplying the British Army during the War of 1812. His son William (LEFT) inherited his land holdings in downtown Toronto and profited from the growth of the city in the mid-1800s. He built a large house at King and Bay in 1853 and lived there until he died in 1880. The building became bank offices after his widow's death and was torn down in 1946. Henry Victor Holton Cawthra, a descendent of Joseph Cawthra, married Ada Austin Arthurs of the Austin family, owners of Spadina. And Anthony Patrick Cawthra Adamson, architectural historian and author of the The Ancestral Roof *and other books, is also a Cawthra descendant.*

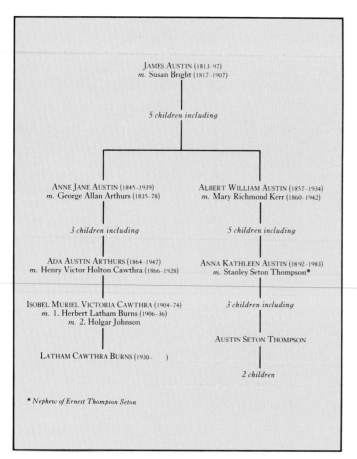

JAMES AUSTIN (1813-97)
m. Susan Bright (1817-1907)

5 children including

ANNE JANE AUSTIN (1845-1939)
m. George Allan Arthurs (1835-78)

ALBERT WILLIAM AUSTIN (1857-1934)
m. Mary Richmond Kerr (1860-1942)

3 children including

5 children including

ADA AUSTIN ARTHURS (1864-1947)
m. Henry Victor Holton Cawthra (1866-1928)

ANNA KATHLEEN AUSTIN (1892-1983)
m. Stanley Seton Thompson*

ISOBEL MURIEL VICTORIA CAWTHRA (1904-74)
m. 1. Herbert Latham Burns (1906-36)
m. 2. Holgar Johnson

3 children including

AUSTIN SETON THOMPSON

LATHAM CAWTHRA BURNS (1930-   )

2 children

* Nephew of Ernest Thompson Seton

One of the most historic houses in Toronto, Spadina was built in 1866 by James Austin on land bought from the Baldwin family, who had had a house there since 1818. James Austin (LEFT) came from County Armagh as a boy and was apprenticed to William Lyon Mackenzie to learn the printing trade. With Patrick Foy he established a prosperous wholesale grocery business and in 1871 became the first president of the Dominion Bank, a position his son Albert Austin also later occupied. Albert built the first street railway in Winnipeg but lost a lengthy legal battle to James Ross and William Mackenzie over the franchise to build an electrified system. Austin Seton Thompson's book, Spadina: A Story of Old Toronto, *tells the story of his family's house, which has been expanded several times but still contains many of the original furnishings. Nearby were built many other impressive houses, including Sir John Eaton's Ardwold, Samuel Nordheimer's Glenedyth (both demolished), and Sir Henry Pellatt's Casa Loma. Anna Kathleen Thompson lived at Spadina until 1982. The house is now owned by the City of Toronto and the Ontario Historical Society.*

Of the nine children of clergyman Featherstone Lake Osler, four were to become prominent: Featherston Lake Osler (1838-1924), a lawyer and judge; Britton Bath Osler (1839-1901), colourful criminal lawyer and member of the prosecuting council in Louis Riel's trial; Sir William Osler (1849-1919), the famous doctor; and Sir Edmund Boyd Osler (1845-1924), shown above. Sir Edmund started the brokerage house of Osler and Hammond, was a backer of the CPR, and became president of the Dominion Bank in 1901. He built a large house in Rosedale called Craigleigh, whose grounds are now a park. His son Hugh joined the Winnipeg firm of Osler, Hammond and Nanton. Oslers are still prominent in law and finance. A grandson of Sir Edmund, Gordon P. Osler, is chairman of Stanton Pipes and was head of Osler, Hammond and Nanton until it was sold in the 1960s. He married Nancy Riley of the Winnipeg Rileys. Another grandson of Sir Edmund is John Harty Osler, a justice of the Ontario Supreme Court. Campbell Revere Osler, partner in the law firm of Osler, Haskin and Harcourt, and Britton Bath and Peter Scarth Osler, partners in Blake, Cassels and Graydon, are grandsons of Britton Bath Osler.

Sir Edmund Walker, president of the Canadian Bank of Commerce, was also the first chairman of the board of trustees of the Royal Ontario Museum (1912-24) and the founder of the Champlain Society.

Sir Joseph Flavelle (1858-1939) was the last Canadian residing in this country to receive a hereditary title. He first became prominent as president of the William Davis Company, pork packers. Later he became one of the richest men in Canada and president of National Trust, chairman of the Canadian Bank of Commerce, chairman of the Grand Trunk Railway, majority owner of Simpsons, and an important governor of the University of Toronto. He had three children: Mina, Clara, and Ellsworth. Mina married Wallace Barrett and Clara married Frank McEachren (Colonel Frank McEachren is their son). Edith Flavelle, Sir Joseph's niece, married J.S. McLean.

Flavelle's house (ABOVE) on Queen's Park now houses the Law Faculty of the University of Toronto. A sign in the baronial main hall warns students, "No bicycles."

The drawing room of Sir William Mortimer Clark's house at 303 Wellington Street West. Clark was president of the Toronto Mortgage Company, a director of the Metropolitan Bank, and a lieutenant-governor of Ontario.

Inconspicuous beneath undistinguished architecture and layers of grime, the Toronto Club lurks on Wellington Street a short walk from Toronto's financial district. Founded by the Family Compact of Upper Canada in 1835 and rescued from insolvency by Bud McDougald in the 1940s, it is Toronto's wealthiest and most exclusive private club.

ABOVE: Government House at King and Simcoe streets in Toronto. This was the official residence of the lieutenant-governor of Ontario until it was demolished in 1912. BELOW: Chorley Park, the grand new chateau-style Government House built in 1916 in North Rosedale overlooking the Don Valley, was closed by the Hepburn government in 1937. It was used as a military hospital until 1956 and was demolished in 1959.

James Stanley McLean (1876-1954) joined the Harris Abattoir Company as a clerk in 1901 and rose to become, in 1927, the first president of the newly formed Canada Packers, which incorporated the Harris Abattoir and three other companies. He was president and chief executive officer until 1954.

An aerial view of the McLean estate on Bayview Avenue in Toronto. J.S. McLean bought the land in 1928 and had the house designed by Eric Arthur. McLean was an enthusiastic supporter of Canadian artists in the 1930s and 1940s and much of his collection hung on company premises. After his death the house was occupied by his wife until her death in 1967. The property is now owned by the Sunnybrook Medical Centre.

Winter Fair, they stayed at the McDougald place, attended an afternoon reception at E.P. Taylor's horse farm near Oshawa, and dined with Doris Phillips (no relation), widow of another Argus partner, Eric Phillips.

Two events, 17 years apart, signify the transformation of Old into New Toronto. The first was the unveiling, on October 28, 1966, of Henry Moore's *Archer*, purchased for the New City Hall by Phil Givens, then Toronto's feisty mayor. On that crisp, clear autumn night, 10,000 Torontonians jammed the city-hall square to cheer as trumpets fanfared, and a *feu-de-joie* marked the statue's unveiling. The other event was the publi-

cation on May 27, 1983, of a photograph in the *Toronto Star* of two middle-aged men, passing a baton one to the other in a 24-hour relay race staged as a fund-raising drive by the Royal Ontario Museum. The two men caught in mid-stride are Sydney Hermant and Eddie Goodman: that two Jews could succeed each other as chairman of the ROM's Board of Trustees without the raising of a single dissenting voice meant that the day of token appointments was over at last. (One Jew had been a previous ROM Chairman: Noah Torno, the president of Jordan Wines, from 1971 to 1974.) Hermant, who owns Imperial Optical and is the largest individual shareholder of the Canadian

The Gooderham and Worts distillery, which still stands near the foot of Parliament Street in Toronto, is shown here in a chromolithograph from the 1890s by A.H. Hider. James Worts started a mill at the mouth of the Don River in 1831 and was joined the next year by his brother-in-law William Gooderham (1790-1881), a Norfolk farmer's son who fought in the Napoleonic Wars. Worts died in 1834 and in 1837 Gooderham added a successful distillery. His nephew, James Gooderham Worts, became a partner in 1845. The Gooderham interests expanded into industry, finance, and railway building. William Gooderham was one of the founders of the Bank of Toronto and in 1865 became its president, as did his third son George, who was president of the bank from 1882 to his death in 1905.

The Gooderhams and Wortses have been mainstays of Toronto club life. The Toronto Society Blue Book of 1935 lists 18 Gooderhams: 10 were members of the Badminton and Racquet Club and there were eight in the Granite Club, 15 in the Ontario Jockey Club, 10 in the Rosedale Golf Club, 14 in the RCYC, and 11 in the Toronto Hunt Club.

Sir Albert Edward Gooderham (1861-1935), son of George Gooderham, also went into the family business. He largely funded the establishment of the Connaught Laboratories and was knighted in 1934. His uncle, William Jr., provided a lump sum of $125,000 to move Victoria University from Cobourg to Toronto, where it was federated with the University of Toronto.

Peter S. Gooderham, Toronto investment dealer, is a director of Hal Jackman's Empire Life Insurance Company and E-L Financial Corporation and chairman of its subsidiary, the Dominion of Canada General Insurance Company.

Bud McDougald with Prince Philip at the Royal Agricultural Winter Fair in 1967.

At a 1983 fund-raising drive for the Royal Ontario Museum, outgoing chairman Sydney Hermant passes the baton to successor Eddie Goodman.

Imperial Bank of Commerce, inspired what may well be the most flowery press release in Canadian journalism. In a handout about Hermant's 1978 appointment to the ROM chairmanship, an anonymous prose-merchant described young Sydney's pose in a picture of the Hart House Debates Committee of 1934-35 as follows: "Among the group were an already well-known historian, a couple of professional men, and several who would make their marks in Canada's diplomatic corps. At the right of seated future Ambassador to Germany Escott Reid and just to the left of standing future Ambassador to the Netherlands Saul Rae, sits 22-year-old Sydney Hermant. His arms, like those of the other sitting members, are akimbo. His immaculately-creased left trouser leg is balanced across his equally immaculately-creased right knee and he is facing the photographer with what, in other circles, might be called an enigmatic, Mona Lisa-style smile."

Hermant, who broke family precedent when he married a staunch Anglican named Margaret Shaw, spent five years as an effective chairman of the Royal Ontario Museum overseeing its expansion and modernization.

Eddie Goodman, his successor, is a wise fox in the ways of politics and the law, never forgoing the touch of social conscience that has distinguished him from many of his colleagues. His most astonishing coup was to obtain a divorce for John Robarts, the former Premier of Ontario, in June 1976 with so little publicity that it was not even mentioned on the court docket.

The fact that these and other telling social events hardly caused a ripple was a welcome sign of Canada's (or, at least, Toronto's) maturity. Unfortunately, materialism had replaced snobbishness, so that McKenzie Porter could write in the *Sun*, with only slight exaggeration: "It does not matter, in Toronto Society, how you earn your money—as long as you earn plenty."

Toronto society is in the process of rapid change.

Rosedale, the leafy residential enclave in central Toronto, almost went to seed with the migration to the suburbs in the 1950s but has since rebounded.

Flavelle's summer house on Sturgeon Point is occupied by civil-rights crusader Clayton Ruby; Timothy Eaton Memorial Church is presided over by a Ukrainian preacher from Whitkow, Saskatchewan; the Canadian representative attending the 26th Annual International Debutante Ball at the Waldorf-Astoria in New York was a construction company owner's daughter from Mississauga; Vincent Massey's birthplace has become one of a chain of steak-and-ale restaurants.

Rosedale has so far survived the onslaught. Named after Mary Jarvis's 1830s garden, Rosedale is still the comfortable place to live. The writer who comes closest to defining the Rosedale ethic is Scott Symons. He concludes that Rosedale

helps energize the national consciousness: "Beyond its evident limitations, its mitigated stuffiness, its snobbery is neither better nor worse than I can find any day in any CBC office. Rosedale, and all the other 'Rosedales' across the country, represent the difference between being merely housebroken, and being civilized. Canada both cherishes and loathes the 'Rosedale myth'. Yet, without it, without its quiet embodiment of decent manners and its sense of family and historical continuity, we might be merely Americans."

Much of the big money resides in Forest Hill, King City, Moore Park, and behind the tailored shrubbery up Bayview way. The most beautiful house in Forest Hill Village belongs to Jimmy Kay (who chairs Dylex, a kind of Jewish Argus Corp.).

The Fredrik Eaton house in Forest Hill was built by Sigmund Samuel, a steel merchant who was a major benefactor to the University of Toronto.

An interior and exterior view of the John Parkin house in the Bayview area.

The architect Barton Myers has designed some of the more fashionable modern houses in Toronto. His trademark style includes light airy interiors and the use of stock industrial hardware such as exposed ductwork. Shown here is the Wolfe House in Rosedale (top) and an interior view of his residence on Berryman Street.

Muskoka, 100 miles north of Toronto, has been the favourite summer place of the city's great families since the days when the trip was made by train and lake steamer. Shown above is the Seagram boathouse on North Bohemia Island. Below are the Whippet, originally owned by Ewart McLaughlin, nephew of R.S. McLaughlin, and still in the family, and (BOTTOM) a fine old day cruiser owned by actor Donald Davis.

Winston's is the favoured lunching spot of Toronto's senior money managers (when they are not at the Toronto Club). Many tables are permanently reserved and owner John Arena, shown here, zealously supervises the seating plan.

The home, which Kay has turned into an exquisitely decorated Cotswold manor house, once belonged to a son of M.J. Boylen, the mining company magnate. (Young Boylen used to sleep with a gun at his bedside. One night, when his wife was reading late, he asked her to switch off the light. She wouldn't, so he shot out the bulb. The scar is still on the wall.)

Apart from their addresses, Toronto's Establishmentarians are known by the charities they keep. In 1980, a peculiar conflict developed when four of the city's major hospitals launched simultaneous campaigns, vying among one another for Establishment funds. The Toronto General collected $12.5 million with Tom Bell, chairman of

Abitibi-Price, in charge and Fred Eaton and Alf Powis lending a hand. The Wellesley raised $9.1 million with J.W. Hamilton (lately of Imperial Oil), Ed Bovey (then of Norcen), and Galen Weston doing the honours. Meanwhile, Shirley (Mrs. Conrad) Black, Alton Cartwright (CEO of Canadian General Electric), and Jim Livingstone (then president of Imperial Oil) concentrated on the hospital's Research Institute. Duncan Lockhart Gordon (Walter's brother) handled most of the charity chores for the Hospital for Sick Children.

The Toronto Establishment has its own medical consultants (Drs. Robert A. Clappison and Jim Paupst); portrait painters (Cleeve Horne and Pietro Annigoni); architects (John C. Parkin and

Ed Ziedler); dress designers (Maggy Reeves, Winston Kong, and anything Eddie Creed imports into his emporium); corporate lawyers (Howard Leighton Beck and Douglas Laidlaw); decorators (The Art Shoppe and Robert Dirstein); money managers (Tim Martin and Chuck Loewen); lunching spots (the Toronto Club and Winston's*); spas (Maine Chance in Phoenix, Arizona, and The Greenhouse in Arlington, Texas); favourite politicians (John Turner and Bill Davis); most-sought-after real-estate agents (Sis Weld, Mary Gordon, and Cecil Hedstrom—all of Johnston & Daniel); and gaming tables (elegant evenings at Larry Heisey's house on Highland Avenue).

A very special lady within the Toronto—and Canadian—Establishment's universe is Zena Cherry, the *Globe and Mail* columnist who chronicles its daily doings and undoings. What makes her column that newspaper's most avidly followed feature is not just that she is the only journalist invited to the social events that really count, but that she has a sixth sense about who is moving up and who is fading from contention. She lives a private life in a Forest Hill Village house filled with a collection of clown models from all over the world. The daughter of a society doctor and brought up in a private school, she is tactful and discreet, and, as one fellow journalist noted, has an "information-retrieval system that IBM itself would envy."

THEY ARE THE PRODUCT of good nutrition, good schools, good camps. Their cheeks glow from eating cream with their cereal. But instead of being like their mothers—who still keep neurotic Lhasa Apsos or Labs, shy away from real work,

Karen Kain in her wedding dress designed by Maggy Reeves for her marriage to actor Ross Petty in 1983.

and always remove their earrings before answering the phone—the new breed of Toronto society women is energetic, gregarious, ambitious, and tough. They may not all "go to business," but those who do—whether in volunteer or paid labour—are incomparably more vibrant than hostesses of the past. Once-dominant organizations such as the Junior League have trouble attracting members.

One mark of acceptance is being known by your first name alone. Any connoisseur of the breed knows that "Dibs" is Mrs. J.A. Rhind; "Mary-O" is Mrs. Richard Rohmer; "Nicki" is either one of

The glory of Winston's never seems to dim. It is the place, like Elaine's in New York, "where public people go to be private in public." But many other restaurants qualify as acceptable meeting spots. Senator Keith Davey likes to entertain at the Inn on the Park's Vintage Room and claims that he carried its waiters for the Liberals during the 1979 election.

Norman Elder, the Establishment's enfant terrible, is shown with artifacts from his many expeditions to the Amazon and New Guinea. His great-grandfather came to Canada from Scotland and established a business in Toronto making delivery wagons and elegant carriages. The Elders today are a well-known equestrian family: Robert Elder (Norman's father) was master of foxhounds at the Toronto and North York Hunt and his brother Jim is on the Canadian Equestrian Team. Norman himself has competed at the Pan-American Games (1967) and was captain of the Three-Day Event Team at the 1968 Olympics in Mexico.

OPPOSITE: Known for her zest and fast-paced lifestyle, Catherine Leggett is one of Toronto's premier hostesses.

two Mrs. Eatons; "Liz" is Mrs. John A. Tory; "Mary" is Mrs. Don Early; "Sharon" is Mrs. T.K. Zuckerman; "Trudy" is Mrs. Tom Bell; "Posie" is Rosemary Chisholm; "Sis" is Harriet Bunting Weld; "Sonja" is Mrs. Tom Bata; and "Catherine" is Mrs. Stephen Leggett.

The Toronto social "set" is not the closed club it once was, but its current leaders include: Sarah Band; Susan Bassett (Doug's wife); Sonja Bata; Shirley Black; Patty Anne Burns; Mona Campbell; Colleen Carmichael; Mary Carr-Harris; Susan Cohon; Marlene (Elia) Del Zotto; Honor de Pencier; Anna Maria de Souza; Sherry Fell; Pat Gray; Kitty Griffin; Catherine Leggett (who also sells

anti-mine equipment for warships around the free world); Peg Mara; Phyllis Matthews; Elizabeth McClelland; Julie Medland; Melanie Munk; Nancy Osler; Helen Phelan; Nancy Phillips; Anna Porter; Loretta Rogers; Heather Thomson; Geills Turner; Ina Weldon; Hilary Weston; and Ivy Willmot. Liz Tory, whose husband masterminds the exponential growth of the Thomson empire, is probably the most sought-after social animator, partly because she is so well organized (serving on a dozen key committees as well as running her own company, Tudor Travel) but mainly because she has an instinct for how group effort can best be meshed into meaningful results.

Zena Cherry, photographed at her Forest Hill house.

Then there is the Rosedale Golf Club Eightsome: Don and Mary Early; Tom and Joyce Mulock; Chuck and Rosemary Rathgeb; and Pauline and Zoltan Tariczky. Rosemary is a Clarke, Pauline is a Just, Joyce is a Morton, and Mary is the heiress to the McColl oil fortune. They go everywhere and do everything together.

IF TORONTO SOCIETY HAS a royal family, it is the Eatons; the monarch is Signy Hildur (Stephenson), widow of John David Eaton. Her family (and it is almost as good to be an Eaton by marriage as an Eaton by birth) is unusually close: Fred and "Nicki" (the daughter of D'Arcy Argue Counsell Martin of Hamilton); John Craig and "Sherry" (the daughter of John Howard Taylor of Toronto); Thor and "Nicki" (the daughter of Jacques Courtois of Montreal); and George and "Terry" (the daughter of T.K. McIntosh). Even though the Eatons try to live ordinary lives, it never quite works. When Thor was attending Forest Hill Collegiate before switching to Upper Canada College, he was heard earnestly complaining that he was the only kid in his class who hadn't had a bar mitzvah.

Commodore Bruce McGowan leads the way as Prince Philip visits Mia's Red Jacket *at the Royal Canadian Yacht Club in 1983. Following the Prince are John Rothwell, vice-commodore, and the crew.*

ABOVE: The cruising schooner Zahra *was Aemilius Jarvis' flagship in 1907. Jarvis was a mainstay of the R.C.Y.C. for nearly 50 years and was described by Commodore George Gooderham as "the greatest yachtsman in the club's history."*

LEFT: The crew of Scrapper, *contender for the George Cup in 1921. Left to right: Norman Gooderham, Walter Windeyer, Arnold Massey, and Jack Townsend. For years members of the Gooderham family have been among the most numerous and active members of the club. Windeyer pioneered the use of the Marconi rig in the club and went on to sail his Dragon,* Tip, *in the Olympics and won the Dragon Gold Cup, emblematic of world Dragon supremacy.*

J.R.

*The R.C.Y.C. was founded in 1852 when, as the club's annals put it, "yachting
was a practical experimental field for naval science, and Trafalgar, only 47
years away, was an event still well within the memory of many original
members." The club received its royal charter in 1854. Its first home was a brick
house on Sir Casimir Gzowski's wharf on the site now occupied by Union
Station. Other homes included a scow, a steamer, and various clubhouses on the
mainland and Toronto Island. The present clubhouse, shown at top, was built in
1922. Shown below is the attractive yacht* Southwind *in the club's sheltered
anchorage.*

George Cuthbertson, dean of Canadian yacht designers and co-founder of C&C Yachts, chats with Shirley Crang in front of the R.C.Y.C. clubhouse.

John Craig is the most outgoing and amiable Eaton but Fred is the most impressive. In charge of the family business since 1977, he has revitalized the operation, with a 1980 net estimated at $60 million on a sales volume of $2 billion.

In Fred's office there is a needlepoint quotation from Chairman Mao: *Parasites who depend on imperialism soon find out that their bosses are not reliable. The whole situation will change when the tree falls and the monkeys scatter.* He believes firmly in the notion of perpetuating Eaton's not only as a lively and efficient enterprise, but also as a private proprietorship, repeating the old Irish proverb that "the best manure in the farmer's field is the farmer's footsteps." In the spectrum of the brothers' instincts for risk-taking, George ranks at the top and Thor at the bottom.

The company has an active board of directors but the four Eatons own all the shares and make the final decisions. Fred and George handle most of the operational chores; George is more involved in the Eaton Bay Financial Services operation while John Craig acts as family spokesman and morale booster among employees. Thor runs his own enterprises (including Grand Entertainment, which lists Nana Mouskouri among its client-

stars), races horses, and runs a farm in Florida. Fred has a house in Caledon, flies to Lyford Cay, shoots at Griffith Island and Long Point, and owns the 1950 Rolls-Royce that once belonged to Sir James Dunn; yet he spends most of his time not on the leisure those belongings suggest, but working hard to make the empire grow.

Their names decorate Toronto's more prestigious charity drives, but their scrubbed good looks appear only occasionally in the social pages. The brothers enjoy their privacy, are determined to demonstrate their business acumen, and seem to have failed at nothing except being playboys.

The ultimate test of social acceptability in Toronto is the ritualistic business of leasing one of the 40 private boxes at the Royal Agricultural Winter Fair. The contest for this privilege has little to do with either the raising or the racing of horses. "Inclusion in the list of box holders at the Royal Agricultural Winter Fair," sociologist Merrijoy Kelner has commented, "confers a social distinction which apparently makes an individual more acceptable as a business associate in the upper echelons of the financial world."

The boxes are so valuable that they become a major item in the list of perks offered the most

The Royal Agricultural Winter Fair brings together more famous faces than any other Toronto social event. The photos on these pages, from various years, were taken in the ring and at receptions in the President's Room.

Princess Anne at the "Royal" in 1979 presenting a trophy to Mark Laskin.

Signy Eaton, widow of John David Eaton, presents a scholarship.

Jim Elder on Immigrant competing in the 1960s.

ALL: COURTESY ROYAL AGRICULTURAL WINTER FAIR

SECTION	BOX	Name
34	L	Abel, Mr. Ted G.
20	B	Addison, Mr. J. Harry
22	B	Addison, Mr. John H.
12	G	Allan, Mr. Duncan M.
38	D	Andison, Mr. George N.
37	D	Angus, Mr. Ian W.M.
19	A	Anstey, Mrs. Susan Jane
19	B	Armstrong, Mr. H. Charles
30	C	Baker, Lt.-Col. Charles
14	G	Ballard, Mr. and Mrs, W.R.
12	H	Bartlett, Mr. Robert
22	N	Bassett, Mr. Douglas
40	A	Bassett, Mr. John
11	E	Bayer, Mr. and Mrs. Edward
23	B	Beeler, Mr. Byron E.
34	H	Beit von Speyer, Miss Ellin
34	A	Bennett, Mrs. Stewart G.
39	D	Bermingham, M.F.H., Mr. C. William
20	J	Bertin, Mr. and Mrs. James
12	L	Biggs, C.D., F.A.I.C., Mr. Everett
35	G	Black, Mr. G. Montegu
14	E	Boehm, Mr. George
9	B	Bolton, Mr. Thomas G.
38	D	Boyd, Mr. John A.
22	H	Boylen, Mr. James A.
2	A	Brickenden, Mrs. G.A.P.
9	J	Broome, Mrs. W.A.
5	E	Brown, Dr. J. Glen
33	C	Bulford, Mr. Michael J.
35	A	Burka, Major and Mrs. A.M.
34	C	Burns, Mr. Latham C.
39	A	Burton, Mr. C. Merrill
19	A	Burton, Mr. Edgar G.
32	A	Burton, D.S.O., E.D., LL.D., K.L.J., Lt.-Col. G. Allan
24	C	Bush, Mr. John R.
15	J	Butler, Mr. Alan C.
14	B	Cakebread, Mr. John C., Sr.
20	K	Callahan, M.D., F.R.C.S. (c.), W.P.
12	A	Campbell, Col. and Mrs. K.L.
28	A	Campbell, Mr. Peter G.
27	C	Canadian Equestrian Federation
2	D	Cardy, Mr. A. Gordon
20	A	Carpenter, Mr. Gordon S.
21	F	Carruthers, Mr. John A.
10	H	Carter, Mr. James H.
22	J	Catto, Mr. Douglas M.
15	D	Chassels, Dr. J.B.
28	D	Coad, Mr. E.H.
4	B	Cochrane, Mr. Frank
38	A	Coleman, Mr. D.C.
10	L	Colhoun, Mr. J.L.A.
15	G	Collard, Mr. Barry D.
10	D	Conron, Dr. and Mrs. A.B.
19	E	Cook, Mr. Allan A.
28	H	Cooke, Mrs. James L.
35	H	Corner, Mr. Dick
12	B	Cottrelle, Mr. J. Elliot
32	B	Crang, Mr. J. Harold
2	E	Crang, Mr. J.H., Jr.
25	D	Cross, Mr. W.B.
22	D	Crothers, Mr. Joseph P.
7	D	Cuddy, Mr. A.M.
13	B	Cudney, Mr. Douglas J.
6	B	Curtis, C.D. Lt.-Col. Wilfred A.
34	D	Dale-Harris, D.S.O., Mr. Robert B.
11	C	Daniel, Mr. C. William
29	H	Darling, Mr. and Mrs. A.J.
28	K	Darrach, Mr. N.C.
32	K	Davidson, Mr. W.P.
3	D	Devlin, Mr. John H.
20	C	Dillingham, Mrs. F.H.
29	J	Dolson, Mrs. Frank
20	G	Douglas, C.D., Major C.R.
13	G	Dow, Mr. and Mrs. J. Carl
30	K	Drew, Mrs. George A.
15	A	Dunlap, Mr. Moffat
22	G	Dunn, Mr. Vincent P.
22	O	Dunton, Mr. D.S.
32	D	Eaton, Mr. A.Y.
32	C	Eaton, Mr. John C.
4	D	Edwards, Mr. C.F.
30	E	Ehrlick, Mr. Allan H.L.
15	C	Elder, Mrs. Robert
20	M	Elder, Mr. R. James
37	B	Emery, Mr. and Mrs. John
20	E	Evely, Mr. and Mrs. Neville
4	C	Faloney, M.F.H., Mr. B.J.
31	A	Fell, Mr. Anthony S.
9	C	Fennell, Mr. and Mrs. Scott
15	E	Ferguson, Mr. and Mrs. J. Cecil
13	J	Ferguson, Mrs. W.B.
14	K	Firestone, Mr. D. Morgan
1	B	Foster, Mr. Harry E.
14	D	Fowler, Mr. and Mrs. E.J.
22	O	Fraser, Mr. James D.
20	H	Freeman, Dr. M.G.
30	L	Gairdner, Mr. James R.
5	A	Gairdner, Mr. and Mrs. J.S.
30	J	Gardhouse, Mr. Reford W.
15	H	Gayford, Major Gordon and Mr. Thomas F.
21	E	Governor General's Horse Guard
10	K	Graham, Mr. and Mrs. Preston
8	G	Grant, Mr. J.C.
2	B	Gray, Mr. Gordon C.
24	A	Gray, Mr. W. Keith
14	L	Green, Miss Adrienne
33	J	Greenspan, Mr. Harry
9	H	Gregg, Dr. W.A.M.
28	E	Gregory, Mr. John R.
30	G	Hamilton, Martha
23	C	Hargrave, Mr. Donald
6	A	Harris, Mr. Peter D.G.
12	E	Harris, Mr. William A.
40	B	Harris, Mr. W.B.
8	A	Hawkes, Mr. R.H.
10	F	Hays, Mr. Thomas E.
37	C	Hazledine, Mr. M.V.
20	F	Heggie, Mr. W.L.
13	H	Heintzman, Mr. John
17	C	Hellyer, Mr. Walter C.
9	D	Henry, Mr. William D.
18	C	Herbinson, Mr. Brian A.
27	F	Hermant, Mr. Sydney
22	B	Hogarth, Mrs. Ann
28	J	Holbrook, Dr. and Mrs. J.G.
5	C	Humphries, Mrs. W.R.B.
32	D	Hunter, Mrs. Donald F.
7	F	Hunter, C.D., Lt.-Col. Peter W.
24	C	Jackson, Mr. Thomas
14	F	Jacobsen, Dr. and Mrs. George
13	E	Jarvis, Mrs. Æmilius
35	E	Johnston, C.D., Q.C., Lt.-Col. J.I.
35	D	Kee, Mr. Charles A.
22	A	Ker, Mr. David S.I.
14	H	Kerr, Mr. James W.
38	C	Kerr, Mr. James W.
7	C	Kierulf, Mrs. Andrea
30	G	Klinger, Elizabeth
8	E	Kneeland, Mr. R. Joseph
7	J	Knight, Mr. Harold A.
8	L	Knowlton, Mr. Austin E.
10	J	Lange-Mechlen, Mr. R.M.
23	J	Larry, Mr. and Mrs. L.J.
13	F	Leckie, Mrs. Arthur E.
29	F	Lederer, Mr. Derek J.M.
7	A	Leitch, Mr. John D.
11	B	Long, Mr. Robert
20	O	MacDonald, Mr. Hugh T.
8	C	MacDougall, Mr. Hartland M.
18	A	Macintosh, Mr. Ian A.
13	D	Mackay, Mr. Allan O.
27	E	MacLaren, Mr. and Mrs. Donald
10	D	Mann, Major General and Mrs. C.C.
28	H	Marran, Mr. Robert C.
28	C	Matthews, Mr. Paul W.
33	H	Medland, Mr. C.E.
23	E	Menzies, Mrs. Brenda Northey
18	D	Millard, Mr. Paul
18	C	Morison, Mr. R.D.
8	H	Morold, Mr. and Mrs. Karl
34	G	Morrow, Mr. Graham
7	G	Moses, Mr. Allan R.
7	B	Murdoch, Mr. John W.
7	H	Murray, Mr. Ralph R.
28	L	McCague, Mr. J. Brian
27	B	McCarthy, Mr. John L.
36	A	McClelland, Mr. John A.
33	F	McCurdy, Mr. H.T.
33	B	McCutcheon, Q.C., Mr. James W.
30	B	McDougald, Mrs. John A.
32	G	McEachren, C.V.O., C.M., E.D., C.D., Col. Frank F.
11	A	McInnes, Mr. S. Roderick
40	D	McKee, Mrs. C.S.
51	B	McKee, Mr. John Angus
5		McLaughlin, Mr. and Mrs. R. Bruce
32	J	McLaughlin, Mr. S.B.
13	C	McLean, Mr. H.A.
8	M	McLean, Mr. W.F.
26	B	New, Mr. C. John
22	C	Newman, Mrs. George D.
26	A	Newman, M.P.P., Mr. William G.
9	G	The Niagara Parks Commission
21	H	Offen, D.C., Mr. Thomas R.
21	C	Ormston, D.F.C., Mr. Ian C.
5	D	Osler, Mr. Gordon P.
7	E	Pabst, Mr. and Mrs. B.V.
12	F	Pady, Mr. Walter J.
1	C	Page, Mr. Donald H.
26	C	Pallett, C.D., Major D.W.
21	B	Palmer, Mr. Douglas
8	F	Patterson, Mr. C.F.
40	C	Pearce, Mr. W.E.
9	E	Pemberton, Mr. J.D.
27	G	Perry, Mr. John H.
22	M	Phillips, Mr. K.B.
14	L	Pirie, Mr. and Mrs. R.S.
8	F	Pitfield, Mr. Ward C.
34	G	Plaxton, Mr. W.J.
4	A	Potter, Mrs. N.F.
33	G	Powell, Mr. and Mrs. Lambert Clay
35	C	Ramsey, Rudy and Suzanne
27	H	Regan, Q.C., Mr. F. Vincent
20	D	Renz, Mr. Hansjörg
11	D	Richardson, Mr. George T.
35	F	Richardson, C.A., Mr. John D.
12	C	Richardson, Mr. Malcolm D.
30	H	Rigby, Mr. John B.H.
34	B	Ritchie, Mr. C.E.
9	A	Ritchie, Mr. William
12	D	Roberts, Mr. E.J.
11	F	Robinson, Mr. and Mrs. James K.
34	E	Rodanz, Mr. George
32	L	Rogers, Mr. Guy W.
36	B	Roman, Mr. Stephen B.
28	G	Rough, Mr. R.H.
34	J	Rowe, P.C., LL.D., Hon. W. Earl
23	D	Rowell, Mr. Bradley R.
27	J	Rumble, Mrs. George
24	B	Rumble, Mr. Robert J.
8	J	Russell, Q.C., Mr. Gordon A.
29	C	Russell, Mrs. W.J.
25	B	Rutherford, M.B.E., C.D., Col. The Hon. Mr. Justice R.C.
23	A	Ryan, Mrs. Frank
28	F	Samuel, Mr. Ernest L.
32	H	Savage, Mrs. Laurence M.
33	D	Schickedanz, Mr. Gustav L.
20	N	Schury, Mr. Rudolph
22	E	Scott, Mr. and Mrs. L.C.
39	B	Scripps, Davis, Mrs. Ellen
14	A	Seabrook, Mr. John M.
37	E	Semler, Mr. John H.
29	G	Sheppard, Mrs. G. Harry
25	C	Sifton, Mrs. June M.
13	A	Sifton, C.D., M.F.H., Col. Michael C.
14	L	Simpson, Mr. J.L.
17	A	Sinnett-Place, Mrs. Claribel. M.
8	K	Sissons, Mrs. Caroline J.
29	D	Smith, Mr. Stephen C.
5	D	Sonshine, Mr. David
50	D	Spence, L.M.C.C.(Ed.), Dr. Magnus
12	J	Sproat, Mr. William John
8	F	Stewart, Mr. William A.
10	A	Stoik, Mr. John L.
17	B	Stoker, Mr. Desmond N.
18	D	Stone, Mr. Melvin
9	F	Stone, Mr. Michael
29	E	Thackray, Mr. J.C.
29	A	Thomson, Mr. Richard M.
12	K	Thomson, Mr. William E.
34	K	Thornbrough, Mr. Albert A.
20	L	Timmins, Mr. Gerald L.
3	D	Tory, Q.C., Mr. John A.
32	E	Toyne, Mr. William E.
8	D	Trollope, M.F.H., Mr. R.W.
35	F	Upjohn, Mrs. Marion
39	C	Vanderplaats, Mr. Tjerk-H.W.
21	D	Van de Water, Mr. George A.
3	A	Wadsworth, Mr. J.P.R.
22	F	Wakefield, Mrs. R.W.
30	A	Wallace, D.S.O., M.C., Brigadier F.C.
33	E	Warren, O.B.E., Mr. Trumbull
22	L	Weaver, Mr. and Mrs. Robert
30	F	Weld, Mrs. Harriet Bunting
29	B	Weldon, Mr. David B.
33	A	Weston, Mr. and Mrs. W. Galen
24	D	Whitaker, D.S.O., E.D., Brigadier W.D.
2	B	White, Mr. Evan W.
12	C	Wigle, Mr. Douglas H.
32	F	Wilder, Mr. W.P.
6	C	Wilkins, Mr. Donald J.
14	J	Wilson, Mrs. Gillian
35	J	Willson, Mr. W.F.
39	C	Wooley, Q.C., Mr. Douglas C.
21	A	Winter, Mr. John R.
15	B	Wood, Mr. and Mrs. N. Peter
33	C	Worsley, Mr. John A.
17	E	Woytowich, Mr. and Mrs. George
1	A	Wright, Mr. and Mrs. Charles C.
14	C	Young, Mrs. Susanne

Mrs. Eric Phillips presenting a trophy.

Russell Harrison with Sheila Rice

Michael Sifton.

Sherry Eaton, wife of John Craig Eaton, presenting a ribbon.

Prince Michael of Kent (LEFT) with H.A. McLean and Galen Weston.

John Eaton and friend.

Ken Thomson with Mrs. G. Allan Burton (Betty Kennedy) and Pauline McGibbon.

ALL: NORM SCUDELLARI

95

(TOP LEFT) Conrad Black at the Royal in 1979.

Ted Burton with his wife and his son Gregory, then a second lieutenant in the Queen's Own Rifles, now serving in Northern Ireland with the 1st Battalion, Light Infantry, in the British Army.

(RIGHT) The G. Allan Burtons, 1982.

(LEFT) Ken Taylor and Mrs. John H. Devlin at the Fair in 1980.

ALL: NORM SCUDELLARI

senior of corporate executives, including bank chairmen. They are passed on from one generation to the next. At the close of the 1979 season, for example, Henry Borden turned Box 4A over to his daughter, Mrs. Norris Frank Potter of King City, Ontario. Box locations are all-important. That same year, Galen Weston made the move from 36A to 8A, while Ted Medland, head of Wood Gundy, inherited 35B from his predecessor, the late Charles L. Gundy.

For eight nights every November since 1922, they have crowded into the Royal in their finery, the men in their hunting pinks hung with medals, their ladies in long gowns, stoles, and diamond tiaras, to watch the horses go through their paces. There are many events, but the highlight is the jumping. (A snooty British major-general once described the origin of horse jumping as "a means of keeping our NCOs amused while we played polo.") Most Winter Fairs are graced by the pres-

D.G. (Bud) Willmot with Steady Growth, the horse that won the 1979 Queen's Plate, at his Kinghaven Farm.

ence of a sprinkling of British dukes, marquesses, earls, viscounts, barons, baronets, and knights who act as judges or decoration or both.

Beyond the socialites who swarm to the Fair, there is a group of genuine equestrians—a British-oriented leisure class whose adherents seem to spend half their lives on the backs of horses and the other half talking about it. The best-equipped and most professional operation in the country is Spruce Meadows in Calgary, which belongs to Ron and Marg Southern. But breeding farms like Jack Leitch's Leitchcroft, the Burns family's homestead at Kingfield, Bud Baker's Northcliffe Farms, the late Conn Smythe's and George Gardiner's Caledon properties, Harold Crang's Glenville Farms at Newmarket, and the Jokers Hill acreage owned by Murray Koffler enjoy more social prestige. One of the most sought-after invitations is to the Kinghaven spread at King City, Ontario, that D.G. Willmot purchased from the late J.S.D. Tory. Bud and Ivy Willmot bred Steady Growth, the thoroughbred that won the 1979 Queen's Plate; the Willmot navy-blue and white racing colours have been carried by an imposing array of other winners. That's quite an achievement for a boy who put himself through university, carrying his lunch to lectures, while his mother took in boarders to help foot the tuition fees.

The largest and most profitable horse-breeding enterprise is E.P. Taylor's Windfields Farms, now run largely out of Maryland by his son, Charles. The senior Taylor first became interested in breeding horses when he set up a small racing stable in 1935 with Jim Cosgrave. Mona Bell, one of his yearlings, placed second in the 1938 King's Plate; Taylor tried to win first place for the next eleven years and finally succeeded with Epic in 1949. During the next decade, eight Taylor-bred horses captured the same honour, five under his own silks. Taylor is, in fact, one of the most successful horse breeders in the world; Northern Dancer, a bay colt born in 1961, went on to win 14 of his 18 starts, including the 1964 Kentucky Derby and the Preakness—and has become the racing world's most successful stud. In 1983, a Northern Dancer colt brought $10.2 million at the Keeneland Yearling sale in Lexington, Kentucky.

E.P. Taylor with Northern Dancer and jockey Bill Hartack in the winner's circle at the 1964 Kentucky Derby. Northern Dancer, the first Canadian-bred horse to win this race, now stands at Windfield Farms in Maryland and is the world's most profitable stud.

The Queen's Plate (or King's Plate), North America's longest-running stakes race, was given royal sanction by Queen Victoria in 1859. First run in 1860, the race was restricted to Ontario horses until 1944. Royalty have attended often, the first being Princess Louise, daughter of Queen Victoria and wife of the governor general, the Marquis of Lorne. Queen Elizabeth and Prince Philip came to the 100th running, but the most frequent royal visitor has been the Queen Mother. In 1939 she and her husband, King George VI, were the first monarchs to attend (shown below) and she has come five times since; her most recent visit was in 1981.

The Seagram stable holds the record for the most wins—20 between 1890 and 1935. Since then, horses owned or bred by E.P. Taylor have dominated the Plate. Owners and senior Jockey Club officials wear morning suits and grey toppers and no woman's outfit is complete without a resplendent hat. The photographs below show Mrs. R. B. Dale-Harris in conversation with a jockey and Malcolm Richardson.

NANCY HALPIN

NANCY HALPIN

NANCY HALPIN

NANCY HALPIN

Royalty, or their representatives, are traditionally driven to the Royal Box (ABOVE) in a landau escorted by the Governor General's Horse Guards. On the left is Lieutenant-Governor John Black Aird with the winning jockey of the 1983 Queen's Plate. The trophy itself is not a plate but a gold cup standing one foot high, topped with a gold beaver.

A meet of the Toronto and North York Hunt in the late 1930s at Eaton Hall farm, the Eatons' King Township estate. Left to right: Mrs. Aemilius Jarvis, Miss Joan Tailyour, Mrs. Timothy Eaton, Miss Margaret Eaton, Tom J. Macabe, Harrison Gilmour, William Levett (the huntsman) in the foreground, the whipper in, unidentified, Miss Phyllis Rawlinson, Robert Brown, H.R. Tudhope, unidentified, Aemilius Jarvis (Master of the Hunt), Robert Elder, Malcolm Richardson, Harold Crang, Robert Hollingsworth (whipper in).

The equestrian set finds every excuse to mix with British royalty. Even though few of England's sporting types are aware of it, Maude ("Jim") McDougald still owns Kingsclere, quietly acquired by her husband, the late Bud McDougald, in 1976. In the historic Hampshire stables' 85 boxes, the McDougald thoroughbreds share space with mounts belonging to the Queen, Paul Mellon, and Colonel Julian Berry, one of the United Kingdom's best-known racers. Eight Derby winners trained at Kingsclere. Its magnificent Park House overlooks a dozen cottages, a well used covered ride and 200 acres of downland gallops on which the McDougald horses (identified by their French-grey and cerise racing colours) can be worked any distance up to two miles.

Meanwhile, back at the ranch, tradition is hale. The Toronto and North York is the city's most prestigious hunt club, dating back to 1843 when British garrison officers first brought over some foxhounds. The club's listing of past Masters of the Hunt comprises a history of the Toronto elite: George Gooderham, James Worts, George Beardmore (whose tenure lasted from 1893 to 1931), D.L. McCarthy, Alfred Rogers, Timothy Eaton, Aemilius Jarvis, Lady Eaton, Clifford Sifton, Robert Elder, Michael Sifton, John Elder, Walter Pady, W.P. Rogers, J. Harold Crang, Jack Leitch, and Murray Koffler. It isn't Hampshire, but that's probably a blessing.

The hounds of the Toronto and North York Hunt in front of Lady Eaton's house on her King estate. Hunting on the property ceased when it was taken over by Seneca College in the early 1970s.

The Toronto and North York Hunt is shown leaving Harold Crang's Glenville Farm in 1957. The huntsman is Mr. Pickford.

BELOW: The Eglinton and Caledon Hunt in action. G. Allan Burton was master of the foxhounds for 23 years. The present MFH is Major Charles Kindersley.

J.R.

The International Polo Series for Charity at the Gormley Polo Centre is held in conjunction with the Toronto Polo Club. Polo is fast, thrilling, and competitive, and the Toronto Polo Club (founded in 1960) is committed to the expansion and development of the game.

J.R.

Presentation of the Rolex Challenge Cup to the winning Toronto team. During the 1983 series teams from Ada, Michigan, Skaneateles, N.Y., Milwaukee, and Chicago competed in this annual charity event. Clifford Sifton was a member of the Toronto team and the Sifton family has done much to further interest in the sport.

Cedric Ritchie, chairman of the Bank of Nova Scotia.

Richard Thomson, chairman of the Toronto-Dominion Bank.

THE WHEELS GO ROUND, and somehow Toronto always ends up in the middle. Even though Canada is becoming politically more and more decentralized, it is being drawn economically ever more tightly within one orbit. Toronto is the only Canadian city where members of the local business Establishment almost automatically qualify for cross-country status. Nearly three-quarters of the certified members of Canada's national business Establishment live in the Toronto commutershed. They can be divided into five main categories: the money men, the corporate men, the professional directors, the media moguls, and the lawyers.

The Money Men. About $1.5 billion in various forms changes hands during the average Toronto working day. Many handle the complex details behind these transactions, but fewer than two dozen make the most important decisions about who is going to get how much money and on what terms. The list is headed (as any Canadian list that sets out the priorities of financial realities must be) by the bankers: Dick Thomson and Robin

Korthals at the Toronto-Dominion; Ced Ritchie and Gordon Bell at the Bank of Nova Scotia; Russ Harrison and Don Fullerton at the Commerce; Bill Mulholland, Bill Bradford, and Hartland Mac-Dougall at the Bank of Montreal; and Allan Taylor and R.G.P. Styles at the Royal.

The most spectacular of the investment dealers is Jimmy Connacher of Gordon Securities, which since 1981 has been responsible for 9 per cent of the total dollar volume on the Toronto Stock Exchange. An outsider whose firm is on the inside in many of the big block trades, the hard-driving Connacher won't talk to reporters and has threatened to fire any of his staff who discuss office business with the press, *Canadian Business* reported in 1983.

Gordon handles the million-share deals and spurns the retail client who buys or sells in small quantities. On September 1 this year, it jumped in size by merging with R.A. Daly & Co. to become R.A. Daly, Gordon Securities Inc. It's more like an aggressive Wall Street operation than its old-

William Dimma (president) and Gordon Gray (chairman) of A.E. LePage, the dominant real-estate company that has carried out land assemblies for some of the largest downtown developments in Toronto.

line Canadian counterparts and has been pushing itself into the underwriting field. On the basis of capital invested in the business, the merged company ranks fourth among Canadian dealers, after Dominion Securities Ames, Wood Gundy and Richardson Greenshields.

The most influential among the investment dealers are still, however, the heads of the established firms: Latham Burns, Jack Lawrence, and Peter Eby at Burns Fry, Ted Medland at Wood Gundy, Ward Pitfield at Pitfield Mackay Ross, Tony Fell at DSA, David Weldon at Midland Doherty, Brian Steck at Nesbitt Thomson, Austin Taylor at McLeod Young Weir, Chuck Loewen at Loewen Ondaatje and Frank Lamont at Richardson Greenshields. Other major financial groups are centred on Hal Jackman's Empire Life collection of companies (Victoria & Grey Trustco, E-L Financial Corp.); Canadian General Securities (Guaranty Trust, Traders Group), headed by

the brothers James and Fred McCutcheon and Alan Marchment; Canadian General Investments, run by Max Meighen and Alex Barron; Norman Short and Gurston Rosenfeld of the Guardian Group; and Andy Sarlos and Barry Zukerman of HCI Holdings.

The Corporate Men. What differentiates this highly influential platoon of chairmen and presidents from other executives is that, through the multitude of seats they hold on other boards, their influence is felt far beyond the confines of their own corporations. Among the most important are Don McIvor (Imperial Oil), Charles Baird (Inco), Peter Gordon (Stelco), Jack Leitch (Upper Lakes Shipping), Conrad and Montegu Black (Argus), John Stoik (Gulf Canada), Don McGiverin (Hudson's Bay Co.), Gordon Gray and Bill Dimma (A.E. LePage), Bill McLean (Canada Packers), Trevor Eyton (Brascan Ltd.), Dean Muncaster (Canadian Tire), Alf Powis and Adam

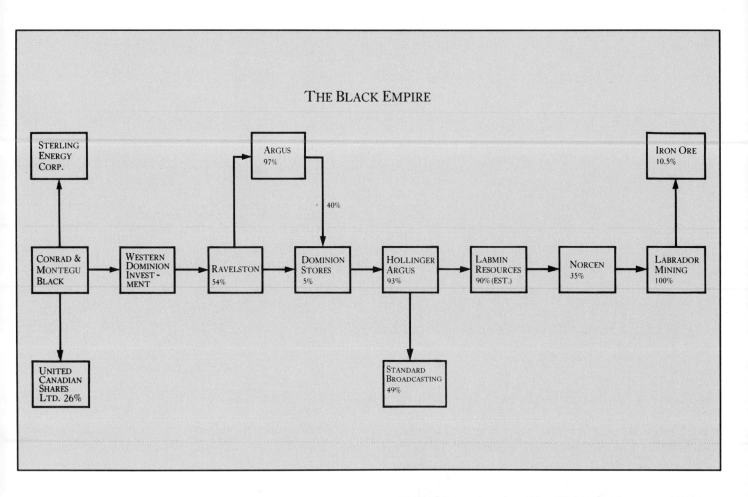

THE BLACK EMPIRE

| STERLING ENERGY CORP. | | | ARGUS 97% | | | | | | IRON ORE 10.5% |

| CONRAD & MONTEGU BLACK | WESTERN DOMINION INVESTMENT | RAVELSTON 54% | DOMINION STORES 5% | HOLLINGER ARGUS 93% | LABMIN RESOURCES 90% (EST.) | NORCEN 35% | LABRADOR MINING 100% |

40%

UNITED CANADIAN SHARES LTD. 26%

STANDARD BROADCASTING 49%

Argus Corp. was formed in 1945 when the four principal shareholders, M. Wallace McCutcheon, E.P. Taylor, Bud McDougald, and Eric Phillips, pooled their holdings and went in search of acquisitions. E.P. Taylor initially held the controlling interest in exchange for folding in his stock in Canadian Breweries, the brewing giant he had put together in the 1930s. The principal holdings through the 1950s were B.C. Forest Products, Dominion Stores, Domtar, Hollinger Mines, Massey-Ferguson, Standard Broadcasting (CFRB in Toronto and CJAD in Montreal), and Canadian breweries (sold to Rothmans in 1968). Under the founding group, the Argus policy was to acquire controlling but not necessarily majority interest in its investments. Under Conrad Black and his brother Montegu, who after the death of Bud McDougald captured control of Ravelston Corp. (the holding company that controls Argus), the Argus holdings have undergone a series of complex reorganizations to transform them from a portfolio of investments into a more tightly knit operating company. Argus relinquished its shares in Massey-Ferguson to the troubled company's pension fund in 1980. The chart shows the present organization and includes the Black brothers' other major holdings.

G. Montegu Black, president of Argus Corp., with E.P. Taylor at the Massey-Ferguson annual meeting, 1980.

The Challenger 600 operated by Sugra (Argus spelled backwards), the aircraft holding company of Argus, for Conrad Black. Sugra also operates a Challenger, registered C-GCIB, for the Canadian Imperial Bank of Commerce.

Conrad Black (BELOW) is chairman of Argus Corp. His father, George Montegu Black, Jr., was an Argus partner and the man who turned Canadian Breweries into a profitable operation for E.P. Taylor. George Montegu Black, Sr., owned Western Breweries of Winnipeg, one of the companies incorporated into Canadian Breweries.

The Argus headquarters at 10 Toronto Street in Toronto was built in 1853 as a post office and was later the Toronto branch of the Bank of Canada. It was refurbished by E.P. Taylor in 1958 (and by Conrad Black in 1980) in the style of a British merchant bank.

Zimmerman (Noranda), Charles Rathgeb (Comstock International), Galen Weston (Weston's), Cliff Hatch and Bill Wilder (Hiram Walker Resources), and Ray Wolfe (Oshawa Group).

The Professional Directors. Rather than being tied to any one large corporation, they move from boardroom to boardroom, offering advice and collecting their director's fees. The most influential among them are Ed Bovey (the country's best fund-raiser and all-round splendid fellow), John Coleman (former deputy chairman of the Royal Bank), John Godfrey (senator, lawyer, and Liberal fund-raiser), W.B. Harris (chairman of Barclays Bank of Canada), Alex MacIntosh (lawyer and corporate mandarin), Beverley Matthews and D.A. McIntosh (lawyers), Allen Lambert (former T-D chairman), William Twaits (former chairman of Imperial Oil), James and John Tory (twin lawyers and corporate directors), A.J. "Pete" Little (former partner in Clarkson Gordon) and George Mara (entrepreneur and Jannock chairman).

The Media Moguls. Among those who run the nation's main communications outlets are John and Doug Bassett (Baton Broadcasting), Donald Campbell and Fred Metcalf (Maclean Hunter), Murray Chercover (CTV), St. Clair Balfour and Gordon Fisher (Southam), Beland Honderich (*Toronto Star*, Harlequin Enterprises), Roy Megarry (*Globe and Mail*), Doug Creighton (*Toronto Sun*), Ken Thomson and John Tory (Thomson Newspapers), Bill Armstrong and Peter Herrndorf (CBC-TV), Ted Rogers (cable TV), Michael de Pencier (magazines), Michael Sifton (publishing and polo), and Allan Waters (CHUM).

Other notables of the Toronto business scene are Conrad Black, Michael Koerner (international investment), John Carmichael (equipment leasing), George Cohon (hamburgers), Peter Allen (Little Long Lac group of mining companies), John C.L. Allen (mining investments, father of Peter), Don McCarthy (food products), Jim Coutts

(politics), Irving Gerstein (Peoples Jewellers), Ron Barbaro (partner in Win-Bar Insurance Agencies), Bill Bremner (chairman, Vickers and Benson), Kenneth McGowen (joint founder of Mac's Milk), Steve Stavro (president, Knob Hill Farms), J.J. Barnicke (realtor), Jamie Gairdner (realtor, Johnston & Daniel), David S. Beatty (financial consultant), D.S. Anderson (corporate director), Ken Andras (stockbroker), Chris Barron and Peter Harris (stockbrokers, Cassels Blaikie), Jack Barrow (corporate director), David Barr (Moore Corp.), Ralph Barford (chairman, GSW Inc.), Major-General Bruce Matthews (corporate director), Tom Galt (chairman, Sun Life), Val Stock (Canada Packers), John Aird (lieutenant-governor), Edmond Odette (Eastern Construction), Jack Stodgell (stockbroker), R.A. Bandeen (Crown Life), V.K. Mason (Construction), R.A. Bird (construction), J.J. Robinette (advocate), C. William Daniel (Shell Canada), J.C. Thackray (Bell Canada), R.C. Scrivener (corporate director), Lionel Schipper (Schipper Enterprises), D'Alton Sinclair (financial consultant), and J.M. Bankes (corporate director).

The Lawyers. The platoons of lawyers active in advising their corporate clients on tax matters and litigation include Allan Beattie, Jake Howard, John Finlay, Allan Findlay, Purdy Crawford, Fraser Fell (who recently deserted the lawyers' ranks to become chairman of Dome Mines), Blair MacAulay, Bill Macdonald, Don Macdonald, Harry Macdonell, Bill Somerville, Richard C. Meech, Garnet Pink, Howard Beck, Doug Laidlaw, the brothers F.A.M. and Edward Huycke, John DesBrisay, Alan Lenczner, Bob Stevens, Rudy Bratty, George Tamaki (who's moved from the Stikeman Elliott office in Montreal to its counterpart in Toronto), J.G. Torrance, Robert Sutherland, Harry Sutherland, Hon. John Turner, J. Chisholm Lyons, Donald Pringle, J.D. Stevenson, Norman Robertson, Donald Wright, Donald Carr, John Bassel, Lou Guolla, Donald Guthrie, Robert Kingston, Ardagh

Kingsmill, N.M. Simpson, Robert Law, and Percy Finlay, who is still active despite his octogenarian status.

Several important investment houses disappeared as independent entities in the 1981-82 crunch, including Greenshields and A.E. Ames, but other groups of moneymen consolidated their positions. They included Arachnae (Fred McCutcheon), Canavest (George Vilim), Connor, Clark (John Clark), First Marathon (Larry Bloomberg), Guardian Group (Norman Short, Gurston Rosenfeld), McCarthy Securities (Leighton McCarthy), Pope & Co. (Joe Pope), Friedberg Mercantile Group (Albert Friedberg), AGF Management (Allan Manford, Warren Goldring), Beutel, Goodman (Austin Beutel, N.E. Goodman, Seymour Schulich), Mackenzie Financial (Alexander Christ), F.W. Thompson Co. Ltd. (Fred Thompson), Bolton Tremblay Funds (David Scott), and Trimark Investment Management (Arthur Labatt, Bob Krembil, Michael Axford).

The most mesmerizing man on Bay Street is still Andy Sarlos, the former Hungarian freedom fighter who made $40 million, lost it, made most of it back—and did it all with a flair that hypnotized his peers. His trades have accounted for at least 10 per cent of the TSE's volume, and his every move became the stuff of rumour and legend. In the spring of 1983 he survived a heart attack and came back to claim his share of the market's values and prognostications.

The Exchange itself moved into new quarters, robbing Canadian capitalism of the symbol of its power. Throughout modern Canadian history, farmers, Social Crediters, prospectors, and hard-shell Baptists have condemned "Bay Street" as a synonym for greed, while its defenders have praised it as the mecca of Canada's free-enterprise system. But Bay Street was Bay Street only because the Stock Exchange was on it; most brokers and investment houses had long ago found other, less symbolic addresses in nearby bank towers.

The health of the investment industry is reflected by the price of the 136 seats on the TSE. Six memberships changed hands in 1982; one bid, of $165,000, was the second-highest ever. As recently as 1978, TSE seats were going for as little as $12,000—a lot less at the time than the cost of a Toronto taxi licence.

At about the time the new TSE building was being inaugurated, a clash of unprecedented proportions was developing inside the cozy cousinhood of the chartered banks and investment dealers. At stake was the $378 million paid out annually in brokerage commissions for trades of shares listed on the TSE.

On one side of the jousting field was the rambunctious duo of Harvard M.B.A.s who head the Toronto-Dominion Bank—Dick Thomson and Robin Korthals—and have turned the smallest of Canada's Big Five banks into a superbly organized, supremely profitable money machine. The two were determined to provide a national investor service with discounts on standard brokerage fees of as much as 64 per cent.

Opposing their initiative was the highly influential lobby of Bay Street's established investment dealers, led by such heavyweights as Ted Medland, chairman of Wood Gundy, and Austin (Firp) Taylor, the 330-pound chief of McLeod Young Weir. Ironically, Taylor had also been the main strategist for Royal Trustco's successful repelling of Robert Campeau's attempted 1980 takeover. Other investment dealers jumped into the battle, viewing the conflict as an issue central to their survival.

What the TD wanted was to introduce its "Green Line Investor Service" which would allow customers to buy and sell stocks as quickly and easily as they could make deposits in their savings accounts. The bank would perform just about every other service—except research—previously provided by the established investment houses.

As revolutionary as the TD's initiative sounded, it was no more than a copy of similar schemes already successful in the United States. Still, it was one of the few instances of a public quarrel within Canada's financial Establishment.

The new trading floor of the Toronto Stock Exchange opened in 1983 and has a greatly increased floor area as well as every possible electronic aid. At left is Murray Howe, vice-president of Richardson Greenshields and chairman of the board of the TSE when the new exchange was built, and at right is J. Pearce Bunting, president of the TSE.

Members of the Royal Ontario Museum board on a visit to Egypt in 1908. Left to right: Charles Cockshutt, Mrs. H.D. Warren, Gordon Osler, Mrs. Gordon Osler, Sir Edmund Osler, H.D. Warren, Mr. Theurer (the guide). The group was visiting Dr. Currelly, ROM curator.

John Labatt (RIGHT), of the London brewing family, was the subject of a famous kidnapping case in 1934. He is shown with his wife Bessie in Bermuda in 1948. After several generations as a family business, the brewery was bought by Brascan, now part of the Peter and Edward Bronfman empire.

The Iveys have been one of the leading families in London, Ontario, for at least three generations. Among the enterprises various family members have financed or owned are Northern Insurance, Empire Brass, the Hotel London, Sparton Radio, and the Ben-miller Inn. Richard M. Ivey, shown here with his wife Beryl, is , like his father and grandfather, a lawyer and a major benefactor to the University of Western Ontario.

IF THERE IS ONE CITY in Canada with a history profoundly affected by a private club, it is Winnipeg. None of this country's elite institutions ever came to symbolize so directly a province's concentration of business and political authority as the Manitoba Club, established (only eight months after the city itself) in 1874. It eventually became not merely the hub of Manitoba's Establishment but the source of its animating spirit.

Gathering place of those who came to be called the Sanhedrin, the club was dominated by John W. Dafoe, the great editor of the *Free Press*, who was a club member in good standing from 1903 until his death in 1944. The circle included, at various times, Tom Crerar, Isaac Pitblado, James (Bogus) Coyne, R.F. McWilliams, Elmer Woods, Culver Riley, Joe Harris, George Ferguson, Bruce Hutchison, Brigadier Richard Malone, David Kilgour, Dick Murray, Frank Walker, and Edgar Tarr, who huddled in a corner of the large lounge and dissected the world, talked up free trade, and spread the gospel of Manchester Liberalism. The late W.L. Morton, the province's historian-laureate, noted that membership in the Manitoba Club remained "the symbol of success and the club itself the centre of the informal exchange of opinion and information access which marks the 'insider'."

But that was long ago. Most of the adventurous Winnipeggers have moved elsewhere; the *Free Press* has been swallowed up by chain journalism, and the Manitoba Club no longer has a waiting list. Winnipeg is an inviting and forgiving place, but it's also something of a ghost town.

No other municipal jurisdiction in Canada has so much history to live up to. No matter how brightly its Chamber of Commerce and other boosters view the present and extrapolate the future, they cannot match the past. Winnipeg is the Vienna of Canada, a city state without an empire, the Chicago of the North that never made it.

ROBIN BRASS

The once-powerful Manitoba Club on Broadway still includes many of Winnipeg's Establishment people but failed to adjust to the changing ethnic mix of the city's business world.

There was a time before the branch plants (and the mentality that accompanied them) took over the Manitoba economy, a time when Winnipeg could boast (and did) of having more millionaires to the acre than any other Canadian city. In its edition of January 29, 1910, the *Winnipeg Telegram* proudly reported that the city had 19 millionaires but that the list "could be extended to twenty-five without stretching the truth," then pointedly added, "the *Telegram's* Toronto correspondent in writing a list of the millionaires of the Queen City put the list at only twenty-one."

It was a time of knighthoods, when Winnipeg's leading businessmen were honoured by the sovereign across the sea. Among them were Sir John Christian Schultz, Sir Daniel Hunter McMillan, Sir Rodmond Roblin, Sir Joseph Dubuc, Sir Doug-

Toronto-born Sir Augustus Nanton (1860-1925) ran the Winnipeg partnership of Osler, Hammond and Nanton, investment dealers. He was also a director of the Dominion Bank and chairman of the Canadian Committee of the Hudson's Bay Company. Shown below is his house on Roslyn Road in 1924.

las Colin Cameron, Sir James Aikins, and Sir Augustus Nanton.

It was, above all, a grand time for the grain trade. The first lake shipment from Port Arthur was delivered by James Richardson & Sons in 1883, and the business spawned the Grain Exchange in 1887. It was there, in the raucous bidding of its trading pit, that the new fortunes were seeded. The grain-merchant families all made their mark — the Bawlfs, Gillespies, Gooderhams, Hargrafts, Heffelfingers, Heimbeckers, Krofts, Leaches, McCabes, McMillans, Meladys, Miseners, Murphys, Parrishes, Patersons, Powells, Purveses, Richardsons, Searles, Sellerses, Smiths, and Vincents.

Formation of the Canadian Wheat Board in 1935 and the unbridled growth of the Wheat

George Montegu Black (1875-1959), grandfather of Conrad Black, established a business empire in Winnipeg after the family moved there from Halifax in 1882. G.M. Black gained control of Drewrys brewery which eventually became Western Breweries Ltd.

Pools of co-ops cut into the families' trading profits, but Winnipeg's residual mystery is that, with the remarkable exception of the Richardsons (and on a smaller scale the Patersons, the Parrishes, and Heimbeckers), these grain businesses have vanished as if they had never existed. Except for one fairly small investment by George Sellers, not one of the great grain merchants or their progeny had looked farther west to grab a stake in the oil and gas fields of Alberta. Most of the Winnipeg money just sat there or was dissipated by the sons and daughters of the original merchant princes. Two of the last individually owned grain compa-

George T. Richardson and his wife Tannis at a reception for Hudson's Bay Company directors at the Manitoba Archives.

Wellington Crescent, which winds for several miles along the south bank of the Assiniboine River, and the adjoining streets make up the finest residential district in Winnipeg.

The Wellington Crescent house of C.S. Riley.

ROBIN BRASS

nies—Federal and National—were sold in 1972 and 1974.

The current generation of the grain clans is scattered, with some, like Noreen Murphy, joining the international jet set and others retiring to the Caribbean. Only a few, such as Richard Kroft, moved out of grain into other lucrative investments. Stewart Searle is chairman of Federal Industries, a conglomerate that includes a railway, aircraft engine maintenance shop and bulk terminals; Wick Sellers heads Spiroll, in which Jim Richardson is a silent partner. Bob Purves is into commodities. Three great-grandsons of Nicholas Bawlf are living in British Columbia, as is George Heffelfinger, who became a loganberry grower outside Victoria.

So much of the city is a shell of its past—the Nanton Building, for example, or the now-quiescent Grain Exchange Building on Lombard Avenue, which houses the Manitoba headquarters of the Victorian Order of Nurses and the offices of the Winnipeg Stock Exchange, perhaps the saddest appurtenance of the city's claim to financial importance. As Winnipeg writer Roger Newman noted in a 1983 article in *Manitoba Business,* the

WSE, founded in 1904, occupies a two-room suite and doesn't need a trading floor—because all trades are executed by phone. The seventeen firms represented deal in only 75 stocks and conduct in total about a million dollars' worth of business *annually.* "If we didn't have the exchange, we'd be Regina," says Robert Stafford, the current WSE president.

The Winnipeg Commodity Exchange, successor to the Grain Exchange (founded in 1887), moved over to the new Trizec centre at Portage and Main in 1980. Its 330 members did a $12-billion trade in commodity contracts in 1982, but WCE memberships were selling in 1983 for about $5,000, down from $14,000 a couple of years earlier. (A seat on the Chicago Board of Trade, the largest commodity futures market in the world, was selling for $250,000 at the same time.)

The problem is that Winnipeg is no longer head-office country. Even the few large-scale institutions that maintain their corporate homes there (such as the Hudson's Bay Company, Great-West Life, and the Investors Group) owe prime allegiance to their owners in the East. Even Winnipeg's lively newer set of movers and shakers—Izzy Asper, Bob Graham, Alan Sweatman, Marty Freedman, Jack Fraser, Arni Thorsteinson, Ted Turton, Randy Moffat, and Neil Baker—are doing many of their deals elsewhere. It's still too easy for the business elite to fly over the city on the way back and forth between Toronto and Vancouver. The money train doesn't stop here any more.

One of the few surviving stalwarts is Conrad Sanford Riley, who heads United Canadian Shares and Canadian Indemnity. A heavyweight in any category he cares to enter, he is a man in calm possession of power, plugged into the country's commercial aristocracy. Frances, his wife, is a granddaughter and great-granddaughter of lieutenant-governors of Manitoba; her sisters married the late R.D. (Peter) Mulholland, a Bank of Montreal president, and George Sellers, of the grain family. A Prairie patriot whose father headed the Canadian Committee of the Hudson's Bay Company, Riley silently laments that both his sons, Conrad Jr. and Dennis, are carving their careers in Toronto.

Winnipeg's one saving economic grace is the continuing primacy of the Richardson family. On December 31, 1980, without anyone in the city being aware of it and with the modest silence that is their trademark, the Richardsons passed a significant milestone. When the totals for the year were added up, the combined revenues of their numerous enterprises zipped above the $1 billion mark for the first time, leaving a net income of $22 million to be divided among the private company's partners: the four Richardsons (George, James, Kathleen, and Agnes, the wife of Senator William Benidickson).

George Richardson has emerged as the most creative and successful member of the clan since the death of James A. Richardson in 1939. In his unassuming, almost diffident way, he goes about quietly expanding his family's empire from atop the 32-story tower at Portage and Main that dominates the Winnipeg skyline. A kind man

whose proudest boast is that many members of his company's 25-year club are third-generation Richardson employees, he has an adventurous side to his nature that only his closest friends know about. He is one of the country's most experienced helicopter pilots, guiding his Bell Jet Ranger across the Canadian landscape. He will put aside four days to fly from Winnipeg to Prince Rupert, British Columbia, visiting Richardson operations along the way—knowing the route well by now, comfortable because he can always follow the pipeline that one of his subsidiaries threw across the Rockies.

With about 400 elevators, its own fleet of ships, and grain terminals at Thunder Bay and on the north shore of Burrard Inlet, the Richardson-owned Pioneer Grain Company dominates Canada's private grain trade. The family's investment operations were impressively enhanced by the 1982 acquisition of Greenshields Inc. of Montreal.

Because the Richardsons can legitimately claim four generations of wealth and influence—back through George's father and mother (who ran the company from 1919 until 1966), to Henry and George A. (who handled corporate affairs from the turn of the century into the First World War) and to the original James Richardson (who established the firm in 1857)—they are in a class by themselves in Winnipeg and in Western Canada.

MONEY AND POWER IN SASKATCHEWAN, Alberta, and British Columbia are still so raw that life and commerce are tinged with that special excitement of being on a frontier, of existing constantly on the edge of undiscovered potential.

Strangers who view the Prairies from commercial or private jets see the isolated glow of cities and a scatter of grain elevators rearing up from the subtle geography of the plains. This physical space is central to the Western psyche. It is not so much the idea of *being* alone as wanting to be *left* alone, of having room to grow, of being one's own person.

When times are good, this sustaining myth of a land with no boundaries gives the impression to outsiders that the successful Westerner feels omnipotent, thinks big, and lives rich. It is a difficult stereotype to overcome, because Westerners, particularly in Calgary and Vancouver, act it out themselves, and never more so than during the petrodollar boom of the mid-1970s. They rode the tide of fast money and even faster bank loans to sci-fi lifestyles, trading up on cars, yachts, jets, and wives in a whiplash of conspicuous spending. This brazen new posse of oilmen, real-estate flippers, high-tech sorcerers, stock-market swifties, and fast-food caballeros shattered the common ethos that until then had united Canada's commercial elite. The women they tend to love and marry, not necessarily at the same time, kept themselves as thin as Patek Philippe wristwatches, their hair swept up in tiers as if whirled in a Cuisinart. Most of these newcomers possessed about as much introspection as freight trains with a schedule to keep. They rejected tradition, welcomed risk, and generally flaunted a very un-Canadian *macho* approach to business.

What only a few of the Westerners realized was that, like every other new economy which depends on raw material exports, theirs is essentially a plasticine culture shaped by outside influences—OPEC, Ottawa, the Soviet grain harvest, Middle East wars, the weather, Brazil's national debt, and Mexico's trade balance. When the roof fell in during 1981-82, the banks panicked, foreclosing the same loans they had been urging on their customers only six months before. Oil prices fell—then kept falling. Almost overnight, it seemed, there was no market for lumber: the American housing industry had slumped. Base-metal prices plummeted to below their Depression lows; the stock market turned sour; the values of real-estate properties hit bottom.

Most Western Canadians found themselves inhabiting a scary Darwinian world in which only the fittest and fastest could stay alive. It was then

that they most regretted not having those tenuous bonds of schools, clubs, and bloodlines that sustain a solidified Establishment through bad times. All the Westerners had going for them was fellowship born out of their determination to survive—that and the fear of irrelevance if they ever again allowed themselves to become so vulnerable.

This was probably the main reason Saskatchewan, Alberta, and British Columbia opted so firmly for right-wing governments and why they fought so hard to get Ottawa on their side. Only with the power of the federal state behind them would they feel safe and impregnable.

THE DIFFERENCES BETWEEN THE Establishments in Saskatchewan and the other Western provinces is immense. Despite its recent turn to the Conservatives, socialist administrations have been in power for most of four decades, so that Saskatchewan has not had a chance to develop much of a private-sector power structure.

Saskatchewan no longer ranks as a have-not province. Its million inhabitants now live in cities rather than on farms and its grain bounties and underground riches of potash and uranium produce record-setting revenues. Oil remains the big question mark. The province's first well was drilled in 1906, but it wasn't until 30 years later that oil was discovered in commercial quantities on the Saskatchewan side of the Lloydminster field.

The province's richest citizen is probably Frederick Walter Hill, head of a family insurance and development business in Regina that has expanded into resources and television. He earned a B.A. at the University of Saskatchewan and an M.B.A. at Harvard, received a medical discharge from the RCAF in 1941 because of a heart murmur, then promptly joined the U.S. Army Air Force instead. Hill served as a pilot in heavy bombers over Italy and was awarded the Distinguished Flying Cross and Air Medal with three oak-leaf clusters. He took over McCallum Hill, the family firm, in 1947, organized Canadian Devonian Petroleums

REGINA LEADER-POST

Fred Hill

Morris Shumiatcher

(later sold to the Keevils of Teck Corporation) and, through the late 1950s into the '60s, developed the 600-acre Hillsdale residential and commercial subdivision on the south side of the city. A director of the Canadian Imperial Bank of Commerce, Hill is involved in many other ventures, spending at least $5,000 a month on long-distance phone calls to keep track of everything. His son Paul, who has degrees from Washington's Georgetown University and from Western Ontario, became president of the family empire in 1978.

In a category by himself is Morris Cyril Shumiatcher, known to one and all as "Shumi." His house in Regina is a veritable museum of Oriental antiques. Son of a Calgary lawyer, he served as an RCAF air gunner, has half a dozen law degrees and is accredited to the bar in all the Western provinces plus the Northwest Territories, has served on several royal commissions, and in the law field is a Renaissance man who seems to enhance every enterprise he touches.

Other significant Saskatchewan players include: Graham Walker (investments), Adrie Schutte (food stores), Jim Balfour (politics, oil),

Lloyd Barber (university president and corporate director), John Davidson (oil and law), Rob Foley (construction), Peter Gundy (investments), Bill Hunter (football), Will Klein (trust company), Ernest and Sam Richardson (real estate), Ross Sneath (life insurance), Ted Turner (wheat), W.E. Bergen (co-operatives), Sidney Buchwold (politics and directorships), John Enns (margarine), Earl Foster (investments), George McNevin (construction), and Herb Pinder (drug store chain and other investments).

"THERE IS SOMETHING OF ISRAEL about Alberta," wrote William Thorsell, of the *Edmonton Journal*. "Both see themselves existing in a milieu where someone is trying to deny their existence."

It was this psychology that had prompted the energy entrepreneurs to build ever-higher office towers, especially in downtown Calgary, unconsciously designing them as forts against outsiders. It didn't work. By mid-1983, seven million square feet of office space stood empty and, for the first time since the North West Mounted Police arrived in 1875 to drive out the whiskey-traders,

Calgary's population dropped significantly. Oil exploration virtually stopped, with three times as much oil being pumped out of the ground as was being discovered.

Only a decade before, when the Arab oil price increases began to take hold in 1973, Alberta's gross provincial product had jumped 40 per cent in one year. The Oil Patch bloomed for the next seven years; then, on Tuesday, October 28, 1980, the Trudeau government announced its National Energy Program. "History will one day record," thundered Ted Byfield, publisher of *Alberta Report*, "that a government of Canada by act of deliberate policy tried to destroy the prosperity of the one section of the country that had escaped the recession and offered the best hope for the whole nation's future. At the same time it indentured the country to the Middle East's oil producers and brought its own oil industry to a catastrophic halt. Historians will be hard pressed to find anywhere an act of government so irresponsible, so vindictive, and so insane as that which was produced last week by Mr. Trudeau and his thugs at Ottawa."

Don Braid of the *Edmonton Journal* summed up the depth of Alberta's alienation from the East: "Many would sneer at a cancer cure if it came from Ontario." Such contempt for Central Canada was hardly new. It dates back at least to the 1930s, when the Depression wiped many struggling Alberta companies off the map, while the combination of windstorms and drought literally blew farms away. By 1932, the price of wheat had dropped to 38 cents a bushel from $2.30 in the 1920s—and that was before the devastating grasshopper plague of 1934 hit the land. Two years later, William Aberhart's Social Credit administration defaulted on its bonds. The federal government did nothing, leaving Albertans with the clear message that both God and Ottawa had deserted them.

Alberta's resources seem always to have been dispatched somewhere else for conversion to cash. The Hudson's Bay Company gathered furs for the London auctions, Pat Burns drove his thundering herds of cattle to distant markets, and the grubby-knuckled discoverers of the fields at Coleman shipped their coal westward to tidewater. Wheat rolled east to be milled in Montreal; oil and gas were pipelined to Ontario, the oil to be refined in Sarnia and Toronto.

TO BE A *REAL* OLDTIMER IN CALGARY means that your roots stretch back before the 1947 oil discovery at Leduc. Those memories provide an enduring camaraderie suffused with the sepia tint of memory. This regret about the devaluation of simplicity and the dilution of the pugnacious individualism that first blossomed here is a recurring theme, often equated with loss of innocence and idealism.

The old guard of the Calgary Establishment includes all manner of men, but pride of place belongs to the ranchers of southern Alberta, currently in their fourth generation. First among them are the Crosses, descendants of A.E. Cross, a judge's son from Montreal who moved to Alberta in 1884 to start ranching. He married a daughter of Colonel J.F. Macleod, who built Fort Calgary as a North West Mounted Police post in 1875. Cross had the A7 Ranch near Nanton, south of Calgary, and became the first brewer in the old North West Territories. He was also one of the Big Four who founded the Calgary Stampede, with Pat Burns, George Lane, and A.J. McLean. The surviving children of A.E. are James B., who raises Herefords at Okotoks and is always looking for the perfect bull; Mary Dover, the handsome doyenne of nearby Midnapore; Sandy, who raises his Shorthorns and Ling cattle; and John, who has the A7 and raises Herefords.

The death of Pat Burns's son, Patrick Michael, in September 1936, five months before the old meatpacker and cattleman died, left Pat without a direct line of descent. Pat's grandnephew, R.J. Burns, a lawyer, and his sons, John and Dennis, are now the principal family members in Calgary.

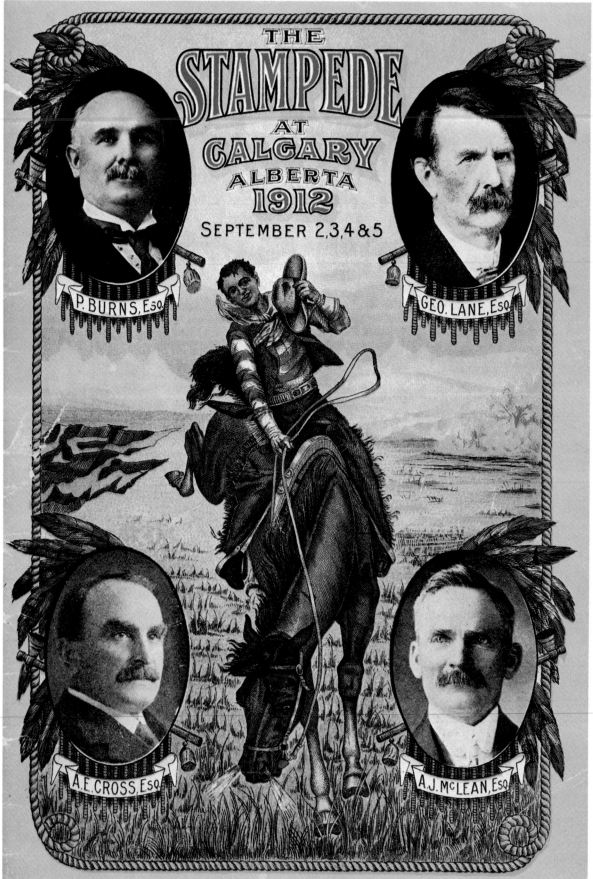

120

Other members of the old guard include Bob Burns (retired construction man and son of an original a partner in Burns & Dutton); Eric Connelly (retired consultant); the Copithornes (who ranch just west of Calgary); Red Dutton (Burns & Dutton and hockey); the Harvies (Dorothy, a matriarchal figure and widow of the philanthropist Eric, and her sons Don, a Bank of Montreal director and chairman of the Devonian group of charitable foundations, and Neil, of the Glenbow Ranch near Calgary and Riske Creek in the Chilcotin country of B.C.); Roy Jennings (a developer and son of the late Reg Jennings, a partner in Burns & Dutton); Frank Lynch-Staunton (Antelope Butte Ranch near Lundbreck); Grant MacEwan (author, former Liberal leader, former mayor, former lieutenant-governor; not an Alberta oldtimer himself, but he writes about the old days); Ken Manning (real estate; grandson of pioneer Alberta and B.C. lumberman Fred C. Manning; son of Clar Manning, founding chairman of the University of Calgary and a former president of the Stampede; Clar now lives near Victoria); Don Matthews (Highland Stock Farms) and his brother, lawyer Dick Matthews; Fred McKinnon (a son of early rancher Lachlin McKinnon); Fred's son Russell (a lawyer with Dick Matthews's firm); Neil and Jim McKinnon (L.K. Resources), sons of Fred's late brother Charlie; Fred Peacock (corporate director and former provincial minister of industry and commerce); Gordon Pearce (economic consultant and community activist); Hugh Planche (the politician); and the brothers Alastair Ross (Allaro Resources, a Liberal bagman who turned in his bag), and Graham Ross (Taro Industries).

An early Calgary Stampede program cover showing the "Big Four" ranchers (Pat Burns, George Lane, A.E. Cross, and A.J. McLean) who founded what is now the world's largest rodeo.

Among the leading Alberta ranchers is Fred Perceval of the Two Dot, who doesn't use his title (11th Earl of Egmont) and runs the place with his son (called Frederick to distinguish him from Fred; he doesn't use the title Viscount Perceval). They're descendants of Spencer Perceval, the British prime minister assassinated in the House of Commons lobby in 1812. Fred's grandfather settled in Alberta after coming up from Missouri in 1890. Fred, identified in the British press in the 1930s as the Cowboy Earl, sold his Midnapore land in 1959 and moved south to the Two Dot, once owned by the Earl of Minto, a governor general. Other Nanton–High River ranchers include the Armstrongs, Bladeses, Cartwrights (of the D Ranch, not the Ponderosa; they also have the EP Ranch, bought from the Duke of Windsor), Chattaways, Gardiners, Wambekes, and Watts. (George Chattaway and Ernie Blades are sons-in-law of Rod McClay, a pioneer Mosquito Creek cattleman.)

Not a Calgarian but a member of ranching's old guard is Stubb Ross of Lethbridge, whose family once had a million acres in southern Alberta. The family's holdings, built up by Stubb's grandfather, Walter, and father, George Graham Ross, are down to fewer than 200,000 acres and the original ranch is split up into various Ross companies—Lost River Ranches, Flying R Ranches, and Milk River Cattle. Stubb launched an airline (Time Air) and his older brothers, Jack and the late George Graham II, became the cattlemen of the family. The Rosses made a successful investment in Central–Del Rio Oils, now PanCanadian Petroleum, and Jack sits on its board.

Although most Calgary oilmen strongly insist that no local Establishment exists, they readily categorize its components. "There were the old families, like the Crosses and the Harvies, who came here several generations ago and founded the place," says Jack Pierce, who heads Ranger Oil and knows nearly everybody. "They keep very substantially to themselves. Then came the

Pat Burns (1856-1937), founder of Burns Foods, was one of the "Big Four" ranchers and Calgary's first millionaire. Born in Oshawa, he moved west in the 1880s to supply beef to railway construction crews. He established a slaughterhouse in Calgary that grew into Alberta's largest private-sector employer. He was appointed to the Senate in 1931. Shown below is a group at his Bow Valley Ranch, Midnapore, around 1900. His spendid Calgary house (ABOVE), designed by Francis Rattenbury, was built in 1901 and demolished in 1956.

GLENBOW ARCHIVES, CALGARY

The Prince of Wales, a frequent visitor to Canada, was an enthusiastic outdoorsman. The prince eventually bought the EP ranch at Pekisko, Alberta, though he visited there only very occasionally. Shown here is a view of the ranch house on the EP and a photograph of the Prince of Wales in action, earnestly helping with the round-up at the Bar-U ranch near High River during his visit to Canada in late summer of 1919.

PUBLIC ARCHIVES CANADA/PA 22322

nouveaux riches of the 1950s, epitomized by Max Bell, Bobby Brown, and Frank and George McMahon. They were like what you see on the TV show *Dallas*, and there was virtually no exchange between that group and their predecessors. Now there is a sort of crossover grouping, people like myself who are close to the original ones. A few of the others in that category are Bob Blair, Jack Gallagher, Fred Mannix, Rod McDaniel, Art Child, Bill Fitzpatrick, and Dick Bonnycastle.''

Much of the Calgary Establishment consists of Saskatchewan farm boys who grew up reading *Star Weekly* for excitement. Digital wristwatches that double as calculators are much in evidence. Oil-company executives deal with problems and decisions directly, seldom fencing themselves off behind pickets of corporate deadwood. Their speech tends to be peppered with expletives in a cadence quite different from the monotone of the investment dealers who still dominate Eastern gatherings.

The most potent status symbol is hiring some of the best legal guns in the West to negotiate deals. Mac Jones, Dick Matthews, John Ballem, Bob Black, Don McLaws, and Jim Palmer lead the pack. Other prominent lawyers include Ron Bell, Bill Britton, Gordon W. Brown, John Burns, Roy Deyell, Bob Dinkel, Major-General W.A. Howard, Joseph Katchen, Richey Love, Stanley Mah

CALGARY HERALD

Jean and Eric Harvie with Gordon Southam (left). Eric Harvie (1892-1975), a lawyer, owned the mineral rights to the land on which Imperial Oil made the famous Leduc strike in 1947 and became one of the richest men in Western Canada. An inveterate collector of Western Canadian historical artifacts, he also acquired such curiosities as Sir Robert Peel's penny-farthing bicycle and the last Model-T Ford ever built. Most of his collection is now in the Glenbow Museum, of which his son Donald Southam Harvie is a director. Dorothy Jean Harvie, Eric Harvie's wife, is a Southam.

MICHAEL BURNS PHOTOGRAPHY

Oilmen Frank McMahon and Max Bell won the Queen's Plate with their horse Merger in 1968. McMahon made his money from Pacific Petroleums; Bell first struck oil in Turner Valley in 1936. He came close to capturing control of the Hudson's Bay Company and the CPR; in 1959, with Victor Sifton of the Winnipeg Free Press, he formed FP Publications.

Toy, John O'Connor, Cliff Rae, Larry Ross, Don Sabey, Jack Smith, David Tavender, and Allan Twa.

Important members of Calgary's geological and consulting community include Don Axford, Bruce Baily, Donald Burtt, Antony Edgington, George Govier, Vernon Horte, Don Mackenzie, Ernie Pallister, John Poyen, and Grant Trimble. The geologist whose reports give any project the automatic imprimatur of success remains Rod McDaniel, who also acts as Peter Lougheed's chief fund-raiser.

A world-scale development operation headquarters in Calgary is Trizec, the Bronfman-Reichmann partnership run by Harold Milavsky, a tough and capable wheeler-dealer who has built the once-frail company into a $3 billion giant. He runs things out of what may well be Canada's only corporate president's office with three (count 'em) corner windows. Other Alberta developers haven't been so lucky. Klaus Springer went bust. Ralph Scurfield did too, but his companies, which

lost more than a quarter of a billion dollars in 1982, were refinanced in a last minute rescue.

Calgary is a business town, and businessmen form its natural Establishment. It's the only place in Canada where the commercial and social elites are as yet indistinguishable.

One of the few oilmen to analyze the social implications of this Calgary phenomenon was Peter Martin Stoddart Longcroft, an Englishman who heads Tricentrol in Canada: "Possibly the most distinct factor which distinguishes the English business and social environment from that of southern Alberta is that in the latter, business and social contacts are largely the same, whereas in the former there tends to be a distinct and purposeful separation."

In Calgary, you are what you do. Social life has become considerably muted since the Recession, but outdoor barbecues remain the favourite form of entertainment, with Dick Bonnycastle's Stampede breakfasts and realtor Gerry Knowlton's annual bash being among the best attended. Fred

In 10 short years Marg and Ron Southern have developed Spruce Meadows into an internationally acclaimed equestrian centre. Each year they host the Spruce Meadows "Masters," with teams from all over the world competing. The Masters offers the most prize money and attracts the largest crowds of any similar outdoor show-jumping event in North America.

Mannix's pheasant shoots and the Jubilee Ball at the Banff School of Fine Arts are also important events. Socially, the couple everyone wants on the guest list are Sir Rodney Touche and his talented wife, Ouida. London-born and Oxford-educated, Touche was a major shareholder of Lake Louise Lifts, and stayed on as general manager when he sold out to Charlie Locke for $20 million. A cultured and interesting couple, the Touches have a circular country Hobbit house built into a hillside with a fireplace on an axle, so that it can be rotated at will.

Much of what happens in social Calgary takes place at Spruce Meadows, the magnificent equestrian complex developed by Ron Southern and his wife, Marg, who is also a director of Shell Canada and Woodward's. Considered to be second in scope only to England's Hickstead, the Southern facilities can house 300 horses. The Spruce Meadows Masters is North America's only outdoor jumping competiton sanctioned by the World Equestrian Federation. The stable is breeding a new strain of show horses (crossing thoroughbreds with Hanoverians) and, to spice up competiton, Southern flies mounts in from Europe.

The status of the only two Calgary clubs that count—the Ranchmen's and the Petroleum—is a matter of lively controversy. "[The Calgary Petroleum Club's] name is redolent of power and money," Frank Wesley Dabbs once commentd in *Calgary* magazine. "It is a pinnacle of social and corporate achievement in a one-industry town. In terms of class and contacts, it ranks with the best in Dallas and Houston.... Like the Christian church, the club no longer embraces the entire constituency from which it takes its name." It is a deadly accurate assessment. Most of the real movers in Calgary eat at their desks; the rank of regular attendees at the Petroleum Club has been lowered, with some exceptions, to the vice-presidential level.

The more exclusive Ranchmen's retains much of its former lustre, but even in its remodelled incarnation it is not the essential institution it once was.

WHAT'S WESTERN ABOUT CALGARY is not that people wear cowboy hats or go around saying "Howdy" to one another. The Western ethic implies that people haven't yet arrived where they're heading, but they're determined to get there. Where you started from or what you did is irrelevant: having a high energy level and being willing to gamble is essential.

The nature of its narrow economic base dictates that Calgary should have at the apex of its economic structure the anonymous and (except for Arne Nielsen at Canadian Superior and Bill Fitzpatrick at Bralorne) largely interchangeable heads of the great transnational corporations.

The gala Banff Centre Jubilee Ball at the Banff School of Fine Arts on Saturday, July 23, 1983. BELOW LEFT: Susanne Palmer, Edmonton barrister and a member of the Banff Centre board, and Frank King, chairman of the XVth Olympic Winter Games Organizing Committee. CENTRE: getting down at the Ball, with jazz vocalist "Big" Miller and the Tommy Banks Big Band. RIGHT: Peter Lougheed with Ann Heisey, wife of Lawrence Heisey, president and director of Harlequin Enterprises and a member of the Banff Centre board of governors.

Some of the more interesting independent-minded entrepreneurs are Gustaaf "Gus" Van Wielingen, Harley Hotchkiss, Dick Bonnycastle, John Masters, Jim Gray, Carl Nickle, Peter Bawden, Verne Lyons, the three Seaman brothers, Alan Graham (insurance), Baron Carlo von Maffei (farming and property), Jack Scrymgeour (oil and plumbing supplies), Ron Southern (mobile homes, power), Bud McCaig (trucking, etc., etc.), Bob Wisener (merchant banking), and John Fleming (petroleum accounting).

In a class by themselves are Arthur Child, the fiscal genius who rescued Burns Foods, and Bob Blair, who more than any one man has become the conscience of the Oil Patch. Child, at 73, still puts in an average of ten hours behind his desk. He has an eclectic mind and has managed to privatize his company, establishing his control in the process.

Child most succinctly summarizes the Calgary ethic: "People are quite happy to go their own ways. We won't let anybody take liberties, but we're not looking for distinction as such. Business is fun to people out here. But we're very realistic, very hard-nosed when it comes not only to our companies' investments but our own portfolios. No real-estate operator, broker, or anybody like that could even get the time of day from me. I make my own decisions."

Blair, another individualist, is an avowed Canadian nationalist, which in these longitudes is as rare as finding a whooping crane with quints. A thoughtful, unpredictable man of many talents, he guided Nova Corp. through the recession with a minimum of troubles. He values his independence above all else, cursing what he calls the Oil

BOTH: FINANCIAL POST

Jack M. Pierce, CEO of Ranger Oil, a Bronfman-affiliated company, and (RIGHT) Arne Nielsen, chairman of Canadian Superior Oil.

Patch's crab-pot syndrome: "When you boil them, any crab that tries to get out of the pot is pulled back by the others."

The only proprietor in Alberta with corporate assets in the billion-dollar class is Frederick Charles Mannix. There is a kind of invisible inevitability about the Mannixes in Alberta. An astonishing line-up of the province's big players are Mannix graduates—Premier Peter Lougheed, who for about five years was an officer of and in-house counsel for the key operating company, Mannix Co. Ltd.; Chip Collins, a Bank of Nova Scotia accountant who was with Mannix Co. Ltd. during Lougheed's time and later handled the company's coal operations before joining Lougheed in government; Dave Wood, in charge of public relations for the Mannix organization for thirteen years, a Lougheed PR and TV advisor who later became vice-president for corporate affairs of Western Cooperative Fertilizers; Harold Milavsky, one-time chief accountant who became controller of Loram International and now heads Trizec Corp.; Fred Wilmot, a veteran of the Mannix construction operations, now running his own Prestige Builders company; Alastair Ross, who presided over the two Mannix petroleum units (Western Decalta and Pembina Pipe Line) before establishing his own oil investment portfo-

lio; Harry Booth, an accountant who left the Pembina presidency in 1969 to head Alberta & Southern Gas, controlled by the giant California-based utility Pacific Gas & Electric; Bill Fitzpatrick, assistant to Pembina president Jim Scott in the late 1950s, who now heads the Bentley family's Bralorne Resources.

Until a recent illness, Mannix divided his time between a golf cottage in Palm Desert, situated on the Eldorado Club polo grounds, and his new $2 million house near Priddis in the foothills 20 miles southwest of Calgary. It was built for his new bride, 40 years his junior, Janice Florendine. His former home, the FM Ranch in the Fish Creek area just south of Calgary, was expropriated for a provincial park. The province offered to pay him $5 million for the property, but Mannix took his demand for $41 million to the courts and won a smaller settlement. His great joys are shooting grouse in Spain and deer in Czechoslovakia, or participating in the annual pheasant shoot he hosts, when hundreds of specially imported birds are released minutes before the hunters wade into the underbrush. Mannix is also one of two Albertans (the other is Baron Carlo von Maffei) who belong to the exclusive Club aux Brigands, a private shooting preserve on Ile aux Ruaux, downstream from Quebec City.

Canoe Cove Manufacturing Ltd. built Cybele III, *a 46-foot cruiser, for Arthur Child, president of Burns Foods in Calgary. A masterwork of functional nautical design and engineering,* Cybele III *looks (as Child puts it) "something like a miniature wartime corvette."*

Mannix's only public presence is as director of the Royal Bank (since 1965), Stelco (since 1968), and the Scripps Clinic and Research Foundation in California (since 1972). He keeps changing company names (from Mannix to Loram to Mancal), as if he could somehow hide his family connections from the public, and hires fresh public relations advisors to keep him out of sight.

The other, still significant, presence in the Oil Patch is Jack Gallagher of Dome. Until he lost the chairmanship of his company early in 1983, he dominated the province's and the country's imagination. From a standing start in 1950, he developed Dome into Canada's largest energy complex—and did it entirely with other people's funds, without paying taxes or dividends in the process.

The long-term source of Gallagher's attraction was that his corporate vision extended well beyond monetary returns. He marched to a different drum corps. The massive technology he created to exploit the frigid depths of the Beaufort Sea was dedicated to uncovering what he willed to be there: a frozen Middle East bursting with 90 billion barrels of oil and other riches. The problem was that, under Gallagher, Dome regularly spent up to three times its cash flow, and it was only by shamelessly tapping the federal treasury that he was able to risk Dome's future among the unforgiving floes that churn off Tuktoyaktuk.

Gallagher's philosophy had been to stress growth from within but, in June 1981, he and his board decided to acquire the 47 per cent of Hudson's Bay Oil and Gas then still in public hands. By the time that fateful decision was implemented, interest rates had skyrocketed. The value of Dome's stock had plummeted; the oil glut and the National Energy Program had wiped out most of the cash flow expected from the HBOG properties; and Dome's debt burden had spiralled to an astronomical $8 billion. Canada's bankers, who held so much Dome debt that they might as well have painted Gallagher's smiling profile on their banknotes, had been content to carry the company's debt on 10-year promissory notes until the HBOG deal. That transaction made them so nervous that they drastically shortened the payout terms, and ended up refusing to refinance Dome

Frederick Stephen Mannix (1881-1951), shown above, was a railway contractor who went into the coal business. His son, Frederick Charles, shown in the photo at top right with Royal Bank chairman Rowland Frazee (who is on the right), took control of the business in the 1940s and built it into an international giant with interests in earth moving, construction, engineering, oil, and coal. Closely controlled by Mannix and his sons Frederick Jr. and Ronald, the organization has expanded to 132 intricately linked companies and is the most powerful company in Alberta. After losing a drawn-out legal battle to save the family ranch at Fish Creek from expropriation, Mannix created a new 1435-acre ranch, Chinook Downs, with private lakes, facilities for horses and cattle, and elaborate electronic security devices. Seen in the lower photo is the house.

unless the federal government provided a safety net. This was promptly done—but part of the salvage price demanded by the bankers was Gallagher's resignation.

In his 30-year rise, Gallagher had transformed Dome into Canada's most important energy con-sortium. He was never very interested in making money for himself or for his shareholders, preferring the less mundane pursuit of altering the world's geography. He managed to accomplish just that. Gallagher understood that the real conflict in Canada is not between East and West, Left and

Jack Gallagher built Dome Petroleum into an energy giant, only to have high interest rates bring it to the brink of bankruptcy. The company began as an oil-exploration off-shoot of Dome Mines, the long-established gold-mining company, but soon outgrew its parent.

Right, or French and English—but between the reactionaries and the rebels, between those who obey authority and those who act on their own imaginations.

What brought Gallagher to ground was an accident of timing, and the Canadian economy thus lost its resident dreamer.

Gallagher's replacement at Dome was a Scottish accountant named J. Howard Macdonald. But that succession involved much more than just another corporate shuffle. It marked the end of risk taking on an empire scale and the death of the dream branded into the soul of every loyal Oil Patcher: that with luck he too could alter his allotted portion of the world.

EDMONTON'S ESTABLISHMENT, more similar to Regina's or Saskatoon's than Calgary's, has a heavy overload of politicians and bureaucrats, led of course by Peter Lougheed, the eternal premier of Alberta. Alone among Canada's premiers, Lougheed is the uncrowned king of his province's business Establishment, but is neither as parochial nor as partisan as his supporters portray him.

His roots run deep. He numbers one governor and one chief factor of the Hudson's Bay Company among his ancestors; his grandfather was one of the last senators appointed by Sir John A. Macdonald and the first Albertan to be knighted.

He runs the province. The premier meets with at least two dozen businessmen in a regular cycle of private lunches. All but the wisest of his guests believe they have exclusive access to Lougheed's ear. None does, yet they all influence his thought processes. Lougheed makes his own final decisions, but among those he consults most frequently are Peter Macdonnell, senior partner of Milner & Steer, Edmonton's largest law firm; Rod McDaniel, the Calgary geologist; Don Getty, one of his former energy ministers; Ron Southern (Atco), Norman Green (a Calgary developer), Joe Healy (an Edmonton car dealer), Bud McCaig (Trimac), Bud Milner (steel fabrication), Stan Milner (Chieftain), Hoadley Mitchell (Edmonton oil consultant), Ken Moore (Supreme Court of Alberta), Doc Seaman (Bow Valley Industries), Harry Van Rensselaer (energy investment consultant), and Arthur Child (Burns Foods).

Two of Edmonton's important oilmen—Stan Milner and Bill McGregor—do not fit the brasher mould of their Calgary equivalents. Saskatchewan-born McGregor is held in highest esteem at the Mayfair Golf and Country Club because so many of its members became considerably richer by buying into Numac Oil & Gas when he launched it in 1963 at the $1.65 offering price. Numac now holds good acreage in the Mackenzie Delta, a major uranium find in Saskatchewan, coal in British Columbia, and part of a North Sea rig.

Younger but just as crusty, Stan Milner of Chieftain has spread his company's influence throughout most of the Western hemisphere, as well as running trucking and car-leasing operations, and has plans for a conveyor system to move coal from the fields in northeastern British Columbia. His most influential outside directorships are Canadian Pacific and Woodward Stores. In 1982,

Don Getty, president of D. Getty Investments, is one of the half-dozen key Lougheed advisors; Getty, an oil millionaire, was at one time Alberta's minister of Energy and Natural Resources and is also a former Edmonton Eskimo quarterback.

Peter Lougheed, shown in a moment of amity with Pierre Trudeau at the PM's residence in Ottawa, dominates the political and economic life of his province as does no other provincial premier.

Edmonton real-estate entrepreneur G. Donald Love, head of the Oxford Development Group.

Edmonton oilman Stan Milner of Chieftain Development.

majority interest in the firm was acquired by the provincially-controlled Alberta Energy Company.

Business aside, Edmonton has a far more vital cultural life than Calgary—with Joe Shoctor's magnificent Citadel Theatre, a first-class symphony orchestra and opera company, an imaginative city art gallery, and the best jazz festival north of Monterey. It's also the roosting place of Mel Hurtig, nationalist publisher and encyclopaedia promulgator. Even if the cliff dwellers in the luxury condominiums that overlook the meanders of the North Saskatchewan River and the occupants of the mansions that line the manicured crescents of Glenora form only a golden minority, their lifestyles rival those of the rich in any Canadian city.

Bill McGregor, president of Edmonton's Numac Oil and Gas.

The Edmonton business establishment has only a handful of significant players and, with the exception of Peter Pocklington, is very quiet money. Some of the important influencers include Louis Desrochers (law and politics), Peter Batoni (Batoni Properties), Don Carlson (Carlson Development Corp.), John Ferguson (Princeton Developments Ltd.), Ralph MacMillan (Edmonton Properties), Ron Dalby (management consulting), Newt Hughes (corporate director), Bob McAlpine (Clarepine Developments), Branny Schepanovich (law, Yugoslav and Liberal politics), William and Dr. A.W. Sereda (Heritage, Canada's first Ukrainian trust company), James R. Shaw (cable TV), Aaron Shtabsky (law), Donald Stanley (engineering and Third World sewage construction), Hal Yerxa (CFCW-Camrose and horse racing), Max Ward (airline), Bob Stollery (construction), Donald Cormie (investments), Dr. Charles Allard (investments), Don Love (real estate), the Ghermezian brothers (real estate and maintaining their cult of mystery), and Peter Pocklington (politics—past and, perhaps, future—and salvaging his financial empire).

Neither suffering from the lows nor benefiting from the same highs as Calgary, Alberta's capital is a pleasant place to live and do business. "Edmonton is like a Marie Osmond in a Dolly Parton body," *Edmonton Journal* cartoonist Edd Uluschak once cryptically explained—and left it at that.

IF THAT'S TRUE, THEN VANCOUVER is the Greta Garbo of Canadian cities: evocative and desirable with hints of hidden hedonism, yet unconquerable, distant, and Nordic in the depths of its mystery. Despite its lotus-land reputation, Vancouver is a city built on appetites as much as dreams, on psychic slippage and sudden urges, on betrayals as much as on beauties.

At night, viewed from Arthur Erickson aeries across the bays and up the cliffs where the city's privileged reside, Vancouver resembles an extra-terrestrial space station. Each office tower breaks the darkness with its own pattern of light, making the downtown area glow like a magic mountain among the foothills.

The reason it has always remained a provincial rather than a world metropolis is that Vancouver politics, commerce, and culture have never quite come together into any recognizable pattern. There is too much emphasis on today, instead of on yesterday or tomorrow, still too much concern with speed instead of quality. Being on the move is the ultimate virtue.

The Establishment, such as it is, exists as an off-the-ramp aggregation of *nouveaux riches* who made it a couple of years ago, and are still around to tell the tale. This attitude of severing roots, of pretending that the past never happened, is the saving grace and motivating force of British Columbia's successful entrepreneurs. It deepens their self-reliance, fosters the illusion that theirs is the land of ultimate freedom, and liberates them from having to repeat past mistakes. Endowed by sun and space, this province on the Pacific has produced a breed of Canadians who know how to adapt the 20th century to their own use.

They feel, therefore they are.

In the late spring of 1983, the jerry-rigged hierarchy that runs the place received an unexpected boost with the electoral coronation of Bill Bennett, who interpreted the voters' rejection of Dave Barrett–style socialism as a mandate to bring back the 13th century. If bloodletting had been approved by the B.C. Medical Association, he would have reintroduced leeches. The voters had supported restraint, but Bennett's purgative seemed to them too harsh a medicine.

By the early summer of 1983, considerable economic recovery had taken place, with B.C.'s gross provincial product headed up again to $43 billion. Lumber sales had surged back as the American housing industry recovered from its slump and it was a tribute to the cost-cutting efficiency of the West Coast's integrated produc-

H.R. MacMillan, founder of MacMillan Bloedel, and (RIGHT) his long-time associate W.J. VanDusen. MacMillan began a modest timber export business in 1919 that by 1935 was a world force in forest products and merchant shipping. VanDusen and MacMillan were among the 10 Vancouver men who established the Vancouver Foundation, now second largest in the country, in 1943.

ers—MacMillan Bloedel, B.C. Forest Products, and Crown Zellerbach—that they were making money at operating rates well below 80 per cent. Metal prices had not recovered completely, but new mines were opening and the Japanese coal export scheme in the northeast was picking up speed. Private capital spending was still down, but housing starts were climbing again. The recent economic devastation was being replaced by murmurs of hope and signs of renewed revelry.

Subdued as always, it was the residue of Vancouver's once-powerful Old Guard Establishment—the families whose members trace their bloodlines back to the original forestry and mining fortunes—that best survived the Great Recession. They gather every Tuesday for lunch at 12:15 in one of the dingy private banquet rooms of the Hotel Vancouver. They call themselves the Round Table and, though the food is nondescript, it's a good opportunity to dissect the latest of Pierre Trudeau's perfidies, to trade gossip about who's moving down to Palm Springs or across to Maui, and, best of all, to relive their glory days. Vaguely modelled on King Arthur's Round Table (in the sense that the jealousies of its members are

watered down because the gathering has no head table and no "knight" can claim precedence over any other), the group was founded in 1923 by Victor Odlum and Richard Bell-Irving. Its first chairman was Chris Spencer, who headed his family's department store. The impressive roll call of guests has included Field Marshal Montgomery, Mike Pearson, Joey Smallwood, Raymond Massey, and Sir Harry Pilkington, the glassmaker. (There have been only five women guests invited over the past 60 years, the first being Margaret Bondfield, Minister of Labour in Ramsay MacDonald's Cabinet.)

The Round Table has no bylaws, no constitution, makes no decisions, and holds to only two traditions: at the end of every meal each member is given two crystal mints; and at its Christmas luncheon, members harmonize on "D'ye ken John Peel?" in memory of an early member, James Pemberton Fell. Recent members include Geoff Andrew, a former master at Upper Canada College and son-in-law of a UCC principal who became secretary of the Wartime Information Board and chairman of the Leon and Thea Koerner Foundation; Harry Boyce, former president of Yorkshire

Czechoslovakian-born Walter C. Koerner (TOP LEFT) co-founded Alaska Pine with his brother, Leon, in 1939, later acquired B.C. Pulp and Paper from I.W. Killam, and sold control in 1954 to Rayonier Canada, of which he was chairman until 1972. Leon, shown at right with his wife Thea, was one of the West Coast's most enlightened philanthropists. Walter's son Michael (LOWER LEFT) manages the family's investments from Toronto.

Trust; Pearley Brissenden, lawyer; Michael Brown, investment man; Tom Brown, who was wounded while fighting with the Irish Fusiliers on the beaches of Normandy and went on to command Odlum Brown, the investment house; Kenneth Caple, retired head of the CBC in B.C. and former chancellor of Simon Fraser University; Jack Clyne, the former judge and ex-chairman of MacMillan Bloedel, whose sense of occasion, connections, and instinct for power gave the Vancouver Establishment an early taste of its national clout; J. Stuart Clyne, lawyer and son of Jack; Ian McTaggart Cowan, former professor of zoology at UBC and former chairman of the Arctic Insti-

tute of North America; Davie Fulton, a former federal justice minister and former member of the Supreme Court of B.C.; Most Rev. Godfrey Gower, retired Anglican archbishop; Bill Hamilton, Postmaster General in the Diefenbaker government and head of the Employers' Council of B.C. until he recently joined Donald Macdonald's royal commission on the economy; David Helliwell, former chairman of B.C. Resources Investment; Tony Hepburn, president of Odlum Brown; Gerry Hobbs, the former boss of the great CPR smelters at Trail; Norman Hyland, corporate director; Arthur Johnson, a Rhodes scholar, lawyer, and governor of St. George's School; D.

The Bell-Irvings are one of British Columbia's leading families. Scottish-born Henry Ogle Bell-Irving was a civil engineer on the CPR from 1882 to 1885 and founded a salmon cannery in Vancouver. His brother Duncan (above) came to Vancouver in 1883. One of the original doctors at the City Hospital (now the Vancouver General), he was also a director of the family enterprises and president of the Vancouver Club. The most notable current member of the family is Henry Pybus Bell-Irving (RIGHT), until 1983 lieutenant-governor of British Columbia. After a distinguished military career, including service during the Second World War in Sicily and northwest Europe, he went into the real-estate business, first as head of Bell-Irving Realty and later as chairman of A.E. LePage Western Ltd. He is honorary colonel of the Seaforth Highlanders of Canada. BELOW: Another member of the family, Colonel Richard Bell-Irving, photographed in an informal moment with his wife while on holiday at Lake Louise in the 1930s.

Lukin Johnson, retired partner of Price Waterhouse; G. Peter Kaye, chairman of the Vancouver Foundation; Stu Keate, the former publisher of the *Vancouver Sun* who turned down a senatorship to stay within his craft; Hugh Keenleyside, former diplomat and former co-chairman of B.C. Hydro; Warnett Kennedy, architect and politician; Walter Koerner, at 85 the last survivor of the great brotherhood of Czech-born lumber barons who permanently altered the character of Vancouver society by moving the city out of its frontier phase into philanthropy and culture; Tom Ladner, lawyer and investor; author, archivist, and former National Librarian W. Kaye Lamb; Larry MacKenzie, a Harvard and Cambridge grad who has collected 25 university degrees and served for nearly 20 years as president of UBC; Murray Newman, president of the Vancouver Public Aquarium Society; John Nichol, retired senator, active at Pearson College; Jack Nicholson, former lieutenant-governor of B.C. and Minister of Forestry in the Pearson government; Roger Odlum, retired insurance broker; Dr. Russell Palmer, whose practice numbered many Establishment families; Peter Pearse, UBC economics professor;

Selwyn Rocksborough Smith, retired social worker; Tony Scott, professor of economics at UBC; Frederic Soward, retired historian; David Tupper, lawyer; George Volkoff, retired dean of science at UBC; and J.O. Wilson, a former Chief Justice of the B.C. Supreme Court.

In a place where anything that happened in the 1950s is regarded as practically antediluvian, the Round Table passes for what's left of the old Establishment. Hugh Martin, who built the Bayshore Inn and headed the federal Liberal Party in B.C. when that was still a meaningful function, once lamented, "all of us were born 50 years too soon. This place didn't start coming into its own until the 1970s, when the really big real-estate fortunes were made."

Martin's reference to "us" means families such as the Farrells (telephones), Wallaces (shipbuilding), Walkems (law and shipbuilding), Bell-Irvings (everything), Grahams (investments), MacMillans (lumber), Reifels (booze), Buckerfields (feeds), Tuppers (law), Hanburys (lumber), Cromies (publishing), Malkins (wholesalers), Spencers (department stores), Brocks (mining), Letsons (machinery), Brookses, Foleys and Langs (newsprint), Hunttings and Laings (lumber), McLennans (hardware), Ceperleys and Rounsefells (real estate), Rosses (stockbroking), Abbotts and Marpoles (CPR), Furbers (property), Hendrys and Hambers (lumber), the McRaes (lumber, mining, politics)—as well as the Dunsmuirs (coal), Rithets, Priors, Pembertons, and Pendrays of Victoria. "Once upon a time," he reminisced, "the Vancouver Establishment really perceived itself as an Establishment. The women—Mrs. Hamber, Mrs. Brooks, Mrs. Laing, and others—arranged the big dinner parties and the Junior League balls. General McRae's wife was the doyenne of them all. Her parties were *de rigueur*—if you weren't invited to her New Year's Eve ball, you were out. As far as the Establishment in those days was concerned, the wives pretty well created the

Harry and Edna Reifel, of the British Columbia brewing and distilling family, on their way to a costume party. The Reifels, like the Bronfmans, made a fortune from liquor that somehow found its way to the United States during Prohibition.

players and boundaries. The men were merely the bricklayers."

Unlike the proprietors of the great fortunes of Eastern Canada, most of whom are three generations removed from the sweat of the individuals who built them up, the old Vancouver families still live with a touch of wilderness in their genes.

Senator John Wallace deBeque Farris, photographed in 1958.

Probably only half a dozen families stretch back beyond three generations of prominence in B.C., and few have attained such note as the Farrises. It was Senator John Wallace deBeque whose distinguished legal-political career brought the Farrises fame and fortune in the province. They rose to the very top of Vancouver society. It became a year-end ritual for the senator and his family to set aglow the Christmas lights on the giant fir tree in the grounds of his estate on Granville hill at Marpole Avenue. The senator, who had taken more appeals to the British Privy Council than any other Canadian lawyer, died at 91 in 1970, and his son John inherited his legal practice, the prestige of his name and reputation.

Young John had all the privileges: attending Harvard Law School, taking over his father's law firm, serving as a director of half a dozen national corporations, and becoming, like his father, one of the few British Columbians to head the Canadian Bar Association. He became Chief Justice of British Columbia in 1973 but fell from grace five years later when prostitute Wendy King revealed that Farris had been one of her clients. The younger Vancouver Establishment's willingness to forgive Farris was tinged with more than a little admira-

tion for the 67-year-old Chief Justice's alleged exploits, but Farris turned out to be his own harshest critic. He would not return to his family law firm, had himself delisted from *Canadian Who's Who*, resigned all his public offices, and sentenced himself to obscurity as inside counsel at the firm of Shrum, Liddle and Hebenton.

A family that retains its low profile is the Rogers clan. Founding father Benjamin Tingley Rogers had just finished school at Phillips Academy in Andover, Massachusetts, in 1883 when his father, the manager of a New Orleans sugar refinery, died a few days after being hit on the head with a brick thrown through his window by an employee on strike. He established a Vancouver sugar company and was eventually succeeded by his four sons, in order of their birth: Blythe Dupuy Rogers (1918-1920), Ernest Theodore Rogers (1920-1939), Philip Tingley Rogers (1939-1953), and Forrest Rogers (1953-1973). Forrest is now a semi-active chairman, but his son Stephen is a highly visible member of the Bennett government. The original Rogers also had three daughters, two of whom up and married two of the three brothers who formed the Cherniavsky Trio, whose Canadian tour brought them to Vancouver in 1916. Mary was wed to Mischel (cello) and Elspeth to Jan (piano). B.C. Sugar is now run by Peter Cherniavsky, the son of Elspeth and Jan, and its board remains a handy roost for the city's most powerful financiers. It is a sign of the times, however, that when a new lieutenant-governor was chosen for the province in the summer of 1983, the appointment went to Robert Gordon Rogers—not a B.C. Rogers at all, but a Montreal-born civil engineer who had gone on to head Crown Zellerbach and the Canada Harbour Place Corp.

In a class by themselves (because their influence continues unabated) are the Woodwards, the Eatons of Vancouver. Former Lieutenant-Governor W.C. Woodward's $2 million house near Butchart Gardens is for sale, but Charles Namby

The Aquilo, *owned by B.T. Rogers, founder of B.C. Sugar, was the first sizable steam yacht on the British Columbia coast, with a length of 127 feet and a beam of 20 feet. Rogers loaned it to the Royal Canadian Navy as a submarine mother ship during the First World War. The photograph at right centre shows the B.T. Rogers house in Vancouver in 1905.*

Current members of the Rogers clan include Forrest Rogers, photographed here with a Pierce-Arrow. He is the fourth son of B.T. Rogers and chairman of B.C. Sugar; his son C. Stephen Rogers (ABOVE) has been, since 1979, a member of the B.C. cabinet.

Walter Nichol, at one time lieutenant-governor of British Columbia and publisher of the Vancouver Province. *Nichol's grandson is Vancouver power broker John Nichol, president of Springfield Investment Co.*

Wynn ("Chunky") Woodward, current chief of the clan, is as influential as ever. Tall and fit, he's not a bit like his nickname. A super skier, one of B.C.'s best fishermen, he trains and rides champion cutting horses, owns Canada's largest ranch (the half-million-acre Douglas Lake spread), and loves to track moose through the wilderness. He is married for the third time, looks like a Marlboro Man with a high IQ, and feels much more at home roaming the Nicola Valley rangeland than lounging around the boardroom of the Royal Bank. Chunky is a totem Establishment figure, the third-generation chairman of the family department store chain, whose annual sales reached $1.1 billion in 1982. His empire of 25 stores (all in B.C. and Alberta) is now run by a cousin, Woody

The legendary Charles Namby Wynn (Chunky) Woodward, skier, fisherman, horseman, hunter, and third-generation chairman of the Woodward department-store chain. He is shown here at his half-million acre Douglas Lake Ranch, accompanied by one of his foremen and arranged among some sample enthusiasms.

MacLaren, who trained at Upper Canada College, UBC, and Price Waterhouse and loves the retail trade.

The institution that caters most attentively to the older generation's fussy demands is the Vancouver Club, a prime-time watering hole where many of those who count still gather for lunch. One of the problems is that the Vancouver Club enforces its rule that no member or his guest can take notes during meals. Most of the new-style entrepreneurs love doodling on tablecloths (which they take with them), napkins, backs of menus. If they tried that within the stuffy confines of the Vancouver Club, the waiters would swoon and the Stilton would crumble.

The thinly disguised prejudices of the Vancouver Club were slightly dented by the 1980 admission of Dr. Chan Gunn, Bob Lee (the city's prime real-estate dealer), and Tong Louie, who runs a large food-marketing operation and is the first Chinese to become a director of the Royal Bank. (Just in case there might be any clucking, Louie's name was put forward by Charles Cecil Ingersoll Merritt, a Vancouver war hero who won the

The venerable Vancouver Club, founded in 1893, was once referred to by columnist Allan Fotheringham as a "varicose-veined reservoir of tasteful tweed dignity."

Bob Lee, Vancouver's prime real-estate dealer shown here with his father, is responsible for channelling large amounts of Far Eastern money into Canadian investments.

FACING: Nathan Nemetz, Chief Justice of British Columbia, in the Arthur Erickson-designed Law Courts in Vancouver.

140

Jack Diamond is head of the B.C. Jockey Club and chancellor of Simon Fraser University. He is shown here in his private aerie above the track at Vancouver's Pacific National Exhibition Grounds.

Victoria Cross at Dieppe.) Louie, whose private company has quietly grown to control a major part of the B.C. wholesale food trade, is the Chinese community's "good old boy"; to emphasize the fact that he bears the burden for no man, he gave his sons and heirs solidly Prussian names: Brandt and Kurt.

The Vancouver Club's anti-Jewish bias was first shattered in 1977 when Chief Justice Nathan Nemetz of the B.C. Supreme Court joined—a request that could hardly be denied, since his sponsors were John Farris (then his senior as Chief Justice of British Columbia) and the late Walter Owen, then the province's lieutenant-governor. The only other Jewish members who followed were Abe Gray and Leslie Raphael. Several of the Jewish community's leading members, including Sam Belzberg, Joe Segal, and Jack Diamond, remain outside the club. Diamond, who was a butcher in Poland, runs the city's largest abattoir and has become an outstanding racehorse breeder.

He made it to chancellor of Simon Fraser University and became a Mason, but he's still not welcome at the Vancouver Club.

MOST OF TODAY'S ACTIVE PLAYERS belong to a new generation that ignores the Vancouver Club. They are self-made and classless, embracing the philosophy of lives as scenarios—eccentric extroverts who dream of creating a new Pacific Rim empire on Canada's West Coast.

Nomads in search of themselves, they feel little obligation to provide for the next generation. Life is lived for the ecstasy of the moment, whether it consists of getting the biggest slice of the biggest financial deal going, beating the pants off a neighbour in racquetball, or sticking your partner for a huge dinner bill at The Mansion, Le Pavillon, or, more likely, at one of Umberto Menghi's marvellous eateries. It is seduction of the flesh that preoccupies them, but it is seduction of their souls that is taking place. They are not a founding people.

The main effect of their arrival has been to transform Vancouver's downtown into an important financial district. Quite apart from the growing number of Canadian companies moving their operations westward, much of the world's flight capital seeking a safe, profitable haven is finding its way to Vancouver. "The high concrete walls of Howe Street," Denny Boyd noted in the *Vancouver Sun* during the autumn of 1980, "are beginning to glow with the rich hues of foreign currency, and its recent flow may be traced right up to the muzzles of Russian guns pointed menacingly at the Middle East oil fields...Perhaps we will see the day when the mark of prestige among Swiss millionaires will be a numbered B.C. bank account." Jacques Barbeau, a graduate of Harvard Law School and son-in-law of Walter Owen, runs the law practice that advises many of the newcomers. "We're deluged with Iranians, Turks, as well as Japanese and Germans trying to invest in B.C.," he notes. "Even the Swiss, who are perhaps the most myopic people in the world, are moving in."

Barbeau recognizes a real change in Vancouver's attitude to the rest of Canada. "We used to have to keep explaining how we can go skiing, play tennis, and sail all in the same day, but that's all becoming redundant now. We can't be bothered having to justify our lifestyles. Besides, most visitors from the East get a false impression watching a lot of people from the financial district going home early. Because of the time-zone difference, our offices start operating at 7:30 A.M. and it takes me precisely eight minutes to drive from my house in Shaughnessy. So you can put a fairly good day's work in and still leave early."

IN MOST CITIES, GREAT HOUSES inspire great parties. In Vancouver, it's the other way around. The mansions most of the new Establishment types occupy are advertisements of their wealth, allowing them to create environments that embody their illusions and mirror their fantasies.

Each house is individual, but they tend to have some denominators in common: a Corinthian lightness and grace in the architecture that blends exteriors with interiors. At least part of the living room can be landscaped, for example; there might be marble bathrooms with skylights through which to count the stars while soaping a lady's back; decks off the bedroom with a mountain and/or ocean view; exposed beams in lofts meant as meditation roosts; an extravagant use of technology and knick-knacks of all kinds, including machines that make julienne French fries; Jacuzzis; solid oak front doors thick enough to double as butcher's blocks; tiled fireplaces with gas jet starters; and conversation pits fitted with remote-controlled Betamaxes for watching reruns of "Wall Street Week."

One great status symbol is to have your house done by Arthur Charles Erickson, the country's most bankable architect and designer of Canada's pavilions at both Expo 67 and Expo 70, of Simon Fraser University, and of Toronto's Roy Thomson Hall. His Zen-like approach to design creates an almost mystical effect.

In a city where the most essential cultural institutions are TV crusader Dr. Jack Webster, pundit Allan Fotheringham, and *Sun* columnist Denny Boyd, the arts do not really provide society's leading edge; the most prized celebrities are visiting entertainers from L.A. and Vegas. But houses are crammed with the costly splashings of West Coast artists.

The most obvious signs of ostentatious spending are cars and yachts. Vancouver abounds with great blue-water sailors. Lol Killam's 73-foot ketch *Graybeard* is probably the best-known racer; the yacht with the best lines is George O'Brien's 12-metre *Endless Summer*. Plenty of those fancy, low-slung Italian coupes with unpronounceable hood markings and 50 coats of hand-rubbed lacquer prowl Stanley Park like mechanical

Shaughnessy was developed by the CPR as an exclusive residential area. (Many of the streets bear the names of CPR directors.)
Shown here is the Tudor-style mansion built by Walter C. Nichol, publisher of the Province, *in 1912.*

panthers. But most of the upscale crowd sticks with a turbo-diesel Mercedes or, preferably, a Rolls. The most expensive model in town is the custom-built $250,000 brown-and-tan Corniche that stock broker Peter Brown bought in 1980; he was so impressed with it that, instead of waiting, he had the car flown from Britain.

A compulsory manifestation of B.C. wealth remains a *pied-à-terre*, usually referred to as "a shack," at Whistler. The economic setbacks of the early 1980s devastated Whistler's real-estate values, but the resort (which includes nearby Blackcomb) boasts North America's longest ski-able vertical drop (4,280 feet), and plans include a glacier lift to bring to fruition skiers' dream of perpetual winter. So many couples who aren't married (to each other) spend weekends at Whistler that tattles about their carryings-on turn the hills into one huge whispering gallery. "There are always rumours in the valley," socialite Valerie Gibson once reported in *Vancouver*. "Kiss a girl at Emerald Estates, and you're divorced by the time you reach the Husky station."

Everybody skis, jogs, sails, or swims. Bob Wyman of Pemberton, Houston, Willoughby has his own swimming pool, but usually drives up to the Hollyburn Country Club because the pool is longer (82 feet). Woody MacLaren of Wood-

Two views of the house designed for Helmut Eppich by Arthur Erickson. The house is considered an outstanding example of Erickson's work.

The first sailing club in Vancouver was the Burrard Inlet Sailing Club, started in 1887 with Henry Bell-Irving as chairman. It disappeared in a few years, as did other early efforts. The Vancouver Yacht Club was founded in 1903, renting premises initially from the Vancouver Rowing Club in Coal Harbour, and received its royal charter in 1906. Shown here are scenes from the annual spring sailpast, which is one of the highlights of the season, and two of the finest yachts in Vancouver: on the facing page, Lol Killam's 73-foot ketch Graybeard and, above, Canada's only other twelve-metre, George O'Brien's Endless Summer, which is a former Australian America's Cup hopeful. Endless Summer is shown off Victoria in the Swiftsure, the premier racing event.

ward's has qualified for Level Three of the Canadian Ski Instructors Alliance. Many of the Establishment types hunt, but without foxes. Instead, the Fraser Valley Hunt follows hounds on the track of a fox-scented sack dragged behind a nimble pony club rider. The problem is that a real fox occasionally blunders onto the course, upsetting the proceedings. At one 1978 hunt, a pack of hounds following the phony fox took after a real fox, then when a deer crossed their trial, some dogs followed it, resulting in three streams of very confused hunters.

THE POWER EQUATIONS in British Columbia are never stable for very long, but some names keep reappearing. The Bentley and Prentice families, who control Canadian Forest Products, are a prime example. Peter Bentley, who heads the company, has emerged as one of the dominant stars of the new generation of Canadian business leaders. He took the firm public in 1983 as Canfor Corp. (it had been called by some the largest privately owned enterprise west of Eaton's), and sold off a third of its equity for $142 million.

Bentley lives quietly and is not burdened with a large ego. He likes upland game shooting, has done some sports-car racing, and enjoys bridge and golf, but nearly all his energies are devoted to business. His only real hobby is being a silent partner in the company that holds the BMW distribution for Canada. Backed by the strong and enlightening presence of Ron Longstaffe, his executive vice-president and one of Canada's most knowledgeable art collectors, Bentley runs most of the company's subsidiaries as if they were divisions. One major exception is Versatile Corp. (acquired in 1974), which is headed by Peter Paul Saunders, a Hungarian-born entrepreneur who may well rank as B.C.'s most capable manager.

Some of the other, more-enduring Vancouver "names" include Morris Belkin (printing and packaging), the Bentalls (land and construction), the Block brothers (real estate), Ron Cliff (corporate director), Graham Dawson (construction), Doug Gardiner (corporate director), Frank Griffiths (broadcasting), Trevor Pilley (banking), John Pitts (management), Ray Peters (broadcasting), Gordon Gibson, Jr. (politics), and Ken Tolmie and Doug Maitland (Whistler). The most interesting power couple: Senator Jack Austin, who has singlehandedly moved the Liberals in B.C. from near masochistic to near plausible, and his wife, writer Natalie Freeman, who has talent to burn.

Until the mid-'70s, Vancouver's financial and social establishments were one and the same. But that longstanding blend fissioned when the new loners achieved fiscal prominence. Jimmy Pattison, Edgar Kaiser, Jr., Peter Brown, Bob Carter, Nelson Skalbania, Sam Belzberg, Norman Keevil, Jr., Joe Segal, David Radler, Herb Doman, and Peter Cundill did not fit any existing category; each man represented a subspecies on his own.

The Great Recession of the early 1980s put a lid on most of their exploits or pushed at least a few of them permanently out of contention. As the banks pulled in the loans on which most of their wealth was pyramided, they were overheard whispering among themselves about yet another buddy who was "into big numbers, receiverwise."

The country's most heroic bankrupt, without a doubt, was real-estate flipper Nelson Skalbania, hit by Ottawa for back taxes of more than $4 million and saddled with lawsuits from creditors for another $3 million. After announcing his fiscal difficulties at a Bayshore hot-dog dinner for a hundred friends, he was granted $90,000 a year in pocket money toward the attempt at repairing his fortunes. Jack Poole, Neil Cook, and the Doumet brothers were in similar difficulties, but Joe Segal, the Belzberg brothers, Herb Doman, Bob Lee, Edgar Kaiser, and the two Norman Keevils (senior and junior) survived the downturn; by the summer of 1983 they were well along the comeback trail. The most dramatic renascence was that of Murray (the Pez) Pezim, a stock promoter who freely admits to being a living legend. The former Toronto butcher was more than once close to bankruptcy, but by mid-1983 he was riding high, controlling 57 companies listed on the Vancouver Stock Exchange.

The dominant personality of the VSE remains Peter Brown, head of Canarim Investment and known to one and all as "the Rabbit." An eternal optimist and one of the smartest money men in the country, Brown traded shares worth $2.5 billion during the first six months of 1983. The Rabbit has a well-earned reputation for high living and plotting complicated pranks. To everything he does he adds a dash of razzle-dazzle. He's creative and unconventional enough that he has managed to turn the prosaic business of being a stock broker into a grand amusement: his trading days, for instance, are measured not in dollar turnover but in terms of bottles of Dom Perignon. ("Hell," he'll exclaim, "that was a five-Dom day!" Or, disconsolately: "No better than a one-Dom day.") The Rabbit has manfully resisted becoming an Establishment figure, insulting one maître d' after another and committing countless outrages against the accepted mores of Canada's moneyed class. Sworn to upholding his individuality, he is energetically dedicated to his particular understanding of life's joys and priorities. But his resistance has been to no avail. As Art Buchwald, the American humorist, once remarked: "When you attack the Establishment, they don't put you in jail or a mental institution. They do something worse: they make you a *member*."

The other Vancouver entrepreneur in danger of becoming a permanent Establishment fixture is Jimmy Pattison, the one-time used-car dealer who has changed his image—lock, stock, and oil barrel—to that of "international merchant banker." Gone are the polka-dot bow ties and powder-blue Cadillacs: Pattison now dons three-piece pinstripe suits, more in keeping with his latest incarnation.

His conglomerate—The Jim Pattison group —is number 103 on the list of Canada's largest

J.R.

Peter (the Rabbit) Brown, flamboyant head of Canarim Investment and one of the powers of the Vancouver Stock Exchange. Brown is dangerously close, despite his best and most stylish efforts to the contrary, to becoming an Establishment figure.

Murray (the Pez) Pezim, stock promoter, former butcher, legend-at-large. His latest bonanza is a share in the Hemlo gold play.

NIGEL DICKSON

Jimmy Pattison, one-time used car dealer and now international merchant banker shown sitting on the bridge of his 77-foot custom-built cabin cruiser, Nova Springs.

companies and is one of the few firms among the top 500 owned 100 per cent by one person. After trying a dozen businesses (and doing well in them all), Pattison turned international with Great Pacific Finance AG, a financing institution at Zug, 25 minutes south of Zurich. The B.C. entrepreneur is also a partner in Anamco, an arbitrage company operating out of the Cayman Islands with London's J. Henry Schroder Bank as partner.

What will forever endear Brown and Pattison to B.C.'s social and fiscal hierarchy is that instead of abandoning competitors who had been hammered by the severe economic downturn they helped keep many of them afloat. In the shifting sands of the province's power structure, keeping a colleague from going "underwater" guarantees the future clout of any man.

Victoria had an Establishment of its own, consisting of colonial administrators and Royal Navy officers, when Vancouver was still covered with forest. Shown here is the Admiral's House, built in 1885, an attractively unpretentious house reminiscent of an English country vicarage.

At the other end of the architectural scale from the Admiral's House is Craigdarroch Castle in Victoria. More monumental than elegant, with towers, parapets, stained glass, and porte cochère, *it was built in the 1880s by Scotsman Robert Dunsmuir, coal millionaire and builder of the Esquimalt and Nanaimo Railway. Dunsmuir died before his castle was completed, but his widow lived there until her death in 1908. Their son James was at different times premier and lieutenant-governor of British Columbia.*

The Hastings House is an elegant country hotel on Saltspring Island, one of the Gulf Islands that with their salubrious climate are a favourite retreat from the hustle—and the rain—of Vancouver. Owned in part by the Cross family of ranching fame, the hotel occupies several buildings on property formerly owned by Warren Hastings, a naval architect who helped design landing craft used on D-Day. Hastings, an Englishman, designed the houses to suit his Elizabethan furniture. Guests arrive by ferry, by yacht (at the hotel's marina), and by floatplane. The wine cellar is well stocked and menus are hand-lettered daily.

DESPITE THE FASCINATION of most Canadians with the extravagant oddities of the West Coast, some of the most interesting rustles of future influence are emanating from the other end of the country. The Hibernia oil find, Sable Island gas strikes, and other less-publicized discoveries have prompted another look at the Atlantic region, the seldom-appreciated back garden of Canada's Establishment. Perhaps the most startling discovery was that life east of the 70th line of longitude could be pleasant without being bucolic, rewarding without becoming hectic.

Home ground for the great Canadian fortunes of Samuel Cunard, Max Aitken (Lord Beaverbrook), and Sir James Dunn, the Maritimes needed most of a century to recover from the twin blows of Confederation and the end of the age of sail. Otherwise realistic men spent their evenings sighing for the days when the tidal terminal of every creek and river was marked by the tall angular silhouettes of great schooners and clipper ships.

Max Aitken (1879-1964), Lord Beaverbrook, was born in Maple, Ontario, and raised in Newcastle, New Brunswick. A brilliant organizer, he put together such companies as Stelco, Canada Cement, and Royal Securities before searching for greater challenges in England. He became a British MP in 1910 and was raised to the peerage in a controversial appointment in 1917, long before his major contribution to public life as a minister in Churchill's war cabinet. He bought the Daily Express in 1917 and went on to acquire other papers. He was a major benefactor to New Brunswick through such institutions as the Beaverbrook Art Gallery in Fredericton. His son, Sir Max Aitken, a distinguished RAF fighter pilot in the Second World War, lives in London and is life president of Express Newspapers Ltd.

Oaklands, built during the 1860s in Halifax by William Cunard, boasted a glass-enclosed winter garden and Italianesque carriage entrance. Halifax-born Sir Samuel Cunard (1787-1865) for many years ran the mail service to and from Halifax, Boston, Newfoundland, and Bermuda. In 1840 he obtained a British contract and subsidy to operate a trans-Atlantic mail service, which became the chief British steamer line on the North Atlantic run. His son Sir Edward inherited his share in the business and was succeeded by brother William.

A 1965 gathering at the presentation of the Eleanor Roosevelt Humanities Award in Saint John. Left to right: K.C. Irving and his wife, Harriet; Mrs. J.M. Franklin; Allan Bronfman; Lorraine Robichaud and her husband, Louis J. Robichaud, then premier of New Brunswick.

PUBLIC ARCHIVES CANADA/MONTREAL STAR COLLECTION/PA 132012

This spiritual defeatism turned Maritimes businessmen toward their governments to form temporary coalitions with the only force they considered powerful enough to bargain effectively with the Central Canadian authorities. The line between public and private enterprise grew increasingly blurred, prompting K.C. Irving's classic comment: "I don't think politics and business mix. New Brunswick is too small for politics."

The Irvings—and, increasingly, the McCains—continue to dominate the feudal structure of New Brunswick. There are a few other important names—the Gagnons, the Blacks, a passle of Olands, plus Pat Rocca, the construction man who is rebuilding downtown Saint John—but most of the great New Brunswick merchant families (the Millers of Campbellton, the Piries of Grand Falls, the McLeans of Charlotte, the Taits of Shediac, the Kents of Bathurst) have vanished from the scene.

The senior Irving fled to the tax haven of Bermuda in 1971, but he controls his empire through his sons, Jack (known as "Gassy"), Jim ("Oily"), and Arthur ("Greasy"). "Every New Brunswicker knows that K.C. Irving is a lot more than just a man," wrote Russell Hunt and Robert Campbell in a biography that referred to K.C. as "a social phenomenon on the same level of importance as a revolution or a war." They commented how difficult his importance is to measure. "You can't do it, for instance, by counting up how much his companies own or how much they earn, because the figures simply aren't available. Nor can the Irving power be neatly or easily measured. If there ever was a company town covering 28,000 square miles, with a population of 600,000, New Brunswick is it; and the company is K.C. Irving Ltd.—a company that was begun by Irving and his father in 1926 as a Ford dealership, but which has grown in less than fifty years to be the single most powerful economic force in Eastern Canada."

Kenneth Colin Irving was born in 1899 at Buctouche, an oyster-fishing village on New Brunswick's east coast. His father operated sawmills and a general store. After brief stints at Dalhousie and Acadia universities, young Irving established the local dealership for the Model-T Ford and became Imperial Oil's agent for Kent

County. By 1924, he was selling so much gas and oil that Imperial unexpectedly disfranchised him to take over distribution for its own account. An outraged Irving got a bank loan, put in storage tanks and built his own service stations, painting them red, white, and blue, the same colours as Imperial's. He was determined to challenge the outsider's supremacy. Within four years, his company was a success and he moved his operations to the five-story garage in Saint John that became his headquarters for the next 43 years. Irving started a construction company to build his stations and moved into shipping, bus lines, and lumber. He also acquired the Saint John Shipbuilding and Dry Dock Company, which in the summer of 1983 was awarded the $3.58 billion contract to build six new patrol frigates for the Canadian navy.

Irving's energy, combined with the country-store clerk's shrewdness that characterized his deals, lengthened the roster of his enterprises. Eventually, he controlled a hundred companies, employing one in every twelve of the province's workers and owning fully one-tenth of New Brunswick's land area. In partnership with Standard Oil of California, he put up a $50 million refinery near Saint John and, with the heirs of Simon Patiño, the Bolivian tin king, financed exploitation of base-metal deposits near Bathurst. His gasoline stations have proliferated into a chain of two thousand outlets; he has acquired every English-language newspaper and most of the important radio and TV outlets in the province. There was no single public stock offering in any of his enterprises, so his personal ownership has remained undiluted and their earnings do not have to be disclosed. His corporate structure, which no outsider has ever managed to disentangle, is so complicated that, in the summer of 1971, when the seamen on one of his tankers, the *Irving Ours Polaire*, wanted to have their union certified, they couldn't figure out the name of the corporation that owned the ship.

The McCain dynasty, rooted in the gracious splendour of their mansions lining River View Drive in Florenceville, is very much more open, a great deal more adventurous, and certainly more international. Two of the McCain brothers—chairman Harrison and president Wallace—have built a world-scale commercial empire based on the lowly French fry. Theirs may well be Canada's ultimate example of free enterprise on the sprout. The McCains' father, Andrew, sowed the seeds of the potato empire by exporting spuds to South America, and with his wife, the spunky Laura Blanche (Perley), founded the McCain dynasty—but it was the two boys who made it what it is. Harrison, who is the more visible of the two (though ownership of McCain Foods is evenly divided), rarely seems to alight, using one or another of his jets to do business on whatever continent he happens to be visiting. The McCain enterprises span 25 factories that turn out frozen foods worth $750 million a year in half a dozen countries, including the United States, most of Western Europe, and the United Kingdom.

Like most other successful New Brunswickers, the two McCains apprenticed under K.C. Irving. By the time he was 30, Harrison held the post of Irving Oil's sales manager for New Brunswick; Wallace, at 23, was already manager of the Irving-owned Thorne's Hardware operation. They both left in 1957. Harrison is married to Billie, daughter of former Liberal Premier and Chief Justice J.B. McNair (who died in 1968). Wallace is married to Margaret, daughter of Senator Margaret Fawcett Norrie of Truro, Nova Scotia.

Intense yet endearing—more like a good old boy out of *Dallas* than a plantation owner from *Gone With the Wind*—Harrison makes the blood pump wherever he goes: always in the passing lane and hardly ever being passed.

A much more elusive and mysterious New Brunswick presence is Reuben Cohen of Moncton. A gentle-voiced lawyer with the persistence of a terrier, Cohen has that special quality of taking people at their face value which distinguishes Maritimers from their more cynical Central-Canadian colleagues. Cohen graduated with honours from Dalhousie Law School, bought out Central Trust in his home town, and merged it first with Nova Scotia Trust Company and later with Eastern Canada Savings & Loan Company of Halifax to form the region's most influential group of financial companies. With his partner Leonard Ellen, a Montreal investment dealer and lumber wholesaler, he waged an eight-year holy war to take over Toronto's controversial Crown Trust. By the summer of 1983, the two financiers were on the verge of capturing control of the Nova Scotia Savings & Loan Company, adding the Halifax-based lending institution with assets of $400 million to their expanding financial stable.

PRINCE EDWARD ISLAND, with a population of only 123,000, has until recently been something of a Third World province—dependent on potatoes and fishing, nurturing past glories but few prospects. But in June 1983, oil exploration worth $28 million was started by Chevron and Texaco off the Island's northeastern shore, holding out the promise that P.E.I. might join Nova Scotia as the eventual site of an energy boom.

Discovery of the $3 billion Ventures field off Sable Island, due to start pumping natural gas to the New England states in 1987, has transformed Halifax and its hinterland. It is a boom of the sort P.E.I. both fears and craves. Out of this one strike alone, the Nova Scotia treasury is due to collect an estimated $22 billion in taxes and royalties. The nine ocean rigs in place off the province's shores in mid-1983 have encouraged the dreams of more gas and oil finds. The total effect has been to lift Halifax into the category of growth region—if not a future Calgary, a miniature Aberdeen in the offing.

Quite apart from its surging economic vigour, Halifax has become a centre of intellectual ferment, with such heavyweight former Upper Canadians as George Grant, Tom Kent, James Eayrs, John Godfrey, George Bain, and Harry Bruce gracing its shores and valleys. Dalhousie Law School continues to exert influence, and King's College is gaining deserved renown.

The Nova Scotia Olands lost their patriarch, Victor, in the summer of 1983 and the family's prestige suffered somewhat from the sale of its brewery to Labatt's, but, along with some other local dynasties, various Olands continue to occupy the favoured corners of the Halifax Club. R.B. Cameron, the Royal Bank's largest shareholder, is as shrewd and mischievous as ever; R.A. Jodrey, who once sat on 56 Canadian boards of directors, has been succeeded by his heirs, John Jodrey and David Hennigar, who in tandem went on to capture control of Extendicare Ltd. and Crown Life Insurance in Toronto. J.E.A. Nickerson has become the province's beleaguered fisheries king; Michael Novak and Ralph Medjuck continue to build Halifax into an urban metropolis. The fastest-growing influence is J. William E. Mingo, a mutton-chopped lawyer with two dozen directorships who also serves as national treasurer for the federal Liberals.

Mingo's mentor and still the central authority of who does what in the province is Frank Manning Covert. Now well into his 70s and spending more time in his beloved ocean-side retreat at Hunts Point in Queens County, Covert graduated from Dalhousie Law School and articled under the late James McGregor Stewart, the great collector of Kipling manuscripts, who became a vice-president and director of the Royal Bank. Covert spent two war years in Ottawa as a lawyer in Munitions and Supply, then joined the RCAF and won the Distinguished Flying Cross. He sat at the feet of Angus L. Macdonald, campaigned for James Ilsley, worked for C.D. Howe, and acted as legal adviser to Roy Jodrey, Fred Manning, George Chase, Ralph Bell, the Sobeys, the MacCullochs, and others. Covert is one of the few Maritimers totally accepted by every branch of the Upper

George W.C. Oland, who came to Canada in the late 19th century, married Ella Y. Bauld of Halifax and went into the brewing business. Oland Breweries was sold by the family to Labatt's in 1971. (Oland cousins in Saint John own Moosehead Breweries, which is still an independent company.)

RIGHT: Lindola, the Oland family home on Young Avenue in Halifax was built in 1905.

BELOW: The Oland crest. "Truth and Honour" is the family motto.

Colonel Sidney Oland (son of George Oland) and his three sons expanded the family business. Left to right: Victor, Bruce, Sidney Oland (seated), and Don. Victor Oland, who died in 1983, was a former lieutenant-governor of Nova Scotia and the driving force behind the building of Bluenose II, *the replica of the famous fishing schooner.*

OLAND

157

Bruce Oland, with his wife, Ruth, at their house in Halifax. He is chairman of Lindwood Holdings, the family holding company.

On the Northwest Arm are found many of the attractive houses where the old families of Halifax still live.

Frank Covert at his country place on the Atlantic in Queens County, Nova Scotia. He is the senior partner in the Halifax law firm of Stewart, MacKeen and Covert and, though he has retired from some of his directorships, remains an influential figure in the Maritimes.

William Mingo at his Halifax home. As well as holding numerous company directorships, he has played a key role in the development of Halifax as a modern container port.

Canadian Establishment. He acts as if he were constantly surprised that anyone should be bothered listening to him—while tossing out, like some bored lover's compliments, prescient advice that has an uncanny way of turning out to be the incisive solution to the issue at hand.

The most interesting family seeking Covert's advice and legal and fiscal counsel is the Sobeys of Stellarton. The dynasty was founded by Frank, who started out as a butcher. He built up a chain of movie theatres and supermarkets and ended up, at one time or another, with dominant blocks of stock in Dominion Textile, Anthes Imperial, Jannock, Canadian Salt, Wajax Ltd., and Halifax Developments Ltd., all held through Empire Co. Ltd., the family's investment trust. The Sobey brothers—Donald, David, and William—sit on 27 boards, are thoroughly involved in natural gas distribution, and have control of Halifax's downtown Scotia Square development jointly with the Jodrey family. Their largest holding remains Sobey Stores, which now has annual sales of more than $544 million—plus substantial interests in Montreal's Provigo Inc. and the Hannaford Brothers food chain in northern New England.

The Sobeys—a subdued yet determined clan of upright citizens on the corporate warpath—represent money power quietly biding its time in the Nova Scotia hinterland.

NEWFOUNDLAND IS ANOTHER MATTER. Very different from other Atlantic provinces, the province has always existed on its own, playing by special rules. It is still caught between the urge to remain a colony of whichever external power is most willing to carry its debts and the drive to match the pride of its people with the elusive dream of economic independence. The traditionally overwhelming influence of the Water Street overlords—the Macphersons, Winters, Harveys, Murrays, Bowrings, Perlins, Ayres, Hickmans, Bells, Collingwoods, Monroes, Crosbies, Steers,

Pratts, and Outerbridges—firmly endures, even if that influence is expressed in businesses now widely divergent from their shared, strictly merchantile beginnings. But not all the families have survived the economic disfranchisement they felt at the time of Confederation in 1949.

The original members of the St. John's aristocracy were provisioners to the British fleets, commissioners who grew rich on Newfoundland's special colonial privileges and tariff barriers, gradually diversifying their holdings into retail outlets, fishing operations, construction, and local politics. They became the island's "black kings," agents with whom the occupying British garrison commanders and governors made their private and profitable arrangements in return for keeping the native population from becoming more than reasonably restless.

All this changed in 1949 when Joey Smallwood brought the island into Confederation. With some notable exceptions, the old families lost their drive, retreating into coupon clipping or leaving Newfoundland altogether. Stores and wholesale operations moved in from the mainland, displacing the Water Street monopolies, but power was scarcely dispensed into new hands.

Geoff Stirling (whose son Scott is the creator of the comic strip *Captain Newfoundland*) is a broadcaster who is as comfortable in a waterfront tavern as searching for theological and extraterrestrial unknowns in Arizona. The Lundrigans of Corner Brook and Harry Steele (who runs Eastern Provincial Airways) man the Newfoundland Establishment's outposts. In some trouble but still dominant through the force of their personalities are John and Andrew Crosbie, heirs to the dynasty founded by Sir John Chalker Crosbie, an exuberant freebooter who became finance minister in Newfoundland's colonial administration of the 1920s. It was Ches, the eldest of his eleven children, who turned the primitive conglomerate left by Sir John into a modern commercial enterprise.

Water Street in St. John's, shown here about 1900, came to symbolize the mercantile aristocrats who dominated the Newfoundland economy.

Job Brothers, the oldest business firm in Newfoundland, is said to have been founded in 1730. The most significant endeavour of this mercantile company was the seal fishery. Job's at one time employed 150 people year-round as well as hundreds of sealers each spring. The photo shows the board of directors in 1946, with Henry Job in the centre. The present chairman is L.H.M. Ayre.

BOTH: PROVINCIAL ARCHIVES OF NEWFOUNDLAND AND LABRADOR

Because of its limited on-shore resources, the island has been dominated by premiers who govern in a Huey Long mode of despotic populism. Alfred Brian Peckford, a former teacher sworn into office in March 1979, rules firmly in that tradition, using Ottawa as his punching bag. With Newfoundland's three chief exports—newsprint, iron ore, and fish—suffering from poor demand in the early 1980s, attention was focused on offshore oil exploration. While physical indications were favourable, especially in the Hibernia field, Peckford's continuing jurisdictional disputes with Ottawa kept a lid on commitments—and secondary on-shore economic benefits remained relatively insignificant.

If this issue could be resolved, the signs are there for the soothsayers to read: Canada's Establishment, that group of power wielders who determine how this country works, is taking on a decidedly Maritime tinge. That tilt toward the East could peter out, or it could become the driving force behind the next wave of newcomers to overwhelm the current lists of the influential. The only certainty is that, as in the past, the Establishment will abide, renewing itself from the heavings of an economy and the evolution of a society still very much in their formative stages.

BECAUSE THE STRUCTURE AND the sources of its authority have become evanescent, the exact anatomy of Canada's Establishment is harder to pin down than it once was—but those who have felt the chill of its exclusions recognize its existence. The primary mission of the Establishment's loyalists, like that of most other elites, is to perpetuate their influence and, despite a politically hostile environment, this country's elite has succeeded in adapting to fit the times. Behind the rustle of *Wall Street Journal* pages in the reading rooms of their private luncheon clubs, within the recesses of the silk-lined boardrooms that perch atop the chartered banks' head offices and around the standing-reservation squash courts where they flex their minds and muscles, they divvy up the world with their usual style. Their greatest ambition is to remain unavailable and unassailable, saying nothing too testy or quotable, even to each other; they assume that their cronies are all fine fellows and that mannerly restraint will resolve most problems.

What is important about the men and women portrayed in this volume is that how an Establishment organizes itself indicates how a nation will ultimately pursue its objectives.

PROVINCIAL ARCHIVES OF NEWFOUNDLAND AND LABRADOR

Ayre's department store, about 1907. The firm of Ayre and Sons dates from 1859, when Charles Ayre, who came from Devon as an apprentice with Benjamin Bowring, went into business for himself. Ayre's wharves were among the busiest in St. John's, catering to thousands of coastal schooners each year.

Christopher Pratt sailing his C&C sloop in heavy weather on St. Mary's Bay, Newfoundland.

LEFT: *The imposing main entrance of Rideau Hall, official Ottawa residence of governors general since 1867. This stone facade and the formal main entrance hall (BELOW) were added in 1914 to the original 1838 house. Hall portraits include (left to right) King George VI in court dress, Edward VII as Prince of Wales in 1863, and Queen Elizabeth II. FACING PAGE, TOP LEFT: The High Commissioner of Uganda, Mrs. A. A. Amailuk, presents her Letters of Commission to Governor General Schreyer in the Grand Ballroom. The painting of Queen Elizabeth II and Prince Philip is by Lemieux.*

Rideau Hall was built by Scotsman Thomas MacKay in 1838. An architectural competition was held for a residence for the Queen's representative but the plans never went ahead and MacKay's stone villa, friendlier than the Victorian designs, has remained in use. The other official residence is the Citadel in Quebec.

RIGHT: The Governor General and Mrs. Lily Schreyer with their children: (left to right) Jason, Karmel, Lisa, and Toban. "Reggie" occupies a place of honour.

LEFT: The oval bedroom of the Royal Suite. BELOW LEFT: The Drawing Room whose tall windows overlook the rose garden. BELOW: The ballroom set for 110 dinner guests. The specatacular chandelier contains 12,650 pieces of crystal lit by 80 bulbs.

II

The Dynasties

Being portraits of twenty-one families that for at least three generations have exemplified prestige and leadership of the Canadian Establishment.

The Bassetts

HE BASSETTS, a family prominent in the communications and sports businesses, particularly in Ontario, have long represented an energetic and particularly photogenic kind of capitalism.

The family's Canadian roots extend back to 1909 when John Bassett (1886-1958) arrived from Northern Ireland and quickly established the family's involvement in the media by becoming a reporter for the Montreal *Witness*. Shortly afterward, he moved to the Montreal *Gazette*, where for many years he was chief parliamentary reporter. After serving with the Governor General's Foot Guards during the First World War and rising to the rank of major, Bassett was named a vice-president of the *Gazette* in 1918; eventually he became its president and publisher. As a private individual he purchased the Sherbrooke *Daily Record*, which later passed from the Bassett family to Conrad Black. In *Duplessis*, Black's biography of the long-time Quebec premier, he characterizes the elder Bassett as having been "political, combative, blustery, pro-French, unscrupulous, shameless—in a word a natural ally of Duplessis."

The leader of the second generation is John White Hughes Bassett, born in Ottawa in 1915. He was educated at Bishop's College School and Bishop's University in the Eastern Townships of Quebec, but moved to Toronto and became a reporter on the *Globe and Mail* in 1938. His

John White Hughes Bassett in the study of his Toronto house.

reporting career, like his father's, was interrupted by war. Bassett served variously with the Royal Highland Regiment (the Black Watch of Canada), the Royal Rifles, and the Seaforth Highlanders; he saw action in North Africa and Italy and, again like his father, emerged as a major. After the war, he worked for the Toronto *Telegram* and in 1952 purchased the newspaper in partnership with the Eaton family.

In the 1950s he became a partner in several sporting concerns: Maple Leaf Gardens, which houses and owns the Toronto Maple Leafs hockey club and was often referred to as the Carlton Street Mint, and the Toronto Argonauts football club. In 1960, the federal Conservative government granted a licence for Toronto's first commercial television station, CFTO. It became the cornerstone of the CTV television network, which Bassett dominates through Baton Broadcasting, a company that also holds several radio stations and other properties.

The late 1950s and early 1960s, however, were not marked only by triumphs for the Bassetts. In 1957, the *Telegram* was unsuccessful in an attempt to convert advertisers and the public to the idea of a Toronto Sunday edition (a scheme subsequently made workable by others) and in 1962 Bassett stood for Parliament as a Conservative in the Toronto Liberal stronghold of Spadina and was soundly defeated.

In the 1970s, apparently wearying of the publishing business, the family withdrew from newspapers entirely. In a controversial 1971 decision, Bassett closed the *Telegram*. A decade later, the

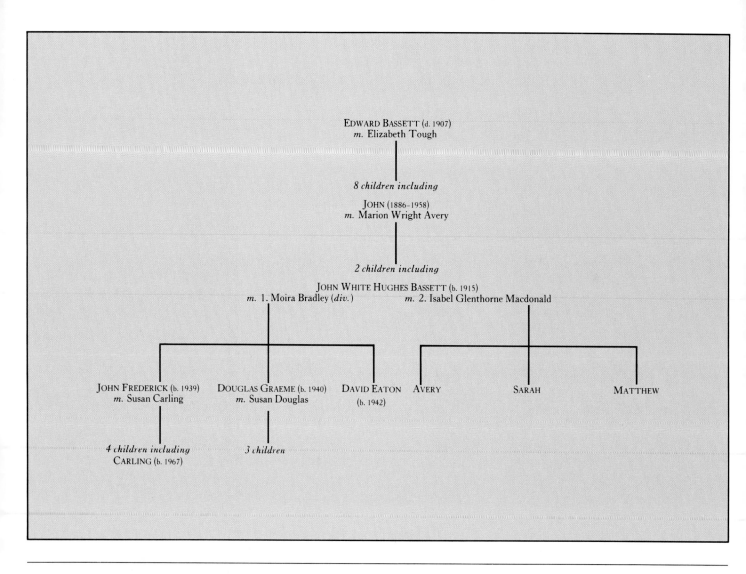

EDWARD BASSETT (d. 1907)
m. Elizabeth Tough

8 children including

JOHN (1886–1958)
m. Marion Wright Avery

2 children including

JOHN WHITE HUGHES BASSETT (b. 1915)
m. 1. Moira Bradley (div.)   m. 2. Isabel Glenthorne Macdonald

JOHN FREDERICK (b. 1939)   DOUGLAS GRAEME (b. 1940)   DAVID EATON   AVERY   SARAH   MATTHEW
m. Susan Carling   m. Susan Douglas   (b. 1942)

4 children including   3 children
CARLING (b. 1967)

Bassetts also sold Inland Publishing, the chain of suburban weeklies that had been run by Douglas Graeme Bassett (b. 1940), the second of John W.H.'s three sons. The business concerns of the youngest son, David Eaton (b. 1942), have not received much public attention. John Frederick (b. 1939) has expanded some of the family's traditional concerns, especially by moving into feature film production and by becoming active in professional sports franchises and real estate in the United States.

While the family business is now largely run by Doug, it is mainly through John F. that the family name has been kept before the public in the fourth and fifth generations. After graduation from the University of Western Ontario, John F. Bassett married Susan Carling of the famous brewing family. Their daughter, Carling Bassett (b. 1967), is among the continent's top-ranked professional tennis players and in 1983 became the first Canadian to make it to the quarter-finals at Wimbledon.

When John W.H. Bassett ruled the *Telegram* from offices on Toronto's Front Street, the poet John Robert Colombo was once moved to write of him as "Lord Bassett of Front." It was a jesting but a thoroughly appropriate tribute to the patriarch of a family long known for flamboyant attention to business and entrepreneurial zeal.

Three generations of Bassetts have slowly shifted their business interests from newspaper publishing to broadcasting. Douglas Bassett continued to operate community newspapers long after the family had abandoned metropolitan daily journalism by closing the Toronto Telegram *in 1971. He is shown here at television station CFTO in Toronto.*

John F. Bassett, eldest of the three Bassett sons, is a feature-film producer and investor in professional sports.

Carling Bassett, the 15-year-old daughter of John F. and Susan Carling Bassett, is one of the world's top-ranked professional tennis players.

Thomas Bata, seen here at Bata International headquarters in Don Mills, heads the Canadian-based company that produces one-third of the shoes sold in the Free World.

The Batas

THE BATAS HAVE been cobblers for an astonishing 11 generations, but it is only recently that they have achieved global pre-eminence to the point where one of every three pairs of shoes sold in the non-communist world is made by the Batas at one of the 100 factories they maintain in almost as many countries. It is more recently still that the Bata dynasty has called Canada home.

The founder of the business was Tomas Bata (1876-1932), a shoe maker in his native Zlín, Czechoslovakia, who began the current multinational corporation with an initial capitalization of only $200. A dedicated proponent of efficiency, Bata was a pioneer in applying time-and-motion studies to manufacturing and even installed a miniature office in the elevator so he wouldn't waste the moments spent travelling between floors. In time, the company grew so large that Zlín became almost a company town.

The founder's son, Thomas J. Bata (b. 1914), was sent as a teenager to erect a factory in Switzerland, which would become the company's European nerve centre. (Along with Bermuda, where the family has two trusts, Switzerland remains the offshore financial base.) The son was already well established in the business when his father was killed in a mysterious air crash in 1932. The intent behind Tom Sr.'s will was that Tom Jr. be groomed for the chief executive's role a bit longer, so control of the enterprise passed to Jan Bata, the founder's half-brother. This precipitated a family feud that ended only with Jan Bata's death a quarter-century later, even though effective power devolved to Tom during the Second World War.

When the Nazis invaded Czechoslovakia, both Batas fled—Jan to the United States and Tom to Canada. Tom had prudently smuggled out plans for shoe-making machinery, as well as much of the family's assets in the form of gold bullion, and was thus able to erect from scratch an entire Ontario town in direct imitation of Zlín. The town was named Batawa. From this new base, Bata built the global empire now run from Don Mills, Ontario.

Just as the first Tom Bata was rather American in his outlook on efficiency, so the present Batas are somewhat Japanese and futuristic in their conception of the privately held company, its style of operation, and its place in the world. Employees are referred to internally as Batamen, and the family name is used as a prefix in names of many of their company towns, not just in Batawa, Ontario. The company's attitude towards Batamen and Batawomen is one of paternalistic good faith, and the firm has a reputation for staff development and for allowing employees to rise to management positions.

In 1946, Tom Bata married Sonja Wettstein (b. 1926), an architect and a member of one of Switzerland's most important families; she quickly became a knowledgeable partner in the ever-growing business. In the past few years, Sonja Bata has emerged as a powerful and prominent business person as well as a significant patron of the arts. She sits on the boards of Alcan Aluminium and Canada Trustco, was once director of the National Design Council of Canada, and is a vital

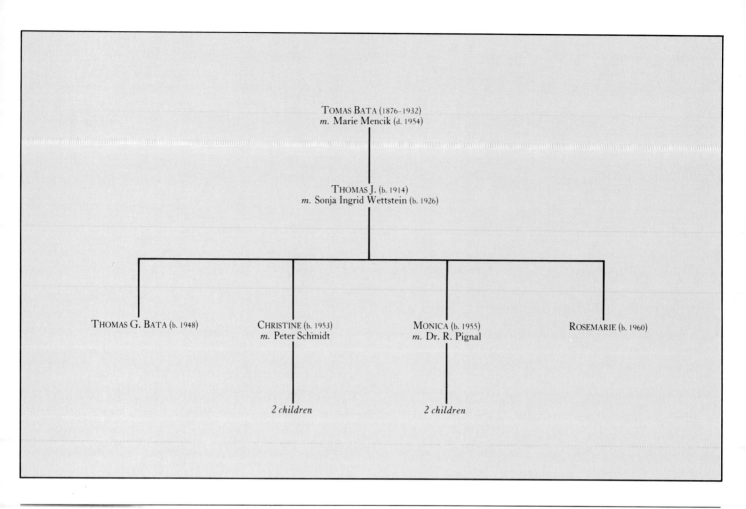

TOMAS BATA (1876–1932)
m. Marie Mencik (d. 1954)

THOMAS J. (b. 1914)
m. Sonja Ingrid Wettstein (b. 1926)

THOMAS G. BATA (b. 1948)

CHRISTINE (b. 1953)
m. Peter Schmidt

MONICA (b. 1955)
m. Dr. R. Pignal

ROSEMARIE (b. 1960)

2 children

2 children

force in the Canadian Council for Business and the Arts. Her sense of design finds an outlet in ever-changing shoe styles and her views and training in architecture, it is rumoured, resurfaced in Bata's Don Mills headquarters building.

The Batas travel extensively from their base in Toronto and are as prominent in international social circles as the Bronfmans. They have made acquaintances within the British royal family. They have four children, one of whom, a son, is expected to succeed his father: Thomas George Bata (b. 1948), a Harvard M.B.A. who has been the company's European regional manager.

Sonja Bata with part of her shoe collection; the Batas operate what is believed to be the only museum devoted exclusively to footwear.

J.R.

Sonja Wettstein Bata was a member of one of Switzerland's most important families when she married the shoe magnate Thomas Bata. An architect by training, she has influenced the dramatic course of the company and given it much of its character.

JIM ALLEN

The Bata corporate headquarters in Don Mills, a building thought to reflect the architectural ideas of Sonja Bata.

J.R.

The Birks

THE BIRKS NAME in Canada is associated with a particular shade of pale blue used on the gift boxes in which fine silver and jewellery come from the stores of Henry Birks and Sons. There are now more than a hundred such stores as well as half again as many Birks-owned shops that operate under other names. Birks is one of the few Canadian businesses that has been passed down through four generations of the same family and is quite probably the only one with fourth-generation employees.

In England, there were Birkses in the cutlery and jewellery trade from Elizabethan times straight through to the early 19th century. That's when John Birks became a pharmacist instead. In 1832, this family oddity left the Sheffield region for Canada. John's choice of career turned out to be a unique deviation from the family pattern, however, for his son Henry (1840-1928) entered the jewellery trade; he apprenticed to a Montreal firm and eventually became a partner. The firm closed and in 1879 he went out on his own. Thus one of the family's hallmarks—a churchwarden pipe, a symbol that had been in use for hundreds of years—once again appeared on fine silver and gold. It was among the insignia used, for example, on church silver which, in Catholic Quebec, accounted for a significant percentage of Birks's business.

Henry was eventually joined by his three sons, who became partners in 1893 when a new store, since expanded several times, opened on Montreal's St. Catherine Street. His sons were William Massey Birks (1868-1950), John Henry Birks (1870-1949), and Colonel Gerald Walker Birks (1872-1950). The Colonel quit the business in 1919 to devote all his time to Methodist good works, particularly the YMCA, but the other two, known as Mr. W.M. and Mr. Henry, served as successive presidents through a long period of growth. Mr. W.M., for example, continued the plan of buying other firms, particularly manufacturing silversmiths, with the result that today Birks makes 85 per cent of the sterling silver and jewellery it sells and is the fourth largest jewellery maker in the world. W.M., who was also one of the instigators of the merger that brought about the United Church of Canada, ran the firm until 1938, when the presidency passed to Mr. Henry, who had been running the company's silver factory. Thereafter control went successively to W.M's sons: Henry Gifford Birks (b. 1892) and Victor Birks (b. 1904).

Since 1972 the president has been Henry Gifford's son Drummond Birks (b. 1919), known to intimates as Drummie, who is the first Birks chief executive to graduate from university (McGill, of course). His most notable accomplishment as president has been expanding into the United States through takeovers of such firms as Shreve's and Long's, both of Boston, and through opening

The Henry Birks who founded the famous silver and jewellery firm in Victorian Montreal was a native Canadian, though his father had come from England where the family were known as cutlers and silversmiths as far back as Elizabethan times. The photo shows Henry Birks and his young family in 1903. When the male offspring were old enough, the company acquired its present name, Henry Birks & Sons.

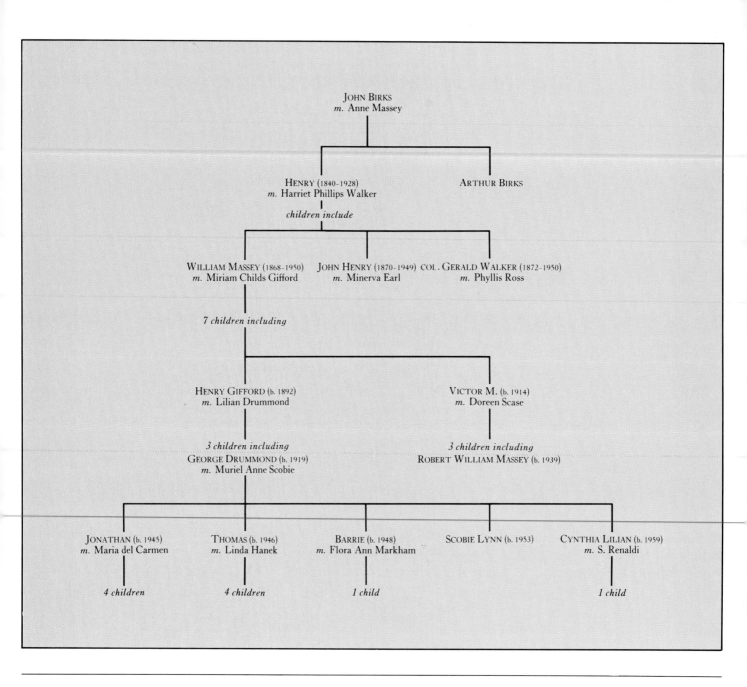

JOHN BIRKS
m. Anne Massey

HENRY (1840-1928)
m. Harriet Phillips Walker

ARTHUR BIRKS

children include

WILLIAM MASSEY (1868-1950)
m. Miriam Childs Gifford

JOHN HENRY (1870-1949)
m. Minerva Earl

COL. GERALD WALKER (1872-1950)
m. Phyllis Ross

7 children including

HENRY GIFFORD (b. 1892)
m. Lilian Drummond

VICTOR M. (b. 1914)
m. Doreen Scase

3 children including
GEORGE DRUMMOND (b. 1919)
m. Muriel Anne Scobie

3 children including
ROBERT WILLIAM MASSEY (b. 1939)

JONATHAN (b. 1945)
m. Maria del Carmen

THOMAS (b. 1946)
m. Linda Hanek

BARRIE (b. 1948)
m. Flora Ann Markham

SCOBIE LYNN (b. 1953)

CYNTHIA LILIAN (b. 1959)
m. S. Renaldi

4 children

4 children

1 child

1 child

Birks stores in American locations such as Baltimore and Philadelphia. By 1985 the firm expects that 25 per cent of its sales volume will be generated south of the border. All told, there are now approximately 120 stores using the Birks name, including many opened in Canadian shopping plazas through the 1960s and 1970s.

Drummie has three sons who work in the business and are expected to carry it on: Jonathan (b. 1945), Thomas (b. 1946), and Barrie (b. 1948). Traditionally the presidency has gone to a Birks son in his 50s. From top to bottom, the business is distinguished by an old-money way of doing things. This *modus operandi* goes beyond a fondness for good manners and discretion bordering on top secrecy. There is also the fact that control is tightly held. Seventy per cent of the shares in the business are owned by the family, the remainder by employees who, if they wish to sell their shares, must sell them only to the Birks family or to other employees. After all, the business is a family affair, and an elegant one at that. The Birks have always believed, on excellent authority and no doubt correctly, that Birks is in the best of taste.

William Birks poses in 1946 with his son Henry Gifford (right), grandson Drummond (centre), and great-grandson Henry Jonathan, all of whom were bred to the business.

Henry's boys William, John, and Gerald in 1940. The first two would each serve as president of the company while Gerald devoted himself to philanthropy.

The company president since the early 1970s has been Drummond Birks (ABOVE). He has boldly expanded the business into the United States while respecting the traditions reflected in the firm's St. Catherine Street shopfront in Montreal with its elaborate clock (LEFT), a landmark for generations.

The Bronfmans

IT IS SOMEHOW typical of this, one of the wealthiest families in North America and until recently one of the most mysterious, that there is some question about where the patriarch, Sam Bronfman, was actually born. One school of opinion holds that he first saw the world in mid-ocean while his parents Ekiel and Minnie Bronfman and siblings—Abe, Harry, and Laura—were emigrating from Russia in 1889. Others contend that Sam arrived after the family had landed and were on their way towards Wapella, a tiny ethnic settlement in eastern Saskatchewan where they eventually lighted. Everyone agrees, however, that in the 1920s Sam, by taking advantage of Prohibition laws in the United States, helped set the Bronfmans on a course that would make them owners of the largest group of liquor companies in the world.

In the early years of the century, the Bronfmans moved busily about the Prairies, first farming, then subcontracting for the Canadian Pacific Railway, next operating small hotels. From this last enterprise, involvement in the liquor trade followed. Unlike the situation in the United States, where booze was banned by constitutional amendment, Prohibition in Canada was a provincial affair: not all of the provinces banned liquor at the same time, if at all. Accordingly, the Bronfmans, initially under Harry's guidance, were able to establish a perfectly legal (and profitable) interprovincial mail-order liquor business.

Their success led them to enter the distilling field as well. In 1924 they erected a small distillery in Quebec and started an importing and warehousing business in Nova Scotia for bringing in liquor from overseas. By then, Prohibition had officially ended in the various provinces, although it would continue in the United States for another nine years. This was the key to their future wealth: it was illegal for Americans to import liquor into their country, but it was not illegal for Canadians to export from theirs. Accordingly, Harry Bronfman, who by now had been joined by brothers Abe, Sam, and Allan, became very prosperous. In 1927 the Bronfmans acquired control of Joseph E. Seagram and Sons, a company much troubled by Prohibition, and merged it with their own firm to form Distillers Corporation–Seagrams, an entity that, following the repeal of Prohibition in the United States in 1933, began taking over what in time became an astounding array of liquor and wine businesses in various countries.

Subsequently, the family moved equally intrepidly into world-wide energy exploration through Texas Pacific and Seaforth Petroleum, then, through Cadillac Fairview, into international real estate. Most of this activity was the doing of Sam Bronfman, who ruled the empire from Montreal. When he died in 1971, he left two daughters—Minda (b. 1925 and now the wife of Baron Alain de Gunzburg of the European banking family) and Phyllis (b. 1927, an architect)—as well as two sons who carried on the family business. The first son is Edgar Bronfman (b. 1929),

Seagram's headquarters, the miniature feudal castle Sam Bronfman built in 1928 at 1430 Peel Street in Montreal.

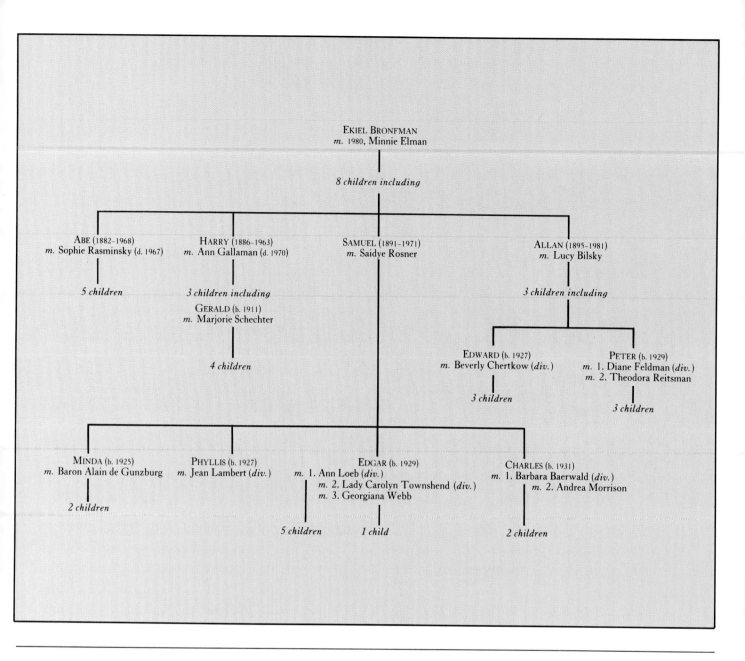

EKIEL BRONFMAN
m. 1980, Minnie Elman

8 children including

ABE (1882–1968)
m. Sophie Rasminsky (d. 1967)

HARRY (1886–1963)
m. Ann Gallaman (d. 1970)

SAMUEL (1891–1971)
m. Saidye Rosner

ALLAN (1895–1981)
m. Lucy Bilsky

5 children

3 children including
GERALD (b. 1911)
m. Marjorie Schechter

3 children including

4 children

EDWARD (b. 1927)
m. Beverly Chertkow (div.)

PETER (b. 1929)
m. 1. Diane Feldman (div.)
m. 2. Theodora Reitsman

3 children

3 children

MINDA (b. 1925)
m. Baron Alain de Gunzburg

PHYLLIS (b. 1927)
m. Jean Lambert (div.)

EDGAR (b. 1929)
m. 1. Ann Loeb (div.)
m. 2. Lady Carolyn Townshend (div.)
m. 3. Georgiana Webb

CHARLES (b. 1931)
m. 1. Barbara Baerwald (div.)
m. 2. Andrea Morrison

2 children

5 children   1 child

2 children

who went to New York in the 1950s and became head of the principal Seagram subsidiary in the United States, later gaining controlling interest, albeit briefly, in MGM. Edgar's son Samuel II (b. 1953) was kidnapped in 1975 and was returned only after his father had paid a ransom of $2.3 million.

The other son of Sam Bronfman is Charles (b. 1931), who was put in charge of Thomas Adams Distillers at 23 and became president of the House of Seagram, Canadian arm of the liquor empire, at 27. He lives in Montreal and controls, among other things, the Expos baseball club. His high

profile, obvious wealth, and power have sometimes caused confusion in the minds of outsiders because of obvious similarities to the so-called "other Bronfmans"—Edgar and Charles's cousins, Edward (b. 1927) and Peter (b. 1929).

The sons of Allan Bronfman, Edward and Peter, have risen from comparatively modest circumstances to the position of having, in a 1978 estimate, holdings of $2 billion. As the 1970s loomed, for instance, this branch of the family owned a Montreal office building and various small businesses such as bowling alleys and it was widely assumed that they were estranged from

Looking like the typical 19th-century European immigrants they were, Ekiel and Minni Bronfman (above and below left) came from Russia to settle in Saskatchewan, where they acquired numerous small businesses. The family became famous and powerful largely through the efforts of their son Samuel (RIGHT), shown with his wife Saidye in the early 1930s. Selling liquor, at first interprovincially and then internationally, led him naturally to the distilling business as well. He took over the Seagram Company and built it into a world-wide organization.

their uncle Sam. The breakthrough, in the eyes of the news media at least, came when they marshalled their resources to try, unsuccessfully as it happens, to take over Great-West Life Assurance of Winnipeg. Subsequently, they have been spectacularly successful and now control Trizec Corporation, whose real-estate holdings include Place Ville Marie in Montreal and major complexes and hotels in the rest of Canada and the Unites States, the Continental Bank of Canada, and Ranger Oil. In 1979, their Edper Equities acquired 50.1 per cent of Brascan—the former Brazilian Traction, Light & Power—for $335 million, a deal that rocked the financial world and seemed to signal a tough new spirit in the corporate wars. Other holdings have included the Montreal Forum and the Canadiens hockey team.

The Bronfmans are far and away the most influential Jewish family in Canadian business and rival the Thomsons in wealth. They are acknowledged as patrons of the arts and are seen to eschew politics outside Quebec. Internationally, theirs is the biggest Canadian name one can drop.

Sam Bronfman in later years, going over blueprints for the Seagram Tower in New York. Designed by Mies Van der Rohe, at the instigation of Sam's daughter Phyllis Lambert, it is one of the landmarks of modern architecture.

A separate and distinct branch of the family is descended from Sam Bronfman's brother Allan, shown here with his wife Lucy and part of their collection of figurines on his 80th birthday.

In recent generations, the Bronfmans have expanded from the liquor business into fields as diverse as entertainment and oil. Edgar Bronfman, one of Sam's sons, has been a major figure in the United States since the late 1950s and heads the American Seagram operation. He is shown with his wife Georgiana and with his son Sam Jr. shortly after the latter's release by kidnappers in 1975.

The Westmount house built by Sam Bronfman.

Of the two Bronfman lines so prominent in Canada today, the first is led by Charles Bronfman of Montreal, shown above left with his daughter Ellen when he received the Golda Meir Leadership Award for his contributions to the State of Israel Bonds Organization, and above with his son Stephen celebrating a victory by the Montreal Expos, one of the many family investments. The other branch is based in Toronto and headed by Charles' cousin Peter Bronfman (TOP RIGHT); it has been a major financial power only since the 1970s.

Phyllis Lambert (TOP), daughter of Sam Bronfman, studied sculpture as a child and was trained in architecture at the Illinois Institute of Technology. She is a prime mover in the conservation and renovation of older buildings in Montreal and was the first president of Heritage Montreal. In 1979 she founded the Canadian Centre for Architecture. Among her own designs is the Saidye Bronfman Cultural Centre in Montreal (ABOVE), one of the many contributions by the Bronfmans to the life of that city.

Sir John Crosbie (FAR LEFT), described by one of his sons as "probably one of the biggest old pirates that ever existed on the face of the earth," started out managing his widowed mother's hotel in St. John's (BELOW) and soon had many other enterprises and was equally busy in politics. He was once the acting premier of Newfoundland, which his son C.A. Crosbie (RIGHT) did not feel should enter Confederation. The younger Crosbie, known as Ches, added such enterprises as aviation to the family's holdings.

The Crosbies

"TO BE A Newfoundland Crosbie," the Montreal economist Dian Cohen has written, "is something like being a Greek Onassis." It's perhaps appropriate to add that there is something Mediterranean in the occasional family feuding within the current generation.

The founder of the dynasty was Sir John Chalker Crosbie (1876-1932), described by his grandson in one of his many memorable one-liners as "probably one of the biggest old pirates that ever existed on the face of the earth." When his father died in 1892, the future knight quit school to run the family hotel, which he had to rebuild the following year when it was destroyed by fire. He had a knack for making money and was soon involved in shipping, construction, fisheries, and insurance—especially insurance and particularly marine insurance—and set up the family holding company, Crosbie & Co., in 1900.

He was also active politically. From 1908 onwards, he held several portfolios in the colonial government, and was acting prime minister of Newfoundland when he received his knighthood in 1918. In 1925, he established a margarine plant in St. John's—the Newfoundland Butter Company—at about the same time that the government imposed new duties on imported butter and margarine. After 1928 he dropped out of public life and died when the family fortunes were at low ebb during the worst days of the Depression.

Sir John and Lady Crosbie had a multitude of children, each destined to distinguish himself or herself in some manner, including marriage to other leading families. Olga Crosbie, for example, married Lewis Ayre of the rich and powerful Water Street family; some of her siblings married into clans whose companies were later gobbled up by the Crosbies. Those children who went directly into the family business included A.H. (Bill) Crosbie (1919-1981), who was awarded the Distinguished Service Order in the Second World War, and the eldest son, Chesley Arthur Crosbie (1905-1962), who succeeded to the presidency on Sir John's death.

It was Ches who upgraded and modernized the family's portfolio, adding, for a time, ownership of Eastern Provincial Airways. He too was active in politics, though not publicly so. He did not share Joey Smallwood's view that Newfoundland should join the rest of Canada, but he supported Smallwood and his Liberal Party both before and after the fateful union in 1949.

Today, the best known member of the family is Ches's eldest son, John Carnell Crosbie (b. 1931), who was finance minister in Joe Clark's short-lived government and ran for the Progressive Conservative leadership in 1983. If press reports are to be believed, he and his brother Andrew C. Crosbie (b. 1933) have an on-again, off-again relationship. John studied law at Queen's and Dalhousie before finishing his education at the London School of Economics; he was judged the top law student in Canada. As a Liberal he held six cabinet posts in the Newfoundland government, but later resigned to sit first as an independent and then as a Tory against Smallwood, his former mentor. In the 1971 election his brother Andrew (to whom he had sold his interest in the business) managed Smallwood's campaign against him.

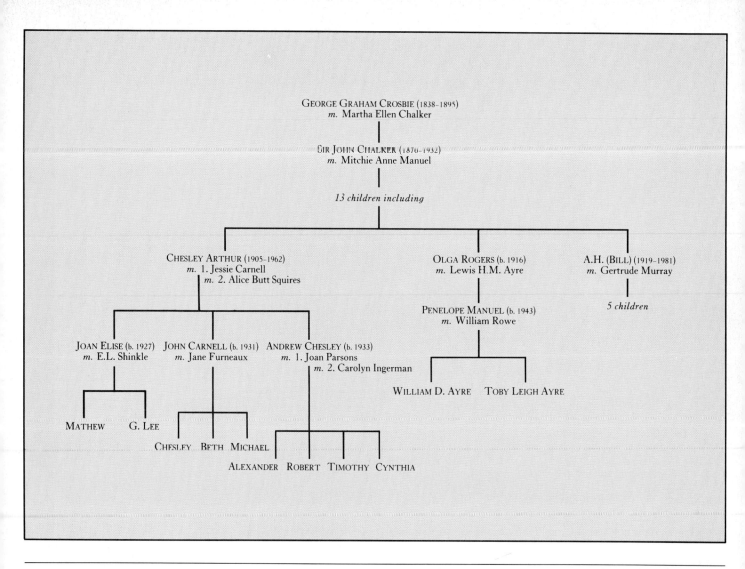

GEORGE GRAHAM CROSBIE (1838–1895)
m. Martha Ellen Chalker

SIR JOHN CHALKER (1876–1932)
m. Mitchie Anne Manuel

13 children including

CHESLEY ARTHUR (1905–1962)
m. 1. Jessie Carnell
m. 2. Alice Butt Squires

OLGA ROGERS (b. 1916)
m. Lewis H.M. Ayre

A.H. (BILL) (1919–1981)
m. Gertrude Murray

5 children

PENELOPE MANUEL (b. 1943)
m. William Rowe

JOAN ELISE (b. 1927)
m. E.L. Shinkle

JOHN CARNELL (b. 1931)
m. Jane Furneaux

ANDREW CHESLEY (b. 1933)
m. 1. Joan Parsons
m. 2. Carolyn Ingerman

WILLIAM D. AYRE   TOBY LEIGH AYRE

MATHEW   G. LEE

CHESLEY   BETH   MICHAEL

ALEXANDER   ROBERT   TIMOTHY   CYNTHIA

As for the company, it is still heavily into insurance. One arm, Mercury International, provides flight-insurance machines and foreign-exchange kiosks in airports. Recently, though, the family has entered new fields such as newspapers, printing, and construction. The most dramatic change was the family's entry into the oil supply business in the early 1970s. During the Recession, there were a few signs of ill health. Chimo Shipping went bankrupt in 1981, followed by the closing of Domac Enterprises, the Crosbies' construction equipment firm. But then, each generation of this Newfoundland family has weathered difficulties in business, and the pattern of successes and failures will no doubt apply to the fourth generation being brought along to assume their places in the Newfoundland Establishment.

ABOVE: John C. Crosbie and his wife, the former Jane Furneaux. FACING: Andrew and Carolyn Ingerman Crosbie in their home in St. John's, from which he manages the family ventures.

A.E. Cross arrived in Calgary in 1881 to work as a bookkeeper. Two years later he was a landed member of the cattle aristocracy. In time he also became an important figure in the brewing and hotel businesses.

The Crosses

THE CROSSES OCCUPY a special place in the social and economic life of Alberta. Not only are they one of the first families of Calgary, with a list of enduring good works and business enterprises to their credit, but they are also a direct link to the original cattle aristocracy so dramatically eclipsed by the later energy fortunes.

The founder of the dynasty was the storied Alfred Ernest Cross (1861-1932). A.E., as he was known, was born in Montreal, the son of a judge whose father had come from Monkland in Scotland. Setting the pattern for the Crosses who were to follow, he attended a wide range of schools: the Montreal Business College, Haileybury College in England, and finally the Ontario Agricultural College (now the University of Guelph). Thus equipped, he moved to Calgary in 1881 to assume a job as a bookkeeper in a ranching operation. Two years later he had his own spread with 3,400 head of cattle and a herd of wild horses. This ranch, called the A7, expanded to the point where, today, it is one of Canada's largest and retains the reputation for quality that A.E., by importing the best British bulls, worked hard to establish.

In 1892, Cross started Calgary Brewing & Malting and actually attended yet another school in order to obtain a brewmaster's certificate. Six years later he was sent as a Conservative to the territorial legislature. He held various outside directorships, including Calgary Gas and Calgary Power. His hobby was polo, which he pursued with dignified abandon.

In 1899, Cross married the daughter of Colonel James Farquharson Macleod of the North West Mounted Police who he had built Fort Calgary, Fort Walsh, and Fort Macleod in the trading-post days. Of their eight children, it was James B. (b. 1903) who became president of the brewery after his father's death. James, too, had gone to the Ontario Agricultural College, not to mention Birmingham University in Britain and the Alfred Jorgensen Institute in Copenhagen. He tended the family's existing companies as well as moving ambitiously into the hotel field in several Alberta cities. He also set up a hatchery to supply trout for Alberta streams and rivers.

A Western loyalist, James Cross once followed the Calgary Stampeders football team to Toronto and demonstrated both his style and his enthusiasm by riding a horse up Bay Street and frying bacon and eggs on the steps of City Hall.

James's sister Mary Dover has been Queen of the Banff Winter Carnival, a soldier, a Calgary alderman, and a rancher. Now in her 80s she lives in Midnapore on acreage once well south of Calgary and now a district of the city. She is turning the property into a garden on the English pattern and is an avid collector of trees. She is proud to have seven of the 11 species of fir that grow in Canada.

James's son Donald (b. 1932) was educated more prosaically than his ancestors, at the University of Alberta and at the University of Western Ontario, where he took an M.B.A. He has remained true to family tradition by pursuing business affairs vigorously and by taking up polo.

Another family tradition, and the one for which the Crosses are best known in Calgary, is their

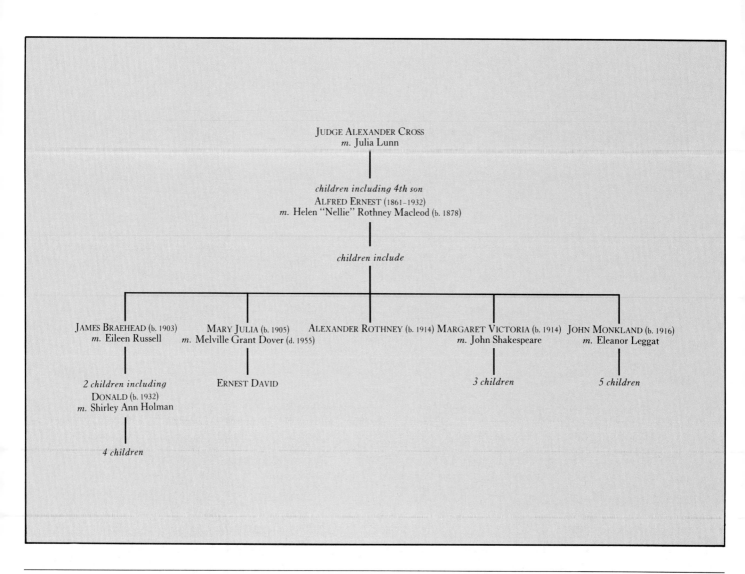

JUDGE ALEXANDER CROSS
m. Julia Lunn

children including 4th son
ALFRED ERNEST (1861–1932)
m. Helen "Nellie" Rothney Macleod (b. 1878)

children include

JAMES BRAEHEAD (b. 1903)
m. Eileen Russell

MARY JULIA (b. 1905)
m. Melville Grant Dover (d. 1955)

ALEXANDER ROTHNEY (b. 1914)

MARGARET VICTORIA (b. 1914)
m. John Shakespeare

JOHN MONKLAND (b. 1916)
m. Eleanor Leggat

2 children including
DONALD (b. 1932)
m. Shirley Ann Holman

ERNEST DAVID

3 children

5 children

4 children

keen commitment to the Stampede. It was A.E. and three fellow ranchers who founded the event in 1912, and both James and Donald have continued to be intimately connected with the annual blowout.

A.E. Cross family group. Left to right: James B.; Alexander R.; Margaret; Mrs. A.E. Cross; Mary.

Princess Elizabeth, on her 1951 tour, alights from a stagecoach assisted by James B. Cross, who succeeded his father both as president of the family brewery and of the Calgary Stampede.

The centrepiece of the Cross holdings was A.E.'s original A7 Ranche, which, even in its earliest days, was run strictly on scientific principles, though the Crosses have always tried to nurture the frontier spirit. Aldersyde district residents square dance in a barn at the A7 as the Cross family celebrates the 70th anniversary of the ranch in 1956. A.E.'s family continue to operate the A7 Ranche, which is now the second-largest such spread in the country.

Moving cattle on Sandy Cross's Rothney Ranch.

GLENBOW ARCHIVES, CALGARY/PHOTO BY KARSH

DERYK BODINGTON

Another noted member of the clan is Mary Cross Dover, during the Second World War the highest-ranking woman in the Canadian Armed Forces.

Mary Dover in her English-style garden.

CALGARY EXHIBITION AND STAMPEDE

Today the family's various enterprises are continued partly by James Cross's son Donald, seen with Governor General Edward Schreyer at the Calgary Stampede.

Taken in the final decade of his life, this portrait of Timothy Eaton, the pious, teetotalling Irish immigrant, gives some hint of the tenacity and dedication to business that would make his family one of the richest in Canada.

The Eatons

"THE EATONS" is the answer most Canadians would give if asked to name a rich and influential family, for it is a fact that they have been visibly wealthy for four generations even while jealously guarding the exact size of their fortune. T. Eaton Co., the firm that runs the famous Eaton's department stores as well as holding valuable downtown real estate in every major Canadian city, remains a private concern. As such it is not called on to disclose much financial information, but sales are estimated at about $2 billion a year.

As famous as the stores in Canadian folklore is the man who founded them, a pious teetotalling Methodist named Timothy Eaton (1834-1907) who immigrated to Canada in 1854 following the Potato Famine in his native Ireland. After a dozen years working as a general merchant and dry-goods dealer, he set up his—and Toronto's—first department store. The revolutionary element of the enterprise was that Eaton would brook no dickering and extend no credit. (The first edict still survives, but the second gave way long ago to T. Eaton Acceptance, which issues credit cards to customers of the retail stores.) Instead, Timothy Eaton offered a wide variety of merchandise for cash only and at fixed prices. He coined and stood by the motto, "Money refunded if goods not satisfactory."

Other innovations followed, including the catalogue business for rural customers (begun in 1884) and integration by means of manufacturing under various house brands. The latter policy held not just for big-ticket items or staples such as clothing, but even extended to schoolbooks. Some provinces purchased their standard texts from Eaton's, which printed them on the company's own presses.

Like subsequent members of the family, Timothy Eaton was well known for his acts of philanthropy. In his case, the philanthropic urge climaxed posthumously when Timothy Eaton Memorial Church was opened in Toronto in 1913. By that time, his son John Craig Eaton (1876-1922) had already succeeded to the presidency of the company following the death of his elder brother Edward (1863-1900).

John Craig, too, was both a business expansionist and a benefactor of the community. He pushed the company further westward, for instance, and planned what later became the College Street block in Toronto, a huge Art Deco development that could have been the inspiration for the Marx Brothers film *The Big Store*. His tireless work for the Allied cause during the First World War brought him a knighthood in 1915, and, since in 1901 he had married Florence McCrae (1881-1970) of Omemee, Ontario, there was now a Lady Eaton—two words that for an astoundingly long time were virtually synonymous with enormous wealth and good works. Presiding over a number of town and country houses, Lady Eaton was, for example, a major patron of the Toronto Symphony Orchestra, the Institute for the Blind, and Children's Welfare.

Sir John Craig's will stipulated that his stock in the company be kept intact until one of his four sons was chosen by the executors to take over the

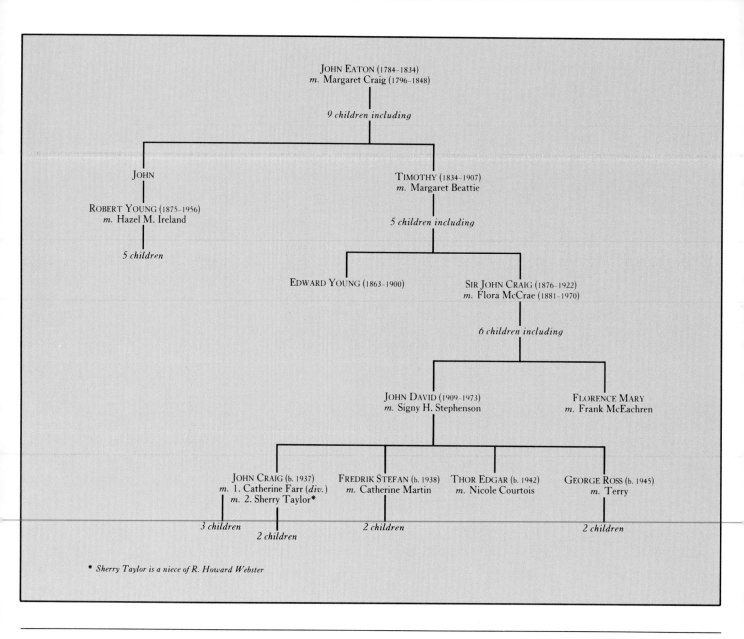

JOHN EATON (1784–1834)
m. Margaret Craig (1796–1848)

9 children including

JOHN

ROBERT YOUNG (1875–1956)
m. Hazel M. Ireland

5 children

TIMOTHY (1834–1907)
m. Margaret Beattie

5 children including

EDWARD YOUNG (1863–1900)

SIR JOHN CRAIG (1876–1922)
m. Flora McCrae (1881–1970)

6 children including

JOHN DAVID (1909–1973)
m. Signy H. Stephenson

FLORENCE MARY
m. Frank McEachren

JOHN CRAIG (b. 1937)
m. 1. Catherine Farr (*div.*)
m. 2. Sherry Taylor*

FREDRIK STEFAN (b. 1938)
m. Catherine Martin

THOR EDGAR (b. 1942)
m. Nicole Courtois

GEORGE ROSS (b. 1945)
m. Terry

3 children

2 children

2 children

2 children

* *Sherry Taylor is a niece of R. Howard Webster*

firm. In the interim, Robert Young Eaton, an Irish-born nephew, became president. After being groomed in lesser posts beginning in 1930, John David Eaton (1909-1973), the executors' choice, was named chief executive in 1942. Under him, the company continued its expansion, particularly into suburban areas, and the family also moved into partnerships involving other businesses as represented in the Eaton's various dealings with John Bassett and his sons. Before he retired in 1969, John David had begun planning the Eaton Centre in Toronto, which would be realized by the next generation in 1977. His favoured charities included the Royal Agricultural Winter Fair, Crippled Children's Centre, Toronto General Hospital, and the Salvation Army.

By his wife, Signy Stephenson Eaton (m. 1933), John David Eaton had four sons: John Craig (b. 1937), Fredrik Stefan (b. 1938), Thor (b. 1942), and George (b. 1945). By mutual consent and design Fred took over the presidency in 1977. His is a much more streamlined and efficent company than the earlier incarnations of his great-grandfather's dream, though the streamlining has come at the occasional expense of tradition. The catalogues so dear to the hearts of rural Canadians were delivered no more after 1976, and in the early 1980s Eaton's announced the phasing out of

Sir John Craig Eaton (centre) and his son John David (in his nurse's arms) at the departure of the Eaton Machine Gun Battery during the First World War.

In the second generation, the Eatons were led by Sir John Craig Eaton (LEFT) and his wife Lady Eaton (RIGHT), on an outing with her daughters in the 1920s. Lady Eaton would symbolize the old order until her death in 1970.

Ardwold, Sir John and Lady Eaton's home in Toronto as it looked shortly after its completion in 1911. The house was so large that it even had a private hospital with its own operating room. The mansion was razed in 1936 and the site was developed as the present Ardwold Gate.

its Christmas parades in Montreal, Toronto, Winnipeg, and Vancouver.

Other traditions remain strong, however. The balance sheets are still kept far from public view and, for good luck, Torontonians still rub the bronze toe of a large statue of Timothy Eaton that long rested in the old Queen Street store and now graces the Eaton Centre. Touching the effigy of an early teetotalling capitalist seems a perfectly appropriate ritual for Toronto, but alas, the rite did not emerge spontaneously: it was originated by Eaton's public-relations department.

In the minds of countless Canadians, the Eatons remain almost synonymous with great family wealth. Shown here is Sir John Eaton's yacht Florence *(named for Lady Eaton) at its slip in Toronto sometime in the 1920s.*

Lady Eaton in her public role, arriving at the opening ceremonies of the family's College Street store in Toronto with her son, John David.

Lady Eaton in her private role riding to hounds with Aemilius Jarvis at Eaton Hall, the family estate in King, north of Toronto.

The Timothy Eaton Memorial Methodist (now United) Church in July 1939. Construction began in 1910 with the east side, which was originally the Sunday-school building. The church on St. Clair Avenue in Toronto was completed in 1914 from plans drawn up by Wickson and Gregg, who also designed Ardwold.

Today Eaton's is run by a fourth generation, the sons of John David and Signy Eaton. Now in their 40s are John and Fred Eaton (TOP), caught by the camera at the Royal Agricultural Winter Fair in Toronto, and their brother George (ABOVE), seen in 1972 pursuing a motor racing championship. He was a first class driver but has severed his connections with the sport completely. Fred Eaton has been the president of T. Eaton & Co. since 1977. RIGHT: Everything about the Eatons is tasteful even when on the grand scale, as with the family mausoleum in Mount Pleasant Cemetery Toronto.

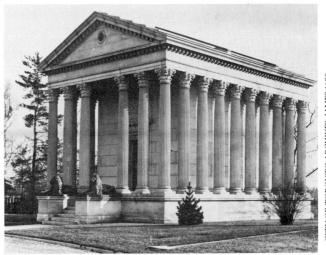

J.R.

The rarely photographed K.C. Irving, creator of an empire crucial to the economy of New Brunswick, where the Irving name—as seen on oil storage tanks—is associated with an astounding array of enterprises. Irving himself now resides in Bermuda.

The Irvings

THE IRVINGS HAVE been capitalists of consequence in the Maritimes for three generations. But it is only K.C. Irving (b. 1899) of the middle generation who has penetrated the national consciousness, albeit as a nebulous character of mythic proportions. "Suffice it to say, then," wrote Russell Hunt and Robert Campbell in their book *K.C. Irving: The Art of the Industrialist*, "that Irving's power, affluence and prestige in New Brunswick and eastern Canada are so immense and pervasive that they cannot adequately be described...."

Kenneth Colin Irving was born in the largely French-speaking town of Buctouche on New Brunswick's north shore where his father, J.D. Irving, the most influential man in the region, owned lumber mills and general stores. The young Irving went to university in Nova Scotia—at both Acadia and Dalhousie—but graduated from neither. Instead, he joined the Royal Flying Corps but got overseas only as the First World War wound down. Returning to New Brunswick, he established himself as a local Ford dealer. It was clear that the Model-Ts he sold were transforming society so he shrewdly got into gasoline as well, acquiring an Imperial Oil distributorship in Kent County, Nova Scotia. When Imperial cancelled the deal in 1924, it unwittingly touched off a long string of entrepreneurial successes for Irving.

The roots of his methodology are illustrated in a story told about him as a boy. When the noise of the pet ducks he was raising in the family yard brought complaints from the neighbours, he had the ducks killed and sold them to the complainants, thereby solving the diplomatic problem and netting himself $100 besides. Much the same spirit followed the split with Imperial Oil. With his distributorship gone, Irving resolved to beat Imperial at its own game. Borrowing what money he could, he purchased an oil storage tank from one supplier in the United States and gas to fill it from another, then set up his own oil company in Buctouche. The venture was formalized in 1928 when, with loans from his father and others, he began Irving Oil Company with headquarters in Saint John. The company was the foundation of all that was to follow.

When he quarrelled with Canadian National Railways over charges for hauling his oil, he started his own fleets of trucks and barges. (Eventually he bought his own railroad as well, but only to get the valuable timber lands it owned.) In time he entered shipping, as his father had done before him. At first his fleet consisted of five surplus naval corvettes, which he converted to tankers. The conversion was handled by a shipyard he had bought to produce landing craft during the Second World War, while a pulp and paper plant he owned turned out wooden aircraft frames.

In peace as in war, Irving was at his best as an integrator. When he built his most publicized project, a $50-million oil refinery in Saint John, the structural steel came from his own steel company. But his consistently most controversial investments have been those that, between about 1945 and 1970, gave him ownership of all of New Brunswick's English-language daily newspapers as well as control of radio and television outlets.

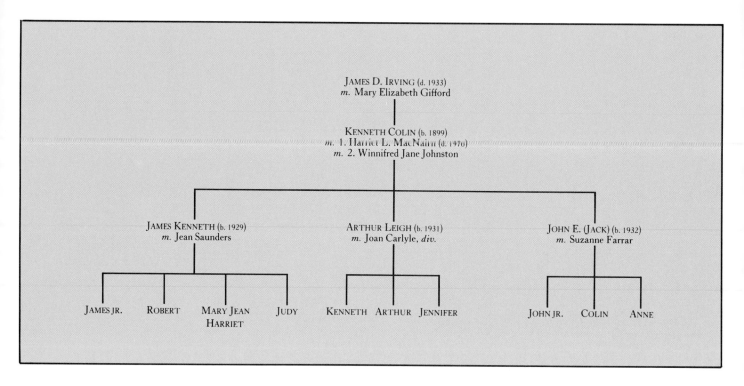

JAMES D. IRVING (d. 1933)
m. Mary Elizabeth Gifford

KENNETH COLIN (b. 1899)
m. 1. Harriet L. MacNairn (d. 1970)
m. 2. Winnifred Jane Johnston

JAMES KENNETH (b. 1929)
m. Jean Saunders

ARTHUR LEIGH (b. 1931)
m. Joan Carlyle, *div.*

JOHN E. (JACK) (b. 1932)
m. Suzanne Farrar

JAMES JR.   ROBERT   MARY JEAN HARRIET   JUDY

KENNETH   ARTHUR   JENNIFER

JOHN JR.   COLIN   ANNE

The 1970 Davey Commission on the Mass Media estimated that Irving's TV stations reached 94.9 per cent of New Brunswick's potential audience.

It is natural and inevitable that rumours should swirl around an industrialist of such eminence and wealth. Significantly, on those rare occasions when he has spoken for the record, Irving has denied any involvement or interest in politics. As he noted, "I don't think politics and business mix. New Brunswick is too small for politics." In 1972, Irving, who was then in his 70s, retired to Bermuda, where he occupies a role similar to that of E.P. Taylor in the Bahamas: the mysterious Canadian of enormous wealth and unknown influence. But it was apparent for years before his departure from New Brunswick that much of the

K.C. Irving with sons Jack, James, and Arthur.

day-to-day control of his empire was already in the hands of his three sons: Jack (b. 1932), James (b. 1929), and Arthur (b. 1931), who are sometimes known behind their backs as Gassy, Greasy, and Olly, respectively, for the particular facet of the petroleum business in which each brother has shone.

"For the three richest young men in New Brunswick," *Maclean's* magazine once observed, "they lead surprisingly unpretentious lives; they don't collect art, they drive Fords and Mercuries, their homes are nothing special, and their visits to the Irving fishing lodge on the Miramichi River are brief and infrequent." But then, flamboyance would not be in character and ostentation isn't necessary; in New Brunswick, to be an Irving is enough.

THE IRVING COMPANIES' HOLDINGS

General Realty Co.
North End Service Stations
Millicen Bros. Ltd.
St. John Propane Gas Co. Ltd.
Eastern Oil and Service Station Ltd.
Domestic Petroleum Co. Ltd.
Irving Steamship Ltd.
Arnfast Propane Ltd.
Keefe Propane Gas
Les Pétroles Inc.
Les Pétroles Irving Inc.
Société Immobilière Irving Ltée.
Gas Outlet (1962) Ltée.
Les Immeubles Loret Ltée.
Les Immeubles Clark Inc.
Irving Realty Co. Ltd.
Atlantic Speedy Propane
Halifax Propane Gas Ltd.
Island Propane Gas Ltd.
Fredericton Propane Gas Ltd.
Moncton Utility Gas Ltd.
Nova Scotia Propane Gas Ltd.
Avelon Oil Co. Ltd.
Rupert Lester Ltd.
Fredericton Fuels Ltd.
Saint Albert and Co. Ltd.
S. Cunard and Co. Ltd.
Dartmouth Fuel Ltd.
Chevron Oils Lté.
Fuel Oil Sales Lté.
Standard Stations Ltd.
S and A Developments Ltd.
Irving Refining Ltd.
Cana-Pari Ltd.
FMR Co. Ltd.
Irving Oil Terminals Ltd.
Chipman Timber Products
Coastal Transport Ltd.
Grand River SoftWoods

Grand Lake Timber Ltd.
MacKay Lumber Co. Ltd.
Atlantic Towing Ltd.
Highland Hardwoods
St. George Pulp & Paper Ltd.
Charlotte Pulp and Paper Ltd.
Hosan Lake Timber
Victoria Forest Products Ltd.
Kent Homes Ltd.
Grand Lake Timber Ltd.
Road & Sea Transport Ltd.
Boston Brook Enterprises Ltd.
Atlantic Truck & Trailer Ltd.
Kent Line Ltd.
Mace Ltd.
St. John Shipbuilding & Dry Dock Ltd.
Marque Construction Ltd.
Atlantic Coast Copper Corp. Ltd.
Barclay's (Nassau) Nominees Ltd.
Key Anacon Mines Ltd.
Northern Canada Mines
Harbour Developments Ltd.
Saint John Iron Works Ltd.
Universal Constructors & Engineers Ltd.
Consolidated Rambler Mines Ltd.
Canada Veneers Ltd.
Canada Veneers (Qué.) Co. Ltd.
D'Auteuil Lumber Co. Ltd.
The New Brunswick Railway
Ocean Steel & Construction Lté.
Ferro Chemicrete Eng. Ltd.
Stres Con Lté.
Sten Enterprises Ltd.
Consolidated Fisheries
Steel and Engine Products Ltd.
Saint John Pulp & Paper Ltd.
Irving Pulp & Paper Ltd.
Kimberley Clark Corporation
Crothers G.A. Ltd.

Tidal Chemicals Ltd.
Chemetics International Ltd.
S.M.T. Eastern Ltd.
Island Motor Transport Ltd.
S.M.T. System Ltd.
Saint John Motor Line Ltd.
New Brunswick Publishing Co. Ltd.
Moncton Publishing Co. Ltd.
New Brunswick Broadcasting Co. Ltd.
Moncton Engraving Ltd.
Brodier Co.
University Press of New Brunswick
Palmer Ltd.
Unipress Ltd.
Brunswick Book (Wholesale Ltd.)
United Sales Ltd.
Brunswick Motors Ltd.
Thorn's Ltd.
Maritime Tire Ltd.
Chemic Ltd.
J.J. Snook Ltd.
Commercial Equipment Ltd.
Thorne's Hardware (1970) Ltd.
F. Wragge Ltd.
Lewis Bros. Hardware
Lewis Brothers 1970
Eastern Home & Auto
Chinic Hardware
Commercial Equipment Inc.
Universal Sales Ltd.
Wood Motors Ltd.
Wood Lumber Co. Ltd.
Sydney & Whitney Pier Bus Service
Auberge du Blvd. Laurier
E.F. Malkin Ltd.
Steel & Engine Products Ltd.
City Transit Ltd.
Interprovincial Coach Lines
Ocean Finance Ltd.

The Lougheeds

HE LOUGHEEDS ARE one of the first families of Alberta—almost literally so, since they were established there a generation before the province was carved out of the old North West Territories in 1905. The roots of the family have been traced back as far as Tudor times in Scotland, though it was from Ireland that the first North American Lougheeds emigrated in 1815. Eventually there would be both American and Canadian branches of the family. The former changed the name and in time founded the Lockheed aircraft fortune in California. The Canadian arm left the spelling unaltered and produced Sir James Alexander Lougheed (1854-1925), one of the most remarkable Albertans of his time.

Born in Ontario, James graduated from Osgoode Hall and was called to the bar in 1881. Two years later, as a lawyer for the Canadian Pacific Railway, Lougheed moved to Calgary, which then consisted of a tent colony along the site of the CPR line. He is said to have arrived in Calgary on a handcar. In an age when inside knowledge was one of the perks of business, Lougheed purchased several parcels of land, which subsequently became the heart of downtown Calgary. In 1884, he married the niece of Donald Smith (the future Lord Strathcona), the largest

shareholder in the Hudson's Bay Company—and later its governor—and a leading backer of the CPR. In 1889, when he was said to be worth $70,000, Lougheed became one of Sir John A. Macdonald's last appointments to the Senate. He was named Senate Tory leader in 1906, was knighted in 1916, and in the early 1920s was minister of the Interior and of Mines in the Meighen government.

Throughout his career, Sir James juggled law and politics (taking in as his law partner the future prime minister, R.B. Bennett) as well as business. He was involved in early oil-well promotions in the Turner Valley, but his principal activity was real estate. During the First World War, it was reported that he was assessed one half of all the taxes in the city of Calgary. He owned an astounding array of downtown office buildings, including ones named after each of his children. Thus, the Edgar Block was named for Edgar Lougheed (1893-1951), a graduate of Western Canada College, McGill University, and Dalhousie University, and, like his father, a lawyer.

Edgar Lougheed served with the Royal Canadian Army Service Corps during the First World War, emerging with captain's rank, and following his father's death was left the unenviable task of shepherding the family assets through the Depression. The fight to maintain this wealth through perilous times was not entirely successful. As though to symbolize the decline, Sir James's mansion, Beaulieu, was sold at auction in 1938. (It is now owned by the province as a historic site.) Edgar Lougheed's sons carried the family name to

James (later Senator Sir James) Lougheed (TOP LEFT) moved west from Ontario in 1883 and bought property in what soon became downtown Calgary. In September 1884, he married Betty Hardisty, a niece of one of the founders of the Canadian Pacific Railway who later reigned in society as Lady Lougheed (TOP RIGHT). Their Calgary home, Beaulieu (BELOW), was a showplace and is now designated a historic site.

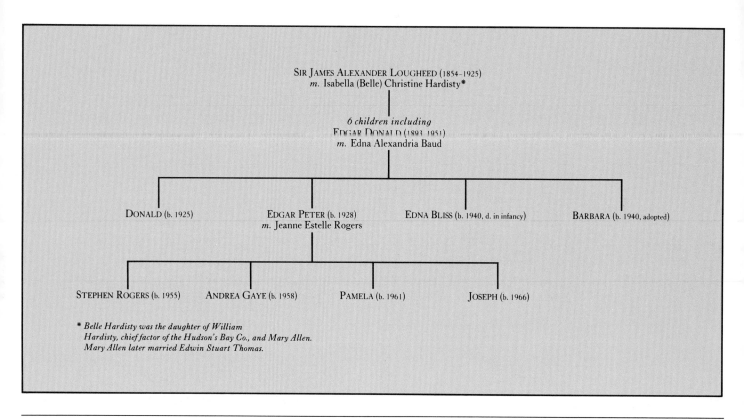

SIR JAMES ALEXANDER LOUGHEED (1854–1925)
m. Isabella (Belle) Christine Hardisty*

6 children including
EDGAR DONALD (1893–1951)
m. Edna Alexandria Baud

DONALD (b. 1925)

EDGAR PETER (b. 1928)
m. Jeanne Estelle Rogers

EDNA BLISS (b. 1940, d. in infancy)

BARBARA (b. 1940, adopted)

STEPHEN ROGERS (b. 1955)   ANDREA GAYE (b. 1958)   PAMELA (b. 1961)   JOSEPH (b. 1966)

* *Belle Hardisty was the daughter of William
Hardisty, chief factor of the Hudson's Bay Co., and Mary Allen.
Mary Allen later married Edwin Stuart Thomas.*

renewed prominence. Donald (b. 1925), a graduate of the University of Alberta, would in time become executive vice-president of Esso Resources Canada, a subsidiary of Imperial Oil. Peter (b. 1928), a graduate of the same institution and of Harvard University, became a third-generation lawyer who moved into business and then into politics, achieving his greatest renown as premier of Alberta.

Following a brief career as a professional athlete (a running back with the Edmonton Eskimos football club), Peter Lougheed became corporate counsel for Mannix Co., the megalithic Calgary-based construction firm founded by Fred Mannix, which built such projects as the Toronto subway system; subsequently he entered private practice as a specialist in construction law, which often related to energy development. In 1964, he became interested in provincial politics and began campaigning for the leadership of the provincial Progressive Conservative Party.

In the 1967 election, Lougheed's Tories took on the Social Credit Party that had governed the province since 1935. They failed to dislodge the government, but they did replace the Liberals as the opposition in the legislature. Four years later they swept into power, taking 49 of the 75 seats. Lougheed's term in office has coincided with an enormous boom in oil and gas development in the province as well as running battles with the federal government over energy and over provincial jurisdictions and powers under a patriated Canadian constitution. Lougheed's regionalist stand and his unswerving belief in private enterprise have made him an immensely popular leader in Alberta. Among his accomplishments is the Alberta Heritage Savings Trust Fund, built up with part of the oil and gas royalties accruing to the provincial treasury; the fund makes loans and grants to educational, medical, and recreational facilities. After more than a decade in power, he remains the undisputed ruler of Alberta and a tacit force in national politics.

Lady Lougheed and daughter Marjorie with chauffeur at Beaulieu (LEFT). Lady Lougheed was the daughter of a Métis woman, Mary Thomas (RIGHT).

Peter Lougheed, grandson of Sir James, has been premier of Alberta since 1971. His tenure has coincided with stepped-up development of oil and gas reserves in the province—which still had a generation to go as part of the North West Territories when his family first settled there. He is shown with his wife Jeanne and son Joe celebrating one of his several crushing electoral victories.

Harrison McCain, chairman of McCain Foods, the fast-growing international concern headquartered in the somewhat unlikely spot of Florenceville, New Brunswick.

The McCains

*I*T SEEMS THAT the farther east one moves in Canada, the more relaxed and down to earth seem the Establishment families—and the more secretive as well. The McCains, who operate an international food-processing and distribution empire from the unlikely centre of Florenceville, New Brunswick, are an example of this phenomenon, particularly the part about lack of pretension.

Appropriately, the McCains' beginnings are as modest as their present circumstances are grand. Originally from Northern Ireland, the family arrived in Canada in 1837 and first came to notice through Andrew D. McCain (1878-1953), who wished to be a doctor but became a farmer instead. He pioneered the export of seed potatoes from Canada and built up a significant business, though it is unclear whether the substantial sum he left his children derived from his land holdings or his prescient way with the stock market. In any event, the sons parlayed the inheritance into McCain Foods—a major multinational food empire.

The sons are Andrew McCain (b. 1921), the president and chief executive officer of McCain Produce Co.; H. Harrison McCain (b. 1927), the chairman of McCain Foods; and G. Wallace McCain (b. 1930), the president of McCain Foods. All continue to live in Florenceville, a company town in practice, if not by design. The sons also married into provincially prominent families. Mrs. Wallace McCain is the daughter of a senator, and

Mrs. Harrison McCain is the daughter of a former premier of New Brunswick. Yet much is made of their being just plain folks. "When you go to a church dinner," says one Florenceville native, "the McCain women will be there cooking and serving just like everyone else." The brothers' political connections remain good. Staunch Liberals like their father, they helped finance Pierre Trudeau's leadership campaign in 1968.

Curiously, the two younger brothers once worked for K.C. Irving, the man who remains synonymous with big business in New Brunswick despite the successes of the McCains. Harrison McCain was Atlantic sales manager for Irving Oil and Wallace McCain once managed an Irving-owned hardware business. In recent years, there has been some ill feeling between the two families, supposedly because of the Irvings' decision to add potatoes and other food products to their portfolio.

But K.C.'s sons will have a long way to go to catch up to the Florenceville family. From owners of a single potato-processing plant 25 years ago, the McCains have become the world's largest producers of French fries, as well as being prominent in many other prepared foods, from fruit juices to pizza. They have made major inroads into the British, Australian, American, and European markets, while back home they have integrated their operations through significant investment in the farm equipment, fertilizer, and trucking businesses. And in the wings are four McCain sons now growing up in the family business.

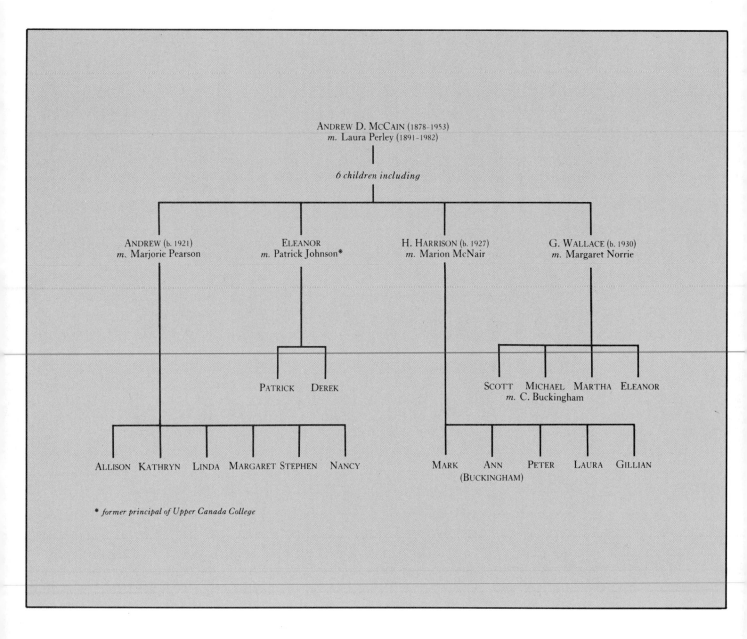

ANDREW D. McCAIN (1878–1953)
m. Laura Perley (1891–1982)

6 children including

ANDREW (b. 1921)
m. Marjorie Pearson

ELEANOR
m. Patrick Johnson*

H. HARRISON (b. 1927)
m. Marion McNair

G. WALLACE (b. 1930)
m. Margaret Norrie

PATRICK   DEREK

SCOTT   MICHAEL   MARTHA   ELEANOR
m. C. Buckingham

ALLISON   KATHRYN   LINDA   MARGARET   STEPHEN   NANCY

MARK   ANN   PETER   LAURA   GILLIAN
(BUCKINGHAM)

* former principal of Upper Canada College

Seldom photographed individually, much less together, the McCain family of New Brunswick here pose in 1973, grouped around the late Laura Perley McCain. McCain Foods sprang from the seed-potato business of her husband Andrew.

A beautiful if not famous Molson, Louisa, at the time of her wedding—an important Montreal social event of 1927.

The Molsons

THE MOLSONS HAVE the deepest roots of any Canadian business dynasty, stretching back to the 18th century and the earliest English settlement along the St. Lawrence. The Molson Companies Limited is now a multimillion-dollar conglomerate active in chemicals, sports, retail lumber operations, and warehousing and distribution. But the sentimental heart of the financial empire (and the most lucrative part of it) remains Molson Breweries of Canada, whose president, Eric Herbert Molson (b. 1937), represents the eighth generation of Molsons in the business.

The brewery was founded in 1786 by John Molson (1763-1836), who arrived in Montreal from England as an 18-year-old orphan and lived to see the family take on its aura of established wealth and prestige. This first Molson was something of a polymath. In 1809, for example, he built the first successful steamboat on the St. Lawrence; its speed gave him an edge in obtaining financial news that helped him increase his fortune during the War of 1812. In 1826 he also became president of the Bank of Montreal following a stint in Quebec's legislative assembly.

The brewery and related enterprises were recast in 1816 as a partnership with John's three sons: John (1787-1860), Thomas (1791-1863), and William (1793-1875).

Each son ultimately ventured into other business interests. John, for example, became president in 1837 of Canada's first railway, the Champlain and St. Lawrence line. Thomas tried, at first unsuccessfully, to branch out into distilling, then moved to Kingston where he and his son John

Henry Robinson Molson (1826-1897) came to run separate liquor businesses, neither of them connected with the Montreal branch of the family enterprise. William Molson, a great benefactor of McGill University, set up Molson's Bank in 1855, an institution that until it merged with the Bank of Montreal in 1925 placed the family in the position of being able to issue its own paper money.

In time, this most complex of families had English- as well as French-Canadian branches, both somehow involved in brewing and other concerns and both noticeably fecund. By the end of the 19th century there seemed to be so many Molsons in Canadian finance and entrepreneurship that few outsiders could get an accurate idea of their influence. An impressive total of 34 Canadian Molsons served in the First World War: five were killed and 13 were wounded. They were awarded two Distinguished Service Orders, six Military Crosses, a Legion of Honour, a Croix de Guerre, and at least four miscellaneous decorations. Such was the Molson name, however, that the medals could add little additional lustre.

The most conspicuous Molson of recent times, and one who personifies the family's traits and concerns, is Senator Hartland de Montarville Molson (b. 1907), who was honorary chairman of Molson Companies, parent of the brewing company, until 1983. Like a surprisingly high percentage of Canada's dynastic offspring (and like many other Molsons) he attended Bishop's College School at Lennoxville in the Eastern Townships of Quebec, followed in his case by the Royal

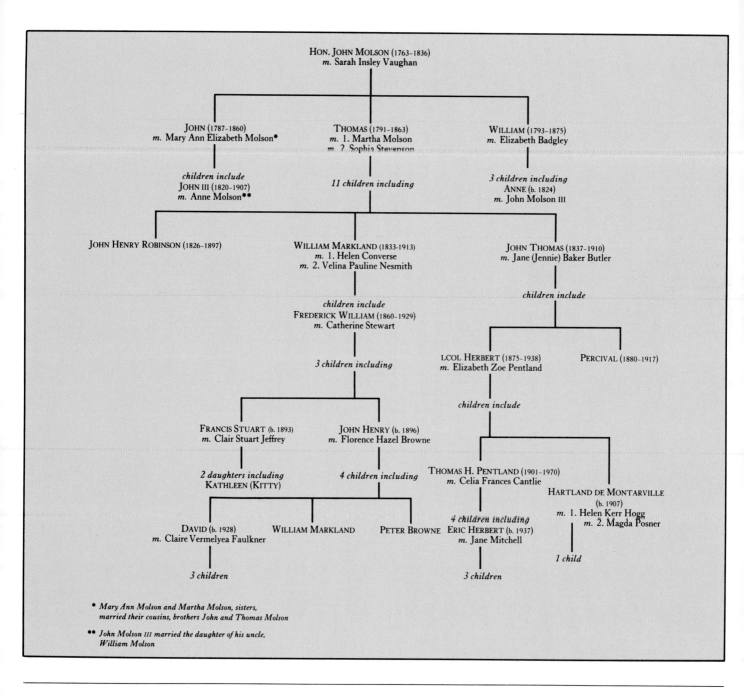

HON. JOHN MOLSON (1763–1836)
m. Sarah Insley Vaughan

JOHN (1787–1860)
m. Mary Ann Elizabeth Molson*

THOMAS (1791–1863)
m. 1. Martha Molson
m. 2. Sophia Stevenson

WILLIAM (1793–1875)
m. Elizabeth Badgley

children include
JOHN III (1820–1907)
m. Anne Molson**

11 children including

3 children including
ANNE (b. 1824)
m. John Molson III

JOHN HENRY ROBINSON (1826–1897)

WILLIAM MARKLAND (1833–1913)
m. 1. Helen Converse
m. 2. Velina Pauline Nesmith

JOHN THOMAS (1837–1910)
m. Jane (Jennie) Baker Butler

children include
FREDERICK WILLIAM (1860–1929)
m. Catherine Stewart

children include

3 children including

LCOL HERBERT (1875–1938)
m. Elizabeth Zoe Pentland

PERCIVAL (1880–1917)

FRANCIS STUART (b. 1893)
m. Clair Stuart Jeffrey

JOHN HENRY (b. 1896)
m. Florence Hazel Browne

children include

2 daughters including
KATHLEEN (KITTY)

4 children including

THOMAS H. PENTLAND (1901–1970)
m. Celia Frances Cantlie

HARTLAND DE MONTARVILLE
(b. 1907)
m. 1. Helen Kerr Hogg
m. 2. Magda Posner

DAVID (b. 1928)
m. Claire Vermelyea Faulkner

WILLIAM MARKLAND

PETER BROWNE

4 children including
ERIC HERBERT (b. 1937)
m. Jane Mitchell

1 child

3 children

3 children

* *Mary Ann Molson and Martha Molson, sisters,*
married their cousins, brothers John and Thomas Molson

** *John Molson III married the daughter of his uncle,*
William Molson

Military College at Kingston. Fittingly for a family with one foot in each culture, Molson's first job was with a banking house in France. Typically, he soon returned and opened his own bush plane service, Dominion Skyways. He also kept up the family's traditional interest in the armed forces and was already a long-service militia officer when the Second World War began. One of the first to volunteer for the RCAF, he was part of a squadron credited with shooting down 75 enemy planes and was himself shot down during the Battle of Brit-

ain. After the war he joined the family brewing business, becoming president in 1953. Two years later he was appointed to the Senate, sitting as an independent. He remains true to family tradition by being associated with the Bank of Montreal and McGill University.

Commercial empires rise and fall, cultures ebb and flow, but after almost two centuries the Molsons remain a living symbol of old Anglo Montreal with its rich overtones of privilege and noblesse oblige.

The Molsons, one of the most remarkable families in Canadian history, derive from John Molson (1763-1836) (LEFT), an English orphan who came to Montreal and founded the brewery that is still the focal point of the clan's varied business interests. Thomas (CENTRE) and William (RIGHT) were two of his sons.

The Molson farm on Lake Memphramagog. This photograph was taken in the late 1800s.

BOTH: PUBLIC ARCHIVES CANADA/MOLSON COMPANIES LTD.

John Thomas Molson commissioned this steam yacht, the Nooya, *from a British shipyard in 1870. It was of 160 gross tons and became, with its maiden voyage, the first private yacht to make the Liverpool-Quebec crossing. John Thomas Molson was the grandfather of the present Senator Hartland de Montarville Molson, O.B.E.*

The next generation of Molsons was led by Colonel Herbert Molson, shown at left in a 1930s caricature; he was once said to speak French "with a Bank of Montreal accent." RIGHT: Percival Molson was one of 34 Molsons who served in the First World War—and one of the five who never returned. He was a leading amateur athlete and Percival Molson Stadium at McGill University was erected in his memory.

Hartland Molson circa 1959 with Maurice (Rocket) Richard of the Molson-owned Montreal Canadiens.

Kathleen (Kitty) Molson, the daughter of F. Stuart Molson (RIGHT), was a prominent society lady of the 1950s. She was married briefly to the racing driver Stirling Moss.

August 1968, Senator Molson (second from left) sold the Canadiens to David Molson (on the left) and the brothers William and Peter Molson.

Eric Herbert Molson, the only person with the famous surname now conspicuous in the management of the eight-generation family empire.

Not the first Richardson, nor even the first James Richardson, but the one who took control of the family enterprises and, until his death in 1939, made them a remarkable force in Winnipeg and the nation, particularly in grain trading, stock brokerage and aviation.

The Richardsons

FOR YEARS THE Winnipeg skyline was punctuated by only one modern skyscraper: the Richardson Building at Portage and Main. This monument to corporate power dominated the city visually almost as much as the Richardsons have long dominated it financially, for, more than a century ago when Winnipeg was still a rollicking frontier town, this remarkable family was already immersed in a complex range of businesses.

Like a surprising number of Canada's other first families, the Richardsons sprang from Irish soil. The founder in this case was the first James Richardson (1819-1892), who came to Canada as a child and soon found himself selling newspapers on the street corners of Kingston. In time, he became a friend of a young local lawyer, John A. Macdonald, and became involved in politics, as the Richardsons—who tend to alternate parties in succeeding generations—are to this day. But James did not neglect his business affairs. By the 1850s, he was a figure of consequence in real estate, potash, and retailing. A public-spirited man, when Kingston needed a new Customs House, Richardson was one of several citizens who acted as guarantors; when the contractor defaulted and cost him a fortune, Richardson headed west and became a full-time grain trader to recoup his losses.

After James's death the firm was run first by one son, George A. (1852-1906), then, on *his* death, another son, Henry W. (1855-1918). Appointed to the Senate in 1916, Henry mixed politics not only with the grain trade but also with his special concerns, mining and shipping. Curiously, only one of Henry's six sons entered the business, so that with his demise control of the company was passed to a cousin, James Armstrong Richardson (1885-1939). This James, who had been born in Kingston, later bought out the rest of the family and became, in the public mind of the time, the one and only Richardson.

James A. Richardson was a mover and shaker on a heroic scale. He made the grain firm an international force, became an important figure in the stock-brokerage business, founded radio stations, bankrolled prospectors, and even helped finance the first successful experiments with colour motion pictures. The field in which he had the greatest impact, however, was aviation. In 1926, he founded Western Canada Airways, which later became Canadian Airways and in turn CP Air. Richardson-trained personnel also helped to found what is now Air Canada.

Richardson was a genuinely farsighted tycoon, and it was he in 1929 who laid the plans for the Winnipeg skyscraper. But this vision was not realized until 30 years after his death when the family empire—somewhat surprisingly for the time—had been run for 27 years not by his sons but by his widow, Muriel Sprague Richardson (1892-1973), a patron of the arts who moved boldly to sell off many unprofitable companies. When she retired in 1966, the power passed to her sons, then in their 40s: James A. (b. 1922) who became chairman, and George T. (b. 1924), who became president.

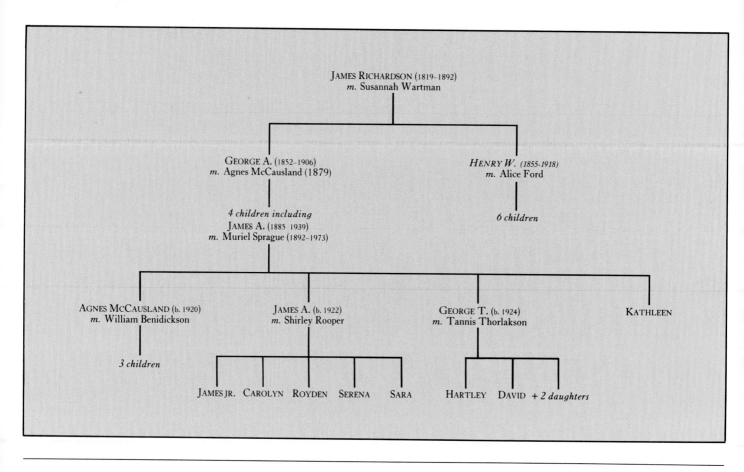

JAMES RICHARDSON (1819–1892)
m. Susannah Wartman

GEORGE A. (1852–1906)
m. Agnes McCausland (1879)

HENRY W. (1855–1918)
m. Alice Ford

4 children including
JAMES A. (1885–1939)
m. Muriel Sprague (1892–1973)

6 children

AGNES MCCAUSLAND (b. 1920)
m. William Benidickson

JAMES A. (b. 1922)
m. Shirley Rooper

GEORGE T. (b. 1924)
m. Tannis Thorlakson

KATHLEEN

3 children

JAMES JR.   CAROLYN   ROYDEN   SERENA   SARA

HARTLEY   DAVID   *+ 2 daughters*

George, who in 1970 became the first Canadian-born governor in the 300-year history of the Hudson's Bay Company, continues to run James Richardson & Sons from atop the Richardson Building, using a private helicopter to commute to a farm that seems to reinforce his fiercely agrarian and Western views. "There's a perspective from Winnipeg that's different, that's clear and unobscured," he once told an interviewer. "Westerners are different, and we're Westerners." Indeed, their grain elevators, distinguished by the word PIONEER in mammoth letters, are the principal landmarks in scores of Prairie towns, where they compete against elevators marked POOL, owned by farmers' co-operatives.

After a traumatic eight years as a minister in the Trudeau government, James Richardson has become the Don Quixote of Canadian politics, campaigning on behalf of a unilingual Canada that never was and never could be.

Of the two daughters of James and Muriel, Kathleen, a director of Gulf Canada and Sun Life,

continues to dominate Winnipeg's cultural and philanthropic scene, and expanded into a new sphere as chief backer of the ultimately unsuccessful Circus Tivoli. Agnes lives in Ottawa and sits on the boards of Mutual Life and National Trust.

In 1982, Richardson Securities of Canada, the family underwriting firm, acquired the old Montreal brokerage house, Greenshields. The deal put the Richardsons, already the country's largest private grain merchants, up there with Dominion Securities Ames and Wood Gundy in the top rank of Canadian investment dealers. It also served to illustrate yet again the westward drift of financial power, a change that, so far as the Richardsons are concerned, is almost certain to intensify in the future.

Taking advantage of that drift will be left to the new generation moving up. James has three daughters and two sons: Royden works as an analyst at Richardson Greenshields and James Jr. runs his own highly successful leasing company. George's branch of the family has Hartley coming

James Richardson's widow, Muriel Richardson, who after his death in 1939 reorganized and ran the empire until the late 1960s, when she passed the reins to her sons, then in their 40s.

James and Muriel Richardson's children: James (once prominent in the Trudeau cabinet), Agnes, George, and Kathleen. Agnes, married to Sen. William Benidickson, is chancellor of Queen's University in Kingston, as was her father.

An Ivan Glassco caricature of James A. Richardson. Charles Vining said of him that he "likes to act as he thinks a Westerner should and tries accordingly to make the handclasp a little stronger."

With his brother in politics, George Richardson dominated the various family businesses and in 1970 became the first Canadian-born governor in the 300-year history of the Hudson's Bay Company. He is shown here in 1973 with then Manitoba Premier (later Governor General) Edward Schreyer, making the province a gift of Bay archives. Behind them, in fur-trader costume, is a modern-day HBC factor.

along in the Richardsons' real-estate division and David, who could be the most impressive member of the new crop; he is a publisher of five business magazines under the Canasus banner and has several other enterprises on the go. But his most important role has been to take the family back to its roots in the grain trade by pioneering a nutritious wheat-rye hybrid cereal strain called triticale. Richardson's is the largest independent triticale contractor in Canada, and the TritiRich subsidiary is the country's biggest producer of the grain.

As dynasties go, the Rileys are an old one by the standards of Western Canada. The founder was Robert T. Riley who came to Canada in 1873 when he was 21 and founded several insurance companies. One of his grandsons, Culver Riley (ABOVE, nearest the camera) inherited not simply his father's tolerance of insurance, but also his love of rowing; he once qualified for the Olympics, though he did not actually take part in the games.

Devotion to rowing seems to be a family trait; further proof is supplied by Derek Riley (ABOVE, foregound), another of Robert T. Riley's eight grandchildren.

The Rileys

HE RILEYS REPRESENT a phenomenon that outsiders studying Canada's elite might assume to be more common than it is: the insurance fortune.

The English-born founder of the dynasty, Robert Thomas Riley (1851-1944), came to Canada in 1873. He was the son of one of the owners of *The Daily Telegraph* in Fleet Street. After working a farm near Hamilton until 1881, he moved to Winnipeg as the agent of an Ontario businessman. With others he founded Great-West Assurance Company in 1892 and, in time, became president of Canadian Fire Insurance Company (1895), Northern Trusts Company (1904), and Canadian Indemnity Company (1912). Over the years, he was also a prolific outside director of various concerns, including the Canadian National Railways. Robert was a Conservative and a Methodist who, if asked, would probably have cited those facts as the reason for his remarkably long life.

Of his children, it was the second son, Conrad Stephenson Riley (1875-1960), who expanded the family business. This Riley was a notable athlete (rowing) who started in the Canadian Insurance Company as a clerk and was named president in 1942. He later held the same title with Canadian

Indemnity and served as chairman of the Canadian committee of the Hudson's Bay Company. Of his eight children, W. Culver Riley (1907-1970) continued his father's twin involvement in insurance and rowing (indeed, he qualified for the Olympics in 1928, a year in which, unfortunately, Canada did not mount a rowing team). Another son, Conrad Sanford Riley (b. 1916), once headed Dominion Tanners and is now the chairman of Canadian Indemnity. His son Conrad Sanford Riley, Jr. (b. 1943), went into the family businesses, as did W. Culver Riley's son, W. Culver Riley, Jr. (b. 1935).

The family's influence in the Canadian Establishment was extended by two of Conrad Stephenson's other children: Jean Elizabeth Riley (1913-1976) and Ronald T. Riley (1909-1959). Jean married George Montegu Black, Jr. (1911-1976) and became the mother of Conrad and Montegu Black; and Ronald married George's sister, Margaret Montegu Black. The latter's son, also named Ronald T. Riley, sold his family holdings to cousins Conrad and Montegu, but remains active in the business world as a vice-president of Canadian Pacific and a director of Argus Corp.

Robert T. Riley.

ROBERT THOMAS RILEY (1851–1944)
m. 1. Harriet Murgatroyd
m. 2. Annie Sinclair

9 children including
CONRAD STEPHENSON (1875–1960)
m. Jean Isabel Culver

8 children including

W. CULVER (1907–1970)
m. Elizabeth F. Hamilton

W. CULVER (b. 1935)

RONALD T. (1909–1959)
m. Margaret Montegu Black*

3 children including
RONALD T. RILEY (b. 1935)

JEAN ELIZABETH (1913–1976)
m. George Montegu Black, Jr. (1911–1976)

GEORGE MONTEGU BLACK III
(b. 1940)
m. Mariellen Campbell

CONRAD MOFFAT
BLACK (b. 1944)
m. Shirley Hishon Walters

2 children

CONRAD SANFORD (b. 1916)
m. Mary Frances
Myrtle Aikins

CONRAD S., Jr. (b. 1943)
m. Joan McKnight

DENNIS A.

2 children

* *Margaret Montegu Black married Ronald T. Riley.*
Her brother, George Montegu Black, Jr., married
Riley's sister, Jean.

DEPT. OF ARCHIVES & SPECIAL COLLECTIONS, THE UNIVERSITY OF MANITOBA

THE CANADIAN INDEMNITY COMPANY

THE CANADIAN INDEMNITY COMPANY

Three Rileys involved with Canadian Indemnity and other concerns: from left to right, Culver Riley (1927–1970), chairman of
Canadian Indemnity until his death; his brother, Conrad S. Riley, Canadian Indemnity's present chairman; and Conrad S. Riley, Jr.,
now in his 40s and recently appointed president of United Canadian Shares, parent of Dominion Tanners and Canadian Indemnity.

Sandy Riley, the grandson of Conrad Stephenson Riley, continues the family's enjoyment of boating. He is shown here sailing a Finn in the 1976 Olympics at Kingston, Ontario.

While still in his 20s, Edward S. Rogers, Jr., known as Ted, bought a tiny FM radio station in Toronto and is now perhaps the single most important figure in the Canadian cable television industry.

The Rogers

Of ALL CANADIAN business dynasties, the Rogers family has the most historic roots as well as the most futuristic, high-tech associations. The name is now practically synonymous with cable television, particularly in Ontario where Rogers Cablesystems dominates the all-important Toronto market, but even 50 years ago the Rogers family was identified with state-of-the-art electronics. All this seems slightly incongruous, yet paradoxically much in keeping with the varied traditions of a family that has made its mark through more centuries in more places and in more fields of endeavour than any other family in the ranks of the Establishment.

The Rogers clan can trace its ancestry back to 1300 when a merchant named Aaron Rogers fled religious persecution in Rome and resettled in London. He apparently recouped his fortune, but the freedom he sought for his family was, in historical terms, relatively short-lived. Aaron's great-grandson, John Rogers, a canon of Old St. Paul's, was burned at the stake in 1555— England's first Protestant martyr. A half-century later Thomas Rogers and his son Joseph, in yet another bid for religious freedom, left for the New World on board the *Mayflower*.

Joseph's son James eventually became a prosperous merchant in Connecticut and the beneficiary of several royal appointments and acts of patronage. From that point forward the family's fortune was inextricably bound up with the society of the American colonies. In the Seven Years' War, Robert Rogers, along with his less famous brother Richard, led Rogers' Rangers, a storied band of irregulars. During the American Revolution, one Rogers had his home burned by the British and another, Ann Rogers, was married to Joseph Hopkinson, a signatory to the Declaration of Independence. Not being loyalists, they had no particular need to flee the new republic, so it was only at the turn of the 19th century that the first Rogers came to Canada. Once again the impetus was religious: the family was now Quaker.

In 1801 Timothy Rogers (1756-1844) came to York County, Upper Canada, as the leader of his own and 40 other Quaker families, settling what became the town of Newmarket near Toronto. (He later founded Pickering as well.) Rogers was virtually the father of the Quaker faith in Toronto and left behind many children, as well as a famous journal covering 50 years of his life on both sides of the border. During his grandchildren's generation, the family divided into two distinct branches.

Elias Rogers (1850-1920) fathered a clan that, though now Methodist, perpetuated Timothy's name and good works and became prominent in Ontario business, primarily through St. Marys Cement Ltd. Another of Timothy's grandsons was Samuel Rogers (1835-1903), whose son Albert (d. 1932) was the father of Edward Samuel Rogers (1901-1939).

It was with this first Edward Samuel that the interest in communications first surfaced. Early in the Depression, he invented the radio tube that made it possible to build receiving sets without batteries, thus drastically cutting the cost of radios and making them far more popular. The patent made him a fortune, which he then invested in the

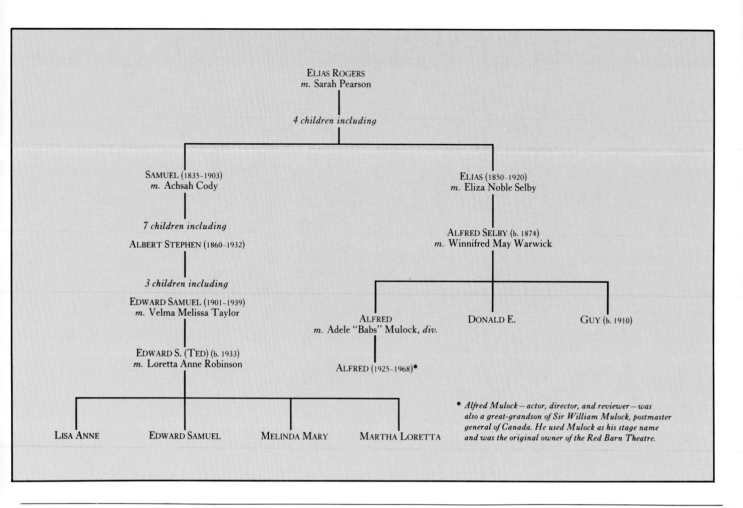

ELIAS ROGERS
m. Sarah Pearson

4 children including

SAMUEL (1835–1903)
m. Achsah Cody

ELIAS (1850–1920)
m. Eliza Noble Selby

7 children including
ALBERT STEPHEN (1860–1932)

ALFRED SELBY (b. 1874)
m. Winnifred May Warwick

3 children including
EDWARD SAMUEL (1901–1939)
m. Velma Melissa Taylor

ALFRED
m. Adele "Babs" Mulock, *div.*

DONALD E.

GUY (b. 1910)

EDWARD S. (TED) (b. 1933)
m. Loretta Anne Robinson

ALFRED (1925–1968)*

LISA ANNE

EDWARD SAMUEL

MELINDA MARY

MARTHA LORETTA

* *Alfred Mulock — actor, director, and reviewer — was also a great-grandson of Sir William Mulock, postmaster general of Canada. He used Mulock as his stage name and was the original owner of the Red Barn Theatre.*

Toronto radio station CFRB, today Canada's largest. But following his early death his widow sold the station. Rogers' original radio tube is now housed in a rosewood case in the home of his son, Edward Samuel (Ted) Rogers Jr. (b. 1933), whose influence on broadcasting has also been profound.

Educated at UCC and trained as a lawyer, Ted Rogers entered the communications field in 1960 when, for a modest $85,000, he bought the tiny Toronto FM station, CHFI. At the time only five per cent of local homes could receive FM signals, but the market, small as it was, was already overcrowded. Rogers improved the odds for success by adding a complementary AM station and then boosting the FM outlet to a 'round-the-clock operation. These were moves that required years of lobbying and some daring financial ploys, and the process was completed only in 1966. At about the same time Rogers became convinced that cable television offered attractive opportunities, and he

moved into that field as well, at first in partnership with the Bassett and Eaton families. The CRTC, however, later forced these other dynasties to sell out to Rogers.

In the early days of cable, most operators seemed content to sit back and let the people wanting American TV programming come to them for service. Rogers was different. He was an aggressive marketer, and he believed in producing his own programmes to sweeten the appeal. In the 1970s he bought out two of his competitors, Canadian Cablesystems and Premier Cablevision, giving Rogers 1.2 million subscribers in the Toronto area and more in several smaller Ontario centres and cities on the West Coast. Subsequently he moved into the United States as well, with operations in Minneapolis, Syracuse, and the lucrative southern California market. Lately he has secured a toehold in the United Kingdom too. From his radio and cable base, Rogers has become

Edward S. Rogers, Sr., who died in 1939, revolutionized radio by his invention of a vacuum tube that made battery-powered receiving sets obsolete. Subsequently he purchased what became, under later ownership, Canada's largest radio station.

involved in other cultural industries, serving as a director of Gage Publishing and the Famous Players chain of movie theatres (of which Rogers Cablesystems once owned 48 per cent).

The family's Quaker associations are long gone now. Ted Rogers is Anglican, particularly clubbable, well liked, and well connected. His wife, the former Loretta Anne Robinson, is the daughter of Lord Martonmere, the veteran British political figure and one-time governor of Bermuda. They have three daughters (Lisa, Melinda, and Martha) and one son (Edward Samuel Rogers III).

John Wright Sifton (1833-1912) was already the third generation of that Irish Protestant family in Canada when he moved to the Prairies, the region with which most later Siftons have been associated in various ways. His son Sir Clfford Sifton, seen below with his family about 1910, was a newspaper proprietor like his father but is best remembered as the federal Immigration minister who helped populate the Canadian West with European immigrants.

The Siftons

THE SIFTONS ARE an extensive, powerful, and exquisitely confusing family of newspaper proprietors and equestrians associated mainly with the Prairie provinces, although the dynasty's corporate headquarters are in Toronto.

Despite stiff competition, the most famous of the family remains Sir Clifford Sifton, the Edwardian statesman who, as Interior and Immigration minister in Sir Wilfrid Laurier's government, opened the West to rapid settlement by recruiting hundreds of thousands of European immigrants whom he characterized as "stout peasants in sheepskin coats."

The Siftons were Irish Protestants from County Tipperary. To Canada in the 1820s came Charles Sifton (1752-1842) and his wife, who were following their sons Bamlet and Joseph. With John Wright Sifton (1833-1912), one of Bamlet's five sons, the family's entrepreneurial and political streak became apparent. J.W. was a farmer and pioneer oilman in Ontario before moving west in 1875, where he contracted to put through railway and telegraph rights-of-way. But he quickly shifted his interests to politics, becoming speaker of the Legislative Assembly of Manitoba as early as 1878. From then until 1902, when he became first a vice-president and finally president of the *Manitoba Free Press*, he lost as many elections as he won, filling the time out of office with various posts in the civil service. It was during his era with the *Free Press* (later the *Winnipeg Free Press*) that the paper became the voice of Western-style agrarian liberalism. With the forceful views of its editor, John W. Dafoe, the paper transcended its provincial boundaries and became a vital force in the nation.

J.W. Sifton's mission was carried on by his two sons, Arthur Lewis (1858-1921) and Sir Clifford (1861-1929), whose knighthood was awarded in 1915 for work on the home front during the First World War. A.L. trained for the law and was called to the North West Territories bar in 1883. He practised in Brandon (for a time in partnership with Clifford) and later at Prince Albert and Calgary. Between 1899 and 1903 he was MLA for Banff and later chief justice of the territorial supreme court—a post that automatically made him the first chief justice of the newly created Alberta supreme court in 1905. Five years later he quit the bench to become the provincial Liberal leader; he served as premier of the new province from 1910 to 1917. In that year he broke with the Laurier Liberals over conscription and entered Borden's wartime coalition government in Ottawa. He was a Canadian delegate to the Versailles peace conference, and at the time of his death was secretary of state.

When A.L. and his brother were young lawyers in Brandon, they were known as keen judges (and prodigious buyers) of horseflesh. But it was left to Sir Clifford to confirm the family trait of being equally keen judges (and purchasers) of newspapers; it was he who brought the *Brandon Sun* under Sifton control.

This talent gained cumulative force with Sir Clifford's sons, especially the significant brothers of the next generation, Clifford (1893-1976) and Victor (1897-1961). These two outdid their elders in many things, especially in the intensity of

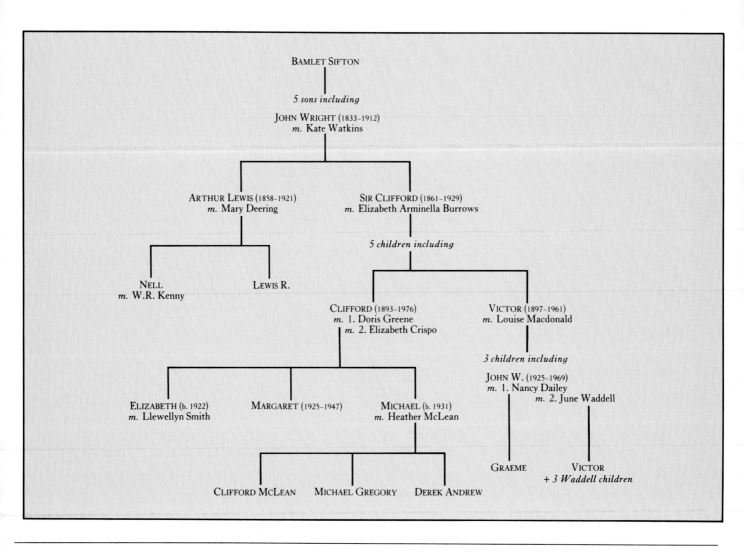

BAMLET SIFTON

5 sons including

JOHN WRIGHT (1833–1912)
m. Kate Watkins

ARTHUR LEWIS (1858–1921)
m. Mary Deering

SIR CLIFFORD (1861–1929)
m. Elizabeth Arminella Burrows

5 children including

NELL
m. W.R. Kenny

LEWIS R.

CLIFFORD (1893–1976)
m. 1. Doris Greene
m. 2. Elizabeth Crispo

VICTOR (1897–1961)
m. Louise Macdonald

3 children including

JOHN W. (1925–1969)
m. 1. Nancy Dailey
m. 2. June Waddell

ELIZABETH (b. 1922)
m. Llewellyn Smith

MARGARET (1925–1947)

MICHAEL (b. 1931)
m. Heather McLean

GRAEME

VICTOR
+ 3 Waddell children

CLIFFORD MCLEAN   MICHAEL GREGORY   DEREK ANDREW

their sibling rivalry. Both Clifford and Victor served in the first war, both rose to the rank of major, and both were awarded the Distinguished Service Order. Clifford, however, ultimately had the greater distinction of being wounded three times. He ran Armadale Corporation, the family holding company, in Toronto, while Victor worked on the Saskatoon *Star-Phoenix* and the Regina *Leader-Post* when the family acquired those papers; he ultimately settled in Regina.

The rivalry between them grew more heated over the terms of their father's will. Sir Clifford had left his estate to his sons, four of whom were still living at the time of his death in 1929. Victor apparently felt it unfair that Clifford should be holding so much of the newspaper empire, when he was inexperienced as a publisher. The situation came to a head years later in 1953 when just the

two brothers were left. Victor purchased Clifford's interest in the *Free Press*, while Clifford got the two newspapers (and, by then, some radio stations as well) in Saskatchewan.

Miraculously, each business prospered. Victor threw the *Free Press* into the kitty that made up the FP Publications newspaper chain, receiving a large slice of FP in return. On Victor's death, this interest was passed to his son, John, and, at *his* death in 1969, to John's son Victor. Or rather, the stock was put in trust for young Victor until 1990, when he will turn 25, a fact that became a major problem at the time of FP's sale to the Thomson family in 1980.

Meanwhile, Clifford Sifton and his first wife Doris Greene Sifton produced three children: Elizabeth (b. 1922), who married Llewellyn Smith, heir to the E.D. Smith jam and jelly fortune;

TOP: PUBLIC ARCHIVES CANADA/PA 28 & 25 : WINNIPEG FREE PRESS

PUBLIC ARCHIVES CANADA/PA 4454

Sir Clifford typified the all-round public man of his times and managed to look the part in this 1917 portrait (TOP LEFT). Everything about him reflected the high style of the man of affairs, including his Ottawa home. The portrait at top right shows Sir Clifford's wife, Lady Sifton.

Margaret (1925-1947); and Michael Clifford (b.1931), the current president of Armadale, who joined his father in upgrading plant and equipment in the Saskatchewan newspapers and radio stations while maintaining residence in the Toronto area.

As the present head of the family, Michael Sifton retains the familial interests in publishing, good works, and horses. He has pointed out that he is "responsible for [the] revival of polo in Toronto" and once counted the world's largest indoor polo field among his possessions. He also once owned *Toronto Life* magazine and still owns Canada's largest privately held airport, the Buttonville Airport north of Toronto. He has not, however, followed the ancestral path into politics. Michael's three sons are expected to eventually assume control of the Sifton empire. The eldest of the sons, inevitably, is named Clifford.

Sir Clifford is said to have inherited from his father J.W. Sifton not only what is now the Winnipeg Free Press *but also a commanding knowledge of horses. Well into advanced years, Sir Clifford (TOP LEFT) would join in the hunt, as seen here in a snapshot circa 1914. Being horsemen gave his sons (TOP RIGHT) unneeded additional social standing. Tension was growing meanwhile between Sir Clifford's line and that of his younger brother Arthur Lewis Sifton (MIDDLE LEFT), who moved farther west, to Alberta, and later Saskatchewan. He and his wife (BOTTOM LEFT) are seen here dressed for George V's coronation in 1911. In a later view, they are making a tour of Egypt with their children Nell and Lewis.*

*Victor Sifton (ABOVE) con-
ducted a long rivalry with his
brother Clifford that resulted in
his acquiring all his brother's
shares in the* Free Press.

*With Victor's death in 1961,
the* Free Press *passed to his son
John. The newspaper is now
owned by Thomson Newspa-
pers Ltd.*

Young Graeme Sifton leaves the
Free Press *after being laid off in a
1982 staff reduction.*

*Publishing has been only one of the interests of Michael Sifton, the current head of the family who is better known as an aviator and avid
sportsman.*

The Sobeys

In 1983, when the CBC produced a television soap opera for adults about 50 years in the life of a Canadian business family, it gave the mini-series the somewhat un-Canadian title *Empire Inc.* One of the reasons the CBC did not use *Empire Ltd.* is that Empire Co. Ltd. is the name of the holding company of the Sobey family of Nova Scotia, one of those remarkable Maritime dynasties (like the McCains, the Olands, and the Jodreys) who dominate and are intensely loyal to their own region, yet little known outside of it.

One business journal has observed that the Sobeys would rather retain an unsuccessful investment than sell it to outsiders from another part of Canada. But this does not indicate any general financial aloofness on their part. Sobey's is a synonym for supermarkets in Nova Scotia, as it has been for decades, but the family has long since expanded into textiles, insurance, shopping centres, property development, oil and gas, even bowling alleys. In 1982 Empire, run from the somewhat unlikely spot of Stellarton, Nova Scotia, had gross sales of more than $554 million.

The roots of this surprising dynasty reach back to John William Sobey (1869-1949), who was brought from England as a boy to a farm in Pictou County, Nova Scotia, then moved on to Stellarton. Shortly after the turn of the century, he bought a credit meat business. In time he was

The elusive Frank H. Sobey, who joined the small credit meat business his father had started in Nova Scotia and helped turn it into Sobeys Stores, a virtual synonym for supermarkets in Nova Scotia. More recently the family has expanded into energy and property development.

joined in the business by his father and then by his own sons, Frank H. (b. 1902) and Harold (1911-1976). There seemed little in the enterprise that was remarkable; more than 20 years would elapse before a second store was added, this one in New Glasgow. But 20 years after *that*, the newly organized Sobeys Stores, through a combination of acquisitions and startups, included 14 credit meat stores and two groceterias, as they were then called. The last two outlets proved so successful that the family decided to abandon the credit meat business and concentrate on the cash-and-carry trade. To this end, Frank H. Sobey oversaw a bond issue that made his name known in financial circles.

Shortly afterwards, firmly established as the head of the family, Frank Sobey began to broaden its interests. Cinemas were one of his prime concerns. He first entered the field during the Depression, then sold out to Odeon following the Second World War. When he decided to re-enter the business, he did so with a vengeance. In 1963, the Sobeys became the partners of the Famous Players organization in cinemas throughout the Atlantic provinces as well as the sole proprietors of almost a score of their own movie houses. In time, Frank Sobey became a minor international figure from his base in the Maritimes, reminiscent in his way of the very young Max Aitken. But, unlike the future Lord Beaverbrook, Sobey remained where he was and retained many regional characteristics, among them a sense of noblesse oblige and an abiding love of community. A member of everything from the Mount Royal Club in Montreal to Lloyd's of

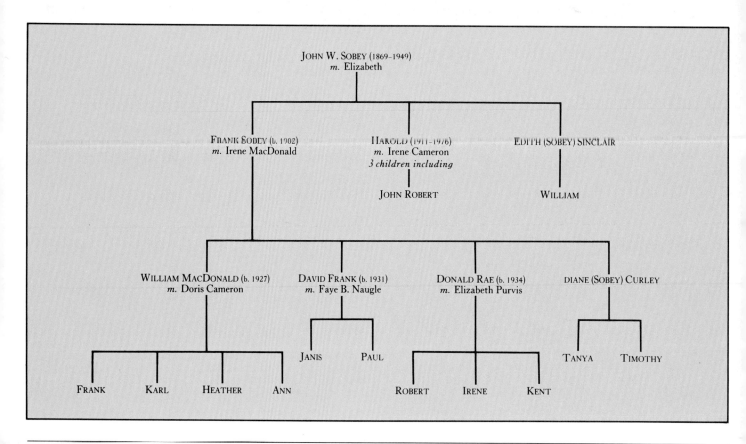

JOHN W. SOBEY (1869–1949)
m. Elizabeth

FRANK SOBEY (b. 1902)
m. Irene MacDonald

HAROLD (1911–1976)
m. Irene Cameron
3 children including

JOHN ROBERT

EDITH (SOBEY) SINCLAIR

WILLIAM

WILLIAM MACDONALD (b. 1927)
m. Doris Cameron

DAVID FRANK (b. 1931)
m. Faye B. Naugle

DONALD RAE (b. 1934)
m. Elizabeth Purvis

DIANE (SOBEY) CURLEY

JANIS   PAUL

TANYA   TIMOTHY

FRANK   KARL   HEATHER   ANN

ROBERT   IRENE   KENT

London, Sobey nonetheless took time to serve as mayor of Stellarton for 22 years (from 1937 to 1959).

The network of business interests, including such recent schemes as Halifax Developments Ltd., developers of the Scotia Square project in that city, is continued by Frank H. Sobey's sons, all of whom continue to live modestly in the Stellarton–New Glasgow area. William (b. 1927) is the chairman and CEO of Sobeys Stores following an apprenticeship with the rival Loblaws chain, which once held an interest in Sobeys. David F. (b. 1931) is president of Sobeys Stores. The most influential of the brothers is probably the youngest, Donald R. (b. 1934), the president of Empire and overseer of the dynasty's wealth.

The Sobey family's complicated network of business interests is now run by Frank Sobey's three sons: David and William (FACING PAGE) and Donald (ABOVE), the president of Empire Company Limited, the family company. All continue to live unpretentiously in the Stellarton area of Nova Scotia.

Mercy Southam, a determined pioneer and the mother of the original William Southam.

The remarkable Southam newspaper family in 1905. Their empire began 28 years earlier when William Southam (white beard, centre) assumed operation of the anemic Hamilton Spectator. *Its turnaround enabled him to despatch sons across the country to run other dailies. Left to right are sons Harry, Gordon, Wilson, Frederick Neal, Richard, and William. Frederick Neal succeeded the patriarch as company president. Seated are his mother, Wilson McNeilage Southam, and sister, Ethel May, who was mother of the present chairman.*

The Southams

THE SOUTHAM FAMILY is the oldest communications dynasty in Canada (if the related Fishers and Balfours are included) and its history illustrates not only the nature of large family businesses but also the way families have traditionally controlled Canada's newspapers. Even today the family, directors, and a few employees of Southam Inc. who in aggregate own 44.9 per cent of the shares, are a tightly knit group: each year they circulate among themselves a privately published book giving the latest details on the family holdings.

The fortunes of the family and those of the publicly traded company are inseparable. Both derive from a manoeuvre in 1877 by which William Southam (1843-1932) and his partner William Carey took over the Hamilton *Spectator*. It was their hope that an imminent return to power by the federal Conservatives would pay dividends in terms of government advertising. It did. The transaction set the pattern for the Southams' politics and for their business practice of taking over key newspapers across the country as they became available rather than starting new publications from scratch.

In realizing his ambitions, William Southam was aided by his sons: Frederick Neal (1869-1946), Wilson (1868-1947), Richard (1871-1937), Harry (1875-1954), William (1877-1957), and Gordon (b. 1886; killed in 1916 during the First World War).

Frederick Neal (known as F.N.), who eventually followed his father into the president's chair, was dispatched to Montreal in 1889 to run a newly acquired printing house; Wilson was put in charge of the recently purchased Ottawa *Citizen* in 1897 and was soon joined there by Harry; while Richard oversaw the family's job-printing operation in Toronto. In time, the Ottawa brothers came to constitute almost a separate bloc.

The fifth son, also named William, spent most of his career running the *Spectator*, which remained strong in the family's affections despite the way other, often more important newspapers were added at regular intervals: the Calgary *Herald* (1908) was followed by the Edmonton *Journal* (1912), the Winnipeg *Tribune* (1920), the Vancouver *Province* (1923), the Medicine Hat *News* (1948), the North Bay *Nugget* (1956), and, beginning in 1969, in a rapid burst of aquisition, the Montreal *Gazette*, the Owen Sound *Sun-Times*, the Prince George *Citizen*, the Brantford *Expositor*, the Windsor *Star*, and the Sault *Star*.

The evolution of the company in these decades is reflected in the changes in the corporate name; from Southam Ltd. of 1904 it became William Southam and Sons (1920), Southam Publishing Co. Ltd. (1927), Southam Co. Ltd. (1938; it went public in 1945), Southam Press Ltd. (1964), and finally the present-day Southam Inc. (1978). During this period the headquarters moved from Hamilton to Ottawa to Montreal and finally to Toronto, where it remains.

Throughout the acquisition process, the Southams have maintained high standards, often substantially improving the publications they have acquired. The chain has retained its own foreign correspondents, built an excellent feature service, invested heavily in plant and equipment, and on

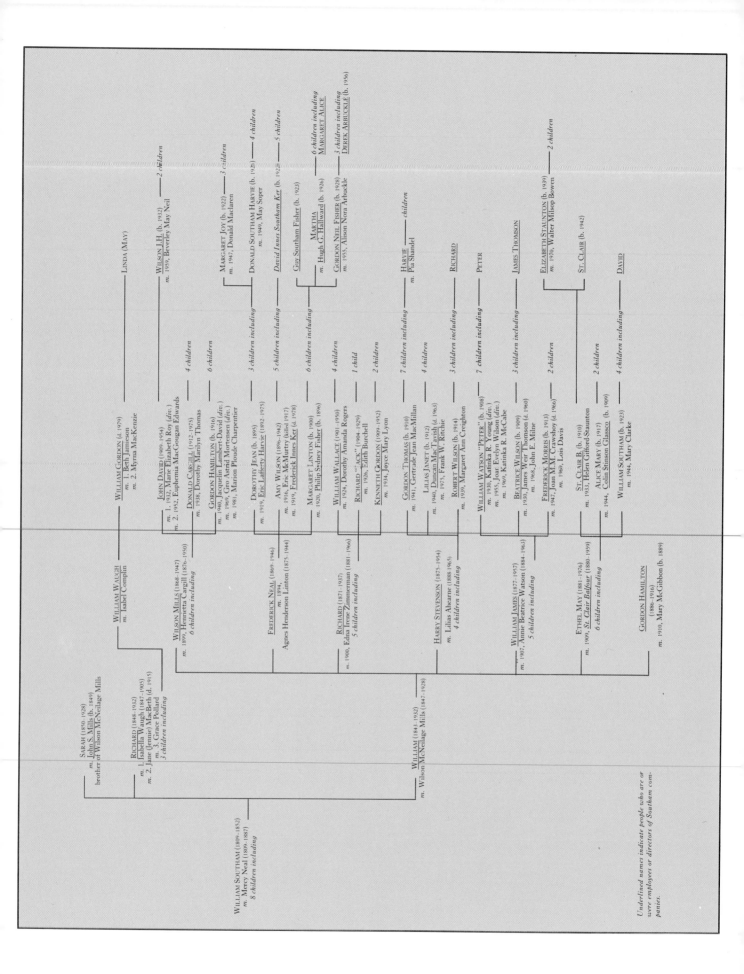

SARAH (1850-1928)
m. John S. Mills (b. 1849)
brother of Wilson McNeilage Mills

RICHARD (1848-1932)
m. 1. Isabella Waugh (1847-1905)
m. 2. Jane (Jennie) MacBeth (d. 1915)
m. 3. Grace Pollard
3 children including

WILLIAM WAUGH
m. Isabel Complin

LINDA (MAY)

WILLIAM GORDON (d. 1979)
m. 1. Beth Jamieson
m. 2. Myrna MacKenzie

WILSON J.H. (b. 1932) ——— 2 children
m. 1959, Beverley May Neil

WILLIAM SOUTHAM (1809-1852)
m. Mercy Neal (1809-1887)
8 children including

WILSON MILLS (1868-1947)
m. 1899, Henrietta Cargill (1876-1950)
6 children including

JOHN DAVID (1909-1954)
m. 1. 1932, Marie Elizabeth Roy (div.)
m. 2. 1952, Euphemia MacGougan Edwards

DONALD CARGILL (1912-1975) ——— 4 children
m. 1938, Dorothy Marilyn Thomas

GORDON HAMILTON (b. 1916) ——— 6 children
m. 1940, Jacquelin Lambert-David (div.)
m. 1969, Gro Astrid Mortensen (div.)
m. 1981, Marion Ploude Charpentier

MARGARET JOY (b. 1922) ——— 3 children
m. 1947, Donald Maclaren

DONALD SOUTHAM HARVIE (b. 1925) ——— 4 children
m. 1949, May Soper

DAVID INNES SOUTHAM KER (b. 1922) ——— 5 children

FREDERICK NEAL (1869-1946)
m. 1894,
Agnes Henderson Linton (1875-1944)

DOROTHY JEAN (b. 1895)
m. 1919, Eric Lafferty Harvie (1892-1975)

AMY WILSON (1896-1942)
m. 1916, Eric McMurtry (killed 1917)
m. 1919, Frederick Innes Ker (d. 1978)

MARGARET LINTON (b. 1900) ——— 3 children including
m. 1920, Philip Sydney Fisher (b. 1896)

GUY SOUTHAM FISHER (b. 1923)

MARTHA ——— 6 children including
m. Hugh G. Hallward (b. 1926) MARGARET ALICE

RICHARD (1871-1937)
m. 1900, Edna Irene Zimmerman (1881-1966)
5 children including

WILLIAM WALLACE (1901-1950)
m. 1924, Dorothy Amanda Rogers

GORDON NEIL FISHER (b. 1928) ——— 3 children including
m. 1955, Alison Nora Arbuckle DEREK ARBUCKLE (b. 1956)

RICHARD "ACK" (1904-1929) ——— 4 children
m. 1926, Edith Burchell

KENNETH GORDON (1909-1952) ——— 1 child
m. 1934, Joyce Mary Lyon

WILLIAM (1843-1932)
m. Wilson McNeilage Mills (1847-1928)

HARRY STEVENSON (1873-1954)
m. Lilias Ahearne (1888-1965)
4 children including

GORDON THOMAS (b. 1910) ——— 2 children
m. 1941, Gertrude Jean MacMillan

HARVIE ——— children
m. Pia Shandel

LILIAS JANET (b. 1912) ——— 7 children including
m. 1940, Duncan MacTavish (d. 1963)
m. 1975, Frank W. Ritchie

RICHARD

ROBERT WILSON (b. 1914) ——— 4 children
m. 1939, Margaret Ann Creighton

WILLIAM WATSON "PETER" (b. 1908) ——— 3 children including
m. 1930, Katinka R. Young (div.)
m. 1955, Joan Evelyn Wilson (div.)
m. 1969, Katinka R. McCabe

PETER

WILLIAM JAMES (1877-1957)
m. 1907, Annie Beatrice Watson (1884-1963)
5 children including

BEATRICE WILSON (b. 1909)
m. 1930, James Weir Thomson (d. 1960)
m. 1968, John E. Milne

JAMES THOMSON ——— 7 children including

FREDERICK MORRIS (b. 1913) ——— 3 children including
m. 1947, Joan M.M. Crawshoy (d. 1966)
m. 1969, Lois Davis

ELIZABETH STAUNTON (b. 1939) ——— 2 children
m. 1970, Walter Milsop Bowen

ETHEL MAY (1881-1976)
m. 1909, St. Clair Balfour (1880-1959)
6 children including

ST. CLAIR B. (b. 1910) ——— 3 children including
m. 1933, Helen Gifford Staunton

ST. CLAIR (b. 1942)

ALICE MARY (b. 1917) ——— 2 children
m. 1944, Colin Stinson Glassco (b. 1909)

GORDON HAMILTON
(1886-1916)
m. 1910, Mary McGibbon (b. 1889)

WILLIAM SOUTHAM (b. 1923) ——— 4 children including
m. 1944, Mary Clarke

DAVID

Underlined names indicate people who are or were employees or directors of Southam companies.

248

The Southam brothers (left to right, F.N., Richard, W.J., Wilson, and Harry), photographed on the roof of their Montreal building in 1927, were still extending their printing and publishing holdings and still keeping matters close to their collective vest, just as the family continues to do today.

occasion found innovative solutions to the problems of an overcrowded market. Such was the case in 1957 when the Southams formed another company, Pacific Press, with the owners of the Vancouver *Sun* (later acquired by FP Publications) so that both the *Sun* and the *Province* could be produced from the same plant while maintaining their independence.

Ultimately, this deal backfired somewhat when in 1980 Southam bought out FP's share after FP had been purchased by the Thomson group. That overall rationalizing of the industry, which included Thomson's closing the Ottawa *Journal* and Southam's closing the Winnipeg *Tribune* the same day, embroiled both chains in a controversy that led to a royal commission on corporate concentration in the newspaper business and to

charges under the anti-combines laws. But the incident was an anomaly in the family's long involvement in the business.

When the founding Southam was followed as president by his son, control was consolidated within the family: F.N. promptly bought out the estate of William Carey, his father's original partner. This consolidation was undone in the strictest sense when F.N. was succeeded by his son-in-law, Philip S. Fisher. The original family line entered the picture once more, however, when Fisher was followed as chief executive by St. Clair Balfour, who is related to the Southams maternally as well as by marriage. When Balfour was elevated to the chairmanship in 1975, Gordon Fisher (the son of Philip Fisher) became president. Thus, the family has, so to speak, Southam-

Gordon Southam of Vancouver, shown in a 1957 portrait, married a daughter of H.R. MacMillan.

Wilson Southam, the president and general manager of The Group at Cox, serves on the board of Southam Inc. and is a son of John David Southam.

ized the outsiders who have married into it. When Fisher in turn moved on to the chairmanship, the presidency was assumed by Wilson J.H. Southam.

Like some other Canadian newspaper families, the Southam-Fishers have been loath to diversify much outside the printing and publishing trades, where their holdings include business publications such as *The Financial Times* and *Executive*. They were broadcasting pioneers in the 1920s, however, when the Edmonton *Journal* started station CJCA, and they still have minority broadcast holdings in London, Ottawa, Edmonton, and Calgary, though their activity in electronic media is constrained by federal regulation. A more recent departure has been the acquisition of the mammoth Coles bookstore chain.

As individuals, the Southam-Fishers are close and not disposed towards personal publicity, except that which attaches to them as patrons of the arts. Aside from those named above, the principal figures in the clan currently include William Watson Southam (b. 1908), Robert Wilson Southam (b. 1914), and Gordon Southam (b. 1916), all retired executives of the newspaper chain, and most particularly G. Hamilton Southam (b. 1916), who after a brief career in journalism joined the Department of External Affairs. He eventually served as Canada's ambassador to Poland and later became director general of the National Arts Centre in Ottawa. In the current generation, Gordon Southam's son Harvey, a grandson of lumber magnate H.R. MacMillan, is publisher of his own business magazine in Vancouver.

J.R.

J.R.

Clockwise, present Southam chairman St. Clair Balfour, who is related to the Southams by both blood and marriage, Gordon Fisher, who became president when Balfour assumed the chairmanship; and G. Hamilton Southam who, through his diplomatic career and leadership in the arts community, is the best known of the clan.

J.R

In 1969, on his 75th birthday, Lord Thomson of Fleet was given a banquet at the Dorchester in London. Flanking him, left to right, are Mrs. Mary Wilson (wife of the British prime minister), the Earl of Snowdon, Princess Margaret, the Duke of Kent, and Prime Minister Harold Wilson.

The present Lord Thomson of Fleet, Kenneth Thomson, is seen here with several of his many Krieghoffs.

The Thomsons

MANY CANADIAN ESTABLISHMENT families have started out in tattier rags than the Thomsons did, but few have ascended to greater riches or done so more quickly. As a successful business family with world-wide interests, the Thomsons are scarcely three generations old, yet the change from genteel poverty to extreme wealth came within one generation—specifically, during the latter half of Roy Thomson's life.

Roy Thomson (1894-1976) was born in Toronto, the son of a local barber. Until well into middle age, he seemed an unlikely candidate for success. As late as 1925 when his auto-parts distributorship collapsed, he and his family were turned out of their modest Toronto house in the neighbourhood where he was born. During the Depression, Thomson hit the road as a travelling salesman, principally in northern Ontario. And it was in that unlikely time and place that opportunity, if it didn't exactly knock, at least beckoned.

Having bought a broken-down radio transmitter for $100 (on credit), Thomson in 1931 began operating a minuscule station in North Bay. Its novelty helped make it a success, and Thomson followed with another station in Timmins. The need to publicize programmes led him in 1934 to purchase the weekly *Timmins Press*, which he transformed into a daily. The *Press* became the unlikely foundation of a newspaper empire that eventually came to include *The Times* of London, 41 of the 115 dailies in Canada, and scores of other newspapers in Britain, the United States, and elsewhere. Added to these holdings were publishing houses, travel agencies, employment bureaus, and disparate other businesses.

The global empire building stemmed from Thomson's involvement in the United Kingdom, which began in the 1950s when he purchased *The Scotsman* of Edinburgh. He later proved successful in getting the franchise for independent television in Scotland, which, he quipped to a Canadian *Time* magazine stringer, was "like having a licence to print your own money." The phrase would later haunt this curious figure, who bore some resemblance to the cartoon character Mister Magoo and was well known for his rough candour and his parsimony. Shortly after acquiring *The Sunday Times* from Lord Kemsley and later *The Times* from the Astor interests, he was created a peer, becoming Lord Thomson of Fleet. The title did much to arouse the ire of fellow newspaper owners, a group into which Thomson never really fit.

As *The Times* was to observe in its obituary of Thomson, he was "an owner who sought profit not power," a fact that put him in contrast to his friend and fellow Canadian, Lord Beaverbrook. Taken to its furthest extreme, Thomson's lack of concern with politics and overwhelming concern with money once led him to make Soviet Premier Nikita Khrushchev an offer to purchase *Pravda*, whose status as an iron-clad monopoly Thomson much admired.

Thomson's career would have been remarkable enough even without the dramatic turn it took in his last years, when one of his British companies became active in petroleum exploration. According to legend, the decision to do so evolved over the years during Thomson's frequent penny-ante poker games with American oil billionaire J. Paul

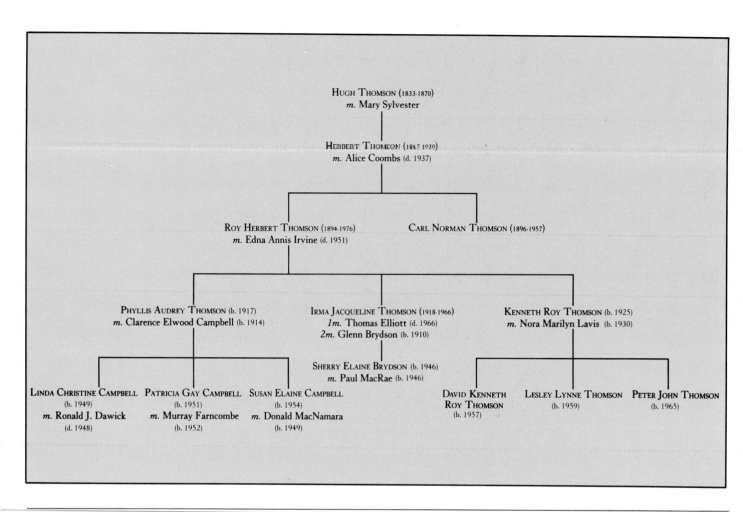

HUGH THOMSON (1833-1870)
m. Mary Sylvester

HERBERT THOMSON (1867-1920)
m. Alice Coombs (d. 1937)

ROY HERBERT THOMSON (1894-1976)
m. Edna Annis Irvine (d. 1951)

CARL NORMAN THOMSON (1896-1957)

PHYLLIS AUDREY THOMSON (b. 1917)
m. Clarence Elwood Campbell (b. 1914)

IRMA JACQUELINE THOMSON (1918-1966)
1m. Thomas Elliott (d. 1966)
2m. Glenn Brydson (b. 1910)

KENNETH ROY THOMSON (b. 1925)
m. Nora Marilyn Lavis (b. 1930)

SHERRY ELAINE BRYDSON (b. 1946)
m. Paul MacRae (b. 1946)

LINDA CHRISTINE CAMPBELL
(b. 1949)
m. Ronald J. Dawick
(d. 1948)

PATRICIA GAY CAMPBELL
(b. 1951)
m. Murray Farncombe
(b. 1952)

SUSAN ELAINE CAMPBELL
(b. 1954)
m. Donald MacNamara
(b. 1949)

DAVID KENNETH
ROY THOMSON
(b. 1957)

LESLEY LYNNE THOMSON
(b. 1959)

PETER JOHN THOMSON
(b. 1965)

Getty, who kept insisting that energy was where the future lay. In 1971, Thomson finally gave in and joined Getty and Armand Hammer, the founder of Occidental Petroleum, in backing exploration in the North Sea. At the time oil sold for under a dollar a barrel. At Thomson's death five years later, it was well on its way to a record high of about $30 a barrel. Since Thomson held about a quarter of the North Sea action, the price rise increased the family's wealth by a multiple probably without precedent in Canadian financial history, leaving Thomson's son Kenneth (b. 1923), the second Lord Thomson, a major figure in Canadian financial affairs.

Known on Bay Street as Young Ken though now into his 60s, Kenneth Thomson is as reserved and cultured as his father was extroverted and earthy. He is a noted art collector as well as being, in the words of one otherwise skeptical Toronto journalist, a person who has

probably never been rude to anyone in his life. In 1981, he donated $4.5 million to the building fund for Toronto's new municipal concert auditorium, which became Roy Thomson Hall. There were public objections that it should not be named for someone who had been so indifferent to music, but the hall's management responded in some desperation that the charge was untrue since Roy, the honorary colonel of the Toronto Scottish Regiment, had in fact been fond of the bagpipes.

Kenneth's cultural pursuits, however, have not meant any diminution in the Thomson devotion to business. In 1979, the Thomsons beat out the Westons for control of the Hudson's Bay Company, paying $640 million for the company not long after the Bay had swallowed the Simpsons department store chain in another well-publicized takeover. In 1980, Thomson Newspapers, the family's principal North American publishing unit, took over FP Publications, the proprietors of,

Kenneth Thomson, shown with part of his ceramic collection, has taken advantage of his stake in North Sea oil development to greatly expand the Thomson fortunes, purchasing such institutions as the Hudson's Bay Company. ABOVE: His Rosedale house is one of the finest pieces of Georgian-style architecture in Toronto.

among other newspapers, the Toronto *Globe and Mail*. Since the Thomsons had earlier sold *The Times* and *The Sunday Times* to Rupert Murdoch on the heels of apparently insoluble labour problems, the *Globe* has become the family's newspaper flagship. Action to close or sell several newspapers in the FP group at the same time as the rival Southam family was rationalizing its newspaper empire led to a royal commission on concentration in the newspaper business, the so-called Kent Commission, whose major concern was the awesome power of the Thomson chain.

The Thomson family has been known for its acquisitiveness, its personal and corporate thriftiness, but also for its fair dealings. The leadership of the family is expected to pass to the next Lord Thomson, Kenneth's son David Kenneth Roy Thomson (b. 1957), who is currently learning the family business. In the meantime, Sherry Brydson (b. 1946), a daughter of Roy's daughter Irma

Thomson Brydson (1918-1966) and thus Kenneth's niece, has given the family an elegant edge by founding an exclusive Toronto women's club and by sponsoring several businesses that grew out of her two years' residence in Thailand, where her journalist husband worked on the *Bangkok Post*, one of the more farflung outposts of the Thomson empire.

Kenneth Thomson's personal wealth is estimated to be more than $1.5 billion, making him a likely candidate to be Canada's richest man. Yet he is reputed to turn to his wife when in need of a haircut, and during the Kent Commission hearings, he turned up to testify with a hole in the sole of one of his shoes, à la Adlai Stevenson. When Sonja Bata asked for the famous shoe for her family's shoe museum, she was told she would have to wait. After all, the other shoe in the pair was still perfectly serviceable.

Governor General Georges Philias Vanier as captured by Karsh of Ottawa. The Vaniers are an old family at home in either of Canada's cultures. Georges married into another such family, the Archers.

The Vaniers

THE VANIERS ARE not a dynastic family in the same way as the others in this volume. They have, at least in recent generations, been conspicuous in good works and diplomacy rather than in business. But as one of the elemental French-Canadian families, the Vaniers are at least as remarkable as any of the others whose callings have lain in more materialistic directions.

Few families can claim longer roots in this country. Guillaume Vanier, who settled in Quebec in the late 17th century, was not the first of the clan to come from France, but was the most storied. He lived in Quebec City and died after accidentally shooting himself following a running battle with the Iroquois. His offspring and immediate descendants went different ways, some heading north as trappers, others settling in Montreal in the 1760s. It was in Montreal that Jean-Baptiste Vanier was born in 1810 and it was there that he raised eight sons, the youngest of whom was Philias Vanier (1862-1938).

Philias was a multifaceted businessman who was particularly successful in real estate. He married the daughter of an Irish immigrant, with whom he had five children. The eldest was George Philias Vanier (1888-1967), who would eventually become governor general and, in the process, become loved by English- and French-speaking Canadians alike—no mean feat.

George Vanier was bilingual from the start, for both languages were spoken in the Vanier home, though, of course, he always considered himself a québecois, but one intensely devoted to the crown and to the federal system. He attended Loyola College and Laval University and studied law, being admitted to the bar in Quebec City in 1911.

He might have remained a lawyer there had not the First World War broken out. Vanier helped organize the Royal 22nd Regiment, the so-called Vandoos (the nickname being a corruption of le vingt-deuxième, or 22nd). This regiment of French-Canadian volunteers performed heroically overseas, and Vanier himself was twice wounded. He lost a leg in the conflict and was awarded the Military Cross and Bar and the Distinguished Service Order. In 1921—the year he married into the old Anglo-Gallic Archer family of Quebec—he was named aide-de-camp to Governor General Lord Byng of Vimy. He then pursued a military career and in time was named commander of his old regiment, headquartered at the historic Citadel in Quebec City before resuming the diplomatic life.

An independent Canadian foreign policy was a new phenomenon in the 1920s and early 1930s, and Vanier's natural talent for diplomacy marked him for a quick rise in the embryonic foreign service. After helping represent Canada at the League of Nations and at the important London Naval Conference, he became, in 1931, unofficial deputy high commissioner to Britain, first under former Ontario Premier Howard Ferguson and later under Vincent Massey. When the Second World War came, his military and diplomatic careers were interwoven through four distinct phases. In 1939-40 he was minister to France. When France was overrun by the Nazis, he became commander of Military District 5 in Que-

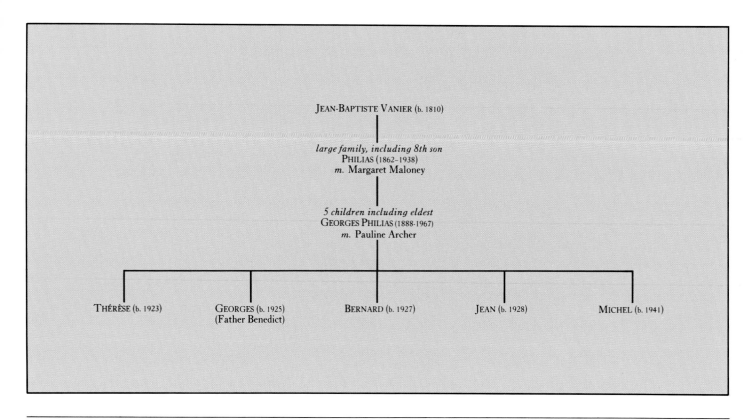

JEAN-BAPTISTE VANIER (b. 1810)

large family, including 8th son
PHILIAS (1862–1938)
m. Margaret Maloney

5 children including eldest
GEORGES PHILIAS (1888-1967)
m. Pauline Archer

THÉRÈSE (b. 1923)   GEORGES (b. 1925)   BERNARD (b. 1927)   JEAN (b. 1928)   MICHEL (b. 1941)
(Father Benedict)

bec City. Later he was ambassador to the Allied governments in London, then was again minister to France from 1944 until 1953 when he retired from diplomacy.

In the 1950s Vanier was director of such institutions as the Bank of Montreal and Crédit Foncier, and began receiving what would become a most intimidating list of degrees, honours, and awards. In 1959 he succeeded Vincent Massey as governor general, becoming only the second native-born Canadian to hold that position.

He and Pauline Vanier remain in the memory of many Canadians the perfect vice-regal couple: tall and erect, white-haired and gracious, beribboned, and genuinely concerned for the welfare of all Canadians. It as as governor general that Georges Vanier (he began using the French form of his given name when installed at Rideau Hall) initiated the Vanier Medal, given annually to recognize achievement in public service, and established the Vanier Institute of the Family to promote the study of the family in society.

In Canada's centennial year, Georges Vanier died, a few short months after making a passionate and eloquent speech pleading with Canadians to stay together through their second century. He was buried in the Citadel at Quebec which, like Montcalm before him, he had once commanded. In 1966 the town of Vanier, near Ottawa, was named in his honour and following his death another community near Quebec City followed suit.

Collectively, Vanier's five children represent as many fields of interest as their father did individually. Thérèse Marie Cherisy Vanier (b. 1923) is a doctor who resides in Britain and specializes in research on blood disease, and Georges (b. 1925) is a priest whose religious name is Father Benedict. Two others live in France: Bernard (b. 1927) is an artist and Jean (b. 1928, the best known of the current generation) is a Catholic theologian who founded and still runs the International Federation of L'Arche, and organization that maintains homes for the severely handicapped. The youngest son, Michel (b. 1941), is a Canadian university professor.

Pauline Archer (TOP LEFT) with her parents in a photograph by Notman circa 1900 and (CENTRE) shortly before her marriage in 1921. BOTTOM LEFT: Georges Vanier during the First World War in the uniform of a major in the Royal 22nd Regiment (the Vandoos), a unit he helped to organize, and (RIGHT) with Pauline, after their marriage.

Georges Vanier with his family about 1930.

That diplomacy has often been a stepping stone to important offices needs no better proof than the photograph at the right, taken in London in 1937. Seated are Vanier and the high commissioner of the day, Vincent Massey, whom Vanier would in time follow as governor general. Behind are Lester Pearson, whose tenure as prime minister would overlap with Vanier's years as governor general, and Ross McLean.

The Vaniers, seen below at Camp Fortune, brought a rare combination of dignity, style and warmth to their vice-regal duties.

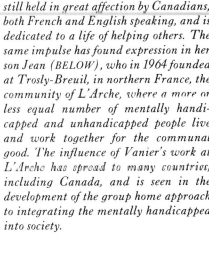

The Vaniers at Rideau Hall in 1964.

Madame Vanier (BOTTOM LEFT) is still held in great affection by Canadians, both French and English speaking, and is dedicated to a life of helping others. The same impulse has found expression in her son Jean (BELOW), who in 1964 founded at Trosly-Breuil, in northern France, the community of L'Arche, where a more or less equal number of mentally handicapped and unhandicapped people live and work together for the communal good. The influence of Vanier's work at L'Arche has spread to many countries, including Canada, and is seen in the development of the group home approach to integrating the mentally handicapped into society.

Garfield Weston's son, Galen, who has modernized and improved the business. He is renowned for his dedication to polo and his love of Ireland, where he maintains one of his several homes.

The Westons

THE WESTONS ARE proprietors of one of the world's largest family-controlled businesses, George Weston Ltd., a multinational food-processing and food-retailing company with 1982 sales of $7.8 billion.

The family's course was set in 1868 when George Weston (b. 1864) arrived in Toronto from Oswego, New York, with his English-born parents. Young Weston attended local schools, then apprenticed to Toronto bakers. At the age of 18 he became an independent businessman by purchasing from his employer one of the bread delivery routes he had been servicing. He quickly added more routes and later entire bakeries, including the so-called Model Bakery, an innovation at the time in hygiene and efficiency, which opened in 1897.

Weston was both an active and a passive player in the game of shakeout and rationalization that affected industries such as baking around the turn of the century. When he started out, neighbourhood bakeries were common in the city, but by 1900 a few large firms, his own included, dominated the scene. In 1903, he sold his bread business to a group that was consolidating to form Canada Bread. Part of the deal was that Weston should refrain from selling bread for 10 years, so for the next decade he concentrated on biscuits and confections.

By 1913, when he could begin making bread again, he had been a Toronto alderman, and was a Methodist church leader and businessman whose name, even at that early date, was synonymous with baked goods. Weston died in 1924, felled by pneumonia incurred, according to legend, when he walked miles through a blizzard rather than spend money for cabfare or overnight accommodation.

By that time, effective control of the company had already passed to his son, W. Garfield Weston, who had been born in 1898 in the family apartment above the Model Bakery. It was he who put the family and the company into the running, nationally and internationally. Weston served with the Canadian Engineers during the First World War, mainly in Britain, where he became enamoured of both British baking methods and British society. Much of the mammoth empire he built would eventually be centred there, run from an office atop Fortnum & Mason.

The global reach of the business really began in 1928 when a public stock offering allowed him to expand Canadian operations nation-wide and to move, tentatively at first, into the American market. Then, as later, most of Weston's ventures were takeovers rather than startups. Indeed, W. Garfield Weston probably holds the world record for successful takeover attempts; in 50 years at the helm of George Weston Ltd., he purchased control of more than 2,000 companies around the world, an average of one acquisition about every ten days. Most of the companies were in Commonwealth nations and operated everything from fishing fleets to traplines. The Depression brought him temporary setbacks, but also quickened his pace because so many company bargains were available. It was in the 1930s, for instance, that he moved boldly into Britain, taking over major bakeries and becoming a public figure there. In 1940,

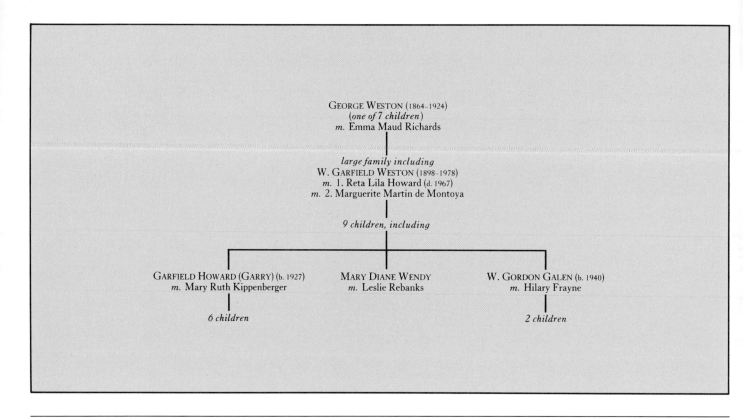

GEORGE WESTON (1864–1924)
(*one of 7 children*)
m. Emma Maud Richards

large family including
W. GARFIELD WESTON (1898–1978)
m. 1. Reta Lila Howard (d. 1967)
m. 2. Marguerite Martin de Montoya

9 children, including

GARFIELD HOWARD (GARRY) (b. 1927)
m. Mary Ruth Kippenberger

6 children

MARY DIANE WENDY
m. Leslie Rebanks

W. GORDON GALEN (b. 1940)
m. Hilary Frayne

2 children

he was elected to Westminster as a Tory MP and throughout the war was involved in government work on both sides of the Atlantic.

It was also during the war that the business took its most unusual turn. Until 1943, Weston had acquired only bakeries and other food-related businesses. That year, however, he persuaded Viscount Bennett, the former Canadian prime minister, to sell his majority interest in the E.B. Eddy paper company. This was the only major departure in the longstanding pattern which brought him control of, for example, the Loblaws supermarket chain (1947), the William Neilson candy concern (1948), and the National Tea Supermarkets in the United States (1956). The Eddy acquisition, however, indicated what later became more than apparent: Weston, although a genius at acquisition, was less gifted at integration. There was little if any visible orchestration of the empire from above, and Weston's companies became notorious for competing against one another and getting in one another's way. This legacy of disorganization was felt by Garry Weston (b. 1927) in Britain and W. Galen Weston (b. 1940) in North America following their father's death in 1978.

While still in his 20s, Galen Weston, using his own funds, built up a chain of supermarkets in Ireland, virtually creating the demand for such establishments there. He also took naturally to real-estate development and department stores. After Garfield's death, Galen and his fresh team of associates resurrected the Loblaws chain and returned it to prosperity; pruned the company of superfluous branches; sold such businesses as the Tamblyn drugstore chain; and made a melodramatic, well-publicized attempt for control of the Hudson's Bay Company but lost out to Kenneth Thomson.

Although as a whole reclusive and hesitant to participate in many outside functions, some members of the family continue to maintain a high standard of international business achievement. Toronto's Galen Weston—whose homes include an Irish manor house and the English castle where Edward VIII abdicated—plays polo in the same league as the Prince of Wales.

George Weston, the Toronto baker and municipal politician, poses with his family in the first decade of this century. His arm is entwined with that of his son Garfield (shown later in life above right) who would become the acknowledged king of corporate takeovers and make George Weston Ltd. a force to be reckoned with in the food business throughout the Commonwealth.

Although George Weston was born in the United States the family had British roots and the old loyalty has been strong throughout the generations. Garfield Weston served for years as a British MP and held imperialist views similar to those of his friend, mentor, and fellow Canadian, Lord Beaverbrook. Garfield also bought the famous British emporium Fortnum & Mason (LEFT). Galen Weston also owns Fort Belvedere, the castle in which Edward VIII abdicated for the love of Wallis Simpson. The castle sits in 59 acres of parkland at Windsor. Note the ring of cannon.

Charles Woodward, the penny-pinching founder of the Vancouver department-store fortune, began business by supplying Indians on Manitoulin Island from a general store built of logs.

Despite early reverses in Cuba, Colonel W.C. Woodward, with his wife (RIGHT), would excel as the financial brains of the family firm; he was once British Columbia's lieutenant-governor.

The Woodwards

THE WOODWARDS, WHO control department stores in Vancouver and other western cities, are a family rife with nicknames and full of fascinating contrasts: in the course of one generation they went from frontier roughness to splendorous wealth, with all the changes in personality and manner such a progression often entails.

The founder of the mercantile empire was Charles Woodward (1852-1937), a farmer born in Hamilton, Ontario, the son of an English immigrant. In 1870 Woodward went to Manitoulin Island and opened a log cabin general store that catered to a mainly Indian clientele. In 1891 he moved on to British Columbia, five years after Vancouver had practically been wiped out in a fire that had created many commercial possibilities. The following year the abstemious, tight-fisted disciple of Calvin opened a shop in the city and did so well that by 1903 he was able to build the department store at Hastings and Abbott streets, a location then considered far to the east of downtown. Extensions were made to the building in 1908, 1914, and irregularly thereafter.

In the early days, Woodward's not only did the sort of retail trade common to department stores but also maintained a brisk mail-order business supplying homesteaders, trappers, bushmen, and Mounties throughout the Northwest in much the same way Eaton's served the needs of rural southern and eastern Canada. But though the two firms were alike in scope and approach, the temperaments of their owners differed markedly. Compared with Charles Woodward's, Timothy Eaton's view of life was positively frivolous and sybaritic. Despite his great wealth, Woodward never owned a car and daily took the trolley to the store where, being always the first to arrive, he would open all the mail himself. Each day he had a cheap shave at the city's barber college, and neither there nor anywhere else did he ever tip more than a nickel. He was even known to sleep in the display beds in the store's furniture department.

Two of Woodward's nine children followed him into the business: Percival Archibald Woodward (1890-1968) and William Culham Woodward (1885-1957). Percival, known as Puggy would rise to handle the merchandising end of the business and "Billy" would be its financial brain despite some early failures in money matters. In 1901 Billy joined the Royal Bank of Canada, which posted him to its operation in Cuba; he later joined a firm of stock brokers there and promptly lost all his savings. But by the time he succeeded to the presidency of Woodward's in 1937, he had learned his financial lessons well. A few years later he was appointed lieutenant-governor of British Columbia, an office in which he served from 1941 to 1946.

Father and son were almost complete opposites. In the early days of the second war Billy Woodward was an executive assistant to C.D. Howe, and survived a mid-Atlantic torpedoing with Howe and E.P. Taylor. Shortly after the war he earned the rank of colonel, by which title he liked to be addressed thereafter. He also enjoyed the good life, touring Africa with a radio, a refrigerator, and a personal servant in his tent, or travelling to other favourite haunts like Hawaii (where he

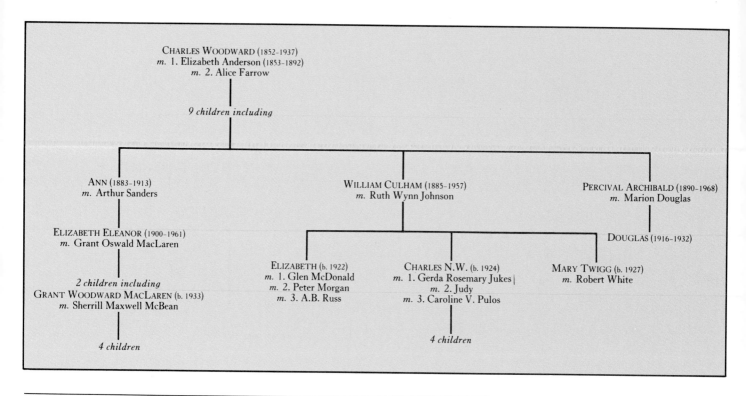

CHARLES WOODWARD (1852–1937)
m. 1. Elizabeth Anderson (1853–1892)
m. 2. Alice Farrow

9 children including

ANN (1883–1913)
m. Arthur Sanders

ELIZABETH ELEANOR (1900–1961)
m. Grant Oswald MacLaren

2 children including
GRANT WOODWARD MACLAREN (b. 1933)
m. Sherrill Maxwell McBean

4 children

WILLIAM CULHAM (1885–1957)
m. Ruth Wynn Johnson

ELIZABETH (b. 1922)
m. 1. Glen McDonald
m. 2. Peter Morgan
m. 3. A.B. Russ

CHARLES N.W. (b. 1924)
m. 1. Gerda Rosemary Jukes
m. 2. Judy
m. 3. Caroline V. Pulos

4 children

PERCIVAL ARCHIBALD (1890–1968)
m. Marion Douglas

DOUGLAS (1916–1932)

MARY TWIGG (b. 1927)
m. Robert White

died) and the family ranches in British Columbia. But Billy Woodward was not all fun. He expanded the size, scope, and profitability of the family business, leaving it that much more complex a job for his son, Charles Namby Wynn Woodward (b. 1924), who is always called Chunky even though he is lean and athletic.

Chunky Woodward mixes business (he began selling boy's apparel) and pleasure. He frequently dresses in cowboy duds and is devoted to the Douglas Lake Ranch—one of the biggest and oldest in North America—which he bought in 1957. Frequently married, he has at least one son who could eventually head the family business.

But another line may possibly be in contention. Since 1979, the president of Woodward's Stores has been Chunky's cousin Grant Woodward MacLaren (b. 1933), who started with the firm in 1957 as an accountant. Woody, who once sold men's wear in the stores, likes vigorous sports such as rugby and scuba diving and is almost as dedicated to the success of the Canadian Heart Foundation as he is to the success of the department stores. His son Douglas may one day run the business.

Colonel W.C. Woodward's children in the 1930s. Left to right, Mary Twigg, Charles, and Sidney Elizabeth. Charles, for some reason known as Chunky, ran the department stores until 1979 and now gives much of his time to ranching.

CITY ARCHIVES, VANCOUVER

Woodwyn, the house built by Colonel Woodward during the Second World War, overlooks Brentwood Bay in Victoria. The property was put up for sale by the family in 1983.

Chunky Woodward (LEFT) remains one of the most colourful and best-known businessmen on the West Coast. His cousin Grant Woodward MacLaren (RIGHT) started with Woodward's Stores as an acountant in 1957 and is now the company president.

III

The Honours List

Being a listing of Canadians of exceptional achievement in the Arts, Architecture, Journalism, Business, Finance, Law, Public Service, the Military, Religion, Academe, Science, and Medicine.

Marks of Honour

By Carl Lochnan

THE ORDER OF CANADA was inaugurated on July 1, 1967, the 100th anniversary of Confederation. For the advocates of an indigenous Canadian system of honours, Centennial Year was an especially propitious time to make a start when the country was celebrating the great achievements of the founders and builders. Hitherto, Canadians had known only imported forms of honour that had their roots and traditions in Europe. Titles of nobility and other marks of royal favour were a familiar element of life from the earliest days of exploration and settlement through the periods of French and British colonial administration.

In the *ancien régime*, governors of New France, intendants, and other important functionaries were usually drawn from the *noblesse*, whose rank was inherited or conferred by the king. While the social structure of the colony followed the Old World pattern, Louis XIV did not try to implant the whole complex apparatus of feudalism in the North American wilderness. To encourage colonization, the land on both sides of the St. Lawrence River was divided into long, narrow strips and the seigneurial system of land tenure was introduced. Because the acquisition of land *en fief* in France was the sure route into the *noblesse*, it is a common misconception that similar dignities accompanied land grants in Canada. Some among the seigneurs of New France, however, were ennobled by letters patent from the king in recognition of services for the development and defence of the colony. Hereditary titles acquired in that way fell into disuse after 1759 and only the title of Baron de Longeuil has been preserved through special dispensation from the British Sovereign.

Honours have sometimes been bestowed for less laudable reasons than merit alone. In the Canadian context it is instructive to consider the baronets of Nova Scotia, a 17th-century creation of James I. When the Stuart kings succeeded to the throne of England on the death of Elizabeth I, they judged themselves to be meanly provided for by Parliament. Casting about for ways to supplement the royal income, James I saw an opportunity to profit from the social aspirations of the middle class. In 1611 he instituted the baronetage, a hereditary honour subordinate to the peerage but ranking above knighthood. A baronetcy could be purchased for a sum sufficient to support 30 troops in Ulster for three years or about £1000. The scheme was so successful that eight years later the baronetage of Ireland was instituted, followed in 1624 by the baronets of Nova Scotia. Ostensibly, the aim of this latter foundation was the colonization of a part of the New World. An applicant for the honour was required to support six colonists for two years or to pay 2000 marks to the King and a further 1000 marks to Sir William Alexander, to whom the colony had been granted. Although the sale contributed little of lasting benefit to the Atlantic province, it produced a handsome return for the royal coffers when, as the king expected, most applicants chose the second option.

When New France came under British rule, a new hierarchy of officialdom took over the principal civil and military offices. Among those who were entrusted with key roles during the century preceding Confederation, many bore titular distinctions. Not so the men who achieved prominence in the public affairs of the emerging provinces. There were no titles among the Fathers of Confederation when they met to devise a formula for union. But a new era began when Confederation was proclaimed on July 1, 1867, and Queen Victoria conferred a knighthood on the first prime minister of the Dominion, Sir John A. Macdonald.

In the matter of honours an uneasy relationship, punctuated by occasional sharp disagreements between Ottawa and Westminster, persisted through the years from Confederation until the First World War. These tensions were due mainly to the inflexible opposition of the Colonial Office to any proposal favouring the exercise of the royal prerogative of honours in Canada by the governor general on the advice of the prime minister. In practice, the two usually conferred informally before the governor general's recommendations were sent to London. Both were frustrated by the erratic and sometimes cavalier way in which these affairs were treated by British ministers. Macdonald himself attached great importance to honours as an incentive to public service. He was amenable to the procedures imposed by the Colonial Office, but he pressed again and again for a more generous allotment for the Dominion.

The Liberal leader, Alexander Mackenzie, prime minister from 1873 to 1878, would accept no honour for himself, but he was irate on learning that the Colonial Secretary meant to include a Canadian in a forthcoming honours list without consulting Ottawa. He lodged a strong complaint, but in London his objections were dismissed.

The recipients of honours in Canada during the years of Macdonald's mandate were engaged chiefly in public affairs, members of the cabinet and the judiciary; some also came from banking, commerce, and railway development.

The Liberal victory in 1896 brought Wilfrid Laurier into office as prime minister. He was immediately offered a knighthood, which he firmly declined. But the following year, when he arrived in England to attend Queen Victoria's Diamond Jubilee, he found that the Colonial Secretary, Joseph Chamberlain, with the agreement of Lord Aberdeen, the governor general, had included his name in the list for Jubilee honours. Laurier was dismayed and objected strenuously but was persuaded to accept—"Not wishing," as he afterwards said, "to mar the harmony of the Jubilee Week." Public reaction in Canada was entirely favourable, but Laurier always saw his title as a political liability.

In 1902 the government attempted once more to gain a voice in the distribution of honours; accordingly, an Order-in-Council was passed declaring that the existing practice of the governor general's making recommendations without the advice of the ministry "is not in harmony with the principles of our constitutional system." The Colonial Office stood firm and the policy remained unchanged.

The year 1911 marked the beginning of the end of the old system of honours in Canada. While Sir Robert Borden was engaged in the election campaign that the Conservative Party won, two expatriate Canadians, both members of the British Parliament, were helping to turn public feeling against titular honours. Andrew Bonar Law who some years later would be the first Canadian to become—if only briefly—a British prime minister, was busy securing a knighthood for his life-long friend, Max Aitken. Before taking up residence in England, Aitken had amassed a fortune in Canada in ways that aroused animosity and suspicion. The governor general, Earl Grey, reported that the news of Aitken's knighthood was greeted across Canada "with a howl of indignation and disgust." In 1916, through an extraordinary piece of political sleight-of-hand, Sir Max Aitken became first a baronet and then a peer, to be known thereafter as Lord Beaverbrook.

In the public view the system was being flagrantly abused: critics cited as examples titles granted on Borden's recommendation during the Great War, including a knighthood for Sam Hughes, his eccentric minister of Militia and Defence, a baronetcy for the Toronto meat packer, Joseph Flavelle, and a peerage for the Montreal newspaper proprietor, Sir Hugh Graham.

When Sir Robert Borden was returned in the general election of 1917 to head the Unionist government, he was preoccupied with the central issue of winning the war. He seemed unaware of the gathering storm until the first squall blew up in the new coalition cabinet early in 1918. An Order-in-Council was pushed thorough reasserting the position taken in 1902 by the previous Liberal administration but going on to direct that Canadians would no longer receive hereditary honours and that those then existing would be extinguished. Britian asked that the question be reserved for discussion at the forthcoming meeting of Dominion prime ministers, but the wind of change quickly reached gale force and on May 22, 1919, the Nickle Resolution, so-called, was adopted by the Commons along with an Address to the King effectively excluding Canadians in future from receiving honours of any kind, whether titular or non-titular.

The new policy remained in effect until 1931, when the Conservative government under R.B. Bennett set aside what British authorities referred to as Canada's "self-denying ordinance." On Bennett's submission several knighthoods and a number of lesser awards were approved in 1934-35.

When the Liberals were returned to office in 1936, Mackenzie King promptly reverted to the former honours policy, which he would undoubtedly have kept in place indefinitely had it not been for the exigencies of war. Under the terms of the Nickle Resolution, Canadian servicemen remained eligible for British military decorations for valour and distinguished service but were excluded from awards in the orders of chivalry. These of course were available to personnel of all the other Commonwealth Forces. It was only late in World War II, following on the favourable recommendation of a parliamentary committee, that the ban was lifted and many service personnel and civilians received non-titular honours for war service.

In consequence of a further recommendation by the committee, the first uniquely Canadian honour was instituted in 1943: the Canada Medal. Officials laboured for some months to prepare an acceptable initial list of recipients, but Mackenzie King rejected the list. In the end, he decided that the Canada Medal should not be conferred on anyone. The whole notion of awards for merit was repugnant to Mackenzie King: he felt that virtue is its own reward. Yet in 1946, when he himself was offered the Order of Merit by King George VI, he contrived, after a brief bout of conscience, to accept that most prestigious honour.

Prime Minister Louis St. Laurent invited the Royal Commission on Arts, Letters and Sciences to make a confidential report on Honours and Awards in 1951. Vincent Massey, chairman of the commission and a tireless advocate of a Canadian order of merit, responded with alacrity. But no further action ensued and the subject passed quietly into limbo for a further 15 years.

ORDER OF CANADA

If Canada now has its own system of honours, the credit must go to Lester Pearson, who had a profound belief in the power of symbols as an expression of national identity and unity. In the face of vociferous opposition from many interest groups and against the advice of some of his colleagues in government, he determined that Canada must have a distinctive flag. Pearson carried that objective to a successful issue in 1965 and embraced the cause of honours with equal fervour. Voices around the prime minister urged caution and he was obliged to accept some compromises, but in the spring of 1967 the Order of Canada was established.

Badge of a Companion of the Order of Canada. It is suspended from a ribbon around the neck. The badges of officers and members differ in detail but follow the same basic design. The badge was designed by Flight Sergeant Bruce Beatty and is derived from a typical snow crystal pattern as seen under a microscope.

The Queen is Sovereign of the Order of Canada and the governor general, as Chancellor and Principal Companion, presides over its affairs with the assistance of an Advisory Council under the chairmanship of the Chief Justice of Canada. Administrative support is provided by the Chancellery of Honours at Government House in Ottawa.

Anyone may propose the name of a Canadian for recognition and all nominations are brought before the Advisory Council. Admission to membership in the Order is based on individual merit and achievement in an important field of endeavour.

There are three categories of membership, limited as follows:

COMPANION: not to exceed 150 in all.
OFFICER: not more than 46 appointments in any one year.
MEMBER: not more than 92 appointments in any one year.

A list of new members is published twice yearly, in advance of Canada Day and New Year's Day.

Regular investitures are held in the spring and autumn at Rideau Hall, when the governor general in his capacity of Chancellor inducts the new appointees and presents each with a scroll and the insignia of membership: the badge of the Order in gold for Companions and in silver-gilt for Officers. These badges are worn suspended from the ribbon of the Order passing around the neck. The badge of Member is in silver and worn on the left breast. For informal daily wear with street clothes members are supplied with a small scale replica in the form of a lapel badge. All members are entitled to have the initials of their rank placed after their names: C.C., O.C., or C.M.

At the outset the Order consisted of two grades, but after five years some modifications were made and a third grade added to bring increased recognition to those who serve at the community level.

Badge of a Commander of the Order of Military merit. The badge of Commander is suspended from a ribbon; those of Officer and Member are worn above the left breast pocket of the uniform.

ORDER OF MILITARY MERIT

In 1972 separate provision was made for the Armed Forces by establishing a parallel Order of Military Merit. The Queen is Sovereign of the Order, the governor general is Chancellor, and the Chief of Defence Staff is Principal Commander. There are three grades of membership: Commander, Officer, and Member, to which appointments are made for outstanding meritorious service in military duties of varying degrees of responsibility.

There is no overall limit of membership, but appointments made in any one year may not exceed 0.1 per cent of the strength of the Armed Forces. Of that number not more than six per cent may be appointed as commanders, not more than 30 per cent as officers, and the remainder as members.

Appointments are made by the governor general on recommendation by the minister of National Defence, who in turn receives proposals developed by an Advisory Committee that reports to the Chief of Defence Staff. Appointees wear the insignia of their respective grades, a neck decoration for Commanders and badges worn at the breast by Officers and Members. Initials follow the names of recipients: C.M.M., O.M.M., and M.M.M. The Chancellor holds investitures for the Order twice each year.

Carl Lochnan is a former Assistant Secretary to the Governor General. Among his responsibilities was the administration of the Honours Secretariat.

Order of Canada

SOVEREIGN
Her Majesty Queen Elizabeth II

CHANCELLOR AND PRINCIPAL
 COMPANION
His Excellency the Right Honourable
 Edward Schreyer, C.M.M., C.D.

EX-OFFICIO COMPANIONS
Madame Jules Léger, Ottawa, Ont.
The Right Honourable Roland Michener, P.C., C.M.M., C.D., LL.D., D.C.L., F.R.S.C. — Toronto, Ont.
Mrs. Roland Michener, Ph.D., LL.D., D. Litt. — Toronto, Ont.
Her Excellency Mrs. Edward Schreyer, Ottawa, Ont.

COMPANIONS (C.C.)
Allard, Le général J.V., C.B.E., D.S.O., E.D., C.D. — Trois-Rivières, Que.
Atwood, Dr. Margaret, LL.D. — Toronto, Ont.
Bata, Mr. Thomas J. — Don Mills, Ont.

Bell, Dr. Robert E., Ph.D. — Montreal, Que.
Bernardi, Dr. Mario, D.Mus. — Ottawa, Ont.
Bertrand, M. le docteur Claude, M.D. — Montreal, Que.
Bird, The Hon. Florence, D.Hum.L. — Ottawa, Ont. (Miss Anne Francis)
Bissell, Dr. Claude T., D.Litt. — Toronto, Ont.
Blais, Mlle Marie-Claire — Montreal, Que.

Bradfield, Dr. John R.,
B.Sc.Eng. — Toronto, Ontario

Brind'Amour, Mme Yvette, D.B.A. —
Montreal, Que.

Bryce, Mr. Robert B., B.A.Sc. — Ottawa,
Ont.

Burns, LGen. E.L.M., D.S.O., O.B.E., M.C.,
C.D. — Manotick, Ont.

Callaghan, Dr. Morley, B.A. — Toronto,
Ont.

Carter, His Eminence Gerald Emmett
Cardinal, L.Th. — Toronto, Ont.

Castonguay, M. Claude, LL.D. — Sillery,
Que.

Chevrier, L'hon. Lionel, C.P.,
C.R. — Montreal, Que.

Choquette, M. Robert, D.Litt. — Montreal,
Que.

Clark, His Grace the Most Reverend
Howard H., D.D. — Toronto, Ont.

Clyne, The Hon. John V. — Vancouver,
B.C.

Colville, Mr. Alexander — Wolfville, N.S.

Copp, Dr. Douglas Harold, M.D. — Vancouver, B.C.

Cormier, Le Révérend Père Clément,
c.s.c., A.R.C. — Moncton, N.B.

Corry, Dr. James A., LL.D. — Kingston,
Ont.

Crump, Dr. Norris R., D.Eng. — Calgary,
Alberta

Culliton, The Hon. Edward Milton, Q.C.,
D.C.L. — Regina, Sask.

Dagenais, M. Camille A., LL.D. — Montreal, Que.

Dansereau, M. le Professeur Pierre,
D.Sc. — Montreal, Que.

David, M. le docteur Paul, M.D.   Mon
treal, Que.

Davidson, Dr. George F., Ph.D. — New
York, N.Y., U.S.A.

Davies, Dr. Robertson, D.Litt. — Toronto,
Ont.

de Grandpré, M. Louis-Philippe,
C.R. — Montreal, Que.

Dextraze, Le général Jacques-A., C.B.E.,
C.M.M., D.S.O., C.D. — Ottawa, Ont.

Douglas, Mr. T.C., D.C.L. — Ottawa,
Ontario

Drapeau, Son Honneur M. Jean,
C.R. — Montreal, Que.

Dunton, Dr. A. Davidson,
D.Sc. — Ottawa, Ont.

Erickson, Dr. Arthur C., B.Arch. — Vancouver, B.C.

Evans, Dr. John Robert, M.D.,
D.Phil. — Toronto, Ont.

Filion, M. Gérard, S.R.C. — Montreal,
Que.

Flahiff, Hiss Eminence Cardinal George
B., c.s.b., D.D. — Winnipeg, Man.

Ford, Mr. Robert A.D., D.Litt. — Paris,
France

Forrester, Dr. Maureen, D.Mus. —
Toronto, Ont.

Fortier, M. le docteur Claude,
M.D. — Quebec, Que.

Frankel, Mrs. Egmont L., — Toronto,
Ont.

Frappier, M. le docteur Armand, O.B.E.,
M.D. — Outremont, Que.

Frye, Dr. H. Northrop, D.Litt. — Toronto,
Ont.

Gale, The Hon. George Alexander, Q.C.,
LL.D. — Willowdale, Ont.

Gascon, Mr. Jean, LL.D. — Ottawa, Ont.

Gaudry, M. Roger, D.Sc. — Montreal,
Que.

Gauvin, M. William H., Ph.D. — Beacons-
field, Que.

Gendron, M. Pierre R., D.Ph. — Hudson,
Que.

Genest, M. le docteur Jacques, M.D.,
LL.D. — Outremont, Que.

Gerin-Lajoie, M. Paul, C.R., D.Ph. — Montreal, Que.

Giguere, M. le Professeur Paul-Antoine,
F.C.I.C. — Quebec, Que.

Gingras, M. le docteur Gustave,
M.D. — Monticello, Ile-du-Prince-
Edouard

Girardin, M. J.-C. Emile — Montreal,
Que.

Giroux, M. Roland — Montreal, Que.

Gordon, The Hon. Walter L.,
P.C. — Toronto, Ont.

Gray, Dr. James Lorne, D.Sc. — Deep
River, Ontario

Guindon, Le Très Révérend Père Roger,
o.m.i., D.Th. — Ottawa, Ont.

Hall, The Hon. Emmett M., Q.C. — Saskatoon, Sask.

Harrison, Dr. James M., D.Sc. — Ottawa,
Ont.

Hébert, Mlle Anne — Paris, France

Herzberg, Dr. Gerhard, D.Sc. — Ottawa,
Ont.

Hicks, The Hon. Henry D., Q.C. — Halifax, N.S.

Hitschmanova, Dr. Lotta,
Ph.D. — Ottawa, Ont.

Hogg, Dr. Helen, D.Sc. — Richmond Hill,
Ont.

Hutt, Dr. William, M.M., D.F.A. — Stratford, Ont.

Ignatieff, Dr. George, LL.D. — Toronto,
Ontario

Keenleyside, Dr. Hugh L., Ph.D. — Victoria, B.C.

Kenojuak — Cape Dorset, N.W.T.

Kerwin, M. le professeur Larkin,
D.Sc. — Sillery, Que.

Koerner, Dr. Walter C., D.B.A. — Vancouver, B.C.

Lacourcière, M. Luc, D.Ph. — Beaumont,
Que.

Laurence, Dr. Margaret, D.Litt. — Lakefield, Ont.

Léger, Son Eminence le Cardinal Paul
Emile, L.Th. — Montreal, Que.

Lemelin, M. Roger — Cap Rouge, Que.

Lemieux, Monsieur Jean-Paul,
A.R.C. — Sillery, Que.

Lévesque, Le Très Révérend Père
Georges Henri, o.p., LL.D. — Montreal,
Que.

Lewis, Dr. Wilfrid B., C.B.E.,
Ph.D. — Deep River, Ont.

Lonergan, The Reverend Bernard,
D.Litt. — Boston, U.S.A.

Lower, Dr. Arthur R.M., Ph.D. — Kingston, Ont.

MacKenzie, Dr. C. Jack, C.M.G., M.C.,
D.Sc. — Ottawa, Ont.

MacKenzie, The Hon. N.A.M., C.M.G.,
M.M., C.D., Q.C. — Vancouver, B.C.

MacLennan, Dr. Hugh, Ph.D. — Montreal,
Que.

McClure, Dr. Robert, M.D.,
D.D. — Toronto, Ont.

McGibbon, The Hon. Pauline M.,
LL.D. — Toronto, Ont.

McLaren, Dr. Norman — Montreal, Que.

Maillet, Mlle Antonine,
D.ès-L. — Outremont, Que.

Manning, The Hon. Ernest C.,
P.C. — Edmonton, Alta.

Marshall, Dr. Lois, LL.D. — Scarborough,
Ont.

Martin, The Hon. Paul, P.C.,
Q.C. — Windsor, Ont.

Martineau, M. Jean, C.R. — Montreal,
Que.

Martland, The Hon. Ronald,
LL.D. — Rockcliffe Park, Ont.

Miller, Air Chief Marshall Frank R.,
C.B.E., C.D. — Charlottesville, U.S.A.

Morgan, Dr. Moses O., C.D., LL.D. — St.
John's, Nfld.

Ouimet, M. J.-Alphonse, B.Eng. — Pointe
Claire, Que.

Outerbridge, Col. The Hon. Sir Leonard
C., Kt., C.B.E., D.S.O., C.D. — St. John's,
Nfld.

Parkin, Mr. John C., D.Eng. — Toronto,
Ont.

Pearkes, MGen. the Hon. George R.,
V.C., P.C., C.B., D.S.O., M.C., C.D. — Victoria, B.C.

Pellan, M. Alfred, D.B.-A. — Laval, Que.

Pepin, L'hon. Jean-Luc, C.P.,
L.Ph. — Ottawa, Ont.

Picard, M. Laurent A.,
B.Sc.A. — Outremont, Que.

Pickersgill. The Hon. J. W., P.C.,
LL.D. — Ottawa, Ont.

Pigeon, L'hon. Louis-Philippe,
C.R. — Ottawa, Ont.

Plummer, Mr. Christopher — Darien,
Conn., U.S.A.

Polanyi, Professor John C.,
D.Sc. — Toronto, Ont.

Pratt, Dr. Christopher, B.F.A. — St.
Mary's Bay, Nfld.

Quastel, Dr. Juda H., Ph.D. — Vancouver,
B.C.

Quilico, M. Louis — Toronto, Ont.

Rasminsky, Dr. Louis, C.B.E.,
LL.D. — Ottawa, Ont.

Regis, Le Révérend Père Louis Marie,
o.p. — Montreal, Que.

Reid, Dr. Escott M., LL.D. — Ste Cécile de
Masham, Que.

Riopelle, Monsieur Jean-Paul — Paris,
France

Ritchie, Dr. A. Edgar, LL.D. — Ottawa,
Ont.

Ritchie, Dr. Charles S.A., D.C.L. —
Ottawa, Ont.

Robertson, Dr. Gordon, LL.D. — Ottawa,
Ont.

Robertson, Dr. H. Rocke, M.D. — Ottawa,
Ont.

Robichaud, L'hon. Louis J., C.P.,
   C.R. — Ottawa, Ont.
Robinette, Dr. John J., Q.C.,
   D.C.L. — Toronto, Ont.
Roblin, The Hon. Dufferin, P.C. — Winnipeg, Manitoba
Rocher, M. Guy, D.Ph. — Outremont,
   Que.
Ronning, Dr. Chester A., LL.D. — Camrose, Alta.
Roquet, Soeur Ghislaine, C.S.C. — Montreal, Que.
Rouleau, M. Alfred, D.Soc. — Levis, Que.
Rousseau, M. Roger — Wellington, New Zealand
Roy, Son Éminence le Cardinal Maurice,
   O.B.E., D.D. — Quebec, Que.
Saulnier, M. Lucien — Ile Bizard, Que.
Scott, The Most Reverend Edward W.,
   D.D., D.C.L. — Toronto, Ont.
Scott, Dr. Francis R., Q.C., LL.D. — Westmount, Que.
Shaw, Dr. Robert F. — Montreal, Que.
Solandt, Dr. Omond M., O.B.E., C.D.,
   M.D., D.Sc. — Bolton, Ont.
Somers, Mr. Harry S. — Toronto, Ont.
Spence, The Hon. Wishart Flett, O.B.E.,
   LL.D. — Ottawa, Ont.
Spinks, Dr. John W. T., M.B.E.,
   Ph.D. — Saskatoon, Sask.
Spry, Dr. Graham, LL.D. — Ottawa, Ont.
Stephenson, Sir William Samuel, Kt.,
   M.C., D.F.C. — Paget N., Bermuda
Thode, Dr. Henry G., M.B.E.,
   Ph.D. — Lynden, Ont.
Thorlakson, Dr. P. H. T., M.D. — Winnipeg, Man.
Twaits, Dr. William O., B.Comm.,
   D.C.L. — Toronto, Ontario
Vachon, Son Excellence Monseigneur
   Louis-Albert, D.Th. — Sillery, Que.
Vanier, L'hon. Madame Georges P.,
   C.P. — France
Vaughan, Mr. Murray — St. Andrews,
   N.B.
Vickers, Dr. Jon S., D.Mus. — Tuckerstown, Bermuda
Vincent, M. Marcel, M.Comm. — Montreal, Que.
Wilson, Dr. J. Tuzo, O.B.E.,
   D.Sc. — Toronto, Ont.

*The list above shows Companions of the
Order of Canada. There are also about
1300 Officers and Members.*

Order of Military Merit

SOVEREIGN
Her Majesty Queen Elizabeth II

CHANCELLOR
His Excellency the Right Honourable
   Edward Schreyer C.C., C.D.

PRINCIPAL COMMANDER
General Gérard C.E. Thériault C.D.

COMMANDERS (C.M.M.)
Allan, VAdm John, C.D.
Baile, BGen Blake, C.D.
Baker, MGen Douglas Roger, C.D.
Barr, MGen John Wilmer Browning, C.D.
Beattie, BGen Clayton Ernest, C.D.
Belzile, Mgén Charles Henri, C.D.
Bennett, Cmdre Ross Taylor, C.D.
Bernatchez, Mgén Joseph Paul Émile,
   C.B.E., D.S.O., C.D.
Berube, Bgén Robert, M.M., C.D.
Boyle, VAdm Douglas Seaman, C.D.
Brodeur, RAdm Nigel David, C.D.
Carr, LGen William Keir, D.F.C., C.D.
Carswell, LGen Harold Allison, C.D.
Charles, RAdm John Alexander, C.D.
Chouinard, Lgén Jacques, C.D.
Cloutier, Mgén Joseph Maurice Gaston,
   C.D.
Collier, VAdm Andrew Laurence, D.S.C.,
   C.D.
Comack, BGen Hugh, C.D.
Cotaras, Cmdre Constantine, C.D.
Creber, MGen Ernest Basil, C.D.
Dare, LGen Michael Reginald, D.S.O.,
   C.D.
Dextraze, Gén Jacques Alfred, C.C.,
   C.B.E., D.S.O., C.D.
Dunn, MGen John Jacob, C.D.
Edwards, Cmdre Gordon Lewis, C.D.
Falls, Adm Robert Hilborn, C.D.
Fulton, VAdm James Andrew, C.D.
Genin, Bgén Jacques Richard, C.D.
Gutknecht, Lgén Joseph Armand René,
   C.D.
Holmes, BGen Donald Ernest, C.D.
Howard, MGen William Arnold, C.D.
Hull, LGen Allan Chester, D.F.C., C.D.
Kinney, MGen Clyton Malcolm, C.D.

Lacroix, Bgén Joseph Lucien Roger, C.D.
Leach, MGen Wilson George, C.D.
Learoyd, Cmdre Douglas Rainsford, C.D.
Legge, MGen Bruce Jarvis, E.D., C.D.,
   Q.C.
Lewis, LGen Kenneth Edward, C.D.
MacKenzie, LGen George Allan, C.D.
Magnusson, MGen Norman Lawrence,
   D.F.C., C.D.
Mainguy, RAdm Daniel Nicholas, C.D.
Manson, BGen Paul David, C.D.
McAlpine, LGen Duncan Alastair, C.D.
McLachlan, LGen Hugh, D.F.C., C.D.
Michener, The Rt. Hon. Roland, P.C.,
   C.D., Q.C.
Mooney, BGen Robert Errington, C.D.
Oxholm, BGen Bendt Alexander O'Neill,
   C.D.
Paisley, MGen William George, C.D.
Paradis, Lgén Jean-Jacques, C.D.
Pickering, BGen Alan, C.D.
Piercey, BGen George Charles, E.D., C.D.
Radley-Walters, BGen Sydney Valpy,
   D.S.O., M.C., C.D.
Robertson, BGen George Burnley, E.D.,
   C.D., Q.C.
Rohmer, MGen Richard, D.F.C., C.D.,
   Q.C.
Romanow, BGen Joseph Roman, C.D.
Senior, MGen Russell Norman, C.D.
Sharp, Gen Frederick Ralph, D.F.C., C.D.

Smith, LGen James Charles, C.D.
Smith, RAdm Thomas Anthony
   McKenna, C.D.
Sturgess, MGen Roy, C.D.
Summers, BGen Jack Leslie, M.C., C.D.
Theriault, Lgén Gérard Charles Édouard,
   C.D.
Thompson, BGen William Rae, C.D.
Thorneycroft, MGen Kenneth John, C.D.
Timbrell, RAdm Robert Walter, D.S.C.
Turcot, Lgén Gilles Antoine, C.D.
Vance, LGen John Elwood, C.D.
Vincent, MGen William Horace, C.D.
Weisman, BGen Mortimer Lyon Aaron,
   C.D.
Withers, Gen Ramsey Muir, C.D.

*The list above shows Commanders of the
Order of Military Merit. There are also
about 1100 Officers and Members.*

Orders of Chivalry

BESIDES THE ORDER OF CANADA and the Order of Military Merit, which are the only orders with official status in this country, there are other orders which have charters generally as charitable organizations but which have their own ranks, observances, knighthoods, decorations, investitures and insignia, and 1000 years of history. The three most significant orders of chivalry are (using the customary abbreviations of their lengthy names) the Order of Malta, the Order of St. John, and the Order of St. Lazarus.

Among members of these orders, it seems to be agreed that Malta and St. John are senior to St. Lazarus, but there the agreement ends. Malta and St. John share a common history up to a point; St. John has been in Canada longer than Malta as a continuous organization and has a larger membership, but Malta came here first with the nobles of France. Many members belong to more than one order and a few to all three (and others).

THE SOVEREIGN MILITARY HOSPITALLER ORDER OF ST. JOHN OF JERUSALEM, RHODES, AND MALTA

The Order of Malta, to use the short form, traces its roots to Christian monks who provided hostels for pilgrims and cared for the sick and wounded in Jerusalem before the Crusades. They wore the eight-pointed white cross of Amalfi, as merchants of that southern Italian republic had built their church and hospital.

After the fall of Acre in 1291, the handful of Hospitallers that survived the massacre escaped to Cyprus. In 1310 they occupied Rhodes, from which they were driven by the Turks in 1522. In 1530 they were granted the island of Malta, which they ruled until they were expelled by Napoleon in 1798. A period of exile and dispersal followed until the knights re-established themselves in Italy and, in 1834, in Rome, where their headquarters remain.

Insignia of a Knight Grand Cross of Magistral Grace of the Order of Malta. It is worn on a collar. The insignia of other classes are similar, with variations in details of the collar, the form of the crown, and so on. Ordinary knights wear the insignia on a plain black ribbon.

The Canadian Association of the Order of Malta was not established until 1953 (though many nobles in New France were Knights of the Order) and it has a rarefied membership of about 150 members, many of them lawyers and senior academics. It is a purely

Catholic Order and much more religious in nature than the others. In the European countries, to become a Knight it is necessary that one's ancestors be nobles. The requirements vary from one country to the next: in Germany and Austria, for example, all 16 great-great-grandparents must be nobles. For this reason Knights tend to come from the same noble families for generation after generation. In Canada such requirements obviously are impossible and knights are admitted on the basis of honourable descent for three generations and a career of public service. Many, however, choose to adopt a coat of arms and apply for letters patent from the College of Heralds in London to take on noble status and smooth the way for their descendants. Members of the Order fall into several levels: Knights of Magistral Grace, Knights of Grace and Devotion, Knights of Honour and Devotion, Knights of Obedience, and the most elevated and rarest of all, Knights of Justice, who have taken religious vows and become monks. These are differences of status of birth or service, not of obligation or authority.

The Order has supported a variety of services to the sick and poor, including ambulance and first-aid services, nursery schools for children of working parents, and a system to identify bed-ridden persons needing rescue in case of fire or other emergency whereby the insignia of the Order is displayed on a door or window. Not to be confused with the insignia denoting membership in the Order are the medals that the Order from time to time bestows on outsiders for distinguished public service.

THE MOST VENERABLE ORDER OF THE HOSPITAL OF ST. JOHN OF JERUSALEM

The Order of St. John shares common origins with the Order of Malta, which was present in England until it was banned and its estates were confiscated by Henry VIII in 1540. The Order was revived in England in 1831 as the result of the efforts of a group of French knights, but headquarters in Rome refused to recognize this Protestant branch of the Order and thenceforth it was free to develop independently as the Order of St. John. Queen Victoria granted a royal charter to the Order in 1888; since then, the reigning monarch has always been its Sovereign Head. From this root developed the branches (priories) in Canada and other former members of the British Empire.

Star of a Dame Grand Cross of the Order of St. John. It is worn on a broad black ribbon that passes over the right shoulder. There are variations in embellishment and in the manner of wearing the insignia to distinguish the different grades of members.

The total membership of the Order in Canada is about 4500, of which about 200 are knights or dames, 375 are commanders, 1075 are officers, and 2850 are serving in the ranks.

Health education, courses in first aid, and support of ambulance services through the St. John Ambulance Association and Brigade are the chief activities of the Order in Canada. The earliest recorded first-aid course in Canada was given by Brigade Surgeon C.M. Douglas in Quebec City in 1883. The first Brigade unit formed was the London (Forest City) No. 1 Ambulance Division in 1909. Since then the Brigade, still a volunteer organization, has become a familiar presence wherever crowds gather. In 1983, for the first time in the history of the Order, a woman, Yvette Loiselle of Montreal, was appointed Chief Commissioner of the St. John Ambulance Brigade in Canada.

In both world wars the St. John Ambulance Association gave thousands of first-aid courses, organized and staffed hospitals, and provided front-line ambulance drivers. On the home front, members of the Brigade have been among the first on the scene at such disasters as the Halifax Explosion and the landslide at St.-Jean Vianney. The year 1983 marked the 100th anniversary of St. John in Canada.

Membership in the Order of St. John (as distinct from volunteering in the St. John Association and Brigade) is by invitation only.

THE MILITARY AND HOSPITALLER ORDER OF ST. LAZARUS OF JERUSALEM

The Order of St. Lazarus traces its origin to the Crusades of the 12th century. It is ecumenical and has branches today on all continents. Traditionally the main object of the Order was the fight against leprosy in the fields of treatment and research — which remains one of its chief concerns—but it has extended its support to other areas of medicine as well.

The Order of St. Lazarus in Canada was incorporated in 1963 under letters patent issued to the Honourable John Keiller MacKay, the Honourable Pierre Sévigny, Colonel Frank F. McEachren, and Lieutenant-Colonel James I. Douglas. It was the first federal charter issued in both official languages. The Order was not new to Canada, having flourished in Quebec during the French regime. It was re-established 200 years later to help further the cause of national unity and undertake charitable work.

For several years two branches functioned in Canada on parallel lines as a result of a division of authority in Europe. In May 1982 they amalgamated; the Honourable Pauline McGibbon, a member since 1967, became Grand Prior of the united priories. This was the first time in the history of the Order that a Grand Priory was headed by a woman. In Canada there are about 600 members who bear various chivalric ranks and titles.

The two European branches are headed by Prince Don Francisco de Borbon y Borbon of the Spanish Royal House and the Duc de Brissac of the ancient French nobility. The spiritual protector of both branches is His Beatitude Maximos V Hakim, Greek Catholic Melkite Patriarch of Antioch and of all the East, of Alexandria and Jerusalem.

Insignia of a Knight of the Order of St. Lazarus. It is worn around the neck on a ribbon. The insignia of the lower orders are somewhat simpler versions, while that of a Knight Grand Cross is like that of a Knight but is worn on a sash on the left hip.

Order of Malta

PRESIDENT
H.E. Bâtonnier Jacques Viau
CHANCELLOR
Bernard LaVigueur
HOSPITALLER
Vladimir Kavan
HONORARY TREASURER
Francis MacCullough
HISTORIAN
Robert Pichette
MASTER OF CEREMONIES
Patrick McKenna
COUNCILLORS
Lanfranco Amato
Hon. Mr. Justice Jules Deschênes

Richard Dubois
Dr. Claude Faribault
Dr. Roger Gaudry
Donald F. McDonald, Q.C.
John MacPherson
LCol Jacques Ostiguy
Rosemary Rathgeb

Order of St. John

SOVEREIGN HEAD OF THE ORDER
Her Majesty the Queen
PRIOR
His Excellency the Rt. Hon. Edward
  Schreyer, C.C., C.M.M., K.St.J., C.D.
BAILIFF GRAND CROSS
BGen C.J. Laurin
DAME GRAND CROSS
Yvette Loiselle
The Priory Chapter is the governing body of the Order of St. John and consists of the Prior, Bailiff, and Dame Grand Cross, executive officers, appointed members of Priory Council, provincial presidents, chairmen of Special Centres, not more

than 16 representative knights/dames, and not more than eight representative commanders (brothers/sisters).

REPRESENTATIVE KNIGHTS/DAMES
Burton D. Colter, N.B.
Dr. William A.J. Donald, Alta.
Dr. Dawson W. Einarson, Ont.
Col Roland Leclerc, Que.
MGen Bruce J. Legge, Ont.
Dr. Henry A. Myers, N.S.
The Hon. Mr. Justice J.D. Taggart, B.C.
Mary A.G. Best, Sask.
Col J.R. Roche, Que.
Brig Eric Snow, N.B.
D.W. Cunnington, Pri
R.G. Loftus, Ont.
Irene Ross McPhail, Fed.dist.
Dr. D.W. Rae, Man.
Dr. R.H. Thorlakson, Man.
Col Paul Vachon, Que.
REPRESENTATIVE COMMANDERS
LCol R. Boucher, Que.
LCol James Breithaupt, Ont.
Evelyn Pepper, Pri.
Dr. Hughes Ferland, Que.
John Cumberford, B.C.
R.G. Douglas, Ont.
PRIORY COUNCIL
Col J.C. Dubuc, *Chancellor*
Frank Brown, *Vice-Chancellor*
Col Frank F. McEachren, *Vice-Chancellor*
A.M. Tattersfield, *Treasurer*
W.G. Burke-Robertson, *Legal Counsel*
BGen H.B. Brodie, *Chief Commissioner*
LCol E.L. Barry, *Dir. of Association*
Dr. J.K. Besley, *Chief Med. Officer*
Dr. B. St.L. Liddy, *Hospitaller*
Yvette Loiselle, *Almoner*
M.H. Rayner, *Registrar*
Judge J.R. Matheson, *Genealogist*
E.J. de Lotbinière, *Dir. of Ceremonies*
Col L.E. Barclay, *D/Chief Commissioner*
C/Supt H.E. Feagan, *D/Chief Commissioner*
Col W.S. Watson, *D/Chief Commissioner*
Dr. M.F.E. Wyile, *Chief Supt.*
Dr. Iain Mackay, *Chief Surgeon*
LCol D. Gogan, *Chief Nursing Officer*
J.G. Aylen, *D/Legal Counsel*
G. Rodger, *D/Dir. of Assoc.*
Dr. W.R. Coleman, *D/Chief Med. Officer*
J.A. Albery, *Chief Cadet Officer*
Col G.F. Blyth, *Pres., B.C. Council*
Lex Blair, *Pres., Sask. Council*
D.V. Reynolds, *Pres., Alta. Council*
N.M. Stewart, *Pres., Man. Council*
Lorne R. Clark, *Pres., Ont. Council*
LCol G.A. Beament, *Pres., Fed. Dist. Council*
Maj J. Poulin, *Pres., Que. Council*
R. Brenan, *Pres., N.B. Council*
D.A. Roscoe, *Pres., N.S. Council*
Dr. Gustave Gingras, *Pres., P.E.I. Council*
Kevin Hutchings, *Pres., Nfld. Council*
Victor Irving, *Pres., N.W.T. Council*
Joan Gordon, *P.R. Advisory Committee*
BGen C.J. Laurin, *Appointed Member*

Dr. Helen K. Mussallem, *Appointed Member*
G.D. deS. Wotherspoon, *Appointed Member*
J.A. Cowan, *Priory Secretary*
plus chairmen of Special Centres

Order of St. Lazarus

GRAND PRIOR
Dame the Hon. Pauline M. McGibbon, C.C., D.G.C.L.J.
PRIOR
Chev. John Parkin, C.C., G.C.L.J.
VICE-PRIOR
Chev. André Tessier, G.C.L.J.
REFERENDARY (MALTA)
Chev. John J. Arena, G.C.L.J.
REFERENDARY (PARIS)
Chev. John H. Sullivan, G.C.L.J.
BAILIFF
Maj C.R. Douglas, C.D., G.C.L.J.
CHANCELLOR
Maj Andrew A. Duncanson, G.C.L.J.
DEPUTY CHANCELLOR, ADMINISTRATION
LCol Jacques W. Ostiguy, D.C.O., C.D., G.C.L.J.
DEPUTY CHANCELLOR, COMMANDERIES
Chev. James Wood, G.C.L.J.
SENATE
BGen J. Guy Gauvreau, D.S.O., E.D., C.D., G.C.L.J.
Chev. John C. Eaton, K.C.L.J.
Col Frank F. McEachren, C.M., C.V.O., E.D., C.D., G.C.L.J.
Col the Hon. Pierre Sévigny, P.C., C.D., G.C.L.J.
VICE-CHANCELLOR & REGISTRAR-GENERAL
MGen Roger Rowley, D.S.O., E.D., C.D., G.C.L.J.
VICE-CHANCELLOR & SECRETARY-GENERAL
Col H.E.C. Price, M.B.E., C.D., K.C.L.J.
VICE-CHANCELLOR, FINANCE
LCdr Ian Morgan, K.C.L.J.
VICE-CHANCELLOR, COMMISSIONS
Sir Arthur Chetwynd, Bt., K.C.L.J.
COMMISSIONER, QUEBEC COMMANDERIES
Chev. Claude Legris, K.C.L.J.
COMMISSIONER, ONTARIO COMMANDERIES
LCol R.G. Douglas, C.D., K.C.L.J.
COMMISSIONER, WESTERN COMMANDERIES
Capt E. Dixon, C.D., G.C.L.J.
COMMANDERS, COMMANDERIES
Chev. Robert Pichette, K.C.L.J., *Acadia*
Chev. George A. Brown, K.L.J., *B.C.*
Chev. A.J. Dixon, K.C.L.J., *Calgary*
LCdr J. Johnson, K.C.L.J., *Edmonton*
Chev. David D. Ruddy, K.C.L.J., *Montreal*
—*Ottawa*
LCol André Therrien, M.C., C.D., K.C.L.J., *Quebec*
BGen J. Neil Gordon, D.S.O., C.D., K.C.L.J., *Toronto*
LCol T.A. Wilder, C.D., K.L.J., *W. Ont.*

RECEIVER GENERAL
Chev. David Irwin, K.C.L.J.
CAPITULAR
Chev. Robert Thomson, Q.C., K.C.L.J.
HOSPITALLER
SgLCdr G.A. Trusler, C.D., K.L.J.
HERALD
Col A. Strome Galloway, E.D., C.D., K.C.L.J.
JUSTICIAR
MGen Bruce J. Legge, Q.C., C.M.M., C.D., K.C.L.J.
MARSHAL
LCol James R. Breithaupt, C.D., K.C.L.J.
ALMONER
Chev. Edmund Bovey, C.M., K.L.J.
SCRIVENER
Chev. David Mundy, C.L.J.
CHAPLAIN
Maj Rev. H.F. Roberts, E.C.L.J.
JUGE D'ARMES
Chev. Robert Pichette, K.C.L.J.
INSIGNIA (MALTA)
Maj Donald Harris, O.L.J.
INSIGNIA (PARIS)
Capt (RCN) Patrick Nixon, D.S.C., C.D., K.C.L.J.
SWORD BEARER
LCol André Therrien, M.C., C.D., K.C.L.J.
STANDARD BEARER
Chev. John R. Woods, K.C.L.J.
ARCHIVIST
Chev. Andrew J. Birrell, M.L.J.
COMMISSIONS CHAIRMEN
Chev. William D. Holford, K.C.L.J., *Ecumenical*
Capt R.B. Hale, K.C.L.J., *Historical*
SgLCdr G.A. Trusler, M.D., C.D., K.L.J., *Medical*
Chev. David Mundy, C.L.J., *National Unity*
Col A. Strome Galloway, E.D., C.D., K.C.L.J., *Communications*

281

The Debrett's Six Hundred

The Editors wish to acknowledge the assistance of consultants in each category in developing lists of individuals considered both eminent and influential within those fields. Most of those selected for inclusion received questionnaires; responses have formed the basis for these biographies. In the absence of subject-provided information, entries either were prepared from original research or consist of name and affiliation alone. The latter form of inclusion *should not* be taken as an indication of rank. Individuals already portrayed in the "Dynasties" section are not included in this list. Politicians were deliberately not included, since their positions are temporary and subject to the mercurial will of the voters.

ACADEME & RELIGION

Bailey, Alfred Goldsworthy

O.C., B.A., M.A., Ph.D., D.Litt., LL.D., F.R.S.C.

Historian. b. March 18, 1905, Quebec City; m. Jean Craig Hamilton; res. Fredericton.

Alfred Bailey is a noted author, poet, historian, anthropologist, and university professor. He received a Royal Society of Canada Overseas Fellowship and was educated at the universities of New Brunswick, Toronto, and London. He began his writing career as a reporter with the Fredericton *Daily Mail* and staff writer with Toronto's *Mail and Empire* before turning to teaching at the University of Toronto and the University of New Brunswick, where he is now Professor Emeritus of History. He was elected a Fellow of the Royal Society of Canada in 1951, is an Officer of the Order of Canada, and has served on the boards of the Beaverbrook Art Gallery, the Saint John Art Club, and the National Library Advisory Council. He has written many articles and poems, including *Songs of the Saguenay and Other Poems* (1927) and *Miramichi Lightning* (1981), as well as academic works such as *The Conflict of European and Eastern Algonkian Cultures* (1937; 2nd ed. 1969).

Barber, Clarence L.

M.A., Ph.D.

Professor of Economics, University of Manitoba, Winnipeg

Barber, Lloyd

O.C., B.A., B.Comm., M.B.A., Ph.D., LL.D.

Administrator. b. March 8, 1932, Regina; m. Muriel Pauline Duna; s. Muir, Brian, David, d. Kathleen, Susan, Patricia; res. Regina.

Now president and vice-chancellor of the University of Regina, Lloyd Barber earned his B.A. and B.Comm. (in administration) at the University of Saskatchewan before heading to the University of California to complete his M.B.A. in marketing in 1955. He returned to the University of Saskatchewan to fill a variety of positions: instructor, professor, associate professor, and dean of commerce, before his current appointment. During this time he also received his Ph.D. from the University of Washington. He was appointed by the Privy Council of Canada to be the Indian Claims Commissioner and Special Inquirer for Elder Indian Testimony and in 1980 he was made Honorary Saskatchewan Indian Chief. In addition to being named an Officer of the Order of Canada (1978), he has also received the Centennial Medal (1967) and the Vanier Medal, awarded by the Institute of Public Administration of Canada (1979). Barber is a director of such companies as Burns Foods, Husky Oil, and the Bank of Nova Scotia and is president of the Association of Universities and Colleges of Canada. He collects Indian and Inuit art and artifacts.

Baum, Gregory Gerhard

B.A., M.A., Th.D.

Theologian. b. June 20, 1923, Berlin; m. Shirley Flynn; res. Toronto.

Dedicated to ecumenism and social justice, Gregory Baum has actively promoted these causes through his many books and articles, teachings, and church and political involvements. "Some people say I work all the time and that I am overly serious; they do not realize how much enjoyment I get out of this intellectual and theological mission," he says. In recognition of his work, he has been awarded honorary degrees from six universities. He majored in mathematics and physics at McMaster University and received his M.A. in math at Ohio State University in 1947. He earned his doctorate of Theology at the University of Fribourg, Switzerland, and has taught at St. Michael's College at the University of Toronto since 1959. He represented the Secretariat for Promoting Christian Unity at the 1961-1965 Vatican Council. He is a member of a number of religious societies and has been editor of *The Ecumenist*, a journal dedicated to Christian unity, for 20 years, while also serving on the editorial committee of *Concilium*, a Catholic theological review published in seven languages.

Belshaw, Cyril S.

M.A., Ph.D.

Anthropologist. b. December 3, 1921, Waddington, New Zealand; widowed; d. Diana Marion, s. Adrian William; res. Vancouver.

Cyril Belshaw was educated in New Zealand and he received his Ph.D. at the London School of Economics in 1949. He then became a Research Fellow at the Australian National University and carried out field work in New Guinea until 1951. In 1953 he was appointed assistant professor of anthropology at the University of British Columbia, where he continues to teach. He has been active in the university's affairs: he sits on close to a dozen committees. He is also a member of a multitude of anthropological societies around the world, acting in various capacities, such as president of the International Union of Anthropological and Ethnological Sciences and the XI International Congress of Anthropological and Ethnological Sciences from 1978 to 1983. Professor Belshaw has been invited to impart his findings by the United Nations, the U.S.S.R. Academy of Sciences, and the Chinese Academy of Social Sciences and has given lectures at cities ranging from Bogota to Peking. Belshaw is the author of a great number of anthropological books, articles, and reports. He is listed in nine biographical collections, including five "Who's Whos."

Bissell, Claude Thomas

C.C., M.A., Ph.D., D.Litt., LL.D., F.R.S.C.

University professor and administrator. b. February 10, 1916, Meaford, Ontario; m. Christina Flora Gray; d. Deirdre; res. Toronto.

Claude Bissell was president of the University of Toronto from 1958 to 1971, a period of great expansion that also included the stormy years of student protests and sit-ins. He is proud of the part he played in building the university's Robarts Library. Bissell first joined the faculty of the university in 1941 as a lecturer in English; he became a professor in 1962. For two years immediately before he assumed the presidency at Toronto, he was the president of Carleton University. He is the author of various articles on Canadian and English literature and of four books, the best-known of which is *The Young Vincent Massey*, co-winner of the City of Toronto Book Award in 1982. He has been president of World University Service of Canada, the National Conference of Canadian Universities and Colleges, and the Carnegie Foundation for the Advancement of Teaching. In 1967-68 he was visiting professor of Canadian Studies at Harvard. He is also a director of Confederation Life. During the Second World War, he served with the Argyll and Sutherland Highlanders of Canada and attained the rank of captain. He was educated at the University of Toronto and Cornell University and has been awarded honorary degrees by 19 universities in Canada, the United States, England, and Scotland. He belongs to the York Club.

Blishen, Bernard Russell, M.A.

Professor of Sociology, York University, Toronto.

Bloomfield, Morton Wilfred

B.A., M.A., Ph.D., D.Litt.

University professor. b. May 19, 1913, Montreal; m. Caroline Lichtenberg; s. Micah, Samuel, d. Hannah Rubins; res. Cambridge, Massachusetts.

Now the Arthur Kingsley Porter Professor of English (Emeritus) at Harvard University, Morton Bloomfield has had a long and distinguished career teaching English at universities across North America. He received his B.A. and M.A. at McGill University, where he lectured for a year before moving to the United States in 1935. His teaching career at the University of Akron was interrupted by the Second World War, in which he served with the U.S. Army as master sergeant and received the Bronze Star. He then taught at Ohio State until 1961, with visiting professorships at Hebrew University in Jerusalem and at the Australian National University, among others. He is a member of various literary societies and a prolific author; he is also on the advisory boards of scholarly journals such as *American*

Speech, New Literary History, and the *Journal of the History of Ideas*. He is a founder of the National Humanities Center in North Carolina. Bloomfield comes from a distinguished family: his brother Arthur is a professor of economics at the University of Pennsylvania; his cousins Bernard and Louis Bloomfield are, respectively, president of the Eldee Foundation and senior partner in the Montreal law firm of Bloomfield and Bloomfield.

Breton, Albert
B.A., Ph.D., F.R.S.C.

Economist. b. June 12, 1929, Montmartre, Saskatchewan; m. Margot Fournier; d. Catherine, Natalie, Françoise, s. Robert; res. Toronto.

Albert Breton, professor of Economics at the University of Toronto, has pursued a career in the research and teaching of economics. He received his B.A. in 1951 from le Collège de St. Boniface of the University of Manitoba and his Ph.D. in Economics in 1965 from Columbia University. His professional positions have varied from lecturer in Economics at the London School of Economics to work for the federal government of Canada as senior consultant in the Prime Minister's Office (1970–79) and vice-chairman of the Federal Cultural Policy Review Committee (1978–82). A Fellow of the Royal Society of Canada since 1976, Breton has also received several Canada Council Research Scholarships and is the author of more than 50 published works. He is a governor of the National Theatre School of Canada.

Brunet, Michel, B.A., M.A., Ph.D.
Professor Emeritus, History, University of Montreal.

Buitenhuis, Peter M., B.A., Ph.D.
Professor of English, Simon Fraser University.

Cairns, Hugh Alan Craig
B.A., M.A., D.Phil., F.R.S.C.

Political scientist. b. March 2, 1930, Galt, Ontario; m. Patricia Ruth Grady; d. Lynn Marie, Wendy Louise, Elaine Barbara; res. Vancouver.

The recipient of a wide range of honours, Cairns has taught at the University of British Columbia since 1960. He studied at the universities of Toronto and Oxford and has been a visiting professor at Memorial University of Newfoundland, the University of Edinburgh, and Harvard (where he was Mackenzie King visiting professor). He has received the Queen's Silver Jubilee medal, the President's Medal from the University of Western Ontario, and the 1982 Molson Prize from the Canada Council. He was president of the Canadian Political Science Association in 1976-77. His most famous studies were published as "Prelude to Imperialism: British Reactions to Central African Society, 1840-1890" and "A Survey of the Contemporary Indians of Canada," which he co-authored.

Careless, James Maurice Stockford
O.C., A.B., A.M., Ph.D., F.R.S.C.

Historian. b. February 17, 1919, Toronto; m. Elizabeth Isobel Robinson; five children; res. Toronto.

One of Canada's most influential and brilliant historians, J.M.S. Careless has devoted a lifetime to interpreting and chronicling Canada's development. His highly regarded textbook *Canada, A Story of Challenge* resulted in his being awarded the Governor General's Medal in 1954 and served as a source of information for more than a generation of young historians. Careless has written many journal articles and books; he received the Governor General's Award for non-fiction for his book *Brown of the Globe* in 1964. He has served on many commissions and acted as director of the Ontario Heritage Foundation from 1975 to 1981. He was a special wartime assistant to the Department of External Affairs, joined the History Department of the University of Toronto in 1945, and has been a professor of History since 1959.

Carter, Gerald Emmett
O.C., B.A., B.Th., L.Th., M.A., D.D., D.H.L., Ph.D., LL.D., D.Litt.

Cardinal. b. March 1, 1912, Montreal; res. Toronto.

His Eminence G. Emmett Carter has been a Cardinal since 1979 and Archbishop of Toronto since 1978. He has held a variety of positions, including chairman of the International Committee for English in the Liturgy, member of the Permanent Council of the Synod, Canadian representative at Consilium for Liturgy in Rome, chancellor of Assumption University, rector of St. Lawrence College, and supervisor for the Montreal Catholic School Commission. He was founder and principal of the St. Joseph Teachers College and a charter member and first president of the Thomas More Institute for Adult Education. Among his publications are *A Shepherd Speaks* and *The Modern Challenge to Religious Education*. He holds numerous honorary degrees. Cardinal Carter comes from a family of eight children, of whom four went into the Church: one of his brothers, Alexander, is Bishop of Sault Ste. Marie. He believes that "the Church can do something about re-instilling in humanity some sense of dedication, some passion for things that are other than material values."

Ch'en, Jerome, M.A., Ph.D.
Professor of History, York University.

Clark, Samuel Delbert
O.C., B.A., M.A., M.A., Ph.D., LL.D., D.Litt., F.R.S.C.

Sociologist. b. February 24, 1910, Lloydminster, Alberta; m. Rosemary Josephine Landry; s. Samuel David, William Edmund, d. Ellen Margaret; res. Agincourt, Ontario.

S.D. Clark pioneered the recognition of sociology as a separate discipline and became the first chairman of University of Toronto's Department of Sociology. He is the author of such major sociological works as *The Social Development of Canada* (1942) and *The Developing Canadian Community* (1962; rev. 1968). He earned his degrees at the universities of Saskatchewan, McGill, and Toronto. He has taught at the University of Toronto and been a visiting professor at, among others, Dartmouth College, the University of California at Berkeley, and the University of Tsukuba, Japan. President of the Royal Society of Canada in 1975, he was awarded the society's Tyrrell Medal for the furtherance of the knowledge of Canada's history. Clark has an extensive collection of antique clocks and watches (120 in all).

Clement, Wallace
B.A., M.A., Ph.D.

Sociologist. b. March 1, 1949, Niagara-on-the-Lake, Ontario; m. Elsie Andres; s. Jeffrey, Christopher; res. Ottawa.

Clement's landmark study *The Canadian Corporate Elite*, published in 1975, updated John Porter's classic work (*The Vertical Mosaic*) on the power structure of the Canadian business establishment and earned its author immediate acclaim. Few knew that Clement was a doctoral student at Carleton University at the time and that the book was his master's thesis. His later studies—*Continental Corporate Power, Hardrock Mining*, and a recent collection of essays, *Class Power and Property*—have made significant contributions to the growing literature of the new political economy in Canada.

Cook, Ramsay, M.A., Ph.D., F.R.S.C.
Professor of History, York University, Toronto.

Cotler, Irwin
B.A., B.C.L., LL.M.

Lawyer, professor of law. b. 1940, Montreal; married; res. Montreal.

Irwin Cotler was elected national president of the Canadian Jewish Congress in 1980. He is deeply concerned about the plight of the Jewish community in the Soviet Union and is "legal counsel" for the imprisoned Anatoly Shcharansky. His monumental brief on the Shcharansky case, which was served on the Soviet ambassador to Canada, is a model followed by Soviet Jewry committees throughout the Western world. Cotler received his law degree at McGill in 1965, went on to earn his LL.M. at Yale the following year, and studied at the Hebrew University in Israel. Before taking up his position with the Canadian Jewish Congress, Cotler was a professor at McGill, specializing in international law; before that he was an associate professor at Osgoode Hall Law School of York University. He is a noted speaker, the author of more than 50 papers, and a legal editor, and has played an active part in such organizations as the Canadian Civil Liberties Association and the Canadian Human Rights Foundation.

Craig, Gerald M., Ph.D.
Professor of History, University of Toronto, Toronto

Cruise, James Edwin
B.A., M.S., Ph.D., LL.D.

Museum administrator. b. June 26, 1925, Port Dover, Ontario; res. Toronto.

Director of the Royal Ontario Museum since 1975 during a period of extensive renovations, James Cruise has an extensive background in botany and taxonomy. He was born in Port Dover, Ontario, and after graduation from high school he was a navigator for the Royal Canadian Air Force. After the Second World War he studied at the University of Toronto and taught botany and taxonomy at Cornell University before accepting a Fellowship at the Philadelphia Academy of Science. For the next 16 years he taught botany at the State University of New Jersey at Trenton, Princeton, and

JOHN SCHREINER

BRIAN WILLER

ABOVE: Lloyd I. Barber. RIGHT: G. Emmett Cardinal Carter. BELOW: James E. Cruise at the Royal Ontario Museum.

J.R.

J.R.

J.R.

ABOVE: Paul Fox at the Principal's house, Erindale College, University of Toronto. The house (BOTTOM) was built in 1880 by descendants of General Isaac Brock. The mantel came from George Brown's house. RIGHT: Northrop Frye.

KEN ELLIOTT

the University of Toronto, where he became associate dean of the Faculty of Arts and Science in 1972 for three years. In addition to his teaching he served for four years as a consultant to the National Science Foundation in Washington and was involved with its summer institutes. He is a past president of the Ontario Society of Biologists and belongs to a number of nature- and museum-oriented societies. He was awarded the Queen's Silver Jubilee Medal in 1977. His favorite pastimes are breeding purebred cattle and ornamental waterfowl at his farm in his home town.

Currie, Arthur W.
Former Moderator, Presbyterian Church in Canada, Toronto.

Davis, Arthur K., B.A., Ph.D.
Professor of Sociology, University of Alberta.

Despland, Michel, Th.D.
Professor of Religion, Concordia University, Montreal.

Dion, Leon, M.A., Ph.D., LL.D., F.R.S.C.
Professor of Political Science, Laval University.

Doern, George Bruce, B.Comm., M.A., Ph.D.
Director, School of Public Administration, Carleton University.

Dulong, Gaston
B.A., Lic.ès.Litt.

Educator. b. March 25, 1919, St-Esprit, Quebec; m. Jeanne-Marie Desfontaines; d. Veronique, Françoise; res. Sillery, Quebec.

The fifth of 14 children, Gaston Dulong has always been fascinated by French-Canadian dialects. This led to the compilation of a 10-volume series entitled *Le Parler Populaire du Québec et de ses Regions Voisines*, published in 1980. Dulong received his education at Collège Bourget in Rigaud and at Laval before attending the Ecole des Chartes in Paris, where he received his Licence-ès-Lettres. Returning to Quebec, he taught French, Latin, and Greek at Collège Classique St-Jean-Eudes in Quebec City and has been professeur titulaire at Laval since 1967. He is a member of the Canadian Linguistic Association and of the Conseil International de la Langue Française. He is married to the daughter of a French general and they periodically visit the Côte d'Azur region of France.

Dupré, J.S., A.M., Ph.D., D.Sc.Soc., LL.D., D.U.
Chairman of Political Science, University of Toronto.

Easterbrook, W.T., M.A., Ph.D., LL.D., F.R.S.C.
Professor of Political Economy, University of Toronto.

Eayrs, James G., A.M., Ph.D., F.R.S.C.
Professor of Political Science, Dalhousie University.

Eccles, William John, M.A., Ph.D.
Professor of History, University of Toronto.

Exner, Adam
Cardinal, Archbishop of Winnipeg.

Flahiff, G.B.
Cardinal, Winnipeg

Fox, Paul Wesley
B.A., M.A., Ph.D.

Educator, political scientist. b. September 22, 1921, Orillia, Ontario; m. Joan Muriel Gladwin; s. Rowley, Bruce, Nicholas; res. Mississauga, Ontario.

Robert Kaplan, Ed Broadbent, Stephen Lewis, and John Tory have something in common—they all took their first course in Canadian politics at the University of Toronto with Paul Fox. Fox has been a teacher of introductory Canadian politics for 25 years to more than 5,000 students and in 1976 became the principal of Erindale College at the University of Toronto. One of his books, *Politics: Canada*, has become a standard university text and is now in its fifth edition. As principal, Fox lives in a house built in 1880 by the family of Major-General Brock on land granted to them by the Upper Canada legislature. His own military involvement was as a lieutenant in the Canadian Infantry Corps during 1944-45. After the war, Fox returned to the University of Toronto, where he had earned his B.A., to continue studies for his M.A. He received a British Council Fellowship for 1947-48 and from 1948 to 1954 he lectured at Carleton College. Fox began his long career at the University of Toronto in 1954 and earned his doctorate from the London School of Economics in 1959. Throughout his career, Fox has taken an active interest in the welfare of the Canadian state. He served on the Royal Commission on Bilingualism and Biculturalism from 1964 to 1968 and the Ontario Advisory Committee on Confederation from 1965 to 1971. He has been president of the Canadian Political Science Association and chairman of the Bilingual Districts Advisory Board in Ottawa. He has also received a Canada Council Leave Fellowship for 1970-71.

Frye, Herman Northrop
C.C., B.A., M.A., D.D., LL.D., D.Litt., D. de l' U., L.H.D., F.R.S.C.

Writer, literary critic, university professor. b. July 14, 1912, Sherbrooke, Quebec; m. Helen Kemp; res. Toronto.

Northrop Frye is unquestionably Canada's most respected literary critic and theoretician. He was raised in Moncton, New Brunswick, and educated at the University of Toronto and Oxford. He was ordained a minister in the United Church of Canada in 1936. His long association with Victoria College in the University of Toronto began in 1939 when Frye began to teach in the English Department there. He was made a full professor in 1948 and chairman of the department in 1952, a post he held until 1959 when he was appointed principal of the College. In 1967 he was made university professor of English Literature and in 1978 chancellor of Victoria University in the University of Toronto. He has received a great number of awards and prizes and holds 30 honorary degrees from universities around the world. Professor Frye won the Molson Prize in 1971 and was made an Honorary Fellow of Merton College of Oxford in 1973. He is much sought after as a guest lecturer by universities everywhere. His first book, *Fearful Symmetry: A Study of William Blake* (1947), secured his reputation as a brilliant and challenging scholar-critic. His next book, the difficult and encyclopedic *Anatomy of Criticism* (1957), made him famous. He has published many other studies and collections of essays over the years, the best-known probably being his *The Bush Garden: Essays on the Canadian Imagination* (1971). His latest book is an ambitious study of the meaning and influence of the Bible as literature called *The Great Code* (1982).

Godfrey, John Ferguson
B.A., M.Phil., D. Phil.

Educator. b. December 19, 1942, Toronto; res. Halifax.

Elder son of Senator John Morrow Godfrey, Toronto lawyer and Liberal fund raiser, John Ferguson Godfrey is the president and vice-chancellor of the University of King's College in Halifax. He was educated at Upper Canada College, Neuchatel Junior College in Switzerland, and received his D.Phil. from St. Anthony's College at Oxford in 1975. Godfrey has been awarded the Queen's Jubilee Medal (1977) and the Vanier Award (1981). He is a member of many organizations, including the Society for French Historical Studies, the North British Society, and the Halifax Board of Trade. An active patron of the arts, he holds directorships with the Atlantic Ballet Company and the National Film Board. He is also a director of the National Council of the Canadian Human Rights Commission. His many collections include lithographs, antique clothes, and hats. He is a member of, among others, the Toronto Badminton & Racquet Club, Osler Bluff Ski Club, and several academic associations. His brother Stephen is a Toronto journalist specializing in the arts.

Grant, George
O.C., B.A., M.A., D.Phil., LL.D., D.Litt., F.R.S.C.

Writer, university professor. b. November 13, 1918, Toronto; m. Sheila; six children. res. Halifax.

Philosopher, political scientist, legendary teacher of comparative religion and "Canadian philosophy," George Grant is the grandson of George Monro Grant, the principal of Queen's University from 1895 to 1902 and father-in-law of Vincent Massey, and the son of William Lawson Grant, the first professor of Canadian history at Queen's and, ultimately, headmaster of Upper Canada College from 1917 to 1935. George Grant was educated at UCC, Queen's University, and Oxford, where he was a Rhodes scholar. From 1947 until 1959 he taught at Dalhousie University; in 1959 he was offered a professorship at the newly established York University, which he accepted and then shortly afterwards resigned because of what he regarded as York's infringement of his academic freedom. Instead he accepted a teaching position at McMaster University where he became, in 1961, chairman of the Department of Religion. In 1980, he left McMaster ("because it had become a research machine" that "eliminated particularity") to return to

Dalhousie (King's College). Grant's first book to bring him recognition was his *Philosophy in the Mass Age* (1959), but it was his *Lament for a Nation: The Defeat of Canadian Nationalism* (1965) that garnered him his reputation as a Red Tory and polarized his readers into passionate defenders and detractors. *Lament for a Nation* was Grant's encoding of the steps by which Canada had come to possess what Grant still thinks of as a branch-plant society, with little independence in matters of defence and foreign affairs. He carried on the argument four years later in *Technology and Empire: Perspectives on North America* (1969). He is currently at work on a new book to be called *Technology and Justice*.

Hamelin, Louis-Edmond

O.C., B.A., M.A., F.R.S.C.

Educator. b. March 21, 1923, St. Didace, Quebec; m. Collette Lafay; s. Philippe, d. Anne-Marie; res. Trois Rivières, Quebec.

Louis-Edmond Hamelin is currently the rector of the University of Quebec at Trois Rivières. His long career of research into and writing about the unique geography of the Arctic and sub-Arctic regions has been recognized by the receipt of the Governor General's Medal in 1975, the Prix Scientifique du Quebec in 1976, and most recently the Molson Foundation Prize in 1982. At various stages of his career, Hamelin has been visiting professor at the universities of Ottawa, Toulouse, and Abidjan.

Hebb, Donald O., M.A., Ph.D., D.Sc., D.H.L., D.C.L., LL.D., F.R.S., F.R.S.C.

Professor Emeritus, Psychology, McGill University.

Helliwell, John F., B.Comm., B.A., D.Phil., F.R.S.C.

Professor of Economics, University of British Columbia.

Henripin, Jacques, B.A., Ph.D., L.es.Sc., Dr. de l'U. Paris

Professor of Demography, Université de Montreal.

Hodgetts, John Edwin

B.A., M.A., Ph.D., D.Litt., LL.D., F.R.S.C.

Political scientist. b. May 28, 1917, Omemee, Ontario; m. Ruth; s. Edwin C., P. Geoffrey, d. E. Anne; res. Newtonville, Ontario.

Ted Hodgetts is generally considered to be the father of the study of public administration in Canada. His long career as a teacher at Queen's University and the University of Toronto has included visiting professorships (Dalhousie, Memorial, Northwestern, Guelph) and a five-year stint as principal and president of Victoria College at the University of Toronto. A Rhodes scholar and Nuffield Fellow, he has served on the Board of the Toronto School of Theology and the Academic Panel of the Canada Council. He has been an editor of *Queen's Quarterly*, has written many books and articles, and has received several honours for his seminal work.

Holmes, John Wendell

O.C., B.A., M.A., LL.D., D.C.L., D.Litt., F.R.S.C.

Professor of international relations, diplomat (retired). b. June 18, 1910, London, Ontario; res. Toronto.

John Holmes's long and remarkable career as diplomat and scholar has centred on Canada's relationship with the world community. He joined the Department of External Affairs in 1943 and served in London, in Moscow, and at the United Nations before becoming assistant under-secretary of state for External Affairs in 1953. He retired from the public service in 1960 and entered academic life, holding positions as a professor of International Relations at Glendon College (York University), Leeds University, and the University of Toronto. He was Claude T. Bissell Professor of Canadian-American Relations at the University of Toronto in 1980-81. Holmes is the author of several books, including *Canada: A Middle-Aged Power* (1976) and *Life with Uncle: The Canadian-American Relationship* (1982). He holds the position of counsellor with the Canadian Institute of International Affairs and is a member of the board of directors of the International Peace Academy.

Horowitz, Myer, B.A., M.Ed., Ed.,D., LL.D.

President and Vice-Chancellor, University of Alberta.

Johnston, David Lloyd, A.B., LL.B., LL.D.

Principal and Vice-Chancellor, McGill University.

Kenny, Douglas Timothy

B.A., M.A., Ph. D.

Professor of Psychology. b. October 20, 1923, Victoria, B.C.; m. Margaret; s. John, d. Kathleen; res. Vancouver.

Dr. Kenny is professor of psychology at and former president of the University of British Columbia, where he studied for his B.A. and M.A. He received his Ph.D. from the University of Washington. At the University of British Columbia he has also held the positions of acting dean and dean of the Faculty of Arts and head of the Department of Psychology. He became president in 1975 and stepped down in 1983. He is a director of the Social Sciences and Humanities Research Council and the Discovery Park Foundation, and belongs to the University Club, the Vancouver Club, and the American Psychological Association.

Kilbourn, William Morley

B.A., A.M., Ph.D., F.R.S.C.

Writer, university professor. b. December 18, 1926, Toronto; m. Mary Elizabeth Sawyer; s. Nicholas, Timothy, Michael, d. Philippa, Hilary; res. Toronto.

William Kilbourn was educated at the University of Toronto, Harvard, and Oxford. After receiving his Ph.D. from Oxford, Kilbourn joined the History Department of McMaster University where he taught from 1951 until 1962 (except for the two years, 1953–55, when he was a Teaching Fellow at Harvard). In 1962, he moved to the newly established York University where he is now professor of History and Humanities. A writer of immensely readable works of history, Kilbourn won the University of British Columbia's President's Medal for biography in 1956 for his first book, *The Firebrand: William Lyon Mackenzie and the Rebellion in Upper Canada*. Four years later he published *The Elements Com-*

bined: *A History of the Steel Company of Canada*. He wrote "The Writing of Canadian History" for *The Literary History of Canada* (1965). In 1966, he produced *The Restless Church* (a response to Pierre Berton's *The Comfortable Pew*) and *The Making of the Nation*; in 1968, *Religion in Canada*, and in 1970, *Pipeline: Trans-Canada and the Great Debate*, along with *Canada: A Guide to the Peaceable Kingdom*. In 1970, Kilbourn became a Toronto alderman. From 1973 on, he was a member of the Metropolitan Council and the City of Toronto Executive Committee. This new commitment to city politics resulted in his publishing *Inside City Hall: The Years of Opposition* (1972) (with David Crombie, Karl Jaffary, and John Sewell), *The Toronto Book* (1976) and *Toronto* (essays and photographs, 1977). Recently, he has returned to writing a more scholarly kind of history with the publication of *C.D. Howe: A Biography* (1979), with Robert Bothwell. Kilbourn is a member of the executive of the Canada Council, a member of the Toronto Arts Council, on the board of the Toronto General Hospital, and a member of the executive of the Canadian National Committee for UNESCO. He belongs to the Canadian Historical Association, the Toronto Historical Board, and the board of radio station CJRT-FM. Professor Kilbourn also paints, collects contemporary Canadian art, and plays pretty good jazz piano.

Kitchen, Martin.

B.A., Ph.D., F.R.Hist.S., F.R.S.C.

Historian. b. December 21, 1936, Nottingham, England; m. Nandita Mitter; res. Vancouver.

The author of a number of books dealing with German history in the 20th century, including *A Military History of Germany*, *The Politics of the German High Command Under Hindenburg and Ludendorff*, and *Germany in the Age of Total War* (with Volker R. Berghahn), Martin Kitchen has taught history at Simon Fraser University for many years. He was educated at Magdalen College, Oxford, and at the School of Slavonic and East European Studies at the University of London. He is a member of the University Club of Vancouver and a Fellow of the Royal Society of Canada.

Klinck, Carl Frederick

O.C., B.A., M.A., Ph.D., D.Litt., F.R.S.C.

Literary historian. b. March 24, 1908, Elmira, Ontario; m. Margaret Elizabeth Witzel; s. David Michael; res. London, Ontario.

Carl Klinck has been a leading figure in the advancement of scholarship in Canadian literary history. The co-author (with R.E. Watters) of the landmark work *Canadian Anthology* and the general editor of the *Literary History of Canada* from 1958 to 1976, he is also an outstanding biographer (of Wilfred Campbell, E.J. Pratt, Tiger Dunlop, and Robert Service). Carl Klinck was dean of Arts at Waterloo College (1942-47) and a professor (and now emeritus professor) of English at the University of Western Ontario. He is an honorary member of the Biographical Society of Canada.

Lacoste, Paul

O.C., B.A., M.A., LL.L., L.Ph., D.U.

University administrator. b. April 23, 1923, Montreal; m. Louise Marcil; d. Hélène, Anne-Marie, s. Paul-André; res. Montreal.

Paul Lacoste in the board room at the University of Montreal. The painting is a Riopelle.

LEFT: John Godfrey at the University of King's College, Halifax, with dancers from the Atlantic Ballet Company. BELOW: David Slater (left), Murray Ross, and Lois M. Wilson.

Paul Lacoste, rector of the University of Montreal, considers his "contribution to the progress of the University of Montreal and to the reform of the education system of the Province of Quebec" as his greatest accomplishment. A graduate of the universities of Montreal, Chicago, and Paris, he has had a career in both philosophy and law. He has been a professor of Philosophy at the University of Montreal since 1946; he was called to the Bar in Montreal in 1960, lectured at the university from 1961 to 1968, and practised law from 1964 to 1966. Made a vice-rector of the university in 1966, he became rector in 1975. He was a moderator and commentator with the CBC's Public Affairs Division from 1950 to 1963. He has been a member of the Royal Commission on Bilingualism and Biculturalism (1965-71), the Council of the City of Montreal and the Montreal Urban Community (1970-74), the Council of Quebec Universities (1969-77), and the Quebec Superior Council of Education (1964-68). He is a past president of the Conference of Rectors and Principals of Quebec Universities (1977-79), and of the Association des universités partiellement ou entièrement de langue française (1978-81). He is currently a director of the Ecole polytechnique de Montréal, the Ecole des hautes études commerciales (Montreal), and the Clinical Research Institute of Montreal. In 1977 he received the Queen's Jubilee Medal and was made an Officer of the Order of Canada. The recipient of an honorary LL.D. from McGill University, he has also earned the Human Relations Award of the Canadian Council of Christians and Jews.

LaFrance, Yvon, B.A., L.PH. D.Ph.
Professor of Philosophy, University of Ottawa.

Lambert, Wallace, M.A., Ph.D., LL.D.
Professor of Psychology, McGill University.

Léger, Paul-Emile
C.C., L.Th. J.C.L., S.T.D., D.C.L., LL.D., D.Hum.Litt, K.H.S.
Priest, missionary. b. April 26, 1904, Valleyfield, Quebec; res. Montreal.

Although Cardinal Léger had been well known as Archbishop of Montreal, he won nationwide fame and admiration when, in 1967, he resigned as Archbishop of Montreal to become a missionary to the lepers and handicapped in Africa. While in Africa he used his influence to draw attention to the suffering he had encountered and to raise money for various humanitarian projects, in particular a rehabilitation centre for the handicapped in Cameroun. He had previously been Canadian representative to Vatican II and was one of the voices advocating reform and a greater role for lay people in the Church. Léger was educated at the Séminaire de Sainte-Thérèse, the Grand Séminaire de Montréal, and l'Institut Catholique de Paris. He is the brother of Jules Léger, Governor General from 1974 to 1979. He has received countless awards and honours, both religious and secular: he holds a dozen honorary degrees from Canadian universities and the Pearson Medal for Peace, is Knight Grand Cross of the Equestrian Order of the Holy Sepulchre of Jerusalem, and has been a papal legate on several occasions. Since returning to Canada in 1979, he has been co-president of he Canadian Foundation for Refugees and has tried to awaken the conscience of Canadians to the plight of the Asian refugees.

LePan, Douglas V.
B.A., M.A., D.Litt., LL.D., F.R.S.C.
University professor, poet, novelist, diplomat. b. May 25, 1914, Toronto; m. Sarah Katharine Chambers; s. Nicholas, Donald; res. Toronto.

Professor Douglas LePan was educated at the University of Toronto and Oxford University. After receiving his B.A. from Oxford (1937), he taught at Harvard University (1938-41) and shortly after that became personal advisor on Army education to Gen. A. G. L. McNaughton, Commander-in-Chief, First Canadian Army, 1942-43. From 1943 until 1945, he saw active service as a gunner with the 1st Canadian Field Regiment, RCHA, in Italy. After the war, LePan began his career in international diplomacy, becoming first secretary on the staff of the Canadian high commissioner in London (1945-48), and upon moving to the Department of External Affairs in Ottawa, special assistant to the secretary of state (1949-51). From 1951 until 1955 he was counsellor and later minister-counsellor at the Canadian Embassy in Washington and from 1955 until 1958, secretary and director of research of the Royal Commission on Canada's Economic Prospects. The next year, he was assistant under-secretary of state for External Affairs, and for a period of five years (1959-64), professor of English Literature at Queen's University. In 1964, Professor LePan was appointed principal of University College, University of Toronto. In 1970, he became university professor and, after his retirement from the university in 1979, university professor emeritus. He has been a senior fellow of the University of Toronto's Massey College since 1970. LePan has published three books of poetry: *The Wounded Prince and Other Poems* (1948), *The Net and the Sword* (1953), for which he received the Governor General's Award for poetry, and *Something Still to Find* (1982). His novel, *The Deserter*, was published in 1964 and won the Governor General's Award for fiction. Professor LePan won the Royal Society of Canada's Lorne Pierce Medal in 1976. In 1979, he published a volume of memoirs, *Bright Glass of Memory*. Douglas LePan has been a member of the Canada Council (1964-70) and president of the Academy of the Humanities and Social Sciences, Royal Society of Canada (1975-79). He belongs to the York Club, the League of Canadian Poets, and the Canadian Institute of International Affairs.

Lévesque, René Jules Albert, B.Sc., Ph.D.
Physicist, Vice-President (Research), University of Montreal.

Lipsey, Richard G.
B.A., M.A., Ph.D., F.R.S.C.
Educator. b. August 28, 1928, Victoria; m. Diana Louise Smart; steps. Mark Alexander Daniels, s. Matthew Richard, d. Joanna Louise, Claudia Amanda; res. Kingston, Ontario.

By combining his unique abilities as a scholar and a textbook writer, Richard Lipsey has achieved a reputation on both sides of the Atlantic. His textbooks *Introduction to Positive Economics*, *Economics* (with P.O. Steiner), and *An Introduction to a Mathematical Treatment of Economics* (with G.C. Archibald) are among the most widely used textbooks in North America and the United Kingdom. Dr. Lipsey has been a visiting professor at the University of California at Berkeley (1963-64), the University of British Columbia (1969), and Yale University (1979-80). He has been Sir Edward Peacock Professor of Economics at Queen's University since 1970. His writings have been widely published in professional journals and he has served on many research and advisory councils.

Lower, Arthur Reginald Marsden
C.C., B.A., M.A., A.M., Ph.D., LL.D., D.Litt., D.C.L., F.R.S.C.
Historian. b. August 12, 1889, Barrie, Ontario; m. Evelyn Marion Smith (deceased); d. Louise Evelyn; res. Kingston, Ontario.

Arthur Lower's landmark study *From Colony to Nation: A History of Canada* has helped define the way two generations of Canadians have seen themselves and their national development. He joined the RNVR in the First World War and served with the Dover Patrol, at the blockade of Ostend, and in the North Sea. After studies at Toronto and Harvard, Lower taught at Tufts, Harvard, and the University of Manitoba before becoming Douglas Professor of Canadian History at Queen's. He has been president of the Canadian Historical Association (1943) and the Royal Society of Canada (1961-62), as well as the winner of the RSC's Tyrrell Medal. He won the Governor General's Medal from the Canadian Authors Association in 1947 and 1955. He has been a visiting professor at Dalhousie, Wisconsin, and Duke universities as well as the University of Glasgow. Other books include *Canadians in the Making* and *A Pattern for History*. He was named a Companion of the Order of Canada in 1968.

McConica, James K., M.A. D.Phil, F.R.H.S.
Professor of History, Pontifical Institute of Mediaeval Studies and Centre for Medieval Studies, University of Toronto.

Macdonald, H. Ian
O.C., K.L.J., B.Comm., M.A., B.Phil., LL.D., K.G.L.J.
Economist, university administrator. b. June 27, 1929, Toronto; m. Dorothy Marion Vernon; s. Gordon, Roy; d. Jill, Anne, Jennifer; res. Toronto.

H. Ian Macdonald, president of York University as well as professor of Economics and Administrative Studies, earned his M.A. at Oxford in 1954 as a Rhodes scholar for Ontario, and his B.Phil. at Toronto in 1955. He taught economics at the University of Toronto from 1953 until 1965, when he left to become chief economist for the government of Ontario. Two years later he became deputy provincial treasurer and deputy minister of economics; in 1972 he became deputy minister for intergovernmental affairs as well. Professor Macdonald left government service in 1974 to assume his present posts at York, but he continues to be a respected and influential economic advisor to government and business. He has served as special advisor to the federal government's Royal Commission on Financial Management and Accountability, director of the Ontario Educational Communications Authority, president of the Couchiching Institute of Public Affairs, a member of the Attorney General's Committee on Securities Legislation, a member of the Economic Council of Canada, chairman of the Advisory Committee on Confederation to the Ontario Government, and director of the Harold Innis Foundation, University of Toronto (1982). His current directorships include London House Association of Canada, Hockey Canada, the North-South Institute, CJRT-FM, Canadian General Electric, Rockwell International, the AGF Group of Funds, Ciba-Geigy Canada, the Canadian Rhodes Scholars' Foundation, the Oxford University Foundation of Canada, and many others. He belongs to the Canadian Economics Association, the American Economics Association, the Royal Economic Society, the Canadian Association for the Club of Rome, the Institute of Public Administration of Canada, the Toronto Association of Business Economists, and other professional associations. He has received many academic and civic honours, including the Governor General's Medal, Cody Trophy, Canada Centennial Medal, and Queen's Silver Jubilee Medal; he has been made an Officer of the Order of Canada, and a Knight of Grace of the Order of St. Lazarus of Jerusalem.

MacGregor, D.C., B.A., F.R.S.C.

Professor Emeritus, Economics, University of Toronto.

MacKay, William Andrew, Q.C., B.A., LL.M., LL.D.

President and Vice-Chancellor, Dalhousie University, Halifax.

Macpherson, Crawford Brough

O.C., B.A., M.Sc., D.Sc, LL.D., D.Litt., F.R.S.C., F.R.Hist.S.

Political scientist. b. November 18, 1911, Toronto; m. Kathleen Margaret Walker; d. Susan Margaret, Sheila Jane, s. Stephen Denis; res. Toronto.

C.B. Macpherson, often considered one of the founding fathers of Canadian political economy, has received many honorary degrees during his career and commands a considerable international reputation. He has taught at the University of Toronto for many years and as professor of Political Science there since 1956. He was appointed university professor at the University of Toronto in 1975 and was invested as an Officer of the Order of Canada in 1976. Along with numerous journal articles, Macpherson has made a substantial contribution to the scholarly community as the author of *Democracy in Alberta* (1953; second edition, 1962), *The Political Theory of Possessive Individualism*, *The Real World of Democracy* (1965), *Democratic Theory: Essays in Retrieval* (1973), and *Burke* (1980). *The Real World of Democracy* (1965), originally one of the CBC Massey Lecture Series, has been translated into several languages and continues to be required reading in many first-year courses in Canadian universities and colleges. Macpherson has travelled extensively and has held visiting appointments at Churchill College (Cambridge), Hebrew University (Jerusalem), Aarhus University Institute of Philosophy in Denmark, Arizona State University, and the

Australian National University. He is an active member of several scholarly associations.

Mandel, Eli

B.A., M.A., Ph.D.

Poet, teacher. b. December 3, 1922, Estevan, Saskatchewan; m. Ann; three children; res. Toronto.

For three decades Eli Mandel has been a major force in both creating and shaping the study of Canadian literature. His achievements as author of such volumes of poetry as the *Minotaur Poems* (1954), *Fuseli Poems* (1960), *Black and Secret Man* (1964), and *An Idiot Joy* (1967) were formally recognized with the Governor General's Award for poetry in 1967. Through close friendships with many of Canada's best-known writers, Mandel has brought a sense of first-hand excitement to his teaching of Canadian literature as professor of English Literature at Collège militaire royale de Saint-Jean (1953-57), the University of Alberta (1957-65), and York University (1965 to now). He has been a participant on many radio and television programs and has written and edited numerous critical works and anthologies.

Marchak, P., B.A., Ph.D.

Professor of Sociology, University of British Columbia.

Ormsby, Margaret A., M.A., Ph.D., LL.D.

Professor Emeritus, History, University of British Columbia.

Paquet, Jean-Guy, B.A.Sc., M.Sc., Ph.D., F.R.S.C.

Rector, Laval University.

Robertson, Harold Rocke

C.C., B.Sc., M.D., C.M., D.Sc., LL.D., F.R.S.C., F.A.C.S., F.R.C.S.(E), F.R.C.S.(C)

Surgeon, university administrator (retired). b. August 4, 1912, Victoria; m. Beatrice Roslyn Arnold; s. Thomas, Ian, Stuart d. Beatrice; res. Mountain, Ontario.

Educated at St. Michael's School, Victoria, B.C., at École Nouvelle, Coppet, Switzerland, and at McGill University in Montreal (B.Sc. 1932, M.D. 1936), Rocke Robertson belongs to a family of eminent scholars and judges. He began his distinguished career in medicine interning at the Montreal General Hospital. In 1938-39, he was clinical assistant in surgery at the Royal Infirmary, Edinburgh. In 1939, he returned to Montreal to become assistant in surgery and then assistant surgeon at the Montreal General. From 1940 to 1944 he served overseas. He rose to the rank of lieutenant-colonel and received a service decoration. In 1944-45, he was chief of surgery for the Vancouver Military Hospital and, from 1945 until 1959, surgeon-in-chief for its successor Shaughnessy Hospital. Dr. Robertson's career as an educator parallels his life as a surgeon. From 1950 until 1959, he was professor of surgery at the University of British Columbia and surgeon-in-chief at Vancouver General Hospital. In 1956 he was visiting lecturer at Harvard University. Two years later, Dr. Robertson was appointed director of the Professional Unit of St. Bartholomew's Hospital in London, England. From 1959 until 1962, he

was once again in Montreal, in the double role of surgeon-in-chief at the Montreal General and chairman of the Department of Surgery in Faculty of Medicine at McGill University. From 1962 until 1970, he served as the University's principal and vice-chancellor. Dr. Robertson holds a number of honorary degrees including honorary archivist, the Royal College of Physicians and Surgeons of Canada. He is a member of the Board of Curators of McGill's Osler Library, past president of the Traffic Injury Reasearch Foundation, past president of the Mont St. Hilaire Nature Conservation Centre, president of the Society of Friends of the Osler Library, and a member of the Friends of the Bodleian Library, Oxford. He was made Companion of the Order of Canada in 1969.

Robertson, Robert Gordon, P.C., C.C., B.A., M.A., LL.D., D.U., F.R.S.C.

President, Institute for Research on Public Policy, Ottawa.

Rocher, Guy, C.C., M.A., Ph.D.

Professor of Sociology, University of Montreal.

Ross, James Sinclair

Writer. b. January 22, 1908, Wild Rose, Saskatchewan; res. Malaga, Spain.

Sinclair Ross's classic novel of the Canadian West, *As For Me and My House*, was published in 1941 while he was employed by the Royal Bank, which he had joined in 1924 at Abbey, Saskatchewan. It was not until he retired in 1968 that *The Lamp at Noon and Other Stories* appeared. He has also written *The Whir of Gold*, *Sawbones Memorial*, and *The Race and Other Stories*. The modesty and anonymity of his career belie his formidable reputation.

Ross, Malcolm, O.C., M.A., Ph.D., LL.D., F.R.S.C.

Thomas McCulloch Professor of English, Dalhousie University.

Ross, Murray George

O.C., B.A., M.A., Ed. D., LL.D., D.C.L., D.Litt., D.U., F.A.S.A.

Educator. b. April 12, 1910, Sydney, Nova Scotia; m. Janet K. Lang; d. Susan, s. Robert; res. Toronto.

Prominent in both the worlds of business and education, Dr. Ross considers the founding of York University in Toronto as his chief accomplishment. Ross was York's first president (from 1960 until 1970) and is now the University's first president emeritus. Educated at Acadia University, the University of Toronto, the University of Chicago, and Columbia University in New York, Ross was awarded a UNESCO Fellowship which enabled him to undertake an ambitious study of the nature of higher education in England, France, Israel, the Soviet Union, and the People's Republic of China. Much of his subsequent work in the sociology of education, management, and community action appears in his steady stream of scholarly books, the best known of which are probably *Community Organization: Theory and Principles* (1955) which has been translated into German, Spanish, Japanese, Korean, Italian, Portuguese, French, and Greek; *New Under-*

standings of Leadership: a Survey and Application of Research (with C.E. Hendry) (1957); The New University (1961); The University: the Anatomy of Academe (1976), for which Ross was awarded the Borden Medal (the American Council on Education's Book Award); and Canadian Corporate Directors on the Firing Line (1980). Murray Ross was made an Officer of the Order of Canada in 1979. He has been awarded Canada's Centennial Medal (1967), and the Queen's Silver Jubilee Medal (1979). In an article in the Globe and Mail (1980) about the nature of corporate democracy, Ross pointed out that in the intimately inter-related world of Canadian big business, corporate leaders have "collected board memberships as boys collect hockey cards." Murray Ross has assuredly collected a few; he is, for example, a director of the Capital Growth Fund, the Continental Group of Canada, McGraw-Hill Ryerson, and director emeritus of Volvo Canada. He is a former director of Time Canada and of the Associates Capital Corp. Extremely prominent in community activities, Ross is currently chairman of the board of trustees of the Ontario Historical Studies Series, a member of the advisory committee for the Quarterly of Canadian Studies, and the honorary director of the national council of the YMCA. He has formerly served as the president of the Canadian Institute on Public Affairs, as chairman of the Task Force on Mental Health for the Ontario Council of Health, as director of the Ontario Mental Health Foundation, and as a member of the board of trustees of the Ontario Hospital Association. Murray Ross is an elected fellow of the American Sociological Association, a member of the American Academy of Arts and Sciences, and a member of the American Academy of Political and Social Science. He belongs to the Arts and Letters Club, the Badminton and Racquet Club, the Hillsboro Club, the Queen's Club and the York Club.

Rotstein, Abraham, B.A., Ph.D.

Professor of Economics, University of Toronto.

Roy, Maurice

C.C., O.B.E., B.A., S.T.D., D.Ph.

Archbishop of Quebec (retired). b. January 25, 1905, Quebec City; res. Quebec City.

The son of the late Honourable Ferdinand Roy, chief judge of the Magistrates Court, His Eminence Maurice Cardinal Roy was educated at the Petit Séminaire in Quebec, where he received his B.A. He was ordained a priest in 1926; after further studies in Rome and Paris, he taught at the Grand Séminaire in Quebec and was chaplain of the students at Laval University. During the Second World War he served with the chaplains' service of the Canadian Army, rising to the rank of colonel and chaplain in chief of the 1st Canadian Army. His involvement with the Canadian Army continued after the war, as he visited troops in Korea and other parts of the world. He succeeded Rodrigue Cardinal Villeneuve at Quebec City in 1947 and became Primate of Canada in 1956. In 1965 he was elevated to the Sacred College of Cardinals and given the titular church of Our Lady of the Blessed Sacrament and the Holy Canadian Martyrs. Among the awards he has received are Officer of the Order of the British Empire, Chevalier of the Legion of Honour, and the Bailiff Grand Cross of Honour and Devotion, Sovereign Order of Malta. From 1966 to 1976 he served as chairman of the Council for the Laity and of the Pontifical Commission for Justice and Peace. He was made a Companion of the Order of Canada in 1971; in 1981 he retired as Archbishop of Quebec.

Sadleir, Richard H.

B.A., M.A.

Educator. b. April 23, 1929, Toronto; m. Joan Robinette; d. Mary, Catherine, s. Thomas; res. Toronto.

Principal of Upper Canada College, one of Canada's most celebrated private schools and the educator of many Canadians who have risen to national and international prominence, Richard Sadleir has the task of maintaining old-school tradition and values in an increasingly technical and bottom-line-oriented society. He was educated at Trinity College, of the University of Toronto and received his M.A. from Trinity College, Cambridge. From 1956 to 1963 he was English Master at UCC, then moved to Trent University, where he served as dean of men and master of Peter Robinson College until 1969. His interest in music led to the directorship of the Peterborough Community Concert Association from 1963 until 1971, during which time he also acted as chairman of the Peterborough Symphony Orchestra Board, with a one-year stint with the Ontario Federation of Symphony Orchestras. From 1969 to 1975 he taught English at Trent, then returned to Toronto to accept the post of UCC's principal. He was elected president of the Canadian Headmasters Association for a one-year term in 1979 and is the recipient of the Centennial Medal. His wife is a daughter of the noted Toronto lawyer J.J. Robinette.

Scott, Edward Walter

C.C., B.A., L.Th., D.D.

Clergyman. b. April 30, 1919, Edmonton; m. Isabel Florence Brannan; s. Douglas, d. Maureen, Patricia Anne, Elizabeth Jean; res. Toronto.

Archbishop and primate of the Anglican Church of Canada since 1971, Edward Scott has fostered an activist spirit in the church, not without misgivings on the part of some of his flock. He began his career in Prince Rupert, B.C., in 1942 and went on to be general secretary of the Student Christian Movement at the University of Manitoba and rector of a church in Winnipeg's south end. Other steps followed, including a period as director of social service and priest-director of Indian work for the diocese of Rupert's Land. He established the first Indian-Métis Friendship Centre and spoke for native land claims. As well as his duties as archbishop, Scott was moderator of the World Council of Churches from 1975 to 1983. He is an ardent proponent of ecumenism.

Simeon, Richard, Ph.D.

Director of the Institute of Intergovernmental Relations, Queen's

Slater, David W.

B.Comm., M.A., Ph.D.

Policy advisor, teacher. b. October 17, 1921, Winnipeg; m. Lillian Margaret Bell; d. Barbara Jane, Gail Patricia, Carolyn Louise, Leslie Anne; res. Ottawa.

The chairman of the Economic Council of Canada since 1980, Dr. David W. Slater has been a teacher and policy advisor since 1946. After serving with the Canadian Army in Britain and Northwest Europe from 1942 to 1945 and receiving mentions in despatches, Slater divided his time between Queen's and Stanford universities as lecturer and instructor in Economics. From 1952 to 1968 he held various positions at Queen's before becoming the dean of Graduate Studies and Research there for two years. He was president of York University in Toronto from 1970 to 1973, after which he went to Ottawa as general director of the Fiscal Policy and Economic Analysis Branch in the Department of Finance. By 1978 Slater had become the director of the Economic Council of Canada and later vice-chairman and acting chairman before taking on the position of chairman.

Smiley, Donald Victor, M.Ed., M.A., Ph.D., F.R.S.C.

Professor of Political Science, York University, Toronto.

Stacey, Charles Perry

O.C., O.B.E., C.D., B.A., B.A., A.M., Ph.D., LL.D., D.Litt., D.Sc.Mil., F.R.S.C.

Historian. b. July 30, 1906, Toronto; m. Helen Kathleen Allen; m. Doris Newton (deceased); res. Toronto.

From the University of Toronto in 1927 C.P. Stacey went on to Corpus Christi College at Oxford, then to Princeton where he received his A.M. in 1931 and his Ph.D. in 1933. During his time at Princeton, Stacey was in the Reserve (1929-40), having served in the ranks of the Canadian Corps of Signals in the old Non-Permanent Active Militia in 1924. He was commissioned in 1925. He taught history at Princeton from 1934 to 1940, returning to active service as historical officer at Canadian Military Headquarters in London from 1940 to 1945 and director of the Historical Section at Army Headquarters from 1945 until 1959, when he retired from the Army. Colonel Stacey taught for many years thereafter as professor of History at the University of Toronto and was appointed university professor (1973-75) and special lecturer (1975-76). He took leave from the university during 1965-66 to be director of the Historical Section at Canadian Forces Headquarters. He has made an outstanding contribution to Canadian military history as the author of many books on the subject. He received the Governor General's Award for academic non-fiction for The Canadian Army, 1939-45 in 1948. However, he is perhaps best known for his work on Mackenzie King, including A Very Double Life: The Private World of Mackenzie King (1976), Mackenzie King and the Atlantic Triangle (1977), Canada and the Age of Conflict, Vol. 1 (1977), and The Mackenzie King Era, Vol. II (1981). His autobiography, A Date with History, was published in 1983. Colonel Stacey has been active in many academic associations as well as military institutions, including as president of the Canadian Historical Association (1952-53) and the Canadian Writers' Foundation (1958-59). He is a member of the American Historical Association and the Canadian Military Institute, of which he is an honorary historian. He and his wife both have officerships of the Order of Canada and honorary LL.D.s.

Story, George Morley, B.A., D.Phil., F.R.Hist.S., F.S.A., F.R.S.C.

Henrietta Harvey Professor of English Language and Literature, Memorial University of Newfoundland, St. John's.

Symons, Thomas H.B.

O.C., B.A., B.A., M.A., LL.D., D.U., F.R.S.C., K.L.J.

Educator. b. May 30, 1929, Toronto; m. Christine Ryerson; d. Mary, s. Ryerson, Jeffrey; res. Peterborough, Ontario.

Thomas Symons was educated at Upper Canada College, the University of Toronto Schools, the University of Toronto, Oxford (Oriel College), the universities of Paris, Leyden, and Rome, and Harvard University. At present Vanier Professor at Trent University, vice-president of the Social Sciences and Humanities Research Council, and special advisor on higher education to the Secretary of State, Professor Symons has been dean of Devonshire House at the University of Toronto, chairman of the Commission on French Language Education in Ontario, chairman of the Ontario Human Rights Commission, chairman of the Association of Commonwealth Universities, chairman of the Commission of Canadian Studies, and founding president of Trent University. He is a member of the Canadian Society for the Study of Higher Education, the Canadian Historical Association, and a Fellow of the Royal Society of Canada; he is chairman of the International Board of United World Colleges, a trustee of Oriel College, Oxford, honorary treasurer of the Association of Commonwealth Universities, a member of the National Library Advisory Board, a member of the Board of the Arctic Institute of North America, a member of the Advisory Committee on Academic Relations of the Department of External Affairs, and past president of the Canadian Association in Support of Native Peoples. He has received many academic awards and honours (including honorary degrees from 10 Canadian universities and colleges) and has been awarded the Canadian Centennial Medal, the Medal of the Ontario Arts Council, the Queen's Silver Jubilee Medal, and the Distinguished Service to Education Award of the Council for the Advancement and Support of Education in Washington. Professor Symons was made a Knight of the Military and Hospitaller Order of St. Lazarus of Jerusalem in 1971 and an Officer of the Order of Canada in 1976. He belongs to the Rideau Club (Ottawa); the Athenaeum (London); the University Club, the Badminton and Racquet Club, and the Albany Club (Toronto); and the Peterborough Club.

Taylor, William E. Jr., A.M., Ph.D., F.R.A.I., F.R.G.S., F.S.A.S., F.R.S.C., LL.D., D.Litt.

President, Social Sciences and Humanities Research Council of Canada, Ottawa.

Tepperman, L., A.M., Ph.D.

Professor of Sociology, University of Toronto.

Thomas, Clara McCandless, M.A., Ph.D.

Professor of English, York University, Toronto.

Tilley, Donald Egerton, B.Sc., Ph.D.

Principal, Royal Military College of Canada, Kingston.

Tremblay, Marc-Adélard

O.C., B.A., L.S.A., M.A., Ph.D., F.R.S.C., D.U.

Anthropologist. b. April 24, 1922, Les Eboulements, Quebec; m. Jacqueline Cyr; s. Marc, d. Geneviève, Lorraine, Colette, Dominique, Suzanne; res. Sainte Foy, Quebec.

Professor Tremblay has led several research teams in the study of Quebec culture and has published many books, articles, and monographs. He has also given a great deal of his time to community service. He was educated at a Jesuit college in Montreal and at the University of Montreal, where he earned a B.A. in agronomy, followed by a Master's degree in sociology at Laval and a Ph.D. at Cornell University in 1954. He was the recipient of scholarships from the Agricultural Research Council, the Carnegie Foundation, the Canada Council, and the Social Sciences and Humanities Research Council. He joined Laval in 1956; he has held a full professorship since 1963, has also served as vice-dean of the Social Science Faculty and, from 1971 until 1979, as dean of the Graduate School. He is a past vice-president of the Institute for Research on Public Policy, past chairman of the Academic Panel of the Social Sciences and Humanities Research Council; he is also past president of the Association of Rehabilitation Services of Quebec, the Service de Réadaptation sociale (Quebec City), and the Fédération des Cooperatives d'Habitations du Québec. He is co-chairman of the Canadian Committee of the International Congress of Anthropological and Ethnological Sciences and president (1981–84) of the Royal Society of Canada. He was the founding president of the Canadian Sociology and Anthropology Association and he is the secretary of l'Academie des Sciences Morales et Politiques. He belongs to the anthropological and sociological societies of France and the United States, as well as many other professional associations. Some of his recent publications are: *Role des organismes communautaires dans la prévention du crime et la réhabilitation des delinquants, La desoccidentalisation de l'ethnographie, Les constructions parallèles de l'identité québécoise et l'acculturation,* and *The Acadian Society of Tomorrow: the impact of technology on the social global structure.*

Tremblay, Rodrigue, Ph.D.

Professor of Economics, University of Montreal.

Trudel, Marcel, O.C., B.A., Ph.D., D.ès.Litt.

Director, Department of History, University of Ottawa.

Warkentin, John, B.Sc., M.A., Ph.D.

Professor of Geography, York University.

Weldon, John, B.A., Ph.D.

Professor of Economics, McGill University, Montreal.

Wilson, Lois M.

B.A., B.D., D.D.

Minister of religion, writer. b. April 8, 1927, Winnipeg; née Freeman; m. Rev. Dr. Roy F. Wilson; d. Ruth Casson, Jeanie Adamson, s. Neil, Bruce; res. Kingston, Ontario.

Dr. Lois Wilson has been the "first woman" in several highly visible positions. She was the first woman to be elected president of the Canadian Council of Churches and the first woman moderator of the United Church of Canada. As a writer, speaker, and self-described "catalytic agent in community affairs," she is a tireless worker for the causes she considers important, such as bringing the agenda of the international community to Canadian churches and the community at large; highlighting the growing gap between the rich and the poor of the world; pressing such issues as the responsible use of earth's resources, the responsible and moral use of technology, the changing roles of women and men, and the changing relationship of Christians to those of other faiths and ideologies. Her goal is to "motivate people to identify their own ethical responsibilities vis-à-vis these issues and others affecting a human future," and she attempts to raise these questions through the use of "all contemporary means." For Lois Wilson this means writing in newspapers, magazines, and books, and speaking and preaching on television, radio, and in person.

Lois Wilson's father, Dr. E.G.D. Freeman, was dean of Theology at Winnipeg's United College (now part of the University of Winnipeg), it was from United College that she received her B.A. in 1947 and her B.D. in 1965. She began her church career as associate minister of First United Church of Thunder Bay, Ontario, then served in churches in Kingston. From 1979 until 1981 she was moderator of the United Church. During the past decade she has had numerous appointments to working units of the World Council of Churches, including Congregational Renewal and Human Rights. She was a delegate to the Sixth Assembly of the World Council of Churches and spokesperson for Canadian Churches and non-government organizations to the United Nations Special Session on Disarmament. She is a member of Amnesty International, Canadian University Services Overseas, the Canadian Civil Liberties Association, the Council of Trustees of the Institute for Research on Public Policy, and the Inter-Church Committee on Human Rights in Latin America. In addition, she has been actively involved in the Elizabeth Fry Society, the National Film Board, Social Planning Councils, Oxfam, the Children's Aid, and various other community service organizations. She has received honorary degrees from several theological colleges. She has travelled widely and met people at all levels of society, including "those most victimized by their society."

Wonders, William Clare

C.D., B.A., M.A., Ph.D., Fil.D., F.R.S.C.

Professor of geography. b. April 22, 1924, Toronto; m. Lillian Johnson; d. Karen, Jennifer, s. Glen; res. Edmonton.

William Clare Wonders was the first geographer ever appointed to the University of Alberta. Before 1953, geography had not been taught at the university level in the province, but under his guidance a department grew up, with a full range of programs and a professional Division of Meteorology. Wonders studied at the University of Toronto and Syracuse University. His first appointment was in 1948 as geography lecturer at Toronto. He moved to the University of Alberta in 1953. During his long association with that university he has received many academic honours and fellowships, including a Canada Council Leave Fellowship, a Fellowship in the Arctic Institute of North America, a Government of Alberta Achievement Award for Excellence, an honorary doctorate from Uppsala University in Sweden, and an Award for Service to the Profession of Geography from the Canadian Association of Geographers. He has been a visiting professor at the universities of British Columbia, Aberdeen, Scotland; Uppsala, Sweden; Oklahoma; and others. Wonders is chairman of the Atlas of Northern Canada Committee; as well, he is a member of the Policy Board of the Canadian Plains Research Centre at the University of Regina, the Alberta Historic Sites Board, the Advisory Committee on Toponomy Research and the Canadian Permanent Committee on Geographical Names, and he is a councillor of the Champlain Society. He is also a member and past president of the Canadian Association of Geographers and he belongs to the Royal Canadian Geographical Society, the geographical societies of Scotland and the United States, as well as the Hudson's Bay Record Society, the Heraldry Society of Canada, and the Heritage Canada Foundation.

ARTS & MEDIA

Adamson, Anthony Patrick Cawthra

O.C., B.A., M.A., LL.D., F.R.A.I.C., M.C.I.P.

Architect, writer. b. October 7, 1906, Toronto; m. Augusta Bonnycastle; s. Adrian, Jeremy, d. Inigo; res. Toronto.

Anthony Adamson was educated in Port Credit, Ontario, and at Wellington College, England, Cambridge University, and the University of London. When he returned to Toronto after post-graduate work in London, he set up a practice as an architect and town planner, eventually becoming a professor of town planning at the University of Toronto (1955–65). He named his consultant company Proteus Limited after "the Greek consultant" Proteus, "an oracle," Adamson says, "who only answered clients he wanted to answer." Adamson was vice-chairman of the National Capital Commission in Ottawa from 1959 to 1967 and served for a decade as an elected municipal officer in the Township of Toronto, on the School Board, and as a councillor (serving as reeve in 1953–54). In 1955–56, he was chairman of the Public Utilities Commission; also in 1956, he became president of the Peel County Children's Aid Society. He was president of the Ontario Welfare Council (1964), and twice president of the Town Planning Institute of Canada (1946, 1951). In 1967–69, he was director of the National Theatre School and, from 1969 to 1974, chairman of the Ontario Council of the Arts. From 1975 until 1981 he was a member of the Heritage Foundation. Recently, he says, he resigned from all of his clubs and associations except for the Arts and Letters Club in Toronto. His awards and prizes include the Coronation and Jubilee medals and the Gabrielle Léger medal presented in 1981 by Heritage Canada. In 1978 he was given the City of Toronto's Award of Merit. He was made an Officer of the Order of Canada in 1974. Adamson is the co-author of a delightful series of books about historical Canadian architecture: *The Ancestral Roof, The Gaiety of Gables,* and *Hallowed Walls* (which received the Governor General's Award for non-fiction in 1975). He has a spectacular garden and collects oriental ivories and woodblock prints.

Anderson, Doris Hilda

O.C., B.A., LL.D.

Journalist, novelist. b. November 10, 1925, Calgary; née McCubbin; divorced; s. Peter David, Stephen Robert, Mitchell Richard; res. Toronto.

President of the National Action Committee on the Status of Women, Doris Anderson has a long history of working for women's rights. She was editor of the influential women's magazine, *Chatelaine,* for two decades; in 1979 she was appointed president of the Canadian Advisory Council on the Status of Women, a position she held for three years. She is an Officer of the Order of Canada, has received the Centennial Medal (1967) and the YWCA Woman of Distinction Award for 1983, and was named to the Canadian News Hall of Fame. Anderson is the author of two novels, *Two Women* (1978) and *Rough Layout* (1981), and is a member of the Writer's Union of Canada, the Metropolitan Children's Aid Society, and the Canadian Association for the Repeal of the Abortion Law. As well as being active on the boards of the Ontario Press Council and the Civil Liberties Association, she is a director of the Toronto Free Theatre and the Roland Michener Foundation. She also collects Canadiana.

Arthur, Paul Rodney

B.A., R.C.A.

Design consultant. b. December 20, 1924, Liverpool, England; m. Dinah Kerr; s. Jonathan, d. Carolyn; res. Toronto.

Paul Arthur, son of the architectural historian Eric Arthur, is credited with developing the systems approach to the design of visual communications in general and having helped to bring signage design to a professional level in North America. To this end he has completed research projects dealing with such diverse topics as the use of holography in visual communications and the psychological use of colour in the work environment. Born in England, he earned his B.A. in English at the University of Toronto and served during the Second World War as a lieutenant with the Royal Canadian Naval Volunteer Reserve. He was assistant editor of *Graphis International,* published in Zurich, from 1951 to 1956, then returned to Canada to become the editor of *Canadian Art* (now *artscanada*), a position he held until 1967. He is now chairman of Newton Frank Arthur Inc. and of Newton Frank Arthur Consulting Ltd., and president of his own company, VisuCom Limited. He is a member of various design organizations across North America and was awarded the Centennial Medal in 1967.

Atwood, Margaret Eleanor

C.C., B.A., A.M., D.Litt., LL.D.

Writer. b. November 18, 1939, Ottawa; m. Graeme Gibson; d. Eleanor Jess Atwood Gibson; res. Toronto.

The author of such memorable novels as *Surfacing* and *Life Before Man,* Margaret Atwood is one of Canada's most notable literary figures. Her poetry, reviews, and critical articles have been published in magazines across North America, and she has received many awards such as the E.J. Pratt Medal and the Governor General's Award, as well as being named a Companion of the Order of Canada. Her childhood was spent in the northern bush of Quebec and Ontario, wintering in Ottawa, Sault Ste. Marie, and Toronto. After earning degrees at the University of Toronto and at Harvard and teaching at universities across Canada, she spent two years in Europe. In 1972 she published *Survival: A Thematic Guide to Canadian Literature,* a work of literary criticism that has profoundly influenced the way Canadians think about themselves and their country. In 1973 she moved to Alliston, Ontario, where she wrote the poetry included in *You Are Happy* and *Two-Headed Poems,* as well as a collection of short stories entitled *Dancing Girls* and her novel *Life Before Man.* A member of ACTRA and CANSCAIP, she is also actively involved in Amnesty International.

Augustyn, Frank

Dancer; Toronto

Bateman, Robert McLellan

Wildlife artist; Milton, Ontario

Beecroft, Norma Marian

Composer, producer, administrator. b. April 11, 1934, Oshawa, Ontario; res. Toronto.

Norma Beecroft attended the Royal Conservatory of Music in Toronto from 1952 until 1958, studying composition with John Weinzweig and flute with Keith Girard. She won a scholarship in 1958 to study composition with Aaron Copland and Lukas Foss at the Berkshire Music Center in Tanglewood, Massachusetts. In 1959, 1960, and 1961 she visited Rome to study at the Academia Santa Cecilia, and took private flute lessons. She became interested in electronic music and attended Myron Schaeffer's electronic music classes at the University of Toronto (1962–63); in 1964, she studied with Mario Davidorsky at the Columbia-Princeton Music Center in New York. She began working for the CBC in 1954 as a script assistant for TV music programs. From 1957 to 1959, she acted as a music consultant to CBC television. After private studies in Germany, England and Italy in

ABOVE: *Marion MacRae and Anthony Adamson, co-authors of* The Ancestral Roof *and* Hallowed Walls.
RIGHT: *Margaret Atwood at her farm north of Toronto.*
BELOW: *Mario Bernardi.*

1960–61, she returned to the CBC in Toronto, this time as national programs organizer for radio. From 1966 to 1969, she produced the series *Music of Today*, *Organists in Recital*, and *RSVP*. In 1969 her documentary, *The Computer in Music*, received an Armstrong Award for excellence in FM Radio broadcasting. In 1975, she produced 13 CAPAC/RCI broadcast recordings ("Music Canada"). From 1965 until 1968, Norma Beecroft was president of the Ten Centuries Concerts and in 1971, co-founder (with Robert Aitken) of the New Music Concerts. Throughout this time Norma Beecroft had, of course, been composing her own music, some examples of which are her "Improvvisazioni Concertanti No.2" (commissioned by the National Arts Centre in 1971), "Rasas II" for contralto, chamber ensemble and tape (commissioned by the CBC in 1972), "Three Impressions From Sweetgrass" (commissioned by the Ontario Youth Society Choir in 1973), and "Hedda," a ballet score for orchestra and tape commissioned by the National Ballet of Canada in 1981.

Bernardi, Mario
C.C.

Symphony and opera conductor. b. August 20, 1930, Kirkland Lake, Ontario; m. Mona Margaret Kelly; d. Julia; res. Toronto.

The son of a blacksmith in a small Ontario mining town, Mario Bernardi studied music at the Conservatory in Venice and at the Mozarteum in Salzburg, receiving diplomas in piano, organ, and composition. He served as music director of Sadler's Wells Opera (now the English National Opera) of London, England, then spent 13 years as music director of the National Arts Centre in Ottawa, where he developed a small orchestra renowned for the brightness and clarity of its playing, especially of the classical repertoire. He is now music director of the Calgary Philharmonic and principal conductor of the CBC Vancouver Orchestra. Bernardi was named a Companion of the Order of Canada and has received several honorary degrees in music. A member of London's Savage Club, he plays chess and reads in his spare time. His father-in-law, Philip Kelly, was an Ontario cabinet minister in the 1950s.

Berton, Pierre
O.C., B.A., LL.D., D.Litt., Doctor of A.U. (Athabasca University)

Author, broadcaster. b. July 12, 1920, Whitehorse, Yukon; m. Janet Constance Walker; s. Peter, Paul, Eric, d. Penny, Pamela, Patricia, Peggy Anne, Perri; res. Kleinburg, Ontario.

Pierre Berton is perhaps the best-known author and broadcaster in Canada. He has written revue sketches for the stage, plays and documentaries for radio, films, and television, a daily newspaper column, a musical comedy for the stage, and 28 books. He appears on two weekly television shows (*Front Page Challenge* and *The Great Debate*) and is heard daily on Toronto's CKEY. He is the only Canadian to win three Governor General's Awards for non-fiction and holds two National Newspaper Awards, both won in the same year. A son of the Klondike, he worked in mining camps during his university years, then spent four years in the army, rising from private to captain/instructor at Kingston's Royal Military College. He joined the Vancouver *News-*

Herald and at 21 became city editor. In 1947 he left the *Vancouver Sun* for Toronto and became an assistant editor of *Maclean's*, Canada's largest consumer magazine. In 1953 he was named managing editor and five years later joined the *Toronto Star* as associate editor and columnist, a position he held until 1962 when he began his own television program, *The Pierre Berton Show*, which ran for 11 years. Among his works are the two-volume history of the construction of the C.P.R. (*The National Dream* and *The Last Spike*), *Klondike*, and *The Secret World of Og*, a popular children's book based on his own offspring. He is a member of ACTRA, the Canadian Civil Liberties Association, and Amnesty International, among others.

Birney, Alfred Earle
O.C., B.A., M.A., Ph.D., LL.D., D.Litt., F.R.S.C.

Writer. b. May 13, 1904, Calgary; divorced; s. William; res. Toronto.

The leading Canadian poet of his generation, Earle Birney has published 22 books of poetry translated into a dozen languages including Russian and Swahili, a play, and two novels. His novel *Turvey*, first published in 1948 and still in print, has sold 50,000 copies and is the basis of a stage play and two musical comedies. He has received the Governor General's Medal for Poetry (1942, 1945) and the Leacock Medal for Humour (1949) and is the subject of five biographies and a National Film Board production. Over the past three decades, he has given 1500 poetry readings in 30 countries. The son of a rancher, Birney still loves the Canadian West. He is working on the second volume of his memoirs and has recorded three albums of his poetry with the percussion band Nexus.

Bloore, Dorothy Cameron
Former art dealer; Toronto

Bloore, Ronald L.
Artist; Toronto

Bobak, Bruno (Bronislaw Josephus) and Bobak, Molly Lamb
Artists. Bruno b. December 28, 1923, Wawelowka, Poland; Molly b. February 25, 1922, Vancouver; s. Alexander, d. Anny; res. Fredericton, New Brunswick.

Bruno Bobak came to Canada with his parents in 1925. He studied on Saturday mornings at the then Art Gallery of Toronto with Arthur Lismer and at Toronto's Central Technical School with Carl Schaefer. Bobak continued to paint while serving in Europe with the Royal Canadian Engineers during the Second World War, winning first prize in the Canadian Army Art Exhibition at the National Gallery of Canada (March 21, 1944). From 1944 to 1946, he served as an official war artist. It was as a war artist that he met his future wife. Molly Lamb also studied art on Saturday mornings at the Vancouver Art Gallery before studying art at the University of British Columbia, with Jack Shadbolt as one of her instructors. She joined the CWAC in 1943 and, coincidentally, won third prize in the same Canadian Army Art Exhibition in which Bruno won first. She was appointed an official war artist—Canada's only female war artist—in 1945, the year she and Bruno Bobak married. After the war, the Bobaks settled in Vancouver where they continued to paint. In 1952–53, Bruno constructed a 29-foot concrete mural for the Vancouver School of Art. In 1956, the Bobaks travelled to New York, sketching all the way. The next year they used Bruno's Royal Society Canadian Government Overseas Fellowship to go to Europe, where Molly in particular produced some of her finest drawings and watercolours. Both exhibited during these years in galleries in London, Leeds, and Bristol. Molly's article in *Canadian Art*, "Leisure to Paint" (May, 1959), charmingly recreates their life in England and on the continent. When they returned to Canada, they settled in Fredericton where they teach at the University of New Brunswick. Bruno is a director of the university's Art Centre as well. Both belong to the Canadian Group of Painters and the Canadian Society of Graphic Art. Bruno Bobak also belongs to the Society of Canadian Painters, Etchers, and Engravers, and the Canadian Society of Painters in Water Colour.

Boggs, Jean Sutherland
O.C., B.A., M.A., Ph.D., LL.D., F.R.S.C.

Art historian, museum director. b. June 11, 1922, Negritos, Peru; res. Ottawa.

Jean Sutherland Boggs is chairman of the Canada Museum Construction Corporation and, in that role, supervisor of the design and construction of the new National Gallery in Ottawa, the Gallery for which she served as director for a brilliant decade (1966-76). Educated at Trinity College, the University of Toronto, and at Radcliffe College, Harvard, Boggs began her career as curator and art historian in Montreal where from 1942 to 1944 she was education secretary for the Art Association of Montreal. She was assistant professor of art at Skidmore College (New York) in 1948-49 and assistant professor of art at Mount Holyoke College (Massachusetts) from 1949 to 1952. From 1954 to 1962 she was first assistant and then associate professor of art history at the University of California. In 1962, she was made curator of the Art Gallery of Toronto (now the Art Gallery of Ontario), a position she held for two years, leaving to take the Steinberg professorship of art history at Washington University in St. Louis. After two years in St. Louis, she accepted the directorship of the National Gallery. In 1976, she left Canada again, this time to become professor of fine arts at Harvard for three years before taking up her present post in Ottawa. Jean Sutherland Boggs holds 12 honorary degrees and was named a Phi Beta Kappa Visiting Scholar in 1974-75. She was made an Officer of the Order of Canada in 1973. Boggs is the author of *Portraits By Degas* (1962), *Drawings by Degas* (1967), *The National Gallery of Canada* (1971), and the article "Picasso, the Last Thirty Years" in *Picasso in Retrospect* (1973). In 1964-65, she gave a series of talks on CBC radio called *Listening Pictures*. She belongs to the Cercle Universitaire in Ottawa.

Boyle, Harry J.
O.C., D.Litt., LL.D.

Writer, broadcaster. b. October 7, 1915, St. Augustine, Ontario; m. Marion McCaffrey; s. Michael, d. Patricia; res. Toronto.

Harry Boyle's long career as a writer began in his native western Ontario, where he was a freelance writer for various newspapers. He worked for the Wingham radio station (1936-41) and was a reporter with the *Stratford Beacon-Herald* (1941-42). He joined the CBC, eventually becoming supervisor of features, and produced many of the leading programs of the day including *CBC Wednesday Night* and the *Project* series. He was vice-chairman of the Canadian Radio-television and Telecommunications Commission from 1968 to 1976 and chairman in 1976-77. He has been a newspaper columnist, playwright, essayist, memorist, and novelist; one of the best-known of his novels bears the pre-emptive title *The Great Canadian Novel* (1972). He is an Officer of the Order of Canada. Among his honours and awards are the Leacock Medal for Humour, honorary doctorates from Trent and Concordia universities, and membership in the Canadian Newspaper Hall of Fame.

Brott, Alexander

O.C., Lic.Mus., Mus.D., LL.D., F.R.S.A., F.R.S.C.

Composer, conductor, violinist. b. March 14, 1915, Montreal; m. Lotte Goetzel; s. Boris, Denis; res. Montreal.

Equally well known as a conductor, composer, and violinist, Alexander Brott began to study the violin at the age of six. He made his professional violin debut in 1928. By 1933, Brott had earned his Licentiate of Music diploma from McGill and his Lauréat from the Académie de Musique de Québec. From 1935 to 1938 he studied at the Juilliard School of Music in New York. There he earned his diploma in orchestration and composition; he also won the Loeb Memorial Award for performance and the Elizabeth Sprague Coolidge Award for his composition *Two Symphonic Movements: Oracle*, performed in 1938 by the Montreal Symphony conducted by Sir Thomas Beecham. In 1939 Brott joined the faculty of McGill as an instructor in violin and orchestration; that same year he founded the McGill String Quartet. From 1945 to 1958 he was concertmaster and assistant conductor of the Montreal Symphony. In 1947 his composition *From Sea to Sea*, commissioned by the CBC's International Service, was broadcast by 800 radio stations worldwide. It was also performed by the Royal Philharmonic Orchestra under Beecham. In 1948, he won an Olympic Bronze Medal for his composition *War and Peace*. In 1950, his *Concerto for Violin and Chamber Orchestra* was performed at Carnegie Hall by Leopold Stokowski. The CBC commissioned him in 1953 to compose *A Royal Tribute* celebrating the coronation of Queen Elizabeth II, a work he eventually conducted himself at the Royal Albert Hall in London. In 1955 he became associate professor and chairman of the Instrumental Department at McGill. A year later, Pierre Monteux conducted Brott's *Analogy in Anagram* (commissioned by Monteux) for the Montreal Symphony. Since 1963, he has been music director of the Kingston Symphony Orchestra and, since 1965, full professor in the Faculty of Music at McGill. Four of his works were commissioned to honour Canada's centennial. He has been conductor-in-residence at McGill since 1974. He was given the Canadian Music Council Medal in 1976 for his contribution to music in Canada and the Queen's Silver Jubilee medal in 1977; in 1978 he was named an Officer of the Order of Canada. He is married to a professional cellist. His two sons are also distinguished musicians: Boris is a conductor and Denis is a cellist with the Or-

ford String Quartet. Alexander Brott is an inveterate collector, with notable gatherings of fossils, stones, and minerals, musical instruments, walking sticks, and "characteristic hats and memorabilia from various lands." He owns a Rolls-Royce, several Cadillacs, a pontoon house boat, "a Pedalo, and other related extravagances."

Callaghan, Morley Edward

C.C., B.A., LL.D., Litt.D.

Writer. b. 1903, Toronto; m. Lorette Florence Dee; s. Michael, Barry; res. Toronto.

Morley Callaghan has been writing seriously for 50 years. He first came to notice as a short-story writer in the days of Hemingway and Fitzgerald when he escaped Toronto's repressive atmosphere for the expatriate life in Paris in the 1920s. His stories were greatly admired by Hemingway and his celebrated boxing match with that writer is still the subject of controversy (Callaghan won). His writing deals with deep moral concerns, but he is above all a skilled teller of sometimes deceptively simple stories. Among his many books are *Such Is My Beloved* (1934), *The Loved and the Lost* (winner of a Governor General's Award in 1951), *The Many-Colored Coat* (1960), and *A Fine and Private Place* (1975). He was made a Companion of the Order of Canada in 1983, having previously declined an officership.

Callwood, June

C.M.

Writer. b. June 2, 1924, Chatham, Ontario; m. Trent Frayne; d. Jill Callwood, Jesse Ann; s. Brant Homer, Casey Robert (deceased); res. Islington, Ontario.

A *Globe and Mail* columnist and former CBC television host, June Callwood is well known as a writer and an outspoken supporter of humanitarian and feminist causes. She was the founder or a founding member of almost a dozen organizations, including the Canadian Civil Liberties Association, the Writers' Union of Canada, Nellie's Hostel for Women, Women for Political Action, and the Writers' Development Trust and has been chairman, president, or vice-president of most of them. At present she is a member of the Ontario Ministry of Health Assistive Devices Committee and a judge of the National Newspaper Awards. She also sits on the National Executive of the Canadian Council of Christians and Jews. In 1969 she was named B'nai B'rith Woman of the Year and in 1974 received the City of Toronto Award of Merit. Her books include *Portrait of Canada* and (with Marvin Zuker) *The Law is Not for Women*.

Campbell, Norman

Writer/producer; Toronto

Casson, Alfred Joseph

O.C., LL.D., R.C.A.

Artist. b. May 17, 1898, Toronto; m. Margaret Petrie; d. Margaret; res. Toronto.

One of the most conservative and stylized of Canada's classic landscape painters, A.J. Casson is the last surviving member of the Group of Seven. He began his career as a commercial

artist, working, for example, for Franklin Carmichael for seven years as an assistant designer. It was at Toronto's Arts and Letters Club where he eventually met the other members of the famous coterie. Casson first exhibited in 1921, with the Ontario Society of Artists. His painting "Clearing" was purchased by the National Gallery two years later. In 1925, Casson, Carmichael, and F.H. Brigden founded the Canadian Society of Painters in Water Colour. A year later, in 1926, Casson became a member of the Group of Seven (which had been left with only six members because of the departure of Franz Johnston). Casson kept up his commercial work for most of his career. During 20 years as vice-president and art director for Sampson Matthews Ltd., he worked with the National Gallery and the Canadian Pulp and Paper Association to develop programs for the finer and more accurate reproduction of the work of Canadian painters. It wasn't until 1959, when he was 61, that Casson had his first one-man exhibition (at Toronto's Roberts Gallery). Since that time, his pictures have been purchased for all the important galleries and major collections in Canada. Casson was awarded honorary doctorates from the University of Saskatchewan in 1971 and the University of Toronto in 1975. He was made an Officer of the Order of Canada in 1978. He maintains an especially fine garden at his Toronto home.

Colville, David Alexander

C.C., B.F.A.

Artist. b. August 24, 1920, Toronto; m. Rhoda Wright; d. Ann Kitz, s. Graham, John, Charles; res. Wolfville, Nova Scotia.

Alex Colville is widely regarded as Canada's pre-eminent realist painter. Educated in Amherst, Nova Scotia, and at Mount Allison University in Sackville, New Brunswick, Colville served with the Canadian Armed Forces from 1942 to 1946, the last two years of his term as an official war artist. When he returned to Canada, Colville began teaching at Mount Allison, where he remained with the faculty of the Fine Arts Department until 1963. In 1967 he was visiting artist at the University of California at Santa Cruz. He is now chancellor of Acadia University in Wolfville. Colville is a meticulous painter and print maker who has been known to spend years on a single picture; rarely does he produce (even working at top speed) more than two or three a year. His pictures are always drawn from the apparently ordinary moments of daily Maritime life but are made to seem so motionless and hieratic that they take on the semi-surrealistic quality of mystery and foreboding that seems to make them so popular. A modest man (he lists as his major achievement having made pictures "which some people think are good"), Colville prefers to remain quietly working in Wolfville and strolling on nearby Evangeline Beach to the life of glamour available to an artist of his stature. In 1983 the Art Gallery of Ontario mounted the first major Colville retrospective exhibition.

Cronyn, Hume

LL.D.

Actor, director, writer. b. July 18, 1911, London, Ontario; m. Jessica Tandy; c. Christopher Hume, Tandy, Susan Tettemer; res. Pound Ridge, New York.

Jean Sutherland Boggs

June Callwood

Morley Callaghan

Alexander Brott with his wife Lotte and son Boris.

ALL: J.R.

Alex Colville on the tidal flats by his Wolfville, Nova Scotia, cottage.

George Cuthbertson on Hiawatha. *Cuthbertson supervised the restoration of this R.C.Y.C launch, which is the oldest registered vessel on the Great Lakes. Also seen is his famous 1966 design,* Mia's Red Jacket, *now owned by P. J. Phelan; this is the vessel that established C&C's international reputation.*

ALL.J.R.

Hume Cronyn has had a long and distinguished career as an actor, director, and writer in Canada, the United States, and Britain. He has appeared on the stage, in films, and on radio and television, often with Jessica Tandy, whom he married in 1942. During the Second World War, he toured military installations for Canada and the United States. In 1953 he attended the opening ceremonies of the Stratford Festival but did not act there until 1969. In 1976 he played Shylock in *The Merchant of Venice* and Bottom in *A Midsummer Night's Dream* at Stratford and became a member of the board. Among the many awards that Cronyn has received are the Barter Theatre Award, American Academy of Dramatic Arts Award for Achievement by Alumni, Leland Power Honor Award, Los Angeles Dramatic Critics Award, Straw Hat Award (for direction), the Obie, and the Tony. Cronyn's father was a London financier and member of Parliament, Hume Blake Cronyn, and his mother belonged to the Labatt family. He was educated at Ridley College and McGill University, and trained as an actor at the New York School of Theatre, the Mozarteum in Salzburg, and the American Academy of Dramatic Art.

Cuthbertson, George Harding

B.A.Sc., R.C.A.

Yacht designer. b. June 3, 1929, Brantford, Ontario; m. Helen Isabella Donaldson; s. Michael Allan, John Kelly, d. Jill Foster; res. Milton, Ontario.

Indisputably the dean of modern yacht design in Canada, George Cuthbertson was born to a family of non-sailors who nonetheless enrolled him in the Royal Canadian Yacht Club's junior club at 14. By the age of 17 he was the club's official measurer and his future as a manipulator of the subtle dimensions of yachts was practically assured. Shortly after graduating from the University of Toronto with an applied-science degree in 1950, he formed a partnership to produce products in a then new material called fibreglass. In 1954 he modified the design of the eight-metre *Venture*, which returned the Canada's Cup match racing trophy to its native soil for the first time since 1903. Cuthbertson eventually moved into the design and brokerage business. In 1961 he took on a minority partner, George Cassian. Among their many successes during the 1960s were *Red Jacket*, a revolutionary design that was the first craft (and crew) from outside the United States to win the Southern Ocean Racing Conference Series in 1968, and *Manitou*, which won the Canada's Cup in 1969. That year, Cuthbertson & Cassian joined forces with three yacht builders to form the public company C&C Yachts. Cuthbertson served as chairman, president, and chief executive officer from 1974 until 1981. During his tenure, he oversaw a company that became a world leader in design and manufacturing innovation as well as in sales volume. Soon after C&C was bought by outside interests, he established his own one-man design office, Motion Yacht Designs. In addition to his interest in yachting, he is an avid flier and owns a small airplane he built virtually out of spare parts. He and his family live in a renovated octagonal farmhouse.

Davies, Michael Rupert Llewellyn

C.M., B.A., F.R.S.A.

Publisher. b. July 22, 1936, Kingston, Ontario; m. Elaine Stephens; s. Gregory, Eric, Andrew, Timothy, d. Jennifer; res. Kingston.

Michael Davies is publisher and owner of the Kingston *Whig-Standard*, which is one of a shrinking number of independent Canadian daily papers and which has been in the Davies family since 1925. He is a nephew of Robertson Davies, who was formerly editor of another Ontario daily, the Peterborough *Examiner*. Michael Davies is past president of the Canadian Daily Newspaper Publisher's Association and a director of Canadian Press. He sits on the Board of Trustees of Queen's University and has served on the boards of a number of cultural institutions, including the Ontario Arts Council and the Stratford Festival. Davies is a keen sailor and has logged between 40 and 50 thousand miles of ocean sailing, half of that on his 67-foot custom-built C&C schooner, *Archangel*.

Davies, Robertson

C.C., B.Litt., D.Litt., D.C.L., LL.D., F.R.S.C.

Writer, university professor. b. August 28, 1913, Thamesville, Ontario; m. Brenda Mathews; d. Miranda, Jennifer, Rosamond; res. Toronto and Caledon East, Ontario.

A man of wide learning and extraordinary energies, Robertson Davies has been an actor (the Old Vic Repertory Company in London), a newspaper publisher (*The Peterborough Examiner*), a university professor, a novelist, an essayist, and playwright. He was master of the University of Toronto's Massey College from its establishment in 1963 until his retirement as emeritus professor of English Literature and master emeritus of the University of Toronto in 1981. He was educated at Upper Canada College, at Queen's University, and at Oxford (Balliol). He holds 17 honorary degrees from Canadian universities. Davies is probably best known as a writer; his books include *Shakespeare's Boy Actors* (1939), *The Diary of Samuel Marchbanks* (1947), *Tempest Tost* (1951), *Leaven of Malice* (1954), *A Mixture of Frailties* (1958), *A Voice from the Attic* (1960), *Fifth Business* (1970), *The Manticore* (1972), *World of Wonders* (1975) — these last three novels together comprise the famous Deptford Trilogy — and *The Rebel Angels* (1981). Among his best-known plays are *Fortune My Foe* (1948), *At My Heart's Core* (1950), *A Jig For The Gypsy* (1954), *Love and Libel* (1960), *Question Time* (1975), and *Pontiac and the Green Man* (1977). Some of his essays and occasional pieces have been collected in *One Half of Robertson Davies* (1977), *The Enthusiasms of Robertson Davies* (1979), and *The Well-Tempered Critic* (1981). Among Davies's awards are the Louis Jouvet Prize for Direction (for *The Taming of the Shrew* at the Dominion Drama Festival in 1949), The Stephen Leacock Medal (1955), the Lorne Pierce Medal of the Royal Society of Canada (1961), and the Governor General's Award for fiction (1973). Robertson Davies served as governor of the Stratford Shakespearean Festival and is now a senator of the Festival. He is also a former member of the board of the National Arts Centre in Ottawa. He is an honorary member of the American Academy and Institute of Arts and Letters (1980), a member of literary societies — including the Powys Society — and an enthusiastic member of the Long Christmas Dinner Club. He lives at Windhover in the hills of Caledon East, a country home that he is making historic, he says, as fast as he can.

Davis, Donald George

B.A.

Actor, director, producer. b. February 26, 1928, Toronto; res. Toronto.

Educated at St. Andrew's College and at the University of Toronto, actor Donald Davis began in 1948 to take an important part in the development of serious theatre in Canada; he became co-founder of and principal director for Toronto's Crest Theatre, acting in and directing many plays in Toronto and in the rest of Canada before devoting much of his time to professional theatre work in Britain (1950-53) and in the United States since 1959. He starred on Broadway in the North American premiere of Samuel Beckett's *Krapp's Last Tape* (1960) and *That Time* (1976) and in 1983 played major roles in the North American premiere of Beckett's *Catastrophe* and the world premiere of his *What Where* in an off-Broadway triple-bill of Beckett's recent works. Davis is a director of the Centre Stage in Toronto. He is a life member of Canadian Actor's Equity. He also belongs to the Canadian Actors' Association, ACTRA, The American Actors' Equity, the Screen Actors' Guild, and AFTRA. A passionate lover of Ontario's Muskoka Lakes region, Donald Davis is co-founder and director of Muskoka's Straw Hat Players and is a member of the Muskoka Lakes Foundation. He has a summer home at St. Elmo in Muskoka and enjoys sailing his boats, the *Heather Belle*, a 37-foot day cruiser built in New York State in the 1890s, and the *Ardmore*, a 28-foot launch, built in Bracebridge, Ontario, in 1925. His sister Barbara is married to Harry Somers, his brother Murray is also involved in theatre, and they are part of the family that owned the Davis Leather business in Newmarket, Ontario.

De Pencier, Michael

B.A., M.A.

Publisher. b. January 19, 1935, Toronto; m. Honor Barbara Bonnycastle; s. Nicholas John, Mark Dumaresq, d. Miranda Augusta; res. Toronto.

In Toronto publishing and business circles, Michael de Pencier is noted for the success of Key Publishers, of which he is president, and for the casual way he runs the company. Among the magazines he publishes are *Toronto Life*, *Canadian Business*, the *Bargain Hunter Press* (a classified advertising tabloid), and *Quill & Quire* (a book trade tabloid published on a break-even basis). De Pencier has a reputation for being able to motivate his staff and work with creative people and for foreseeing changes in the market. He is a strong supporter of Canadian publishing: he was active in the formation of the Canadian Periodical Publishers Association and the National Magazine Awards Foundation. He was educated at Trinity College School, the University of Toronto, and the University of Michigan, where he also taught philosophy. His wife is the sister of Richard Bonnycastle.

Diamond, Abel Joseph

B.Arch., M.A., M.Arch., F.R.A.I.C., A.R.I.B.A., N.C.A.R.B.(Cert.), C.I.P., A.I.P., R.A.A.

Architect. b. November 8, 1932, Piet Retief, South Africa; m. Gillian Mary Huggins; s. Andrew Michael, d. Alison Suzanne; res. Toronto.

After receiving his education at the universities of Capetown, Oxford, and Pennsylvania, A.J. Diamond worked in Sir Hugh Casson's London office before coming to Canada in 1965. The firm of A.J. Diamond and Barton Myers designed the Ontario Medical Association building, York Square, and Beverley Place in Toronto, student housing in Edmonton, and the offices of Alcan Aluminium in Toronto, Montreal, and Cleveland, among other major projects. Diamond has taught at the universities of Toronto, York, Texas, and Pennsylvania and is a Fellow of the Royal Architectural Institute of Canada and a member of the Royal Academy of Arts. He is a collector of Canadian contemporary art and 19th-century English lithographs. He and his family live in the original Moore farmhouse in the Moore Park area of Toronto.

Dickson, Horatio Henry Lovat
O.C., B.A., M.A., LL.D., D.Litt., F.R.S.C.

Writer, publisher. b. June 30, 1902, Victoria, Australia; m. Marguerite Brodie; s. Jonathan Lovat, res. Toronto.

Lovat Dickson's life is best recounted in his own superb two-volume autobiography, *The Ante-Room* (1959) and *The House of Words* (1963). He came to Canada with his parents from Australia and attended the University of Alberta. In 1929 he was in England, editing *The Fortnightly Review* in London (1929-32). In 1932, he established his own publishing company in London, Lovat Dickson Limited, for which he acted as chairman and managing director until 1938 when he became the editor of General Books for Macmillan and Company. In 1941 he was made Macmillan's editorial director—a position he held until 1964. Dickson is also the author of *H.G. Wells, His Turbulent Life and Times* (1969), *Wilderness Man: The Strange Story of Grey Owl* (1973), *Radclyffe Hall at the Well of Loneliness* (1975), and several other books. Lovat Dickson is past president of the Canadian University Society (1962-66), a member of the Arts and Letters Club in Toronto, and a member of the Writers Union of Canada. He collects antiquarian books.

Doyle, Kevin

Editor-in-chief, Maclean's magazine; Toronto

Doyle, Richard James
O.C., LL.D.

Newspaper editor. b. March 10, 1923, Toronto; m. Florence Chanda; d. Judith, s. Sean; res. Toronto.

Richard Doyle was editor-in-chief of the *Globe and Mail* until he stepped down in 1983. He went to school in Chatham, Ontario, and served as a flying officer with a Bomber Command Squadron of the RCAF during the Second World War. After the war he worked as city editor with the *Chatham Daily News* and as assistant city editor and managing editor of the *Globe* before assuming the chief editorial post. Dic Doyle is the author of *The Royal Story* (1952), a popular history of the British monarchy. He has honorary degrees from St. Francis Xavier University and from King's College of Dalhousie University. He was made an Officer of the Order of Canada in 1983. He summers in Springhurst Beach on Nottawasaga Bay in Ontario and winters in Fort Myers, Florida.

Edinborough, Arnold
M.C., B.A., M.A., LL.D., Litt.S.D., F.R.S.A.

Journalist. b. August 2, 1922, Donington, England; m. Letitia Mary Woolley; s. Alastair Michael, d. Christine Ann, Sarah Jane; res. Toronto.

President and chief executive officer of the Council for Business and the Arts in Canada, Arnold Edinborough has been involved with the development of Canadian culture in various capacities: theatrical director, amateur actor, professional radio and television performer, arts administrator, board member. After serving as a captain with the Royal Artillery during the Second World War (for which he received the Military Cross), he returned to Cambridge for his B.A. He then emigrated to Canada and taught English at Queen's University in Kingston, where he also earned his M.A., and in 1954 he became editor of the Kingston *Whig-Standard*. Four years later he took over as editor and publisher of *Saturday Night* magazine, a position he held until 1970. Since then he has been president of his own company, Edina Productions, chairman of Dyatron Canada, and chairman of the International Scholarship Foundation. His arts-related involvement includes being a vice-president of Massey Hall and Roy Thomson Hall and senator of the Stratford Shakespearean Festival Foundation. He has edited and written five books, acted as host of four television series, and was a radio commentator for 15 years.

Ellis, Mark

Yacht designer; Oakville, Ontario

Erickson, Arthur Charles
C.C., B.Arch., D.Eng., LL.D., A.R.C.A., F.R.A.I.C., F.A.I.A., M.R.I.B.A.

Architect. b. June 14, 1924, Vancouver; res. Toronto and Vancouver.

World traveller and internationally recognized architect and designer, Arthur Erickson studied at the University of British Columbia and saw service in the Second World War as a captain in India and Malaya with the Canadian Army Intelligence Corps. His early ambition to be a painter resulted in the not insubstantial recognition of two honourable mentions in the B.C. Artists' Annual Exhibition at the Vancouver Art Gallery in 1941. By 1950, he was engaged in the first of his international wanderings in search of architecture and design ideas (an exotic kind of free-form education Erickson has always engaged in) in the Middle East, the Mediterranean, Scandinavia, and Britain (1950-53), after which he took up the teaching of architecture (at the same time as he began to build the first of the buildings that would bring him fame): he was an assistant professor at the University of Oregon in 1955-56 and at UBC in 1956-61 (and an associate professor at UBC in 1961-64). In the early 1960s he began winning awards for his designs (especially for a series of spectacular private houses like the Graham House built in Vancouver in 1963 and the house he built for painter Gordon Smith in

1964): the Western Houses Special Award (1961) and the Pan Pacific Citation of the American Institute of Architects (Hawaiian Chapter) in 1963. In 1961 he received a Canada Council Fellowship for architectural research in Japan and the Far East and in 1963 won (with architect Geoffrey Massey, son of the late Raymond Massey, with whom Erickson ran his firm at the time) the Simon Fraser University Competition for his spectacular open light-filled plan for the new university in Burnaby, B.C.; his complex of university buildings eventually won three Massey medals for architecture. He won a prodigious number of design and architecture awards over the next two decades, including the Canada Council's Molson Prize (1967) and the Royal Bank Award (1971). His major architectural commissions include Vancouver's MacMillan Bloedel Building (1969), the Museum of Anthropology at the University of British Columbia (1972), Robson Square and the Law Courts Complex in Vancouver (1973), the Royal Bank of Canada headquarters in Ottawa (1976), the Yorkdale Subway Station in Toronto (1977), the University of Lethbridge in Alberta (1971), the Canadian Pavilion of Osaka's World Fair (1970), California Center, Bunker Hill, Los Angeles (1980), and Roy Thomson Hall in Toronto (1982). Arthur Erickson is a Fellow of the Royal Architectural Institute of Canada, a member of the Institute for Research on Public Policy, and an Honorary Fellow of the American Institute of Architects. He was made an Officer of the Order of Canada in 1973 and a Companion in 1981. Erickson has been described by architecture critic Edith Iglauer in her *Seven Stones, a Portrait of Arthur Erickson, Architect* (1981) as a "witty, semi-mystical, not at all humble man" who once told her "Where I am or what I am is no concern of mine. I am concerned with what our civilization is all about, and expressing this in buildings. Everything I do, everything I see, is through architecture."

Faibish, Roy Abraham

Public servant, broadcasting executive. b. August 14, 1928, Regina; divorced; s. Leonard Jack, Lee David; d. Kristina Leslie; res. London.

Roy Faibish has had a varied career in business, government, and the military. At present he is an advisor to the government of the United Kingdom on broadband services. His previous positions include policy advisor to the Leader of the Opposition (John Diefenbaker), commissioner on the Canadian Radio-television and Telecommunications Commission (CRTC), and Ottawa editor of the television program *This Hour Has Seven Days*. He has also been executive vice-president of Bushnell Communications and vice-president (Europe) of Rogers Cablesystems. He was a co-director and co-writer of a CBC television documentary on China entitled *The 700 Million*. He was a flying officer in the RCAF Primary Reserve. Faibish's non-business activities include writing poetry, collecting books, buying claret for his wine cellar, travelling, curling, and walking. He considers his chief accomplishment to be "influencing public policy since 1954."

Fairley, Barker
O.C., B.A., M.A., Ph.D., D.Litt., LL.D., F.R.S.C., F.B.A., R.C.A.

Writer, painter, university professor. b. May 21, 1887, Barnsley, Yorks, England; m. Margaret Adele Keeling; d. Ann Schabas; m. Nan Elizabeth Laurin; d. Elizabeth, Joan, s. William, Tom; res. Toronto and Wellington, Ontario.

Internationally respected for his scholarly contributions to the study of German literature and, also, during the past 10 years, for his landscape and portrait painting, Barker Fairley grew up in Yorkshire, went to Leeds Grammar School and the University of Leeds, and to the University of Jena where he earned his Ph.D. in German literature and began his long and successful career as a university teacher. Professor Fairley came to Canada in 1910 to teach at the newly established University of Alberta in Edmonton. He left Alberta in 1915 to begin his long association with University College in the University of Toronto where, except for a brief sojourn in Manchester as head of the Department of German Literature (1932–36), he taught and served as chairman of the German Department until his retirement as professor emeritus in 1957. He published the first of his many books in 1926 — a study of and tribute to the great English epic poet and travel writer Charles M. Doughty. This was followed by his ground-breaking works about Goethe — *Goethe as Revealed in his Poetry* in 1932 and his classic *A Study of Goethe* in 1947. Other books include studies of Heinrich Heine (1954) and the German novelist Wilhelm Raabe (1961). The University of Toronto Press published Fairley's prose translation of Goethe's *Faust* in 1970. Fairley is the author of numerous articles on German and English literature in scholarly journals. In 1920, he was instrumental in founding *The Canadian Forum*, to which he contributed columns and articles for half a century (many of the early ones being spirited and convincing defenses and explications of the paintings of Fairley's friends, the then much-misunderstood Group of Seven). Fairley began painting on his own in the 1930s, quickly developing a sparse stylized way with landscape and portraiture that has, over the years, brought him a wide public and inclusion in many important collections. A collection of his portraits was published in 1981 (*Barker Fairley Portraits*).

Findley, Timothy Irving Frederick
D.Litt.

Writer, actor. b. October 30, 1930, Toronto; divorced; res. Cannington, Ontario.

Timothy Findley began his career by studying at Toronto's Royal Conservatory of Music (drama, voice) and the Sterndale-Bennett School of Drama before heading for England to study at London's Central School of Speech and Drama. On his return to Canada in the late 1940s he began working as a professional actor, appearing in plays in Kingston, Toronto, and Stratford — where he was a charter member of the newly formed Stratford Shakespearean Festival (1953). During these years he acted in London as well, and at both the Edinburgh and Berlin drama festivals. In 1955, he played in *Hamlet* in Moscow. He also played that year on Broadway. Findley began to write novels in the 1960s. In 1967 he wrote *The Last of the Crazy People* and two years later *The Butterfly Plague*. His memoir-like novel, *The Wars*, (1977) won him that year's Governor General's Award for fiction. His most recent novel is the best-selling *Famous Last Words* (1981).

Findley was playwright-in-residence at Ottawa's National Arts Centre (1974-75) and writer-in-residence at the University of Toronto (1979-80). His play *Can You See Me Yet?* was performed at the National Arts Centre in 1976. Another play, *John A. Himself*, was produced by Theatre London in 1979. Findley has written extensively for radio and television as well, having scripted (with William Whitehead) the acclaimed *The National Dream* (for which he and Whitehead won an ACTRA award in 1975), *Dieppe, 1942* (which won them an Anik award in 1979), and the episodes *Newcomers 1911* and *Newcomers 1832* from the television series *The Newcomers* produced in 1977-78 by the production company of Neilsen Ferns. He has, in addition, written documentary films, short stories, and a host of magazine pieces. He was the subject of an entire issue of the scholarly periodical *Canadian Literature* (Winter 1981). Findley lives in a house built in 1840 as a pharmacy. He draws, paints, and collects blue glass and character dolls.

Firestone, Otto John
M.A., D.J.R.P.D.

Economist, university professor, art collector. b. January 17, 1913, Austria; m. Barbara Ann MacMahon; steps. Patrick, Peter; m. Isobel Toronto; s. Bruce, Peter, d. Brenda, Catherine; res. Ottawa.

Equally well known as an economist and as the originator of the Ontario Heritage Foundation Firestone Art Collection, Jack Firestone was educated at McGill University, the London School of Economics, and the University of Vienna. He has an honorary degree from Hanyang University, Korea (1975). From 1942 until 1960, he worked as an economist for the Canadian government, serving as a research assistant and then as director of economic research and economics advisor to C.D. Howe, Minister of Trade and Commerce. Firestone proudly points out that he served Howe longer than any other senior officer. In Howe's ministry Firestone helped originate "economic policies relating to post-war reconstruction, and high levels of employment and income." His writings during this period include *Residential Real Estate in Canada* (1951) and *Canada's Economic Development, 1867-1953* (1958). Since 1960, he has been professor of Economics at the University of Ottawa (and, since 1978, professor emeritus of Économics). Among Dr. Firestone's publications are the books *Problems of Economic Growth* (1965), *Broadcast Advertising in Canada, Past and Future Growth* (1966), *The Economic Implications of Advertising* (1967), *Industry and Education, a Century of Canadian Development* (1968), *The Public Persuader* (1970), *Economic Implications of Patents* (1971), and a great number of articles, studies, and books written with other historians and economists. From 1961 to 1965, Firestone served as a member of the Royal Commission on Health Services, which recommended the universal program of medicare subsequently adopted by the federal government and the provincial legislatures. During the busy years as an economist and government adviser, Firestone collected over a thousand important Canadian paintings, drawings, and pieces of sculpture. In 1972 he donated the collection and the house in which it is exhibited to the Ontario Heritage Foundation. He is, fittingly, the curator of the collection. His books, *The Firestone Art Col-*

lection (1978) and *The Other A.Y. Jackson* (1979), grew out of his interest in Canadian art and his longstanding friendships with many of the artists whose works he collected. Dr. Firestone has received the Queen's Coronation Medal.

Forrester, Maureen
C.C., LL.D., D.Litt., D.Mus.

Contralto. b. July 25, 1930, Montreal; m. Eugene Kash; d. Paula, Gina, Linda, Susanna, s. Daniel; res. Toronto.

Respected internationally for her fine musicianship and for her majestic contralto voice, Maureen Forrester has given countless pleasure to Canadian music lovers and lovers of great music everywhere through her concerts, recitals, TV and radio appearances, and recordings. She was educated at William Dawson School in Montreal and studied music privately. Forrester received the Banff School of Fine Arts National Award in Music in 1967, the Harriet Cohen International Music Award in 1968, and the Canada Council's Molson Prize in 1972. She is a Fellow of Stong College at York University and was appointed a member of the Board of Trustees for the National Arts Centre Corporation in 1973. She was made a Companion of the Order of Canada in 1967.

Fotheringham, Allan
Journalist, Vancouver

Franca, Celia
O.C., LL.D., D.C.L., D.Litt.

Dancer, director. b. June 25, 1921, London, England; m. James W. Morton; res. Ottawa.

The founder of the National Ballet of Canada, Celia Franca studied ballet at the Guildhall School of Music and the Royal Academy of Dancing before performing with Ballet Rambert, the Three Arts Ballet, the International Ballet, and the Sadler's Wells Ballet (now the Royal Ballet). In 1947 she joined the Metropolitan Ballet as soloist and ballet mistress and began choreographing for television, creating the first two ballets ever commissioned by the BBC. In 1951 she was invited to Canada to investigate the possibility of starting a ballet company. Ten months later the National Ballet made its debut and began touring a year later. Performing herself during the company's early years, Franca decided in 1959 to concentrate on the management of the growing company and on the new National Ballet School, which she founded with Betty Oliphant. Under her direction the National Ballet has blossomed into an internationally respected dance company which emphasizes the classics while also stressing Canadian choreography. Officially retired since 1974, Franca remains actively involved as a coach, producer, and character dancer and is a guest teacher for the Vancouver Ballet Association, the Quinte Dance Centre, and the School of Dance (Ottawa). In 1978 and 1980 she was invited by the Chinese Ministry of Culture to teach classical ballet technique. She wrote of her experiences in *The National Ballet of Canada: A Celebration* (1978). She is the recipient of numerous awards and honorary degrees. In 1967 she was named Officer of the Order of Canada. Her husband is the principal clarinetist of the National Arts Centre Orchestra.

Robertson Davies

RIGHT: Michael Davies' Archangel, a 67-foot C&C schooner launched in 1980, is seen at Hamilton Harbour, Bermuda.

ABOVE: Arthur Erickson at home in Vancouver. The reflecting table is made from the curtain wall material used in the Canadian Pavilion at the Osaka World's Fair. LEFT: Donald Davis on board his 100-year-old day cruiser in Muskoka. The boat, originally steam-powered, was renovated by Davis and makes a pleasant launch for picnic parties on the lake.

Arnold Edinborough

V. Tony Hauser

J.R.

O. J. Firestone in the A. Y. Jackson guest room of his Ottawa home and (below) seated before Jack Shadbolt paintings in the lounge.

J.R.

Maureen Forrester

Celia Franca at home in Ottawa.

Murray and Barbara Frum with some of their collection of primitive art.

Mira Godard

Fraser, John Anderson

B.A., M.A.

Journalist. b. June 5, 1944, Montreal; m. Elizabeth Scott MacCallum; d. Jessie, Kathleen; res. Toronto.

Now national editor of the Toronto *Globe and Mail*, John Fraser has a colourful background in journalism and literature. He was the *Globe*'s dance critic during the period Canadian dance came of age (1971-1975), he was involved in the defection of Mikhail Baryshnikov in Toronto, he was Peking correspondent during the Xidan Democracy Movement, and he is the author of two books, *Kain and Augustyn* (1977) and *The Chinese: Portrait of a People* (1980), which has been published in seven languages. Fraser was educated at universities in Newfoundland, Oxford, and Norwich, and is a grandson of John Alexander Fraser, one of the founders of Dominion Securities (the training ground of the late Bud McDougald). He has won a National Newspaper Award three times in six years (1975, 1977, 1979), the Queen's Jubilee Medal, and the Governor General's Award for non-fiction in 1980. He is married to the granddaughter of Dr. James MacCallum, a patron of Tom Thomson and the Group of Seven, and belongs to the Champlain Society and the Writers' Union of Canada. He enjoys playing tennis and the piano, and collects antique Chinese furniture, a hobby that began during his travels in China for the *Globe*.

Freedman, Harry

Composer. b. April 5, 1922, Lodz, Poland; m. Mary Morrison; res. Toronto.

Born in Poland and raised, from the age of three, in Medicine Hat, Alberta, Harry Freedman—like a number of other Canadian musicians—wanted to be a painter. He enrolled at the Winnipeg School of Art when he was only 13, but was lured away from painting (though it has remained a powerful influence on his music) by big-band jazz, for which he began training (as a clarinetist) when he was 18. It was through his studies in jazz that he was gradually led to the world of symphonic music. Freedman served with the RCAF in the Second World War. After the war, he began to study composition in Toronto with the renowned John Weinzweig. He joined the Toronto Symphony Orchestra in 1946 as English horn and stayed with the orchestra for 25 years, becoming the orchestra's composer-in-residence during his last year with the TSO. Freedman composed a great deal of music for the TSO, including new settings for "O Canada" and "God Save The Queen" and his ambitious *Graphic 1 ("Out of Silence...")*, composed for the orchestra's 50th anniversary. Since that time, he has devoted himself almost entirely to composing. Much of his work employs variations on the 12-tone serial technique and frequently involves allusions to the visual arts (his *Tableau*, *Images*, and *Klee Wyck*, for example). He abandoned the 12-tone system in 1953 for his *First Symphony* (premiered in 1961 by the CBC Symphony Orchestra), but returned to it in different ways in subsequent work—primarily in his *The Tokaido* (1964). During the 1960s Freedman wrote scores for the movies and for television, including *Pale Horse, Pale Rider*, *The Pyx*, *Lies My Father Told Me*, and *Act of the Heart*. He has also written incidental music for the Stratford Shakespeare-

an Festival, Toronto Arts Productions, and Festival Lennoxville. He was commissioned to write three scores for the Royal Winnipeg Ballet (*Rose Latulippe*, 1966, *Five Over Thirteen*, 1969, and *The Shining People of Leonard Cohen*, 1970). He helped to found the Canadian League of Composers in 1952 and was its first secretary; from 1975 to 1978, he was its president. He has also served on the advisory board of Pollution Probe. Harry Freedman is an associate of the Canadian Music Centre. In 1980, the Canadian Music Council named him Musician of the Year.

French, William Harold

B.A.

Literary critic. b. March 21, 1926, London, Ontario; m. Margaret Jean Rollo; s. Mark, Paul, d. Jane, Susan; res. Toronto.

William French describes his chief achievement as "responding to the challenge of documenting and commenting critically on the flowering of Canadian literature between 1960 and the present." This he has done admirably in his thrice-weekly column in the *Globe and Mail* and in his lectures as a part-time instructor at Ryerson Polytechnical Institute's School of Journalism. He began working for the *Globe* as a general reporter soon after his graduation from the University of Western Ontario (with honours in journalism). In 1954-1955 he held a Nieman Fellowship at Harvard University and then returned to the *Globe* to become, eventually, its literary editor. He won National Newspaper Awards for Critical Writing in 1978 and 1979, and is the author of *A Most Unlikely Village: A History of Forest Hill* (1964). He is an avid amateur photographer and often goes camping in Cape Breton Highlands National Park.

Frum, Barbara

O.C., B.A.

Broadcaster, journalist. b. September 8, 1937, Niagara Falls, Ontario; née Rosberg; m. Murray Bernard Frum; s. David, Matthew, d. Linda; res. Toronto.

Barbara Frum is well known to most Canadians as host of CBC's *The Journal* and as the host, from 1971 until 1981, of the popular CBC radio current affairs program *As It Happens*. She grew up in Niagara Falls, and studied history at the University of Toronto. After graduating, she worked for CBC radio as a freelance writer and commentator, contributing items to such programs as *Trans-Canada Matinee* and *Audio*. She began writing for magazines and newspapers about the same time, contributing articles to *Maclean's*, *Chatelaine*, *Saturday Night* (for which she wrote a television column), the *Globe and Mail*, and the *Toronto Star*, where she wrote a radio column. She made her TV debut in 1967 as co-host of *The Day It Is* (which became *Weekday*), eventually hosting her own television show, *The Barbara Frum Journal*. Other tasks at the CBC during the past 10 years include contributions to *The Way It Is*, *Quarterly Report*, and commentary for two federal election campaigns, one royal tour, the 1976 Progressive Conservative convention, the 1980 Quebec Referendum, and the 1981 royal wedding. Frum has received four ACTRA

awards, the National Press Club of Canada Award for Outstanding Contribution to Canadian Journalism (1975), and The Canadian Press's Woman of the Year award in 1976. That same year she published a memoir of her experiences in broadcasting called *As It Happened*. She was made an Officer of the Order of Canada in 1979. Barbara Frum and her husband, developer Murray Frum, own a large and distinguished collection of primitive art.

Fulford, Robert Marshall Blount

Writer, editor, broadcaster. b. February 13, 1932, Ottawa; m. Jocelyn Dingman; s. James, d. Margaret; m. Geraldine Sherman; d. Rachel, Sarah; res. Toronto.

Robert Fulford has been a journalist since 1949, the year he began to write for the *Globe and Mail*. He wrote for the *Globe* in 1949-53 and again in 1956-57. In 1958 he moved to the *Toronto Star*, where he wrote with considerable panache about the visual arts and related cultural matters. He has written on and off for the *Star* over the last 25 years (in 1958-62, in 1964-68, and at present) as a literary columnist. In 1955, Fulford was assistant editor of *Canadian Homes and Gardens*, in 1956 assistant editor of *Mayfair*, and in 1962-64 assistant editor of *Maclean's* magazine. He has been the editor of the monthly *Saturday Night* magazine since 1968. Fulford is also a popular radio and television commentator and interviewer. His books include *This Was Expo* (1968), *Crisis at the Victory Burlesk* (1968), *Marshall Delaney at the Movies* (1974), *The Drawings of Harold Town* (text, 1969), *An Introduction to The Arts in Canada* (1977), and, with Joan Murray, *The Beginning of Vision: The Drawings of Lawren Harris* (1982). His latest book is *Canada: A Celebration* (with photographer John de Visser, 1983). Robert Fulford has won the University of Western Ontario's President's Medal for magazine writing twice and has won the National Magazine Award twice. In 1981, he received the *Prix d'honneur* of the Canadian Council of the Arts.

Gascon, Jean

C.C., LL.D.

Actor, director. b. December 21, 1921, Montreal; m. Marilyn Gardner; one daughter, two sons; res. Montreal.

Jean Gascon, the mercurial director of Théâtre for the National Arts Centre in Ottawa, formed his first theatre-group in 1951, Le Théâtre du Nouveau Monde of Montreal. In 1960, he became the co-founder and a director of the National Theatre School and subsequently the school's general director. In 1964, after directing productions at Stratford, he was made associate director of the Shakespearean Festival Foundation. In 1967, he became the Stratford Festival's artistic director, a post he held for the next decade. Gascon is a member of the Administrative Council of the National Film Board and has been awarded the Canadian Drama Award, the Canada Council's Molson Award (1965–66), and the Royal Bank Award (1974). He was made an Officer of the Order of Canada in 1967 and elevated to Companion of the Order of Canada in 1975.

Gelber, Arthur Ellis
O.C., LL.D.

Business executive, public servant. b. June 22, 1915, Toronto; m. Esther Salomon; d. Nancy Joan Bjarnason, Patricia Susan Rubin, Judith Ann, Sara Beth; res. Toronto.

Now chairman of the Ontario Bicentennial Advisory Commission, Arthur Gelber has long been involved with the arts in Canada. His list of chairmanships includes such organizations as the Ontario Arts Council, the Board of Trustees of the National Arts Centre in Ottawa, the National Ballet of Canada, and the Ontario Conference of the Arts. He has also been on the Board of Directors of the Shaw Festival and the Canadian National Exhibition. He is a Director of the National Theatre School of Canada, the American Council for the Arts, and the Encyclopaedia of Music in Canada. In recognition of his contribution to the arts and to the community (he is also active in the Canadian Jewish Congress and the United Jewish Welfare Fund), Gelber was named an Officer of the Order of Canada (1972), awarded the City of Toronto's Order of Merit (1973), the Centennial Medal, and the Queen's Silver Jubilee Medal and the *Diplôme d'honneur* (1979). Gelber is a life member of both the Art Gallery of Ontario and the Royal Ontario Museum. On top of all these activities he runs the family textile business.

Godard, Mira Marina
B.Sc., M.Sc., M.B.A.

Art dealer, publisher. b. January 31, 1932, Bucharest, Romania; m. Reginald S. Bennett; res. Toronto and Montreal.

Mira Godard's father was the president of a Romanian subsidiary of a Swiss machinery company; her family left Romania for Switzerland in 1948, then moved to Paris where she attended the Sorbonne and eventually earned her *certificat de mathématiques supérieures.* In 1950 she moved with her family to Montreal. She studied at Sir George Williams University (now Concordia University) and McGill, where in 1958 she received her M.B.A. A year later she became a supervisor of the precision measurement labs at Montreal's Aviation Electric. In 1961, Mira Godard purchased the Agnes Lefort Gallery in Montreal and began her distinguished career as an art dealer, showing both radical kinds of contemporary painting (Borduas was a gallery mainstay) and giving their first one-man exhibitions to both Jean-Paul Lemieux and Arthur Lismer. She eventually closed her Montreal gallery (Gallery Godard-Lefort) to open (in partnership with international art mogul Frank Lloyd of Marlborough in New York) the Marlborough Godard Gallery in Toronto in 1972. Godard severed her partnership with Lloyd in 1977 after Mark Rothko's daughter sued him over the handling of her father's estate. Godard became the sole owner of the Mira Godard Gallery. She opened a Calgary branch in 1981. She is now the exclusive Canadian dealer for such artists as Alex Colville and Christopher Pratt (whose work she helped to publish in a sumptuous limited edition produced by the Quintus Press, of which she is one of the five directors). Naturally, she collects—including archaic and prehistoric ceramics, of which she has over 300 examples. She has commissioned a house in Toronto by architect Arthur Erickson and is eagerly awaiting its completion.

Grosskurth, Phyllis
B.A., M.A., Ph.D.

Biographer, literary critic, university professor. b. March 16, 1924, Toronto; née Langstaff; divorced; s. Christopher, Brian, d. Anne; res. Toronto.

Phyllis Grosskurth was educated at St. Clement's School, the University of Toronto, the University of Ottawa, and the University of London, which awarded her a Ph.D. in 1962. She is well-known for her biographies, the first of which, a life of the 19th-century English author John Addington Symonds, was published in 1964 and won both the University of British Columbia's award for biography and a Governor General's Award for non-fiction (1965). Her major biography of Victorian sage and pioneer sexologist Havelock Ellis was published in 1980. She is currently at work on a full-scale biography of psychoanalyst Melanie Klein and her place in the psychoanalytic movement in the first half of this century. Grosskurth has taught at Carleton University and the University of Toronto, where she is a professor in the Department of English Literature. She has received two Guggenheim fellowships, two Laidlaw fellowships, a Rockefeller fellowship, and two Killam scholarships to assist her with her work as a biographer. She is a member of the Toronto Psychoanalytic Society. She collects 14th-century Persian ceramics.

Gustafson, Ralph Barker
B.A., M.A., D.Litt., D.C.L.

Poet. b. August 16, 1909, Lime Ridge, Quebec; m. Elisabeth Renninger; res. North Hatley, Quebec.

Poet Ralph Gustafson was educated at Sherbrooke High School, Sherbrooke, Quebec, and at Bishop's University and Oxford. He began to write poetry early, and won the Venerable Archdeacon Scott's Prize for Poetry while an undergraduate at Bishop's. Gustafson's teaching career includes a term as music master at Bishop's College School in 1930, a time as master at St. Alban's School in Brockville, Ontario, and many years as professor of English Literature and poet-in-residence at Bishop's University (1963-79). A tireless world traveller, he has journeyed, as he puts it, "from Samarkand to Bangkok, from the North Cape to Manapouri," and found in the process "why I live where I do": he is passionately fond of his life in North Hatley, in the scenic Eastern Townships. His first book, *The Golden Chalice* (1935), won the Quebec government's Prix David. Gustafson has published 20 books of poetry, including *Rivers Among Rocks* (1960), *Sift in an Hourglass* (1966), *Ixion's Wheel* (1969), and *Fire on Stone* (1974), which won the Governor General's Award for poetry and the A.J.M. Smith Award of the International Studies Program, Michigan State University. A collection of his selected poems, *The Moment is All*, was published in 1983. Gustafson has also published short stories. His collection, *The Brazen Tower*, was published in 1974; his *The Vivid Air*, in 1980. Gustafson was poetry delegate to the United Kingdom in 1972, to the Soviet Union in 1976, to Washington in 1977, to Italy in 1981 and 1982. He is a founding member of the League of Canadian Poets and a life member of the Keble College Association, Oxford. An enthusiastic musician, he has a fine collection of classical piano music. His favourite summer place, he says, is home; his favourite winter place, "anywhere there is sun." He doesn't have any pastimes: life is too short, he maintains, to go out of your way to pass time.

Gwyn, Richard and Sandra
Journalists; Ottawa

Hailey, Arthur
Writer. b. April 5, 1920, Luton, England; m. Sheila Marjorie Dunlop; d. Jane, s. Roger, John, Mark, Steven; res. Nassau, Bahamas.

Arthur Hailey is the author of numerous best-selling novels that have sold approximately 120 million copies published in 30 languages. The well-known titles include *In High Places* (1962), *Hotel* (1965), *Airport* (1968), *Wheels* (1971), *The Moneychangers* (1975), and *Overload* (1979). Hailey was a pilot in the RAF from 1939 to 1947, leaving as a flight lieutenant. At that time he emigrated to Canada and worked in Toronto as editor of a trade magazine. Many of his novels have been transformed into successful motion pictures—*Airport* (1970) and *Wheels* (1978), for instance—and he is the author of 12 television plays. He is a member of the Authors League of America and the Writers Guild of America and has an honorary life membership in the Association of Canadian TV and Radio Artists. He also enjoys yachting in the Bahamas on his 38-foot Bertram cruiser, *Sheila 11.*

Hall, Amelia
Actor; Toronto

Harper, J. Russell
O.C., B.A., M.A., D.Litt., F.R.S.C.

Art historian. b. April 15, 1914, Caledonia, Ontario; m. Elizabeth Goodchild; d. Jennifer; res. South Lancaster, Ontario.

Russell Harper, Canada's distinguished art historian, attended Hamilton Teacher's College and McMaster University. After spending the years 1942–46 in the RCAF, he entered Victoria College at the University of Toronto. While still a graduate student, he became curator of the Lee Collection in Hart House (1947–50). From 1948 to 1952 he was chief cataloguer for the Royal Ontario Museum in Toronto. In 1952 he became archivist for the New Brunswick Museum in Saint John. From 1957 until 1959, he served as curator of the Lord Beaverbrook Art Collection in Fredericton. In 1959 Harper was made curator of Canadian Art for the National Gallery, a post he held for four years. After this he became curator of the McCord Museum in Montreal. From 1967 to 1979 he taught in the art department of Sir George Williams University in Montreal. Professor Harper is the author of a great many books about Canadian art, the best known of which are his *Painting in Canada: A History* (1966), *Paul Kane's Frontier* (1971), *A People's Art* (1974), and *Krieghoff* (1979). Harper is a fellow of the Royal Society of Canada. He was made an Officer of the Order of Canada in 1975.

Herrndorf, Peter
Broadcasting executive, Toronto

J.R.

Ralph Gustafson at North Hatley, Quebec. Besides being a poet and scholar of English literature, he has a fine collection of classical piano scores and 78 rpm records.

J.R.

Arthur Gelber in his Rosedale house.

Amelia Hall, shown here with Alec Guinness in the 1953 Stratford production of Richard III. She was the first woman to appear on the Festival stage.

Hirsch, John
O.C., Litt.D., LL.D.

Director. b. May 1, 1930, Siofok, Hungary; res. Stratford, Ontario.

Appointed artistic director of the Stratford Festival Theatre in 1980, director John Hirsch has made an energetic and inventive (and often controversial) contribution to almost every aspect of theatre in Canada. He was educated in Budapest and Winnipeg, and has produced and directed plays in Canada and internationally, including work for the Manitoba Theatre Centre, the Crest Theatre in Toronto, Jean Gascon's Théâtre du Nouveau Monde in Montreal, the Lincoln Center Repertory Theater in New York, the Habimah-National Theatre of Israel, the Tyrone Guthrie Theater in Minneapolis, the New York City Opera, the Mark Taper Forum in Los Angeles, the St. Lawrence Centre in Toronto, and, of course, the Stratford Shakespearean Festival. He has been a CBC-TV producer and from 1972 to 1974 was head of CBC-TV Drama. He was founder of Winnipeg's Rainbow Stage and in 1979–80 consulting artistic director for the Seattle Repertory Theater. Mr. Hirsch has been given the Outer Circle Critics Award, the Los Angeles Drama Critics Circle Award, an Obie Award, and the Canada Council's Molson Prize (1977). He was made an Officer of the Order of Canada in 1967. He has honorary degrees from the University of Manitoba and the University of Toronto.

Horne, Arthur Edward Cleeve
R.C.A.

Painter and sculptor. b. January 9, 1912, Jamaica, West Indies; m. Jean Mildred Harris; s. Robert Cleeve, Arthur William, Richard Rowley; res. Toronto.

Cleeve Horne studied at the Ontario College of Art in Toronto. He served in the Second World War and retired with the rank of captain. Best known for his formal portraits of people prominent in business, industry, the military, and government, Horne has also been active as an arts administrator: he has worked to bring together the arts, industry, and government in order to originate important commissions for Canadian artists. He was directly responsible for much of this kind of early art patronage in this country. Horne was president of the Ontario Society of Artists from 1949 to 1951, president of the Arts and Letters Club from 1955 to 1957, and vice-president of the Royal Canadian Academy of Arts Trust Fund. Cleeve Horne's awards include the R.A.I.C. Allied Arts Award (1963), the R.C.A. medal (1965), the Centennial Medal (1967), and the Queen's Silver Jubilee Medal (1977).

Hutchison, Bruce
Writer/journalist; Victoria

Hutt, William
Actor; Stratford, Ontario

Hyland, Frances
Actor; Stratford, Ontario

Isaacs, Avrom
Art dealer; Toronto

Juneau, Pierre
O.C., B.A., LL.D., F.R.S.C.

Public servant. b. October 17, 1922, Verdun, Quebec; m. Fernande Martin; s. André, Martin, d. Isabelle; res. Ottawa.

Pierre Juneau was appointed president of the Canadian Broadcasting Corporation on August 1, 1982. He was educated at the Collège Sainte-Marie in Montreal (B.A., 1944) and at the Sorbonne and the Institut catholique de Paris (graduating as a licentiate in philosophy in 1949). In 1949, he helped found the periodical *Cité libre*. During the early 1950s, he helped to establish La fédération des mouvements de jeunesse au Québec and was its fifth president. He was one of the founders of the Montreal International Film Festival and was the Festival's President from 1959 to 1968. Juneau joined the National Film Board in 1949 and remained with the Board until 1966. He began as the NFB's Montreal district representative and became assistant regional supervisor for Quebec; in 1951 he became chief of International Distribution and, in 1952, assistant head of the European Office in London. In 1954, he was appointed secretary of the NFB and from 1964 to 1966 was senior assistant to the commissioner and director of French Language Production. In 1966, he was appointed vice-chairman of the Board of Broadcast Governors and, in 1968, chairman of the Canadian Radio-television and Telecommunications Commission, a position he held until 1975, when he became minister of Communications. After being defeated in a by-election that year, he served as advisor to the Prime Minister and was made Chairman of the National Capital Commission (1976) and under-secretary of state (1978). In 1980, he was appointed deputy minister of Communications. Juneau is a member of the Board of Directors of the National Arts Centre and of the National Film Board.

Kain, Karen
Dancer; Toronto

Karsh, Yousuf
O.C., D.C.L., LL.D., D.H.L., O.F.A., M.F.A., F.R.P.S., R.C.A.

Photographer. b. December 23, 1908, Mardin, Armenia-in-Turkey; m. Solange Gautier; m. Estrellita Nachbar; res. Ottawa.

In 1924, photographer George Nakash brought his nephews Yousuf and Malak Karsh to Canada. The young Yousuf Karsh attended school in Sherbrooke, Quebec, and then studied in Boston with photographer John H. Garo. In 1932, he opened his now world-famous Ottawa studio. Karsh photographed Winston Churchill in Ottawa in 1941. The photograph appeared on the cover of *Life* magazine and later on postage stamps throughout the countries of the Commonwealth. Karsh's international reputation was secured. Many of his portraits of prominent world figures were reproduced in Karsh's first book, *Faces of Destiny* (1946). Karsh was the first photographer to have a one-man exhibition at the National Gallery (1959) and the only artist to have a one-man exhibition at Expo 67. The Expo show, entitled Men Who Make Our World, was so successful that it has been in more or less continuous circulation ever since. In 1968 it was shown in Montreal and in Boston; in 1969 it went to Detroit and Seattle; during 1971–79, it toured Europe; it was finally (in response to a Japanese request) presented to Japan by the Canadian government, and is now in the permanent collection of the Museum of Modern Art in Tokyo. In 1973, it was exhibited by the National Gallery of Australia; in 1975, by the government of Alberta. Karsh's many publications include *Portraits of Greatness* (1959), *This is the Mass* (1958, 1959), *This is Rome* (1959), *This is the Holy Land* (1960), *These are the Sacraments* (1962), *In Search of Greatness* (an autobiography, 1962), *The Warren Court* (1965), *Faces of Our Time* (1971), *Karsh Portraits* (1976), and *Karsh Canadians* (1978). Karsh has, of course, received many prizes, awards, and honours, such as the Centennial Medal in 1967, the Canada Council Medal in 1969, and the Medal of Service of the Order of Canada in 1968. Karsh is a trustee of the Photographic Arts and Sciences Foundation, an Honorary Fellow of the Royal Photographic Society of Great Britain and a member of the Royal Canadian Academy of Arts. He holds honorary degrees from Queen's University, Carleton University, Mount Allison University, Dartmouth College, Ohio State University, Bishop's University, Emerson College (Boston), the University of Massachusetts, the University of Hartford, Tufts University (Medford, Mass.) and Dawson College (Montreal).

Kattan, Naim
F.R.S.C.

Writer, arts administrator. b. August 26, 1928, Baghdad, Iraq; m. Gaétane Laniel; s. Emmanuel; res. Ottawa and Montreal.

Naim Kattan studied at the Alliance Israélite Universelle Baghdad (Tafayoudh College, Baghdad), the University of Baghdad, and the Sorbonne. At present head of the Creative Writing and Publishing Section of the Canada Council, Kattan has published novels, short stories, and essays. Most of his books have been published in French. *Le réel et le théâtral* (1970) won the Prix France-Canada in 1971, and was published in an English translation in 1972. Other works include *La mémoire et la promesse* (1978), *Ecrivains des Amériques, Tome I Les Etats-Unis, Tome II Le Canada Anglais, Tome III L'Amérique latine* (1980), *La discrétion et autres pièces* (1974), *Dans le désert* (1975), *La Traversée* (1977), *Le Rivage* (1979), *Adieu Babylone* (1976, published in English as *Farewell, Babylon*, 1976), *Les Fruits Arrachés* (1978), and *Le Sable de l'île* (1981). Other titles in English include *Paris Interlude* (1979) and *The Neighbours And Other Stories* (1982). Naim Kattan is a Fellow of the Royal Society of Canada and the Société des Cent Associés.

Keate, James Stuart
O.C., B.A.

Journalist, publisher. b. October 13, 1913, Vancouver; m. Letha Katherine Meilicke; d. Kathryn Jane, s. Richard Stuart; res. Vancouver.

Stu Keate started as a reporter with the Vancouver *Province* and *Toronto Star* and his career in journalism was interrupted only during the war years when he served as a lieutenant-commander in the RCNVR. He worked for

John Hirsch

Karsh by Karsh

Cleeve Horne surrounded by portraits in his Toronto studio.

J.R.

J.R.

Kenojuak at Cape Dorset

TOM SKUDRA

Bruce Kirby with Canada 1 *at Newport.*

BRIAN WILLER

Anton Kuerti at his summer home in Parry Sound, Ontario.

Time in the post-war years and in 1950 was appointed publisher of the *Victoria Daily Times*, leaving in 1964 for a 14-year career as publisher of the *Vancouver Sun*, during which time his paper won the Michener Award "for all-round excellence" and the MacLaren Award for Design as well as numerous national awards for reporting and photography. His autobiography, *Paper Boy*, was published in 1980. During his publishing career he was president of the Canadian Press and of the Canadian Daily Newspapers Association. He has received various honours for his services as a fund raiser. His clubs include the Union in Victoria and the Vancouver.

Kenojuak Ashevak
C.C.

Artist. b. 1927, Ikirisaq, Northwest Territories; m. Johnniebo; six children; res. Cape Dorset, Northwest Territories.

Kenojuak spent the early years of her life living on the land and travelling from camp to camp on south Baffin Island and in northern Quebec. While living in Quetuk in the late 1950s she and her husband began to draw and carve in soapstone, with the encouragement of James Houston. Since then she has gained an international reputation and her work has been featured in several special projects such as the World Wildlife Portfolio (1978) and the Commonwealth Print Portfolio (1978). The recently released book entitled *Graphic Arts of the Inuit: Kenojuak* focuses on her life and art. Other accomplishments include collaboration on a mural that hung in the Canadian Pavilion at Expo 70 in Osaka, Japan, reproduction of her print "Enchanted Owl" on the stamp commemorating the Northwest Territories' centennial, and a trip to Rotterdam in 1980 to attend an Inuit print exhibition. Kenojuak has been awarded several honours; in 1967 she was appointed an Officer of the Order of Canada and in 1982 a Companion.

Kenyon, Walter
Curator, Royal Ontario Museum; Toronto

Kirby, Bruce Robert William
Yacht designer. b. January 2, 1929, Ottawa; m. Margo Dancey; d. Janice Kelly; res. Rowayton, Connecticut.

The man who designed the Laser and *Canada 1* has had no formal training in yacht design. A Canadian citizen living and working in Rowayton, Bruce Kirby arrived at his occupation by way of journalism. After serving as a reporter for the Ottawa *Journal* from 1950 to 1956 and as a copy editor for the *Montreal Star* from 1956 to 1964, he assumed the editor's post at the American-based *Yacht Racing Magazine*. He began designing boats on the side and built a firm reputation among dinghy sailors. The design that made him a household name in nautical circles was the Laser, a high-performance, one-man sailboat, of which there are now approximately 125,000 world-wide. (Kirby owns the first, a definite collector's item.) His commissions have increased in size since his switch to full-time designing. In 1981, with Kirby (a member of Canada's 1968 Olympic sailing team) at the helm, the 40-foot *Runaway*, the largest yacht he had yet created, led the three-boat Canadian team to a sixth-place

finish at England's prestigious Admiral's Cup series. It was the best performance by a Canadian team in the history of the trophy. Soon after, Kirby was asked to design the 63-foot *Canada 1*, Canada's first challenger for the America's Cup in over 100 years, which competed off Newport in the summer of 1983. He is a member of the Society of Naval Architects and Marine Engineers, the Royal Canadian Yacht Club of Toronto, the New York Yacht Club, the Britannia Yacht Club of Ottawa, and the Noroton Yacht Club of Darien, Connecticut. He is the only Canadian among the 20 people world-wide elected to the Yacht Racing Hall of Fame in Newport, Rhode Island.

Kritzweiser, Kay
Art critic/journalist; Toronto

Kuerti, Anton Emil
B.Mus., F.R.H.C.M.

Pianist, teacher, composer. b. July 21, 1938, Vienna; res. Toronto and Parry Sound, Ontario.

Anton Kuerti arrived in the United States in 1944 and, after studying in Boston with Edward Goldman, made his debut when he was only nine playing the Grieg A Minor Piano Concerto with the Boston Pops Orchestra. He studied at the Longy School, Cambridge, Mass., 1948–52; at the Peabody Institute where he studied composition with Henry Cowell, 1952–53; at the Cleveland Institute with Arthur Loesser, 1953–55 (Clevelanders persist in claiming him as theirs); and at the Curtis Institute, where he studied with Rudolf Serkin—whom he lists as one of his most influential teachers—and with the venerable Mieczyslaw Horszowski. While he gave many solo recitals during his student years, and performed annually at the Marboro Festival (1953–56), his professional career really began in 1957 when he won the Philadelphia Orchestra Youth Prize, the National Music League Award, and the prestigious Leventritt Award, which includes engagements with major American orchestras. Anton Kuerti first played with the Toronto Symphony in 1961 as a last-minute replacement for Dame Myra Hess. He settled in Canada in 1965, and since then has performed with most of the world's great orchestras. Although he is an enthusiastic supporter of new music, he is still best known as an authoritative interpreter of Mozart, Beethoven, Schubert, and Mendelssohn, whose music he plays with an intensity and visionary originality that either alienates his listeners or, much more often, has them scrambling for superlatives. Already favourably compared to the legendary pianists of the century, like Kempff, Schnabel, and Horowitz, Kuerti possesses technique that has enormous energy combined with superb control. Kuerti's long association with the University of Toronto began in 1965, the year of his arrival in Canada, when he became pianist-in-residence. In 1968 he was made an associate professor (until 1972) and thereafter the University of Toronto's artist-in-residence. In 1971, Kuerti returned to the composing he had begun as a student. His *Linden Suite* for piano was written that year, and followed by *Magog* for cello and piano (1972), *String Quartet No.2* (1972), *Symphony "Epomeo"* (1973), *Violin Sonata* (1973), and *Six Arrows* for piano (1973). His current project is his Festival of the

Sound at Parry Sound, on Georgian Bay, an international-class summer music festival that Kuerti is gradually building and fine tuning.

Laing, Blair
Art dealer; Toronto

Landry, Roger D.
Newspaper publisher. b. January 26, 1934, Montreal; m. Suzanne Shepherd; s. Charles, d. Johane, Geneviève; res. Montreal.

Roger Landry's route to the position of president and publisher of the Montreal newspaper *La Presse* was an unconventional one by way of junior hockey in the Canadiens organization, studies at the London School of Economics, marketing at Bell Canada, and the Quebec Provincial Police. He was an inspector with the QPP from 1963 to 1965, responsible for transport and communications. He was a deputy director of Expo 67 and in 1970 set up a public relations company, which he left in 1975 to join Rayonier Québec, a subsidiary of ITT. In 1977 he took charge of marketing and public affairs for the Montreal Expos baseball club and in 1980 he joined *La Presse* as executive vice-president, becoming president and publisher at Quebec's largest daily in 1981.

Lansdowne, James Fenwick
Wildlife artist; Victoria

Laurence, Margaret
C.C., B.A., D.Litt., LL.D., D.Litt.S., F.R.S.C.

Writer. b. July 18, 1926, Neepawa, Manitoba; divorced; d. Jocelyn, s. David; res. Lakefield, Ontario.

Margaret Laurence is one of Canada's most distinguished writers. She was educated at United College (now part of the University of Winnipeg). In 1949 she moved to Africa, living for a time in Somaliland and in Ghana. Her experiences in Africa led to her first books: *A Tree of Poverty* (1954), an anthology of Somali literature; *The Prophet's Camel Bell* (1963), an account of her life in Somaliland; *The Tomorrow-Tamer* (1963), a collection of short stories set in Ghana; and her first novel, *This Side Jordan* (1960), which won the Beta Sigma Phi First Novel Award for 1961. Her book of critical writings, *Long Drums and Cannons* (1971), is a study of Nigerian literature. In 1957, Margaret Laurence left Africa to live in England, and from 1957 until 1970 divided her time between England and Canada. In 1970 she settled in Lakefield, near Peterborough. Her novel *The Stone Angel* (1964) is an acknowledged classic, though she may still be better known for her *A Jest of God* (1966), which won the Governor General's Award for fiction in 1967 and was filmed in the United States as *Rachel, Rachel*. In 1969 she published *The Fire-Dwellers*, in 1970 *A Bird in the House* (a collection of interrelated short stories), and in 1974 *The Diviners*—for which she was given her second Governor General's Award for fiction (1975). Margaret Laurence has written extensively for children as well, including *Jason's Quest* (1969), *The Olden Days Coat* (1979), *Six Darn Cows* (1979), and *The Christmas Birthday Story* (1980). Laurence was awarded the President's Medal of the University of Western Ontario in 1961,

Margaret Laurence

All the people in this photo were acting at the Stratford Festival in 1956, but the reason for the picture is that they had all worked with Amelia Hall during her time as artistic director of the Canadian Repertory Theatre in Ottawa. Back row, left to right: William Shatner, Christopher Plummer, Richard Easton, Donald Davis, William Hutt. Front row: David Gardner, Max Helpmann, Amelia Hall, Eric House, Bruce Swerdfager (now general manager of the St. Lawrence Centre in Toronto). Immediately behind Amelia Hall is Ted Follows.

Blair Laing at his Bloor Street, Toronto, gallery with a Monet from his personal collection.

312

1962, and 1964. She was made a Fellow of the Royal Society of Canada in 1977. She has received 13 honorary degrees from Canadian universities. From 1981 to 1983 she was chancellor of Trent University.

Layton, Irving

O.C., B.Sc., M.A., D.C.L., D.Litt.

Poet. b. March 12, 1912, Neamitz, Romania; m. Harriet Bernstein; d. Samantha Clara; m. Aviva Cantor; s. David; m. Betty Frances Sutherland; s. Max, d. Naomi; res. Oakville, Ontario.

Irving Layton was brought to this country by his parents in 1913. He was educated at Baron Byng High School in Montreal and at McGill University. An enormously prolific poet, Layton published his first volume, *Here and Now*, in 1945. Since then he has produced over 30 volumes, including *Red Carpet for the Sun* (which won the Governor General's Award for poetry in 1960), *Balls for a One-Armed Juggler* (1963), *For My Brother Jesus* (1976), and *The Gucci Bag* (1983). In 1963 he edited a volume of Canadian love lyrics called *Love Where the Nights Are Long*, with pictures by Harold Town. His poems have been translated into Romanian, Polish, Russia, Korean, Spanish, and Italian. In 1982, he was nominated by Italy and Korea for the Nobel Prize in Literature. Irving Layton has been poet-in-residence or writer-in-residence at the University of Guelph, Concordia University, the University of Ottawa, and the University of Toronto. He is at present professor of English Literature at York University. Layton lists "social intercourse" as his favourite recreation and suggests that his "helping to make Canadians less stuffy and repressed" is his chief achievement, along with "inspiring countless young Canadians to forsake their religious, political, and social superstitions."

Lemelin, Roger

C.C., LL.D., Litt.D., F.R.S.C.

Writer, publisher. b. April 7, 1919, Quebec City; m. Valéda Lavigueur; s. Pierre, Jacques, André, d. Diane, Sylvia; res. Cap-Rouge, Quebec.

Roger Lemelin, appointed president and publisher of Montreal's *La Presse* in 1972, left the paper in 1981 to devote his time entirely to his writing career. The eldest in a family of 10 boys, he left school at the age of 15 and from that time on relied totally on self-education. He is the author of numerous novels, short stories, and essays and is perhaps best known for *Les Plouffes* (1948). He transformed his Plouffe family saga into a weekly bilingual CBC series (1953-59), as well as a film and a television mini-series. Lemelin has been honoured with doctorates from the University of Windsor and Laurentian University. He has also received two Guggenheim fellowships, the Prix de la Langue Français (France), is a Fellow of the Royal Society of Canada (1949), a Canadian member of l'Académie Goncourt (1974), and a Companion of the Order of Canada (1980). He is an avid chess player and was responsible for organizing the 1979 chess tournament at Man and His World in Montreal, which pitted the world's top 10 chess players against each other for the most prize money ever awarded to a chess champion.

Lemieux, Jean-Paul

C.C., R.C.A.

Artist. b. November 18, 1904, Quebec City; m. Madeleine Desrosiers; d. Anne, Sophie; res. Charlevoix, Quebec.

Admired widely for his haunting depictions of man alone in a sometimes inhospitable universe, Lemieux received his early training in Montreal, at Loyola College and at L'Ecole des Beaux-Arts, where he studied for three years under Charles Maillard and Edwin Holgate. In 1929, while visiting Paris, Lemieux met Quebec artist Clarence Gagnon who was then working on his illustrations for *Maria Chapdelaine*. Lemieux decided to live and work near Gagnon in Montparnasse. In 1930 he returned to Montreal, set up a commercial art studio (which the Depression summarily closed down again), and in 1934 began teaching at his alma mater, L'Ecole des Beaux-Arts. After a brief sojourn at the nearby Ecole du Meuble, Lemieux moved to teach at L'Ecole des Beaux-Arts de Québec in Quebec City, and began to paint more seriously. In 1941, he painted his now famous *Lazare* (owned by the Art Gallery of Ontario). This painting started him in the direction he would follow for the next decade: a sort of mock primitivism with overtones of social and religious criticism and unrest that would come to be regarded as quintessentially québecois. In 1954 Lemieux won a Canada Council Scholarship to study in France for a year, but he felt that the year was unaccountably wasteful and unproductive. When he returned gratefully to Quebec City, he began to paint the lonely and poignant figures in the landscape on which his reputation now rests. About them he once said, "I am especially interested in conveying the solitude of man and the ever-flowing passing of time. I try to express in my landscapes and my figures this solitude, this silence in which we all move." In 1965, Lemieux finally retired from teaching to spend his time painting—mostly near Ile-aux-Coudres, Quebec. In 1967, the Montreal Museum of Fine Arts mounted a lavish retrospective consisting of 108 of his pictures. A year later he was made a Companion of the Order of Canada.

Letendre-Eloul, Rita

R.C.A.

Artist. b. November 1, 1928, Drummondville, Quebec; m. Kosso Eloul; res. Toronto.

Rita Letendre is one of Canada's most prolific painters and one of the most frequently commissioned as a decorator of large public spaces. She studied at the Ecole des Beaux-Arts in Montreal and later with Paul-Emile Borduas, with whose Automatistes she was at first linked. Her later work has become increasingly clean and geometric and deals almost exclusively with the effects of wedges of pure colour in hot juxtaposition. Large outdoor commissions include her mural "Sunforce" at California State University at Long Beach (1965) and her famous (and highly visible) "Sunrise" at Toronto's Ryerson Polytechnical Institute (1971). One of her best-known works is a skylight dome mural that comprises the entire roof of the Glencairn Station of the Toronto subway system (1977). Rita Letendre is represented in the collections of Canada's public galleries and in many important private collections. She has received awards and prizes, including Le Prix Rodolphe de Repentigny

(Montreal, 1960), the Canadian National Exhibition First Prize in Painting (1968), and the Festival International de Peinture Cagnes sur Mer (Prix National, 1970). She is married to internationally known Israeli sculptor Kosso Eloul. She also cultivates orchids and creates gourmet meals.

Lightfoot, Gordon

Singer/songwriter; Toronto

McClelland, John Gordon

O.C., B.A.

Publisher. b. 1922, Toronto; m. Elizabeth Matchett; s. Robert, d. Sarah, Anne, Suzanne Drinkwater, Carol McCabe; res. Kleinburg, Ontario.

Jack McClelland is Canada's best-known publisher—both because he has been unfailingly supportive of new Canadian writers (many of whom have become, over the years, the country's senior writers) and because he has been supportive of Canadian writing in extraordinarily flamboyant ways. Determined to put Canadian books on the map—financially as well as esthetically—he has piloted his often beleaguered company, McClelland and Stewart Limited, with the same verve and abandon he did as a motor torpedo boat commander during the Second World War. As a publisher, he has "sailed his leaky ship of a company through seas that would sink anyone else," to quote his crony, Farley Mowat. Educated at St. Andrew's College in Aurora, Ontario, and at the University of Toronto, in 1952 Jack McClelland took over the publishing business begun in 1906 by his father, John McClelland. He resigned from the presidency of M&S in 1982 but stayed on as chairman. He is also president of the paperback publishing company Seal Books. McClelland has been awarded the Banff Medal, the Centennial Medal, and has been made an Officer of the Order of Canada. He belongs to the Granite Club and the Muskoka Lakes Golf & Country Club.

McConnell, Robert

Vice-President, Product Development, Southam Inc., Toronto

MacLennan, Hugh

C.C., B.A., M.A., Ph.D., D.Litt., D.C.L., L.L.D., F.R.S.C.

Writer, teacher. b. March 20, 1907, Glace Bay, Nova Scotia; m. Frances Aline Walker; m. Dorothy Duncan (deceased); res. Montreal.

Hugh MacLennan was educated at the Halifax Academy and Dalhousie University. He was a Rhodes scholar representing Canada at large (1928). He received his M.A. from Oxford and his Ph.D. from Princeton. MacLennan was a Guggenheim Fellow in 1943-44, and was awarded an LL.D. from Dalhousie University in 1955 — the first of nineteen honorary degrees from Canadian universities. He was made Companion of the Order of Canada in 1967. He has written seven novels, most of which have been translated into a variety of languages. He is probably best known for his novel about the great Halifax explosion, *Barometer Rising* (1941), his study of English-French tensions in Quebec, *Two Solitudes* (1945), and for his vast panoramic novel about life and politics in Montreal during the days of the Spanish Civil

War, *The Watch That Ends the Night* (1959)—for which he was given his third Governor General's Award. His other novels are *The Precipice* (1948), *Each Man's Son* (1951), *The Return of the Sphinx* (1967), and *Voices in Time* (1980). His non-fiction works include *Oxyrhynchus: An Economic and Social Study* (1935), *Cross Country* (1954), *Thirty and Three* (1954), *Scotchman's Return and Other Essays* (1960), *Seven Rivers of Canada* (1961), and *The Colour of Canada* (1967). In 1952, he was awarded the Lorne Pierce Gold Medal for literature by the Royal Society of Canada, of which he is an Associate Fellow. Hugh MacLennan is Professor Emeritus in the Department of English Literature at McGill University. He spends his summers in North Hatley, in the Eastern Townships of Quebec. He is a connoisseur of roses and is fond of sailing. He regards winning the tennis singles championship of the Maritime provinces as his chief achievement—in addition to his writing and 31 years of teaching at McGill.

McMichael, Robert Alliston
C.M., D.Litt.

Art administrator. b. July 21, 1921, Toronto; m. Signe Kirstin Sorensen; res. Belfountain, Ontario.

Robert McMichael grew up in Toronto and in 1940 was the co-founder of the *Canadian High News*, a paper aimed at secondary schools. After service with the Royal Canadian Navy from 1943 to 1946 he went into direct-mail advertising; in 1954 he began to assemble the vast collection of classic Canadian landscape paintings, most of which were by Canada's famous Group of Seven, and works of Canadian native art that is today known as the McMichael Canadian Collection. The collection is housed in a large gallery of eccentric and homespun design in Kleinburg, Ontario, where it has been a popular mecca for tourists. McMichael is now the gallery's director emeritus. He was made a Member of the Order of Canada in 1974. He is also a Fellow of the Ontario College of Art, a lifetime member of the Ontario Society of Artists, and an honorary patron of the Sculptor's Society of Canada. His honorary doctorate is from York University in Toronto.

Maillet, Antonine
Writer; Montreal

Mansouri, Lotfollah
Musician, opera director. b. June 15, 1929, Tehran, Iran; m. Marjorie Anne Thompson; d. Shireen; res. Toronto.

Lotfi Mansouri came to North America in 1950 from his native Iran when, as he puts it, a childhood passion for unashamed Hollywood entertainments. He enrolled at UCLA at 21 and, as he possessed a good tenor voice, began to study singing. As an undergraduate, he worked as a "super" in west-coast opera productions and enjoyed himself as a performer in cabaret (a couple of times with the equally young Carol Burnett). He also began to direct. In 1957 Mansouri appeared in a made-for-television movie about Enrico Caruso. A year later, he was in Europe, determined to hear grand opera at its best. In 1959, Mansouri became assistant to Herbert Graf, head of the Zurich Opera. In 1966, he became chief stage director of the

Geneva Opera—a post he held until 1975 when Herman Geiger-Torel of Canada's Royal Conservatory of Music hired him to work with the burgeoning Canadian Opera Company (which had just celebrated its 25th anniversary). In 1977, Mansouri succeeded Geiger-Torel as the COC's general director. A mercurial and innovative showman as well as a businessman, Mansouri led the COC into a series of demanding contemporary works (Alban Berg's *Wozzeck* in 1978 and his *Lulu* in 1980). He delighted music lovers by persuading Birgit Nilsson to sing in North America for the first time in five years and by luring Dame Joan Sutherland to make her first appearance in Toronto in *Norma*. Sympathetic to the struggles of operatic newcomers, Mansouri established the Canadian Opera Company Ensemble in 1981. The Ensemble pays its young members a year-round salary. Recently Mansouri staged and directed the opera house sequences for MGM's film *Yes, Giorgio!* starring Luciano Pavarotti. He is the co-author (with Aviva Layton) of his autobiography *Lotfi, An Operatic Life* (1982). Mansouri is an indefatigable party-giver and enjoys cooking Iranian specialties for his guests. He loves old movies, Broadway shows, and all show business.

Mirvish, Ed
Patron of the performing arts; Toronto

Mitchell, William Ormond
Writer; Calgary

Moore, James Mavor
O.C., B.A., D.Litt., LL.D.

Playwright, actor, producer, critic, university professor, arts administrator. b. March 18, 1919, Toronto; m. Alexandra Browning; d. Jessica; m. Phyllis Langstaff Grosskurth; m. Darwina Faessler; d. Dorothea, Rosalind, Marieli, Charlotte

Mavor Moore is an entertainment polymath whose interests range from Shakespeare to musical comedy. He attended the University of Toronto Schools and then the University of Toronto; he received his B.A. in 1941. That year, Moore became a feature producer with CBC radio, leaving only to take up his duties as captain with Canadian Army Intelligence (psychological warfare officer). In 1944-45, he worked in the CBC's International Service and in 1946 became a senior producer for the CBC's Pacific Region. In 1947 he was connected with the United Nations' Information Division, becoming in 1948 chairman of the Radio Section of UNESCO's World Seminar on Education. In 1950 Moore began working in television. It was in the 1950s as well that he seems to have become most absorbed by theatre. In 1949, he wrote the musical review *Who's Who*. From 1948 to 1957 (and then again in 1961-65), Moore produced and directed the famous annual *Spring Thaw* reviews. In 1959-60 he wrote a regular column of drama criticism for the *Toronto Telegram* and in 1960 became the founding chairman of the Canadian Theatre Centre. He was also a member of the first Board of Governors for the Stratford Shakespearean Festival. In 1964 he helped to establish the Charlottetown Festival as founding director. Two years later he became general director of the Cultural Committee for the National Centennial Conference (1966-67)

and from 1965 to 1969 was general director of Toronto's St. Lawrence Centre. In 1974 he was appointed a member of the Canada Council (of which he became chairman). In 1977, he founded the Guild of Canadian Playwrights. He is the author—with various composers—of musical comedies and musical reviews. Moore's writings for the stage include *Sunshine Town* (1954), *The Best of All Possible Worlds* (1956), *The Ottawa Man* (1958), *Johnny Belinda* (1966, with composer John Fenwick), the opera *Louis Riel* (1967, with composer Harry Somers), *Abracadabra* (1978, with composer Harry Freedman), and *Fauntleroy* (1980, with composer Johnny Burke). Moore was awarded the Centennial Medal in 1967 and was made an Officer of the Order of Canada in 1973. Not unexpectedly he lists music as his favourite recreation and belongs to the Arts and Letters Club. He has somehow contrived to live on Moore Avenue in Toronto.

Moriyama, Raymond
B.Arch., M.Arch., LL.D., D.Eng., F.R.A.I.C., M.C.I.P., R.C.A., F.R.S.A.

Architect. b. October 11, 1929, Vancouver; m. Sachi Miyauchi; s. Mark-Michi, Jason-Jun, Adrian-Keiju, d. Murina-Lei, Selena-Midori; res. Toronto.

Ray Moriyama began his career in 1958 after studying architecture at the University of Toronto and McGill. Known for his imaginative and original blending of occidental and oriental design ideas (his Japanese Cultural Centre in Don Mills, Ontario, is an important example), Moriyama has established as his trademark buildings with a delicate and pervasive use of light and a refreshingly intimate sense of space (even in buildings in which the volumes are immense). Among his best-known buildings are Toronto's Ontario Science Centre (1969), Scarborough Civic Centre (1973), and Metropolitan Toronto Library (1977). He has won numerous architectural and design awards, including the Canadian Architects Award of Excellence, the Prestressed Concrete Institute Award, and the Ontario Masons' Relation Council Award. He has won the Governor General's Award for architecture and the Civic Award of Merit from the City of Toronto. Moriyama is in considerable demand as a speaker and has lectured at universities in Canada, the United States, and Japan. He is a member of the Ontario Association of Architects and a director of MTV, Toronto's multilingual television station. He is also a talented painter.

Mowat, Farley
O.C., B.A., D.Litt.

Writer. b. May 12, 1921, Belleville, Ontario; m. Claire Angel Wheeler; m. Frances Elizabeth Thornhill; s. Robert Alexander, David Peter; res. Port Hope, Ontario, and River Bourgeois, Nova Scotia.

Farley Mowat is one of Canada's most widely read writers. He was educated at public and high schools in Trenton and Windsor in Ontario, in Saskatoon, and at the University of Toronto. Mowat served in the Second World War in the Canadian Infantry as a platoon commander and intelligence officer with the Hastings and Prince Edward Regiment in Sicily and in Northwestern Europe. He described the experience in an early book, *The Regiment* (1955), and again in his war memoir, *And No*

Jack McClelland

Hugh MacLennan

Lotfi Mansouri

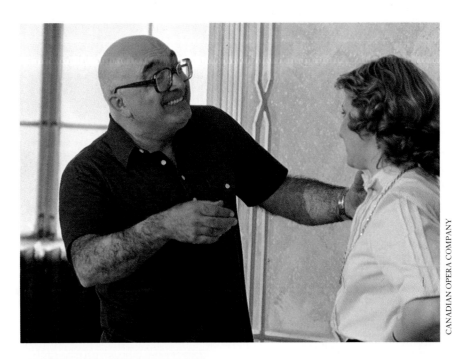

Mavor Moore

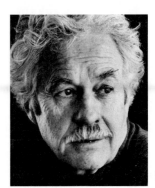

W.O. Mitchell

Farley Mowat

Birds Sang (1979). He began to write steadily after a trip to the Canadian Arctic in 1947-48. The first result was his still popular *People of the Deer* (1951). *The Regiment* followed, and, after that, a book for young readers called *Lost in the Barrens*, which won the Governor General's Award for juvenile literature in 1956. In 1957 Mowat wrote the first of his series of charming, small-scale comedy-memoirs, *The Dog Who Wouldn't Be*, following it with *The Grey Seas Under* (1958). After that his books, many of them quite ambitious studies in popular anthropology and cultural history, appeared with dizzying frequency: *Coppermine Journey* (1958), *The Desperate People* (1959), *Ordeal by Ice* (1960), *Owls in the Family* (1961), *The Serpent's Coil* (1961), *The Black Joke* (1962), *Never Cry Wolf* (1963), *Westviking* (1965), *The Curse of the Viking Grave* (1966), *The Polar Passion* (1967), *Canada North* (1967), *The Rock Within the Sea* (with John de Visser, 1968), *The Boat Who Wouldn't Float* (1969, winner of the Stephen Leacock Award for Humour), *Sibir* (1970), *A Whale for the Killing* (1972), *Wake of the Great Sealers* (1972, with artist David Blackwood), *Tundra* (1973), *The Snow Walker* (1975), *Canada North Now* (1976), *And No Birds Sang* (1979), *The World of Farley Mowat* (1980, an anthology of Mowat's best writing). Mowat spends his summers in River Bourgeois, where the boat who wouldn't float still doesn't.

Munro, Alice

Writer; Clinton, Ontario

Murray, Anne

O.C., B.P.E., D.Litt.

Singer. b. June 20, 1945, Springhill, Nova Scotia; m. William Langstroth; s. William Stewart, d. Dawn Joanne; res. Thornhill, Ontario.

One of Canada's most popular entertainers, Anne Murray is also well known for her TV commercials for the Canadian Imperial Bank of Commerce. After graduating from the University of New Brunswick, she taught high-school physical education in Summerside, P.E.I. In 1966 she joined CBC Halifax's *Singalong Jubilee* as a member of the chorus. Her rise to stardom began in 1970 with the success of her recording "Snowbird." With three Grammy Awards, 19 Juno Awards, a star in Hollywood's Walkway of Stars, and numerous CBC and American network television specials, Murray has garnered an international following. She has been honoured in Canada with a Vanier Medal as an outstanding young Canadian and is an Officer of the Order of Canada (1974). Her production company promotes the careers of other Canadian entertainers, including her brother Bruce and John Allan Cameron. She is the honorary chairperson of both the Canadian Association for the Mentally Retarded and the Canadian Save the Children Fund.

Myers, Barton

B.Sc.Eng., M.Arch., F.R.A.I.C., A.I.A., R.C.A.

Architect. b. November 6, 1934, Norfolk, Virginia; m. Victoria George; d. Suzanne Lewis; res. Toronto.

Barton Myers attended the Norfolk Academy and the U.S. Naval Academy, became a jet fighter pilot for the U.S. Air Force (1956-61), and after receiving his Master's degree in archi-tecture in 1964 from the University of Pennsylvania, worked in Philadelphia with the late Louis Kahn. He moved to Canada in 1968 to join the Faculty of Architecture at the University of Toronto. He was a principal in the Toronto firm of Diamond and Myers, Architects and Planners (1968-75) and founded Barton Myers Associates in 1975. Among the significant projects of Barton Myers Associates are the Seagram Museum in Waterloo, Ontario, the Multicultural Center in Los Angeles (one of the new cultural buildings sited in Exposition Park as part of the 1984 Olympics), and Edmonton's award-wining Citadel Theatre. Myers is the director of the team of 10 leading architects collaborating on the Maguire Partners Proposal for the Bunker Hill Competition for downtown Los Angeles; he is also the designer of the proposed project's 40-story condominium garden tower and terraced housing units. Myers pioneered the development in Toronto in "infill housing," the low-rise, high-density public housing which preserves 19th-century houses (as in the Sherbourne Lanes project). A sought-after teacher, Myers is a professor in the Graduate School of Architecture and Planning at the University of California at Los Angeles; he has been a visiting professor at the Harvard Graduate School of Design, has taught at the University of Pennsylvania, the University of Waterloo, and at the Ontario College of Art. He has also been appointed Thomas Jefferson Professor of Architecture at the University of Virginia. Myers has been an editor for *Architecture Canada*, a member of the Advisory Committee for Design, National Capital Commission, Ottawa; he edited "Vacant Lottery" (an issue of the Walker Art Centre's *Design Quarterly*), and was a founding director of Canada's late architectural review, *Trace*. He is a member of the Royal Canadian Academy of Art, Heritage Canada, and the Society of Architectural Historians.

Nankivell, Neville J.

Editor-in-chief, The Financial Post; Toronto

Oliphant, Betty

O.C., LL.D., F.I.S.T.D.

Ballet teacher, arts administrator. b. August 5, 1918, London; divorced; d. Gail Marion, Carol Ann; res. Toronto.

At present artistic director and ballet principal for the National Ballet School, Betty Oliphant attended the Queen's and St. Mary's College Schools in London, then studied ballet with Tamara Karsavina in London from 1925 to 1933. She was a dancer and dance arranger for dance companies in London before founding her own ballet school there in 1936. She came to Toronto in 1947, establishing the Betty Oliphant School of Ballet in Toronto (1948-49) and becoming ballet mistress for the National Ballet of Canada (1951-62), for which she was associate artistic director from 1962 to 1975. She established the National Ballet School in 1959 and has remained its president. In 1967, she was invited to reorganize the Ballet School of the Royal Swedish Opera. In 1978 she was asked to do the same for the Ballet School of the Royal Danish Theatre. In 1969 she attended the First International Ballet competition in Moscow as the guest of honour of the Soviet Union and in both 1977 and 1981 was a member of the jury for the competition. She has received numerous awards and honours including honorary degrees from Queen's University, Brock University, and the University of Toronto. She was awarded the Centennial Medal and the Molson Prize of the Canada Council (1978). She was made an Officer of the Order of Canada in 1973 and was given the *Diplôme d'honneur* of the Canadian Conference of the Arts in 1982.

Onley, Norman Anthony

R.C.A.

Artist. b. November 20, 1928, Douglas, Isle of Man; m. Yukiko Kageyama; m. Mary Burrows; d. Jennifer, Lynn; m. Gloria Knight; s. James Anthony; res. Vancouver.

Toni Onley began his career in Canadian art in the early 1960s as an abstract-expressionist, making his earliest reputation with large vigorous free-form canvas collages. Only in the late 1960s did he begin to make the delicate naturalistic watercolours (simplified, but atmospherically accurate) of the Canadian North and the far West on which his high reputation rests. Onley received his earliest art training in the Isle of Man. In Canada, he studied at the Doon School of Fine Art near Kitchener, Ontario, in 1951. He received a scholarship in 1956 to study in Mexico. As skillful a print maker as he is a painter, Onley has incorporated in all his pictures (especially, perhaps, in his silkscreens) a kind of sparseness and deftness that is partly a result of his admiration for oriental art techniques and philosophies. As enthusiastic a pilot as he is a delineator of the poetic emptiness of the Canadian wilderness, Onley uses his airplanes (he owns two) to fly to remote locations for sketching and for making *plein air* watercolours. He is represented in a number of important art collections (including the Tate Galley and the Victoria and Albert Museum). It was in 1980, Onley likes to point out, that his entire collection of his own works was sold privately for a record-breaking $930,000, a sale he is sure the largest single sale of works by a living artist. "This was not an artistic achievement," Onley noted, "but the money bought me a great deal of time to paint." It also bought him a 1980 Silver Shadow II Rolls-Royce. His favourite summer place he says, is Georgian Bay; he lists his favourite winter place as "somewhere to dry my watercolours in the sun."

The Orford String Quartet

The Orford String Quartet was formed in 1965 by four men who had met at the Orford Art Centre of the Jeunesses Musicales on Mount Orford in Quebec. The Quartet was made up of Andrew Dawes (first violin), Kenneth Perkins (second violin), Terence Helmer (viola), and Marcel St-Cyr (cello). In 1980, Marcel St-Cyr was replaced by Denis Brott. The quartet gave its auspicious first concert at the Orford Art Centre on August 11, 1965. This was followed almost immediately by an ambitious schedule of successful recitals all over Canada and in major music centres abroad. An extremely well-received concert at Carnegie Hall in New York on November 23, 1967, marked the beginning of the Quartet's international career. The Quartet was invited to play at Expo 67. In 1968 it became the quartet-in-residence at the University of Toronto. In 1976, the Quartet played at the

Toni Onley and his wife Yukiko. The aircraft is a Polish Wilga 80 equipped for glacier flying.

John Parkin in the new Bell Canada building on Bay Street in Toronto. The sculpture is by Gino Lorcini.

J.R.

J.R.

Christopher Pratt with model Donna Meaney of St. Mary's Bay.

CANAPRESS PHOTO SERVICE

Oscar Peterson

BRIAN WILLER

Mordecai Richler

Montreal Olympics and in 1977 it appeared at the Musicanada festival in London. From 1971 to 1974, the members of the Quartet served as faculty at the Kelso Music Centre near Toronto. The Quartet also continued to give both classes and concerts at the Orford Art Centre. The Orford String Quartet received the Molson Prize in 1975. In 1976, it appeared at the United Nations' Habitat Conference in Vancouver. Best known for its superlative readings of Beethoven string quartets and later for the quartets of Mozart, the Orford String Quartet has accumulated an impressive repertoire of both traditional and contemporary works. Typical of the enthusiasm it generates is John Pearce's remark in *Maclean's* magazine (April 18, 1983) that their "fusion of the instruments is so intense that the music appears seamless, the product of one heart and mind." Their playing "has a fastidious cleanliness, a natural pulse and a classical poise and elegance."

Papineau-Couture, Jean
O.C., B.A., B.Mus., D.Mus., LL.D.

Musician, composer, educator. b. November 12, 1916, Montreal; m. Isabelle Baudouin; d. Nadia, Ghilaine, s. François; res. Montreal.

Jean Papineau-Couture is the grandson of Guillaume Couture, one of Canada's first composers and conductors. Papineau-Couture's musical training began in 1940 at the famous New England Conservatory in Boston and during 1941–43 with Nadia Boulanger at the Longy School in Cambridge, Massachusetts, where he composed his first serious work, his *Eclogues*, 1942. In 1945 he returned to Montreal to take up a teaching post at Brébeuf College (in charge of piano studies), switching the next year to the newly established Conservatoire de musique du Québec à Montréal. From 1951 on, he was also a member of the faculty at the University of Montreal, where he taught until 1963. From 1968 to 1973 he was dean of Music at the University of Montreal, and a "pioneer in the development of a course on musical acoustics based on the physical principles of resonance reapplied to the evolution of musical composition." From 1976 until 1978, Papineau-Couture was vice-president and then president of the Humanities Research Council of Canada. He has been active in music and arts administration in Quebec over the past 40 years: in 1962-63, he was president of the Académie de musique de Québec; from 1956 to 1964, President of the Montreal Branch of the Jeunesses musicales du Canada; founder of the Canadian Music Centre (and its president in 1973-74); president (1957-59 and 1963-66) of the Canadian League of Composers; and founder-member (and president, 1966-72) of the Société de musique contemporaine du Québec. In 1962, he was awarded the Prix de musique Calixa-Lavallée and in 1973 the Canadian Music Council's Medal. He was made an Officer of the Order of Canada in 1969. He has an honorary doctorate of music from the University of Chicago (1960) and an LL.D. from the University of Saskatchewan (1967). Gilles Manny's recording of Papineau-Couture's Piano Concerto was awarded the Prix du Festival du disque canadien in 1969.

Parkin, John Cresswell
C.C., B.Arch., M.Arch., D.Eng., D.Sc., P.M.L.J., F.R.A.I.C., F.R.I.B.A., R.C.A.

Architect. b. March 24, 1922, Sheffield, England; m. Jeanne Warmith; s. John Cresswell Jr., Geoffrey Cresswell, d. Jennifer Ann Cresswell; res. Toronto

Educated at the University of Manitoba and at Harvard University, John C. Parkin established his architectural practice in Toronto in 1947. From then until 1968, he was partner-in-charge of design for John B. Parkin Associates (headed by an unrelated namesake); from 1968 until 1971, senior and managing partner for Parkin Architects, Engineers, Planners. Best known for a long series of public buildings in Canada, the Parkin firm designed and oversaw the construction of, for example, both terminals of the Toronto International Airport, the Art Gallery of Ontario, Ottawa's Union Station, Toronto's Humber Memorial Hospital, and the refurbishing of Parkin's alma mater, the University of Manitoba. John Parkin is a Companion of the Order of Canada, a Fellow of the Royal Architectural Institute of Canada, a Fellow of the Royal Institute of British Architects, and a Fellow of the Royal Society of Arts. He is a life member of the Association of Canadian Industrial Designers, past president of the Canadian Conference of the Arts (1955–58), an associate member of the Board of Trustees of the Art Gallery of Ontario, and was chairman of the Architects Advisory Board of Expo 67 in Montreal. He is founding chairman and co-author of enabling legislation for the National Design Council (1959-61) and was a member of the jury for the government of the United Kingdom Commonwealth Competition for the addition to the Houses of Parliament at Westminster in 1968-72. He is past president of the Royal Canadian Academy of Arts (1970-80). Parkin is an ardent supporter of the arts (especially the visual arts) in Canada and lists among his leisure activities the tending of a large collection of North American paintings, drawings, and sculptures. He is the recipient of a number of honorary degrees and awards including an honorary doctorate in science from McGill University (1979) and an honorary doctorate in Engineering from the Technical University of Nova Scotia in Halifax (1977). He was awarded the Centennial Medal in 1967, the Queen's Silver Jubilee Medal in 1977, and the Royal Canadian Institute's Gold Medal in 1979. Since 1982, he has been Prior for Canada of the Military and Hospitaller Order of St. Lazarus of Jerusalem. He belongs to the York Club and the Granite Club in Toronto, the Rideau Club in Ottawa, and the Mount Royal Club in Montreal, among others.

Pellan, Alfred
C.C., LL.D., Litt.D.

Artist. b. May 16, 1906, Quebec City; m. Maddalena Poliseno; res. Auteuil, Laval, Quebec.

Alfred Pellan (born Pelland) has had a long and splendid career. It began early: in his third year as a student at the Ecole des Beaux-Arts in Quebec City, his painting "Coin du vieux Quebec" was purchased by the National Gallery of Canada. By 1925 he was off to Paris, having won a Quebec government bursary for study abroad. While there, Pellan attended the Ecole supérieure nationale des Beaux-Arts de Paris, where in 1928 he received the school's First Prize for painting. When his Quebec bursary expired, Pellan nevertheless stayed on in Paris until 1940. During his years of independent study there, he managed to win first prize for his "Composition abstraite en rouge et noir" entered in the Salon de L'Art mural de Paris (a competition also entered by both Picasso and Léger). He also kept body and sensibility alive through graphic design, eventually turning his hand to everything from designing a perfume bottle for Rouillon to painting directly onto the fabric of one-of-a-kind dresses for Schiaparelli. He had his first New York exhibition in 1941. In 1943, he painted two large murals for the Canadian Embassy in Rio de Janeiro. When Pellan finally returned to Canada in 1943 he joined the staff of the Ecole des Beaux-Arts in Montreal where, despite some acute and theatrical conflicts with his department heads (notably Charles Maillard), he remained until 1952. It was during his years as a teacher in Montreal that he split with the other great pole of Quebec modernism, Paul-Émile Borduas, preferring his own brand of surrealist-based art codified within his own "Prisme d'Yeux" group of followers to the purist strictures of Borduas' "Automatistes." In 1952, Pellan shook off this rather arcane conflict and returned to France via a Royal Society of Canada Fellowship. In 1954 he mounted a one-man exhibition in Paris that was highly praised by André Breton. A year later he was given a major retrospective by the Musée National d'Art Moderne. He returned to Quebec in 1956. He was finally honoured by a Canadian retrospective in 1960 — an ambitious show co-sponsored by the National Gallery, the Art Galley of Ontario, and the Montreal Museum of Fine Arts.

Pellan has pictures in the important Canadian museums and in many collections around the world. He is as well known as a muralist as he is an easel painter and has important murals in the Winnipeg Airport, Place des Arts in Montreal, and the National Library and Archives in Ottawa. He has won innumerable prizes, including the Molson Prize in 1972. He is the subject of six critical and biographical monographs. Pellan was awarded the Centennial Medal in 1967; he has four honorary degrees and was made a Companion of the Order of Canada in 1967.

Peterson, Oscar Emmanuel
O.C., LL.D.

Jazz pianist. b. August 15, 1925, Montreal; divorced; s. Oscar Emmanuel Jr., Norman Raymond, d. Lynn Cheryl, Sharon Vivian, Gaye Carol; res. Mississauga, Ontario.

The son of a CP railroad porter, Oscar Peterson began playing the piano at the age of eight under the guidance of his sister, Daisy. At the age of 15, he won an amateur contest and began his own radio show, *Fifteen Minutes Piano Rambling*. He has performed worldwide since 1950; his concerts and recordings have garnered an international reputation for excellence. His best-known composition, *Canadiana Suite* (1963), received a National Academy of Recording Arts and Sciences Grammy nomination. He has since won three Grammys, in 1975, 1979, and 1980. Peterson is the president of Regal Recordings and the honorary president of the Toronto Jazz club. He has won numerous awards and has been presented with honorary doctorates from several Canadian universities. In 1973, he was made an Officer of the Order of Canada.

Pratt, Christopher

O.C., B.F.A., LL.D.

Artist. b. 1935, St. John's; m. Mary West; s. John, Edwyn, d. Anne, Barbara; res. St. Mary's Bay, Newfoundland.

For a man who is now one of Canada's most distinguished painters, it is curious that he first regarded painting merely as a hobby. It was only after studying engineering at Memorial University and medicine at Mount Allison that he was persuaded by a fellow student, painter Mary West (whom he would later marry) to switch his studies to Fine Arts. After their marriage in 1957, Christopher and Mary Pratt decided to study art in Glasgow, sailing there in 1957 on the freighter *Nova Scotia*. When they returned two years later, Pratt finished his B.F.A. degree at Mount Allison and accepted a position running the art gallery at Memorial University and teaching at the university at night. Not until 1963 did he begin to paint full time. His paintings — which are spare and lean and so highly finished that he normally paints only two or three a year — are both evocations of daily Newfoundland life and, at the same time, serene propositions dedicated to the abstract truths Pratt seems to find lurking beneath a clarified natural world. A lavish monograph limited to 279 copies devoted to his work was published by the Quintus Press; it was reprinted as a popular edition in 1982. Pratt has always been an enthusiastic sailor; he bought his first boat in 1961. His best-known vessel was the *Dry Fly*, a 43-foot Cuthbertson & Cassian sloop which he sold in 1980 to purchase a smaller craft. He still delights in sailing all the way from Newfoundland to Toronto in order to attend the openings of his one-man exhibitions at the Mira Godard gallery. Christopher Pratt has honorary doctorates from both Memorial University (1972) and Mount Allison (1972). He was made an Officer of the Order of Canada in 1973.

Quilico, Louis, C.C.

Opera singer; Montreal

Reaney, James C.

Writer; London, Ontario

Reid, Kate

Actor; Toronto

Richler, Mordecai

Writer. b. January 27, 1931, Montreal; m. Florence Wood; s. Daniel, Noah, Jacob, d. Emma, Martha; res. Montreal.

Mordecai Richler grew up in that district of Montreal known as "The Main" where his father was a junk dealer. Much of his subsequent writing has been drawn from his knockabout early life in this gamy, less-than-affluent neighbourhood. Richler's novels include *The Acrobats* (1954), *Son of a Smaller Hero* (1955), *Choice of Enemies* (1957), the world-famous *The Apprenticeship of Duddy Kravitz* (1959), *The Incomparable Atuk* (1963), *Cocksure* (1968), *St. Urbain's Horseman* (1971), and *Joshua Then and Now* (1980). In addition to his fiction, Richler has published works of criticism (*Hunting Tigers Under Glass*, 1968) and a popular children's book (*Jacob Two-Two Meets the Hooded Fang*, 1976). He has edited numerous anthologies of short stories and has written screenplays, including the screenplay for his own Duddy Kravitz — which was awarded The American

Screenwriters' Guild prize for best comedy, the ACTRA award for best Canadian screenplay, an Academy Award nomination for best comedy screenplay, and a Golden Bear award at the Berlin Film Festival. Mordecai Richler was writer-in-residence at Sir George Williams University in Montreal (1968-1969) and at Carleton University, Ottawa, in 1972-1973. In 1977, he was appointed to the Editorial Board of the Book-of-the-Month Club in New York. He belongs to no club more distinguished than the Canadian Automobile Association and something called The Owl's Nest Society of Mansonville, Quebec. He says his favourite pastime is playing poker.

Rideout, Patricia

Musician, opera singer. b. March 16, 1931, Saint John, New Brunswick; res. Toronto.

Contralto Patricia Rideout studied at the Royal Conservatory Opera School in Toronto from 1952 until 1955. In 1954-55 she performed as a soloist in operatic productions at the Banff School of Fine Arts. Her career can be said to have begun in earnest, however, when in 1955 she sang the part of Annina in the production that year of *La Traviata* by the Opera Festival Association (later the Canadian Opera Company). In 1956 Rideout made her recital debut at the Art Gallery of Ontario and played Bianca in the Stratford Festival's production of Benjamin Britten's opera *The Rape of Lucretia* (with Regina Resnik, Jennie Tourel, and Jon Vickers). She was an original member (1956) of Canada's Festival Singers, singing with that renowned group until 1968. Patricia Rideout has sung *Carmen*, the part of the Sandman in *Hansel and Gretel*, and Mauyra in the Canadian premiere (1958) of Vaughan Williams' opera *Riders to the Sea* (with Teresa Stratas). She has also been a distinguished Suzuki in various productions of *Madame Butterfly* (1960, 1962, 1971). She has performed in opera for the Canadian Opera Company, Stratford Festival productions, the Guelph Spring Festival, and the CBC. In 1975, she and Glenn Gould mounted Schoenberg's difficult *Pierre Lunaire* for CBC-TV and followed that production two years later with Krenek's *Wanderlied Im Herbst*. She gave Distinguished Artists' Recitals with the Toronto Symphony in 1968, 1969, 1970, and 1974. She has performed in various choral works with most of Canada's symphony orchestras. Her most distinguished overall achievement is usually taken to be her enthusiastic support of contemporary music. In 1972, for example, she performed in the European premiere of Harry Somers's *Evocations*. In 1977, she sang John Cage's *Five Songs for Contralto* and his *The Wonderful Widow of Eighteen Springs* for the New Music Society's special birthday concert for Cage in Toronto.

Riopelle, Jean-Paul

Artist. b. October 7, 1923, Montreal; res. Paris.

Jean-Paul Riopelle was a student of Paul-Emile Borduas during that painter's famous and troubled tenure at Montreal's Ecole du Meuble. Riopelle was an early convert in Canada to entirely abstract painting, joining Borduas' influential group of esthetic revolutionaries, "Les Automatistes," and even contributing the cover design for Borduas's incendiary manifesto of esthetic freedom, *Refus Global*. By 1946

Riopelle had moved to Paris, where he began to paint the pictures that have made him world famous; large canvases loaded heavily with thick chunks of oil paint in what are usually hot primary colours trowelled onto the pictures with a palette knife. One of his best-known paintings is a large triptych in the National Gallery of Canada called *Pavanne*, painted (or trowelled) in 1954. Riopelle is also a print maker of considerable reputation.

Rombout, Luke

B.F.A.

Museum director. b. May 4, 1933, Amsterdam, Netherlands; m. Maxine Dawe; d. Melissa, Tanya; res. Vancouver.

Luke Rombout received his formal education in the Netherlands. He came to Canada in 1954 to work in radio and film, first in Montreal and then in Saint John, New Brunswick. In 1960 Lord Beaverbrook appointed him Assistant Curator of the Beaverbrook Art Gallery in Fredericton. From 1965 to 1967 he was Acting Curator at the Owens Art Gallery, Mount Allison University, became Curator in 1967, and was made the Gallery's Director (1968-1971). He became the first Director of the Canada Council Art Bank (which was essentially his own creation) in 1972, and was appointed Head of the Canada Council's Visual Arts and Film Section in 1974. Since 1975, he has been the Director of the Vancouver Art Gallery. Rombout has lectured at Canadian universities including York University, the University of Ottawa, Mount Allison, and the Nova Scotia College of Art and Design. He organized the fine arts and crafts exhibition for the Atlantic Pavilion at Expo 67 in Montreal. He has been a member of the Canada Council's Arts Advisory Panel, the Canadian Museums Association, the Fine Arts Committee of the Department of External Affairs, and the American Association of Museum Directors. He is also a director of Vancouver's Anna Wyman Dance Theatre. Not surprisingly he collects art.

Ronald, William

R.C.A.

Artist. b. August 13, 1926, Stratford, Ontario; m. Helen Higgins; d. Suzanne, Dianna; res. Toronto.

As well known for his personal flamboyance and epic energies as he is for his hectic abstract-expressionist painting, William Ronald was a founding member of Canada's pioneer group of abstract painters, Painters Eleven (1953) and, by the time he was 31, one of the stars of the highly competitive New York art world. Best known for his large hotly-coloured "central image" abstractions, Ronald had six successful one-man shows in a row at New York's Kootz Gallery (1957-63) before returning to Canada to solidify his achievement and to begin to work as a radio and TV broadcaster. Ronald had been a regular panelist on a New York late-night radio panel show; the main topic of discussion, Ronald notes ruefully, was the nature of UFOs: he recalls one intense discussion with two people who had recently been to Jupiter, Mars, and Venus. Back in Toronto, Ronald devised and hosted an experimental TV program on the arts, *The Umbrella* (1966-1967). From 1969 to 1972, he hosted the popular CBC network current affairs radio program, *As It*

J.R.

ABOVE: Luke Rombout supervised the reconstruction of the old Vancouver Court House as the new home of the Vancouver Art Gallery.

LEFT: William Ronald in his Toronto studio.

J.R.

J.R.

Kate Reid.

Happens. For two years after that, he hosted and supervised a pleasantly chaotic free-access TV show called *Free For All* for Toronto's CITY-TV.

As an artist, Ronald has had 34 important one-man exhibitions. In 1975, the Robert McLaughlin Gallery in Oshawa, Ontario (the permanent home for the work of Painters Eleven and its archives) gave Ronald a major retrospective exhibition which subsequently toured Canada. He has paintings in an astonishing number of major museums in Canada and around the world, including the Brooklyn Museum, the Carnegie Institute, Pittsburgh, New York's Museum of Modern Art, the Albright-Knox Art Gallery in Buffalo, the Art Institute of Chicago, Princeton University Museum, the Montreal Museum of Fine Arts, the Art Gallery of Ontario, and the National Gallery of Canada. His largest single work is an enormous mural covering most of the lobby of Ottawa's National Arts Centre. Ronald is an avid sports fan and is especially fond of boxing—about which he has an encyclopedic knowledge.

Roy, Jean-Louis

B.A., M.A., Ph.D

Publisher, academic. b. 1941, Normandin, Quebec; married; two children; res. Montreal.

The remarkable Quebec daily *Le Devoir* maintained its tradition of going outside the newspaper business to choose a publisher when Jean-Louis Roy was named in 1981 to succeed Claude Ryan, who had left nearly three years earlier to enter politics. Roy was a historian, poet, civil libertarian, and professor of French-Canadian studies at McGill University. The newspaper he took charge of reaches a small (50,000 or so) but influential readership in the social, political, and cultural establishment of Quebec. As *Saturday Night* has said, "*Le Devoir* is the national newspaper of Quebec in a way the *Globe and Mail* will probably never be in English Canada." The paper was founded by Henri Bourassa in 1910.

Schaefer, Carl Fellman

C.M., C.D., D.Litt., R.C.A., F.R.S.A.

Artist. b. April 30, 1903, Hanover, Ontario; m. Lillian Marie Evers; s. Mark, Paul; res. Toronto.

Best known for his classic evocations of the Ontario countryside, Carl Schaefer studied at the Ontario College of Art in Toronto under Arthur Lismer and J.E.H. MacDonald, where from 1956 until 1968 he was chairman of the Department of Drawing and Painting. During 1968-70, he was the Department's chairman emeritus. An internationally respected painter, he exhibited with the Group of Seven in 1928 and in 1931. He was represented in "A Century of Canadian Art" at London's Tate Gallery in 1938, at the 11th International Exhibition of Water Colour at the Brooklyn Museum in 1941, and, that same year, at the Art Institute of Chicago. Schaefer showed at the New York World's Fair in 1939, at London's National Gallery in 1944, and at the Museum of Modern Art in Paris in 1946. He was Canada's entry in the first Biennial in São Paulo, Brazil (1951-52). Many regard Schaefer's work from the 1930s as his finest. Indeed, he is frequently

cited as the single most important delineator of Canadian life and culture during that difficult decade. He served as an official war artist with the RCAF from 1943 to 1946 and was wounded twice. Schaefer was awarded the Queen's Coronation Medal in 1953, the Centennial Medal in 1967, and the Queen's Silver Jubilee Medal in 1977. He is a life fellow of the International Institute of Arts and Letters, a Fellow of the Ontario College of Art, and a Fellow of the Royal Society of Arts. A member of the Canadian Group of Painters, the Canadian Society of Graphic Art, and the Canadian Society of Painters in Water Colour, he is a Member of the Order of Canada and the Royal Canadian Academy.

Schafer, Raymond Murray

L.R.S.M., LL.D.

Composer. b. July 18, 1933, Sarnia; m. Phyllis Mailing; m. Jean Elliott; res. Bancroft, Ontario.

Murray Schafer is one of Canada's most inventive and intellectually adventurous composers. His musical training began in 1952 when he first came to the University of Toronto and the Royal Conservatory of Music, and ended in 1955 when he left again, disillusioned about the nature of academic training in music and restless for a more widely integrated collage of experience drawn from literature, philosophy, and linguistics. He left Canada in 1956 to study on his own in Germany. After two years there, he settled in England, where he studied composition and supported himself by journalism and by mounting Ezra Pound's opera about the life of François Villon, *Le Testament*, broadcast by the BBC in 1960. He returned in 1961 to Toronto, where he organized and directed the Ten Centuries Concerts and began a period of teaching in Canada, first at Memorial University (1963-65), as artist-in-residence, and then (1965-75) at Simon Fraser University. While he was at Simon Fraser, he set up the World Soundscape Project, "dedicated to the study of man's relationship to his acoustic environment." In 1975 he moved to a farm near Bancroft, where he continued to compose and where, in 1976-77, he finished a project in the works for 16 years, a complete edition of the musical writings and musical works of Ezra Pound. Among Schafer's best-known compositions are his *Protest and Incarceration*, *Canzoni for Prisoners*, *Loving* (a bilingual opera for television), *Requiems For a Party Girl* (winner of the Fromm Foundation Prize for 1968), *The Crown of Ariadne*, *Lustro*, and his spectacular 12-hour environmental opera *Ra* (premiered at and through the Ontario Science Centre in 1983). Schafer is also a fresh and invigorating writer. His teaching pamphlets—"The Composer in the Classroom," "Ear Cleaning," "The New Soundscape," "When Words Sing," and "Rhinoceros in the Classroom"—are eccentric and compelling handbooks to generate students' esthetic perception. His books include *The Book of Noise* (1970), *E.T.A. Hoffmann and Music* (1975), *Creative Music Education* (1976), *Smoke: A Novel* (1976), and his magnum opus, *The Tuning of the World* (1977). In 1977, Murray Schafer received the Canadian Music Council's first Composer of the Year Award. He was given the Jules Léger Prize for New Chamber Music in 1978 for his *String Quartet No. 2*. In 1980, he received the Prix International-Arthur Honegger for Quartet No. 1.

Scott, Francis Reginald

C.C., Q.C., B.A., B.Litt., B.C.L., D.C.L., LL.D., D. es Jur., D.Litt., F.R.S.C.

Poet, university professor. b. August 1, 1899, Quebec City; m. Marian Mildred Dale; one son; res. Montreal.

Although he is probably best known as a poet, F.R. Scott has had a long and distinguished career in education and jurisprudence as well. He was educated at Bishop's College in Lennoxville and at Oxford (Magdalen College) where he was a Rhodes scholar and earned a B.A. in 1922 and a B.Litt. a year later. He returned to Canada to attend McGill University, where he earned his law degree in 1927. In 1928, Scott became a full-time teacher in McGill's Faculty of Law; he was dean of the Faculty from 1961 to 1964. Frank Scott was co-founder with historian F.H. Underhill of the League for Social Reconstruction and a member of the National Executive of the Canadian Institute for International Affairs from 1935 to 1950. From 1942 to 1950 he was the national chairman of the Co-operative Commonwealth Federation and was advisor to the Saskatchewan government at the Constitutional Conferences of 1950 and 1960. In 1955 he was chairman of the Canadian Writers Conference and in 1960 President of Academy II of the Royal Society of Canada. Scott has been an indefatigable editor of important Canadian magazines: in 1925-27, he was co-editor of the *McGill Fortnightly Review*; in 1928, co-editor of *The Canadian Mercury*; in 1936-39, he edited *The Canadian Forum*; in 1942-45, *Preview*; and in 1945-47, *The Northern Review*. Scott was chairman of the Legal Research Committee of the Canadian Bar Association (1954-56). From 1956 to 1964 he was counsel in important civil liberties cases before the Supreme Court of Canada. He was Guggenheim Fellow in 1940 and was made an honorary foreign member of the American Academy of Arts and Sciences in 1967. In 1978, he was made a corresponding fellow of the British Academy. From 1963 until 1971, Scott was a member of the Royal Commission on Bilingualism and Biculturalism. He has been appointed visiting professor to many Canadian and American universities, many of which have granted him honorary degrees. (He holds 15 of them.) He was given the Lorne Pierce Medal of the Royal Society of Canada in 1964 and the Canada Council's Molson Prize for 1965-66. He was made a Companion of the Order of Canada in 1967. In 1975, he retired from teaching and was made professor emeritus at McGill. F.R. Scott's first book of poems appeared in 1945 and was appropriately titled *Overture*. It was followed in 1954 by *Events and Signals* and in 1957 by *The Eye of the Needle*. Other works (including translations) include *Poems of Garneau and Hébert* (1962), *Signature* (1964), *Selected Poems* (1966), *Trouvailles* (1967), *The Dance Is One* (1973), and *Poems of French Canada* (1977), which won a Canada Council award for translation. His prose works include *Canada Today: Her National Interests and National Policy* (1938), *Civil Liberties and Canadian Federalism* (1959), and *Essays on the Constitution* (1977), for which he was given the Governor General's Award. Professor Scott is also co-editor with A.J.M. Smith of *The Blasted Pine, an Anthology of Satire, Irreverent and Disrespectful Verse* (1957).

Shadbolt, Jack
C.M., LL.D.

Artist. b. February 4, 1909, Shoeburyness, England; m. Doris Kathleen Meisel; res. North Burnaby, British Columbia.

Jack Shadbolt is best known for his intelligent abstractions from nature and for his aesthetic interest in the spiritual power of natural forms and totemic art (an interest traceable to his admiration for the art of the Indians of the Pacific Northwest). Shadbolt received his early education in England and his art education at the Art Student's League in New York (1928 and 1948), the André L'Hôte School of Art in Paris (1937), and the Euston Road Art School in London. He was, for a time, head of the Drawing and Painting section of the Vancouver School of Art and has taught frequently at the University of British Columbia. His work has been included in exhibitions all over the world — including exhibitions at London's Tate Gallery, the Venice Biennale, the São Paulo Biennale in Brazil, the Carnegie Institute, and the Brussels and Seattle world fairs. He has had many one-man shows in New York, San Francisco, Seattle, Montreal, Toronto, and Vancouver, and has been given major retrospective exhibitions both by the National Gallery and by the Vancouver Art Gallery. He has undertaken important commissions, including a large mural for the Edmonton International Airport, the CBC Building in Vancouver, the National Arts Centre in Ottawa, and Confederation Centre in Charlottetown. He received a Guggenheim International Award in 1957, the University of Alberta's National Painting Award in 1969, and the Molson Prize in 1978. Shadbolt has written widely about his own art and about the work of other artists in whom he is interested. In 1968 he published his *In Search of Form* and in 1973 a book of ruminative poems and drawings called *Mind's I*. His latest book is a lavishly produced essay in art methodology and personal mythologizing called *Act of Art* (1981). Jack Shadbolt was made a Member of the Order of Canada in 1972.

Sinclair, Lister Shedden
B.A., M.A., LL.D., D.Litt., Litt.D.

Actor, playwright, broadcaster, director. b. January 9, 1921, Bombay, India; m. Alice Mather, s. Andrew; m. Margaret Watchman, s. Peter; res. Toronto.

Lister Sinclair received his formal education in England at Colet Court and St. Paul's School, London. He went on to study at the University of British Columbia (B.A.) and the University of Toronto (M.A.). Sinclair is a man of enormous intellectual range and diversity of interests. It is entirely typical of him, for example, to have become a member of the University of Toronto's Department of Mathematics shortly after he was asked to teach at Toronto's Royal Conservatory of Music. Eventually, he resigned from both academic appointments to devote himself wholly to freelance writing and broadcasting. He wrote more than 700 dramas for radio, television, and the stage, the best-known probably being his adventure in Canadian gothicism called *The Blood Is Strong*. Sinclair is a resourceful and inventive radio and TV producer as well and has received more than two dozen international awards for distinguished achievement in communications. At one time the Executive Vice-President of the CBC and Vice-President of Program Policy and Development, he is now Executive Producer for the CBC's TV Drama Department. Lister Sinclair is President of the Canadian Conference of the Arts and a member of the Board of Directors for Toronto's Mainly Mozart Festival. He holds honorary degrees from Mount Allison University, the University of British Columbia, Sir Wilfrid Laurier University, and Memorial University in St. John's. He is co-author, with Jack Pollock, of *The Art of Norval Morriseau* (1979).

Smith, Gordon Appelbe
R.C.A., LL.D.

Artist. b. June 18, 1919, Brighton, England, m. Marion K. Fleming; res. West Vancouver.

Gordon Smith came to Canada in 1934 when he was 15. His first art training in this country was at the Winnipeg School of Art where he studied with LeMoine FitzGerald. In 1940, he enlisted in Princess Patricia's Canadian Light Infantry and was wounded in Sicily in 1943. He returned to Canada a year later, continuing his art education at the Vancouver School of Art where he taught from 1946 until 1956. In the early 1950s he began experimenting with semi-abstract images on carefully gridded backgrounds. His "Pruned Trees" of 1955 was purchased by the National Gallery of Canada — and can be said to have anticipated the cool, essentially geometric approach to landscape that Smith maintains to this day. Since 1956, he has been a member of the Faculty of Education, University of British Columbia, where he is now a full professor. In 1968, Smith stopped exhibiting his paintings for a period of five years, during which time he worked with Canadian architect Arthur Erickson on Erickson's Canadian Pavilion for Expo 70 in Osaka, Japan. Smith's contribution to the pavilion included a set of large highly coloured vinyl spinners for the courtyard, each of them 60 feet high and 45 feet wide, the whole constituting a design and installation project that took over two years to complete. In 1970, Smith had a show of prints at the Martha Jackson Gallery in New York. That same year he was named head of painting at the Banff School of Fine Arts. Since 1973 he has been regularly exhibiting large-scale landscapes in muted, rather serene colours. His work can be seen in major museums in Canada and abroad. Smith has represented this country in biennial exhibitions in Yugoslavia, Germany, Spain, France, and Norway. His honorary doctorate is from Simon Fraser University in Vancouver (1973). He has also been awarded the Allied Arts medal of the Royal Canadian Architectural Institute. He lives in a house designed by Arthur Erickson and purported to be one of Erickson's favourites among all of his buildings. He owns a 33-foot sailboat and lists sailing as his principal hobby.

Somers, Harry
O.C., D.Mus., LL.D., D.Litt.

Composer. b. September 11, 1925, Toronto; m. Catherine Mackie; m. Barbara Chilcott; res. Toronto.

One of the few Canadian composers to receive international recognition, Harry Somers came to music in 1939 when he began to study piano, progressing rapidly enough to find himself giving concerts and recitals through the 1940s. In 1941, he joined John Weinzweig's classes in composition at the Conservatory in Toronto, remaining his student (except for a stint with the RCAF in 1943-45) until 1949. That year, Somers won a Canadian Amateur Hockey Scholarship that enabled him to study for a year in Paris with Darius Milhaud. It was in 1948 that Somers decided against a career as a pianist in order to devote himself to composing. Much of his first music was commissioned by the CBC for which he was host of a televised series of youth concerts in 1963 and the CBC's radio series *Music Of Today* from 1965 to 1969. That year he received a substantial grant from the Canadian Cultural Institute in Rome that allowed him to live and work there until 1971. It was in Rome that he completed two of his best-known experiments in vocal writing: *Voiceplay* and *Kyrie*. Somers has written for the stage as well as for film and television. Stratford commissioned his *Five Songs For Dark Voice* for Maureen Forrester; the Floyd S. Chalmers Foundation commissioned his opera *Louis Riel* for the Canadian Opera Company; the National Ballet of Canada commissioned his scores *The Fisherman and his Soul*, *Ballad*, and *The House of Atreus* (the latter with sets and costumes by Harold Town). Somers' *Music For Solo Violin* was commissioned jointly by the Canada Council, the Guelph Spring Festival, and master violinist Yehudi Menuhin, who gave it its premiere. Among his awards are the Critics' Award of the Cava dei Tirreni Summer Festival (1965) and the William Harold Moon Award (1976). He holds honorary degrees from the University of Ottawa, the University of Toronto, and York University. He was made an Officer of the Order of Canada in 1971.

Stevens, Murray
Schooner builder; Lunenburg, Nova Scotia

Symons, H.B. Scott
Writer; Morocco

Templeton, Charles
Writer/broadcaster; Toronto

Tennant, Veronica
Dancer; Toronto

Thom, Ronald
Architect; Toronto

Tisseyre, Pierre
Book publisher; Montreal

Tovell, Vincent Massey
B.A., M.A., R.C.A.

TV producer, director, and writer. b. July 29, 1922, Toronto; res. Toronto.

In the course of his distinguished career in Canadian letters, Vincent Tovell has lectured in English literature at the University of Toronto, served as director of the University of Toronto's Hart House Theatre (1947-48), and, since the early 1950s, has been a producer, writer, and performer for CBC-TV. He is now an executive producer for CBC-TV's Arts, Music, and Science Department. Among his best-known productions are his *The Masseys: Chronicles a Canadian Family* (1978), *The*

ABOVE: *F.R. Scott*

LEFT: *Jack Shadbolt in his Vancouver studio.*

Miriam Waddington

Harold Town

J.R.

Harold Town (ABOVE) in one of the studios at his home near Peterborough and (RIGHT) the main hallway of the house.

J.R.

Owl and the Dynamo: A Portrait of George Grant (1980), and *Must Freedom Fail? The Declaration of Rights – Thirty Years Later.* Tovell is a trustee of the Art Gallery of Ontario and of the National Ballet School of Canada and was chairman of the National Ballet's 25th Anniversary International Seminar (1976). He is a member of the National Theatre School in Montreal. From 1966 to 1970, he was chairman of the Advisory Arts Panel of the Canada Council and has served as vice-president of the Royal Canadian Academy of the Arts. He received the Centennial Medal in 1967 and the Queen's Silver Jubilee Medal in 1977. He is the son of Dr. Harold Murchison Tovell and Ruth Lillian Massey.

Town, Harold Barling

O.C., Litt.D., R.C.A.

Artist, writer. b. June 13, 1924, Toronto; m. Trudella Carol Tredwell; d. Heather, Shelley; res. Toronto and Peterborough.

Harold Town was an early and extremely visible member of Canada's first group of self-acknowledged abstract painters, Painters 11, showing with them in Canada and at New York's Riverside Museum in 1956, the year he also represented Canada at the Venice Biennale. Since then, he has exhibited widely in this country and throughout the world. He has won many prizes and awards and is represented in all of the major galleries in Canada and in the Tate Gallery in London; the Metropolitan Museum, the Museum of Modern Art and the Guggenheim Museum in New York; the Stedelijk Museum in Amsterdam; the Cleveland Museum; and the Museum of Modern Art in São Paulo. His commissions include his 39-foot mural in 1957 for the St. Lawrence Seaway project in Cornwall, Ontario, a two-part mural and a brass screen for Toronto International Airport, as well as murals for the Queen's Park project and Toronto-Dominion Centre in Toronto. He designed the costumes and decor for the National Ballet of Canada's *House of Atreus* (1963-64) and the banners for Founders College at York University in 1965. Town's list of publications is almost as long as his list of important exhibitions: he provided drawings for what was considered in 1962 a very racy book of Canadian love poetry called *Love Where the Nights Are Long* (with Irving Layton) and in 1964 published a handsome book of his puzzling surrealistic drawings, *Enigmas*. *The Drawings of Harold Town* (with a text by Robert Fulford) was published in 1969. His hymn to the movies, *Silent Stars, Sound Stars, Film Stars*, appeared in 1971. When his old friend and sometime mentor painter Albert Franck died in 1973, Town wrote a touching and graceful memoir of him called *Albert Franck: Keeper of the Lanes* (1974). He was co-author with David Silcox of *Tom Thomson: The Silence and the Storm* (1977) – which became a Canadian bestseller. In 1980, filmmaker Christopher Chapman made a film of Town's suite of drawings called *The Vale Variations* ("Pyramid of Roses"), which was shown to considerable acclaim in Cannes. Since 1976 he has been at work on another vast suite of drawings (more than 1000 of them so far) called *The Toy Horse*. He maintains two painting studios, a separate print-making studio, and two drawing studios. His leisure time (if it could be described that way) is spent in redesigning and running his Old Orchard Farm near Peterborough, Ontario. Town was made an Officer of the Order of Canada in 1968.

Vickers, Jon

Singer; New York City

Waddington, Miriam

B.A., M.A., M.S.W., D.Litt.

Writer, educator. b. December 17, 1917, Winnipeg; née Dworkin; divorced; s. Marcus Frushard, Jonathan John Francis; res. Toronto.

Miriam Waddington has degrees in both English literature and social work. She was a case worker for the Jewish Family Service in Toronto from 1942 to 1944 and was assistant director of the Jewish Child Service in Montreal in 1945-46. From 1946 until 1949 she was a lecturer and supervisor of fieldwork at the McGill School of Social Work. Between 1950 and 1964 she was a case worker for the Montreal Children's Hospital Speech Clinic, the John Howard Society, and the North York Family Service in the Toronto suburb. By this time Waddington had already published three volumes of poetry (her first appeared in 1945) and had decided to devote herself to writing and the teaching of literature. In 1964 she began to teach at York University where she was made a full professor in 1973. The author of 11 books of poetry – including *Say Yes* (1969), *Driving Home* (1972), and *The Price of Gold* (1976) – she has also written a critical study of the work of Montreal poet A.M. Klein (1970), edited *The Collected Poems of A.M. Klein* (1974), and edited a selection of the critical writings of John Sutherland (1972). Her first collection of short stories, *Summer at Lonely Beach*, was published in 1982. She is a popular lecturer and gives many public readings of her poetry; she read at the International Poetry Evenings in Struga, Yugoslavia, and has been invited on four occasions to work at Yaddo, the writer's retreat near Saratoga Springs, New York. In 1974, she gave the annual E.J. Pratt memorial lecture at Memorial University in St. John's. In 1980, she was Canada Council exchange poet to Wales. She belongs to a number of professional societies and was awarded an honorary doctorate by Lakehead University in Thunder Bay, Ontario, in 1975. She is currently the editor of *Poetry Toronto*.

Weaver, Robert

Executive Producer, Literary Projects, CBC; Toronto

Webster, Norman

Editor-in-chief, The Globe and Mail; Toronto

Whittaker, Herbert William

O.C., D.Litt.

Columnist, drama critic. b. September 20, 1911, Montreal; res. Toronto.

Now Drama Critic Emeritus for the *Globe and Mail*, Herbert Whittaker's career has touched all phases of theatrical life in Canada. Educated at Montreal's École des Beaux Arts, he served as drama critic for the Montreal *Gazette* and, from 1949 until his official retirement in 1975, as drama critic for the *Globe and Mail*. He has directed plays for the Montreal Repertory Theatre, for both Trinity College Playhouse and Hart House, University of Toronto, and for Toronto's Crest Theatre. As a stage designer, he has worked with the Shakespeare Society of Montreal, university drama societies, and for the Canadian Players. He is twice winner of the Louis Jouvet Trophy for stage direction and the Martha Allan award for Design. His publications include *The Stratford Festival 1953-58, Canada's National Ballet* (1967), and a host of articles for newspapers and magazines around the world. He was a member of the Executive committee of the Dominion Drama Festival (1957-1968), a member of the Board of Trustees for the National Arts Centre in Ottawa (1976-1982), First Chairman of the Drama Bench (1972-75), and First National Chairman of the Canadian Theatre Critics Association (1980). Herbert Whittaker is a member of the American Newspaper Guild, the first life member of the Canadian Actors' Equity Association (1976), a life member of the Associated Designers of Canada, and an honorary member of the Association for Canadian Theatre History. He serves on the advisory boards for the Shaw Festival in Niagara-on-the-Lake, Ontario, and for the Concordia University Drama Division. He belongs to the Order of Canada and has received both the Centennial of Canada Medal (1967) and the Queen's Silver Jubilee Medal (1977). He has a large collection of theatrical portraits, prints, playbills, and books about the theatre – and theatre going is still among his favourite pastimes.

Wilson, Ronald York

R.C.A., O.S.A.

Artist. b. December 6, 1907, Toronto.; m. Lela May Miller, d. Virginia June; res. Toronto.

York Wilson's long and illustrious career as a painter, print maker, tapestry maker, and muralist has taken him to more than 30 different countries during the past 40 years. His work appears in most of the world's great museums including the Musée d'Art Moderne, Paris, the Musée de Dijon in France (for which a Wilson picture was purchased by André Malraux), the Museo Eduardo Westerdahl, Spain, the Birla Academy Museum, India, and the Tanake Museum, Japan, and the Uffizi Gallery in Florence. His work is, of course, in Canada's National Gallery and in major collections across Canada. Wilson showed at the New York World's Fair in 1939 and since then has had over 60 solo exhibitions and has been represented in over 500 group shows throughout the world. He is considered, he admits, "the world's foremost living muralist." He was President of the Ontario Society of Artists from 1946 to 1948, President of the Canadian Group of Painters in 1967 and is now on the Board of Directors for the Art Gallery of Ontario. It was as President of the CGP that he commissioned Paul Duval's award-winning study of Canadian Art, *Four Decades* (1972). In 1978, Duval published a handsome limited edition book about Wilson himself. When he is not working in his Toronto studio-home, York Wilson spends his time either in San Miguel de Allende, Mexico, or in Tenerife in the Canary Islands.

Withrow, William John

C.M., C.D., B.A., M.A., M.Ed.

Art administrator. b. September 30, 1926, Toronto; m. June Roselea Van Ostrom; three sons, one daughter; res. Toronto.

William Withrow received his education at the University of Toronto, where he studied art and archeology. He began his career as a secondary school teacher (1951-60), spending his Saturday mornings directing the Ontario Department of Education's Saturday morning art classes for artistically gifted adolescents at the Ontario College of Art (1957-59). In 1960, he was appointed associate director of the Art Gallery of Ontario (then the Art Gallery of Toronto). He became the gallery's director in 1961. Under Withrow's direction, the gallery's collection increased from 3400 works to over 8000. During his directorship, the Gallery organized and presented such important exhibitions as *Picasso and Man*, *Mondrian*, *Puvis de Chavannes and the Modern Tradition*, *Turner and the Sublime*, *Vincent Van Gogh and the Birth of Cloisonism*, and *Gauguin to Moore*. He also oversaw the AGO's presentation of the popular *Treasures of Tutankhamun*. It was during his tenure as well that Henry Moore donated to the Gallery his superb collection of drawings, prints, and sculptures from his private collection. In 1971, the AGO began its restoration of the Grange and launched a $25 million expansion program, the first major enlargement program since 1935. William Withrow is a charter member and was first president of the Canadian Art Museum Directors Organization (CAMDO) and is a member of the Canadian Museums Association, the Association of Art Museum Directors, the Canadian National Committee for the International Council of Museums, and the International Society of Education Through Art. His publications include *Sorel Etrog/ Sculpture* (1967) and *Contemporary Canadian Painting* (1972). He was awarded Canada's Centennial Medal in 1967 and was made a Member of the Order of Canada in 1980.

Woodcock, George

Writer, editor, critic. b. May 8, 1912, Winnipeg; m. Ingeborg Hedwig Elisabeth Linzer; res. Vancouver.

One of Canada's most dedicated and prolific writers and critics, George Woodcock was taken to England by his parents a few months after his birth; the Woodcocks had emigrated only a few years before. He grew up in Shropshire and the Chilterns and, refusing his grandfather's offer to send him to Cambridge if he became an Anglican clergyman, found himself in the early 1940s deeply involved in the literary life of London — becoming friends with such libertarian and anarchist luminaries as George Orwell and Herbert Read. In 1940 Woodcock published the first of his more than 50 books (more than 80 when the books he has edited are included), a book of poems called *The White Island*. Another book of verse followed — *The Centre Cannot Hold* — then in 1946 his first biography, *William Godwin*. In 1948, Woodcock published a second biography, *The Incomparable Aphra* (a life of the redoubtable Mrs. Aphra Behn) and a critical study called *The Writer and Politics*. In 1949, Woodcock returned to Canada: "It was time," he has said, "to go away and find my real voice." Woodcock settled with his wife on Vancouver Island and began to farm, all the while continuing to turn out the ambitious and elegantly written books that would make his reputation. He began teaching at the University of British Columbia in 1956 and remained there until 1963, when he resigned his academic position to devote himself full-time to his writing. While at the university, he founded the critical magazine *Canada Literature*, which he edited from 1959 until 1977. Among his best-known works are *The Anarchist Prince: a biographical study of Peter Kropotkin* (1950), *Pierre-Joseph Proudhon* (1956), *To The City of the Dead: Travels in Mexico* (1956), *Incas and Other Men* (1959), *Anarchism: A History of Libertarian Ideas and Movements* (1962), *Faces of India* (1964), *The Greeks in India* (1966), *Asia, Gods and Cities* (1966), and *The Crystal Spirit*, a study of George Orwell's work, which won the Governor General's Award for non-fiction in 1966. He has also written a biography of Gabriel Dumont, a history of the Hudson's Bay Company, a history of the Doukhobors, two collections of essays on Canadian literature (*Odysseus Ever Returning*, 1970, and *The World of Canadian Writing*, 1980), a meditation on contemporary history called *Who Killed the British Empire?* (1974), a history of Canada (*The Canadians*, 1980), a critical study of painter Ivan Eyre (1981), and the first volume of an autobiography (*Letter to the Past*, 1982). He won the Canada Council's Molson Prize in 1973 and declined membership of the Order of Canada.

Zeidler, Eberhard Heinrich

Dipl.Ing. LL.D., F.R.A.I.C., R.C.A., F.A.I.A., LL.D.

Architect. b. January 11, 1926, Braunsdorf, Germany; m. Phyllis Jane Abbott; d. Margaret, Kate, Christina, s. Robert; res. Toronto.

Educated in Weimar and at T.H. Karlsruhe University in Germany, Eberhard ("Eb") Zeidler came to Canada in the early 1950s to practise architecture. His firm, the Zeidler Roberts Partnership, has been responsible for some of Canada's most daring and imaginative buildings and structures, including the spectacular Ontario Place complex in Toronto where the buildings, as airy and diaphanous as spacecraft, hover on stilts and hang from cables over the waters of Lake Ontario, and Toronto's Eaton Centre where people shop under a huge arched, glassed-in galleria almost as splendid as the original in Milan. Other distinguished Zeidler buildings include the McMaster University Health Sciences Centre (deemed obsolescence-proof by the 1969 World Hospital Congress), Fanshawe College of Applied Arts and Technology in London, Ontario, Dumont Hospital in Moncton, Young People's Theatre in Toronto, Queen's Quay Terminal in Toronto's Harbourfront, Discovery Bay in Hong Kong, Endicott Center in St. Petersburg, Florida, Canada Place in Vancouver, Metroplex Centre in Kuala Lumpur, and Forum Centre in Singapore. Zeidler has garnered over 60 awards and prizes, including a number of Massey medals for outstanding achievement in Canadian architecture, National Design Awards (1962, 1967, 1972), Awards of Excellence from *Canadian Architecture* magazine, the Prestressed Concrete Institute Award, the American Iron and Steel Institute Award, the Progressive Architecture Design Award, the Ontario Association of Architects Design Award, and dozens more. He won two Governor General's medals for Architecture in 1982 alone. Zeidler is also a prolific writer of articles about architecture and design, many of which have appeared in the world's leading architectural magazines (over 200 of them so far). He has served on many architecture and design juries and has lectured at universities in Canada, the United States, Japan, and Germany. Zeidler is an enthusiastic collector of works of Contemporary Canadian art and is a member of the Contemporary Collections Committee of the Art Gallery of Ontario. He has an honorary doctorate from McMaster University. He belongs to the Badminton and Racquet Club, the Toronto, the Osler Bluff Ski Club, and the Royal Canadian Yacht Club.

BUSINESS

Abbott, Anthony C.

P.C., B.A., LL.B.

Lawyer, politician. b. November 26, 1930, Montreal; m. Naomi Siddall Smith; s. Douglas Chisholm, Timothy Alexander, d. Hilary Smith; res. Ottawa.

Tony Abbott, son of former Liberal cabinet minister and Supreme Court judge Douglas Abbott, was educated at Bishop's University and Osgoode Hall. He was a Liberal MP from 1974 to 1979, serving as minister of Consumer and Corporate Affairs and minister of National Revenue. Since 1979 he has been a business consultant. He is a director of Debrett's Peerage Ltd. and a member of the Rideau Club.

Amato, Baron Lanfranco di Campolevrini

C.M., K.M., K.C.L.J., F.R.S.A.

Business executive. b. April 19, 1922, Rovereto, Italy; m. Liliana Conte; s. Sergio; res. Downsview, Ontario.

Lanfranco Amato is president and chief executive officer of Riello Canada, former president and CEO of Olivetti Canada and L. Amato Associates, a consulting firm, and a director of several companies, including the Banca Commerciale Italiana of Canada. He has been a director of the Toronto Symphony, the Canadian Opera Company, the National Youth Orchestra Association of Canada, and the Canadian Council of Christians and Jews. During the Second World War he served with the Italian Army and the United States Army and was mentioned in despatches. He has received countless awards and honours from several countries: for example, he is a Fellow of the Royal Society of Arts of Great Britain, a Knight of Obedience of the Sovereign Military Order of Malta, and a Grand Officer of the Order of Merit of the Republic of Italy.

Arena, John

Restaurateur, Toronto

Armstrong, John Archibald

B.Sc., B.Sc., LL.D.

Management consultant. b. March 24, 1917; Dauphin, Manitoba; m. June Keith; s. David, Douglas, Drew; res. Toronto.

As chairman and chief executive officer of Imperial Oil, Jack Armstrong, now retired, headed Canada's largest integrated oil company. Joining the company as geologist in Regina, he then became exploration manager of the Edmonton District, general manager of the Producing Department, and director of Marketing Operations in Toronto. He was made executive vice-president in 1966, president in 1970, chief executive officer in 1973, and chairman in 1974. He has a B.Sc. from both the University of Manitoba (Geology, 1937) and Queen's University (Chemical Engineering, 1942), and an honorary LL.D. from the universities of Winnipeg (1978) and Calgary (1980). Since retiring from Imperial Oil, Jack Armstrong serves as a management consultant to Dsbarjco Inc. His clubs include the York, the Granite, and the Rosedale Golf and Country.

Asper, Israel Harold
Q.C., B.A., LL.B., LL.M.

Business executive, lawyer. b. August 11, 1932, Minnedosa, Manitoba; m. Ruth Miriam Bernstein; s. David, Leonard, d. Gail; res. Winnipeg.

The son of a local showbiz entrepreneur, "Izzy" Asper has applied some of his father's dash to his business dealings. This has resulted in his present position of chairman of the board and chief executive officer of CanWest Capital Corporation, a Winnipeg-based holding company with close to $3 billion in assets. He is also chairman of several CanWest affiliates and of Global Communications Limited. After receiving his law degree from the University of Manitoba (with honours and as class valedictorian), he joined the law firm Drache, Meltzer, Essers, Gold and Asper, then in 1959 became a senior partner in his own Asper and Company and subsequently in Buchwald, Asper, Henteleff. He was appointed Queen's Counsel in 1975. In addition to actively being involved in community organizations, Asper was elected leader of the Liberal Party in Manitoba in 1970, a position he held for five years until he decided to return to the world of business. He has lectured on various aspects of the law at universities across Canada, and has written a column dealing with taxation for the Toronto *Globe and Mail* for 11 years. He also wrote *The Benson Iceberg: A Critical Analysis of the White Paper on Tax Reform in Canada* (Clarke, Irwin). He plays a pretty hot jazz piano and collects George Gershwin memorabilia.

Ayre, Lewis H.M.
C.M.

Business executive. b. 1914, St. John's; m. Olga Crosbie; s. Miller H.; d. Penelope M. Rowe; res. St. John's.

A member of a prominent merchant family of St. John's, Lewis Ayre, chairman of Ayre & Sons (established in 1859), joined the firm in 1931. He is director of numerous corporations including the Bank of Nova Scotia and Dominion Stores, and is chairman of Newfoundland Telephone Company and Blue Buoy Foods Limited. Ayre's activities are not exclusive to Newfoundland: he is member of the Toronto Club and the Canadian Club in New York. Interested in conservation, he is also a member of the St. John's Heritage Foundation and the Heritage Foundation of Canada. His wife is a member of the well-known political family. Lewis Ayre is a member of the Order of Canada.

Baird, Charles F.
B.A., LL.D.

Business executive. b. September 4, 1922, Southampton, Long Island, New York; m. Norma Adele White; d. Susan, Nancy, s. Stephen, Charles Jr.; res. Toronto.

Now chairman and chief executive officer of Inco, Charles Baird studied economics at Middlebury College in Vermont and graduated with a B.A. in 1944. He served with the U.S. Marine Corps from 1943 to 1946 and from 1951 to 1952, rising to the rank of captain. He joined Standard Oil of New Jersey (now EXXON) in 1948. From 1955 to 1958 he served in London and became assistant treasurer in 1958. From 1962 to 1965 he was a director and member of the Executive Committee in Paris. In 1965 he returned to the U.S. Navy as assistant secretary of financial management and then as undersecretary of the Navy (1967–69). He received the United States Navy Distinguished Civilian Service Award in 1969. He then joined Inco as vice-president of finance. He is a director of the Bank of Montreal, ICI Americas, and Aetna Life & Casualty, and a governor of the Olympic Trust of Canada. He belongs to the Toronto Club, the Short Hills Club in New Jersey, the Chevy Chase Club in Washington, and the International Lawn Tennis Club. He is also a member of business-oriented organizations such as the Business Council on National Issues, the Ontario Business Advisory Council, and the Economic Club of New York.

Bandeen, Robert Angus
O.C., B.A., Ph.D., LL.D., D.C.L., K.St.J.

Business executive. b. October 29, 1930, Rodney, Ontario; m. Mona Helen Blair; s. Ian Blair, Mark Everett, Robert Derek, Adam Drummond; res. Toronto

Born on a farm in southern Ontario, Robert Bandeen became the youngest president of Canadian National Railways. Through efficient reorganization and cost cutting measures, Bandeen demonstrated his ability to lead large-scale corporations and made CN one of the world's few profitable national railways. He left CN in 1982 and is currently chairman, president, and chief executive officer of Crown Life Insurance. Receiving his education at the University of Western Ontario (B.A., 1952), Bandeen continued his studies in economics at Duke University (Ph.D., 1959). He has received four honorary degrees. His directorships include those of Consolidated-Bathurst, C-I-L, BP Canada, and Extendicare; he is a senator of the Stratford Shakespearean Festival Foundation, chairman of the Bach Festival (Centre-Stage Company), and chancellor of Bishop's University. An enthusiastic skier, Bandeen is also on the Canadian Ski Council. He is an Officer of the Order of Canada and a Knight of the Order of St. John.

Barclay, Ian A.
Chairman, B.C. Forest Products Ltd., Vancouver

Barr, David W.
Chairman, Moore Corp., Toronto

Barron, Alex E.
President, Canadian General Investments, Toronto

Beaubien, Philippe de Gaspé II
O.C., B.A., M.B.A., LL.D.

Business executive. b. January 12, 1928, Montreal; m. Nan Bowles O'Connell; s. Philippe III, François, d. Nanon; res. Westmount, Quebec.

Philippe de Gaspé Beaubien was educated at the University of Montreal and at Harvard, where he was a graduate of the School of Business Administration. He became the founding president of Beaubien Distribution and president of Télémedia (Québec), and is now chairman of the board and chief executive officer of Télémedia Communications and chairman of the board and publisher of TV Guide/TV Hebdo. He was director of operations and then mayor of Expo 67. He was the founder and continues as honorary chairman of Participaction, which drew Canadians' attention to the fact that fitness can and should be fun as well as healthy. He is a director of the Canada Development Corporation, Bombardier Inc., Reitman's (Canada), Canadian Satellite Communications, and McDonald's Restaurants of Canada, as well as the Banff School for Continuing Education, the Chief Executive Organization of Florida, and the York University Advisory Committee. Other activities include the Harvard-Radcliffe Parents Fund Committee, the Toronto French School, and the Canadian Centre of Films for Children. He has received the Order of Canada, the Canadian Centennial Medal, the Czechoslovak Gold Medal, and the B'nai B'rith Award of Merit. He belongs to the Mount Royal Club and the Saint-Denis Club in Montreal and York Club in Toronto.

Beaudoin, Laurent
O.C., B.A., M.Comm.

Business executive. b. May 1938, Laurier Station, Quebec; m. Claire Bombardier; s. Pierre, d. Nicole, Elaine, Denise; res. Knowlton, Quebec.

Laurent Beaudoin became president and chief executive officer of Bombardier at 28. He received his B.A. from the Collège Ste. Anne in Nova Scotia in 1957 and from the University of Sherbrooke he obtained a Master's degree in Commerce (1960). Beaudoin married the daughter of inventor and company founder J. Armand Bombardier. Bombardier's goal under the direction of Beaudoin has been to develop a balance between transportation and recreation—hence its development of both energy-conscious mass-transit vehicles and the Ski-Doo, a vehicle that provides recreation for thousands and that has changed the mode of transportation in the Canadian North. Before joining Bombardier as controller in 1963, he practised for two years as a chartered accountant in Quebec City with the firm of Beaudoin, Morin, Dufresne, and Associates. As well as holding directorships in many companies (including the National Bank of Canada and Celanese Canada), Beaudoin is a member of such clubs as the Saint-Denis, the St. James's, and Mount Royal. He became an Officer of the Order of Canada in 1973.

Beigie, Carle E.
Economist, Montreal

Robert Bandeen

Philippe de Gaspé Beaubien II

Robert Bonner

Peter Bentley at the Vancouver head office of Canadian Forest Products.

Bélanger, Michel Ferdinand

B.A., B.Sc.

Banker. b. September 10, 1929, Lévis, Quebec; m. Hélène; six children; res. Montreal.

When Michel Bélanger left the Montreal Stock Exchange to become a bank president in 1976, he announced that it was because "it's nice to start at the top." In November 1979 he orchestrated the merger of Banque Canadienne Nationale and the Provincial Bank of Canada, creating the National Bank of Canada of which he is now president, chairman of the board, and chief executive officer. He received a B.A. from the College de Lévis and a B.Sc. in economy from Laval University; as well, he was awarded a scholarship by the Central Mortgage and Housing Corporation for post-graduate studies at McGill (1952-54). He joined the Department of Finance in Ottawa in 1954, was with the Economic and International Affairs Division from 1957 to 1960, served as economic advisor for the Quebec Department of Industry and Commerce in 1966 after five years as assistant deputy minister. In 1969 he was economic advisor to the Quebec Executive Council and from 1973-76 Bélanger was president and chief executive officer of the Montreal Stock Exchange. His directorships include those of Power Corp. and Simpsons-Sears.

Bell, Joel I.

B.A., B.C.L., LL.M.

Business executive. b. February 20, 1941, Montreal; res. Ottawa.

Joel Bell left his position as the senior vice-president of finance for Petro-Canada to become the president and chief executive officer of the Canada Development Investment Corporation in 1982. He has served in an advisory capacity for numerous government organizations including the Prime Ministerial Task Force on Labour Relations (1967-68), consultant to the Economic Council of Canada (1967-69), staff consultant to the Canadian Department of Labour (1965-70), special advisor to the Ministry of Consumer and Corporate Affairs (1969-72), chairman of the Working Group on Foreign Investment (1970-73), special counsel to the CRTC (1973), special advisor to the Department of Energy, Mines, and Resources (1973-74), and economic advisor to the Prime Minister (1974-76). He was educated at McGill University (B.A., 1962; B.C.L., 1965), and before attending Harvard University (LL.M., 1967), he was a member of the law firm of Riel, LeDain, Bissonette, Vermette, & Ryan. Joel Bell is also the author of many articles on legal matters.

Bell, John Alexander Gordon

LL.D.

Banker. b. August 16, 1929, Rivers, Manitoba; m. Charlene Elizabeth McCabe; res. Toronto.

Gordon Bell is deputy chairman of the board, president, and chief operating officer of the Bank of Nova Scotia, president and chairman of Scotia Ventures, chairman of Scotia Mortgage, and vice-chairman of Scotia Realty. He has been with the Bank of Nova Scotia since 1948: since then he has been posted to London, Jamaica, and Halifax. He is also chairman of the Council for Canadian Unity and vice-president of the Boys and Girls Clubs of Canada. He belongs to the Toronto, the National, and the Granite clubs.

Bell, Thomas Johnston

B. Comm., LL.D.

Business executive. b. June 26, 1914, Southampton, Ontario; m. Gertrude Harshman; two sons, four daughters; res. Toronto.

Chairman of Abitibi-Price since 1967, Tom Bell is a powerful corporate man with widespread influence. He is also a director of the Royal Bank, Simpsons, Canada Cement Lafarge, and Fiberglas Canada; a trustee of Toronto General Hospital; and past president of the Canadian Arthritis and Rheumatism Society. During the Second World War he served in the 12th Field Regiment of the Royal Canadian Artillery and for six years immediately following the war was lieutenant-colonel of the 11th Field Regiment (Reserve). Bell was educated at Ridley College and the University of Toronto. He belongs to the Toronto, the York, and the Mount Royal clubs.

Belzberg, Sam

B.Comm.

Business executive. b. June 26, 1928, Calgary; m. Frances Cooper; one son, three daughters; res. Vancouver.

One of the three Belzberg brothers (the others are Hymie and Billy), Sam Belzberg began his financial career selling used cars after forgoing a career in law as being unprofitable. With a revolving $15,000 bank credit underwritten by his father, he got into oil leasing and began investing in real estate. In response to a need for real-estate development financing in Western Canada, he founded City Savings and Trust (now First City Trust) in 1962. The company now has assets of over $2 billion and 25 offices across Canada, with subsidiary offices in the United States, and is involved in all aspects of commercial financing. In 1969 he formed Western Realty Projects by consolidating the family's property holdings. The family's controlling interest was sold in 1973 for $48 million. He remains a director of First City Properties, as well as American Eagle Petroleums, and Aberford Resources, but since 1968 he has devoted more and more of his time to charitable organizations such as the United Jewish Appeal, the Canada-Israel Foundation for Academic Exchanges, and the Canadian Council of Christians and Jews. In 1977 he established the Dystonia Medical Research Foundation (and continues to serve as its president) and the Simon Wiesenthal Center for Holocaust Studies at Yeshiva University in Los Angeles. He is a member of advisory councils of the university of British Columbia and Rockefeller university.

Bentley, Peter John Gerald

O.C.

Business executive. b. March 17, 1930, Vienna; m. Sheila Farrington McGiverin; d. Barbara Ruth, Susan Patricia, Joan Katherine, Lisa Maria, s. Michael Peter; res. Vancouver.

Peter Bentley is president and chief executive officer of Canadian Forest Products Limited, which, until it went public in July of 1983, was one of the largest family-owned companies in Canada. As well as continuing to run Canfor (and Canfor Investments), Bentley is a director of Shell Canada and the Bank of Montreal. He is also one of the two Canadian directors (the other is Jean de Grandpré of Bell Canada) on the international advisory board of the Chemical Bank of New York. Canadian Forest Pro-

ducts was founded by Peter Bentley's father, Leopold Bentley, whose interest in big-game hunting had brought him to Canada from Austria as a visitor before the Second World War; when the war seemed inevitable in 1938, he moved his family to British Columbia, where he started a small veneer factory in New Westminster with 20 employees. Canfor now employs 6400 people in the company's logging, forestry, manufacturing, and marketing concerns. In addition to piloting Canfor, Bentley is a sports enthusiast: he made the Pacific Northwest Junior tennis finals and he played on the UBC golf team. He also enjoys shooting and sports-car racing (having recently migrated in his affections from Ferrari to BMW). He is an honorary director of the Canadian Professional Golfers Association and was part of the consortium that brought the Vancouver Canucks into the National Hockey League. Bentley is chairman of the Vancouver General Hospital Foundation and a Trustee of the British Columbia Sports Hall of Fame. Among his clubs are the Vancouver Lawn Tennis and Badminton Club, the Vancouver Gun Club, the Capilano Golf and Country Club, the Vancouver Club, and the Royal and Ancient Golf Club of St. Andrews, Scotland.

Bisson, André

C.M., B.A., M.S.C., M.B.A.

Banker. b. October 7, 1929, Trois Rivières, Quebec; m. Reine Lévesque; d. Isabelle, Hélène; res. Baie d'Urfé, Quebec.

André Bisson has helped adapt the Bank of Nova Scotia, a largely English-speaking institution, to the changing economic and social needs of Quebec. As senior vice-president and regional manager, he has made the bank a stronger force in the Quebec business community. The son of Roger Bisson, a judge of the Quebec Provincial Court, André Bisson studied at Laval and then at Harvard, where he received his M.B.A. In 1962 he returned to Laval to become its director of research and later director of the department of business administration. In 1966 he served for a year as the director of education of the Canadian Bankers Association, then became the director of the Institute of Canadian Bankers until 1971, when he joined the Bank of Nova Scotia. In 1982 he received the medal *Gloire de l'Escolle* of the Laval University Alumni Association and was made a Member of the Order of Canada. He is a director of Conseil du patronat du Québec, the Canadian Institute of Chartered Accountants, and the Fondation de l'Université du Québec à Montréal, among others, and acted as general campaign chairman of Centraide Montreal in 1975. He is a member of the Harvard Business School Association of Montreal, and such clubs as the Saint-Denis, the Mount Royal, and the St. James's.

Black, Conrad Moffat

B.A., M.A., LL.L., Litt.D., LL.D., K.L.J.

Business executive. b. Aug. 25, 1944, Montreal; m. Shirley Hishon Walters; one son, one daughter; res. Toronto.

When Conrad Black and his brother, G. Montegu Black, gained control of Argus Corp. in 1978, the event was more than another corporate takeover: it signified the passing of power from one generation of the economic elite to the next. As Argus chairman he succeeds E.P. Taylor and Bud McDougald, two of the most astute and bold corporate builders in Canadian business history, yet his approach to running one of the country's most important pools of wealth and influence is entirely his own. He is still in the midst of a reorganization of the Argus empire to turn it from a loose group of holdings controlled by interlocking directorships into a more tightly knit operating company, at the same time liberating great amounts of cash to finance further takeovers. Black's father, George Montegu Black, was one of the original Argus partners and his mother was a Riley of the Winnipeg family. Conrad Black went to school at Upper Canada College, Trinity College School, and Thornton Hall. He studied history and political science at Carleton, law at Laval, and earned his M.A. at McGill, writing a thesis on Maurice Duplessis that was later published as a book. One of his earlier enterprises was his purchase in 1969 with partners of the Sherbrooke *Record*, the only English-language daily newspaper in the Eastern Townships. This was the beginning of Sterling Newspapers, a group of about 20 papers in small to middle-sized towns that is still part of his holdings. Black had always followed affairs at Argus closely and his push to acquire control came after the death of Bud McDougald. Among the major moves since he took over have been parting with the near-bankrupt Massey-Ferguson and an attempted takeover of Hanna Mining Co. Black has been a member of the Toronto Club since he was 21 and belongs to the Mount Royal.

Black, James Thompson

C.A.

Business executive. b. July 16, 1925, Montreal; res. Oakville, Ontario.

James Black is chairman and chief executive officer of The Molson Companies and a director of Rio Algom, Petro-Canada, and Mutual Life of Canada. He has been with Molson's since 1949. He is also treasurer of the Canadian Manufacturers' Association, a director of the Council for Canadian Unity, and a trustee of the Fraser Institute. During the Second World War he served with the RCAF as a navigator with the rank of Flying Officer.

Blair, Sidney Robert

B.Sc., LL.D., LL.D., Ph.D.

Business executive. b. August 13, 1929, Port-of-Spain, Trinidad; divorced; s. James, Robert, Martin, d. Megan, Charlotte; res. Calgary.

Bob Blair has numerous critics on both sides of the energy fence: multinationals despair of his "leftist" tendencies of supporting environmentalist, nationalist, and feminist concerns (his company, Nova, employs the highest-placed woman executive in all of Canada's oil companies), while independents criticize his manipulation of Nova's original provincial charter to gain a competitive edge under the banner of free enterprise. Blair blithely ignores all controversy and has pushed Nova from its origins as Alberta Gas Trunk Line in 1954 to a billion dollar concern. Blair earned his degree in chemical engineering at Queen's University and worked as a field engineer and construction supervisor on pipelines, refineries, and operations before moving into management. Passionately involved with his business, he relaxes at his ranch only after putting in long hours at the office. He may well be the only executive of a major oil company ever to visit the towns

likely to be affected by his company's dealings to talk with the inhabitants to find out their concerns and to revise his plans should they prove too hazardous to the environment. He has no time or patience for the oilmen's club-and-golf course circuit, preferring instead to settle deals over a cup of coffee in a local eatery.

Bonner, Robert William

Q.C., C.D., B.A., LL.B.

Lawyer. b. September 10, 1920, Vancouver; m. Barbara Newman; s. Robert York, d. Barbara Caroline, Elizabeth Louise; res. Vancouver.

Robert W. Bonner was educated at public schools in Vancouver and at the University of British Columbia, from which he graduated in 1942 with a B.A. in economics and political science. He joined the Canadian Army after graduating and saw action with the Seaforth Highlanders of Canada in Britain, North Africa, Sicily, and Italy, where he was wounded; he retired from active service in 1946 with the rank of major and was appointed a lieutenant-colonel in the Reserve, commanding the UBC contingent of the COTC until 1953. He was called to the Bar in British Columbia in 1948 and practised law in Vancouver before entering the B.C. government in 1952 as attorney general, a post he held until 1969 (during which time he also held other portfolios, including Education, Industrial Development, Trade and Commerce, and Commercial Transport). He then joined MacMillan Bloedel as a senior vice-president, eventually being appointed president, chief executive officer, and chairman. Since 1976, he has been chairman of the B.C. Hydro and Power Authority. Among his other directorships are Inco, Montreal Trust Company, SCOR Reinsurance Company of Canada, Terramar Resource Corporation, and the Energy Supplies Allocation Board. He is a director of the Canadian Council of Christians and Jews, and Advisory Board member of the Salvation Army, governor of the Vancouver Opera Association, and a patron of the International Foundation for the Arts. Bonner is a life bencher of the Law Society of British Columbia, a member of the Canadian Bar Association, the Vancouver Board of Trade, and vice-president of the Institute of International Affairs. He belongs to the Union Club, the Vancouver Club, and the Capilano Golf and Country Club. His favourite recreation is sailing his Hans Christian '43.

Bonnycastle, Richard Arthur Norwood

B.Comm.

Investor, financial consultant. b. September 26, 1934, Winnipeg; res. Calgary.

As chairman of Harlequin Enterprises, Rupertsland Resources, and chairman and president of the Cavendish Investing Group, Dick Bonnycastle's business interests are vast and varied. He was educated at Ravenscourt School and Trinity College School, and received a B.Comm. from the University of Manitoba. He worked initially at Great-West Life Assurance and was with James Richardson and Sons from 1963 to 1970. During this same time period he helped his parents build up Harlequin Enterprises. His first venture in oil and gas was with Bob O'Connor of Pinnacle Petroleum in Calgary. His directorships now include Sulpetro, Rostland Corporation,

Commercial Oil and Gas, Gulch Resources, Pagurian Corp., and Ducks Unlimited. A thoroughbred enthusiast, he is director of the Canadian Thoroughbred Horse Society (Alberta Division) and Steward of the Jockey Club of Canada. In 1981, in partnership with George Gardiner, he bought the racing and breeding stock of the late Conn Smythe. His sister, Honor, is married to Michael de Pencier, the president of Key Publishers. His memberships include the St. Charles Country, the Royal Canadian Yacht, and the Ranchmen's clubs.

Bovey, Edmund Charles

C.M.

Business executive. b. January 29, 1916, Calgary; m. Margaret Snowdon; s. Charles, d. Myra; res. Toronto.

Retired chairman of Norcen Energy Resources Limited, Ed Bovey was the power behind its rise to one of Canada's largest integrated energy companies. He was educated in British Columbia and his first managerial position was that of assistant general superintendent of Burns & Company. His directorships include those of Abitibi-Price, Canada Packers, Canadian Imperial Bank of Commerce, and Argus-controlled companies, including Norcen. He was one of the instigators of the Japan-Canada Businessmen's Cooperation Conference. His keen interest in the arts—especially ballet, the symphony, and visual arts—led to his chairmanship of the Art Gallery of Ontario Foundation and the Council for Business and the Arts in Canada; he is also a member of the Board of Governors of Massey Hall. He was named a Member of the Order of Canada in 1978.

Brown, Peter MacLachlan

Investment dealer. b. December 15, 1941, Vancouver; m. Joanne Lee Crighton; s. James Mason, Jason Brenton; res. Vancouver.

The freewheeling and adventurous president of the Canarim Investment Corporation of Vancouver (Canarim is a combination of "Canada" and "Pacific Rim"), Peter Brown (known as "The Rabbit") gained spectacular entry into the Canadian Establishment both by the runaway success of his investment firm and by his almost single-handed reform of the Vancouver Stock Exchange. In *The Acquisitors*, Peter C. Newman calls him "as much a fiscal choreographer as a stock broker"; *Vancouver Sun* columnist Denny Boyd describes him as "so bright he makes your eyes water." Brown entered the University of British Columbia at 15; he left five years later and joined Greenshields in Montreal to learn the rudiments of underwriting. He returned to Vancouver in 1968, just as the Vancouver Stock Exchange's "speculative orgy," as Newman puts it, was getting under way. Brown founded Canarim in 1972 and has guided it (during the swashbuckling 13-hour days he puts in) to its present position of financial apotheosis. He appears to enjoy what he does. He loves to party and moves among the international financiers of his acquaintance—and he seems to know them all—with assurance and panache, sometimes with boyish glee. He owns 70 pairs of Gucci loafers (more, no doubt, by the time this is in print), a 1980 6.9 Mercedes-Benz, a 1983 Rolls-Royce Corniche, a Cadillac limousine, and a jeep. He also owns four boats, including a fully restored 1967 mahogany Riva Super Ariston. Brown

G. Allan Burton, seen below with his wife (known professionally as Betty Kennedy) and with one of his grandchildren, lives in the historic Limestone Hall, one of the most attractive country houses in southern Ontario.

ALL: J.R.

owns five per cent of the Vancouver Whitecaps soccer team, and a one-fifth interest in a Whistler Mountain ski resort. He is also part of a $200-million consortium called Realwest Energy. Brown is past president of the Vancouver Stock Exchange, a member of the National Executive Committee of the Investment Dealers Association of America, past chairman of the Accounting Research Advisory Board, and a member of the Institute of Chartered Accountants. He is vice-chairman of Expo 86, a governor of St. George's School, and a trustee and member of the Executive Committee of the Vancouver Art Gallery. In 1981 he was the Vancouver Chamber of Commerce's Businessman of the Year.

Bunting, John Pearce
B.Comm.

Business executive. b. September 6, 1929, Toronto; m. Stephanie Elizabeth Keeley; s. Mark, Charles, d. Elsa, Harriet, Alexandra; res. Toronto.

President of the Fédération Internationale des Bourses de Valeurs and president and chief executive officer of the Toronto Stock Exchange, J. Pearce Bunting studied at McGill University before joining his father in the firm of Alfred Bunting & Co. Ltd., of which he eventually became president. He is a director of Canadian General Tower Ltd., a member of the Board of Governors of Appleby College, chairman of St. John's Hospital, and president of the Lakeland Conservation Association. He belongs to the University, the Canadian, and the Empire clubs, the Board of Trade of Metropolitan Toronto, and the Osler Bluff Ski Club.

Burns, James William
B.Comm., M.B.A.

Business executive. b. December 27, 1929, Winnipeg; m. Barbara Mary Copeland; s. James, Alan, d. Martha; res. Montreal.

James Burns has been president of Power Corp. since 1979 and is president of Trans-Canada Corporation Fund and Shawinigan Industries, chairman of Great-West Life Assurance, and a director of various other companies including Consolidated-Bathurst, Genstar, IBM Canada, Investors Group, and Montreal Trust. He is also a director of the Conference Board of Canada, the Canadian Council of Christians and Jews, and the Arthritis Society. He is honorary lieutenant-colonel of the Queen's Own Cameron Highlanders of Canada. Burns was educated at the University of Manitoba and the Harvard School of Business Administration before joining Great-West Life in 1953. Among his clubs are the Manitoba, the Toronto, and the Mount Royal.

Burns, Latham Cawthra
B.A.

Investment dealer. b. June 26, 1930, Toronto; m. Patricia Annette Higgins; s. Reed, Holton, d. Farish, Cawthra, Ainsley; res. Toronto.

Latham Burns is chairman of the investment firm of Burns Fry and a nephew of the founder of the company's predecessor, Burns Bros., which he joined in 1952. His great-great-grandfather, James Austin, founded the Dominion Bank and his mother was a member of the mercantile Cawthra family, once considered Toronto's richest. He is among the most influential of the investment dealers who run

the Toronto capital market. He is also a director of five other companies, and of St. Michael's Hospital and Bishop Strachan School. Burns was educated at Trinity College School, Collegiate School in New York, and Cornell University. Among his clubs are the Toronto, the York, and the Badminton and Racquet.

Burton, G. Allan
D.S.O., E.D., K.L.J., LL.D.

Business executive. b. January 20, 1915, Toronto; m. Betty Kennedy; m. Audrey Caro Syer (deceased); s. James, d. Gail, Lynn, Janice; res. Milton, Ontario.

Allan Burton has had a multifaceted career, which includes business, community service, the military, art, and sports. For 11 years, until he retired in 1979, he was chairman and chief executive officer of Simpsons Ltd., where he began as a stockboy 44½ years earlier. (His father C. L. Burton was also president and chairman of the firm.) His community service activities included chairmanship of the Toronto Redevelopment Advisory Council (which he helped to found and for which he was responsible for the creation of $1 billion of downtown renewal and development in its first 10 years). He was also president of the Toronto Board of Trade (1962) and chairman of the Business Advisory Group of the University of Western Ontario (1976-80) and of the Metro Toronto Industrial Commission (1967-70). He served with the Governor General's Horse Guards from 1936 to 1970, rising to honorary colonel, and was decorated with a Distinguished Service Order and an Efficiency Decoration. He has served on the Ontario College of Art's Council and is a "reasonably competent" watercolourist. While on the National Industrial Design Council he created the Design Awards to Industry. His main sports interest is horses: he has been for 23 years MFH at the Eglinton & Caledon Hunt Club and he is president of the Royal Agricultural Winter Fair. He is also a member of the Toronto, the York, and the Mount Royal clubs. In 1976 Burton married broadcaster Betty Kennedy, who brought four of her own children and four stepchildren to join Burton's own four children.

Cameron, Peter

President, Canadian Corporate Management, Toronto

Campbell, Donald Graham
F.C.A.

Business executive. b. August 14, 1925, Toronto; m. Audrey Irene Reid; s. David, Marc, Reid, Craig, Scott; res. Islington, Ontario.

Donald Campbell is one of Canada's influential figures in communications in his capacity of chairman and chief executive officer of Maclean Hunter. He studied to be a chartered accountant and, during the Second World War, became a flying officer with the Royal Canadian Air Force in Europe. On his return to Canada he joined Price Waterhouse. In 1950-51 he was treasurer of Noma Lites. He was secretary-treasurer of Atomic Energy of Canada from 1952 to 1957, when he joined what was then Maclean-Hunter Publishing Co. Ltd.; he became president in 1970. He is a director of the Toronto-Dominion Bank, Steinberg Inc., and Maclean Hunter's recent acquisition, Toronto Sun Publishing Corp. He is a

member of the Board of Trustees for the Hospital for Sick Children, the Advisory Committee for the School of Business Administration of the University of Western Ontario, and the Toronto Redevelopment Council, and is past chairman of the Canadian Section of the Commonwealth Press. He belongs to the York Club in Toronto.

Campeau, Robert
D.U.

Real-estate developer. b. August 3, 1923, Sudbury; m. Ilse Luebbert; six children; res. Toronto.

Robert Campeau is the aggressive chairman and chief executive officer of Campeau Corporation who made headlines in 1980 with his unsuccessful attempt to take over Royal Trustco, Canada's largest trust company. Since its formation in 1953, the company has built some 17,000 houses as well as apartment and commercial buildings, shopping centres, and such complexes as Les Terrasses de la Chaudière in Hull, Place de Ville in Ottawa, and Harbour Square in Toronto. It has expanded into Alberta, Texas, Florida, and California and has invested in three Canadian high-tech companies. Robert Campeau began his career in Ottawa in 1949 by taking advantage of the post-war housing shortage and by diversifying his building company through the acquisition of subsidiaries, including a building supply company and a lumber milling operation. He and his family own 70 per cent of the company and 90 per cent of the voting shares. He is on the Board of Governors of Ashbury College in Ottawa and was a charter member of the Board of Regents of Laurentian University in Sudbury. In 1981 the University of Ottawa made him Doctor of the University. Among his clubs are the Rideau in Ottawa and the Mount Royal in Montreal.

Chalmers, Floyd Sherman
O.C., LL.D., Litt.D., B.F.A.

Business executive (retired), patron of the arts. b. September 14, 1898, Chicago; m. Jean Boxall; s. Wallace, d. Joan; res. Toronto.

Floyd Chalmers began his career as a reporter on the Toronto *World* in 1916. He joined the *Financial Post* in 1919 and rose through the ranks to become president of Maclean-Hunter (1952-1964) and chairman (1964-1969). He has been honorary chairman since 1978. He grew up in Orillia and Toronto, served with the 1st Canadian Tank Battalion in the First World War, and attended Khaki College in England. Honoured for his professional ability (he was inducted into the Canadian News Hall of Fame, received four honorary degrees, and was named a Fellow of the International Institute of Arts & Letters), Chalmers is equally renowned in Canada's cultural community. He is the recipient of the Centennial Medal, the Queen's Jubilee Medal, the Diplome d'Honneur of the Canadian Conference of the Arts, and the Toronto Drama Bench Award for Distinguished Contribution to Canadian Theatre, and was the first person to receive the Canadian Music Council Special Award and the Medal of Appreciation from the Ontario Arts Council. He is an Officer of the Order of Canada. The Floyd S. Chalmers Foundation, established to promote and develop the performing arts in Canada, commissioned the opera *Louis Riel* and annually presents the

Edmund Bovey with some of his collection of contemporary art.

Floyd Chalmers with memorabilia from his long career in journalism and the arts.

Chalmers Award of $5,000 to the best drama mounted in Canada during the previous year. Chalmers was also a founder of the Canadian Opera Company and president of the Stratford Shakespearean Festival, and somehow managed to find the time to write a biography of John Bayne Maclean (*A Gentleman of the Press*). His autobiography, *Two Sides of the Street*, was published in the fall of 1983.

Charron, André
Q.C., B.A., LL.L.

Investment dealer, lawyer. b. December 10, 1923, Montreal; m. Louise Mongeau; s. André, Guy-Philippe, d. Caroline, Fannie; res. Montreal.

André Charron is president and member of the Executive Committee of the Montreal investment firm of Lévesque, Beaubien, founded by J.-Louis Lévesque. He is also chairman of Industrial Life, vice-chairman of Northern Life and North West Life, and a director of several companies including Campeau Corp., National Trust, Steinberg Inc., and Atomic Energy of Canada; and a former Chairman of the Montreal Stock Exchange. He was admitted to the Bar of Quebec in 1947. He is a director of l'Hôpital Marie Enfant and belongs to the Mount Royal and the Saint-Denis clubs.

Child, Arthur James Edward
B.Comm., M.A., F.C.I.S.

Business executive. b. May 19, 1910, Guildford, Surrey, England; res. Calgary.

Arthur Child is one of the most important non-oil businessmen in Alberta. Since becoming president and CEO of Burns Foods in 1966, he is credited with saving the company from bankruptcy and making it into the second-largest meat packer in the country. He owns 25 per cent of the company's shares and is chairman of the company's five subsidiaries, president of four other companies, and director of, among others, La Vérendrye Management Corporation. He is a founder and chairman of the Canada West Foundation. Unlike most other members of the Alberta business elite, Child speaks French and feels at home in Quebec. He is noted for his dedication to business: he works 10 hours a day, seven days a week. He is a member of the Royal Canadian Military Institute and the International Institute for Strategic Studies, has a large military library, and believes in applying military techniques to business management. He is also the author of *Economics and Politics in U.S. Banking*. Child has flown his own Gypsy Moth and has made many long voyages at the wheel of a series of motor launches called *Cybele*. He was educated at Queen's University, Laval, the Harvard Business School, and the University of Toronto. Among his clubs are the Mount Royal, the St. James's, the Vancouver, the University (Toronto), the Royal Canadian Yacht, and the Ranchmen's.

Clarke, George F.S.
B.Comm., F.S.A., F.C.I.A.

Business executive. b. February 1, 1921, Govan, Saskatchewan; m. Elsa Marian McLeod; m. Sheila Stewart (deceased); d. Georgia; res. Toronto.

George Clarke is president of Sun Life and a director of Royal Trustco. He is a director of the Canadian Cancer Society and sits on the Board of Governors of the University of Waterloo. During the Second World War he served with the RCAF in Britain, the Middle East, India, and Ceylon and attained the rank of flight lieutenant. He was with Manufacturers Life from 1950 to 1967, when he joined Sun Life as an actuary. He became executive vice-president in 1972 and president in 1978. Among his clubs are the Mount Royal and the Toronto.

Clarke, Lawrence D.
LL.B.

Business executive. b. June 12, 1925, London; married; res. Toronto.

Larry Clarke is founder, chairman, chief executive officer, and major shareholder of Spar Aerospace, the company that built the Canadarm used in the American Space Shuttle. Previously a vice-president of de Havilland, Clarke created Spar in 1967 by buying the Special Products and Applied Research Branch of de Havilland. Since then, he has diversified the company by acquiring a manufacturer of aircraft gear boxes, the space electronics unit of Northern Telecom, and the Montreal satellite and communications plant of RCA Canada.

Clyne, John Valentine
C.C., K.G.St.J., B.A., LL.D.

Business executive. b. February 14, 1902, Vancouver; m. Betty Somerset; s. John Stuart, d. Valentine; res. Vancouver.

Jack Clyne ruled the burgeoning forest products empire of MacMillan Bloedel for 16 years. During this time MacBlo's sales shot up from $160 million to $966 million. Fatherless from an early age, Clyne spent his teenage summers working as a cowboy and a placer miner to earn university tuition. Following postgraduate studies in London, he was admitted to the bar in British Columbia in 1927; soon thereafter he began a 20-year association with Macrae, Duncan and Clyne as a specialist in shipping and admiralty law. In 1947 he was named chairman of the Canadian Maritime Commission and three years later was appointed to the Supreme Court of British Columbia and served on the bench until 1957, when he resigned to join MacMillan Bloedel as chairman and chief executive officer. He also served as sole Royal Commissioner in three public inquiries, including that of the province's milk industry in 1954, and his recommendations paved the way for the current provincial legislation governing that industry. A member, director, or honorary member of many professional and business associations, he has given numerous speeches on the Canadian Constitution and Canadian unity, as well as on institutional and political reform. His out-of-town clubs include the Mount Royal (Montreal), Rideau (Ottawa), and the Bohemian (San Francisco).

Cohen, H. Reuben
C.M., Q.C., B.A., LL.B., D.C.L.

Lawyer. b. July 11, 1921, Moncton; m. Louise Glustein; d. Debra, Natalie; res. Moncton.

One of the Maritimes' most powerful businessmen, Reuben Cohen first began his law career in 1945 after graduation from the Dalhousie Law School. He has gradually put together a broad financial network that encompasses large holdings and/or accompanying directorships in such companies as Central Trust Company, the Maritime Life Assurance Company, the Mortgage Insurance Company of Canada, MICC Investments, United Financial Management, Enheat Inc. LifeSurance Corporation, and Inter-City Gas Corporation. He is chairman of the Investment Committee of the Board of Governors of Dalhousie University and is trustee of the Canadian YMCA Retirement Fund. He was appointed a Member of the Order of Canada in 1979 and is a member of the Halifax Club, the Canadian Bar Association, and the barristers' societies of New Brunswick and Moncton. He owns a large private art collection.

Cohon, George A.
B.Sc., J.D.

Business executive. b. April 19, 1937, Chicago; m. Susan Silver; s. Craig, Mark; res. Toronto.

Raised in Chicago, George Cohon graduated from Drake University in Iowa with a B.Sc. and from Northwestern School of Law with a Juris Doctorate in law. From 1961 to 1967 he practised law with the firm of Cohon, Raizes & Regal and then moved to Toronto, where he became the licensee of McDonald's Corporation for Eastern Canada. He rapidly expanded the food chain and became the corporation's largest licensee by 1970, when McDonald's acquired his license agreement. He stayed on with the company as president of McDonald's Restaurants of Ontario and is now president of McDonald's Restaurants of Canada, which numbers over 425 units across Canada and has sales of $650 million a year. His most famous philanthropic works include founding the Ronald McDonald House of Canada Foundation and being the rescuer of Toronto's popular Santa Claus parade. He has received Israel's highest public service award, the Prime Minister's Medal, as well as the B'nai B'rith Canada 1983 Humanitarian Award and the Promises of Hope Award from the Canadian Children's Foundation. He owns a 1938 Cadillac limousine and a 1967 Chevrolet Impala convertible.

Cormie, Donald Mercer
Q.C., B.A., LL.B., LL.M.

Business executive, lawyer. b. July 24, 1922, Edmonton; m. Eivor Elisabeth Ekstrom; s. John Mills, Donald Robert, James Mercer, Neil Brian, Bruce George, Robert Ekstrom; d. Allison Barbara, Eivor Emilie; res. Edmonton

Chairman, president, and chief executive officer of Principal Group Ltd., a financial services company, Donald Cormie is also responsible for the development of the largest purebred-cattle establishment in Canada using a computer genetic selection program. (A Simmental bull named Signal from this project has the largest number of living offspring in the world.) Educated at the University of Alberta and Harvard, Mr. Cormie began his career as a partner at Smith, Clement, Parlee & Whitaker and has been senior partner at Cormie Kennedy since 1954. He holds numerous directorships and is a member of several clubs and organizations, including the Edmonton and the Royal Glenora clubs and the World Business Council. A collector of early Canadian and Group of Seven art, he also enjoys travelling up the British Columbia coast to Alaska on his 48-

foot Cheoy Lee motor yacht, which can do 35 knots.

Cowpland, Michael C.J.

President, Mitel Corp., Nepean, Ontario

Crang, James Harold

Investment dealer (retired), b. January 11, 1902; m. Dorothy K. Ritchie (deceased); s. James Harold Jr.; m. Margaret Alice Dunlap; res. Toronto

At age 81, active sportsman James Crang reports a catch of 35 salmon in 1983. In 1956 he established a world skeet shooting record of 781 kills in 44 minutes, 58 seconds! He hunted with the Eglinton and Caledon for 60 years. Born in Toronto, Crang attended Upper Canada College. He is now honorary chairman of Crang and Ostiguy and president of Glenville Dairy. He was a major with the 7th Toronto Regiment in 1942 and became Director of Artillery, Canada, 1943-44, and Deputy Director General, Army Technical Development Board. He is a director of the Atlantic Salmon Association, the Toronto and North York Hunt, honorary life director of the Canadian Equestrian Federation, and honorary president of the Eglinton and Caledon Hunt. He raises Guernsey Cattle at his Newmarket farm.

Crawford, Allan

Chairman, Anatek Electronics, North Vancouver

Crump, Norris Roy

C.C., M.E., K.St.J., D.Eng., D.Sc., LL.D., D.C.L.

Business executive (retired). b. July 30, 1904, Revelstoke, British Columbia; m. Stella Elvin; d. Anne Louise, Janice; res. Calgary.

The former chairman, president, and chief executive officer of Canadian Pacific Limited was instrumental in the gradual patriation of CP from less than one-tenth Canadian ownership to more than two-thirds in 1982. During this time CP—Canada's largest private-sector company—began to diversify its rail holdings from transportation (CP Hotels, CP Telecommunications, and CP Air, among others). The son of a railwayman, Buck Crump attended Purdue University, where he studied engineering, after starting to work for Canadian Pacific in 1920. Later he earned an M.A. from Purdue. He rose through the ranks to become president of CP in 1955. He has served on the boards of many major companies such as the Bank of Montreal and Inco. His great interest in Indian lore led to his fellowship of the Glenbow Museum and membership of the Kainai, a blood tribe of Alberta, in addition to many community service activities. He is a Companion of the Order of Canada and a Knight of the Order of St. John and has eight honorary degrees. Now retired, he spends summers on his farm and reads about ancient history and archeology, when not enlarging his gun and antique collections.

Culver, David Michael

B.Sc., M.B.A.

Business executive. b. December 5, 1924, Winnipeg; m. Mary Cecile Powell; s. Michael, Andrew, Mark, d. Diane; res. Montreal.

Since 1979, David Culver has been president and chief executive officer of Alcan Alumini-

um, which he joined in 1949. He is also a director of Canadair, MacMillan Bloedel, and American Express; chairman of the Canada Japan Business Co-operation Committee; and a governor of McGill University. During the Second World War he served with the Canadian Infantry Corps. Culver was educated at Selwyn House, Lower Canada College, Trinity College School, McGill University, the Harvard Business School, and the Centre d'Études Industrielles in Geneva. His wife is the daughter of a former president of the Aluminium Co. of Canada, Alcan's largest subsidiary. Among his clubs are the St. James's and the Mount Royal.

Dagenais, Camille A.

C.C., Eng., B.A.Sc., LL.D., D.Sc., D.A.Sc., F.E.I.C., F.C.S.C.E.

Engineer. b. November 12, 1920, Montreal; m. Pauline Falardeau; s. Guy, Alain, Claude; res. Montreal.

Considered one of Canada's foremost engineers, Camille Dagenais was educated at the Ecole Polytechnique de Montréal, where he received his B.A.Sc. in 1946. He then worked in various engineering capacities on different projects until 1953, when he joined Surveyer, Nenniger & Chênevert Inc. as project engineer. Now chairman of the board of the SNC Group, as it is now known, he has numerous megaprojects under his belt, including studies of the power potential of large Quebec rivers; design of the Daniel Johnson Dam (Manic 5), the world's highest multiple-arch dam; design of the Idukki Dam and Hydroelectric Development in India; and rehabilitation of the heavy-water plant at Glace Bay, Nova Scotia. Among the awards he has received are the Julian C. Smith Medal of the Engineering Institute of Canada, the Medal of Merit of the Association des Diplômés de l'Université de Montréal, and honorary degrees from the Royal Military College of Canada and the universities of Sherbrooke and Laval. He has acted as president or vice-president of various engineering societies such as the Canadian Society for Civil Engineering, the Association of Consulting Engineers of Canada, and the Canadian Nuclear Association, and also served as president of the International Commission on Large Dams. He is a director of the Royal Bank of Canada and Spar Aerospace Ltd., among others, and is a member of the Saint-Denis, Mount Stephen, and Mount Royal clubs.

d'Aquino, Thomas Paul

B.A., LL.B., LL.M.

Lawyer. b. November 3, 1940, Nelson, British Columbia; m. Susan Marion Peterson; res. Ottawa.

Tom d'Aquino was educated at the University of British Columbia, Queen's, and the universities of London and Paris in law and political science. Most of his career has been in or close to government. He was executive assistant to James Richardson (1968–69) and special assistant to Pierre Trudeau (1969–72). He has been a legal advisor and consultant since 1972 and is president of the Business Council on National Issues, president of Intercounsel Ltd., and professor adjunct in the Faculty of Law at the University of Ottawa, where he teaches law of international business transactions. He is a member of the Law Society of British Columbia, Canadian Bar Association, International

Bar Association, Institute of Public Administration of Canada, and the Rideau Club. He lives in a house designed and formerly owned by Hart Massey and drives a 380 SLC Mercedes.

Daniel, C. William

O.C., B.A.Sc., LL.D., P.Eng.

Business executive. b. February 17, 1925, Toronto; m. Ruth Conway; s. David, Robert, d. Colleen, Karen; res. Toronto.

William Daniel has had a long career with Shell Canada, beginning when he graduated from the University of Toronto with a degree in mining engineering in 1947. Since then he has held a variety of positions, serving in petroleum-engineering assignments in Shell branches in the United States, the Netherlands, Venezuela, and Canada; managerial assignments in Canada and Trinidad; and his present position of president and chief executive officer of Shell Canada, which he has held since 1974. He has served on the Council for Canadian Unity and was also vice-chairman and director of the Conference Board of Canada. A trustee of the Ontario Science Centre and of the Toronto School of Theology, he is also a director of Junior Achievement of Canada and a member of the Business Council on National Issues. He belongs to the Toronto, the Rideau, and the Goodwood clubs.

de Grandpré, Albert Jean

O.C., Q.C., B.A., B.C.L., Ph.D., D.U.

Business executive, lawyer. b. September 14, 1921, Montreal; m. Hélène Choquet; s. Jean-François, d. Liliane, Suzanne, Louise; res. Outremont, Quebec.

Jean de Grandpré was educated at Collège Jean de Brébeuf and McGill and was called to the Bar of Quebec in 1943. He practised law with Tansey, de Grandpré, Bergeron and Monet until 1966, when he was appointed general counsel with Bell Canada. He rose within the company through several vice-presidential positions to become president in 1973 and chairman and chief executive officer in 1976. His clubs include the Mount Royal and the Saint-Denis and he is a director of some of the largest businesses, including the Toronto-Dominion Bank, Chrysler, Stelco, and Seagram's.

Desmarais, Paul

O.C., B.Comm., LL.D.

Business executive. b. January 4, 1927, Sudbury; m. Jacqueline Maranger; two sons, two daughters; res. Montreal.

"I think," Paul Desmarais has said, "I've proved that a French Canadian can make it in the business community." Desmarais, who is chairman and chief executive officer of Power Corp., started on a brilliant career of free-wheeling corporate takeovers when he left Osgoode Hall Law School in 1951 to return to his home town to assume the running of his grandfather's calcified bus company. In the words of the *Financial Post's* Amy Booth, he has "been redeploying assets ever since." The acquisition of other bus lines in Ontario and Quebec eventually resulted in the Transportation Management Corp., which subsequently added the holding company Gelco Enterprises, the Imperial Life Assurance Co., and the Investors Group. Desmarais reverse takeover technique,

ABOVE: *Jack Diamond, chairman of the B.C. Jockey Club, at the track.*
BELOW LEFT: Russell Harrison in the boardroom of the Canadian
Imperial Bank of Commerce. BELOW: Paul Desmarais with his family in
1969. The elder son, Paul, is now a vice-president of Power Corp. André
is married to a daughter of Jean Chretien.

in which the smaller company takes over the larger, has been aptly referred to as "the fish swallowing the whale technique" and is his specialty. Eventually, Desmarais took over J.-Louis Lévesque's Trans-Canada Corporation Fund; a few years later, Desmarais acquired his controlling position within Power Corp. Desmarais now heads a major corporate empire with a financial wing consisting principally of the Investors Group, the Great-West Life Assurance Company, the Montreal Trust Company; a resources-area holdings wing (Consolidated-Bathurst); and a media wing consisting of *La Presse* and three other Quebec newspapers. Lately Desmarais has been turning his empire-building attentions to Canadian Pacific. Desmarais is a member of the Business Council on National Issues, the Canada-China Trade Council, the Clinical Research Institute of Montreal, the Fraser Institute, the Hudson Institute, the C.D. Howe Research Institute, the Institute for research on Public Policy, and the Board of the Montreal Museum of Fine Arts. His clubs include the Mount Royal, the Rideau, the Toronto, the Eldorado Country (Palm Desert, California), the Bath and Tennis (Palm Beach, Florida), the St. Andrews (Delray Beach, Florida), and the 21 Club in New York. His son André married France Chrétien, daughter of federal cabinet minister Jean Chrétien.

Diamond, Jack
O.C., LL.D.

Business executive. b. April 9, 1909, Poland; m. Sadie Mandleman; s. Charles, Gordon; res. Vancouver.

Jack Diamond's history would give one the impression of his having the Midas touch: everything he has become interested in has been virtually guaranteed to succeed. A butcher in his native Poland, Diamond purchased the failing Pacific Meat Co. after he arrived in Canada and turned the company into the largest independent meat-packing company in Western Canada before he sold the business in 1964. Later that year he founded West Coast Reduction, of which he is chairman and which is now the largest reduction plant and exporter of tallow and rapeseed oil in Western Canada. His love of horses resulted in organizational success that paralleled his business efforts: he became president of B.C. Turf before its amalgamation with the Ascot Jockey Club in 1960 to become the British Columbia Jockey Club, which now operates the second largest racetrack in Canada. He was chosen Man of the Year by the Jockey's Benefit Association of Canada and inducted into Canada's Horse Racing Hall of Fame; he has received the second annual Sovereign Award of the Jockey Club of Canada. He is a life member of the B.C. Thoroughbred Horse Society and the Horsemen's Benevolent and Protective Association. Among the various honours he has received are first honorary mayor of Marpole, Good Citizen Award (1955) of the Native Sons of British Columbia, and honorary member (and past president) of the Rotary Club of South Vancouver.

Dimma, William Andrew
B.A.Sc., P.Eng., M.B.A., D.B.A., K.C.L.J.

Business executive. b. August 13, 1928, Montreal; m. Katherine Ash; d. Katherine, Suzanne; res. Toronto

Now chairman of the board of Polysar Limited and the president of A.E. LePage (one of Canada's largest real-estate concerns), William Dimma's career has combined education and business. He first studied chemical engineering at the University of Toronto, then business administration at York University before entering Harvard's middle management program. Then, in 1967 he became executive vice-president and director of Union Carbide Canada; in 1974 he returned to York to become dean of Administrative Studies. He was president and director of the giant Torstar Corporation and Toronto Star Newspapers Limited from 1976 to 1978 before joining Polysar. During this time he returned to Harvard to receive his Doctorate in Business Administration. He is a director of such companies as the Continental Bank of Canada and Simpsons-Sears and was on the Board of Governors of Bishop Strachan School (1977 to 1980) and the Economic Council of Canada (1978 to 1981). Dimma remained a member of the Liberal Party "through thick and thin (and without danger pay!)" and he chaired the 1981 Confederation Dinner in honour of Canada's Prime Minister. He is the author of *Canada Development Corporation: Diffident Experiment on a Large Scale* and is married to Katherine Ash, daughter of W.M Vacy Ash, president of Shell Canada from 1948 to 1967. He is a Knight Commander of the Order of St. Lazarus and collects toy soldiers and military figures.

Dlouhy, Dominik

President, Maison Placements Canada Ltd., Montreal

Dobrin, Melvyn

Chief Executive Officer, Steinberg Inc., Montreal

Dobrin, Mitzi
B.A., LL.B.

Business executive. b. 1931, Montreal; née Steinberg; m. Melvyn A. Dobrin; d. Terry Dobrin-Minzberg, s. Lewis, Ronald; res. Montreal.

Mitzi Dobrin, eldest daughter of Sam Steinberg, is credited with having revitalized the Miracle Mart discount stores owned by her father's supermarket chain and saved them from bankruptcy. In 1973, when she was appointed vice-president and general manager, the company was on the verge of bankruptcy; by 1975 it was breaking even and by 1976 it was in the black. By the early 1980s it was not the most profitable division of Steinberg Inc., but it was holding its own. Before taking over Miracle Mart, Dobrin had completed a law degree at McGill and done a little legal aid work, but had had no experience in business. In 1976 she became the first woman director of the Royal Bank; in 1978 she became the first woman to sit on the council of the Montreal Board of Trade in its 150-year history. In 1983 she was named as Steinberg Inc.'s vice-president of legal and corporate affairs. Her husband, Melvyn Dobrin, is chairman and chief executive officer of Steinberg Inc., which he had joined in 1950. The Dobrins collect Canadian art, including Group of Seven paintings.

Drummond, Brian Paul
B.A., M.B.A.

Investment dealer. b. February 17, 1931, Montreal; m. Althea McQueen; s. Jeffrey Sise, d. Kim Ann, Willa McQueen; res. Westmount, Quebec.

Chairman of the Montreal Stock Exchange and vice-chairman of Richardson Greenshields of Canada, Brian Drummond studied at Dalhousie University and the University of Western Ontario, where he received his M.B.A. He then joined the sales department of Aluminum Co. of Canada in Montreal and Windsor, and began working in the Underwriting Department of Greenshields Inc. in Montreal in 1958. He rose to his present position of vice-chairman of Richardson Greenshields, which was formed by a merger with Richardson Securities of Canada in 1982. He is a director of several companies notable in the financial community and his community service activities encompass the Canadian Council of Christians and Jews, the Montreal General Hospital, Lower Canada College, and the School of Business Administration of the University of Western Ontario. He is a descendant on his maternal side of the Sise family, who established the company that is now Bell Canada. He belongs to the Mount Royal Club, St. James's Club, and XPO (Ex-Young Presidents' Organization), and is married to the daughter of Archibald McQueen, a former general manager of the Bank of London and South America in Caracas, Venezuela.

Duncan, James Stuart
C.M.G., LL.D.

Manufacturer, b. 1893, Paris; m. Victoria Martinez Alonzo; one son, two daughters; res. Paget, Bermuda.

Known in his time as "the saviour of Massey-Harris," James Duncan joined the company in Berlin in 1909, came to Canada in 1911, and rose to become president in 1941, then chairman and president in 1949, positions that he held until he resigned in 1956. He was a director of many other companies, including the Bank of Commerce, Argus Corp., Odeon Theatres, and Inco. In the year of the opening of the St. Lawrence Seaway, he was chairman of the Hydro-Electric Power Commission of Ontario (now Ontario Hydro). During the First World War he served as a captain with an artillery unit of the British Army and was mentioned in despatches. During the Second World War he was acting deputy minister of Defence for Air and in charge of the British Commonwealth Air Training Plan. He is an honorary air commodore and was made a Chevalier of the French Legion of Honour; he also received the Cross of Lorraine and the King Haakon VII Cross of Lebanon. He is the author of various publications, including *Russia's Bid for World Supremacy* and *A Businessman Looks at Red China*. He speaks German, French, and Spanish fluently. He belongs to the York Club and the Royal Bermuda Yacht Club.

Eyton, John Trevor
Q.C., B.A., LL.B.

Lawyer, business executive. b. July 12, 1934, Quebec City; m. Barbara Jane Montgomery; s. Adam Tudor, Christopher Montgomery, d. Deborah Jane, Susannah Margaret, Sarah Elizabeth; res. Toronto.

President and chief executive officer of the massive Brascan and a partner in the distinguished law firm of Tory, Tory, DesLauriers & Binnington, Trevor Eyton is one of the more powerful figures in Canada's business community. He earned his degree in law at the University of Toronto (receiving an Honours

ABOVE: John V. Clyne in the Chancellor's office, University of British Columbia with the university mace carved by artist Bill Reid.

Trevor Eyton

Reva Gerstein

James Gray

J.R.

Medal and the Dean's Prize in his first year of law) and began working for Tory, Tory, DesLauriers & Binnington after graduating in 1960. He became a close associate of Edward and Peter Bronfman, whose Edper Investments took over Brascan in 1979. Eyton was appointed president shortly afterwards; by the end of 1979 he had increased the company's net income four times over. He is a member of various "Establishment" clubs, including the Toronto, the Empire, and the Canadian. Eyton holds directorships in a diverse group of major companies, including the Bank of Montreal, Hume Publishing, and Scott Paper. He is also involved with charitable institutions such as the Arthritis Society (Ontario Division), Sunnybrook Medical Centre Institute, and the Canadian Council of Christians and Jews.

Farrar, Geoffrey

President, Barclay's Bank of Canada, Toronto

Farris, J. Haig de B.

Ventures West Capital Ltd., Vancouver

Fell, Anthony Smithson

Investment dealer. b. February 23, 1939, Toronto; m. Shari Helen Graham; d. Annabelle Elizabeth, s. Graham Charles, Geoffrey Allen; res. Toronto.

Chairman, president, and chief executive officer of Dominion Securities Ames Ltd., Anthony Fell is in charge of Canada's largest underwriters of government and corporate securities. Educated at St. Andrew's College in Aurora, Ontario, Fell remains on the board of governors there. He holds directorships in several organizations, most notably Goodyear Canada, Kellogg Salada Canada, and the Canadian Arthritis and Rheumatism Society. His brother Fraser left the Toronto law firm of Fasken & Calvin in 1983 to become chairman of CEO of Dome Mines; Fraser Fell is on the board of Royal Trustco, Dome Petroleum, and Excelsior Life. The brothers are sons of C.P. Fell, president of Empire Life from 1934 to 1937. Anthony Fell is a member of the Toronto and the York clubs.

Frazee, Rowland Cardwell

B.Comm.

Banker. b. May 12, 1921, Halifax; m. Marie Eileen Tait; d. Catherine, s. Stephen; res. Town of Mount Royal, Quebec.

Chairman and chief executive officer of Canada's largest financial institution, the Royal Bank, Rowland Frazee—like his father before him—has made banking a lifelong career. After seeing active service with the Carleton and York Regiment in Britain and Europe during the Second World War, he left the Army with the rank of major and returned to the bank (which he had joined in 1939 at St. Stephen, New Brunswick) and Dalhousie University, graduating in 1948 with his Bachelor of Commerce degree. He moved steadily up the corporate ladder with the Royal Bank, culminating with the appointment to his present position in October 1980. Frazee acts as a director of many organizations, most notably the Business Council on National Issues, the Sports Fund for the Physically Disabled, and the Council for Canadian Unity. He is a governor of McGill University, a director of several companies

(including Power Corp. and Imasco Ltd.), and a member of eight clubs, including the Lyford Cay, the Toronto, the Rideau, the St. James's, and the Mount Royal.

Gallagher, John Patrick

O.C., D.Sc.

Business executive. b. July 16, 1916, Winnipeg; m. Kathleen Stewart; s. James Stewart, Thomas Patrick, Frederick Michael; res. Calgary.

The flamboyant son of a real estate agent, "Smilin' Jack," now retired, was the moving force behind Dome Petroleum from its beginnings as an offshoot of Dome Mines, the major gold producer. He received his B.Sc. in geology in 1937 and became an exploration geologist with Shell Oil the following year. A few months later he began working in the same capacity for Standard Oil of New Jersey, inspecting oil fields in the Middle East, Africa, South America, and Canada. In 1950 he persuaded five groups (one of which was Dome Mines) to put a total of $250,000 at 16 cents a share into his new oil exploration venture. The very next year the small company (Gallagher and a secretary running the show) got its first wildcat strike; Gallagher was then able to sell 500,000 shares at $10 each. Since then, Dome Petroleum has not looked back and its successful forays into the Beaufort Sea region have indicated great promise for oil and gas in the Arctic. In 1982, however, Dome's debt load became enormous because of huge acquisitions in 1981 and high interest rates, but Gallagher was able to persuade the federal government to provide Dome with temporary loan guarantees. A few months later, satisfied that Dome was running on course, Gallagher stepped down as Dome's chief executive officer. Although his favourite pastime is found in one word — "Work!" — Gallagher will now be able to ski and golf, for which he never used to have the time. He was made an Officer of the Order of Canada in 1983.

Galt, Thomas M.

Chief Executive Officer, Sun Life Assurance, Toronto

Gardiner, George Ryerson

B.Comm., M.B.A.

Stock broker, business executive. b. April 25, 1917, Toronto; m. Helen McMinn; d. Judith, Christine, s. Michael; m. Anne Dumstrey; s. Percy; res. Toronto.

Educated at the University of Toronto Schools, the University of Toronto (B.Comm., 1939), and Harvard Business School (M.B.A., 1941), George Gardiner is now chairman of the Gardiner Group Stockbrokers Inc., Scott's Hospitality Inc. (which includes Commonwealth Holiday Inns), Ryerson Oil and Gas, and chairman of the Executive Committee for Rostland Corporation. Prior to formation of the Gardiner Group, he was chairman of the brokerage firm of Gardiner Watson. He still finds time to operate a large thoroughbred breeding and racing stable in the Caledon Hills as well as collect art and ceramics. During the 1970s Gardiner Farms was frequently the leading money-winning stable in Canada and George Gardiner serves as vice-president of the Ontario Jockey Club. In recent years he has devoted much energy and time to his art collection and the George R. Gardiner Museum of

Ceramic Art, housing one of the world's finest collections of Meissen china, will open in 1984 in Toronto. He winters in Miami Springs and is a member of the Badminton and Racquet Club and the Queen's Club. His sister, Helen Doris Gardiner, is married to Paul Phelan.

Gerstein, Reva

O.C., B.A., M.A., Ph.D., LL.D., D.Litt.

Psychologist. b. March 27, 1917, Toronto; née Appleby; m. David Raitblat; m. Bertrand Gerstein; s. Irving, Ira; res. Toronto.

Reva Gerstein has had considerable experience as a member of numerous federal, provincial, and municipal task forces and as a member of provincial post-secondary commissions on education. She was educated at the University of Toronto, where she taught and became chairman of University Affairs. She was chairman of the Mayor's Task Force on Discharged Psychiatric Patients and a member of Emmett Cardinal Carter's Panel on Ethics and the Economy. She was named an Officer of the Order of Canada, Woman of the Year by B'nai B'rith, and is the recipient of honorary degrees and the Centennial Medal. She serves as a director of McGraw-Hill Ryerson, Inco, and CJRT-FM. Gerstein is also involved with the Hospital for Sick Children, the National Council of Christians and Jews, and the Canadian Human Rights Foundation. She is a member of psychology-related organizations as well as the Royal Ontario Museum, the Primrose Club, and the Toronto Symphony, and is a Senator of the Stratford Festival. She was a founder and president of the Hincks Treatment Centre and the Canadian Council on Children & Youth.

Getty, Donald

M.L.A., B.A.

Business executive. b. August 30, 1933, Westmount, Quebec; m. Margaret Inez Mitchell; s. Dale, David, Darin, Derek; res. Edmonton.

President of D. Getty Investments Ltd., Don Getty is a former minister of Energy and Natural Resources in Peter Lougheed's Alberta cabinet. After graduating in Business Administration at the University of Western Ontario, he went on to an outstanding 10-year career as quarterback with the Edmonton Eskimos of the Canadian Football League. He simultaneously began his business career, joining Imperial Oil in 1955. Getty's involvement in politics began as the Conservative MLA for Strathcona West in 1967. He has gone on to become chairman and chief executive officer of Nortek Energy as well as chairman of Interprovincial Steel and Pipe. He is a director of Nova, the Royal Bank, Genstar, Brinco, and several other companies. He is also a member and former governor of the Petroleum Club and a director of Hockey Canada.

Gordon, John Peter George

B.Sc., LL.D.

Business executive. b. November 14, 1920, Toronto; m. Joan Muriel MacPherson; one son, one daughter; res. Mississauga, Ontario.

Following wartime service with the Royal Canadian Electrical and Mechanical Engineers—in which he attained the rank of captain—in Canada, Britain, and Northwest Europe, Peter Gordon joined the Steel Company of Canada (now Stelco), where he has spent his entire career, becoming chief executive officer in 1973 and chairman in 1976. His humanitarian services include service as a director of the Canadian Council of Christians and Jews and Junior Achievement of Canada, as a governor of the Olympic Trust of Canada and McMaster University, and membership in the National Council of the Canadian YMCA and the National Advisory Council of the Boys' and Girls' Clubs of Canada. He received the Human Relations Award of the Canadian Council of Christians and Jews in 1977. He is a director of the Bank of Montreal, The Molson Companies, Bell Canada Enterprises, Sun Life, and Gulf Oil Corporation. His clubs include the Hamilton, Toronto, York, Mount Royal, and Tamahaac.

Gordon, L. Lamont
B.A.

Investment executive. b. April 29, 1932, Harriston, Ontario; m. Barbara Warren; d. Katharine Elizabeth, Deborah Joane, Pamela Suzan, Jennifer Brook, s. James Neil; res. Toronto.

Monty Gordon, president of Almark Resources Ltd., is the successful creator of several companies including Westgrowth Petroleums, Gordon Securities, and Gordon Lloyd Price Investments. After receiving his B.A. in 1955 from the University of Western Ontario's School of Business Administration, Gordon travelled to Europe, where an avid interest in bobsledding developed. He was one of the founding members of the Canadian Bobsledding Association and a member of the 1964 Olympic gold medal team. He began his business career with Nesbitt Thomson and Co. Ltd. in 1957, became a director of that investment firm in 1964, and left in 1969 to found Gordon Securities. In 1977 he sold his interest in the company, then went into partnership with John Lloyd-Price in a merchant-banking firm. A member of the Canadian Club in New York, Gordon also retains his athletic interests as director and vice-president of the Canadian Amateur Bobsleigh and Luge Association.

Gray, Gordon Cecil
F.C.A., B.Comm., C.A.

Real-estate agent. b. October 24, 1927, Copper Cliff, Ontario; m. Patricia Godson; s. Donald, David, Douglas, d. Diane, Deborah; res. Richmond Hill, Ontario.

The son of a banker, Gordon Gray attended Queen's University before joining A.E. LePage Ltd. in 1955 as controller. Nearing the 30-year mark in his career with the company, Gray kept pace with the burgeoning firm, which is now the second-largest real-estate firm in the world, and advanced through various executive positions to his present title of chairman and chief executive officer. He is a director of such companies as Hiram Walker Resources, Rogers Cable systems, and McDonald's Corporaton; also, he serves as a trustee for the Hospital for Sick Children, the Art Gallery of Ontario Foundation, and the Canadian Robert F. Kennedy Memorial. The Grays live in a house built circa 1840.

Gray, James
Canadian Hunter Exploration Ltd., Toronto

Griffin, Anthony George Scott
Business executive. b. August 15, 1911, Langley, Bucks, England; m. Kathleen Lockhart Gordon; s.

Scott, Ian Gordon, Peter Mackenzie Gordon, Timothy Kirkfield, d. Ann McCall; res. Toronto.

Well known as a "professional director" and as a core figure in the Toronto Establishment, Tony Griffin has retired from about 20 directorships. He is a former chairman of Home Oil Co. Ltd., Scurry-Rainbow Oil Ltd., Halifax Insurance Co. Commercial Life Insurance Co. of Canada, Triarch Corp. Ltd., and Toronto & London Investment Co. Ltd. He considers one of his chief achievements the development of Triarch Corp., a private banking firm. He is a grandson of the railway builder Sir William Mackenzie, who with his partner, Sir Donald Mann, put together the Canadian Northern Railway, now part of Canadian National. He served in the RCN from 1910 to 1915, commanding a corvette and a frigate and as a staff officer, retiring with the rank of commander. He was the 1981 recipient of the Human Relations Award of the Canadian Council of Christians and Jews. Tony Griffin has been chairman of St. Michael's Hospital, president of the National Ballet of Canada, a governor of the National Theatre School, manager of the Canadian Olympic Sailing Team (1976), commodore of the Canadian Albacore Association, president of the International Albacore Association, vice-chairman of the London House Association of Canada, a governor of the Royal Life Saving Society, a governor of the National Film Board (1973-79), secretary of the Wartime Prices and Trade Board (1945-47), and secretary of the Royal Commission on Prices (1948-49). He is a member of the Toronto Club, the Royal Canadian Yacht Club, Badminton & Racquet Club, Osler Bluff Ski Club, Royal Cruising Club, Zeta Psi Fraternity, the Canadian Institute of International Affairs, the International Institute of Strategic Studies, the Canadian Institute of Strategic Studies, and the Advisory Committee (and formerly the Steering Committee) of the Bilderberg Group, an international think tank.

Hampson, H. Anthony
Canada Devlopment Corp., Vancouver

Harrington, Conrad Fetherstonhaugh
C.D., B.A., B.C.L., K.St.J., C.T.C.I.

Business executive. b. August 8, 1912, Montreal; m Joan Roy Hastings; s. Conrad, d. Jill, Susan; res. Westmount, Quebec.

Educated at McGill University and the University of Beçanson in France, Conrad Harrington had a distinguished military career during the Second World War, which included service medals and being twice mentioned in despatches while he was with the Royal Canadian Artillery. His association with the military continued until 1976, as he belonged to the 34 and 37 Field Regiments in Montreal and received the Canadian Forces Decoration Centennial Medal. He was called to the bar of Quebec in 1937 and practised law in Montreal until 1939. In business, he joined the estates department of the Royal Trust Company in 1945 and rose to become the company's chairman of the board until his retirement in 1978. He is now chancellor of McGill University, which follows his chairmanship of the McGill Development Program from 1973 to 1978, during which he raised approximately $35 mil-

lion. He is a director of Royal Trustco and its many offshoots, and has been involved with the Salvation Army, the Montreal Museum of Fine Arts, the Boy Scouts of Canada (Montreal Region), and the McCord Museum. He is a member of the Mount Royal and St. James's clubs in Montreal as well as the York and Toronto clubs.

Harris, W.B.
Chairman, Barclay's Bank of Canada, Toronto

Harrison, Russell Edward
Banker. b. May 31, 1921, Grandview, Manitoba; m. Nancy Doreen Bell; one son, one daughter; res. Toronto.

Russell Harrison joined the Canadian Bank of Commerce in 1945 after serving in the Second World War and rose to become, in 1973, president and chief operating officer and, in 1976, chairman and chief executive officer of its successor, the Canadian Imperial Bank of Commerce. His directorships include Royal Insurance of Canada, Falconbridge Ltd., TransCanada Pipelines, and MacMillan Bloedel. Among his public service activities he is a governor of Massey Hall and national chairman of the Ministries Enrichment Program of the Salvation Army. Among his clubs are the Toronto, the Mount Royal, and the Ranchmen's.

Hart, G. Arnold
Chairman, Canadian Investment Fund Ltd., Montreal

Harvie, Donald S.
Chairman, Devonian Group of Charitable Foundations, Calgary

Hatch, H. Clifford
President, Hiram Walker-Gooderham Worts, Windsor, Ontario

Hawke, J. Howard
Chief Executive Officer, Bache Securities Inc., Toronto

Heisey, W. Lawrence
B.A., M.B.A.

Publisher. b. May 29, 1930, Toronto; m. Barclay Ann Smith; d. Janet Elizabeth, s. Mark Alexander; res. Toronto.

Lawrence W. Heisey is chairman and chief executive officer of Harlequin Enterprises, publishers of the extraordinarily omnipresent Harlequin Romances. Educated at Trinity College of the University of Toronto and at the Harvard School of Business, Heisey regards his chief achievement as having "built a rather small Canadian paperback publisher into the largest paperback publisher in the world, selling over 200,000,000 books annually in 13 languages." In addition to manning the helm of Harlequin, Heisey is a director of Mills & Boon in London, Torstar Corp. in Toronto, Miles Kimball Co. in Oshkosh, Wisconsin, and Cavendish Investing in Toronto. He is also a director of the Banff Centre for Continuing Education, the Toronto Chamber Players, the Miles Kimball Foundation, and an honorary

ABOVE: Lawrence Heisey. RIGHT: Beland Honderich in his office at the Toronto Star.

ABOVE: Sol Kanee, Winnipeg miller, is a former chairman of the Royal Winnipeg Ballet and a leading figure in Winnipeg's Jewish community. RIGHT: Financier Hal Jackman in his Toronto office.

director of the Toronto French School. Heisey enjoys sailing; he owns "a rather nice Bertram yacht." He also collects Impressionist and Post-Impressionist paintings and sculpture as well as antique carpets.

Hennigar, David

Burns Fry Ltd., Halifax

Hermant, Sydney

B.A., LL.D.

Business executive. b. December 27, 1912, Toronto; m. Margaret Lewis Marshall; s. Peter, John, Adam, Andrew; res. Toronto.

Sydney Hermant was educated at Upper Canada College and the University of Toronto, where he received his law degree in 1935. He is chairman of the family-owned Imperial Optical, one of the world's major manufacturers of eye glasses. He has worked for such organizations as the Empire Club and the Toronto Board of Trade, of which he was president in 1950-51 and in 1959-60, respectively. He is a director of North American Life Assurance and Peoples Jewellers, and a director emeritus of the Canadian Imperial Bank of Commerce. Formerly chairman of the Board of Trustees of the Royal Ontario Museum, he is an important fund raiser and a benefactor to Toronto's cultural life.

Honderich, Beland Hugh

LL.D.

Publisher. b. November 25, 1918, Kitchener, Ontario; m. Agnes Janet Hutchinson; s. John Allen, David Beland, d. Mary Elizabeth; res. Toronto.

Beland Honderich is chairman and publisher of Toronto Star Newspapers and chairman and chief executive officer of Torstar Corporation, which owns the *Toronto Star*, Canada's largest-circulation paper. The son of a printer in a Mennonite family, Honderich quit high school during the Depression to help support the family and got a job as a stringer for the Kitchener *Record*. In 1943 he joined the *Star* and was with the paper during the height of its circulation wars with the *Telegam*. His promotion to finance editor in 1945 was due to a series of articles that he wrote about Tommy Douglas's CCF government in Saskatchewan, the first socialist government in North America. After becoming editor-in-chief in 1955, Honderich hired writers of the calibre of Ralph Allen, Robert Fulford, Nathan Cohen, Pierre Berton, and Ron Haggart, and possibly the best political cartoonist in the world — Duncan Macpherson. Since the demise of the *Tely*, the *Star* has made several, mostly unsuccessful attempts at diversification and once again finds itself in a circulation war — this time with the *Globe and Mail* and the *Sun*. Honderich belongs to the York Club.

Hopper, Wilbert Hill

B.Sc., M.B.A.

Business executive. b. March 14, 1933, Ottawa; m. Patricia Marguerite Walker; s. Sean Wilbert, Christopher Mark; res. Calgary.

Chairman and chief executive officer of Petro-Canada, Bill Hopper received his B.Sc. in Geology from American University in Washington and his M.B.A. from the University of Western Ontario. His entire career has been spent in the petroleum industry, including his appointment as senior advisor on energy policy to the Department of Energy, Mines and Resources and culminating with the appointment to his present position in 1979. (He had become president and CEO in 1976.) A member of many clubs and associations — including both the Canadian and American Economics associations, the Canadian Institute of Mining and Metallurgy, the Canada-China Trade Council, the Rideau Club, the Ranchmen's Club, the Petroleum Club and Le Cercle Universitaire d'Ottawa — Hopper also holds directorships in Syncrude Canada, Panarctic Oils, and Westcoast Transmission. The *Globe and Mail* Report on Business named him Man of the Year in 1980.

Jackman, Henry Newton Rowell

B.A., LL.B., O.St.J., K.C.L.J.

Business executive. b. June 10, 1932, Toronto; m. Maruja Trinidad Duncan; s. Henry, Duncan, d. Maria Victoria, Consuelo, Trinity; res. Toronto.

The son of financier H.R. Jackman, Hal Jackman is chairman and president of E-L Financial Corp., whose subsidiaries include Empire Life Insurance, Dominion of Canada General Insurance, and the Casualty Co. of Canada. He is also chairman of the Algoma Central Railway, the Economic Investment Trust, and Victoria & Grey Trustco and is director of Hiram Walker Resources, Massey-Ferguson, and Standard Broadcasting, among others. He went to school at Upper Canada College and the University of Toronto Schools, before attending the University of Toronto and the London School of Economics. He is married to a daughter of James Duncan, the former chairman of Massey-Ferguson and a former Federal deputy minister of Defense for Air.

Jeffery, Captain Joseph

Thames Valley Investments, London, Ontario

Jodrey, John J.

Chairman, Minas Basin Pulp and Power Co., Hantsport, N.S.

Jones, R.H.

Investors Group, Winnipeg

Kanee, Sol

Chairman, Soo Line Mills Ltd., Winnipeg

Kay, James

Chairman, Dylex Ltd., Toronto

Keevil, N.B. Jr.

Chief Executive Officer, Teck Corp. Ltd., Vancouver

Koerner, Michael M.

President, Canada Overseas Investments Ltd., Toronto

Koffler, Murray Bernard

C.M., Phm.B., Ph.C., Ph.D.

Business executive. b. January 22, 1924, Toronto; m. Marvelle Seligman; s. Leon, Tom, Adam; d. Theo, Tiana; res. Willowdale, Ontario.

Murray Koffler, chairman of Shoppers Drug Mart, began his career as a pharmacist at the family-owned Koffler Drug Stores after obtaining his Phm.B. from the University of Toronto in 1946. He was instrumental in introducing the ideas of self-service, mass merchandising, and franchising into the retail drug business, which resulted in the development of Shoppers Drug Mart from one store in 1963 to 441 in 1983. He is a director of Four Seasons Hotels, the Canada Development Corporation, Manufacturers Life, and Imasco Ltd., which in 1978 acquired Koffler Stores (which franchises Shoppers Drug Mart outlets). Actively involved in the community, Koffler is founder and chairman of the Council on Drug Abuse as well as director of Mount Sinai Hospital and the Canadian Council of Christians and Jews. His club memberships include the Toronto & North York Hunt, the Craigleith Ski, and the York Tennis. Among the many honours he has received are the Order of Canada (1977) and the Canadian Council of Christians and Jews Humanitarian Award (1974). He collects Canadian art and is the chairman of the Jokers Hill Horse Trials.

Kolber, Ernest Leo

B.A., B.C.L.

Business executive. b. January 18, 1929, Montreal; m. Sandra Maizel; s. Jonathan, d. Marna Lynne; res. Westmount, Quebec.

President of Cemp Investments and chairman and chief executive officer of Cadillac Fairview, McGill-trained lawyer Leo Kolber is one of the most powerful people in the empire held by the heirs of distiller Sam Bronfman, having masterminded the investment of the family's personal capital in real estate during the construction boom of the 1950s and 1960s. He is, naturally, a director of Seagram's and of the Toronto-Dominion Bank. He is also president of Toronto-Dominion Centre, the Mies Van der Rohe–designed complex in Toronto that is one of Cadillac Fairview's major investments. He is a director of the Royal Victoria and Jewish General hospitals and is a member of the Mount Royal Club.

Lahn, Mervyn

President, Canada Trustco, London, Ontario

LeClair, J. Maurice

O.C., B.Sc., M.D., C.M., M.Sc., D.Sc., LL.D., F.R.C.P. (C), F.A.C.P.

Business executive. b. June 19, 1927, Sayabec, Quebec; m. Pauline Héroux; d. Suzanne, Marie, Nathalie, s. François, Manon, Guy; res. Westmount, Quebec.

President and chief executive officer of Canadian National, J. Maurice LeClair originally studied medicine at McGill University and at the University of Minnesota. He has acted as vice-president of the Medical Research Council of Canada and of the Association of Canadian Medical Colleges, and as president of the Medical Deans' Commitee of Quebec. He is a director of the Montreal Heart Institute Research Foundation and of the Montreal Clinical Research Institute, and chairman of six railways, including Grand Trunk Corp., Detroit, Toledo & Ironton Railroad, and CN (France). He belongs to the Mount Royal and Saint-Denis clubs of Montreal, and collects antique clocks and watches.

LEFT: Murrary Koffler in the Four Seasons, Toronto, which he, Eddie Creed, and Izzy Sharp own. BELOW: Dennis McDermott in his office at the Canadian Labour Congress headquarters in Ottawa.

J.R.

J.R.

J.R.

LEFT: Frank McEachren at home in Forest Hill.

Lévesque, Jean-Louis

C.M., D.C.Sc., D.P.Ec., LL.D., D. Soc.Sc.

Business executive. b. April 13, 1911, Nouvelle, Quebec; m. Jeanne Brisson; two daughters, one son; res. Toronto.

J.-Louis Lévesque is chairman of the Montreal investment house of Lévesque, Beaubien, which he founded. He is a successful racer of thoroughbred horses, an interest continued by his son, Pierre-Louis, who heads North American Bloodstock Agency in Toronto and is chairman of Windsor Raceway Holdings. Less well known is his J.-Louis Lévesque Foundation, one of the largest in the country set up by a person who is still alive, with assets over $10 million, which gives large amounts of money for medical research, sports, and education. Lévesque has received honorary degrees from Laval and the University of Montreal, among others, and is a Member of the Order of Canada and a Knight of Magistral Grace in the Order of Malta.

Leitch, John D.

President, Upper Lakes Shipping Ltd., Toronto

Light, Walter Frederick

B.Sc., LL.D., D.A.Sc.

Business executive. b. June 24, 1923, Cobalt, Ontario; m. Margaret Anne Miller; d. Elizabeth, Janice; res. Toronto.

Walter Light, a Queen's University graduate and RCAF veteran, rose to the top position of Northern Telecom (formerly Northern Electric) from the ranks of senior management in engineering at Bell Canada. An executive vice-president, operations, at Bell Canada in 1969, he became president of the Bell high-tech subsidiary in 1974, and chief executive officer as well in 1979. Since 1982 he has been chairman and chief executive officer Northern Telecom. He is also a director of Bell Canada, Genstar Corp., Inco, Northern Telecom, Procter & Gamble, the Royal Bank, and Moore Corp. On the public service front, he is a director of Canadian Executive Service Overseas, governor of the Montreal Museum of Fine Arts, an associate of Carleton University, and vice-chairman of the board of trustees of Queen's University. In addition to belonging to several engineering organizations, he is a member of the C.D. Howe Research Institute, the Board of Trade of Metropolitan Toronto, the Mount Royal Club, the Forest and Stream Club of Dorval, the Granite Club, the Toronto Club, and the York Club. He considers his chief achievement to be "the leadership role achieved by Northern Telecom in high technology."

Longstaffe, John Ronald

B.A., LL.B.

Business executive. b. April 6, 1934, Toronto; m. Jacqueline Holyoake; s. Grant, d. Sherry, Brandy; res. Vancouver.

Ronald Longstaffe is the executive vice-president of Canadian Forest Products, which until it went public in 1983 as Canfor Corp. was regarded as Canada's second largest privately owned company after Eaton's. He went to school at Upper Canada College and the University of British Columbia, where he received his LL.B. in 1958. In 1966 he joined Canadian

Forest Products as its secretary, but left in 1969 to act as director of corporate planning for Reed International Ltd. of London. He returned to a vice-presidency with Canadian Forest Products and is also a director of the company and such affiliates as Canfor Investments, Canfor Ltd., Yorkshire Trust Company, Bralorne Resources, and Versatile Corp. He is a trustee and chairman of the Project Building Committee of St. Paul's Hospital and is a member of the Vancouver Economic Advisory Commission and the Law Society of British Columbia. He has received the Award of Merit from the Canadian Museums Association and the Silver Jubilee Medal. A highly respected art investor, he has a large collection of contemporary Canadian art and international graphics.

Love, G. Donald

Chairman, Oxford Development Group Ltd., Edmonton

Lundrigan, Arthur Raymond

Business executive. b. July 13, 1922, Blaketown, Newfoundland; m. Ida Amanda Johnson; d. Ingrid, Astrid, Sigrid, Gudrid; res. Corner Brook, Newfoundland.

Arthur Lundrigan is president of Lundrigans Ltd., the company that he and his father, William James Lundrigan, built into one of the Atlantic provinces' largest contracting operations. Its main construction subsidiaries include Comstock International, Lundrigans Concrete, Atlantic Concrete, and Atlantic Gypsum, as well as companies in other fields such as printing, engineering, and car and truck dealerships. He is also a director of Sobeys Stores and Maritime Life Assurance.

McDaniel, Roderick Rogers

B.Sc., P.Eng.

Engineer. b. March 18, 1926, High River, Alberta; m. Marilyn Bouck; d. Nancy, Leslie; res. Calgary.

An important member of Calgary's geological consulting community, Rod McDaniel is described by Peter Newman as the man "whose reports give any project the imprimatur of success." Educated in Calgary and at the University of Oklahoma, he was chief reservoir engineer for Imperial Oil before establishing his consulting firm in 1955. McDaniel is chief fund raiser for Peter Lougheed's Conservatives and serves as chairman of Pacific Western Airlines. He is a director of First City Trust and Prudential Steel Ltd. and president of Penny Lane Market Mall Ltd. He has served as president of the Calgary Chamber of Commerce and as a director of the Canadian Chamber of Commerce. He is currently a director of the Calgary Exhibition and Stampede and an associate of the Heritage Park Society. His memberships include Calgary Petroleum, Ranchmen's, Calgary Golf & Country, Outrigger Canoe Club (Honolulu), and the Calgary Highlanders Regiment.

McDermott, Dennis

Labour leader. b. November 3, 1922, Portsmouth, England; m. Mary Caza; s. Michael, Mark, Patrick, William, d. Maureen; res. Kanata, Ontario.

Perhaps Canada's best-known labour leader, Dennis McDermott left England after serving

in the Royal Navy from 1939 to 1946 to become an assembler and welder at the Toronto plant of Massey-Harris, now Massey-Ferguson. After six years at the plant, he became an international representative of the United Automobile Workers of America in 1954, a post he held for 14 years. From 1968 to 1978, he served as the UAW's Canadian director and international vice-president. Since 1978, he has been head of the Canadian Labour Congress. He is chairman of the board of directors of the Labour Education and Studies Centre, of the board of governors of the Labour College of Canada, and of the Commonwealth Trade Union Council. In addition, he is a vice-president of the International Confederation of Free Trade Unions, an executive board member of the Inter-American Regional Organization of Workers (ORIT), and director of the Canadian Civil Liberties Association. He belongs to the UAW, the Association of Canadian Television and Radio Artists, and, consistent with his belief that labour should play a greater role in the electoral process, the New Democratic Party. McDermott has received the Centennial Medal.

McEachren, Frank Flavelle

C.V.O., C.M., E.D., C.D., B.A., K.St.J., G.C.L.J.

Business executive. b. June 6, 1918, Woking, Surrey, England; m. Florence Eaton; s. Gilbert, d. Signy E. Farncomb; res. Toronto.

Frank McEachren was educated at St. Andrew's College in Aurora and received his B.A. from Trinity College at the University of Toronto in 1940. He served with the 48th Highlanders of Canada during the Second World War and had various staff appointments with the Canadian militia thereafter, until 1968. Since 1951 he has acted as aide-de-camp, senior aide-de-camp, and now military secretary to the lieutenant-governors of Ontario. In 1977 he was made a Commander of the Royal Victorian Order by the Queen for his role *in loco parentis* for Prince Andrew while he studied at Lakefield College. From 1958 to 1967 Colonel McEachren served as co-ordinator of royal tours in Ontario, and he is a member of the National Council and past president (1975 to 1981) of the Duke of Edinburgh's Award in Canada. Married to the daughter of Sir John Eaton, he acted as the T. Eaton Co.'s public relations manager and is now chairman of the Eaton Foundation. He has many community interests and became the first layman to serve as a vice-president of the Geneva-based International Union Against Cancer. In 1965 he was awarded the Canadian Public Relations Society's Shield of Public Service National Award for distinguished and dedicated service to the public welfare.

McEntyre, Peter Michael

B.Comm., C.A., C.F.A.

Chartered accountant. b. August 15, 1917, Westmount, Quebec; m. Katherine Margaret Creelman (deceased); s. David, d. Nancy; res. Westmount, Quebec.

One of the true members of Montreal's anglophone business elite, Peter McEntyre is president of Comtrust Holdings and chairman of the board for Canada Cement Lafarge. He is closely associated with the enormous estate of John

Wilson McConnell, which holds a large block of Canada Cement Lafarge stock. The estate also has large holdings in St. Lawrence Sugar Refineries, where McEntyre was secretary from 1948 to 1963. After receiving his Bachelor of Commerce degree from McGill University in 1939, he joined Creak, Cushing and Hodgson, where he became a partner in 1947. From 1941 to 1946, he served in the Royal Canadian Navy and was mentioned in despatches. After leaving St. Lawrence Sugar in 1963, he became president of the McConnell family's Commercial Trust Company, a position he held until 1969. McEntyre also became active in politics, serving as an alderman and commissioner of finance for the City of Westmount from 1962 to 1968, and as mayor from 1969 to 1971. He is a director of Lafarge Coppée S.A. (France), Lafarge Corporation and General Portland (U.S.A.), and International Atlantins (Bermuda). As well, he is governor of Concordia University and chairman of the Boys' and Girls' Clubs of Canada Endowment Fund. He holds club memberships at the University (Montreal), Mount Royal, St. James's, Montreal Badminton and Squash, and Mount Royal Curling.

McGiverin, Donald Scott
B. Comm., M.B.A., K.C.L.J.

Business executive. b. April 4, 1924, Calgary; m. Margaret Ann Weld (deceased); s. Richard (deceased), d. Mary; res. Toronto.

In 1945, Donald McGiverin, a Commerce student at the University of Manitoba, received two scholarships while on his way to a Master's program in Business Administration at Ohio State. The first was the University of Manitoba Gold Medal; the other was the Walter P. Zeller Fellowship in Retailing. Thirty-three years later, McGiverin proved to be a most appropriate recipient of the retailing fellowship. As president of the Hudson's Bay Company, he acquired the store chain founded by Walter Zeller and placed a takeover bid with the shareholders of Simpsons. After a furious bidding war, Simpsons and a large block of stock in its affiliate, Simpsons-Sears, became the property of The Bay in late 1978. Soon after, The Bay was swallowed up by Ken Thomson and the Canadian newspaper empire. McGiverin remained with the company for which he had left a vice-presidency and directorship with the T. Eaton Co. in 1969. He became The Bay's governor in 1982. He is now, in addition, chairman of Simpsons, deputy chairman of Markborough Properties; a director of Zellers, Noranda Mines, Roxy Petroleum, Du Pont Canada, Manufacturers Life Insurance; and a member of the international advisory board of R.J. Reynolds Industries, the Canadian Industrial Renewal Board, and the board of governors of Olympic Trust of Canada. McGiverin is a member of the Beta Gamma Sigma honorary society of Ohio State and the Phi Kappa Pi fraternity. He also holds club memberships at the York, Toronto, Granite, Rosedale, Lambton Golf and Country, St. Charles Country (Winnipeg), Mount Royal, and Lyford Cay (Bahamas). He has been appointed Knight Commander of The Military and Hospitaller Order of St. Lazarus of Jerusalem. A collector of Canadian paintings and sculpture, he is the owner of an original settler's log house and a 1930 Model-A coupé.

McKeough, William Darcy
B.A., LL.D.

Business executive. b. January 31, 1933, Chatham, Ontario; m. Margaret Walker; s. Walker, James; res. Cedar Springs, Ontario.

For 15 years, Darcy McKeough was one of Ontario's most prominent provincial politicians. A graduate of the University of Western Ontario in 1954, he entered the political fray in 1959 with his election to the City Council of Chatham, Ontario. After his re-election in 1961, he set his sights on a career at Queen's Park, and became a member of the legislature in 1963. Re-elected four times, he held a continuous string of ministerial appointments: minister without portfolio, 1966; minister of Municipal Affairs, 1967; treasurer and minister of Economics and chairman of the Treasury Board, 1971; concurrently minister of Municipal Affairs and treasurer and minister of Economics and Intergovernmental Affairs, 1972; parliamentary assistant to the Premier with special responsibilities in energy policy (following his resignation as treasurer), 1973; Ontario's first minister of Energy, 1973; treasurer and minister of Economics and Intergovernmental Affairs, 1975. He resigned his ministerial duties and his seat in the legislature in 1978 to enter the private sector. He is the president and chief executive officer of Union Gas, chairman and director of Redpath Industries, and a director of Algoma Central Railway, Canadian Imperial Bank of Commerce, Consumers Glass, McKeough Sons Co., Noranda Mines, Numac Oil & Gas, and Precambrian Shield Resources. He is on the board of governors of Ridley College (of which he is a graduate) and Wilfrid Laurier University; he is second vice-president of the Stratford Shakespearean Festival, a member of the Canadian Group and the Trilateral Commission. McKeough holds memberships in the Kent Club in Chatham and three clubs in Toronto — the Toronto, the Albany and the Badminton and Racquet.

MacDonald, Pierre
Senior Vice President, Bank of Montreal, Montreal

Macdonnell, Peter L. P.
Partner, Milner & Steer, Edmonton

Maclaren, Donald
James Maclaren Industries Inc., Ottawa

McLaughlin, W. Earle
Company director; Montreal

McLean, William F.
Vice President, Cndn. Imperial Bank of Commerce, Toronto.

Malone, Richard Sankey
O.B.E., E.D.

Consultant. b. September 18, 1909, Owen Sound, Ontario; m. Princess Iona Soutzo; stepd. Princess Marina Sturdza; m. Helen Cook; s. Richard, Robert, d. Deirdre; res. Toronto.

Now a director of Dunrick Ltd., Brigadier Malone is best known for his long career in journalism, which culminated in his positions as publisher and editor-in-chief of the *Globe and Mail* (1974-78) and president of FP Publications (1975-79). After attending the University of Toronto Schools and Ridley College, he began his newspaper career with the *Toronto Daily Star* in 1927. From 1929 to 1933, he wrote for the *Leader-Post* in Regina and then the *Star-Phoenix* in Saskatoon. After a stint with the Parliamentary Press Gallery, in 1936 he began a long association with the *Winnipeg Free Press*. During the Second World War he served with Princess Patricia's Canadian Light Infantry and as staff secretary to the minister of Defence in 1940. He was elevated to Brigade Major, and was wounded and mentioned in despatches during the invasion of Sicily in 1943. He also served as Personal Liaison Officer to Field Marshal Montgomery in Italy, took charge of press and psychological warfare for the Canadian Army during the Normandy campaign, and headed the Canadian mission to General Douglas MacArthur's headquarters in the Pacific theatre. Among the first to enter Paris, Brussels and Tokyo, he was present when peace was signed aboard the USS *Missouri*. Malone also founded the Canadian army newspaper, *Maple Leaf*. He has been publisher of the *Winnipeg Free Press* (1961-74), vice-president Sun Publishing Co. (*Vancouver Sun*), chairman of the *Ottawa Journal*, and a director of four other Canadian newspapers. He is currently a director of the Max Bell Foundation, the Gurkha Appeal, and the Carolyn Sifton Foundation. Malone was honorary aide-de-camp to the governor general in 1946, and is honorary colonel of the Royal Winnipeg Rifles and trustee of the Queen's Own Rifles. He is a member of the Toronto Club, York Club, Royal Canadian Military Institute, and the Institute of Strategic Studies (U.K.). For relaxation, he writes, studies history and economics, golfs, fishes, and paints. He is the author of *Missing from the Record* and *A Portrait of War*.

Mannix, Frederick Charles
Business executive. b. October 21, 1913, Edmonton; m. Janice Christine Florendine; m. Margaret Ruth Broughton; s. Frederick, Philip, Ronald, d. Maureen; res. Priddis, Alberta.

Fred Mannix heads a network of 132 companies whose principal activities are earth moving, building dams, highways, pipelines, and industrial plants; international oil exploration; and coal mining. The chief companies are Loram International, Manalta Coal (largest producer in the country), Techman Engineering, and Pembina Resources (the only publicly traded company in the group, but majority-controlled by the family). The structure of the organization is as secret as its power is great; alumni of the Mannix companies occupy senior positions in the Alberta government, most notably Peter Lougheed and Chip Collins. Mannix began his career in the construction camps of his father, Frederick S. Mannix. His father sold control to Morrison-Knudsen of Boise, Idaho, in the 1940s, but the younger Mannix recovered control and went on to build the organization to its present size. Frederick C. Mannix is a director of the Royal Bank and Stelco. One son, F.P., is a director of Siemens Electric; another, Ronald, is a director of the Bank of Montreal.

J.R.

Alan Marchment

Donald McGiverin   *Ted Medland*

J.R.

NIGEL DICKSON

Mara, George Edward
Chairman, Jannock Ltd., Toronto

Marchment, Alan Roy
B.A., F.C.A., C.T.C.I., K.St.L.

Business executive. b. May 29, 1927, Toronto; m. Patricia Vanstone; d. Fay Alana Jensen, s. Stephen, Scott; res. Toronto.

The chairman and chief executive officer of Guaranty Trust Company of Canada and Traders Group, Alan Marchment received his B.A. in philosophy at the University of Toronto and then studied to be an accountant. After serving with the Royal Canadian Navy as a lieutenant, he joined the accounting firm of Clarkson Gordon as an auditor in 1950. He left five years later to become secretary-treasurer of Pacific Finance Corporation of Canada and chief agent of the Olympic Insurance Company in Toronto. In 1960 he moved to Los Angeles to become Pacific Finance's assistant treasurer and assistant secretary, but three years later again uprooted himself to take the position of president and director of Transamerica International S.A. in Paris, where he remained for two years. He then returned to Toronto to join Eaton's where he rose to a vice-presidency before taking on the presidency of Guaranty Trust in 1973. He is chairman of the Trust Companies Association of Canada and of the Ontario Provincial Courts Committee, and is a member of the Toronto Redevelopment Advisory Council and director of the Navy League of Canada (Ontario Division). He belongs to the Toronto and York clubs, and hunts, fishes, and practises karate in his spare time.

Martin, Paul Edgar
B.A., LL.B.

Business executive. b. August 28, 1938, Windsor, Ontario; m. Sheila Cowan; s. Paul, Robert, David; res. Montreal.

A University of Toronto graduate whose studies included philosophy, history, and law, Paul Martin is president and chief executive officer of the CSL Group. For many years, he was a key figure in Paul Desmarais's Power Corp. empire. Like a number of other Power executives, past and present, Martin has associations with the federal Liberal government. In 1968, he managed the Liberal leadership campaign of his father, the Honourable Paul Martin, a former Canadian High Commissioner to Great Britain. Martin became Desmarais's executive assistant in 1966. In 1969 he was made a Power Corp. vice-president, and in 1971 he became vice-president, special projects of Consolidated-Bathurst, a Power subsidiary. He was appointed vice-president, planning and development, of Power in 1973. Martin became president of Canada Steamship Lines in 1974. The company was renamed the CSL Group in 1980. In 1981 Martin and Laurence Pathy, president of Fednav, bought the CSL Group from Power. Martin is a director of the CSL Group, Domglas, the Canada Development Investment Corp., the Canada Development Corp., Calvert-Dale Estates, Redpath Industries, and Fednav. He is a member of the Law Society of Upper Canada and the C.D. Howe Institute Policy Analysis Committee. He also

belongs to the Mount Bruno Country Club, the St. James's Club, the University Club of Montreal, and the Mount Royal Club. Since CSL owns Kingsway Transports, a highway carrier, and Voyageur Enterprises, a bus operation, Martin is involved in a host of committees and associations concerned with shipping and transportation. He is a governor of Concordia University and a collector of Canadian paintings. He farms at Knowlton, in the Eastern Townships of Quebec.

Masters, John A.
B.A., M.S.

Geologist, business executive. b. September 20, 1927, Shenandoah, Iowa; m. Lenora; s. Charles, Alan, Robert, d. Barbara, Jennifer; res. Calgary.

A colourful, self-confessed "roughneck," John Masters has an instinct for discovering large mineral deposits. He was educated at Yale and the University of Colorado and, on graduation in 1951, joined Kerr-McGee Corp. Four years later he discovered the largest uranium lode in the United States, New Mexico's Ambrosia Lake. He followed up this discovery by finding the first oil field in Arizona and two large offshore fields in the Gulf of Mexico. In 1966 he came to Calgary as head of Kerr-McGee's Canadian operations, where he met his future partner, Jim Gray. They struck out on their own in 1973, forming Canadian Hunter Exploration, which became one of the most successful oil and gas companies in Canada and which discovered the largest gas field in Canada, the Elmworth Basin, in 1976. Masters is now the principal investor in CNG, a company that will convert part of the world's auto fleet to compressed natural gas. The author of several geological scientific papers and *The Hunters*, a book on the history of his company, he has also taught courses in petroleum geology at the University of Calgary.

Matthews, Major-General A. Bruce
President, Matthews & Co. Inc., Toronto

Matthews, Terence H.
Chairman, Mitel Corp., Kanata, Ontario

Mayhew, Logan
Gentleman, entrepreneur, Victoria

Medland, Charles Edward
B.A.

Investment dealer. b. July 6, 1928, Toronto; m. Julia Winsor Eby; d. Virginia, Zoe, steps., Brian, Stephen; res. Toronto.

Ted Medland is chairman and chief executive officer of Wood Gundy, the major Toronto investment house for which he has worked since 1950. His directorships include International Thomson Organisation, Seagram's, Interprovincial Pipe Line, and Abitibi-Price. He is also chairman of Clover Meadow Creamery and a governor of Wellesley Hospital in Toron

to. Medland's clubs are the Toronto, the Toronto Golf, the Badminton & Racquet, Craigleith Ski, the Rosedale Golf, the York, and the Mount Royal.

Megarry, Archibald Roy
Publisher, The Globe and Mail, Toronto

Meighen, Michael A.
Lawyer/company director, Toronto

Meighen, Colonel Maxwell, G.D.
Chairman, Canadian General Investments Ltd., Toronto

Melzack, Louis
Bookseller, Toronto

Milner, Stanley A.
President, Chieftain Development Co. Ltd., Edmonton

Mingo, James William Edgar
Q.C., B.A., LL.B., LL.M., LL.D.

Lawyer. b. November 25, 1926, Halifax; m. Edith P. Hawkins; s. James A., Charles H., d. Sarah M., Johanna E., Nancy S.; res. Halifax.

William Mingo has been a member of the Halifax law firm of Stewart, MacKeen and Covert since 1950. After being a boy seaman on the *Empress of Scotland* in the Second World War, he studied law at Dalhousie University, winning the University Medal in Law in 1949. His more than 20 business directorships include the Royal Bank, Sun Life, Canada Development Investment Corporation, Maritime Telegraph and Telephone Co., Mines Basin Pulp and Power, Bowater Mersey Paper Co., and National Sea Products. Other activities include directorships of the Law Foundation of Nova Scotia and the Forum for Young Canadians. He is chairman of the National Treasury Committee of the Liberal Party of Canada. He was chairman of the Halifax-Dartmouth Port Commission from 1960 to 1983, during the period when the Port of Halifax became an important world port in handling containerized cargo. With his many directorships, his influence in the legal community, and his community activities, Mingo is a key member of the Eastern-Canadian Establishment.

Morley, H. Keith
Chairman, Costain Ltd., Toronto

Mulholland, William David
A.B., M.B.A., LL.D.

Banker. b. June 16, 1926, Albany, New York; m. Nancy Louise Booth; s. William David III, Charles Douglas, James Andrew, John Alexander, Bruce Henry, d. Elizabeth Helen, Madeline Louise, Sarah Alexandra, Caroline Marie; res. Georgetown, Ontario.

Paul E. Martin

Northern Dancer, Ron Turcotte up.

Jean Ostiguy in his Place Ville Marie, Montreal, office. Beside him hangs a photograph of his grandfather.

Born and raised in the United States, Bill Mulholland served in the Philippines in the Second World War in the U.S. Army, after which he earned his M.B.A. at the Harvard Business School. He joined the Morgan Stanley investment banking firm in New York in 1952 and came to Canada in 1969 to become president of Brinco and chairman of Churchill Falls (Labrador) Corp. He returned to banking with his appointment as president of the Bank of Montreal in 1975 and became chairman in 1981. He is the most internationally oriented of Canada's big five bankers, being vice-chairman of the Frankfurt-based Allgemeine Deutsche Credit-Anstalt and a director of Standard Life Assurance Co. of Edinburgh and of the Upjohn Co. in the United States. He is a member of the Mount Royal, Saint-Denis, and the Toronto clubs, among others.

Muncaster, Joseph Dean

President, Canadian Tire Corp. Ltd., Toronto

Nichol, John L.

President, Springfield Investment Co. Ltd., Vancouver

Nickle, Carl O.

President, Conventures Ltd., Calgary

Nielsen, Arne R.

Chairman, Canadian Superior Oil Ltd., Calgary

Northern Dancer

Stud, former racehorse. b. May 27, 1961, Oshawa; s. & d. (champions) Dance Act, Nijinsky II, Viceregal, Minsky, Nice Dancer, The Minstrel, Giboulee, Dance In Time, Try My Best, Nureyev, Storm Bird, Woodstream, Danzatere, Franfreleuche, Lauries Dancer, Nice Dancer, Broadway Dancer, Northernette; res. Maryland.

Bred by E.P. Taylor and born on Taylor's Windfields Farm, as a short stocky colt he was passed over by prospective buyers at the September 1962 yearling sales. Carrying the silks of Windfields Farm, Northern Dancer became a hero on May 2, 1964, when he won the Kentucky Derby — the first Canadian horse to win such an honour. He followed this achievement by winning the Preakness and the Queen's Plate in the same year. After moving to Maryland (1969), Northern Dancer was syndicated for $2,400,000. Canadians buying shares in the syndicate included George Gardiner, J.-Louis Levesque, Garfield Weston, and D.G. Willmot. Through his maternal line, Northern Dancer is related to Sunny's Halo, the Canadian-bred 1983 winner of the Kentucky Derby. Northern Dancer's sire, Nearctic, also born at Windfields, was the 1955 Horse of the Year. His grandsire, Nearco, bred in Italy, was retired to stud an undefeated champion and was one of the few horses in England to have his own bomb shelter during the Second World War. Northern Dancer is known today as the world's leading sire of

stakes winners as well as the world's most expensive sire. His offspring are fetching record-breaking prices and in July 1983 Sheik Mohammed paid $10.2 million at the Keeneland yearling sales for a Northern Dancer colt. Other progeny include Viceregal, Canadian horse of the Year; Nijinsky II, an English Triple Crown winner; The Minstrel, winner of the Derby at Epsom; Franfreleuche, another Canadian Horse of the Year; and more than 400 other offspring.

Offman, Allan E.

Business executive, Toronto

Ostiguy, Jean P.W.

O.C., LL.D.

Investment dealer. b. March 4, 1922, Montreal; m. Michelle Bienvenu; s. Marc, Claude, d. Denise, Danielle, Suzanne; res. Montreal.

Now the honorary chairman of Richardson Greenshields of Canada, Jean Ostiguy followed his father's footsteps into the field of finance after serving three years overseas during the Second World War. In 1948 he joined Casgrain & Co. Ltd., a firm of stock brokers and investment dealers, and became a vice-president and director. He founded Morgan, Ostiguy & Hudon in 1956 and served as its president until 1972, when he became president and chief executive officer of Craig & Ostiguy, which, after a series of mergers with Bankers Securities of Canada, Greenshields, and Richardson Securities of Canada, became Richardson Greenshields of Canada, the largest employer among Canadian investment dealers in North America, Europe, and the Orient. He is a director of such companies as the Canadian Imperial Bank of Commerce (serving on its Executive and Pension Fund committees), Ford of Canada, and Canadian Pacific Air Lines, and has served as president of the Investment Dealers' Association of Canada and co-chairman of the Montreal Stock Exchange and Canadian University Service Overseas, as well as many community organizations. Among the awards he has received are the Queen's Jubilee Medal, the Centennial Medal, and the Eleanor Roosevelt Humanities Award. His wife's father, Achille Bienvenu, was president of Catelli Food Products.

Outerbridge, Sir Leonard Cecil

C.C., Kt., C.B.E., D.S.O., C.D., K.St.J., B.A., LL.B., LL.D.

Merchant. b. May 6, 1888, Asheville, North Carolina; m. Dorothy W. Strathy; d. Nancy; res. St. John's.

A member of one of Newfoundland's old Establishment families, Sir Leonard Outerbridge was lieutenant-governor of Newfoundland from 1949 to 1957, chairman of A. Harvey and Co. (established in 1767), and a director of various other companies. He was educated at Bishop Feild College in St. John's, Marlborough College in England, the University of Toronto, and Osgoode Hall. During the First World War he served with the 35th and 75th Battalions of the Canadian Expeditionary Force and was a staff captain with the 1st Canadian Infantry Brigade; he was awarded the Distinguished Service Order and was twice

mentioned in despatches. He is a son of Sir Joseph Outerbridge, a merchant and philanthropist who represented Newfoundland in tariff negotiations in Ottawa in 1879. He was knighted in 1946 and named a Companion of the Order of Canada in 1967.

Paré, Paul

B.C.L.

Business executive. b. May 30, 1922, Montreal; m. Mary Audrey Drury, s. Victor, Ronald; d. Jane, Cathy; res. Montreal.

Paul Paré is chairman and chief executive officer of Imasco, the giant tobacco, food, and retailing company built on Imperial Tobacco. With roughly half the Canadian cigarette market, the Imperial Tobacco division is the largest element in the company, but other well-known units include Unico Foods, Shoppers Drug Marts, United Cigar Stores, and Collegiate Sports. Paul Paré served in the Royal Canadian Navy during the Second World War and left as a lieutenant-commander. He earned his law degree at McGill and was called to the Bar of Quebec in 1949. He joined the legal department of Imperial Tobacco that year and, except for periods as executive assistant to the Minister of National Defence and as president of Canadian Tabacofina, has remained there since. He became president of Imasco in 1966 and chairman in 1979. His directorships include the Royal Bank, Canadian Pacific Ltd., IBM Canada, and the SNC Group. Among his community activities, he is a governor of the Montreal General Hospital and a member of the Canadian Council of Christians and Jews. He is a member of the Mount Royal Club.

Pattison, James Allen

Entrepreneur. b. October 1, 1928, Saskatoon; m. Mary Ella Hudson; s. James Jr., d. Mary Ann, Cynthia; res. West Vancouver.

Jimmy Pattison is the dynamic owner and president of the Jim Pattison Group of 30 or so companies. The group includes GM and Toyota car dealerships, leasing and finance companies, outdoor advertising companies (including Claude Neon), recreational vehicles, office and residential development, computer services, soft drinks (Crush Canada), magazine distribution, radio station CJOR, Overwaitea supermarkets, and the Air BC floatplanes that fly between Victoria and Vancouver Harbour. He also owns the Vancouver Canadians baseball club and hopes soon to obtain a major league franchise. Pattison is also chairman of Expo 86, the world's fair to be held in Vancouver on the theme of transportation and communications. Pattison started his empire in 1961 when he purchased a GM dealership. He is renowned for his long working hours and effervescent spirits. He has several houses which he hardly has time to use but does enjoy entertaining aboard his immaculate 85-foot motor yacht. He is a member of the Vancouver Club and of the Canyon Country Club in Palm Springs, where he goes from time to time in the winter.

Phelan, Paul James

Business executive. b. September 10, 1917, Toronto; m. Helen Gardiner; s. Paul David, d. Helen Gail Regan, Sharon, Rosemary; res. Toronto.

Paul Phelan aboard Mia's Red Jacket *in Toronto harbour.*

Alfred Powis

ABOVE: Chuck Rathgeb with the Canadair CL-41 Tutor in which he took part in the London-Victoria Air Race during the British Columbia centennial celebrations. It was the lightest jet ever to fly across the Atlantic. ABOVE RIGHT: The Canadian Olympic Bobsled Team of 1964. Standing, left to right: David Hobart, Victor Emery, Charles Rathgeb, John Emery, Lamont Gordon, Doug Connor. Kneeling, left to right: Stan Hamer, Gordon Currie, Peter Kirby, Chris Ondaatje. Missing from this photo is Doug Annakin. Crew of the gold-medal winning sled were: V. Emery, driver; Annakin, number 2; J. Emery, number 3; Kirby, brakeman. Crew of Canada 2: Gordon, driver; Hobart, number 2; Ondaatje, number 3; Currie, brakeman. Chuck Rathgeb was team manager, Connor was coach and Hamer was mechanic.

Henry Rhude at the Central Trust head office in Halifax.

After having attained the rank of squadron leader with the RCAF, P.J. Phelan joined his family firm as clerk in 1945. In 1961 he purchased the outstanding shares of the Canada Railway News Company and its subsidiary Aero Caterers from 40-odd family shareholders, and formed Cara Operations. For 100 years Cara has been a family-owned firm and a pioneer in the food-service industry: from humble beginnings operating news stands on the Grand Trunk Railway to present-day airline catering, Cara has continued to serve the travelling public. Considering himself "lucky to graduate" from De La Salle College, he is now president of Cara Holdings Ltd. and chairman of Cara Operations. Also known for his contributions to Canadian yachting, P.J. as he is known in sailing circles, has campaigned yachts in the Southern Ocean Racing Conference, the Onion Patch Series, including the famous Newport to Bermuda Race, and the Canada's Cup. His current yacht, *Mia's Red Jacket*, designed by George Cuthbertson, is the only Canadian yacht to win the SORC, which it did in 1968. In 1983 Phelan was instrumental in Canada's challenge for the America's Cup, earning him the official title of "Honorary Commodore at Sea." He also represents Canada on the permanent committee of the International Yacht Racing Union, the governing body of international yacht racing. He is a member of the Toronto Club, the York Club, the Royal Canadian Yacht Club, the Queen's Club, and the Osler Bluff Ski Club.

Phillips, Edwin Charles

Business executive. b. October 19, 1917, Saskatoon; m. Elizabeth Johnston; s. Glen, Earl, d. Diane, Carol, Jane, Sue; res. Vancouver.

President and chief executive officer of Foothills Oil Pipe Line Ltd., and chairman or vice-chairman and director of nine related companies (including Foothills Engineering Ltd.), Ed Phillips began his business career as an assistant buyer for Loblaw Groceterias in Toronto. After a stint as a flying instructor with the RCAF in the Second World War, he worked with Canada & Dominion Sugar and Consumers' Gas, then joined Trane Company of Canada as an assistant general manager. He became the company's president in 1966. Two years later he headed for British Columbia and became vice-president of Westcoast Transmission and held various executive positions until his retirement from the company as chairman in April 1983. He is most proud of his 41-year marriage and his six children, and is an enthusiastic horseman at the Southlands Riding & Polo Club. He also belongs to the Vancouver Club and the Shaughnessy Golf and Country Club.

Pierce, J.M.

Chairman, Ranger Oil Ltd., Calgary

Pitfield, Ward Chipman

B.Comm.

Investment dealer. b. September 6, 1925, Montreal; m. Diana Sutherland; s. Chipman, John, David, d. Elizabeth, Sally; res. Toronto.

As chairman and chief executive officer of the investment firm of Pitfield Mackay Ross Ltd.,

Ward Pitfield (brother of Senator Michael Pitfield) is one of the most influential of the investment dealers who operate in the Toronto capital market. He is a director of a number of other companies and of the Hospital for Sick Children Foundation. He is also a trustee of the Ontario Jockey Club. During the Second World War he served with the RAF Transport Command. He was educated at Bishop's College School and McGill University.

Powis, Alfred, III

B.Comm.

Business executive. b. September 16, 1930, Montreal; m. Lousie Margaret Finlayson; s. Timothy Alfred, Charles Robert, d. Nancy Alison; res. Toronto.

Educated at McGill University, from which he received his B.Comm. in 1951, Alf Powis joined Noranda Mines Limited in 1956 after working for Sun Life of Canada as an investment analyst. He became president in 1968 and took the additional post of chairman in 1977. After engineering a successful takeover of MacMillan Bloedel, he headed a bitter struggle to save his own company from takeover by Brascan. Although the battle was unsuccessful and Brascan took over Noranda in the summer of 1981, Powis remains at the head of Noranda. His many directorships include the Canadian Imperial Bank of Commerce, Gulf Canada, Simpsons-Sears, Ford of Canada, the Conference Board of Canada, and Toronto General Hospital. A member of the York, Toronto, and Mount Royal clubs, he also enjoys spending time at his farm.

Rathgeb, Charles Irwin

Business executive. b. December 2, 1921, Three Rivers, Quebec; m. Rosemary Clarke; res. Toronto.

Chuck Rathgeb is one of the Establishment's more flamboyant personalities; his out-of-office accomplishments rival his successful direction of Comstock International, which, under his "benevolent dictatorship," became Canada's largest contracting company. It was sold in 1979 to the Lundrigan interests of Newfoundland. He first became seriously involved in sports while attending Upper Canada College, when he represented Canada on the Commonwealth Cricket Team in 1935. He spent two years in the Arctic as an RCMP constable before joining the Royal Canadian Navy for the Second World War, receiving Campaign medals for the Battle of the Atlantic, and the Invasion of Europe and the Norwegian War Medal. In addition to mountaineering, offshore powerboat racing, bobsledding (gold medal in the 1964 Olympics), airplane racing (he holds the record for crossing the Atlantic in the lightest jet aircraft), ballooning, and motor racing (he became the first Canadian to race the Targa Florio event in Sicily, finishing 10th out of 80 entries), he has also been awarded the "Big Six" by the Explorers' Club in London for his big-game successes. He is a director of the Royal Bank of Canada and other companies, president of the Rathgeb Foundation, and is married to one of the shipping Clarkes. He belongs to the Cresta Club in St. Moritz, the Lyford Cay Club in Nassau, and the Indian Creek Club in Miami, in addition to the York, the Toronto, and the Mount Royal clubs.

Reekie, C. Douglas

President, CAE Industries Ltd., Toronto

The Reichmanns—Paul, Albert, Ralph

Land developers.

One of the world's largest development companies, the Reichmanns' Olympia & York Developments Ltd. began humbly with the purchase of a floundering Montreal plastic tile business. This was the Reichmanns' introduction to the construction industry; they proved to be quick learners, as Olympia Floor & Wall Tile Co. became one of the largest in Canada with sales of around $50 million. (It is still run by Ralph.) The Reichmann family originally came from Hungary, where the father, Samuel, was an egg distributor. They fled to Austria in the 1920s because of the threat of a Communist takeover in Hungary, then moved to France and later to Tangier, where Samuel established a banking house. In the 1950s the family headed for Canada. Sons Albert and Paul gradually moved into real-estate development; in 1962 they branched into office-tower development. They first bought land at bargain prices on the outskirts of Toronto and constructed Olympia Square, which broke the trend toward the concentration of office development in the downtown core. Their next major coup came in 1977, when they purchased eight Manhattan office buildings to become the second-largest private owner of office buildings in New York City. Their investment has since tripled in value, from $350 million to $1 billion. Other deals followed in quick succession: the Reichmanns now own 100 per cent of Block Brothers Industries of Vancouver, a real-estate brokerage firm; 50.1 per cent of Brinco Ltd., an oil and gas producer; 100 per cent of English Property Corp. Ltd., Britain's third-largest property company, which holds 49.9 per cent of the Bronfmans' Trizec Corp. Ltd.; 94 per cent of Abitibi-Price; and 10% of MacMillan Bloedel. Recently they sold their 23 per cent holding in Royal Trustco, Canada's largest trust company, to the Brascan interests of Edward and Peter Bronfman for $144 million. In spite of this great expansion, the Reichmanns remain a very private family and are relatively unknown to most Canadians. They do not belong to any clubs or organizations and keep their business and personal lives strictly separated. As the brothers all have large families, continued private ownership of the Olympia & York empire seems assured.

Reuber, Grant Louis

B.A., A.M., Ph.D., L.L.D., F.R.S.C.

Banker, author, public servant. b. November 23, 1927, Mildmay, Ontario; m. Margaret Louise Julia Summerhayes; d. Allison Rebecca, Barbara Susanne, Mary Margaret; res. Montreal.

After 30 years as an outstanding economist, academic, administrator, author, and banker, Grant Reuber, the son of a farmer from Mildmay, Ontario, became the deputy chairman and deputy chief executive of the Bank of Montreal in 1981. Reuber took his M.A. in Economics from Harvard in 1954—where he had received the John B. Thayer Scholarship—and went on to Cambridge as a research student for 1954-55, having been awarded both a Social Science

LEFT: Lucien Rolland

RIGHT: Stephen Roman. BELOW: Two successive Gulfstream aircraft belonging to Denison Mines have borne the registration CF-SBR, for Stephen B. Roman. Other cute registrations include 'RBC, the Royal Bank of Canada's Lockheed Jetstar; 'KCI, Irving Oil Transport's HS 125; 'JLL, Jean-Louis Lévesque's Israel Westwind; and 'NTL, Northern Telecom's Falcon 20F.

RIGHT: Andrew Sarlos in his Bay Street office.

Research Scholarship and a Sir Arthur Currie Scholarship to Cambridge as well. By 1957 he had obtained a doctorate in Economics from Harvard. During his student years, Reuber held positions with the Bank of Canada's Economics Research Department and the Department of Finance, both in Ottawa. In 1957 Reuber returned to the University of Western Ontario where he had received his B.A. in Economics in 1950 and began a long association there as professor and administrator. He moved from assistant professor in Economics to the head of the department, eventually becoming the vice-president (Academic), provost, and member of the Board of Governors. During his term as vice-president, Reuber was also chairman of the Ontario Economic Council. He found time to write many monographs in economics and contribute to university and banking publications. His banking career started in 1978 when he held the position of senior vice-president and chief economist with the Bank of Montreal for a year. He left to become Canada's deputy minister of Finance until 1980. He returned to the Bank of Montreal as executive vice-president and was appointed the deputy chairman in 1981. Reuber has maintained his connection with the University of Western Ontario by sitting on the Advisory Committee of the School of Business and the National Alumni Advisory Council. He is a member of a number of committees and director of various foundations; in 1983 he became the chairman of Montreal's YMCA. A Fellow of the Royal Society of Canada and an honorary recipient of an LL.D. from Wilfrid Laurier University in 1983, Reuber takes an interest in his collection of prints.

Rhude, Henry Burton

D.F.C., Q.C., LL.B.

Business executive. b. November 11, 1923, Halifax; m. Elsie Foster; s. David, John, Michael; res. Halifax.

Chairman and chief executive officer of the Central Trust Company, Harry Rhude received his LL.B. from Dalhousie University in 1950 and was called to the Nova Scotia Bar in 1951. He served as a navigator in the Bomber Command of the RCAF from 1941 to 1945 and was awarded the Distinguished Flying Cross. He holds directorships in several companies, including Sobeys Stores, Atlantic Shopping Centres, and Exco Corporation. He is also a member of the Canadian Bar Association and the Nova Scotia Barristers Society. Rhude is a former partner in the Halifax law firm of Stewart, MacKeen & Covert. He holds memberships in the Halifax and Saraguay clubs.

Rice, Victor Albert

Business executive. b. March 7, 1941, Hitchin, Hertfordshire, England; separated; s. Greg, Jonathan, d. Kristin; res. Toronto.

Victor A. Rice was elected chairman and chief executive officer of Massey-Ferguson on May 26, 1980, at the age of 39. Before taking the helm of Massey-Ferguson, he had served in a variety of financial positions in the United Kingdom with Ford, Cummins Engine, and Chrysler. In 1970 he joined Massey-Ferguson's Perkins Engines Group as comptroller, North European Operations, based in Peterborough, England. Following his appointment

as the Group's director of finance, he served as Perkins' director of sales operations in 1974. In 1975 he moved to Toronto as comptroller of the world-wide company; in 1977 he was appointed vice-president in charge of staff operations. The following year, he was named president and chief operating officer. Victor Rice is a firm believer in the need for communication between people at all levels of the company, so he logs more than 150,000 miles a year to attend management meetings and to visit Massey-Ferguson plants and offices around the world. He is a director of the Farm and Industrial Equipment Institute, a member of the Board of Trade of Metropolitan Toronto, the President's Association of the American Management Association, the Young Presidents' Organization, the British Institute of Marketing, and the Institute of Corporate Directors in Canada. His clubs include the Toronto Club, the Royal Canadian Yacht Club, the Toronto Golf Club, and the Carlton Club of London.

Ritchie, Cedric E.

O.C.

Banker. b. August 22, 1927, Upper Kent, New Brunswick; m. Barbara Binnington, res. Toronto.

Chairman and chief executive officer of the Bank of Nova Scotia, Cedric Ritchie began his banking career after graduating from high school in Bath, New Brunswick, in 1945. He rose steadily through the ranks, transferring to Toronto in the process, and was appointed president in 1972. Two years later he became chairman. He is also chairman and director of many of the bank's trust companies scattered around the world and serves as a director of Mercedes-Benz Canada, Beatrice Foods, Canada Life, Moore Corp., Canadian Executive Service Overseas, and the Canadian Council of Christians and Jews, among other organizations. He is governor of Junior Achievement of Canada and the Olympic Trust of Canada and is a trustee of Queen's University. In 1981 he was made an Officer of the Order of Canada. Among his clubs are the Mount Royal, the Toronto, and the York.

Rogers, Forrest

Chairman, B.C. Sugar Refinery Ltd., Vancouver

Rolland, Lucien Gilbert

B.A., B.A.Sc., C.E., D.C.Sc., O.St.G.

Business executive. b. December 21, 1916, St-Jérôme, Quebec; m. Marie de Lorimier; s. Nicolas, Stanislas, Etienne, David, d. Natalie, Dominique, Christine; res. Montreal.

After studying at the Ecole Polytechnique of the University of Montreal, Lucien Rolland began working at the family-owned Rolland Paper Co. Ltd. in 1942 as an engineer. In 1952 he became president of the company, whose name was changed in 1972 to Rolland Inc. The company is a leading producer of fine papers and was founded in St. Jérôme by Jean Baptiste Rolland, Lucien's great-grandfather. Lucien Rolland is the sixth Rolland to be president of the company. He is also a director of the Bank of Montreal, Bell Canada, and Canadian Pacific and sits on the boards of the

Montreal Symphony Orchestra, the Atlantic Salmon Association, and the Montreal Board of Trade. He is an honorary member of the board of directors of Notre-Dame Hospital and of the University of Montreal as well as an honorary vice-president of the Canadian Red Cross Society. He belongs to the Mount Royal and Saint-Denis clubs.

Roman, Stephen B.

LL.D., K.C.S.G.

Business executive. b. April 17, 1921, Slovakia; m. Betty Gardon; s. Stephen, Paul, John, David, d. Helen, Angela, Anne; res. Unionville, Ontario.

Stephen Roman emigrated from Slovakia to Canada when he was 16 years old. His first big mining stake was at Elliot Lake, north of Lake Huron, where he discovered uranium deposits. Following this initial success, he put together $59 million and built Denison Mines, a leading world supplier of uranium. As well as being chairman and chief executive officer of Denison Mines, he is chairman of Roman Corp. and Lake Ontario Cement, president of Romandale Farms, and his directorships include Crown Life Insurance, Guaranty Trust of Canada, and St. Michael's College Foundation. He is president of the Slovak World Congress and has honorary LL.D.s from the universities of Toronto (1967) and St. Francis Xavier (1967). On his large farm outside of Toronto he breeds Holstein Friesian cattle; one of his animals made the Guinness Book of Records when it was sold for $65,000. Roman is also a director of the John G. Diefenbaker Foundation and an honorary director of the Royal Agricultural Winter Fair Association. His clubs include the Engineers, Lyford Cay, and Capitol Hill. He was made a Knight Commander of the Order of St. Gregory the Great by Pope John XXIII.

Sarlos, Endre

Investor. b. November 24, 1931, Budapest; m. Mary Fennes; s. Peter; res. Don Mills, Ontario.

Former Hungarian freedom fighter Andy Sarlos is one of the Bay Street's most closely watched investors. Born into a middle-class Budapest family, Sarlos came to Canada in 1957. He studied accounting and spent a decade as chief accountant for Canadian Bechtel, eventually serving on the financial task force planning the giant Churchill Falls power project. After a period with Acres Ltd. in which he masterminded its takeover of the Traders Group and a brief stint with Sam Belzberg, he set out on his own. He has headed HCI Holdings (formerly the Hand Fireworks Co.), the vehicle for his bold investment ventures that have shaken up Bay Street. However, the stock market bust of 1981 shook up HCI, which was sorely overextended and came close to bankruptcy. The company has since made a remarkable recovery. In 1983 Sarlos and his associate Barry Zukerman sold their shares in HCI to Aitken Hume Holdings, an investment company controlled by heirs of Lord Beaverbrook.

Schwartz, Gerald W.

President, CanWest Capital Corp., Winnipeg Entrepreneur; Toronto

Sharwood, Gordon Robertson
B.A., B.A., M.A.

Merchant banker. b. February 26, 1932, Montreal; divorced; s. Robert, Brian, d. Alexandra; res. Toronto.

President of Sharwood and Company as well as vice-chairman of the pay-TV channel First Choice Canadian Communications Corporation, Gordon Sharwood attended Selwyn House School, Bishop's College School, and then McGill, Oxford (where he studied law), and Harvard. He began his financial career in 1956 with the Canadian Imperial Bank of Commerce, where he held numerous positions in branch and general management until 1968, when he was named chief general manager. In 1970 he entered the financial consulting field and became the moving force behind a large and imaginative financial conglomerate that included Guaranty Trust, Acres Ltd., Traders Group, Canadian General Securities, Canadian Insurance Shares, and Aetna Factors Corporation. He is a director of the C.D. Howe Institute, Dover Industries, Canadian Pacific Transport, Nabob Foods, and the Niagara Institute, and belongs to the Toronto Club and the Alpine Ski Club. He is the son of a former vice-president of C-I-L, Robert Sharwood.

Shrum, Gordon M.
Retired scientist, professor, executive, Vancouver

Simard, Arthur
Chairman, Trust Général du Canada, Ste. Anne de Sorel, Quebec

Sinclair, Ian David
O.C., Q.C., B.A., LL.B., LL.D., D.B.A., D.C.L.

Business executive. b. December 27, 1913, Winnipeg; m. Ruth Beatrice Drennan; s. Ian, Donald, d. Susan, Christine; res. Oakville, Ontario.

Ian Sinclair is chairman of Canadian Pacific Enterprises, vice-president of the Royal Bank, and a director of 19 other companies, including CP Air, Canadian Pacific Ltd., Marathon Realty, and Sun Life of Canada. He joined CP as assistant solicitor in the Winnipeg law department in 1942 after five years with the law firm of Guy, Chappell and Co. He is a leading figure in the Canadian business establishment and one of the country's most powerful corporate men. Sinclair considers his greatest achievement to be the "restructuring of corporations and the development of transnational multifaceted natural resource units." He belongs to the Rideau and the Mount Royal clubs.

Southern, Ronald D.
B.Sc., LL.D.

Business executive. b. July 25, 1930, Calgary; m. Margaret Visser; d. Nancy, Linda; res. Calgary.

Ron Southern's entrepreneurial career began when he was 16, when he joined his father, a Calgary fireman, in starting a tiny utility trailer rental outfit called Alberta Trailer Co. Atco has since become a huge concern with interests in companies around the world, ranging from residential housing and building supply to travel consulting. In 1980 Atco purchased 58 per cent of Canadian Utilities Limited, which sup-

plies 80 per cent of Alberta's gas consumption. It has sales in excess of $1 billion per annum and employs approximately 8,000 people. Atco's president and chief executive officer (his father is chairman), Ron Southern also sits on the boards of Nova, Crown Zellerbach, Pacific Western Airlines, and Royal Insurance, among others. He is an honorary associate of the Calgary Exhibition and Stampede Board, governor of the Olympic Trust of Canada, and a charter member of the Young Presidents' Organization. He is married to Margaret Visser, a director of Shell Canada and Woodward Stores, who developed the equestrian complex Spruce Meadows, the top facility in Canada for the sport.

Stewart, David Macdonald
C.M., C.St.J., K.L.J., F.R.S.A., F.H.S.(C), LL.D., D.B.A.

Business executive. b. September 16, 1920, Montreal; m. Liliane Spengler; one son, five daughters; res. Montreal.

President of the Macdonald Stewart Foundation and a director of RJR-Macdonald Inc., one of Canada's largest tobacco firms, David Stewart inherited the company from his father, who had served as Sir William Macdonald's secretary for 50 years and who (with Walter's brother) was rewarded with the company on Macdonald's death. The younger Stewart sold Macdonald Tobacco to the R.J. Reynolds interests of Winston-Salem, North Carolina, in 1974, six years after taking control, remaining a vice-chairman for a time. Educated at Ashbury College in Ottawa and McGill University, his interests include Himalayan cats and one of the world's finest collections of toy soldiers. He is a member of the Mount Royal, the St. James's, and the Saint-Denis clubs.

Strong, Maurice F.
Business executive. b. April 29, 1929, Oak Lake, Manitoba; m. Hanne Marstrand; s. Frederick, Kenneth, d. Maureen, Mary Anne, Alice; res. Tsawwassen, British Columbia.

Maurice Strong's fascination with the exotic and his compelling entrepreneurial instincts have resulted in an extraordinarily varied and successful business career. At 17 he was apprentice to a fur trader at Chesterfield Inlet, Northwest Territories, where he learned the Inuit language. By the time he was 23 he was executive assistant to Jack Gallagher at Dome Petroleum, a position he resigned after two years to form his own company. He went to Africa, where he established service stations in Kenya and Zanzibar and a graphite mine in Tanzania, and took the time to learn Swahili. His formal education consisted of night courses taken during this extremely busy early period of his career, but he has received 23 honorary degrees from universities in Canada, the United States, and Europe. In 1965 he came back to Canada, rejoined Dome, then left for Power Corp., of which he became president in 1966. Soon after that Prime Minister Lester Pearson asked him to head the Canadian International Development Agency, and the international experience he gained there led to his appointment as key organizer for the 1972 United Nations Conference on the Human Environment. While the conference was still in the planning stages, Mr. Strong was made under-

secretary general to the United Nations in Geneva. In Switzerland, he established the Société Générale pour l'Energie et les Ressources. Later, he became the first president and chairman of the board of Petro-Canada, a post he left to assume his present role as chairman of the Canada Development Investment Corporation.

Mr. Strong is also vice-chairman of Tosco Corporation, chairman of the International Energy Development Corporation, and director of and a member of the executive committee of the Canada Development Corporation. Other directorships include the United Nations University; the North-South Energy Round Table (chairman); the International Council of Asia Society, New York; the International Foundation for Development Alternatives, Switzerland (founding co-chairman); the International Council of the World Wildlife Fund; the Aspen Institute (trustee); the Lindisfarne Association; and the International Honorary Committee of the Dag Hammarskjold Foundation. He belongs to the Rideau Club in Ottawa, the Ranchmen's Club in Calgary, the Farmer's Club in the United Kingdom, the Yale Club in New York, the Denver Petroleum Club in Colorado, and the Canadian Club in New York. He has received many honours and awards, including an officership in the Order of Canada in 1976; Henri Pittier Order in 1977; Commander of the Order of the Golden Ark, 1979; the Charles A. Lindbergh Award, 1981; and the UNEP Gold Environmental Leadership Decade Award, 1982.

Sweatman, Alan
Q.C., B.A., LL.B.

Lawyer. b. December 9, 1920, Winnipeg; m. Lorraine MacDonald; s. Alan, Wynn, Paul, Scott, d. Margaret, Elizabeth; res. Winnipeg.

One of Winnipeg's pillars of the Establishment, Alan Sweatman is a director of the Toronto-Dominion Bank and sits on the boards of half a dozen major companies; as well, he is a partner of the law firm Thompson, Dorfman, Sweatman. His studies at the University of Manitoba were interrupted by the Second World War, in which he served with the Royal Canadian Naval Volunteer Reserve, leaving with the rank of lieutenant in 1945. He then returned to university, received his law degree, and read law with the celebrated Isaac Pitblado. His strong sense of justice extends into his private life: he resigned as president of the St. Charles Country Club when his efforts to lift the ban on Jewish members were frustrated. He was a close advisor to Bob Graham, whose successful Inter-City Gas has developed from a tiny distributor in

Taylor, Austin G.E.
President, McLeod Young Weir Ltd., Toronto

Taylor, Charles Plunket Bourchier
B.A.

Writer, horse breeder. b. February 13, 1935, Toronto; m. Marina Sacy; s. Edward, d. Nadina; res. Toronto.

The only son of tycoon and horse breeder E.P. Taylor, Charles Taylor has recently taken the reins of his ailing father's $100 million thoroughbred racing-breeding complex, Windfields Farms, still regarding the managing of

356

ABOVE: Gordon Shrum, now in his 80s, has had a distinguished career in science, the military, academic life and business. He was head of the physics department at UBC for many years, was instrumental in the founding of Simon Fraser University, and is a former chairman of B.C. Hydro. ABOVE RIGHT: E.P. Taylor on one of his saddle horses at Windfields. RIGHT: Maurice Strong, chairman of the Canada Development Investment Corporation.

his inheritance as "moonlighting from his real calling: the writing of finely crafted, semiautobiographical books" (from Sylvia Fraser, in "Bloodlines," a portrait of Charles Taylor in *Toronto Life* magazine, March 1983). Although he is now vice-president of Windfields and actively involved in the direction of the Taylor enterprises, Charles Taylor is best known as the author of four books: *Reporter in Red China* (1966), *Snow Job: Canada, the United States, and Vietnam, 1954-1973* (1974), *Six Journeys: A Canadian Pattern* (1977), and *Radical Tories: The Conservative Tradition in Canada* (1982). He was educated at Trinity College School in Port Hope, Ontario, and at Queen's University. He graduated in 1955 and within a month was working in London for the Reuters News Agency, writing despatches during the day and labouring at the first of his five unpublished novels during the evenings. In 1962 he was chosen by the *Globe and Mail*'s editor-in-chief, Dic Doyle, to go to Hong Kong and then to Peking as the *Globe*'s Far East correspondent, an 18-month sojourn that resulted in his first book. A month in Vietnam for the *Globe* was the beginning of his *Snow Job*, a virulent attack on Canada's Vietnam policies. Taylor went on to cover the Arab-Israeli Six Day War in 1967 and after that reopened the *Globe*'s Nairobi bureau. He returned to Toronto in the early 1970s to take a fuller part in running the Taylor empire (however unlikely a choice for such a role he fancies himself to be) and to continue to write, turning out works that are regarded as paradoxically anti-Establishment in subject matter and tone.

Taylor, Claude I.

President, Air Canada, Montreal

Taylor, Edward Plunket

C.M.G., B.Sc., LL.D.

Industrialist, financier, horse breeder. b. January 29, 1901, Ottawa; m. Winifred Thornton Duguid; d. Judith Winifred Mappin, Louise (deceased), s. Charles Plunket Bourchier; res. Toronto and Lyford Cay, New Providence, Bahamas.

The legendary business tycoon and breeder of thoroughbred racehorses was born in Ottawa, son of Lieutenant-Colonel Plunket Bourchier Taylor and Florence Gertrude Magee. He was educated at Ottawa Collegiate Institute and at McGill University where he earned a B.Sc. in mechanical engineering in 1922. While still in his early 20s, he established the Yellow Bus Company in Ottawa's west end and, shortly afterwards, founded the first metred taxicab company in Ottawa. In 1923, only a year after he'd left university, he became a director of Brading Breweries Ltd. and joined the Ottawa office of the investment house of McLeod, Young, Weir & Co. Ltd. (His father, who had just retired from the Royal Bank, was manager of the office.) E.P. became a director of MYW in 1929 but resigned the following year to found Brewing Corporation of Ontario, which took the name Brewing Corporation of Canada later in the year. In the next few years the new company took over Ontario breweries (among them Brading's in Ottawa, Carling's in London, Kuntz's in Waterloo, Taylor & Bate in St. Catharines, and Cosgrave's and O'Keefe's in Toronto); they were all eventually welded into Canadian Breweries Ltd. Taylor's other great adventures in corporate agglomeration were his consolidation and expansion of the Ontario

Jockey Club and the establishing of Argus Corp. The Jockey Club had been founded in 1881 by Joseph Duggan, T.C. Patteson, and Sir Casimir Gzowski (later to be run by William Hendrie and Joseph Seagram). By 1947 Taylor had been made a director of the OJC and rapidly became its largest stock holder. By buying up the charters of many of the smaller and less successful tracks in the province, he consolidated racing into fewer and greatly improved facilities (including, for example, Woodbine in Rexdale, a Toronto suburb, which opened in 1956). This controlling interest in the Jockey Club dovetailed conveniently with Taylor's interest (and spectacular success) in the breeding of thoroughbreds at his Windfields Farms, which was formed in 1950 when Taylor purchased Colonel R.S. McLaughlin's Parkwood Stables horse farm near Oshawa, Ontario. Windfields' greatest triumph has assuredly been the breeding and racing of Northern Dancer, the first Canadian racehorse to win both the Kentucky Derby and the Queen's Plate (1964). This legendary horse went on to sire many champions, including Nijinsky, who won the English Triple Crown in 1970. Taylor worked hard and impressively for Canada during the Second World War: he was one of C.D. Howe's dollar-a-year men, serving as director-general of Munitions and Supply, president of War Supplies Ltd. in Washington, then president of the British Supply Council of North America based in Washington as well. In 1943, he resumed his career in business, joining Lieutenant-Colonel W. Eric Phillips and Wallace McCutcheon to form Argus Corp. on September 24, 1945. (Major stocks held by Argus included Canadian Breweries and Massey-Harris.) Taylor's last major enterprise has been the exclusive club and residential development he founded at Lyford Cay in the Bahamas. Both Lyford Cay and Windfields Farms are now run by Taylor's son Charles. E.P. Taylor is director emeritus of the Thoroughbred Racing Association Inc. in New York. He was awarded McGill University's first Gold Medal for distinguished service to Canadian society in 1957. He belongs to the Toronto Club, the York Club, the Rideau Club, the Metropolitan Club (New York), the Turf Club (London), the Lyford Cay (Bahamas), and the East Hill (Bahamas).

Thomson, Richard Murray

B.A. Sc., M.B.A.

Banker. b. August 14, 1933, Winnipeg; res. Toronto.

Dick Thomson is chairman and chief executive officer of the Toronto-Dominion Bank, a position he has held since 1978. Educated at the University of Toronto (B.A.Sc., 1955), at the Harvard Business School (M.B.A., 1957), and at Queen's University (Fellow's Course in Banking, 1958), Thomson joined the Toronto-Dominion in 1957, serving in numerous branches in Toronto and Montreal and becoming assistant to the president by 1963. After that, his rise to the top was rapid: he became chief general manager in 1968; vice-president, chief general manager, and director in 1971; president in 1972; and president and chief executive officer in 1977. Thomson is also a director of Cadillac Fairview, Canadian Gypsum, Eaton's, S.C. Johnson & Son Ltd., the Prudential Insurance Company of America, and Union Carbide Canada. He is also vice-chairman of the Hospital for Sick Children in Toronto. His astute and aggressive policies have made

the T-D Bank a powerhouse in the corporate-loans business.

Torno, Noah

M.B.E.

Business executive. b. November 27, 1910, Toronto; m. Rose Laine; steps. Michael; res. Toronto.

A member of a family very much involved in the arts, Noah Torno is vice-chairman of Consumers' Gas and a director of Canada Trust, Hiram Walker Resources, and the World Wildlife Fund. After serving as a lieutenant in the Royal Canadian Navy during the Second World War, he plunged into the family wine business and has continued the family tradition by becoming a member of the Canadian Guild of Crafts and a life member of the Art Gallery of Ontario. He is past chairman of the Royal Ontario Museum.

Tory, John A.

Q.C., B.A., LL.B.

Lawyer, business executive. b. March 7, 1930, Toronto; m. Elizabeth Bacon; s. James, William, d. Ann, Mary; res. Toronto.

A partner in the law firm of Tory, Tory, DesLauriers & Binnington, John Tory now rules the Thomson empire as president of the Thomson Corp., Thomson Equitable Corp., and the Woodbridge Corp. He is a deputy chairman of International Thomson Organisation and Thomson Newpapers. He is a director of the Royal Bank, Sun Life Assurance, Rogers Cablesystems, Rogers Telecommunications, Abitibi-Price, and the Hudson's Bay Company, among others. He works with the Canadian Mental Health Association and is a trustee of the Clarke Institute of Psychiatry. His twin brother, James M. Tory, is a partner in the law firm and a director of several major companies. Their father, the late J.S.D. Tory, was a leading corporate lawyer.

Turmel, Antoine

O.C., D.B.A.

Business executive. b. 1918, Thetford Mines, Quebec; s. André, Jean-François, d. Hélène, Marie-Josée; res. Westmount, Quebec.

Antoine Turmel has become one of Quebec's most successful businessmen through his innovative approach to grocery wholesaling. In essence, his company, Provigo, became highly successful by helping small independents to fight big business. In just five years the company had sales of $2.5 million, and began snowballing with Turmel's skillful handling of increasing sales, mergers, and acquisitions. This culminated in 1977, when Provigo took over M. Loeb Ltd., a merchandising company twice its size, which resulted in Provigo's sudden jump from a Quebec-based business to one that spreads across North America, with a very strong base in California. Turmel, now chairman and chief executive officer of Provigo Inc., was named the French-Canadian Man of the Year in 1967 and sits on the boards of such companies as the National Bank of Canada, Shell Canada, and Noranda Mines.

Van Wielingen, Gustaaf André

B.Sc.

Business executive. b. 1924, Laren, Holland; res. Calgary.

Chairman and chief executive officer of Sulpetro, Gus Van Wielingen was born and raised in Holland. With the coming of the Second World War, he joined the U.S. naval air service (his mother was an American citizen), then transferred to the Dutch armed forces as an intelligence officer. After the war he earned his degree in mechanical engineering at university and began working in Indonesia for Standard Oil of New Jersey before being called up by the U.S. Navy for the Korean War. After his tour of duty, he joined Gulf Canada in Calgary. Over the next few years he worked for Progas Ltd. and J.C. Sproule & Associates, started up two unsuccessful propane-extraction plants, and served on the Royal Commission on Energy. He founded Sulpetro with a borrowed $250,000 in 1967, shortly afterwards, the company struck it big drilling for gas in east-central Alberta. In 1975 he sold out to Hudson's Bay Oil & Gas and invested the profit in 50 per cent of Mesa Petroleum's acreage and an interest in Canadian Hunter Exploration, which ran up his assets to $100 million. The purchase in 1981 of CanDel Oil doubled Sulpetro's Canadian reserves and led to exploration efforts around the world. He was the first Canadian oilman to participate in Petro-Canada's exploration program and now has a 10 per cent interest in East Coast activities. He speaks four languages and has often hosted Prince Philip on his visits to Canada. Along with Dick Bonnycastle, a principal in the Harlequin empire, he shares an interest in thoroughbred horse racing and was a partner with him in the purchase of the late Conn Smythe's racing and breeding stock. He is a good friend of Peter Lougheed and was one of his first clients when Lougheed began his law career. He has been known to refuse bank directorships because he is "too busy" to make the rounds of boardrooms, although he sits on the boards of various Canadian, American, and European public and private corporations. He is a past governor of the Canadian Petroleum Association and a past director of the Independent Petroleum Association.

Wadsworth, Jeffery Page Rein

Business executive. b. July 27, 1911, Toronto; m. Elizabeth Cameron Bunting; one daughter; res. Toronto.

Page Wadsworth joined the Canadian Bank of Commerce in 1928 after studying at Lakefield College School and Upper Canada College. He rose through the ranks to become chairman and chief executive officer of the Canadian Imperial Bank of Commerce until he retired in 1976 and became chairman of the Executive Committee of Confederation Life. He is an honorary chairman of the Board of Governors of Lakefield College School, a member of the Board of Governors of the Lester B. Pearson College of the Pacific, and chairman of the Board of Governors of the University of Waterloo. He belongs to the Mount Royal, the York, and the Toronto clubs, and sails with the Royal Canadian Yacht Club.

Ward, Maxwell W.

O.C.

Business executive, pilot. b. November 22, 1921, Edmonton; m. Marjorie Dorothea Skelton; d. Gai, Blythe, Kim, s. Blake; res. Edmonton.

Max Ward began his aviation career in the RCAF in 1940. After the war he took his savings to de Havilland Canada and made a down payment on a Fox Moth biplane, with which he went into the charter business in Yellowknife as Polaris Charter Co. Other aircraft and several brushes with financial disaster followed, as his enterprise grew into Wardair International, a giant in the charter business whose fleet includes several jumbo jets, not to mention a replica of the first Fox Moth. The company is no longer in the northern bush flying business and is pushing to break into the scheduled business dominated by Air Canada and CP Air. Max Ward is a winner of the McKee Trophy (1973) for his contributions to aviation and is a member of the Canadian Aviation Hall of Fame. His wife is secretary-treasurer and a director of Wardair International.

Warren, Robert Michael

B.Comm.

Business executive. b. April 10, 1937, Montreal; separated; s. Stephen Gregory, Scott Edward Kenneth, d. Victoria Claire; res. Ottawa.

Michael Warren attained national prominence when he was appointed the first president and chief executive officer of Canada Post Corporation in 1981 in the hope that he would succeed in reducing the Post Office's deficits. He was already well known as chief general manager of the Toronto Transit Commission and a director of Gray Coach Lines (1975-81), and a deputy minister in the Ontario Government (1962-75). Warren is also a director of the MDS Health Group. He was educated at Sir George Williams University in Montreal.

Webster, Donald C.

President, Helix Investments Ltd., Toronto

Webster, Lorne C.

Chairman, Prenor Group Ltd., Montreal

Webster, R. Howard

President, Imperial Trust Co., Montreal

Weldon, David Black

B.A.

Investment dealer. b. June 27, 1925, London, Ontario; m. Ina Perry; d. Susan, Mardie, Kate, s. Douglas, Anthony; res. Arva, Ontario, and Toronto.

David Weldon is chairman of the Toronto investment firm of Midland Doherty and a director of several companies including Guaranty Trust, Silverwood Industries, Grafton Group, and Emco. He is also vice-president and director of Goderich Elevators, and is considered one of the most influential of the investment dealers who run the Toronto capital market. He is a member of the advisory board of the University of Western Ontario Business School, trustee and chairman of the finance committee of Toronto General Hospital, and past president and director of the Royal Agricultural Winter Fair. During the Second World War, Weldon served in the Canadian Infantry. His favourite pastimes are breeding standardbred horses and Aberdeen Angus cattle, fishing, golf, and tennis. Among his clubs are the Albany, the York, the London, the

Royal and Ancient Golf Club of St. Andrews, the Griffith Island, and the Ristigouche Salmon Club.

White, Kenneth Alan

K. St. J., C.D., C.T.C.I., F.I.B.A.

Business executive. b. April 5, 1914, Toronto; m. Joan Frankish Crombie; s. D. David R. Alan, Kenneth R.; res. Oakville, Ontario.

As chairman of Royal Trustco and other companies in the Royal Trust Group, as well as a director of many companies including Canadian Pacific, Dominion Textile, and Stelco, Kenneth White is a leading member of the Canadian business establishment. He is also on the Quebec and Ontario councils of the St. John Ambulance, and is a director of St. Mary's Hospital Foundation, the Royal Victoria Hospital in Montreal, and the Montreal Children's Hospital. During the Second World War, White served overseas with the Toronto Scottish, rising to the rank of lieutenant-colonel; he did post-war duty with the Reserve Army. His favourite holiday place is the Eastern Townships of Quebec. Among his clubs are the Toronto, the York, the Mount Royal, and the Rideau.

Wilder, William Price

B.Comm., M.B.A.

Financier. b. September 26, 1922, Toronto; m. Judith Ryrie Bickle; d. Martha Helen, s. William Edward, Thomas Bickle, Andrew Murray; res. Toronto.

William Wilder is deputy chairman of Hiram Walker Resources, chairman of Consumers' Gas, and director of 10 other companies, including Hiram Walker–Gooderham & Worts, John Labatt, the Royal Bank, Canada Life, Noranda Mines, Maclean Hunter, and Simpsons-Sears. From 1972 to 1976, he was the chairman and chief executive officer of Canadian Arctic Gas Study Ltd. His M.B.A. is from the Harvard Business School, and he is credited with having introduced Harvard management techniques to Bay Street when he became executive vice-president of the Wood Gundy investment firm in 1961. He was president of Wood Gundy from 1967 to 1972. He sits on the executive and advisory committees of the School of Business Administration at the University of Western Ontario and on the board of trustees of the Hospital for Sick Children in Toronto. During the Second World War, Wilder was on loan to the Royal Navy from the RCNVR and served in destroyers in the English Channel and on the North Sea. Among his clubs are the York, the Toronto, the Badminton and Racquet, the Rideau, the Tadenac Fishing Club, and Brooks's in London, England.

Willmot, Donald Gilpin

B.A.Sc.

Business executive. b. March 7, 1916, Toronto; m. Ivy Vivien Sutcliffe; s. Michael, David, d. Wendy; res. King, Ontario.

Honorary chairman of The Molson Companies, Bud Willmot moved from the presidency of Anthes Imperial Ltd. of St. Catharines to the post of chief executive officer at Molson's in 1968 when the brewing company bought out Anthes, a foundry and metal-fabricating business. After receiving his B.A.Sc. from the Uni-

William Wilder

David Weldon in his office at Midland Doherty.

Austin Taylor in the Toronto office of McLeod Young Weir.

RICHARD PIERRE

Charles P.B. Taylor

J.R.

Bud Willmot at Kinghaven.

Gordon Wotherspoon at his farm east of Toronto.

J.R.

versity of Toronto, Bud Willmot joined Canadian SKF in Toronto as an engineer. He joined Anthes in 1939; in 1942 he moved to Atlas Steels in Welland. He left in 1948 as assistant to the vice-president and general manager to rejoin Anthes, this time as president. His directorships include the Bank of Nova Scotia (of which he is also a vice-president), Inco, Jannock, and Crown Life. He is a trustee of the Toronto Western Hospital and a governor of Ridley College. He is also vice-president and a trustee of the Ontario Jockey Club and the owner of one of the finest thoroughbred farms in Ontario, out of which several winning horses have been produced, including the 1979 Queen's Plate winner, Steady Growth.

Wisener, Robert A.

Co-chairman, The MerBanco Group, Calgary

Wolfe, Ray D.

C.M., B.A.

Business executive. b. August 3, 1917, Toronto; m. Rose Senderowitz; s. Jonathan, d. Elizabeth; res. Willowdale, Ontario.

Ray Wolfe is chairman of the board and president of the Oshawa Group and owns controlling interest in the business. (The Oshawa Group is the major supplier to IGA stores and owns Towers department stores.) He is a director of the Bank of Nova Scotia, Canadian Pacific Enterprises, Canadian Pacific Ltd., Confederation Life, and several other companies. He is also a director of the Bayview Centre for Geriatric Care and the Canadian

Council of Christians and Jews, and a governor of Mount Sinai Hospital in Toronto. Wolfe has received the Human Relations Award of the Canadian Council of Christians and Jews and the Ben Sadowsky Award of Merit. He is a graduate of the University of Toronto, and he served in the RCAF.

Wotherspoon, Gordon Dorward deSalaberry

D.S.O., K.St.J., E.D., C.D., D.Mil.Sc., Q.C.

Lawyer, businessman, military officer. b. January 12, 1909, Port Hope, Ontario; m. Margaret Trumbull Warren; s. Richard Hugh deSalaberry, Michael Trumbull, Douglas Gordon, d. Margaret Duchesnay; res. Uxbridge, Ontario.

Brigadier-General Wotherspoon's distinguished military career has spanned more than 40 years and has included service with the Reserve Force, the Governor General's Horse Guards and the Royal Canadian Armoured Corps. During active service in Europe in the Second World War, he was mentioned in despatches and was awarded the Bronze Lion of the Netherlands, among other awards. He was educated at Trinity College School, Royal Military College, and Osgoode Hall. A longtime associate of the Eatons, he is a director of Eaton Bay Financial Services and the Eaton Bay Group of Mutual Funds. He is past chairman of the board and honorary trustee of the Royal Ontario Museum and honorary director of the Wellesley Hospital in Toronto. Wotherspoon considers his chief accomplishments to be "the current expansion of the Royal Ontario Museum and commanding the South Alberta

Regiment when it, with supporting troops, closed the last escape route for the two German armies caught in the Falaise Gap with odds at least 25 to 1 in manpower against us." His clubs include the Toronto, the York, the Bonaventure Salmon, and Osler Bluff.

Zimmerman, Adam Hartley, Jr.

B.A., F.C.A.

Business executive. b. February 19, 1927, Toronto; m. Janet Lewis; d. Barbara, Mary, Kate, s. Thomas; res. Toronto.

The president and chief operating officer of Noranda Mines, Canada's largest copper producer and the world's top zinc miner, Adam Zimmerman engineered the company's takeover of forestry giant MacMillan Bloedel, further diversifying its interests into manufacturing, forestry, and mining. He was educated at Upper Canada College, Ridley College, and the Royal Canadian Naval College; he graduated with a B.A. from the University of Toronto's Trinity College in 1950. He began working for Clarkson Gordon as student-in-accounts and rose to the position of supervisor before leaving for Noranda in 1958 to become assistant comptroller. Since 1982 he has been president and COO. He is also a director of Southam Inc., the Toronto-Dominion Bank, Royal Insurance, and the C.D. Howe Institute. He is chairman of MacMillan Bloedel and vice-chairman of Canada Wire & Cable. Among his outside interests, he is trustee for the Hospital for Sick Children, a member of the Advisory Board of the Faculty of Forestry at U of T, and a former chairman of Branksome Hall, a girls' school.

PUBLIC SERVICE & MILITARY

Aird, John Black

O.C., Q.C., B.A., LL.D.

Lieutenant-Governor. b. May 5, 1923, Toronto; m. Lucille Jane Housser; s. Hugh Housser, d. Lucille Elizabeth, Jane Victoria, Katherine Black; res. Toronto.

John Aird, Ontario's 23rd lieutenant-governor, was educated at Upper Canada College; at the University of Toronto (Trinity College), where he received his B.A. in 1946, after serving as a lieutenant with the RCNVR (1942–45); and at Osgoode Hall. He read law with Wilton & Edison and continued to be associated with the firm from 1949 to 1953. From 1953 until his appointment as the lieutenant-governor of Ontario in 1980, he was a partner, founder, and developer of what became Aird & Berlis, a leading legal firm in Toronto. He was a member of the Senate from 1964 to 1974, when he resigned to head the Institute for Research on Public Policy. During this time he was also chairman of the Canadian Section of the Canada–United States Permanent Joint Board on Defence (1971–79) and a member of the Committee of Nine of the North Atlantic Assembly. The grandson of Sir John Aird, who headed the Bank of Commerce, he is a patron of a great number of organizations, including Variety Village, the National Ballet of Canada, and the Canadian National Institute for the

Blind. He is a member of the Toronto and York clubs and collects Canadian art and antique boats—he owns a 1933 Minett-Shields called *Black Beauty II* and a 1928 Disappearing-Propeller sport model called *Gem*.

Argue, Hazen Robert

P.C., B.Sc.

Farmer, politician. b. January 6, 1921, Moose Jaw, Saskatchewan; m. Eugenia Ignatescue; d. Lynda, Susan, Dawn, s. Gregory; res. Ormiston, Saskatchewan.

Appointed minister of state for the Canadian Wheat Board in March 1980, Hazen Argue has a long history of involvement with the political aspects of farming and agriculture. The son of a farmer, he attended the University of Saskatchewan and graduated with distinction in Farm Management in 1944. The next year he was elected to the House of Commons, which soon became his second home as he was re-elected in general elections for five more terms, the last beginning in 1962. In 1960 he was chosen the leader of the CCF at the party's national convention in Regina, and six years later, after the CCF had become the New Democratic Party and he had switched to the Liberals, Argue was appointed to the Senate. He was chairman of the Standing Senate Committee on Agriculture from 1972 to 1979, which he had established to serve the interests of the farming community in the Canadian government. He commutes frequently between Ottawa and his farm in Saskatchewan.

Austin, Jacob

P.C., Q.C., B.A., LL.B., LL.M.

Senator. b. March 2, 1932, Calgary; m. Natalie Freeman; d. Edith, Sharon, Barbara; res. Vancouver.

After studying at the University of British Columbia, Harvard Law School, and the University of California (Berkeley), Jack Austin read law with Nathan T. Nemetz and taught at UBC before being made a partner of Nemetz, Austin & Co. In 1963 he became executive assistant to the Minister of Northern Affairs and National Resources in Ottawa; he returned to Vancouver in 1966 to practise law again. Two years later he became president of Giant Mascot Mines and then of Brameda Resources. From 1970 to 1974 he served as deputy minister for the Department of Energy, Mines and Resources, then acted as principal secretary to the Prime Minister for a year. He was named a Q.C. in 1970 and appointed to the Senate in 1975. In 1982 he was chairman of the Ministerial Sub-committee on Broadcasting and Cultural Affairs. He is the author of "Canadian–United States Practice and Theory Respecting the International Law of International Rivers" and the co-author of "Canadian View of Territorial Seas and Fisheries." He belongs to Vancouver's University Club and New York's Canadian Club as well as the Cercle Universitaire d'Ottawa. Now minister of state for Social Development, he divides his time between his home in Vancouver and his office in Ottawa.

John Black Aird was photographed with family and boats at Muskoka. On the bow of his speedboat, Black Beauty, which he likes to regard as his official barge, he flies the lieutenant-governor's flag. Shown above is the rather exclusive licence plate of his limousine.

ALL: J.R

Baile, Brigadier-General B., C.D.

Commander, Northern Region, Canadian Forces, Ottawa.

Bell-Irving, Henry P.

Former Lt. Gov. of British Columbia, Victoria.

Belzile, Lieutenant-General C.H., C.M.M., C.D.

Commander, Mobile Command, Canadian Forces, Ottawa.

Bouey, Gerald Keith
O.C., B.A., LL.D.

Banker, economist. b. April 2, 1920, Axford, Saskatchewan; m. Anne Margaret Ferguson; d. Kathryn Anne, s. Robert Gerald; res. Ottawa.

Gerald Bouey has been governor of the Bank of Canada since 1973 and in that capacity he helped bring in the high interest rates of the late 1970s and early 1980s as a policy intended to restrain the growth of the money supply and thereby reduce inflation. He is also a director of the Federal Business Development Bank, the Export Development Bank, and the Canada Deposit Insurance Corporation. During the Second World War, he served overseas with the RCAF; on his return to Canada, he studied economics at Queen's University. He has been with the Bank of Canada since 1948.

Bryce, Robert B.
C.C., B.A.Sc., M.A., LL.D., F.R.S.C.

Public servant, economist. b. February 27, 1910, Toronto; m. Frances Robinson; two sons, one daughter; res. Ottawa.

During his 35 years as a government adviser, Robert Bryce became Canada's most powerful civil servant. Among the positions he held were deputy minister of Finance, clerk of the Privy Council and secretary to the Cabinet, economics advisor to the Prime Minister on the constitution, and chairman of the Royal Commission on Corporate Concentration. He was also executive director of the International Monetary Fund. In 1939 he was instrumental in having Keynesian policies adopted by the government of Canada. Son of R.A. Bryce, a noted mining figure, Bryce was educated at the University of Toronto, Cambridge University, where he became a disciple of John Maynard Keynes, and Harvard. At present he is writing a history of the finance department.

Burns, Eedson Louis Millard
C.C., D.S.O., O.B.E., M.C., LL.D

Military officer (retired). b. June 17, 1897, Westmount, Quebec; m. Eleanor Phelan (deceased); d. Mary Eleanor; res. Manotick, Ontario.

Educated at Lower Canada College and the Royal Military College, E.L.M. (Tommy) Burns has had a distinguished military career that spanned two world wars and led to UN peacekeeping duties in the 1950s and later a post as a government advisor. He was commissioned in the Royal Canadian Engineers in 1915 and was awarded the Military Cross in 1916. He rose through brigade and divisional commands in the Second World War, assuming command of the 1st Canadian Corps in March 1944 during operations that led to the capture

of Rimini. In 1955 General Burns was lent to the United Nations for appointment as chief of staff of the UN Truce Supervision Organization in Palestine and latterly commander of the UN Emergency Force from November 1956 to the end of 1959. Following UN duties, General Burns advised the Canadian government on disarmament. Before his retirement in 1975 he was professor of Strategic Studies at Carleton University. He is the author of *Between Arab and Israeli* (1962), *Megamurder* (1966), *General Mud* (1970), *A Seat at the Table* (1972), and *Defence in the Nuclear Age* (1976).

Butler, Esmond Unwin
C.V.O., B.A., C.St.J.

Public servant. b. July 13, 1922, Wawanesa, Manitoba; m. Georgiana North; s. Mark, d. Clare; res. Ottawa.

From 1955 to the present, Esmond Butler has served the Queen and five governors general, and provided administration, resources, and advice for each governor general. He has also participated in the planning of all major royal visits to Canada during this time. He studied at Trinity College at the University of Toronto, and at the University of Geneva and the Institute of International Studies in Switzerland. He began working in Geneva as a staff correspondent for United Press, then became the assistant secretary general of the International Union of Official Travel Organizations before returning to Canada in 1955. In 1972 he was made a Commander of the Royal Victorian Order; he has also been made a Commander Brother of the Order of St. John of Jerusalem. He is a member of the National Council of the Duke of Edinburgh's Awards in Canada and he serves on the advisory board of the Salvation Army. His favourite pastimes are collecting antique books and prints, and restoring early Canadian furniture. He lives in Rideau Cottage at Government House in Ottawa.

Camp, Dalton Kingsley
B.A., M.Sc.

Publicist, political commentator, columnist. b. September 11, 1920, Woodstock, New Brunswick; m. Linda Atkins; s. David Kingsley, Michael George Harold; d. Linda Gail, Constance Marilyn, Cheryl Ann; res. Cambridge, New Brunswick.

Dalton Camp attained nation-wide prominence as president of the National Progressive Conservative Party from 1964 to 1969 and as a candidate (unsuccessful) in the federal elections of 1965 and 1968. He remains a powerful backroom member of the party and an informed and witty commentator on the national political scene. In the early 1970s he was a member of the Ontario Royal Commission on Book Publishing and chairman of the Ontario Commission on the Legislature. At the same time he has had a successful career in advertising and public relations, has been a columnist for the *Toronto Star* and the *Toronto Sun*, and has written several books, including *Points of Departure* (1979). He has also been chairman of the Canadian Civil Liberties Association and a member of the Board of Governors of Acadia University. During the Second World War he served in the Canadian Army. He was educated at the University of New Brunswick, Columbia University, and the London School of

Economics. He plays tennis and belongs to the Albany Club and the Badminton and Racquet Club in Toronto.

Cohen, Marshall Albert

Lawyer, civil servant. b. 1935, Elizabeth, New Jersey; m. Judith Loeb; s. Richard, d. Jessica, Jillian, Jennifer, Amanda; res. Ottawa.

Mickey Cohen, a 1960 graduate of Osgoode Hall Law School, is noted for his rapid rise to deputy minister of Finance in the federal government. Before being hired in 1970 to work on tax reform, Cohen had spent 10 years as a tax lawyer with the Toronto law firm of Goodman & Carr. Since joining the public service, he has been assistant deputy minister of Finance for tax policy; deputy minister of Energy Mines and Resources; and deputy minister of Industry, Trade and Commerce. He is thought to have had a moderating influence on the National Energy Program. In 1977-78 he spent a sabbatical year studying economics at Harvard.

Collins, A. F.
C.D.

Civil servant. b. 1916, High River, Alberta; married; six children; res. Edmonton.

A close advisor of Premier Lougheed of Alberta, Chip Collins is deputy treasurer of Alberta and secretary of the Treasury Board. He has the responsibility for investing the Alberta Heritage Savings Trust Fund, into which oil and gas royalties flow. He was with the Mannix Group of Companies at the same time as Peter Lougheed and was president of Alberta Coal (now Manalta Coal, the largest coal mining company in the country) from 1968 to 1971. During the Second World War he served overseas as a captain with the Canadian Army and remained in the militia as a major until 1956.

Côté, Jean-Pierre
P.C.

Lieutenant-Governor. b. January 9, 1925, Montreal; m. Germaine Tremblay; s. Gilbert, Robert, Paul, d. Andrée, Danielle, Hélène, Jocelyne, Isabelle; res. Sillery, Quebec.

The son of a postal clerk, and originally trained as a dental technician at Longueuil College and Technical School of Dental Technology, Jean-Pierre Côté was sworn in as lieutenant-governor of Quebec on April 17, 1978. Prior to this he served as a Liberal member of the House of Commons for Longueuil, as postmaster general, and as minister of National Revenue. He was appointed to the Senate in 1972. Always keenly interested in community affairs, he has occupied various positions in the Boy Scout movement.

Davey, Douglas Keith
B.A.

Senator. b. April 21, 1926, Toronto; m. Dorothy Elizabeth Speare Petrie; s. Douglas, Ian, d. Catherine; res. Toronto.

After graduation from the University of Toronto, Keith Davey was the sales manager of radio station CKFH in Toronto for 11 years before venturing into Canadian poiltics. In 1961 he became the national organizer of the

Esmond Butler at Rideau Hall

Rear-Admiral Gordon Edwards, shown below at the Maritime Forces Pacific base in Victoria, was a signalman earlier in his career and keeps up his proficiency (ABOVE) with a light installed on the lawn near his house.

ALL: J.R.

Liberal Party of Canada and the next year was the party's campaign director, positions he held until the mid-1960s. During Canada's centennial year he served as commissioner of the Canadian Football League, then chaired the Special Senate Committee on Mass Media until 1972. During the elections of 1974, 1979, and 1980 he acted as co-chairman of the National Campaign committee and was bestowed the title of "The Rainmaker" by columnist Scott Young for the uncanny accuracy of his predictions of the outcome of federal elections. In 1966 he was appointed to the Senate. He is a member of the Toronto General Hospital's Board of Governors and a director of the Shaw Festival and the Canadian Sports Hall of Fame.

Dextraze, Jacques Alfred

C.C., C.B.E., C.M.M., D.S.O., C.D., LL.D.

Military officer (retired). b. August 15, 1919, Montreal; m. Frances Helena Paré; s. Jacques, Robert, John; res. Ottawa.

General J.A. Dextraze, chairman of Canadian National Railways from 1977 to 1982, comes from a military family and has himself had a long and distinguished military career. He joined the Fusiliers Mont-Royal in 1939, served in Europe, Korea (1950-52), and the Congo (1963), and won the Distinguished Service Order in 1944 and a Bar to his D.S.O. in 1945. In 1972, he was promoted to full general and from 1972 to 1977 was chief of the Defence Staff of the Canadian Armed Forces. At that time, General Dextraze retired and saw the realization of a long-time dream in the creation of the Special Service Force, an elite infantry force. His sons have continued the family military tradition: one is a captain in the Canadian Forces and one gave his life fighting in Vietnam. A strong believer in Canadian unity, General Dextraze wrote the bilingualism policy for the Armed Forces. He is active in community affairs as a member of the Atlantic Council of Canada, The Canadian Amateur Boxing Association, and the Royal Canadian Legion. His clubs include the Mount Royal, the Saint-Denis, the St. James's, and the Rideau clubs.

Doiron, Joseph Aubin

B.A., D.D.S., H.D.H., LL.D., DR.SC.So., F.I.C.D.

Lieutenant-Governor, dentist. b. June 10, 1922, North Rustico, Prince Edward Island; m. Bernice Gallant; s. Paul, Robert, Pierre, Omer, Marc, d. Simonne, Colette; res. Charlottetown.

Dr. Doiron, Prince Edward Island's lieutenant-governor since 1980, received his D.D.S. degree from the Faculty of Dentistry at the University of Montreal in 1951. Since that time he has maintained a dentistry practice in Summerside, P.E.I., while also being active in Acadian affairs. He is the founding president and chairman of the Acadian Mardi Gras Association and a charter member and president of the Acadian Museum Association. He is also a member of La Société Saint-Thomas d'Aquin, a cultural organization that represents Acadians in Prince Edward Island. A past president of the Dental Association of P.E.I., Dr. Doiron also served on the board of the Canadian Dental Association. Among the many organizations he is involved in are Summerside Kinsmen, K-40 Club, Knights of Columbus, St. Paul's Parish Council, and the P.E.I. Heritage Foundation.

Edwards, Gordon Lewis

C.M.M., C.D.

Naval officer. b. January 25, 1931, Medicine Hat, Alberta; m. Claire Maureen Campbell; d. Alison, Gretchen; res. Victoria.

The son of a CPR engineer, Gordon Edwards was educated at Carleton University and at the NATO Defence College in Rome. His career with the navy, which has so far spanned 35 years, has taken him from ordinary seaman to rear admiral. During this time he flew five different types of fighter aircraft from five carriers flying the flags of three countries, surely a record of some kind. The most prestigious of his decorations is Commander of the Order of Military Merit from the Canadian Armed Forces. He has served as Commander of Maritime Forces Pacific, the Victoria Search and Rescue Region, and the Standing Naval Force Atlantic, as well as being director of General Military Plans and Operations. He is a past president of Toastmasters and is involved with the activities of the Boy Scouts and the Salvation Army. His list of recreational activities is long and varied: tennis, painting, hiking, sailing, reading, hockey, basketball and stained glass. He is a collector of coins and naval memorabilia, and lives in Victoria's historic Admiral's House, built in 1885.

Forsey, Eugene Alfred

O.C., B.A., M.A., Ph.D., LL.D., D.C.L., D.Litt., F.R.S.C.

Political scientist (retired). b. May 29, 1904, Grand Bank, Newfoundland; m. Ina Harriet Roberts; d. Margaret Sybil Anna, Helen Louise; res. Ottawa.

An authority on constitutional law, Eugene Forsey was educated at McGill University and, as a Rhodes scholar, at Oxford. His father was secretary of the Toronto-based Mexican Light and Power Co. Ltd. From 1942 to 1966, the younger Forsey served as director of research for the Canadian Congress of Labour and its reincarnation, with the Trades and Labour Congress, as the Canadian Labour Congress. He was twice a candidate of the Co-operative Commonwealth Federation (predecessor to the New Democratic Party) for the House of Commons. In 1970 he was appointed by the Liberal government to the Senate, where he sat until his mandatory retirement in 1979. He was one of the authors of the Regina Manifesto, the party platform of the CCF, and wrote *The Royal Power of Dissolution of Parliament in the British Commonwealth* (1943; reissued 1968) and *Freedom and Order* (1974), a collection of essays. He is an honorary life member of the Canadian Historical Association.

Galloway, Andrew Strome Ayers Carmichael

E.D., C.D., O. St. J., K.C.L.J., F.H.S.C.

Military officer (retired), writer. b. November 29, 1915, Humboldt, Saskatchewan; m. Jean Caroline Love; d. Jean Caroline Blackburn, Rosemary Dawn; res. Ottawa.

Strome Galloway was educated at schools in Ontario and Quebec, the Canadian Army Staff College, and the National Defence College. He was commissioned in the Canadian Militia in 1934, serving in the Second World War in Britain, Tunisia (with the British Army), Sicily, Italy, and Northwest Europe. He was appointed to the regular Army in 1946 with the rank of major. He became a lieutenant-colonel in 1951 and a colonel in 1962. He retired in 1968, then served as an honorary lieutenant-colonel with the Governor General's Foot Guards until 1979. From 1955 until 1957, Colonel Galloway was commanding officer of the 4th Battalion Canadian Guards; he was commander of Fort Churchill during 1962-64, and from 1965 to 1968 was Military, Naval, and Air attaché for the Canadian Embassy in Germany. Since his retirement, he has been able to devote himself full time to his interest in heraldry. He is at present — and has been since 1971 — honorary editor of *Heraldry in Canada*. He is also a director of the Heraldry Society of Canada (of which he was made a Fellow in 1975). Colonel Galloway is a member of the Cavalry and Guards Club in London and the Royal Canadian Legion, the Ottawa branch of the Monarchist League, and the United Services Institute of Ottawa. He has received the Centennial Medal and the Queen's Jubilee Medal. He is president of the Ottawa and District Garrison Sergeants' Association and a Standard Bearer (Banner Man) to the 30th Chief of the Clan Carmichael. Colonel Galloway is the author of an autobiography, *The General Who Never Was* (1981), *Beddoe's Canadian Heraldry* (1981), *A Regiment at War* (1979), *The White Cross in Canada* (1983), *Some Died at Ortona* (1983), and a column entitled "Brave Yesterdays" that has appeared monthly in *Legion Magazine* since 1974.

Gauvin, Michel

O.C., C.V.O., D.S.O., B.A., B.L.

Diplomat. b. April 7, 1919, Quebec; m. Nguyen Thi Minh Huong; s. Jean, Marc, d. Kim; res. Peking.

Currently Ambassador of Canada to the People's Republic of China, Michel Gauvin has spanned the globe during his diplomatic career after graduation from Laval and Carleton universities and his subsequent distinguished military service. He served with the Canadian Army in the United Kingdom, France, Belgium, Holland, and Germany during the Second World War and rose to the rank of major by the time of his release in 1947. On loan from the Canadian Army and the Department of External Affairs to the Prime Minister's Office from 1946 to 1950, he then became executive assistant to the Under-Secretary of State for External Affairs for one year before being posted to Ankara, Lisbon, Saigon, Caracas, Buenos Aires, and Leopoldville for two or three-year terms. In 1963 he returned to Canada and worked at the National Defence College in Kingston, Ontario, for one year, when he was sent on a special mission to Kenya, Ethiopia, and the Congo during the Stanleyville crisis and then on to the Dominican Republic in 1965. He then served for three years as the Ambassador to Ethiopia with accreditation to the Republic of Somalia and Madagascar, and to Portugal (1969-70) and Greece (1970-75). In 1973 he served as head of the Canadian Delegation to the International Commission for Control and Supervision at Saigon and was then Canadian secretary to the Queen and co-ordinator of royal visits to the Montreal Olympics and the Queen's Jubilee. Before his present posting, Gauvin was ambassador to Morocco. He is the author of *La Geste du Régiment de la Chaudière*.

Goldenberg, H. Carl

O.C., O.B.E., Q.C., B.A., M.A., B.C.L., LL.D.

Lawyer. b. October 20, 1907, Montreal; m. Shirley Block; s. Edward Stephen, d. Ann Helen Bergman; res. Westmount, Quebec.

One of Canada's foremost mediators, Carl Goldenberg was educated at McGill University, where he also taught economics, political science, and municipal government after his graduation. In the 1946 King's Honours List he was made an O.B.E. for war services. He practised law in Montreal for several years and was named Q.C. in 1952. From 1968 to 1971 he served as special counsel to the Prime Minister on the Constitution, after which he was appointed to the Senate, from which he retired in 1982. Over the course of his career he has served on many federal, provincial, and municipal commissions of inquiry and as an arbitrator in major labour-management disputes in Canada and the West Indies. He has written articles and books dealing with labour relations and has received honorary doctorates from five Canadian universities. He is married to Shirley Block, Professor of Industrial Relations at McGill University.

Gordon, Walter Lockhart

P.C., C.C., F.C.A., LL.D., D.Litt.

b. January 27, 1906, Toronto; m. Elizabeth Marjorie Leith Counsell; s. John Counsell Lockhart; d. Jean Montagu, Jane Glassco; res. Toronto.

Honorary chairman of Canadian Corporate Management (Cancorp), Walter Gordon is a fervent nationalist who was instrumental in the founding of the company in 1945. Formed not only to make a profit but also to prevent the takeover of small Canadian firms by American companies, Cancorp has grown into a conglomerate with more than 30 subsidiaries. Over 90 per cent of the shareholders are Canadian. After being educated at Upper Canada College and Kingston's Royal Military College, in 1927 he became the fifth generation of Gordons to join the family firm of Clarkson, Gordon & Co., which had been established in 1864. He became a partner in 1935 and a partner in Woods, Gordon & Co., the associated firm of management consultants, in 1940. His nationalistic tendencies began to surface at this time with his concern over growing foreign investment in Canada. He began his career in government with his appointment as special assistant to the deputy minister of Finance. After the Second World War he headed several royal commissions: on Administrative Classifications in the Public Service (1946), on Canada's Economic Prospects (1955), and on the Organization of Government in Ontario (1958). In the federal elections of 1962, 1963, and 1965 Gordon was chairman of the Liberal Party's National Campaign Committee and was elected to Parliament. When the Liberals regained power in 1963 he was named minister of Finance; he resigned from cabinet in 1965. He was appointed president of the Privy Council in 1967, but resigned from cabinet a second time in 1968. As well as being one of the founders of the Committee for an Independent Canada (1970), he is the author of several books, including *A Choice for Canada — Independence or Colonial Status* (1966), and *What Is Happening to Canada* (1978). In the early 1980s he was instrumental in establishing the Canadian Institute for Economic Policy.

Gotlieb, Allan E.

O.C., B.A., M.A., B.C.L., LL.B.

Public servant. b. February 28, 1928, Winnipeg; m. Sondra Kaufman; s. Marc, d. Rebecca, Rachel; res. Washington.

Since his appointment in 1981, Allan Gotlieb has been one of Canada's most high-profile ambassadors to the United States, due to both the political issues at hand and a personal style of lobbying and entertaining that has made his residence a key stop on the Washington social circuit. After obtaining his B.A. degree from the University of California in 1949, he attended Oxford University, where he was a Rhodes scholar and from which he obtained his B.C.L. and M.A. degrees. He graduated from Harvard Law School with an LL.B. in 1954, and was on the Board of Editors of the *Harvard law Review*. From 1954 to 1956 he was a Vinerian Law Scholar, a Fellow of Wadham College, and a University Lecturer in Law at Queen's University. He was called to the bar of England in 1956. Since then he has been a special lecturer at Queen's University and a visiting and adjunct professor at Carleton University. He joined the Department of External Affairs in 1957, and became alternate delegate to the United Nations General Assembly in 1967-68. He was then appointed the first deputy minister of the Department of Communications. He chaired a federal inquiry into telecommunications in 1969 and 1970, and in 1971-72 co-chaired a government task force on Privacy and Computers. From 1973 to 1977 he was deputy minister of Manpower and Immigration. In 1976, he was named chairman designate of the Canadian Employment and Immigration Commission. He was appointed under-secretary of state for External Affairs in 1977, and in 1981 was the Prime Minister's personal representative at the Ottawa Summit Economic conference. He is married to a novelist and winner of the Stephen Leacock Prize for humour in 1979. He is an avid art collector; in addition to writing four books and several articles on law and government, he has authored a monograph on the prints of the 19-century French artist James Tissot. He holds an honorary LL.D. from the University of Windsor and was made an Officer of the Order of Canada in 1983.

Gutknecht, René

C.M.M., C.D., B.A.

Military officer. b. July 23, 1930, Montreal; m. Claire Forget; s. Eric; res. Brussels.

Now a lieutenant-general and the Canadian military representative to the NATO Military Committee in Permanent Session, René Gutknecht has also held the positions of commanding officer of Lord Strathcona's Horse in Germany, commander of the 5th Brigade and Base at CFB Valcartier, chief of Land Doctrine and Operations at National Defence Headquarters, and deputy commander of Mobile Command at St. Hubert over his 31 years with the Canadian Forces. The son of the late Herman Gutknecht, vice-president of Henry Birks & Sons, he received his B.A. from McGill University before joining the Forces. He has also served in Vietnam as a member of the Truce Commission, in India and Pakistan as chief operations officer of the UN India-Pakistan Observation Mission, and in Fort Knox at the U.S. Army Armor School. He is the only Canadian to have received the Order of Military Merit at Buckingham Palace from the Queen. His interest in auto racing is evident in his choice of cars: a classic BMW 3.0 litre coupé and a Jaguar XJ6 3.8.

Head, Ivan Leigh

Q.C., B.A., LL.B., LL.M.

Public servant. b. July 28, 1930, Calgary; m. Anne Price; four children; res. Ottawa.

A graduate of the University of Alberta and the Harvard Law School where he was a Frank Knox Memorial Fellow, Ivan Head practised law in Calgary for six years before joining the Foreign Service office of the Department of External Affairs in 1960. He was assigned to Southeast Asia, where he served as third secretary in the Canadian High Commission in Kuala Lumpur, Malaya (now Malaysia), and was subsequently accredited to Burma and Thailand with some responsibility for Singapore. He returned home to become a professor of law at the University of Alberta in 1963. In 1967 he became associate counsel to minister of Justice Pierre Trudeau on constitutional matters. When Trudeau became Prime Minister in 1968, Head became his legal assistant. In 1970 he was appointed Trudeau's special advisor on foreign affairs, a post he would hold for the next eight years. During his tenure, he was credited with restoring the British Commonwealth to prominence in foreign affairs. In 1978, he was appointed president of the International Development Research Centre, which supports research projects in developing countries with grants designed to encourage the creation of indigenous research capability.

Ignatieff, George

C.C., B.A., M.A., LL.D., D.C.L., D. Litt. S.

Diplomat. b. December 16, 1913, St. Petersburg, Russia; m. Alison Grant; s. Michael, Andrew; res. Toronto.

A son of Count Paul Ignatieff and Princess Natalie Mestchersky, George Ignatieff brings an air of grace and the exotic to the chanceliorship of the University of Toronto. After studying political science and economics at the University of Toronto, he was awarded a Rhodes scholarship and received his M.A. at Oxford. During the Second World War he volunteered for the Oxford and Bucks Light Infantry and was posted to intelligence duties until he was transferred, at the request of the Canadian government, to Canada House. Since then he has been a permanent representative of Canada to NATO and the UN and its agencies, assistant under-secretary of state for External Affairs, deputy high commissioner in London, and counsellor at the Canadian Embassy in Washington, among other positions. In addition to his duties as chancellor, he is also chairman of the Board of Trustees of the National Museums, governor of Heritage Canada, and national president of the United Nations Association.

Leather, Sir Edwin Hartley Cameron

Kt., K.C.M.G., K.C.V.O., K.St.J., LL.D.

Corporate director, writer. b. May 22, 1919, Toronto; m. Sheila Adeline Alexie Greenlees; d. Hope, Sarah; res. Paget, Bermuda.

Lieutenant-General René Gutknecht

Carl Goldenberg with grandchildren at his Westmount home.

George Ignatieff in his Chancellor's robes at Convocation Hall, University of Toronto.

Sir Edwin Leather   *Vice-Admiral Daniel Mainguy*   *Pearl McGonigal*

Pauline McGibbon with memorabilia from her years in public life.

One of Canada's most distinguished expatriates, Sir Edwin Leather was governor of Bermuda from 1973 to 1977. At present he is vice-president of N.M. Rothschild of Bermuda and a director of the Menuhin Foundation of Bermuda. He has been a director of various companies, including the Hogg Robinson Group. From 1950 to 1964 he was Conservative member of Parliament for North Somerset at Westminster. He has also been chairman of the Horder Centres for Arthritics. He is the author of three novels. After attending Hillfield School in Hamilton, Trinity College School at Port Hope, and Royal Military College in Kingston, he served with the Canadian Army in the Second World War. He has received many honours, including the Royal Canadian Legion Medal of Merit and the Gold Medal of the National Institute of Social Sciences. He is especially proud of being one of the few Canadians to have been a colonial governor and having founded the Bermuda Festival of the Arts. His clubs include the Carlton in London, the York in Toronto, and the Royal Bermuda Yacht.

Lynch-Staunton, Frank C.

B.Sc., LL.D., K.St.J.

Lieutenant-Governor. b. March 8, 1905, Pincher Creek, Alberta; m. Monica Adam (deceased); s. Hugh, d. Betty Lowe, Marina Field; res. Antelope Butte Ranch, Lundbreck, Alberta.

Sworn in as the province's lieutenant-governor in 1979, Frank Lynch-Staunton is a southwestern Alberta rancher with a long history of community service. After graduating in engineering from the University of Alberta in 1927, he spent two years working for Imperial Oil, then entered a ranching partnership with his father. The ranch, which covers 11 sections in the foothills and has 78 miles of fences, is now a family corporation managed by his son, Hugh. He is a founding member and director of Community Auction Sales, a past councillor of the Municipal District of Pincher Creek, a past senator of the University of Lethbridge, and a past member of the Claresholm Auxiliary Hospital. He was a member of the Pincher Creek Council from 1959 to 1965 and has served on the boards of the Glenbow Foundation and Government House. From 1933 to 1943 he was part of Canada's Reserve Army and achieved the rank of major. He is a Knight of Grace of the Most Venerable Order of the Hospital of St. John of Jerusalem, chancellor of the Alberta Order of Excellence, and the recipient of an honorary LL.D. from the University of Alberta. Lynch-Staunton lives in a ranch house built by his father, Richard, in 1901 — before Alberta was a province — and raises Herefords.

McGibbon, Pauline Mills

C.C., B.A., LL.D., D.U., D.Hum.L., D.Litt.S., B.A.A.(Theatre), Hon. F.R.C.P.S.(C), D.St.J., D.G.C.L.

b. October 20, 1910, Sarnia, Ontario; née Mills; m. Donald Walker McGibbon; res. Toronto.

Pauline McGibbon was lieutenant-governor of Ontario from 1974 to 1980. At present she is chairman of the National Arts Centre, the Toronto International Festival, and of the du Maurier Council for the Performing Arts. She is a dedicated supporter of education and a patron of the arts; at various times she has been chairman of the board of governors of the National Theatre School, a member of the Canada Council, president of the Canadian Conference of the Arts, president of the Dominion Drama Festival, chancellor of the University of Toronto and later of the University of Guelph. She has served as chairman of the Board of Governors of Women's College Hospital and as national president of the IODE. Pauline McGibbon is an honorary life member of the Royal Canadian Military Institute, a life member of the National Club, the Albany Club, the Toronto Ladies' Club, the University Women's Club, the Business and Professional Women's Club, Zonta, Pilot, the Canadian Legion, and the Ontario Chamber of Commerce. Her business connections include the posts of chairman of the board of Murray G. Bulger and Associates, and director of George Weston Ltd. and Mercedes-Benz Canada. Her arts and community service directorships include the Mount Sinai Institute, Donwood Institute, Massey Hall–Thomson Hall, Canadian Opera Company, and Stratford Summer Music. Among the many honours and titles she has received are: Companion of the Order of Canada; Grand Prior of the Order of St. Lazarus of Jerusalem (she is the first woman in 900 years to hold this position), the Canadian Centennial Medal, the Silver Jubilee Medal, Canadian B'nai B'rith Humanitarian Award (1980), the Eleanor Roosevelt Humanities Award, Prix au Mérité from the J.-Louis Lévesque Foundation, and 12 honorary degrees. She is the first woman to be made an honorary colonel of the 25 (Toronto) Service Battalion. Pauline McGibbon collects Canadian art.

McGonigal, Pearl Kathryne

LL.D., D.St.J.

Lieutenant-Governor. b. June 10, 1929, Melville, Saskatchewan; née Kuhlman; m. Marvin A. McGonigal; d. Kimberley; res. Winnipeg.

In 1969 Pearl McGonigal, daughter of a CN machinist, became the first woman elected to the City Council of St. James–Assiniboia. In 1971 she was elected to the Greater Winnipeg City Council. In 1979 she was the first woman to be elected deputy mayor and chairman of the city's Executive Policy Committee, and in 1981 she was sworn in as the province's lieutenant-governor, another first for a woman. She holds several awards for public speaking, wrote the *Frankly Feminine Cookbook* in 1975, and from 1970 to 1981 penned a weekly column for suburban newspapers. A strong supporter of the arts, she is a member of the board of directors of the Red River Exhibition and the Rainbow Stage and an ex-officio member of the Manitoba Theatre Centre. She is active in the Manitoba Environmental Council, the Winnipeg Convention and Visitors' Bureau, and sits on the boards of management of the Winnipeg Home Improvement Program and the Grace General Hospital. Her chairmanships include the advisory board of the Salvation Army Catherine Booth Bible College and the advisory committee of the Grace General Hospital's School of Nursing. She is a member of the St. James Business and Professional Women's Club, the Winnipeg Lionelles (of which she is past president), the Manitoba Club, St. Andrew's Anglican Church, and the Winnipeg Winter Club. She has been awarded the Order of St. John, has received an Honorary doctorate of Laws from the University of Manitoba, and is an honorary colonel of the 735 Communications Regiment.

McIntosh, Cameron Irwin

K.St.J.

Journalist. b. July 1, 1926, North Battleford, Saskatchewan; m. Barbara Aylesworth; s. William, d. Beckie, Jean Ann; res. North Battleford.

Sworn in as lieutenant-governor of Saskatchewan in 1978, C. Irwin McIntosh possesses a background in publishing and a great interest in the outdoors. After leaving the University of Saskatchewan without completing a degree program in 1949, he became a salesman with the printing and publishing company of his father, Cameron Ross McIntosh, an MP for northern Saskatchewan from 1925 to 1940. (His mother, Pearl Susanne McIntosh, was a pioneer nurse in northwestern Saskatchewan.) In 1951, at the age of 25, he became editor of the *North Battleford News*, which became the *News-Optimist* in 1953. After the death of his father in 1971, he assumed the publisher's post as well. McIntosh is the founder and publisher of *Western Canada Outdoors*, as well as a past vice-president of publicity for the Saskatchewan Ski Association and a former editor of the *Saskatchewan Ski Journal*. He served as a trustee of the North Battleford school board 16 years and is a former chairman of the Table Mountain Regional Park Authority, the province's first regional winter park. In addition to many community and newspaper association posts, he is a member of the Outdoor Writers of Canada, the International Weekly Newspaper Association, The Elks Club, and the Masonic Temple. He has received the Paul Harris Fellowship from Rotary International and is a Knight of Grace of the Venerable Order of St. John of Jerusalem.

Mackenzie, Donald C.

C.D., B.Comm.

Military officer. b. May 27, 1931, Mexico City; m. Margaret Thistle; s. Scott, Donald; res. Colorado Springs, Colorado.

Lieutenant-General Donald Mackenzie was the commander of the first RCAF reconnaissance aircraft that successfully photographed U.S.S.R. activities on an ice island in Arctic waters north of Canada in 1954. He attended Trinity College School in Port Hope, Ontario, and graduated with a Bachelor of Commerce degree from the University of Alberta, receiving numerous awards (including the T. Eaton Co. Gold Medal in Commerce) in the process. He entered the Royal Canadian Air Force in 1950. In 1972 he became the first Canadian military attaché accredited to Spain, where he remained for three years. In 1976 he became the commander of the Air Transport Group, which was responsible for Canadian Forces airlift and search and rescue missions, and effected significant improvements in this capacity and as co-chairman of the interdepartmental committee on search and rescue. He became deputy chief of staff, Plans, of NORAD in 1981 and is now deputy commander in chief. He is a member of the Canadian Aeronautics and Space Institute and the Canadian Institute of Strategic Studies.

Lieutenant-General Paul Manson

BRUNO ENGLER

Roland Michener atop Mount Michener in the Rockies.

John Meisel at Colimaison, his spiral house designed by Wilfred Sorensen.

371

Mainguy, Daniel Nicholas
C.M.M., C.D.

Military officer. b. December 2, 1930, Victoria; m. Susan Wainwright; s. Nicholas, d. Sarah, Barbara; res. Ottawa.

Vice-Admiral Daniel Mainguy joined the Royal Canadian Navy in 1950, fresh out of Royal Roads, a naval training establishment in British Columbia. In 1966 he was appointed commanding officer of HMCS *Annapolis*, and then became chief staff officer of the Standing Naval Force Atlantic (1968-69), director of strategic plans (1970-72) commanding officer HMCS *Protecteur* (1972-74), and commander of Standing Naval Force Atlantic (1975). His most recent postings were as chief of staff to the commander-in-chief Western Atlantic (1979-82), and deputy chief of the Defence Staff. He became vice-chief of the Defense Staff in July, 1983. He is a member of the Chesapeake Club and the Men's Canadian Club. His father, Vice-Admiral E. Rollo Mainguy, was chief of staff of the RCN from 1951 until his retirement in 1956, and later became president of the Great Lakes Waterways Development Association.

Manson, Paul David
C.M.M., C.D., B.Sc., P.Eng.

Military officer. b. August 20, 1934, Trail, British Columbia; m. Margaret Nickel; s. Robert, Peter, d. Catherine, Karen; res. Winnipeg.

In 1983, Lieutenant-General Paul Manson was recognized for his 31 years of service as a fighter pilot and was named top airman in the Canadian Forces. Among the positions he has held are commanding officer of the 441 Reconnaissance Squadron in Germany; base commander of the Canadian Forces Base in Chatham, New Brunswick; program manager of the New Fighter Aircraft Program, which led to the procurement of CF-18 aircraft; commander of the 1st Canadian Air Group in Germany; chief of Air Doctrine and Operations at National Defence Headquarters; and his present position as commander of Air Command at CFB Winnipeg. Over the years he has attended a variety of military colleges and in 1957 he received his B.Sc. in electrical engineering from Queen's University. He is a foundation member of the Billy Bishop Heritage Foundation and a director of the Royal Canadian Air Force Benevolent Fund. He also collects Indian artifacts and programs his home computer.

Marchand, Jean
Speaker of the Senate, Ottawa.

Massé, Marcel
B.A., LL.B., B.Phil., LL.D.

Civil servant. b. June 23, 1940, Montreal; m. Josée M'Baye; s. Bernard, Xavier, Stephane, d. Myriam; res. Aylmer, Quebec.

Now under-secretary of state for External Affairs, Marcel Massé was president of the Canadian International Development Agency in Ottawa from 1980 to 1982. He studied at the University of Montreal and McGill, where he received his Bachelor of Law, and then earned a Diploma in International Law at the University of Warsaw in Poland. He was awarded a

Rhodes scholarship in philosophy, history, and economics (1963) and a Nuffield College scholarship in economics at Oxford in 1966. His first position was in the administration and economics division of the World Bank in Washington, D.C., which he held from 1967 to 1971, when he moved to Ottawa as economic adviser to the Privy Council Office. Since then he has held a variety of high-level positions in the federal government and the Privy Council. He is a member of the board of directors of the National Film Board of Canada.

Meisel, John
B.A., M.A., Ph.D., LL.D., F.R.S.C.

Educator, political scientist. b. October 23, 1923, Vienna, Austria; m. Murie Augusta Kelly; res. Tichborne, Ontario.

Educated in Czechoslovakia, Great Britain, Haiti, and at Pickering College (Newmarket, Ontario), the University of Toronto, and the London School of Political Science and Economics (which awarded him the Ph.D. in 1959), John Meisel can lay claim to a background of exotic internationalism. In 1949 professor Meisel joined the faculty of Queen's University where he eventually became head of Political Studies and Hardy Professor of Political Science. He was visiting professor of Political Science at Yale University in 1976-77 and Commonwealth distinguished visiting professor to Great Britain in 1978. He is past president of the Social Science Research Council of Canada and has served on a number of Royal Commissions and Task Forces including Bilingualism and Biculturalism, National Unity, and the Status of Women. The author of over 50 articles in various learned journals, Prof. Meisel is also author of *The Canadian General Election of 1957* (1962), *Working Papers on Canadian Politics* (three editions, 1972, 73, 75), and *Cleavages: Parties and Values in Canada* (1974). He is, as well, co-author of *Ethnic Relations in Canadian Voluntary Associations* and has edited a collection of pieces called *Papers on the 1962 Election* (1964). He is editor of the *International Political Science Review* and a member of the advisory boards of a number of political science reviews in North America and in Europe. He is a member of the Canadian Political Science Association, the American Political Science Association, the International Political Science Association, the International Institute of Communications, the International Association for Mass Communication Research, the Royal Commonwealth Society, the Cercle Universitaire, Ottawa, and the Royal Society of Canada. Professor Meisel is best known to the public as the beleaguered chairman of the Canadian Radio-television and Telecommunications Commission (CRTC), a demanding and increasingly complex post which he held from 1980 to autumn 1983.

Michener, Roland
P.C., C.C., C.M.M., C.D., Q.C., B.A., B.A., M.A., B.C.L., D.C.L., LL.D.

Lawyer, politician. b. April 19, 1900, Lacombe, Alberta; m. Norah Evangeline Willis; d. Joan Rohr, Diana Schatz, Wendy (deceased); res. Toronto.

Roland Michener has had a long and distinguished career in public affairs that culminated in his seven years as governor general from 1967 to 1974. He has also been a member of the Toronto law firm of Lang, Michener; a

member of Parliament; speaker of the House of Commons; and Canadian high commissioner to India and ambassador to Nepal. At present he is an honorary director of several mining and financial companies. He has been general secretary for the Canadian Rhodes Scholarships Trust and chancellor of Queen's University; as well, he is a director of Lester B. Pearson College of the Pacific, the Young Naturalist Foundation, and a trustee of the Royal Ontario Museum. In 1918 he served in the Royal Air Force and during the Second World War as a reserve officer in the Royal Canadian Artillery. Among his many honours are honorary degrees from 20 universities. In 1979 a mountain in the David Thompson Range of the Rockies was named after him; three years later he climbed the last 1500 feet to the summit. He considers his main achievements to be his work in public affairs, in particular as speaker of the House and governor general. He is a proponent of physical fitness.

Osbaldeston, Gordon Francis
O.C., B.Comm., M.B.A.

Public servant. b. April 29, 1930, Hamilton; m. Geraldine Keller; s. Stephen, David, Robert, d. Catherine; res. Nepean, Ontario.

Gordon Osbaldeston was appointed clerk of the Privy Council and secretary to the Cabinet in December 1982. Immediately before that appointment he had served as under-secretary of State for External Affairs. Earlier posts were deputy minister of Consumer and Corporate Affairs, secretary of the Treasury Board, deputy minister of Industry, Trade and Commerce, and secretary to the Ministry of State for Economic Development. In December 1981 he was made an Officer of the Order of Canada; he also received the Outstanding Achievement Award for the Public Service for 1981. He was educated at St. Jerome College in Kitchener, the University of Toronto, and the University of Western Ontario. He won the St. Michael's College Scholarship for 1951 (awarded to the top student in Commerce and Finance), the 1953 J. William Horsey Fellowship, and the 1954 Gold Medal for the top student in second-year M.B.A. class. He is a member of the Board of Directors of the Niagara Institute and a member of the Advisory Committee of the School of Business Administration at the University of Western Ontario.

Ostry, Sylvia
O.C., B.A., M.A., Ph.D., LL.D.

Economist, civil servant. b. June 3, 1927, Winnipeg; née Knelman; m. Bernard Ostry; s. Adam, Jonathan; res. Toronto.

Trained as an economist at McGill and at Cambridge, Sylvia Ostry lectured at McGill from 1948 until 1954, after which she became research officer in the Institute of Statistics at Oxford University (1955-57). From 1962 until 1964, she was assistant professor of Economics at the University of Montreal. Her career as a civil servant began with her appointment in 1964 as director of Special Manpower Studies at the Dominion Bureau of Statistics (now Statistics Canada). From 1969 until 1972, Ostry was director of the Economic Council of Canada. She was chief statistician for Statistics Canada (1972-75) and Canada's deputy minister of Consumer and Corporate Affairs (1975-78). She has written numerous articles for pro-

FACING: Gordon Osbaldeston in his Langevin Block office, Ottawa

fessional journals and is co-author (with Mahmood A. Zaidi) of *Labour Economics in Canada* (third edition, 1979). Until 1983 Ostry was head of the Economics and Statistics Department of the Paris-based Organization for Economic Co-operation and Development. Ostry has received 12 honorary degrees from Canadian universities (including her alma mater, McGill) and is a Fellow of the American Statistical Association, a member of both the American and Canadian economic associations, a member of the International Industrial Relations Research Association, and the Royal Economic Society; she is a consulting member of the Niagara Institute and a director of the Centre for European Policy Studies in Brussels. Ostry was made an Officer of the Order of Canada in 1978. She is married to Ontario's deputy minister of Industry and Trade. She collects 18th-century English furniture and English Art Nouveau artifacts.

Paddon, William Anthony
Lieutenant-Governor of Newfoundland and Labrador, St. John's

Pearson, Geoffrey A.H.
B.A.

Diplomat. b. December 25, 1927, Toronto; m. Landon Mackenzie; five children; res. Moscow.

Geoffrey Pearson is Canada's most recent ambassador to Moscow, having being appointed in 1980 after a 30-year career in the Department of External Affairs. His most recent previous position was as advisor on disarmament and arms control. He has had postings in Paris, Mexico, and New Delhi, but his Moscow posting is his first appointment as an ambassador. Pearson spent much of his youth abroad in the Canadian embassies in London and Washington, where his father, Lester Pearson, was posted before he entered politics. He was educated at the University of Toronto, where he majored in English, and decided on a career in the foreign service after passing the Department of External Affairs examinations.

Pelletier, Gérard
P.C., C.C., B.A.

Diplomat. b. June 21, 1919, Victoriaville, Quebec; m. Alexandrine Leduc; d. Anne-Maria, Louise, Andrée, s. Jean; res. New York City.

Educated at the University of Montreal, Gérard Pelletier worked as a journalist for the influential Montreal daily *Le Devoir* and then as editor of the much larger *La Presse* before entering federal politics in 1965. Along with Jean Marchand and Pierre Trudeau, the "three wise men of Quebec," he was recruited by Lester Pearson and was appointed to the cabinet as minister without portfolio in 1968. Later that year he became secretary of state, a position he held until 1972, when he became minister of Communications. He served as the ambassador to France from 1975 to 1981, when he was appointed ambassador to the United Nations. His goal in life has been "to make myself useful (I hope) to my fellow men." He continues to be interested in books and writing, and is a member of the Canadian Club of New York.

Pitfield, Michael
Senator, Ottawa.

Reisman, Sol Simon
Financial executive, former civil servant, Ottawa.

Richard, François
C.D., B.A., O.St.J.

Military officer. b. February 19, 1934, Quebec City; m. Marie de Gonzague, s. Pierre, Charles, d. Louise; res. Hull, Quebec.

Now a lieutenant-general in the Canadian Armed Forces, François Richard attended the Collège des Jésuites in Quebec City while also serving with the Militia and the COTC. On graduation in 1955 he joined the Forces, where he has remained ever since, including one- or two-year intervals at the Canadian Army Staff College and the Naval Defence College. From 1969 to 1971 he was commanding officer of the 1st Battalion of the Royal 22nd Regiment in Germany; from 1976 to 1979 he served the Privy Council Office. He then became commander of the 5th Brigade Group of Canada and in 1981 was made commander of the Canadian Forces in Europe. He has received the Canadian Forces Decoration and the Jubilee Medal and was named an Officer of the Order of St. John. He is a member of the Garrison club in Quebec, the Canadian Institute of Strategic Studies, and the International Institute of Humanitarian Law, and his interest in cross-country skiing led to his membership with the Biathlon Division of the Canadian Ski Association.

Rogers, Robert G.
Lieutenant-Governor, b. 1920, Montreal; m. Elizabeth Hargrave; two daughters, one son; res. Vancouver.

Before succeeding Henry Bell Irving as British Columbia's lieutenant-governor, Robert Rogers served with forestry giant Crown Zellerbach Canada for over two decades, rising to the position of chairman before his retirement in 1982. He was educated at the University of Toronto Schools and studied civil engineering at U of T until the outbreak of the Second World War. He served with the Canadian Armoured Corps and took part in the D-Day invasion of France. After the war he joined Philip Carey Ltd. of Montreal and in 1950 he was hired by Crown Zellerbach. Since 1976 he has held the position of chairman of the board of the Canada Harbour Place Corporation of Vancouver. He has served as director of the Canadian Council of the International Chamber of Commerce; chairman of the Canadian Forestry Advisory Council; and is a member of the Canadian Pulp & Paper Association's Executive Committee and the Canada-Japan Business Cooperation Committee.

Sauvé, Jeanne
P.C., M.P., D.H.L., D.S., D.L.

Broadcaster, journalist, politician. b. April 26, 1922, Prud'homme, Saskatchewan; née Benoit; m. Maurice Sauvé; s. Jean-François; res. Montreal.

Jeanne Sauvé has the distinction of being the first woman speaker of the House of Commons, a position she assumed in 1980. As speaker, she was responsible for reforming the administration of the House. She has been a Liberal member of Parliament since 1972, first for Ahuntsic in Montreal and subsequently for Laval-des-Rapides. As minister of state for Sci-

ence and Technology, she negotiated a scientific exchange agreement with China and was instrumental in securing funds for Telidon and the Canadarm. She has also held the portfolios of Environment and Communications. Her husband, an MP from 1962 to 1968, held the Forestry portfolio. From 1952 to 1972, Sauvé worked as a freelance broadcaster and journalist, and for three years before being elected to Parliament she was a director of Bushnell Communications, radio station CKAC (Montreal), and Télémedia. She is a founding member of the Institute of Political Research, a past president of L'institut canadien des affaires publiques, and has been on the board of the Montreal YMCA. She was educated at the universities of Ottawa and Paris, and holds honorary degrees from the University of Calgary, the University of New Brunswick, and Mount Saint Vincent University.

Schreyer, Edward Richard
C.C., C.M.M., C.D., B.A., M.A.

Governor General. b. December 21, 1935, Beauséjour, Manitoba; m. Lily Schulz; d. Lisa, Karmel, s. Jason, Toban; res. Ottawa.

Since 1979, the Right Honourable Edward Schreyer has been Governor General of Canada. His appointment marked the first time that someone unconnected with the British, English-Canadian, or French-Canadian Establishment was chosen. From 1969 to 1978, he was leader of the Manitoba New Democratic Party and spent all but the last of those years as premier of the province. At various times he held the portfolios of Industry and Commerce and Finance and was the minister responsible for hydro development. From 1962 to 1965 he was professor of Political Science and International Relations at the University of Manitoba. When first elected to the legislature in 1958, Schreyer was the youngest member. He was elected to a federal seat in 1965 and 1968, then stepped down to lead the provincial party. In 1975 he received the Vanier Award as "Outstanding young Canadian of the year." He was educated at the University of Manitoba.

Shaffner, John Elvin
B.A., D.C.L.

Business executive. b. March 3, 1911, Lawrencetown, Annapolis Co., Nova Scotia; m. Nell Potter; d. Susan, Margaret; res. Port Williams, Nova Scotia.

Prior to his appointment as lieutenant-governor of Nova Scotia in 1978, John Shaffner served as the agent general for Nova Scotia in the United Kingdom and Europe for five years. He received his B.A. from Acadia University in 1931, then began working as a junior audit clerk with a Halifax accounting firm. In 1934 he became the manager of the family's retail business; he joined M.W. Graves & Co. Ltd. of Bridgetown, Nova Scotia, as an accountant in 1941. His responsibilities rapidly grew to encompass full management of the beverage company and its subsidiaries until their sale in 1961; he stayed on as president and director. In 1958 he was appointed president of the Nova Scotia Liberal Association for a two-year term. He is a past chairman of T.P. Calkin Ltd., past vice-president of Evangeline Investments, and a past director of Rothmans of Pall Mall Canada, Carling O'Keefe, and Canada Permanent Trust, among others, and is an outport member of the Royal Nova Scotia Yacht Squadron.

Simmonds, Robert

RCMP commissioner. b. 1926, Keatley, Saskatchewan; divorced; s. Robert, d. Elizabeth; res. Ottawa.

In his role as RCMP commissioner, Robert Simmonds has held the Force together during difficult times of critical provincial and royal commissions, internal misbehaviour, and increasing public cynicism. His rural background provided the basis for his general philosophy of the community working hand in hand with law agencies, an ideal he carried through to his dealings with the federal government. At the age of 18, fearing he might miss the war, he cycled nearly 100 miles to Saskatoon to sign up for the Royal Navy, where he learned to fly as a member of the Fleet Air Arm. Two years later he was back home and he responded to an ad for RCMP pilots. His first duty was to attend a training academy at Depot Division in Regina, renowned for its paramilitary discipline — in his words, "a quick maturing process." His first 10 years as a Mountie were spent in one- or two-man detachments across Alberta, where he invariably left a legacy of respect and trust that his successors were hard put to match. In 1957 he received the first of many promotions with a posting to Calgary for plainclothes work. In 1975, his skillful handling of a Mount Currie Indian Band blockade and subsequent report analyzing Indian problems impressed his superiors and resulted in his vault to the position of deputy commissioner, then two years later to commissioner. In this capacity he initiated major changes that he felt were necessary to counteract the somewhat tarnished image the Mounties had acquired. He did a lot of "house cleaning," rerouted a great deal of decision making to his office, gave substance to the RCMP grievance procedures, and worked long and hard to improve relations with the government, an involvement his predecessors had avoided to the detriment of the RCMP. The McDonald Commission in 1980 increased pressure on him; this strain, added to that of running a force of 20,000 people, soon began to tell on Simmonds. However, he willingly began implementing some of the Comission's recommendations and continues to re-establish the Force as a respected institution, using the same down-home beliefs that have characterized his career.

Smallwood, Joseph Roberts

P.C., D.C.L., LL.D., D.Litt.

Politician (retired). b. December 24, 1900, Gambo, Newfoundland; m. Clara Oates; s. Ramsay, William; d. Clara; res. St. John's.

One of Canada's most flamboyant and at times most controversial politicians, Joey Smallwood is well known across the country for his earthiness and impatience with conservative Easterners. Educated at Littledale Academy, Centenary Hall, and Bishop Feild College in Newfoundland and at the Rand School of Social Science in New York City, he began his career as a reporter with newspapers in St. John's, Halifax, Boston, New York, and London. As a reporter he gained a great deal of experience with trade unions and co-operative organizations. To staunch Newfoundlanders he will remain the turncoat who led the Confederation-with-Canada movement and was elected as premier of Newfoundland in 1949. His at times dictatorial and partisan leadership did not seem to deter voters from re-electing him to consecutive terms until 1972. He re-

entered politics in the fall of 1975 as leader of the Liberal Reform Party and rejoined the Liberal Party the following year. He retired from his seat in June 1977. The author of six volumes of *The Book of Newfoundland* and other books dealing with Newfoundland, he was the subject of the play *Joey*, which was performed in theatres across Canada.

Smith, Thomas A.M.

C.M.M., C.D., B.A.

Naval officer, business executive. b. August 3, 1927, Leamington, Ontario; m. Olga Seradoka; d. Mary-Lynn, Mary-Michele, Mary Roberta, Mary Geraldine; s. Thomas Michael, Christopher John, Mark Timothy, Patrick Xavier, Charles Matthew, Michael Adrian, D. Daniel; res. Windsor, Ontario.

Thomas Smith is chief of reserves for the Canadian Armed Forces, and with his appointment as rear-admiral in 1983 became the first admiral (reserve) in Canada's history. He joined the Navy in 1946 and, among other duties, has taught ship handling and commanded several naval vessels. In civilian life, Smith is senior training manager at Imperial Oil. He is also on the board of directors of the Canadian Corps of Commissionaires and has been on the Board of the Windsor United Way. Among the honours and decorations he has received are the Commander of the Order of Military Merit, the Jubilee Medal, and three Canadian Forces Decorations. He is proud of having instituted several programs in employee development and of being in demand as a public speaker by the Canadian Forces Colleges, teachers' groups, and industrial and college groups. Smith's recreational interests are gardening, sailing and automobiles. He collects Gagnon prints and paintings, stamps, and military artifacts. His large family, most of whom are professional or professionals in training, holds promise of illustrious Smiths to come.

Stanfield, Robert Lorne

P.C., Q.C., B.A., LL.D.

Politician (retired). b. April 11, 1914, Truro, Nova Scotia; m. Anne Austin; m. Mary Hall (deceased); m. Joyce Frazee (deceased); d. Sarah, Judith, Miriam, s. Robert, Maxwell; res. Ottawa.

Now retired, Robert Stanfield has had a long and distinguished political career with the Progressive Conservative Party. Born and raised in Truro, where the Stanfield family manufactures underwear, he attended Dalhousie University, where he received high honours in economics and political science, then Harvard University, where he obtained his LL.D. with honours. He was called to Nova Scotia's Bar in 1940. In 1949 he was elected to the Nova Scotia Legislature in a general election and also appointed leader of the Opposition, a position he held until 1956. After an 11-year tenure as premier and minister of Education, he was elected leader of the Progressive Conservative Party of Canada. He was the leader of the Opposition in the House of Commons until 1976. He then semi-retired, acting as a special representative of the government of Canada to the Middle East and North Africa from July 1979 to February 1980. After the hubbub of political life, he now enjoys gardening at his home in Rockcliffe, a quiet section of Ottawa. He is a member of the Halifax and Albany clubs.

Stanley, George Francis Gillman

O.C., B.A., M.A., M.Litt., D.Phil., D.es.L., LL.D., D.Litt., D.C.L., D.U., C.St.J., F.R.Hist.S., F.R.S.C.

Lieutenant-Governor, historian. b. July 6, 1907, Calgary; m. Ruth Lynette Hill; d. Della Cromwell, Marietta McAtamney, Laurie; res. Fredericton.

When eminent Canadian historian George Stanley submitted a design for use as Canada's flag to Parliament in 1964, he had little idea it would become the country's national emblem a year later. For the lieutenant-governor of New Brunswick, this has been only one in a long line of achievements. Before his current appointment in 1982, Stanley had been director of Canadian Studies at Mount Allison University in Sackville, New Brunswick, from 1969 to 1975. His career in the study of Canadian history began in 1925 when he attended the University of Alberta for his B.A., winning a Rhodes scholarship in 1929 and a Beit Senior Research Scholarship in Colonial History for M.A. studies at Oxford. He was a Royal Society of Canada Scholar in 1934 and later won Guggenheim and Canada Council fellowships. By 1938 Stanley was a lieutenant in the Canadian Militia and served in the Second World War, ultimately as a lieutenant-colonel, and remained in the Reserve for 20 years after his retirement from active service. Stanley's first teaching post after the war was at the University of British Columbia as professor of History. Two years later, he became head of the History Department at Royal Military College in Kingston and 10 years later chairman of the Arts Division and Dean of Arts of RMC, a position he held until going to Mount Allison. A member of various historical societies including the Royal Historical Society and the Canadian Historical Association, Stanley was also part of the Massey Commission on the Arts, Letters, and Sciences in 1950-51. He is the author of *The Birth of Western Canada* (1936), *Louis Riel* (1963), and *The Story of Canada's Flag* (1965).

Steinhauer, Ralph

O.C.

Indian leader, former lieutenant-governor. b. June 1905, Morley, Alberta; m. Isobel Davidson; four daughters, one son; res. Saddle Lake Indian Reserve, Alberta.

The Honourable Ralph Steinhauer has worked long and hard in the interests of Native Indians across Canada. A Treaty Indian (Cree) and great-grandson of the missionary Henry Bird Steinhauer, he spent 34 years as councillor of the Saddle Lake Indian Band and three years as its chief. He is a past president of the Indian Association of Alberta, which he helped to establish, and a member of the Saddle Lake Centennial Development Association, which he also helped to launch. In 1963 he was nominated as the Liberal candidate for Vegreville riding and he became Alberta's tenth lieutenant-governor in 1974. He was involved in the Alberta Rural Development Authority and the Federal Indian Economic Development. He is an honorary patron of more than 30 different organizations and the recipient of the Canadian Centennial Medal, and was named an Officer of the Order of Canada. He and his family live on a farm near Brosseau, Alberta, on the Saddle Lake Indian Reserve.

It is unlikely any Canadian family can boast a longer record of military, legal and political service than the Panets. Seven generations ago Jean Claude Panet settled in Quebec City in 1740 and enlisted as a soldier. Later he became an attorney and a judge. His son Jean Antoine and grandson Philippe were both lawyers, soldiers and Quebec M.P.P.s. His great grandson Charles Eugène was colonel of the 9th Royal Rifles of Quebec and Deputy-Minister of Defence, 1875-1898. Of Charles Eugène's seven sons, six became soldiers, the most notable being Maj. Gen. Edouard de B. Panet, who was much decorated in the First War and retired as general officer commanding the Montreal area at the end of the Second World War. The others were Maj. Gen. Henri A Panet, Brig. Gen. Eugène Panet, Col. A. de Lotbinière Panet, Col. Arthur Panet and Col. Charles Panet. The seventh son, Philippe, was a lawyer in Windsor, Ont. Of the next generation, Brig. Gen. Henri Panet, son of Brig. Gen. Eugène, is retired in England; Major A. de Lotbinière Panet, son of Col. A. de L. Panet, is retired in Ottawa; and Lt. Col. H. de Lotbinière Panet, son of Col. Charles Panet, is dead. Of the present generation, Major Charles Panet, son of Lt. Col. H. de L. Panet, has retired from Army HQ and Lt. A. de L. Panet Jr., an Ottawa lawyer and accountant, is a reserve officer.

The group photograph shows Col. Charles Eugène Panet (seated) with five of his six military sons. Standing, left to right: Arthur, Henri, de Lotbinière, Eugène and Charles. The separate photo shows the sixth, Edouard.

Lieutenant-General François Richard

LEFT: Jeanne Sauvé

Vice-Admiral James Wood

Teschke, William
B.A., M.B.A.

Civil servant. b. 1929, Winnipeg; married; res. Ottawa.

Recently appointed to the joint post of deputy minister of Industry, Trade and Commerce and of the Department of Regional Economic Expansion, William Teschke brings with him a reputation as a top-notch administrator from his days as secretary of the Ministry of State for Economic and Regional Development and previous senior posting in Industry, Trade and Commerce and the Privy Council. He spent 15 years with the armed forces after the RCAF helped put him through school, then worked as an accountant in three federal departments before moving to the Privy Council in 1972, rising to deputy secretary under Michael Pitfield.

Thériault, Gérard Charles Edouard
C.M.M., C.D., B.A.

Military officer. b. June 5, 1932, Gaspé, Quebec; married; s. Dwight, Pierre; res. Ottawa.

Appointed chief of Defence Staff in 1983, General Gérard Thériault began his career with the RCAF in 1951 when he enrolled as a pilot. He saw duty with various jet fighter squadrons through the Cold War period at Canadian bases in Europe, becoming in 1966 commanding officer of 444 Squadron at Baden-Soellingen, West Germany. In 1967 he became vice-commandant at Collège militaire royal de Saint-Jean and in 1970 he took command of the College. Other appointments followed, including a period as commander of 1st Canadian Air Group in Lahr, West Germany. In 1975 he became chief of staff operations at Air Command HQ, rising to commander of Air Command. He joined National Defence HQ in 1977.

Vance, Lieutenant-General John E.,
C.D.

Assistant Deputy Minister, Dept. of National Defence, Ottawa.

Wightman, Major-General David P.,
C.D.

Commander, Canadian Forces Europe, Ottawa.

Withers, Ramsey Muir
C.M.M., C.D., B.Sc., P.Eng., C.St.J.

Military officer, civil servant. b. July 28, 1930, Toronto; m. Jean Allison Saunders; s. James Scott, d. Leslie Susan Schultz, Deidre Ann Hunter; res. Ottawa.

Ramsey Withers is deputy minister of Transport in the federal government, a position he assumed in 1983 after three years as chief of the Defence Staff. He began his military career in 1952; from 1976 to 1980 he was commander of Canadian forces in Europe. General Withers was educated at the Royal Military College and Queen's University. He is vice-patron of the Royal Canadian Military Institute, honorary vice-president of the Royal Canadian Legion, and secretary of the National Council of Boy Scouts of Canada.

Wolfe, Major-General J.P., C.D.

Judge Advocate Gen., Canadian Forces, Ottawa.

Wood, James Crilly
C.D.

Naval officer. b. August 29, 1934, Charlottetown; m. Joan Fay Cameron; s. Michael, Stephen, d. Susan; res. Ottawa.

Commander of Maritime Command since 1983, Vice-Admiral J.C. Wood has had a naval career of 32 years' standing. His previous positions include chief of Maritime Doctrine and Operations. From 1972 to 1979 he was commanding officer of the 1st Canadian Submarine Squadron and has commanded the submarine *Ojibwa* and HMCS *Protecteur*. Wood was educated at Prince of Wales College in Prince Edward Island and at Royal Roads in Victoria. He is active in the church and scouting. He plays squash and tennis and enjoys skiing, doing house renovations, fishing, and, of course, sailing.

LAW

Agrios, Jack N., Q.C.

Barrister & Solicitor; Edmonton

Arthurs, Harry William
B.A., LL.B., LL.M., F.R.S.C.

Professor of Law. b. May 9, 1935, Toronto; m. Penelope Milnes; s. Joshua William, Gideon Jude; res. Toronto.

Although he regards his inclusion in the ranks of the Establishment as "somewhat mysterious, and a little uncomfortable," Harry Arthurs has nevertheless had significant influence. He has served as a member of the Economic Council of Canada, the United Auto Workers Public Review Board, and the Governing Council of the Ontario College of Art. He was also vice-chairman of the Ontario Education Relations Commission, chief adjudicator of the Public Service of Canada, and president of the Canadian Civil Liberties Association. After receiving his B.A. and LL.B. from the University of Toronto, he received his LL.M. from Harvard in 1959. He was a visiting professor or visiting fellow at the universities of Toronto, McGill, Cambridge, and Oxford and served as dean of Osgoode Hall Law School from 1972 to 1977. He has also frequently acted as an arbitrator and/or mediator in labour disputes. Arthurs has helped shape and stimulate legal education and research, contributed to the development of labour relations law and policy, and participated in public debate and policy formation on a broad range of social and legal issues. He is the author of articles on administrative law, legal history, the legal profession, and legal education and is a member of the Canadian Civil Liberties Association and the Royal Society of Canada.

Ballem, John Bishop
Q.C., B.A., M.A., LL.B., LL.M.

Lawyer, author. b. February 2, 1925, New Glasgow, Nova Scotia; m. Grace Louise Flavelle; s. Flavelle Bishop, John Flavelle, d. Mary Mercedes; res. Calgary.

In addition to his duties as a senior partner of the law firm of Ballem, McDill & MacInnes, John Ballem has been a host or narrator of various special television programs and is the author of seven novels and a textbook on oil and gas law. The son of a surgeon, Ballem saw service in the Second World War as a pilot in the Fleet Air Arm of the Royal Navy. He earned his law degree at Dalhousie University in 1949, continuing his education at Harvard Law School, where he received his Master of Law. He then taught for two years at the University of British Columbia before joining Imperial Oil as a solicitor in 1952. In 1956 he was appointed general counsel of Westcoast Transmission and Pacific Petroleum, a position he held for five years before starting his own law firm. He was appointed Queen's Counsel in 1966 and served as vice-president of the Canadian Bar Association that year. He is a member of Calgary's prestigious Ranchmen's and Petroleum clubs, among others, and is a director of Sulpetro and Scotia Oils.

Barbeau, Jacques Gilles
B.A., LL.B., LL.M., C.G.A.

Lawyer. b. May 20, 1931, Montreal; m. Margaret Ann Owen; s. Jean, Paul, d. Jacqueline, Monique; res. Vancouver and Point Roberts.

Jacques Barbeau is a transplanted Montrealer who has successfully entered the tightly knit Vancouver Establishment. A graduate of the University of British Columbia and Harvard, Barbeau spent five years in Ottawa with government taxation divisions and as a director of research for the Canadian Tax Foundation. He opened his own practice in Vancouver in the early 1960s; today Barbeau, McKercher, Collingwood & Hanna deals with clients around the world. Barbeau divides his time between his heritage house in Vancouver's Shaughnessy district and a summer residence in Point Roberts, Washington. He collects Leica cameras and the works of Canadian artist E.J. Hughes and is a member of the Vancouver Club.

Beetz, Jean
B.A., M.A., LL.L., LL.D., D.C.L., F.R.S.C.

Judge, Supreme Court of Canada. b. March 27, 1927, Montreal; res. Ottawa.

Jean Beetz is one of Canada's foremost students of constitutional law. He received his law degree from the University of Montreal. After practising law in Montreal for two years, he was awarded a Rhodes scholarship in 1951 to attend Pembroke College at Oxford University, where he earned a B.A. and an M.A. He then taught civil law at the University of Montreal from 1953 to 1959. From 1959 to 1973 he taught constitutional law and was dean of law from 1968 to 1970. Beetz served as assistant secretary to the federal cabinet from 1966 to 1968, after which he was appointed special counsel to the Prime Minister on constitutional matters; he spent three years in this capacity. In 1973 Beetz was appointed a Judge of the Quebec Court of Appeal; the next year he

Justices of the Supreme Court of Canada: front, Chief Justice Bora Laskin. Justices (right to left): first row, Roland A. Ritchie, Brian Dickson; second row, Jean Beetz, Willard Z. Estey; third row, William R. McIntyre, Julien Chouinard; fourth row, Antonio Lamer, Bertha Wilson.

joined the Supreme Court of Canada. He is a fellow of the Royal Society of Canada and a member of the Cercle Universitaire of Ottawa.

Boland, Janet Lang
Q.C., B.A., LL.B.

Judge. b. December 6, 1928, Kitchener, Ontario; s. Michael Frederic, Christopher John, Nicholas James; res. Toronto.

With her appointment as a judge of the Trial Division of the Supreme Court of Ontario in 1976, Janet Boland became the first woman judge of the Supreme Court of Ontario. She had been appointed a judge of the County of York in 1972 and had previously been a partner in the Toronto law firm of Lang, Michener, Farquharson, Cranston and Wright. She was educated at Waterloo College, the University of Western Ontario, and Osgoode Hall Law School. She began her private law practice in 1950; she joined White, Bristol, Beck & Phipps in 1958, then became a partner at Lang, Michener, Farquharson, Cranston & Wright in 1968.

Borden, Henry
O.C., C.M.G., Q.C., B.A., D.C.L., LL.D.

Lawyer, company director. b. September 25, 1901, Halifax; m. Jean Creelman MacRae; s. Robert, John, Henry, d. Ann; res. King City, Ontario.

Henry Borden's varied career in law and business has spanned more than half a century. Among many other positions, he has been chairman of the Wartime Industrial Control Board, chairman of the Royal Commission on Energy, president of Brazilian Traction, Light and Power (now Brascan), chairman of several insurance companies, a senior member of the Toronto law firm of Borden, Elliot, Kelley and Palmer, and a lecturer on corporation law at Osgoode Hall Law School. He was joint author of the *Handbook of Canadian Company Law*. He is director emeritus of the Bank of Commerce, honorary director of Massey-Ferguson and Canada Trustco, and a past president of the Royal Agricultural Winter Fair. He is a Rhodes scholar and a nephew of Prime Minister Sir Robert Borden, whose memoirs and letters he edited. He was educated at McGill and Dalhousie Law School. Among his clubs are the York and the Canadian.

Borovoy, Alan A.
General Counsel; Canadian Civil Liberties Association; Toronto

Bowlby, John D., Q.C.
Barrister & Solicitor; Bowlby, Luchak; Hamilton

Chipman, David R., Q.C.
Barrister & Solicitor; Stewart, McKeen & Covert; Halifax

Chouinard, Julien
O.C., C.D., LL.L., M.A.

Judge, Supreme Court of Canada. b. February 4, 1929, Quebec City; m. Jeannine Pettigrew; s. Julien, d. Lucie, Nicole; res. Ottawa.

Julien Chouinard studied at Laval University and was awarded a Rhodes scholarship in 1951. After receiving his M.A. at Oxford, he worked in the law firm of Prévost, Gagné, Flynn, Chouinard and Jacques from 1953 to 1965; he also taught corporate law at Laval University. He was Quebec's Deputy Minister of Justice for three years, then the Secretary General of the Quebec cabinet until 1975. From 1975 to 1979, when he was appointed a judge of the Supreme Court of Canada, he sat in the Quebec Court of Appeal. Chouinard was active in the militia; from 1965 to 1968 he commanded the 6th Field Regiment of the Royal Canadian Artillery. In 1972 he received the Vanier Medal from the Canadian Institute of Public Administration and was named an Officer of the Order of Canada in 1974. He has also received the Centennial Medal and the Queen's Jubilee Medal. He was a member of the Royal Commission on Bilingual Air Traffic Services in Quebec from 1976 to 1979.

Cohen, Maxwell
O.C., Q.C., B.A., LL.B., LL.M., LL.D., D.C.L.

Professor of Law, Barrister, Judge ad hoc International Court of Justice. b. March 17, 1910, Winnipeg; m. Isle Sternberg, d. JoAnne; res. Ottawa.

A judge at the International Court of Justice and Scholar in Residence and Professor of Law at the University of Ottawa, Max Cohen has had years of involvement in the cause of human rights, which led to the creation of the Quebec Advisory on the Administration of Justice and the Canadian Human Rights Foundation. He has served as chairman of the Ministry of Justice Special Committee on Hate Propaganda, the Middle Eastern Policy Committee of the Canadian Jewish Congress, and the Canadian Zionist Federation. He received his law degree from the University of Manitoba before continuing his studies at Northwestern University in Chicago and then Harvard Law School as a research fellow. He served with the Canadian Army during the Second World War, rising to the rank of major, and taught at the Khaki University of Canada in England. On his return to Canada in 1946 he started teaching at McGill University and is now Emeritus Professor; he was Dean of Law, 1964-1969.

Courtois, Edmond Jacques
Q.C., B.A., LL.B.

Lawyer, business executive. b. July 4, 1920, Montreal; m. Joan Miller; d. Nicole, s. Jacques, Marc; res. Montreal.

Jacques Courtois is a partner in the Montreal law firm of Stikeman, Elliott, Tamaki, Mercier & Robb, which he joined after leaving Courtois, Clarkson, Parsons and Tetrault in 1982. He is also a vice-president of the Bank of Nova Scotia and Canada Life and director of several companies including various Eaton Bay funds, McGraw-Hill Ryerson, Trizec Corp., Norcen Energy Resources, and Brinco Ltd. He is fund raiser for the Progressive Conservative Party and has close connections with the Eatons. He is on the boards of the Montreal Children's Hospital and the Reddy Memorial Hospital. During the Second World War, Courtois served with the RCNVR. He was educated at the University of Montreal.

Covert, Frank Manning
O.C., O.B.E., Q.C., B.A., LL.B., D.Eng.

Barrister and solicitor. b. January 13, 1908, Canning, Nova Scotia; m. Mary Louise Stewart, s. Michael, Peter, d. Susan, Sally; res. Halifax.

Although modestly playing down his influence and usually crediting others with his accomplishments, Frank Covert is recognized as a leading force in Nova Scotia's business establishment. Now retired from all but a handful of local directorships, Covert spent 27 years on the board of the Royal Bank and 17 years with Sun Life, as well as his many years as a partner of Stewart MacKeen & Covert of Halifax. He was also on the board of Dalhousie University and served as chairman of Nova Scotia's Technical University. He earned his law degree at Dalhousie University. During the Second World War, Covert served as a navigator with the RCAF and was awarded a Distinguished Flying Cross. He is also an Officer of the Order of Canada and of the Order of the British Empire. After 50 years of practising law, he plans to retire to his summer residence at Hunts Point, Nova Scotia.

Cox, William A., Q.C.
Barrister and Solicitor; Cox, Downie; Halifax

de Grandpré, Louis-Philippe
C.C., Q.C., B.C.L.

Lawyer. b. February 6, 1917, Montreal; m. Marthe Gendron; s. Michel, Ivan, d. Sylvie, Francine; res. Town of Mount Royal, Quebec.

Louis-Philippe de Grandpré began his long career in law in 1938, when he joined the firm of Brais, Campbell as an associate just after receiving his B.C.L. from McGill. In 1944 he became an associate with Létourneau, Tansey, Monk, de Grandpré, Lippé & Tremblay, where he remained for five years before starting his own firm, Tansey, de Grandpré, de Grandpré. In 1974, he was appointed a judge in the Supreme Court of Canada, a position he held until October 1977, when he returned to practising law as a senior partner of Lafleur, Brown, de Grandpré. The brother of Jean de Grandpré, chairman of Bell Canada, he is a director of Montreal Life Insurance Company, the Guardian Insurance Company of Canada, and the Montreal Trust Company, as well as the Société de Gestion Katerina Inc. He served as president of the Bar of Montreal (1968–69), the Bar of the Province of Quebec (1968–69), and the Canadian Bar Association (1972–73), and was made a Companion of the Order of Canada in 1972. He is married to the daughter of the Honourable L.H. Gendron, a minister in the federal cabinet in 1935, and is a member of the Mount Royal Club.

Deschênes, Jules
B.A., LL.M., LL.D., F.R.S.C.

Lawyer, judge. b. June 7, 1923, Montreal; m. Jacqueline Lachapelle; s. Pierre, Yves, Jean-François, d. Louise, Mireille; res. Montreal.

The author of numerous books and articles dealing with Canadian law, Jules Deschênes began his law career in 1946 after receiving his Master of Laws from the University of Montreal. From 1966 to 1972 he was a senior partner of Deschênes, de Grandpré, Colas, Godin & Lapointe, and was appointed a judge of the Quebec Courts of Appeal in the latter year. The following year he became the Chief Justice of the Quebec Superior Court, a post he relinquished in 1983. He has lectured on private and international law at the University of Montreal. He has received the Governor Gen-

Jacques Barbeau at his house in Shaughnessy, Vancouver.

Leonard Kitz at his home in the Northwest Arm area of Halifax.

Constance Glube with her family aboard their Erickson 47 in Halifax Harbour.

ALL: J.R.

eral's Medal and Lieutenant-Governor's Medal and was made a Fellow of the Royal Society of Canada (1977) and a Knight of the Order of Malta (1978). Deschênes has served as president of associations such as the Quebec Advisory Council on Justice, the Quebec Branch of the Canadian Bar Association, and the World Association of Judges' Committee on Expanding the Jurisdiction of the International Court of Justice, among others. He is a member of a variety of national and international law-related organizations.

Dickson, R.G. Brian

B.A., LL.B., LL.D., D.Cn.L.

Judge. b. May 25, 1916, Yorkton, Saskatchewan; m. Barbara Melville Sellers; s. Brian, Peter, Barry, d. Deborah; res. Dunrobin, Ontario.

Mr. Justice Brian Dickson studied law at the Manitoba Law School, where he received his Bachelor of Law in 1938. He was called to the Bar of Manitoba in 1940. Shortly afterwards he joined the Royal Canadian Artillery and served until his return to Canada in 1945. He practised law with Aikins, MacAulay & Company until 1963, during which time he also lectured at the Manitoba Law School (1948-54) and was named Q.C. (1953). He was appointed to the Court of Queen's Bench of Manitoba in 1963; 10 years later he was appointed to the Supreme Court of Canada. He is a life bencher of the Law Society of Manitoba. From 1971 to 1973 he was chairman of the Board of Governors of the University of Manitoba; from 1960 to 1971 he was chancellor of the Anglican Diocese of Rupert's Land.

Ducharme, M. Claude, Q.C.

Barrister & Solicitor; Desjardins, Ducharme, Desjardins & Bourque; Montreal

Eagleson, R. Alan

Q.C., B.A., LL.B., LL.M.

Lawyer. b. April 24, 1933, St. Catharines, Ontario; m. Nancy Elizabeth Fisk; s. Trevor Allen, d. Jill Anne; res. Toronto.

One of Canada's flamboyant impresarios, Alan Eagleson was chairman of Team Canada 1972 (the first Russia-NHL series) and of the Canada Cup of Hockey for 1976 and 1981, a role he will again play in 1984. He grew up in a suburb of Toronto and attended the University of Toronto, where he received his law degree, and Osgoode Hall Law School. In 1960 he became a partner of Blaney Pasternak Smela Eagleson and Watson, where he was to remain for 15 years. During this time he was elected a member of the Ontario legislature and served two four-year terms as president of the Ontario Progressive Conservative Association. Since 1975 he has been a sole practitioner and is president of Sports Management, executive director of the National Hockey League Players Association (which he organized), and chief negotiator of Canadian International Hockey. In addition to his hockey interests, he is also a director of the Big Brothers of Metropolitan Toronto, the Queensway and Etobicoke General Hospitals, and Ronald McDonald House, and devotes much of his time to raising funds for charitable organizations. In addition to four university awards, he has received the Vanier Award as one of Canada's five outstanding young men (1968). He

spends his free time at the family's 1870 log cabin in Thornbury, Ontario, winters in Palm Beach, and collects the arts of Lemieux, Bush, and Danby.

Elliott, Roy Fraser, Q.C.

Barrister & Solicitor; Stikeman, Elliott, Tamaki, Mercier & Robb; Montreal & Toronto

Estey, Willard Zebedee

LL.B., LL.M., LL.D.

Judge. b. October 10, 1919, Saskatoon; m. Marian Ruth, s. Wilfred (Bill), John, Paul, d. Eleanor; res. Rockcliffe, Ontario.

Willard Zebedee Estey followed in the footsteps of his father, J. Wilfred Estey, to the Supreme Court of Canada. He was educated at the University of Saskatchewan and at Harvard, where he received his Master of Laws in 1946. During the Second World War, he served in the Canadian Army and in the Royal Canadian Air Force. On his return he became a professor at the College of Law, University of Saskatchewan. He then moved to Toronto, where he practised law until 1972 and lectured at Osgoode Hall Law School from 1947 to 1951. In 1960 he was appointed Q.C.; in 1973 he was appointed to the Court of Appeal of the Supreme Court of Ontario. Two and a half years later he became Chief Justice of the High Court, then Chief Justice of Ontario in 1976. Since 1977 he has been a judge of the Supreme Court of Canada. He is a member of various legal associations and has served as honorary chairman of the Canadian Judges Conference and vice-president of the Canadian Institute for Advanced Legal Studies. He is also chairman of Hockey Canada and an honorary lifetime member of the Board of Governors of York-Finch General Hospital.

Finlayson, George D., Q.C.

Barrister & Solicitor; McCarthy & McCarthy; Toronto

Fortier, Yves, Q.C.

Barrister & Solicitor; Ogilvy, Cope, Porteous; Montreal

Freedman, Samuel

B.A., LL.B., D.C.L.

Judge. b. April 16, 1908, U.S.S.R.; m. Claris Brownie Udow; d. Susan R., Phylis C., s. Martin H.; res. Winnipeg.

Chief justice of Manitoba since 1971, Samuel Freedman came to Canada in 1911. He received his B.A. and LL.B. from the University of Manitoba and was called to the Bar in that province in 1933. He practised law until his appointment to the Court of Queen's Bench for Manitoba in 1952. He was appointed to the Court of Appeal in 1960. Chief Justice Freedman served as president of the Manitoba Bar Association in 1952. He has also been active in community work through the Civil Liberties Association, the Community Chest, Jewish Welfare Fund, and the Canadian Institute of International Affairs. He was awarded the Human Relations Award of the Canadian Council of Christians and Jews in 1956.

Gibson, Ronald Dale

B.A., LL.B., LL.M.

Professor of law. b. May 17, 1933, Winnipeg; m. April Lee Patterson; s. Alan Scott, d. Kristin Lee Lercher; res. Winnipeg.

A law professor at the University of Manitoba since what he calls "the dawn of time" (actually 22 years), Ronald Gibson received his law degree there in 1958, then studied for his Master's at Harvard the following year. He is the author of numerous articles and books dealing with the law, the Canadian Charter of Rights and Freedoms, the Canadian Constitution, and human rights. He was a founding editor of the *Manitoba Law Journal* (1962-65) and acted as constitutional consultant for the governments of Canada and Manitoba, and chairman for a Study Group on the Canadian Constitution (1970-75). Since 1968 he has been chairman of the Legal Research Institute of the U of M, and from 1970 to 1980 he was a director of the Archives of Western Canadian Legal History. More recently, he has been involved in human rights, serving on the Tribunal Panel of the Canadian Human Rights Commission.

Glube, Constance R.

Q.C., B.A., LL.B.

Judge. b. November 23, 1931, Ottawa; née Lepofsky; m. Richard H. Glube; s. John, Harry, Joseph, d. Erica Kolatch; res. Halifax.

Constance Glube has achieved firsts in her career: first female city manager in Canada (Halifax) and first female Chief Justice in Canada (Trial Division of the Supreme Court of Nova Scotia). She was educated at McGill and Dalhousie Universities and became a senior solicitor in the City of Halifax's Legal Department before becoming city manager. She is a member of a number of law societies, including the Canadian Institute for the Administration of Justice, the Canadian Judges Conference, and Nova Scotia Women in Law. She is a former director of the Institute of Public Administration of Canada and a former vice-president of the Canadian Association of Municipal Administrators. Her community involvements include co-chairmanship of the Canadian Council of Christians and Jews (Atlantic region) and presidency of the Women's League of the Shaar Shalom congregation. She was appointed Queen's Counsel in 1974 and received the City of Halifax Medal in 1977. She is a member of the Royal Nova Scotia Yacht Squadron and likes to sail aboard the family's Ericson 47 and drive her BMW 530-I. Her husband is associate professor of business administration of Dalhousie University. She is the daughter of the late Ottawa lawyer Samuel Lepofsky.

Goodman, Edwin Alan

Q.C., B.A., LL.B.

Lawyer. b. 1918, Toronto; m. Suzanne Dorothy Gross; d. Joanne Ruth, Diana Selena; res. Toronto.

Though best known to the public as a backroom Conservative Party power broker, Eddie Goodman has had a long and distinguished legal career as a partner in Goodman and Goodman. After active service in the Second World War, in which he was wounded twice and mentioned in despatches, he read law in the firm of his father, David B. Goodman, and was called to the Bar of Ontario in 1947. His business directorships include Baton Broadcasting and Cadillac Fairview. He is a former chairman of the Committee for an Independent Canada and is, among many public service activities, a director of the National Ballet Guild of Canada, the United Jewish Welfare Fund, and the New Mount Sinai Hospital and chairman of the Royal Ontario Museum. His club memberships include the Albany and the Primrose.

Goodman, Wolfe D., Q.C.

Barrister & Solicitor; Goodman & Carr; Toronto

Greenspan, Edward Leonard
Q.C., B.A., LL.B.

Lawyer. b. February 28, 1944, Niagara Falls; m. Suzy Dahan; d. Julianna, Samantha; res. Willowdale, Ontario.

Perhaps Canada's most widely known criminal lawyer, Eddie Greenspan has become familiar to Canadians both in and out of the court room. He is an educator and speaker in the field of the administration of justice. Since 1982 he has hosted and narrated *Scales of Justice*, a CBC radio docudrama series. He has written numerous articles on criminal justice for magazines and professional journals. He acted as defence counsel in such famous cases as the Hamilton Harbour dredging trial, the Gordon Allen murder trial, and the Sterling Hayden drug case. He studied at the University of Toronto and received his law degree from Osgoode Hall Law School in 1968, and is now a senior partner in the law firm of Greenspan, Rosenberg. He is a member of law societies across North America and is a director of the Advocates Society, the Medical-Legal Society, and the Canadian Civil Liberties Association. He has also served as editor or associate editor of law-related publications and is a member of the Editorial Board of the Canadian Charter of Rights Annotated. He drives a Checker Marathon.

Hanson, Horace A., Q.C.

Barrister & Solicitor; Hanson, Hashey & Scott; Fredericton

Harradence, A. Milton

Justice of the Court of Appeal of Alberta, Edmonton

Henderson, Gordon F., Q.C.

Barrister & Solicitor; Gowling & Henderson; Ottawa

Hnatyshyn, Ramon John
P.C., Q.C., M.P., B.A., LL.B.

Lawyer, politician. b. March 16, 1934, Saskatoon; m. Gerda Andreasen; s. John Georg, Carl Andrew; res. Saskatoon, and Ottawa.

Since graduating with a law degree from the University of Saskatchewan in 1956, Ray Hnatyshyn has enjoyed a distinguished career as both a lawyer and an MP. In 1958, after two years of practice in Saskatoon, he was appointed private secretary and executive assistant to the government leader of the Senate, the late W.M. Aseltine. In 1960 he returned to Saskatoon to practise law with his father, Senator John Hnatyshyn, and he became an active member of many community organizations including the YMCA, the United Community

Funds of Saskatchewan, and the Kinsmen Club. He served as a bencher of the Law Society of Saskatchewan from 1970 to 1974 when he was elected president. In addition to his practice and his work on numerous associations, he was lecturer in law at the University of Saskatchewan. His parliamentary career began in 1974 with his election as MP for Saskatoon-Biggar. He was a member of many House of Commons standing committees and in 1976 he was appointed deputy house leader of the Opposition. Re-elected in 1979 in the riding of Saskatoon West, he was appointed minister of Energy, Mines and Resources and minister of state for Science and Technology in the Progressive Conservative government of Joe Clark. He was re-elected in 1980 and became chairman of the Justice and Legal Affairs Committee of the House of Commons, as well as the justice critic in the Progressive Conservatives' shadow cabinet.

Howland, William Goldwin Carrington
B.A., LL.B., LL.D.

Judge. b. March 7, 1915, Toronto; m. Margaret Patricia Greene; res. Toronto.

The present chief justice of Ontario graduated from Osgoode Hall in 1939 and was called to the Bar of Ontario. Except for the war years 1942-45 when he served with the Royal Canadian Army Service Corps, William Howland practised law with the Toronto firm of Rowell Reid Wright & McMillan (the forerunner of McMillan Binch) from 1939 to 1975. During his time at the Bar, he served as treasurer of the Law Society of Upper Canada (1968-70) and president of the Federation of Law Societies of Canada (1973-74). He was appointed a judge of the Ontario Court of Appeal in 1975 and became chief justice of Ontario in 1977. He is chairman of the Ontario Judicial Council, the Council of Judges of the Supreme Court of Ontario, and of the Ontario Courts Advisory Council; in addition, he is a member of the Board of Governors of Upper Canada College, the Advisory Council of the Toronto Symphony, the University College Committee of the University of Toronto, and a trustee of Wycliffe College (University of Toronto). Chief Justice Howland has made noteworthy contributions in the field of legal education and played a particularly important role in the affiliation of Osgoode Hall Law School, Canada's largest institution of legal education, with York University in the 1960s. Chief Justice Howland comes from a family with a long record of public service — his great-grandfather, Sir William Pearce Howland, C.B., K.C.M.G., was the only American-born Father of Confederation and served as minister of Finance, minister of Internal Revenue, postmaster general, and lieutenant-governor of Ontario; his grandfather and great-uncle were both mayors of the city of Toronto.

Hughes, Charles J.A.

Chief Justice of New Brunswick; Fredericton

Ivey, Richard M., Q.C.

Barrister & Solicitor; Ivey & Dowler; London, Ontario

Kelleher, Stephen Frederick Danby
B.A., LL.B.

Lawyer. b. May 10, 1947, Belleville, Ontario; m. Heather Jane McNamara; s. David; res. North Vancouver.

Stephen Kelleher is a lawyer who as a public servant is making an outstanding contribution to the administration of justice in British Columbia. He is at present chairman of the province's Labour Relations Board and has previously served as its vice-chairman. Kelleher attended Sir George Williams University (Montreal) and the University of British Columbia, receiving a B.A. in 1968 and an LL.B. in 1973. After his call to the Bar of British Columbia in 1974, Kelleher practised law with the Vancouver firm of Munroe, Fraser & Kelleher until 1980. He has been an elected member of the executive of the Vancouver Bar Association (1977-78) and a member of the Committee of Special Advisors to the B.C. Minister of Labour (1979-81) as well as a participant in the programs of the Continuing Legal Education Society of British Columbia.

Kitz, Leonard Arthur
Q.C., LL.B., D.C.L.

Lawyer. b. April 9, 1916, Halifax; m. Janet Brownlee; s. John, Alan, d. Hilary; res. Halifax.

Leonard Kitz is a former mayor of Halifax (1955-57) and is now a senior partner in the law firm of Kitz, Matheson, Green & MacIsaac. He attended Dalhousie University and began practising law after graduation. Over the years he has held executive positions in a wide variety of companies and organizations, including president of Provincial Realty Co. Ltd. and chairman of the Art Gallery of Nova Scotia and of the John Howard Society. He is a past president of the Nova Scotia Barristers' Society and is a trustee of the National Arts Centre. During the Second World War he served as a captain with the Princess Louise Fusiliers. He collects 18th-century furniture and belongs to the Royal Nova Scotia Yacht Squadron, the Saraguay Club, and the Ashburn Golf and Country Club.

L'Heureux-Dubé, Claire
B.A., LL.L., LL.D.

Judge. b. September 7, 1927, Quebec City; m. Arthur Dubé (deceased); s. Pierre, d. Louise; res. Sillery, Quebec.

After receiving her law degree from Laval in 1951, along with the Turgeon Award in Civil Law and the Beaulieu Award in Labour Law, Claire L'Heureux began practising as a partner in the firm Bard, L'Heureux & Philippon. She was a senior partner of L'Heureux, Philippon, Garneau, Tourigny, St-Arnaud & Associates from 1969 until 1973, when she was appointed a judge of the Superior Court of Quebec. Over the next three years she also acted as commissioner of a board that investigated matters relating to the Department of Manpower and Immigration in Montreal. The board's report was filed and published in 1976. On November 2, 1979, Claire L'Heureux-Dubé was sworn in as a judge of the Quebec Court of Appeal. She is president (since 1980) of the International Society on Family Law, and vice-president of the Association québecoise pour l'étude comparative du droit (since 1982). She also belongs to the Canadian Bar Association and the International Federation of Women Lawyers.

J.R.

Edward Greenspan with his Checker Marathon.

GEORGE WHITESIDE

John J. Robinette

William Howland at Osgoode Hall, Toronto.

J.R.

Lamer, Antonio
B.A., LL.L., LL.D.

Judge. b. July 8, 1933, Montreal; m. Suzanne Bonin; s. Stéphane; res. Ottawa.

Antonio Lamer was educated at the Collège de Saint-Laurent and the University of Montreal. From 1957 until 1969 he worked as a barrister. In 1969 he became a judge of the Superior Court for Quebec. He served as vice-chairman (1971–75) and later as chairman (1975–78) of the Law Reform Commission of Canada. In 1978 he was appointed judge of the Court of Appeal for Quebec, then in 1980 justice of the Supreme Court of Canada. Through most of these years he was also a professor of law at the University of Montreal. He is currently a member of the Cercle Universitaire d'Ottawa, the Canadian Bar Association, the international legal fraternity Phi Delta Phi, the Canadian Institute for the Administration of Justice, the Canadian Human Rights Foundation, and the Oriskany (fishing and hunting) Club—of which he is an honorary member.

Laskin, Bora
P.C., B.A., M.A., LL.B., LL.M., LL.D., D.C.L., Ph.D., L.Hum.D., F.R.S.C.

Chief Justice of Canada. b. October 5, 1912, Fort William, Ontario; m. Peggy Tenenbaum; s. John, d. Barbara; res. Ottawa.

Canada's foremost authority on constitutional law and most honoured legal mind, Bora Laskin was educated at the University of Toronto, Osgoode Hall Law School, and Harvard Law School and was called to the Bar of Ontario in 1937. He was a lecturer in Law and an assistant professor of Law at the university from 1940 to 1945, a lecturer in Law at Osgoode Hall from 1945 to 1949, and a professor of Law at the U of T from 1945 to 1965. He was appointed Queen's Counsel in 1956. His first judicial appointment, to the Ontario Court of Appeal, came in 1965. In 1970 he was the first Jew appointed to the Supreme Court of Canada, something of a breakthrough in the higher corridors of power, and became Chief Justice of Canada in 1973. His responsibilities outside the courtroom have been many. He was president of the Association of Canadian Law Teachers (1953-54); president of the Canadian Association of University Teachers (1964-65); chairman of the Board of Governors of the Ontario Institute for Studies in Education (1965-69); member of the Board of Governors of York University (1967-70) and of Carleton University (1970-73); and chancellor of Lakehead University (1971-80). He was a Corresponding Fellow of the British Academy and a member of the Council of Management of the British Institute of International and Comparative Law in 1972. He served as associate editor of the *Dominion Law Reports* and *Canadian Criminal Cases* from 1943 to 1965. He is a member of the National Academy of Arbitrators and an honorary bencher of Lincoln's Inn in London. He has been much published in legal periodicals and has written several books dealing with land law and Canadian constitutional law. (The fifth edition of his *Canadian Constitutional Law* was published in 1975.) He was Hamlyn Lecturer in 1969 on the British Tradition in Canadian Law; a Lionel Cohen Lecturer in 1972 on the Institutional Character of the Judge; a Bentham Lecturer in 1976 on English Law in Canadian Courts

since the Abolition of Privy Council Appeals; and a Cecil Wright Memorial Lecturer in 1982, in which he recounted a personal memoir of the noted Toronto law professor. A Fellow of the Royal Society of Canada, Bora Laskin has received honorary LL.D.s from 20 universities world-wide; honorary D.C.L.s from the universities of New Brunswick, Windsor, and Western Ontario; an honorary Doctor of Philosophy from the Hebrew University of Jerusalem; and an honorary L.Hum.D. from the Hebrew Union College of Cincinnati.

Legge, Laura Louise
Q.C., B.A., R.N., LL.B.

Lawyer. b. January 27, 1923, Delhi, Ontario; née Down; m. Bruce Jarvis Legge; d. Elizabeth Meanwell, s. John, Bruce; res. Toronto.

After eight years as a bencher, Laura Legge reached a milestone in her career in 1983 when she was elected treasurer of the Law Society of Upper Canada, making her the first woman chief executive officer of the body that governs Ontario's 16,000 lawyers. She obtained a B.A. from the University of Western Ontario and trained as a nurse at Toronto General Hospital before turning to the study of law, graduating from Osgoode Hall in 1948. She has combined her legal practice, conducted in partnership with her husband, with a directorship of the Home Care Program of Metropolitan Toronto, membership on the Council of the Ontario College of Art, a vice-presidency of the Ontario Safety League, and the chairmanship of the Admissions Committee of the Law Society of Upper Canada. Her husband, Major-General Bruce Legge, is a former chief of reserves of the Canadian Armed Forces and was chairman of the Ontario Workmen's Compensation Board from 1965 to 1973.

Létourneau, Roger
Q.C., LL.L., LL.D.

Lawyer. b. October 6, 1907, Quebec City; m. Marcelle Mercier; d. Michelle, Marie; res. Quebec City.

Roger Létourneau is senior partner in Létourneau, Stein & Amyot, the largest law firm in Quebec City, employing 37 advocates. He is also a noted fund raiser in the cause of education, who has served as national chairman of the Laval University Capital Funds Campaign. He himself was educated at Laval and at Columbia University in New York City. Besides his legal activities, Létourneau has held directorships of the Bank of Montreal, the Molson Companies, Price Co., Domtar, Mattagami Lake Mines, Tele-Capital, and Consumers Glass. He was also on the Quebec Advisory Board of Royal Trust Co. He belongs to the Canadian Bar Association, the Quebec Bar Association, the Garrison Club, the Mount Royal Club, the Cercle Universitaire, and the Club de Golf de Cap Rouge.

Levine, Michael A.
Barrister & Solicitor; Goodman & Goodman; Toronto

Lewis, P.J., Q.C.
Barrister & Solicitor; Lewis & Sinott; St. John's

McAlpine, John D.
Barrister & Solicitor; McAlpine, Roberts & Hordo; Vancouver.

MacDonald, A. Webster
Barrister & Solicitor; MacDonald & Co.; Calgary

MacDonald, James C., Q.C.
Barrister & Solicitor; MacDonald & Ferrier; Toronto

McGee, Robert Bruce
Q.C., B.A., LL.B.

Lawyer. b. December 3, 1937, Toronto; m. Jean Philp; d. Mary, Wendy; res. Toronto.

A graduate of Osgoode Hall Law School in Toronto, Robert McGee prosecuted many important murder cases in his 16 years as assistant and deputy crown attorney of the City of Toronto. Now in private practice, he is active in the John Howard Society, and was a member of the Task Force on Violence Against Women. He belongs to the Advocates Society, the Medical-Legal Society, the Lawyers Club, the County of York Law Association, the Upper Canada Law Society, and the Criminal Lawyers' Association.

MacIntosh, Alexander John
Q.C., B.A., LL.B.

Lawyer, business executive. b. July 10, 1921, Stellarton, Nova Scotia; m. Katherine Elizabeth Allen; s. Donald Alexander; res. Toronto.

Alexander MacIntosh belongs to the ranks of professional directors, those men who offer advice to various boardrooms without being strongly identified with any particular company. A farmer's son who was a gold medalist at Dalhousie Law School and served in the RCNVR from 1942 to 1945 (leaving with the rank of lieutenant), he is a partner of Blake, Cassels & Graydon, Canada's largest law firm with more than 130 lawyers. But he is also deputy governor of the Hudson's Bay Company, chairman of Canadian Corporate Management Co., as well as director of the Canadian Imperial Bank of Commerce, Torstar Corporation, Fluor Canada, Honeywell, Markborough Properties, Simpsons, Lower Churchill Development Corp., George Wimpey Canada, John Labatt, and Stelco. He is a trustee of Brock University and a member of the Toronto and York clubs.

McIntyre, William Rogers
B.A., LL.B.

Judge of the Supreme Court of Canada. b. March 15, 1918, Lachine, Quebec; m. Hermione Elizabeth Reeves; d. Elizabeth Pauline, s. John Stuart; res. Ottawa.

Mr. Justice McIntyre is the current representative from British Columbia on the bench of the Supreme Court of Canada, having been appointed in 1979. He was educated at the University of Saskatchewan. After serving with the Canadian Army in Britain, Italy, and Northwest Europe during the Second World War, he was called to the Bars of both Saskatchewan and British Columbia in 1947. A distinguished career in practice was followed by his appointment to the Supreme Court of British Columbia in 1967 and to the Court of Appeal for that province in 1973. While on the bench both in British Columbia and in Ottawa, Mr. Justice McIntyre has made a notable contribution to the development and interpretation of Canadian criminal law. He is a member of the Rideau Club (Ottawa) and the Union Club (Victoria).

Maloney, Arthur

Q.C., B.A., LL.B., LL.D.

Lawyer. b. November 26, 1919, Eganville, Ontario; m. Lillian Labine; d. Mary Martha, s. Matthew Joseph; res. Toronto.

Arthur Maloney is one of Canada's most celebrated trial lawyers. He received his education at St. Michael's College of the University of Toronto and at Osgoode Hall; in addition, St. Dunstan's University awarded him a Doctor of Laws in 1961. Maloney was called to the Ontario Bar in 1943. He was elected a bencher of the Law Society of Upper Canada in 1956 and has served as chairman of the Criminal Justice Committee of the Canadian Bar Association and director of the Canadian Society for the Abolition of the Death Penalty. Maloney was first elected to the House of Commons in 1957 as Progressive Conservative member for Parkdale, a Toronto riding, and was appointed parliamentary assistant to the minister of Labour during the Diefenbaker years; he was defeated in the 1962 federal election. His career was capped by his service as the ombudsman for Ontario (1975-78). Maloney is a member of the Toronto Lawyers Club, the Cercle Universitaire (Ottawa), the Newman Club, the Albany Club (Toronto), and the Knights of Columbus.

Matas, David

B.A., M.A., B.A., B.C.L.

Lawyer. b. August 29, 1943, Winnipeg; res. Winnipeg.

David Matas studied law at Princeton and Oxford before returning to Canada in 1968 to become a law clerk to the Chief Justice of Canada. In 1971 he became special assistant to the Solicitor General of Canada, where he remained for a year before beginning his own practice and lecturing on constitutional law at McGill University. In 1980 he became a special advisor to the Canadian Delegation to the UN General Assembly, then a member of the Immigration Task Force. A believer in human rights, he is a member of Amnesty International (and acts as its legal co-ordinator), the League for Human Rights, and is also active in the War Crimes Legal Committee and the Canadian Jewish Congress.

Mendes da Costa, Derek

Q.C., LL.B., LL.M., S.J.D., LL.D.

Lawyer, academic. b. March 7, 1929, London; m. Barbara Prevost; d. Virginia Murdoch, s. Philip; res. Toronto.

Legal scholarship owes much to the brilliant contributions of Derek Mendes da Costa; however, legal academics and enlightened students are not the only beneficiaries of his work. As a member of the Ontario Law Reform Commission (most recently as chairman), he has shaped innovative developments in family and land law that have benefited the citizens of the province. He was educated at King's College (University of London), the University of Melbourne, and Harvard. He holds an LL.D. from the University of London. His teaching career began at the University of London in 1955 and continued in Australia until he moved to Ontario where he has taught at the Osgoode Hall Law School and the University of Toronto. He has combined his various university activities, which include being vice-chairman of the York University Senate, chairman of the University of Toronto Faculty Association Grievance Committee, and chairman of the Graduate Committee of the Faculty of Law, with extensive public service commitments such as being chairman of the Pilot Conciliation Project of the Ontario Provincial Court (Family Division), a member of the Canadian Institute for Advanced Legal Studies, and chairman of the attorney-general's committee on the Representation of Children. His lengthy list of publications represents essential reading for the law student, teacher, and legal practitioner.

Mifflin, Arthur S.

Chief Justice of Newfoundland; St. John's

Mullin, John A., Q.C.

Barrister & Solicitor; Fraser & Beatty; Toronto

Nemetz, Nathaniel Theodore

B.A., LL.D.

Judge. b. September 8, 1913, Winnipeg; m. Bel Newman; s. Peter; res. Vancouver.

Nathan Nemetz practised law from 1937 until 1963, when he was appointed to the Supreme Court of British Columbia. During his distinguished career in practice, he acted as special counsel to the B.C. Public Utilities Commission at the Natural Gas Inquiry, counsel to the province at the Commission on Expropriation, and special advisor in Labour Relations to the municipalities of Vancouver, Burnaby, and New Westminister. He served as a member of the Senate and Board of Governors of the University of British Columbia from 1957 to 1968; he served as chancellor from 1972 to 1975. In addition, he has been chairman of the Board of School Trustees (University District) and past president of the Vancouver Institute. In 1968 he was elevated to the Court of Appeal and in 1973 became chief justice of the B.C. Supreme Court. In 1979 he assumed his current position as chief justice of the Court of Appeal. He is the recipient of honorary degrees from UBC, Notre Dame University of Nelson, and the University of Victoria. Chief Justice Nemetz enjoys playing billiards. He is a past president of the Vancouver University Club and is a member of the Vancouver Club.

Oliver, Herbert Arnold Dimitri

Q.C., K.St.J.

Lawyer. b. June 11, 1921, England; m. Jean Hilda King; s. David, Mark, d. Alexandra; res. Vancouver.

One of British Columbia's foremost trial lawyers, H.A.D. Oliver is senior partner of the Vancouver law firm of Oliver, Waldock. Oliver was educated in England at the London School of Economics and London's School of Law of the Law Society. During the Second World War, he was with the Royal Norfolk Regiment of the British Army and in 1945-46 he served on the Control Commission for Germany. In addition to practising law, Oliver has been appointed vice-chairman of the Forensic Psychiatric Services Commission of British Columbia and consul-general of Liberia. His honours include the Croix de Guerre (France), Knight Grand Cross of the Order of African Redemption (Liberia), Officer of the Federal Order of Merit (West Germany), and Knight of Grace of the Order of St. John of Jerusalem (Denmark). He is a Fellow of the International Academy of Trial Lawyers, a former governor (1973-82) of the Association of Trial Lawyers of America, a past president of the Alliance Française for the Province of British Columbia, past vice-president of the Vancouver Art Gallery Association, former secretary general of the Consular Corps in British Columbia, and a current member of many bodies including the Trial Lawyers Association of B.C., the National Academy of Defense Lawyers (U.S.A.), and the Consular Law Society (New York). His club memberships include the Vancouver, the Royal Vancouver Yacht, the Union (Victoria), and the East India (London). He is an editor of *Western Weekly Reports*, the major law-reporting service for lawyers in Western Canada.

Porter, Julian, Q.C.

Barrister & Solicitor; Porter & Posluns; Toronto

Remillard, G.

Department of Law, Université Laval, Quebec

Richard, Guy André

Chief Justice of the Court of Queen's Bench, Fredericton

Ritchie, Roland Almon

Q.C., D.C.L., LL.D.

Judge of the Supreme Court of Canada. b. June 19, 1910, Halifax; m. Mary Wylde; d. Elizabeth; res. Ottawa.

Mr. Justice Ritchie was one of Nova Scotia's leading legal practitioners (1934-40 and 1945-59) prior to his elevation to the Supreme Court of Canada. He received his education at University of King's College in Halifax and Oxford and is an honorary Fellow of Pembroke College at Oxford. During the Second World War, he served with the Canadian Army Artillery. He lectured in law at Dalhousie University (1958-59), was vice-president of the Nova Scotia Barristers' Society (1958-59) and also chancellor of the University of King's College. Mr. Justice Ritchie is a director of the International Grenfell Association and a member of the Royal Nova Scotia Yacht Squadron, the Halifax Club, the Rideau Club, and the Royal Ottawa Golf and Country Club. His brother,

TOP: *Laura Legge in the Osgoode Hall Library, Toronto.* LEFT: *H. Heward Stikeman in his Cessna Skymaster above the Toronto Islands.* ABOVE: *Richard Rohmer.*

A.L.L.J.R.

Charles S.A. Ritchie, served as Canadian ambassador to the United States and high commissioner to Britain.

Robertson, George B., Q.C.

Barrister & Solicitor; McInnes, Cooper & Robertson; Halifax

Robinette, John Josiah

C.C., Q.C., B.A., D.C.L., LL.D.

Lawyer. b. November 20, 1906, Toronto; m. Lois Walker; d. Joan, Wendy, Dale; res. Toronto.

J.J. Robinette is probably the most distinguished lawyer in Canada. His father Thomas C. Robinette was a leading counsel in Toronto in the early years of this century. J.J. Robinette received his education at the University of Toronto and Osgoode Hall and has been admitted to three provincial Bars—Ontario (1929), Manitoba (1961), and Nova Scotia (1963). He has been a bencher since 1946 of the Law Society of Upper Canada, the governing body of Ontario lawyers, and served as treasurer (or head), of the Society from 1958 to 1962. He gained public prominence as defence counsel for Evelyn Dick, who was tried and acquitted of murder in the most sensational Canadian murder case of the 1940s. He has acted in many other celebrated matters, both civil and criminal, including combines investigations in which he represented business entities controlled by E.P. Taylor and K.C. Irving. Special-interest groups—such as those opposing the Spadina Expressway in Toronto and the international airport at Pickering, Ontario—have retained Robinette as counsel, as has the federal government in several important constitutional cases, including the 1981 Reference to the Supreme Court of Canada concerning the Constitutional Resolution. He is a fellow of the American College of Trial Lawyers, and a member of the Canadian Bar Association and The Advocates Society (Toronto). Robinette is the recipient of honorary degrees from the University of Toronto, the University of Western Ontario, and Queen's University. He was created a Companion of the Order of Canada in 1973.

Rohmer, Richard

C.M.M., D.F.C., C.D., Q.C., B.A., LL.D., C.St.J.

Lawyer, novelist. b. January 24, 1924, Hamilton; m. Mary Whiteside; d. Catherine, Ann; res. Toronto.

A best-selling novelist, Richard Rohmer has had a distinguished career in the Armed Forces and in the field of law. He served with the RCAF from 1942 to 1945 as a fighter pilot and took part in the Normandy invasion. In 1950-53 he flew Vampire jet fighters with the RCAF Reserve; Rohmer retired from the Reserves in 1981 as a major-general. Among his military decorations are the Distinguished Flying Cross and Commander of the Order of Military Merit. He received his law degree from the University of Windsor (of which he is now chancellor) and served as a member of Council of the then Municipality of North York from 1957 to 1958. From 1970 to 1972 he was chairman of the Royal Commission on Book Publishing, then acted as counsel to the Royal Commission on Metropolitan Toronto (1975 to 1977). He is the creator of the Mid-Canada Development Corridor concept, which foresaw the development of Canada taking place in a belt of land

extending across the country immediately north of the major cities. He is the founder of the Thompson House, a home from the aged in Don Mills, and is chairman of the Don Mills Senior Citizens Foundation. He is a member of the Royal Canadian Military Institute, the Canadian Institute of Strategic Studies, and the Canadian Club in Toronto. He is a collector of the paintings of R. Gemmell Hutchison of the Royal Scottish Academy and now practises law with Macaulay, Lipson & Joseph.

Romanow, Roy John

Q.C., B.A., LL.B.

Lawyer. b. 1938, Saskatoon; m. Eleanore Boykawich; res. Saskatoon.

Roy Romanow is a lawyer who has achieved national stature in politics. During the period leading up to the patriation of Canada's Constitution in 1982, while Romanow was a senior minister in Saskatchewan, he and Jean Chrétien, his federal counterpart, played a role of inestimable importance in steering the contentious issues arising out of patriation through the federal-provincial bargaining process. Romanow was educated at the University of Saskatchewan and was first elected to the Saskatchewan Legislative Assembly in 1967 for Riverside. He was a member of the New Democratic Party government from 1971 to 1982, serving at different times as provincial secretary, deputy premier, attorney general, minister of Intergovernmental Affairs, and minister-in-charge of the Potash Corporation. He was defeated in the 1982 ouster of the Blakeney government. In addition to his achievements on the Constitution, Romanow was responsible for the shaping of Saskatchewan's recent policies in the field of natural resources and for farsighted reform of many of the province's legal institutions. He is a member of the Canadian Bar Association, International Commission of Jurists, Canada West Foundation, Public Legal Education Association, Mendel Art Galley (Saskatoon), SPCA (Saskatoon), Saskatoon Heritage Society, and Saskatoon Riverside Tennis and Badminton Club. He is also a member of the Canadian Medical Association Task Force on Allocation of Health Service. He teaches at the College of Law at the University of Saskatchewan.

Sheppard, Claude-Armand, B.A., B.C.L.

Barrister & Solicitor; Robinson, Cutler; Montreal

Shoctor, Joseph H.

C.M., Q.C., B.A., LL.B., LL.D.

Lawyer, theatre promoter. b. Edmonton; m. Kayla Wine; s. Ian, Marshall, d. Naomi Gail; res. Edmonton.

The driving force behind Edmonton's nationally acclaimed Citadel Theatre, Joseph Shoctor has successfully combined a strong interest in the arts with a busy law career. He has produced or co-produced a number of Broadway and off-Broadway shows, and was heavily involved in the 1969 national tour of *Hamlet*. He was the originator of *Downtown Edmonton*, the city's first entertainment paper, and served as chairman of the New Citadel Theatre's Campaign from 1975 to 1977. A director of numerous Alberta companies in the development and service industries, he was also one of the founders and the first secretary-manager of the Edmonton Eskimos of the Canadian Foot-

ball League. He has been an executive of many charitable organizations, including the Edmonton Jewish Community Council and the Federal Zionist Organization, and has received awards such as the B'nai B'rith Citizen of the Year (1966), the Province of Alberta's Achievement Award in Recognition of Outstanding Service in Theatre Arts, and the Prime Minister's Medal of the State of Israel (1978). He is a senior partner in the firm of Shoctor, Hill, Mousseau & Starkman.

Shumiatcher, Morris Cyril

O.C., Q.C., B.A., LL.B., LL.M., S.J.D.

Lawyer, writer. b. September 20, 1917, Calgary; m. Jacqueline Fanchette Clay; res. Regina.

Morris (Shumi) Shumiatcher is a dedicated believer in physical fitness, who has run four miles a day since 1960, "when it was generally regarded as an aberration." Founder of the Regina Polar Bear Club, he has shared its annual New Year's Day run with the Honorary Polar Bear Paw, Roland Michener, who, when he was Governor General and visiting Regina, would run with Shumiatcher and a party including "his aide and a few of his YMCA friends," reports Shumi, "all of whom would repair to my house where my wife would serve an aperitif of hot rum and a hearty breakfast." Shumiatcher was educated at Mount Royal College, Calgary; the University of Alberta, where he received his B.A. and LL.B.; and the University of Toronto, where he earned his LL.M. and S.J.D. He was awarded the Japan Times Travelling Scholarship to Japan, the Rowell Fellowship in Law, and the Rt. Hon. R.B. Bennett Award. Since 1949 he has been engaged in private practice. He has also held the positions of counsel to the Cabinet of Saskatchewan, assistant to the Premier, counsel to the Labour Relations Board; counsel to and a member of the Economic Advisory and Planning Board. At present he is senior partner in the firm Shumiatcher-Fox, honorary consul general of Japan, and dean of the Consular Corps of Saskatchewan. He is a member of the law societies of Alberta, British Columbia, Saskatchewan, Manitoba, and the Northwest Territories; several law-related associations; and the Canadian Club. He is a director of the Saskatchewan Centre for the Arts, and director and past president of the Regina Symphony Orchestra, the Norman Mackenzie Art Gallery, and the Chamber Music Society. In his capacity as a jurist, Mr. Shumiatcher secured the passage of Canada's first Bill of Rights (Saskatchewan). He has also undertaken civil rights cases in the courts, both in the Supreme Court of Canada and in the Judicial Committee of the Privy Council in London, when it was Canada's court of last resort. He has written and lectured on legal and philosophical subjects, and recently established the Morris Shumiatcher lectures on Law and Literature at the University of Saskatchewan. He is the author of many articles and *Man of Law: a Model; Welfare: Hidden Backlash*, and *Assault on Freedom*.

Simons, Sidney B.

Barrister & Solicitor; Vancouver

Southin, Mary F., Q.C.

Barrister & Solicitor; Swinton & Co.; Vancouver

Stikeman, Harry Heward

Q.C., B.A., B.C.L., D.S.

Lawyer. b. July 8, 1913, Montreal; m. Mary Gertrude Wilson; d. Roben Jane; m. Virginia Eloise Guy; d. Virginia, Ann, Elizabeth, Jane; s. Harry; res. Montreal and Shefford Mountain, Quebec.

H. Heward Stikeman with R. Fraser Elliott founded and created the first international Canadian law firm, with offices in Montreal, Toronto, Ottawa, Hong Kong, London, and one soon to open in New York City. He is also the author of many definitive Canadian legal texts and services on taxation, including *The Canada Tax Service* and *Canada Tax Cases*; he is also general editor for Richard DeBoo Ltd. McGill University recently honoured him with a scholarship in his name for students showing excellence in taxation studies. He studied at McGill and at the Université de Dijon in France. Since 1953 he has been a senior partner in Stikeman, Elliott, Tamaki, Mercier & Robb of Montreal and Hong Kong and of Stikeman, Elliott, Robarts & Bowman of Toronto, Ottawa, and London. He has also served as assistant deputy minister of National Revenue in Ottawa. He is a director of the Mercantile Bank of Canada, AMCA International Ltd., CAE Industries Ltd., and Federal Commerce and Navigation Ltd. He is a trustee of the International Bureau of Fiscal Documentation at The Hague, and past governor of the Canadian Tax Foundation. His recreations include sailing his C&C sloop and flying his twin-engine Cessna. He collects modern sculpture and works of the painters of the Fauve School. He lives in one of the first United Empire Loyalist houses in Quebec's Eastern Townships. His clubs include the Lyford Cay in Nassau, the Mount Royal, the Rideau in Ottawa, and the Toronto.

Tarnopolsky, Walter S., Q.C.

Professor, Faculty of Law, University of Ottawa; Ottawa

Teed, Eric Lawrence

Kt. C.D., Q.C., B.Sc., B.C.L., B.A.

Lawyer. b. May 19, 1926, Saint John; m. Lois A. Smith; s. Robert, Peter, Christopher, Terrence, David; res. Saint John.

Eric Teed is a senior partner in the law firm of Teed, Teed and McPhee and honorary consul of Denmark. From 1970 to 1974 he was a member of the Legislative Assembly of New Brunswick and Master of the Supreme Court, and from 1960 to 1961 he was mayor of Saint John. He sits on the University of New Brunswick Board of Governors and is a director of the New Brunswick Historical Society and the Canadian Civil Liberties Association. He has served in the New Brunswick Scottish Regiment and the Royal New Brunswick Regiment. Teed considers that his greatest achievements have been in "public service and law reform with an emphasis on civil liberties and the rights of the individual." He belongs to the Union Club and several law-related associations.

Tellier, Claude, Q.C.

Barrister & Solicitor; Desjardins, Ducharme, Desjardins & Bourque; Montreal

Thurlow, Arthur Louis

Chief Justice, The Federal Court of Canada; Ottawa

Tory, James M.

Barrister & Solicitor; Tory, Tory, DesLauriers & Binnington; Toronto

Turner, John N., Q.C.

Barrister & Solicitor; McMillan, Binch; Toronto

Tweedy, G. Gordon

Q.C., B.A., B.C.L.

Lawyer. b. June 4, 1936, Charlottetown; m. Caroll Ann Mackenzie; s. David, John; res. Charlottetown.

A founding member of a leading Charlottetown law firm, G. Gordon Tweedy is proud to describe himself as a barrister and solicitor in general practice. Since earning a B.C.L. from the University of New Brunswick in 1963, he has practised law in partnership in Charlottetown. He holds directorships in Canadian National Trust and Loan, Industrial Trust, Interprovincial Trust, and Confederation Trust. He is past president of both the P.E.I. branch of the Canadian Bar Association and the Law Society of Prince Edward Island. He is an active Rotarian.

Verchere, Bruce

Barrister & Solicitor; Verchere, Noel & Eddy; Montreal

Wakim, A. Samuel, Q.C.

Barrister & Solicitor; Toronto

Weiler, Paul Cronin

B.A., M.A., LL.B., LL.M.

Law professor. b. January 28, 1939, Port Arthur, Ontario; divorced; d. Virginia, Kathryn, s. John, Charles; res. Cambridge, Massachusetts.

Paul C. Weiler is the author of the first book-length study of the Supreme Court of Canada, *In the Last Resort: A critical study of the Supreme Court of Canada*. Currently professor of Labour Law at Harvard Law School, he received his B.A. and M.A. from the University of Toronto, his LL.B. from Osgoode Hall, and his LL.M. from Harvard University. He began his teaching career as professor of Law at Osgoode Hall at York University in 1965. From 1974 until 1978 he was chairman of the British Columbia Labour Relations Board, where he made valuable contributions to the development of labour legislation. In 1978 became Mackenzie King Professor of Canadian Studies at Harvard. He was appointed to his present position in 1981. He is also a member of the Public Review Board of the United Auto Workers and the National Academy of Arbitrators in the United States and has acted as counsel to the government of Ontario in the reform of the Workers' Compensation Act. He is also credited with inspiring interest, within the Harvard scholarly community, in the development of Canadian legal policy, especially in the areas of constitutional federalism and employment.

Wells, Robert, Q.C.

Barrister & Solicitor; Wells, O'Dea; St. John's

Wilson, Bertha

Q.C., B.A., LL.B.

Judge of the Supreme Court of Canada. b. September 18, 1923, Kirkcaldy, Scotland; m. John Wilson; res. Ottawa.

Madam Justice Wilson is the first female appointee to Canada's Supreme Court. She was also the first woman to sit on the highest court of a province, having been appointed to the Ontario Court of Appeal in 1975. She arrived in Canada in 1949 from Scotland with her husband, a Presbyterian minister. She attended Dalhousie Law School in Halifax during the time her husband was serving as a chaplain in the Royal Canadian Navy and was admitted to the Nova Scotia Bar in 1958. She joined the prestigious Toronto law firm of Osler, Hoskin and Harcourt and became that firm's first female partner. On the Bench, Madam Justice Wilson has combined a sharp, probing intelligence with a simple, genuine courtesy that has earned her a rare degree of affection among practising lawyers. She has been a member of the Board of Trustees of the Clarke Institute of Psychiatry in Toronto, chairman of the United Church of Canada's committee to review the status of women, a trustee of the Toronto School of Theology, and chairman of the Rhodes Scholarship Committee for Ontario.

SCIENCE & MEDICINE

Banks, Peter John

M.D., D.Sc., F.R.C.P., F.R.C.P.(C)., F.R.C.P.I., F.A.C.P.

Physician. b. June 12, 1922, England; m. Mary Way; s. Christopher, Nicholas, d. Anthea; res. Victoria.

Peter Banks is a respected medical internist but is more widely known for his substantial contributions to organized medicine. He is a past president of the British Columbia Medical Association and was president of the Canadian Medical Association *and* the British Medical Association at the same time. He has also served on various medical advisory boards in British Columbia and was instrumental in negotiating a medicare plan with the provincial government. He was a member of the first Canadian medical group to visit China (in 1973) after the 1949 revolution. Dr. Banks received his education at St. Bartholomew's Hospital at the University of London and served in the Royal Air Force during the Second World War.

Bates, David Vincent

M.D., F.R.C.P., F.R.C.P.(C), F.A.C.P., F.R.S.

Physician, university professor. b. May 20, 1922, West Malling, Kent, England; m. Gwendolyn Margaret Sutton; s. Andrew Vincent, d. Anne Elizabeth, Joanna Margaret; res. Vancouver.

David Bates has gained a national and international reputation for his work in internal medicine, especially in thoracic and respiratory diseases. He has published 180 scientific papers on lung function and disease; his "Citizen's Guide to Air Pollution" received a special citation from the Canadian Meteorological Society. From 1973 to 1979 he served on the Science Council of Canada and acted as chairman of a Royal Commission on uranium mining. He received the Cooper Medal from the American Academy of Allergy and the Queen's Jubilee Decoration. The son of an English doctor, Bates was educated at Pembroke College in Cambridge and trained at St. Bartholomew's Hospital. After serving with the Royal Army Medical Corps in India, Japan, and Malaya during and after the Second World War, he held various positions at McGill University in Montreal. He was invited to teach at Harvard, Melbourne, Dalhousie, and Nancy, France. From 1972 to 1977 he was dean of the Faculty of Medicine at the University of British Columbia, where he now teaches medicine and physiology at the Acute Care Hospital. Bates enjoys spending summers at the family cottage on Sechelt Peninsula and is an avid collector of antique maps of his birthplace, Kent.

Bean, Irwin W., M.D.

Family physician; Head, Family Practice Teaching Unit, Wellesley Hospital, Toronto.

Bigelow, W.G., M.D.

Heart surgeon; Toronto

Bocking, Douglas, M.D.

Clinician; Vice-President, Health Science, University of Western Ontario, London

Bois, Pierre, M.D.

Internist; President, Medical Research Council, Outremont

Bourns, Arthur Newcombe

O.C., B.Sc., Ph.D., D.Sc., LL.D., F.C.I.C., F.R.S.C.

Scientific and educational consultant. b. December 8, 1919, Petitcodiac, New Brunswick; m. Marion Harriett Blakney; s. Robert Evans, Brian Hugh, d. Barbara Ellen, Susan Kathleen; res. Brantford, Ontario.

Now a consultant, Arthur Bourns has had a long career with McMaster University which began with his position as a professor of chemistry in 1947. Over the next three decades he helped to develop McMaster from a small liberal-arts college to a major graduate-study and research centre recognized around the world; he has also contributed to the development and support of university research in Canada. While continuing to teach chemistry, he held administrative positions, which culminated in his presidency and vice-chancellorship from 1972 to 1980. He was elected a Fellow of the Chemical Institute of Canada (1954) and of the Royal Society of Canada (1964) and is a director of the Natural Sciences and Engineering Research Council and the Canadian Institute for Advanced Research. In 1982 he was named an Officer of the Order of Canada.

Bown, Herbert G.

B.Sc., M.Sc.

Business executive. b. February 22, 1943, Badger's Quay, Nova Scotia; divorced; s. Stephen, Michael, David; res. Ottawa.

The inventor and developer of Telidon, Herbert Bown studied at Nova Scotia Technical College in Halifax and at the Memorial University of Newfoundland. After completing his degrees in electrical engineering, he worked with the Department of Communications, where he became director-general of information technology. He is now a director and vice-president of marketing and sales for Norpak Corp. in Kanata, Ontario. He was also involved with the early research and development of Bliss-symbols, a means of communication for severely handicapped people, and with the initial development of captioning equipment for CCDA. He owns a 20-year-old mahogany pleasure boat and collects paintings.

Cameron, Douglas George

O.C., M.C., B.Sc., B.Sc., M.D.C.M., F.R.C.P. (London), M.A.C.P., F.R.C.P. (Glasgow [Hon.]), F.R.A.C.P. (Hon.).

Physician. b. March 11, 1917, Folkestone, England; m. Jeanne Sutherland Thompson; s. George, Bruce, d. Jane, Heather, Nancy, Marian; res. Town of Mount Royal, Quebec.

Douglas Cameron was raised and educated in Swift Current, Saskatchewan, and followed the family tradition of enrolling at McGill University, whence his father, a dental surgeon, and his grandfather had graduated. After serving with the RCAMC during the Second World War and earning the Military Cross, he took advantage of a Rhodes scholarship awarded to him in 1940 and travelled to Oxford with his wife, Jeanne. Having earned his second B.Sc., he returned to Canada in 1948 to the Montreal General Hospital, where he had interned, and began a long relationship with the hospital which continues to this day. During his career he has written or co-authored more than 70 scientific papers on hematology and gastroenterology and acted as president of numerous medical societies, including the Royal College of Physicians and Surgeons of Canada; as well, he became Physician-in-Chief at Montreal General and the chairman of McGill's Department of Medicine.

Church, Robert Bertram

B.Sc., M.Sc., Ph.D., Dip. of Transplant

Professor, rancher. b. May 7, 1937, Calgary; m. Joyce Mary-Anne Brown; s. Jeffrey Robert, d. Eileen Alexa; res. Airdrie, Alberta.

A distinguished speaker and author of more than 120 scholarly works, Robert Church is head of the Department of Medical Biochemistry and the Associate Dean of Research of the Faculty of Medicine at the University of Calgary. He is also the owner of Lochen Luing Ranches and president of a livestock consulting firm, as well as being a director of various agricultural and research associations and a member of many scientific committees, such as the Natural Sciences and Engineering Research Council Executive Committee. He studied at the universities of Alberta, Edinburgh, and Uppsala, and was a research associate at the University of Washington before returning to the University of Calgary to teach. He has

assisted in the creation of a world-class medical centre at the university and helped establish the first and most successful embryo transfer company in the world. An avid rodeo fan, he is a director of the Calgary Exhibition and Stampede; he is also a collector of Western art.

Cochrane, William A.

M.D., F.R.C.P.(C), F.A.C.P., LL.D.

Physician, business executive. b. March 18, 1926, Toronto; m. Phyllis Winifred Potts; res. Toronto.

In addition to his busy practice, Dr. Cochrane was instrumental in the planning and development of the I.W. Killam Hospital for Children in Halifax, the Health Science Centre and Medical Faculty at the University of Calgary, and the Health Centre at the Morley Indian Reserve in Alberta. He has also served as president of the Canadian Society for Clinical Investigation and the Canadian Pediatric Society. He received his M.D. at the University of Toronto in 1949 and has held various teaching and administrative positions at Dalhousie University and the University of Calgary. In 1973 he was Alberta's Deputy Minister of Health, and since 1978 he has been chairman and chief executive officer of Connaught Laboratories. In addition to other awards, he has been named Medicine Chief of the Stoney Indian Band of Morley, Alberta.

Copp, Harold, M.D.

Physiologist, endocrinologist; Vancouver

Cumming, W.A.

Executive Vice-President, National Research Council, Montreal

David, Paul B.

O.C., B.A., M.D.

Medical director. b. December 25, 1919, Montreal; m. Yvette Lemire; m. Lili Maillard (deceased); s. Pierre, Charles, d. Françoise, Thérèse, Anne-Marie, Hélène; res. Montreal.

Founder and medical director of the Montreal Heart Institute since 1954, Dr. David has been awarded numerous honours for his work in cardiology. He has received the Archambault Medal of the French Canadian Association of the Advancement of Science and the Annual Awards of the University of Montreal Alumni Association, the Quebec Hospital Association, and the Canadian Heart Association, and was also named Great Montrealer of the Year 1981 and Officer of the Order of Canada. The University of Lyon in France, awarded him an honorary degree in 1970. The son of a longtime Liberal politician, Senator Athanase David, Paul studied for his B.A. at the University of Paris, then graduated *summa cum laude* from the University of Montreal. In addition to his position of medical director of the Montreal Heart Institute, Dr. David has also been president of the Montreal Cardiovascular Society, the Canadian Cardiovascular Society, the Interamerican Society of Cardiology, the Association of French-Language Physicians of Canada, and the Health Forum of Quebec Christians, the latter post he still holds. He has served as vice-president of the International Cardiology Foundation and as Regional Director of the Canadian College of Health Service Executives, and has been an associate professor of medicine at the University of Montreal since 1957.

Dickson, Robert Clark

O.C., O.B.E., C.D., Q.H.P., M.D., LL.D., M.A.C.P., F.R.C.P., F.R.C.P.(C)

Physician. b. September 24, 1908, St. Marys, Ontario; m. Constance Fraser; s. William, d. Shelagh, Jane; res. Vancouver.

Acknowledged as one of Canada's outstanding educators in medicine, Dr. Dickson received his degree at the University of Toronto before heading off to join the Royal Canadian Army Medical Corps in 1939. Rising from the rank of captain to lieutenant-colonel, he served in the United Kingdom, North Africa, and Italy and was made an O.B.E. for his efforts. On his return to Toronto he became an associate professor of medicine at the University of Toronto, then physician-in-chief at the Wellesley Hospital before moving to Halifax, where he taught at Dalhousie University for many years and where he now holds the title of professor emeritus. During his years at Dalhousie he developed the school's Department of Medicine. His involvement with the Royal College of Physicians and Surgeons of Canada, which included a period as its president, resulted in the establishment of a single standard of training. In 1980 the Robert Clark Dickson Wing of Halifax's Victoria General Hospital was opened as an acknowledgment of his efforts in medical education in Canada. He is the son of William Dickson, a federal deputy minister of labour, and has served as a director of the Grenfell Labrador Medical Mission and the Canadian Corps of Commissionaires, along with his involvement with the Victorian Order of Nurses.

Drake, Charles, M.D.

Neurosurgeon; Professor and Chairman, Dept. of Surgery, University of Western Ontario, London

Evans, John Robert

C.C., M.D., D.Phil., LL.D., F.R.C.P.(C), F.A.C.P., F.R.C.P.

Physician, educator. b. October 1, 1929, Toronto; m. Gay Glassco; four sons, two daughters; res. Toronto.

John Evans's later career as president of the University of Toronto (1972-78) and his unsuccessful foray into politics as Liberal candidate in the Rosedale by-election in 1978 have somewhat overshadowed his distinguished career as a doctor and medical educator. He received his M.D. at the University of Toronto and interned at Radcliffe Infirmary of Oxford University on a Rhodes scholarship. He held positions in various Toronto hospitals and was appointed the first dean of Medicine at McMaster University (1965-72). Until 1982 he was a health advisor at the World Bank in Washington; he is now chairman and chief executive officer of Allelix Inc., a joint venture of John Labatt Ltd., Canada Development Corp., and the Ontario government to pursue research into the commercial possibilities of biotechnology. His directorships include Dofasco and Crown Life; he is also a trustee of the Rockefeller Foundation.

Fallis, Fred. B., M.D.

Past President, College of Family Physicians of Canada; Associate Dean of Medicine, University of Toronto

Feeley, James

Director General, Informatics Applications Management, Communications Research Centre, Ottawa

Feindel, Wm. H. M.D.

Neurosurgeon; Director, Montreal Neurological Institute and Hospital

Fortier, Claude

C.C., B.A., M.A., M.D., Ph.D., LL.D., D.U., F.R.C.P.(C), F.R.S.C.

Medical scientist. b. June 11, 1921, Montreal; m. Eliso Gouin, d. Anne, Michèle, Nicole, Nathalie; res. Ste-Foy, Quebec.

Claude Fortier has had a long and distinguished academic and research career and has received recognition all over the world. After studying at the University of Montreal, where he received his M.D. (*summa cum laude*) and Ph.D., he became a Research Fellow for the National Research Council and the American Heart Association, among others, until 1955. He then taught physiology and was director of the Neuroendocrinology Laboratory of Baylor University's College of Medicine in Houston, Texas, for five years. Since that time he has been involved with Laval University in many capacities: Director of the Endocrine Laboratory, Professor of Experimental Physiology, and Chairman of the Department of Physiology of the School of Medicine, and consulting physician of the university's Centre Hospitalier. He has held the position of chairman or vice-chairman with the Science Council of Canada (and its Task Force of Research in Canada, 1975-1978), the Canadian Federation of Biological Societies, and the Medical Research Council of Canada and he has served as president of the Royal Society of Canada. He is a member of many distinguished medical and research societies, and has been a director of organizations such as the Medical Advisory Board and the Muscular Dystrophy Association of Canada. Named a Companion of the Order of Canada in 1970, he has received a great number of awards for his work, which includes over 200 scientific publications. A photography buff, he also collects Precolumbian ceramics, early Egyptian sculpture, and old Japanese prints.

Genest, Jacques

C.C., B.A., M.D., LL.D., D.Sc., M.A.C.P., F.R.C.P.(C), F.R.S.C.

Clinical investigator. b. May 29, 1919, Montreal; m. Estelle Deschamps, s. Paul, Jacques Jr., d. Suzanne, Marie, Hélène; res. Montreal.

A leading authority on hypertension, Dr. Genest has received many awards for his research and for his contribution to medicine in Canada. He established the Clinical Research Institute of Montreal (of which he is scientific director); the Nephrology-Hypertension Service of the University of Montreal, one of the largest and most active research and clinical groups in hypertension; and the first bioethic centre in Canada within a biomedical research institute. He attended Collège Jean de Brébeuf and studied at the University of Montreal Medical School, while also taking summer courses at Harvard. He then worked as a research assistant at Johns Hopkins Hospital and the Rockefeller Institute for Medical Research.

Since 1952 he has headed the Clinical Research Institute of Montreal. Dr. Genest is the president of the Fondation Lionel Groulx, which studies the French history of North America, and is the editor of *Hypertension*, a textbook distributed internationally. He has eight honorary degrees.

Gingras, Bernard A., M.D.

Chemist; National Research Council, Ottawa

Gingras, Gustave, C.C., M.D.

Physician; Founder, The Rehabilitation Institute, Montreal; Past President, Canadian Medical Association, Charlottetown

Gold, Phil

O.C., B.Sc., M.Sc., M.D., Ph.D., F.R.C.P.(C), F.R.S.C, F.A.C.P.

Physician. b. September 17, 1936, Montreal; m. Evelyn Katz; s. Ian Jeffrey, Joel Todd, d. Joselyn Sue; res. Montreal.

Dr. Gold is physician-in-chief and professor of Medicine at Montreal General Hospital and McGill University. He studied at McGill and received numerous scholarships for his scholastic achievements, including the First Place High Aggregate Standing in Final Year. He has made significant contributions in cancer research — Gold and Samuel Freedman discovered the carcinoembryonic antigen in 1965 — for which he has received many awards and medals, and is the first recipient of the Terry Fox Medal. He is the author and co-author of dozens of books and articles dealing with cancer and is a member of scientific and research support organizations across North America.

Goldbloom, Victor Charles

B.Sc., M.D., LL.D.

Physician. b. July 31, 1923, Montreal; m. Sheila Barshay; s. Michael, Jonathan, d. Susan Restler; res. Westmount, Quebec.

Victor Goldbloom was educated at Selwyn House and Lower Canada College in Montreal and at McGill University. He received his postgraduate training in pediatrics at Montreal Children's Hospital and at the Babies' Hospital in Columbia-Presbyterian Medical Center in New York City. During the Second World War he served with the Royal Canadian Army Medical Corps. From 1950 to 1966 he was a practising pediatrician and served as governor and vice-president of the Quebec College of Physicians and Surgeons. He then was elected as a Liberal member of the National Assembly of Quebec, where he remained until 1979. He was appointed Minister of the Environment in 1970 (an office he held until 1976), Minister of Municipal Affairs (1973 to 1976), and Minister Responsible for the Olympic Installations Board (1975 to 1976). His greatest personal achievement was the passage of Quebec's Environment Quality Act and the foundation of Quebec's Environment Protection Services. He was one of Canada's six delegates to the United Nations "Habitat" Conference on Human Settlements. He is now the president and chief executive officer of the Canadian Council of Christians and Jews and president of the International Council of Christians and Jews.

Gutelius, John R., M.D.

Surgeon; Professor and Chairman, Department of Surgery, Queen's University

Hallenberg, Charles H., M.D.

Clinician; Professor of Medicine, University of Toronto

Herzberg, Gerhard

C.C., Dr.Ing., D.Sc., LL.D., F.R.S.C., F.R.S.

Physicist. b. December 25, 1904, Hamburg, Germany; m. Monika Elisabeth Tenthoff; m. Luise (deceased); s. Paul Albin, d. Agnes Margaret; res. Ottawa.

A Nobel Prize winner in chemistry "for his contributions to the knowledge of electronic structure and geometry of molecules, particularly free radicals," Dr. Herzberg received his training at the Darmstadt Institute of Technology and carried out post-doctorate work at the University of Göttingen and Bristol University. From 1930 to 1935 he lectured at Darmstadt, then came to Canada to be a research professor of physics at the University of Saskatchewan until 1945. After a three-year stint at the Yerkes Observatory of the University of Chicago, he began working for the National Research Council of Canada, culminating in his position as Distinguished Research Scientist of the Herzberg Institute of Astrophysics. The author of over 200 papers in scientific journals and six books which have been translated into Russian, Italian, Japanese, German, and Yugoslavian. He has also received over 30 honorary degrees from universities around the world, including Oxford and Cambridge, as well as other awards and honorary memberships in scientific organizations world-wide.

Jones, Robert Orville

O.C., B.Sc., M.D., F.A.P.A., F.R.C.P.(C), D.Eng., F.A.C.P., F.R.C. (Psych.)

Psychiatrist. b. March 31, 1914, Digby, Nova Scotia; m. Mary Eleanor Allen; s. David Robert, d. Louisa Ethelwyn Jones-Dupont; res. Halifax.

Robert Jones has been a leader in the development of psychiatric education at the Dalhousie Medical School and the Maritime School of Social Work in the teaching of theologians, nurses, engineers, and lawyers in the Atlantic provinces. Until the late 1970s, nearly all of the psychiatric personnel in the Maritimes were former students of Dr. Jones; among them, five have been presidents of the Canadian Psychiatric Association. His efforts to join the psychiatric and general-medicine fields proved successful with his appointment to the presidency of the Canadian Medical Association, the first psychiatrist to be so honoured. He studied at Dalhousie and received a Certificate in Psychiatry from Maudsley Hospital in London in 1939. Under a Rockefeller Fellowship he worked at the Henry Phipps Psychiatric Clinic at Johns Hopkins Hospital in Baltimore, then returned to teach at Dalhousie. A life or honorary member of several psychiatric associations, he was also a member of the Canadian Representative Committee of the World Psychiatric Association. He has received a number of awards, including the C.M.A.'s Medal of Service, the Centennial Medal, and the Queen's Jubilee Medal.

Keon, Wilbert Joseph

B.Sc., M.Sc., M.D., F.R.C.S.(C), F.A.C.S.

Surgeon. b. May 17, 1935, Sheenboro, Quebec; m. Anne Jennings; s. Ryan, Neil, d. Claudia; res. Ottawa.

One of Canada's best-known cardiovascular surgeons, Dr Keon studied at Carleton, Ottawa, McGill, Toronto, and Harvard universities. He is professor and chairman of both the Department of Surgery and the Division of Cardiovascular and Thoracic Surgery at the University of Ottawa. He is also the director of the university's Cardiac Unit, which he helped plan and set up, and surgeon-in-chief of the Cardiothoracic Surgery Division at the Ottawa Civic Hospital. He is a member of numerous medical associations, a past director of the Ontario Heart Foundation, past president and vice-president of the Canadian Association of Clinical Surgeons, chairman of the Canadian Heart Foundation Medical Advisory Committee, a founding member of the Canadian Association of General Surgeons, and a member of the board of governors of the University of Ottawa. Dr. Keon collects books on the history of medicine.

Kerwin, Larkin

C.C., B.Sc., M.Sc., D.Sc.

Physicist, administrator. b. June 22, 1924, Quebec City; m. Maria Turcot; d. Lupita, Rosa-Maria, Guillermina, s. Alan, Larkin, Terence, Gregory, Timothy; res. Ottawa.

Dr. Larkin Kerwin, president of the National Research Council of Canada, obtained a B.Sc. from St. Francis Xavier University (1944), an M.Sc. from the Massachusetts Institute of Technology (1946), and a D.Sc. from Laval (1949). He stayed on to teach at Laval University, becoming a full professor in 1956, chairman of the Physics department in 1961, vice-dean of the Faculty in 1967, and vice-rector in 1969. He was the rector of the university from 1972 to 1977. In 1980 he was appointed to a five-year term as president of the National Research council, where he has tried to build up national awareness of the importance of research and development. In July 1982, Prime Minister Pierre Trudeau appointed him to be Canada's representative on a working group set up as a result of the June 1982 Economic Summit. This group studies how research and development can be used to create jobs and help the recovery of the world economy, and is made up of representatives of the seven Economic Summit nations and the European Economic Community. Dr. Kerwin has received 10 honorary degrees and numerous awards and medals, including the Governor General's Medal and the Gold Medal of the Canadian Association of Physicists. He has been named a Fellow of the American Institute of Physics and a Companion of the Order of Canada. He is the author of many articles and a book dealing with atomic and molecular physics and is a member of numerous scientific and professional societies.

Laidlaw, John C., M.D.

Clinician and researcher; McMaster University, Hamilton

Lapp, Philip Alexander

B.A.Sc., S.M., Sc.D.

Business executive, engineer. b. May 12, 1928, Toronto; m. Caulyne Byers; s. David, Douglas; d. Aimee; res. Thornhill, Ontario.

After attending Malvern Collegiate in Toronto, Philip Lapp studied at the University of Toronto, where he won the Harvey Aggett Memorial Scholarship (1948) and earned a B.A.Sc. degree. He then went to Massachusetts Institute of Technology where he received a Goodyear Fellowship (1951). He worked as a research associate while continuing his studies, won Gamma Alpha Rho and Sigma Xi awards, and in 1955 was granted the degree of Sc.D. He returned to Canada and joined de Havilland Aircraft in 1954, beginning as a systems engineer, becoming chief engineer in 1960, and director of technical operations in 1965. From 1967 until 1969 he was senior vice-president and director of Spar Aerospace Products; he left that position to assume the post of consultant to the Committee of Presidents of Universities of Ontario, and director of the Study of Engineering Education in Ontario. Since 1970 he has been president of his own company, Philip A. Lapp Ltd. He is the author of numerous studies on technical and educational aspects of the engineering profession in Canada, including the Science Secretariat group report, *Upper Atmosphere and Space Programs in Canada*; *Ring of Iron*, a study of engineering education in Ontario, *Prospects for Man: Communications Technology*, and *Arctic Systems*. He is the current president of the Association of Professional Engineers of Ontario. He belongs to numerous other professional associations and industry and government study groups, including the Canadian Aeronautics and Space Institute, the Task Force on National Surveying and Mapping, and the Interdepartmental Study Group on Ocean Information Systems.

Lowy, Frederick H.

B.A., M.D., C.M., F.R.C.P.(C), F.A.C.P., F.A.C.P.N.

Educator, psychiatrist. b. January 1, 1933, Grosspetersdorf, Austria; m. Mary Kay O'Neil; s. David, Eric, Adam, d. Sarah; res. Toronto.

The present dean of the Faculty of Medicine at the University of Toronto, Frederick Lowy has always made it his aim to "humanize" medical education. This principle helped to develop the Clarke Institute of Psychiatry, Toronto, into an internationally recognized centre under his leadership. Dr. Lowy received his own medical education at McGill University. He has held several important teaching and psychiatric posts since then, beginning as staff psychiatrist at the Allan Memorial Institute and Royal Victoria Hospital in 1965. In the intervening years he has been professor of psychiatry at McGill University and the University of Ottawa, chief of psychiatry at the Ottawa Civil Hospital, and from 1974 until 1980, director and psychiatrist-in-chief at the Clarke Institute. From 1974 until 1977, he was editor of the *Canadian Journal of Psychiatry*. He is a fellow of the American Psychiatric Association, the American College of Psychiatrists, and the American College of Psycho-analysts. He is a director of the Hospital Council of Metropolitan Toronto, the Ontario Cancer

Helen Mussallem in the Helen K. Mussallem Library at the Canadian Nurses Association headquarters in Ottawa.

Dr. J. Fraser Mustard at McMaster University.

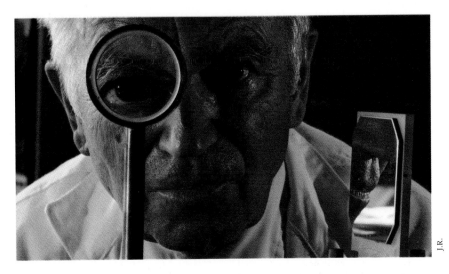

Dr. Gerhard Herzberg in his office at the National Research Council, Ottawa.

Dr. J. Tuzo Wilson at the Ontario Science Centre.

Dr. Theodore Rasmussen.

Institute, the Sunnybrook Medical Centre, and the National Cancer Institute. He belongs to the University Club and the Faculty Club, Toronto, and to numerous medical and psychiatric associations.

Lyon, E. Kirk
M.B., F.A.C.S., F.R.C.S.

Surgeon. b. October 1, 1901, Huron County, Ontario; m. Marion Lowe (deceased), s. Robert (deceased); res. Leamington, Ontario.

One of Canada's most respected medical administrators, E. Kirk Lyon graduated in medicine from the University of Toronto in 1923 at the age of 21. After three years of postgraduate studies, he served as a ship's surgeon in 1926, and then practised briefly in Hamilton and Stratford before setting up his Leamington practice that continued uninterrupted for 45 years. His administrative career began in 1945 with the councillor's post for the Ontario Medical Association's District #1. During his chairmanship of the Leamington District Memorial Hospital Board from 1947 to 1950, a 50-bed hospital was established. Dr. Lyon was chief of the Surgical Department of this hospital from 1950 to 1969. Among many other responsibilities, he has been chairman of both the Canadian Council on Hospital Accreditation and the Canadian Medical Association committee on Hospital Accreditation, the Canadian Medical Association delegate to the World Medical Association in 1955 and to the British Commonwealth Medical Conference in 1959, deputy to the president-elect of the Canadian Medical Association in 1958, and chairman of the Canadian Medical Association's Study of Group Practice committee from 1963 to 1967. Since his retirement from active practice in 1972, Dr. Lyon has been an inspector for the College of Physicians and Surgeons of Ontario. He has received the Centennial Medal, the Canadian Medical Association Medal of Service, and the Queen's Silver Jubilee Medal.

McClure, Robert Baird, M.D.
Missionary, surgeon; Toronto

Macdonald, John Barfoot
D.D.S., M.S., Ph.D., F.A.C.D., A.M.

Professor. b. February 23, 1918, Toronto; m. Liba Bocek; s. Grant, Scott, d. Kaaren, Linda, Vivian; res. Toronto.

Chairman of the Addiction Research Foundation and vice-chairman of the Ontario Council of Health, Dr. Macdonald graduated from the University of Toronto with an honours degree in Dental Surgery in 1942. After a two-year stint as a captain in the Canadian Dental Corps, he studied bacteriology at the University of Illinois and became an assistant professor of bacteriology at the University of Toronto in 1949. He was elevated to associate professor in 1953 after receiving his Ph.D. in Bacteriology from Columbia University, and became chairman of the University of Toronto's Division of Dental Research. He then moved to the United States, serving as director of Boston's Forsyth Dental Infirmary (1956 to 1962), and professor of microbiology (1956 to 1962) and director of post-doctoral studies (1960 to 1962) at the

Harvard School of Dental Medicine. He returned to Canada to serve as the president of the University of British Columbia from 1962 to 1967 and as the executive director of the Council of Ontario Universities from 1968 to 1976. He became a professor of bacteriology at the University of Toronto in 1976, as well as president of the Addiction Research Foundation. He has received five honorary doctorates of Law, two honorary doctorates of Science, an honorary Fellowship of the Institute of Canadian Dentists, and an honorary Fellowship of the Royal College of Dentists. He is a director of the Banff School of Advanced Management, the Association of Universities and Colleges in Canada, the Donwood Foundation, and the Addiction Research Foundation.

McGregor, Maurice, M.D.
Physician; Professor of Medicine, McGill University, Montreal

MacInnis, Joseph Beverly
C.M., M.D., LL.D., F.R.C.S., F.R.C.G.S.

Ocean consultant, writer. b. March 2, 1937, Barrie, Ontario; m. Deborah; d. Tracy, Lara, Jordann, s. Jeff; res. Toronto.

Dr. Joe MacInnis has been studying the relationship of humankind and the sea for over 20 years. He is the first man to dive and film beneath the North Pole; also, he designed the world's first polar dive station, built beneath the floating ice of the Northwest Passage, almost a 1000 kilometres north of the Arctic Circle. In 1969 he established Sublimnos, Canada's first underwater manned station program and over the next 12 years he led 16 scientific expeditions into the Arctic. *Sub-Igloo*, the first polar dive station, was established on the third expedition. In 1975 he took Prince Charles on a 30-minute dive under the ice of Resolute Bay. He is the author of over 30 scientific papers on diving medicine, of many articles for *Scientific American* and *National Geographic*, and of two books about the sea, *Underwater Images* and *Underwater Man*. In 1980 he led the search team that located the remains of HMS *Breadalbane*, the world's northernmost known shipwreck and the subject of his next book, *The Breadalbane Adventure*. He has lectured all over the world and hosted a 15-part CBC television series entitled *The New Wave*. He is president of Undersea Research Ltd.

MacNabb, Gordon M.
President, Natural Sciences and Engineering Research Council, Ottawa

McLean, Lloyd D., M.D.
Surgeon; Professor of Surgery, McGill University; Surgeon-in-chief, Royal Victoria Hospital, Montreal

McLeod, Lionel E., M.D.
Clinician; Dean, Faculty of Medicine, University of Calgary

Morin, Yves, M.D.
Cardiologist; Dean of Medicine, Laval University, Quebec

Mussallem, Helen Kathleen
O.C., B.N., M.A., Ed.D, LL.D., D.Sc., D.St.J., F.R.C.N.

Nurse, health consultant. b. Prince Rupert, British Columbia; res. Ottawa.

Canada's most distinguished nurse is at present a consultant to the World Health Organization. Helen Mussallem saw active service in the Second World War as a lieutenant (nursing officer) in the Royal Canadian Army Medical Corps in Canada and overseas. Beginning as a staff nurse at the Vancouver General Hospital, she rose to become director of Nursing Education. In 1957 she was commissioned to do a survey of nursing education across Canada and in 1962-63 was seconded to the Royal Commission on Health Services. She was executive director of the Canadian Nurses Association from 1963 to 1981 and is a member of the board of directors of the International Council of Nurses. An expert on health care in developing countries, she has carried out assignments in more than 30 countries and has written many articles on health care. She also has a collection of artifacts from the countries her work has taken her to. She was recently invested as a Dame of Grace in the Order of St. John. She is a member of a B.C. family widely involved in public service. Her father, Solomon, was mayor of the Fraser Valley municipality of Maple Ridge for 22 years. Her brother, George, stepped down in 1983 as a Social Credit MLA. Another brother, Nicholas, a provincial judge in Vancouver, died in 1979.

Mustard, James Fraser
M.D., Ph.D., F.R.C.P.(C), F.R.S.C.

Surgeon, medical researcher. b. October 16, 1927, Toronto; m. Christine Elizabeth Sifton; s. Cameron, Jim, John, Duncan; d. Anne, Christine; res. Toronto.

One of Canada's foremost heart surgeons and cardiovascular researchers (especially in the area of hypertension), Dr. Fraser Mustard is the president and senior fellow of the recently formed Canadian Institute for Advanced Research (1982). After graduating from the University of Toronto Medical School in 1953, where he was a member of the Varsity Blues football team, he interned at Toronto General Hospital and went on to Cambridge University, from which he obtained his Ph.D. in 1956. He joined the Faculty of Medicine at McMaster University in 1966, became dean of the Faculty of Health Sciences in 1972, and moved to vice-president of Health Sciences in 1980. Dr. Mustard has won widespread recognition for his work in the research field, including a Gairdner Award for Medical Research (1967) and election to a fellowship in the Royal Society of Canada (1976). A member of many medical associations, including the International Society on Thrombosis and Haemostasis (president, 1981), he also holds directorships in many organizations, among which are the Ontario and Canadian heart foundations. Dr. Mustard enjoys spending his leisure time with his family at his farm, Scamperdale.

Naimark, Arnold, M.D.
Physician; President, University of Manitoba

Paupst, James C., M.D.
Physician; Toronto

Perey, Bernard J., M.D.

Surgeon; Chairman, Department of Surgery, Dalhousie University, Halifax

Polanyi, John Charles

C.C., Ph.D., D.Sc., LL.D., F.R.S., F.R.S.C.

Scientist. b. January 23, 1929, Berlin; m. Anne Ferrar (Susie) Davidson; s. Michael, d. Margaret; res. Toronto.

John Polanyi is university professor at the University of Toronto and one of Canada's most eminent chemists. His Hungarian parents left Germany for England in 1934. Raised in Manchester, he studied chemistry at Manchester University, coming to Canada as a postdoctoral fellow at the National Research Council in 1952. He went to Princeton in 1954 and came to Toronto in 1956. He has many awards and honours, including honorary degrees from McMaster, Carleton, and Harvard. He has published over 100 scientific papers; as well, he is deeply concerned with the role of science and the control of nuclear armaments. He is a Companion of the Order of Canada. His father, Michael Polanyi, who died in England in 1976, was a celebrated physical chemist and philosopher of science; he resigned from the Kaiser Wilhelm Institute as a protest against the Nazis.

Rasmussen, Theodore Brown

B.S., M.B., M.D., M.S., F.R.C.P., F.R.C.S.

Physician, educator. b. April 28, 1910, Provo, Utah; m. Catherine Archibald; s. Donald, d. Ruth, Mary, Linda; res. Montreal.

Dr. Rasmussen was educated at the University of Minnesota, at the Mayo Clinic in Rochester, Minnesota, and at Montreal Neurological Institute of McGill University. He served with the U.S. Army Medical Corps during the Second World War and rose to the rank of lieutenant-colonel. He became a lecturer and resident fellow of McGill University in 1946 and professor of Neurosurgery at the University of Chicago (1947-54). He returned to Montreal in 1954 as deputy director and neurosurgeon for the Montreal Neurological Institute, becoming the Institute's director in 1961, a post he held until 1972. He was, at the same time, neurologist and neurosurgeon-in-chief at Montreal's Royal Victoria Hospital. Dr. Rasmussen has received many important awards and honours—among them Outstanding Achievement awards from both the University of Minnesota (1958) and the University of Chicago (1973). In 1979, he received the Ambassador Award from Epilepsy International and a year later was made a professor emeritus at McGill. The Canadian League Against Epilepsy awarded Dr. Rasmussen the Wilder Penfield Award for 1982. A frequent contributor of articles and papers to learned journals, Dr. Rasmussen has also published *The Cerebral Cortex of Man* (with Wilder Penfield, 1950), and *Functional Neurosurgery* (with Raul Marino, Jr., 1979). He is a member of more than 40 national and international neurological and neurosurgical societies and associations.

Rice, Donald I., M.D.

Family physician; Executive Director, College of Family Physicians of Canada, Toronto

Roy, Augustin, M.D.

President, Professional Corporation of Physicians of Quebec, Montreal

Rusted, Ian E.L.H.

M.D., F.R.C.P.(C), F.A.C.P.

Physician. b. July 12, 1921, Upper Island Cove, Newfoundland; m. Ellen Hansen; s. Christopher, Brian; res. St. John's.

Dr. Rusted studied medicine at the University of Toronto; at McGill University, where he received a National Research Council grant to support research at the Royal Victoria Hospital in Montreal; and at the Mayo Foundation, where he was awarded a Fellowship in Medicine. He is now vice-president (Health Sciences and Professional Schools) and pro-vice-chancellor of Memorial University. He was medical consultant to the Newfoundland Department of Health from 1952 until 1967. In 1953, he joined the St. John's General Hospital as physician and director of Medical Education. He was for several years a member of the Board of Regents of Memorial University and from 1966 until 1974 was director of the university's Research Unit at St. John's General. In 1967 he became chairman of the Department of Medicine at the hospital as well as professor and dean of Medicine at Memorial, holding all three positions at once. He belongs to the Royal College of Physicians and Surgeons of Canada, the Association of Canadian Medical Colleges, the American College of Physicians, the Canadian and Newfoundland Medical Associations, the Canadian Diabetic Association, the American Thyroid Association, and the Canadian Society of Endocrinology and Metabolism. Dr. Rusted is an honorary member of the College of Family Physicians of Canada. He has been visiting professor at the universities of Toronto and Laval and he has received an honorary LL.D. from Dalhousie University. He belongs to the Rotary Club of St. John's and the St. John's Hospital Council.

Salter, Robert B., M.D.

Surgeon; Head of Orthopaedic Surgery, University of Toronto; Senior Orthopaedic Surgeon, Hospital for Sick Children, Toronto

Sawchuk, William

Scientist; Communications Research Centre, Ottawa

Scriver, Charles R.

B.A., M.D.C.M., F.R.S.C.

Medical scientist, educator. b. November 7, 1930, Montreal; m. Esther Katherine Peirce; d. Dorothy Ellen, Julie Boyd, s. Peter Carleton, Paul Pierce; res. Montreal.

Renowned for his work in the field of genetics, Charles Scriver is a professor of Biology, Genetics, and Pediatrics at McGill University. After graduating *cum laude* from McGill in 1955, he spent two years at University College Hospital in London. He has been instrumental in the identification and control of many diseases and mutatives. His development of screening methods to identify biochemical diseases in newborns is an internationally recognized model. Dr. Scriver has been honoured with numerous awards, including election to the Royal Society of Canada (1973), the Queen's Jubilee Medal (1977), the Gairdner International Award (1979), and the R.S.C.'s McLaughlin Medal (1981). His many memberships include the Canadian Pediatric Society, the New York Academy of Sciences, and the governing council of the Positive Action Committee. He has travelled throughout the world as a guest lecturer and visiting professor. Dr. Scriver is an avid photographer, with one exhibition to his credit. His mother, Jessie Boyd Scriver, was pediatrician in chief at Montreal's Royal Victoria Hospital from 1958 to 1965; his father was physician in chief at that hospital from 1969 to 1974.

Scriver, Jessie Boyd

B.A., M.D.C.M., D.Sc., F.R.C.P.(C)

Pediatrician (retired). b. 1895, Montreal; m. Walter Scriver (deceased); s. Charles; res. Montreal.

Renowned for her work with children, especially premature infants, Jessie Boyd Scriver is still an active force in the community. Dr. Scriver graduated from McGill University in 1922 with the first class that allowed women, despite the protests of the male students. She published several medical articles in the late 1920s, set up her own practice during the Depression, and went on to become chief of pediatrics at the Royal Victoria Hospital. She was elected president of the Canadian Paediatric Society in 1952 (the first woman president of a specialist section of the Canadian Medical Association), received an honorary Doctorate of Science from McGill in 1979, and was presented with the Ross Award from the Canadian Paediatric Society for distinguished service to children in 1982. Dr. Scriver continues to be an active patron of the performing arts.

Smith, Stuart Lyon

B.Sc., M.D., F.R.C.P.(C)

Science administrator, politician. b. May 7, 1938, Montreal; m. Patricia Ann Springate; d. Tanya, s. Graig; res. Burlington, Ontario.

Educated at McGill University in Psychiatry and active in student politics, Stuart Smith became associate professor of Psychiatry at McMaster University. He went into Ontario provincial politics when he was elected from Hamilton West in 1975. He was leader of the Ontario Liberal Party from 1976 to 1982, when he resigned the position and his seat to become chairman of the Science Council of Canada, a key organization in determining science policy and channelling funds into research.

Solandt, Omond McKillop

C.C., O.B.E., C.D., B.A., M.A., M.D., M.A., D.Sc., D.Eng.

Scientist. b. September 2, 1909, Winnipeg; m. Vaire Olive Wollaston; d. Sigrid, Katharine; res. Bolton, Ontario.

Dr. Omond Solandt set out to be a researcher in clinical cardiology, but his talent as an administrator soon led him far from his chosen field. Having studied under Dr. Charles Best, who steered him into medical research, he received his medical degree (and Gold Medal) from the University of Toronto in 1936. He was studying and interning in England when war broke out and he was made director of the South

West London Blood Supply Depot. He was subsequently superintendent of the Medical Research Council Physiological Laboratory (studying physiological problems of tank crews) and superintendent of the Canadian Army Operational Research Group (with the rank of colonel). He was about to take up the post as scientific advisor to Lord Louis Mountbatten when the war ended. He became the first chairman of the Defence Research Board (1947-56), vice-president of Research and Development for Canadian National Railways (1956-63), and vice-president of Research and Development for de Havilland Canada (1963-66). He was chancellor of the University of Toronto (1965-71), chairman of the Science Council of Canada (1966-72), and vice-chairman of Erco Chemicals Ltd. (1966-70). Such a cursory list of Solandt's major appointments gives no indication of the innumerable boards, commissions, and committees he has served on, dealing with matters as diverse as urban transit, agricultural research, the environment, engineering, and medicine. He has been a director of Expo 67, a public governor of the Toronto Stock Exchange, and research advisor to the royal commission investigating the Ocean Ranger disaster. He counts his chief achievement as his success in leading teams, large and small, that have done important things. Now "retired," he is a keen world traveller and advises a number of international research centres in developing countries.

Stewart, Chester Bryant

O.C., C.D., B.Sc., M.D.C.M., LL.D., D.Sc., M.P.H., Dr. P.H., F.R.C.P.(C), F.A.P.H.A., M.C.F.P.(C).

Medical educator (retired). b. December 17, 1910, Norboro, Prince Edward Island; m. Kathleen French; d. Joan, Moira; res. Halifax.

Dr. Stewart began a distinguished career dedicated to medical knowledge with his participation in 1938–39 with Sir Frederick Banting in the first survey of medical research in Canada (and he directed the second survey in 1948). Dr. Stewart was educated at Prince of Wales College in Charlottetown, Dalhousie University, and Johns Hopkins University. He was awarded the Anderson Gold Medal, the Gold Medal in Medicine, and the Rockefeller Fellowship in Public Health (1945–46). During

the Second World War he was a wing commander in the RCAF and won a Canadian Forces Decoration. Dr. Stewart then joined Dalhousie University, where he was Professor of Epidemiology for 30 years. His achievements during that time included improvements in medical education and research at Dalhousie, notably financing and planning the Sir Charles Tupper Medical Building as Nova Scotia's centennial memorial in 1967; pioneer research in aviation medicine on decompression sickness; and the adaptation of epidemiological techniques to the study of hospital and health manpower requirements under comprehensive insurance. He also has written many articles on medical research and medical education. Dr. Stewart also served as president of the Association of Canadian Medical Colleges (1961–63), president of the Canadian Public Health (1968–69), and director of the Canada Sickness Survey (1949–50).

Thomas, Gordon W., M.D.

Surgeon; former Professor of Clinical Surgery, Memorial Hospital, Saint John, New Brunswick

Thomson, R. Kenneth, M.D.

Physician, Edmonton

Wilson, Donald R., M.D.

Clinician; Professor of Medicine, University of Alberta

Wilson, Donald Laurence

M.A., M.D.C.M., F.R.C.P. (C), F.A.C.P.

Physician, educator. b. October 2, 1921, Hamilton; m. Mary Isobel Pierce; d. Mary Barbara Kimball, Judith Isobel Ganton, Helen Elizabeth, s. John Alexander, Peter Pierce, Donald Bruce; res. Kingston, Ontario.

The dean of the Faculty of Medicine at Queen's University, Kingston, D. Laurence Wilson is considered one of Canada's top clinicians and medical educators. After completing his education at Queen's, he served in Canada with the RCAMC in 1945, leaving with the rank of captain in 1946. Dr. Wilson joined

the staff of Queen's in 1951 as an assistant professor of Medicine. In 1977, he was presented with the Queen's Jubilee Medal. Dr. Wilson is a member of several medical associations, including the Ontario Medical Association (president, 1973-74), the Canadian Medical Association (president, 1979-80), and the American College of Physicians (governor for Ontario, 1982), and is the author of several scientific articles.

Wilson, John Tuzo

C.C., O.B.E., B.A., M.A., Sc.D., Ph.D., LL.D., F.R.S.C., F.R.S.

Geologist. b. October 24, 1908, Ottawa; m. Isabel Jean Dickson; d. Patricia, Susan; res. Toronto.

J. Tuzo Wilson is an internationally respected scientist whose contributions to glacial geology and the theory of plate tectonics have won him many prizes and honours, including 14 honorary doctorates and 12 gold medals. His work has won widespread acceptance for the theory of continental drift. He was educated at Ashbury College, University of Toronto, Cambridge (where he was a Massey Fellow), and Princeton. Between 1936 and 1939 he was an assistant geologist for the Geological Survey of Canada. During the Second World War he served in the Canadian Army (beginning as second lieutenant and achieving the rank of colonel), and was made an Officer of the Order of the British Empire and an Officer of the U.S. Legion of Merit. In 1946 he assumed the post of professor of Geophysics at the University of Toronto; he was appointed principal of Erindale College in 1967. He also planned the buildings for the Erindale Campus. Since 1974 he has been the director-general of the acclaimed Ontario Science Centre, which he describes as "the largest science laboratory for the public anywhere." He is a member and past president of the Royal Society of Canada and of the International, American and Canadian Geophysical Unions. He belongs to the York Club and the Arts and Letters Club. Dr. Wilson summers at Go Home Bay on Georgian Bay in Ontario, where he sails an unusual boat: a Hong Kong junk. He has written several books and articles about his extensive travel in all parts of the world.

Canadians with British Titles

Sir Max Aitken, Bt., D.S.O., D.F.C.
London, England
The Right Honourable the Lord Ashtown
Hamilton, Ontario
The Right Honourable Althea,
Lady Aylmer
Victoria, British Columbia
Sir Fenton Aylmer, Bt.
Westmount, Quebec
Lady Margaret Ayre
Pointe Claire, Quebec
Sir Christopher Barlow, Bt.
St. John's, Newfoundland
The Right Honourable
the Lady Beaverbrook
Saint Andrews, New Brunswick
Sir Harold Boulton, Bt.
Ottawa, Ontario
Sir Alexander Boyd, Bt.
Vernon, British Columbia
Sir Lauder Brunton, Bt.
Guysborough, Nova Scotia
Sir Herbert Burbridge, Bt.
Surrey, British Columbia
Lord Burghley
100 Mile House, British Columbia
Sir Michael Butler, Bt., Q.C.
Brentwood Bay, British Columbia
Dorothea, Lady Cave-Brown-Cave
Vancouver, British Columbia
Sir Robert Cave-Brown-Cave, Bt.
Vancouver, British Columbia
Lady Marina Cecil
100 Mile House, British Columbia
The Right Honourable
the Viscount Charlemont
Cumberland, Ontario
The Right Honourable the Lord Chatfield
Williamstown, Ontario
Sir George Chaytor, Bt.
Chilliwack, British Columbia
Sir Arthur Chetwynd, Bt.
Toronto, Ontario
Sir John Davis, Bt.
Toronto, Ontario
Sir Derek Hart Dyke, Bt.
Hamilton, Ontario
The Right Honourable the Earl of Egmont
Nanton, Alberta
The Most Honourable
the Marquess of Ely
London, England; Port Hope, Ontario

The Most Honourable
the Marquess of Exeter
100 Mile House, British Columbia
Lady Eileen Fitton
Vancouver, British Columbia
Sir David Flavelle, Bt.
Clarkson, Ontario
The Right Honourable
the Viscount Galway
London, Ontario
Sir Christopher Gibson, Bt.
Richmond, British Columbia
Lord Roderic Gordon, M.B.E.
Bentley, Alberta
The Right Honourable Lord Greenhill,
M.D., D.P.H., F.R.C.P.
Edmonton, Alberta
The Honourable Catherine Greenhill
Edmonton, Alberta
The Right Honourable
the Viscount Greenwood
Qualicum Beach, British Columbia
Sir Robert Gunning, Bt.
Peace River, Alberta
The Right Honourable
the Viscount Hardinge
London, England
The Right Honourable Margaret,
Viscountess Hardinge
Montreal, Quebec
Sir Edwin Leather, K.C.M.G., K.C.V.O.
Bermuda
Lady Livingston
Duncan, British Columbia
General Sir Charles Loewen,
G.C.B., K.B.E., D.S.O.
Mansfield, Ontario
Viscount Loftus
Calgary, Alberta
Sir Allan Mackenzie, Bt.
Cobble Hill, British Columbia
Sir Robert Morris, Bt.
St. Chrysostome, Quebec
Sir Leonard Cecil Outerbridge,
C.C., C.B.E., D.S.O., C.D.
St. John's, Newfoundland
Lady Geraldine Perceval
Nanton, Alberta
Viscount Perceval
Nanton, Alberta
Sir Christopher Philipson-Stow, Bt.,
Thornhill, Ontario

Sir Charles Piers, Bt.
Duncan, British Columbia
Lady Anne Poirier
Comox, British Columbia
Sir Francis Price, Bt.
Edmonton, Alberta
Sir John Robinson, Bt.
Sir Charles Rugge-Price, Bt.
St. Albert, Alberta
Maeve, Lady Rugge-Price
St. Albert, Alberta
The Right Honourable
the Lord Shaughnessy
London, England; Calgary, Alberta
Sir John Simeon, Bt.
North Vancouver, British Columbia
Sir William Stephenson
Bermuda
Lady Alison Stewart-Patterson
Senneville, Quebec
Sir Phillip Stonhouse, Bt.
Medicine Hat, Alberta
Sir John Stracey, Bt.
Montreal, Quebec
Sir Phillip Stuart, Bt.
Winnipeg, Manitoba
Sir Robert Synge, Bt.
Langley, British Columbia
The Right Honourable
the Countess of Tankerville
San Francisco, California
The Right Honourable
the Lord Thomson of Fleet
London, England; Toronto, Ontario
Lady Ann Tottenham
Lord Richard Tottenham
Newmarket, Ontario
Lord Timothy Tottenham
Sir Rodney Touche, Bt.
Calgary, Alberta
Lady Ouida Touche
Calgary, Alberta
Sir Charles Tupper, Bt.
West Vancouver, British Columbia
Sir Charles Wells, Bt.
Toronto, Ontario
The Right Honourable Earl Winterton
Delta, British Columbia
Sir Garnet Wolseley, Bt.
Brantford, Ontario

Appendix
The Family Foundations

THE POWER OF MAJOR fortunes lives on long after the creators have died. This table shows the 25 largest charitable foundations based on family or personal wealth. There are also corporate, community, and special-interest foundations, the largest of which are the Vancouver Foundation (assets about $99 million in 1982; G. Peter Kaye, chairman), the Hospital for Sick Children Foundation, Toronto (assets $65 million; Duncan L. Gordon, chairman), and the Law Foundation of British Columbia (assets about $60 million; L.M. Little, chairman). Forty-three of the 50 largest foundations are based on family or individual fortunes.

Other large family foundations include the Sir James Dunn Foundation (assets about $9 million; Lady Beaverbrook, president), Mr. and Mrs. P.A. Woodward's Foundation (about $9 million; W. Gordon Skinner, president), the McLean Foundation, based on the wealth of J.S. McLean (about $7 million; William F. McLean, president), the Gladys and Merrill Muttart Foundation of Edmonton (about $7 million; Dr.

R.E. Ivany, president), and the Faye and Joseph Tanenbaum Foundation (about $8 million; Joseph Tanenbaum, president).

Joseph Tanenbaum, whose wealth is derived from real estate, construction, and investments, is (like his late brother Max) a major contributor to Jewish causes. The five foundations based on his wealth have combined assets of about $35 million and make grants each year of somewhere over $3 million. Joseph Tanenbaum himself is president of all five foundations and the boards include other family members and associates, including Albert Reichmann and Rabbi Nota Schiller.

There are seven Bronfman family foundations, the Samuel and Saidye Bronfman Foundation being by far the largest (see table). The total assets of all seven are about $24 million and they make grants each year of about $4 million. The figure for grants is high in relation to assets because some of the foundations have little in the way of assets, being channels for year-to-year giving on the part of family members.

Foundation and Source	Assets ($1000s)	Annual Grants ($1000s)	Officers and Directors	Areas of Interest
J.W. MCCONNELL/GRIFFITH *Estd. 1937, Montreal (McConnell). Estd. 1967, Toronto (Griffith)* J.W. MCCONNELL (1877-1963), industrialist (St. Lawrence Sugar, Montreal Star)	$179,009 *(1981)*	$7,958 *(1981)*	Derek A. Price (pres.), Jacqueline Prévost (sec.-treas.), Michael G. McConnell (v-p), Peter M. Laing, Mrs. Peter M. Laing, Mrs. W.B. Hyndman, Mrs. Peter A. Leus, Mrs. D.A. Price, Peter McEntyre	The Griffith Foundation gives all its income to the J.W. McConnell Foundation for distribution and has the same board of directors. Projects funded include educational equipment, educational buildings and research, libraries, hospitals, medical research, museums, performing arts, conservation, studies of crime and delinquency, the handicapped, and youth agencies.
DONNER CANADIAN *Estd. 1950, Toronto* WILLIAM H. DONNER (1864-1953), U.S. industrialist in tin and steel	$56,000 *(1982)*	$4,584 *(1982)*	Donald S. Rickerd (pres.), Gerald Wright (v-p), Joseph W. Donner, Robert Donner, Jr., Ross Goodwin, Dr. Guy MacLean, William Donner Roosevelt, Thomas Shoyama, Dr. Ronald L. Watts, Curtin Winsor, Jr.	Law reform and corrections, foreign policy studies, native peoples, the North. Recent contributions include $200,000 to Carleton University for studies in peacekeeping, $400,000 to McGill to train Inuit teaching assistants for the N.W.T., and $225,000 to the World Wildlife Fund for research on whales.

This table is based in part on information from the *Canadian Directory to Foundations and Granting Agencies* (Allan Arlett, editor), published by the Canadian Centre for Philanthropy.

Foundation and Source	Assets ($1000s)	Annual Grants ($1000s)	Officers and Directors	Areas of Interest
KAHANOFF *Estd. 1979, Calgary* SYDNEY KAHANOFF (*1922-80*), *oilman, founder of Voyager Petroleums*	$25,993 (*1980*) Now about $50,000	$210 (*1980*)	W. Fern Kahanoff (pres.), Alan C. Moon (exec.dir.), Clement W. Dumett, Jr., A. Barry Beaven, Frank Kettner, George M Plewes, Joseph B. Katchen	Supports charitable projects, mainly in Alberta, in health and social welfare, education, medical and scientific research, artistic and cultural organizations. (The figure for grants is low in relation to assets because the foundation received most of its funding in 1980-82.)
MACDONALD STEWART *Estd. 1967, Montreal* Sale of Macdonald Tobacco by DAVID STEWART to R.J. Reynolds Industries	$44,866 (*1980*)	$4,212 (*1980*)	David Macdonald Stewart (pres.), Liliane Stewart (v-p), Kathleen Mather (sec.), Beatrice M. Molson (treas.), Paul Britton Paine (v-p), J.K. Finalyson (v-p), Leo Lavoie (v-p), J.P. Carroll (asst.sec.)	Education, medicine, humanities, museums, heritage. The foundation has made many contributions to preservation and museums in Montreal particularly. It owns the former Louis Forget house on Sherbrooke Street.
R. SAMUEL MCLAUGHLIN *Estd. 1951, Toronto* R. SAMUEL MCLAUGHLIN (*1871-1971*), *chairman of General Motors of Canada*	$38,000 (*1982*)	$3,038 (*1982*)	J.G. Hungerford (pres.), G.D. deS. Wotherspoon (v-p), P.J. Sewell (sec.), J.L.A. Colhoun, Dr. E.A. Sellers	A variety of charities including medical education, libraries, humanities, heritage, social agencies, alcohol and drug addiction, and the handicapped. One of its best-known contributions is the McLaughlin Planetarium, Toronto.
MAX BELL *Estd. 1965, Toronto* G. MAX BELL (*1912-72*), *Calgary businessman (oil,* CPR, FP *Publications)*	$29,846 (*1981*)	$2,682 (*1981*)	George R. Gardiner (pres.), George N.M. Currie (v-p), Pegi Dover (sec.), Richard S. Malone, James A. Richardson, Roland Michener, Diane Marra	The foundation gives grants in the following areas: health services, media, fitness and sports, veterinary medicine, oceans and inland waters, and relations between Canada and the Asian Pacific.
J.P. BICKELL *Estd. 1951, Toronto* J.P. BICKELL (*1884-1951*), *financier and mining executive*	$28,240 (*1982*)	$2,700 (*1982*)	R.G. Darling (chmn.), P.J. Sewell (sec.), E.H. Heeney, D. McNab, A.J. Little	Half the income goes to the Hospital for Sick Children, Toronto. The rest goes to support medical research (10 per cent), scholarships in mining and related areas (5 per cent), and charitable and educational organizations (35 per cent).
W. J. VANDUSEN *Estd. 1970, Calgary* W.J. VANDUSEN (*1889-1978*), *partner of H.R. MacMillan of MacMillan Bloedel*	$26,000 (*1982*)	$1,900 (*1982*)	D. McLaws (pres.), D.J. Warren (sec.), J.T. McDougall	Education—mainly B.C. economics, forestry, conservation—welfare, medical research, and theological education in the United Church.
ELDEE *Estd. 1961, Montreal* *Based on wealth of* SIR MORTIMER DAVIS (*1864-1928*), *named for* LADY DAVIS	$23,547 (*1980*)	$1,680 (*1980*)	Bernard M. Bloomfield (pres.), Louis M. Bloomfield (v-p), Harry J.F. Bloomfield, Abraham Shurem, Peter K. Johnson (sec.-treas.)	Grants to charitable organizations and institutions in Canada, primarily those maintained for the benefit of Jews.
F.K. MORROW *Estd. 1944, Toronto* F.K. MORROW, *industrialist, founder of Dover Industries*	$20,034 (*1979*)	$1,531 (*1979*)	Audrey Loftus (pres.), Sister Laura Anne Hickey (v-p), Cecil W. Wake (treas.), Sister Marguerite Walters	Supports religious, charitable, and educational institutions, mainly the Sisters of St. Joseph in the diocese of Toronto and Upper Canada.
THE MOLSON FAMILY *Estd. 1958, Montreal* T.H.P. MOLSON (*1901-70*) *and* HARTLAND DEM. MOLSON	$20,000 (*1981*)	$991 (*1982*)	Hartland deM. Molson (pres.), Eric H. Molson (v-p), Stephen T. Molson (sec.), Rolland A. Peloquin (treas.), C.F. Harrington, M.G. Huband	Supports innovative projects mainly in health and welfare, education, social development, and the humanities.

Foundation and Source	Assets ($1000s)	Annual Grants ($1000s)	Officers and Directors	Areas of Interest
SAMUEL AND SAIDYE BRONF-MAN FAMILY *Estd. 1952, Montreal* SAMUEL BRONFMAN *(1891-1971) and family*	$19,000 *(1980)*	$2,500 *(1980)*	Saidye Bronfman (pres.), Charles R. Bronfman (v-p), Phyllis Lambert (treas.), Philip F. Vineberg (sec.), Baroness Minda Bronfman de Gunzburg, Edgar M. Bronfman, Barbara Bronfman, Dr. Peter C. Swann (exec.dir.)	Supports a wide range of charitable activities. Some recent major contributions went to the McGill Centre for Children with Learning Problems, the Canadian Arctic Resources Committee, and St. Thomas University Chair in Gerontology.
ATKINSON CHARITABLE *Estd. 1942, Toronto* JOSEPH E. ATKINSON *(1865-1948), owner and publisher of the* Toronto Daily Star	$18,530 *(1982)*	$1,737 *(1982)*	Ruth Atkinson Hindmarsh (pres.), Norman Bishop (sec.), Bertram O. Warner (treas.), William J. Campbell, Catherine Atkinson Crang, Harry A. Hindmarsh, Beland H. Honderich, Burnett M. Thall	Gives grants for religious, charitable, and educational purposes in Ontario. Recent major grants have been made to the University of Western Ontario School of Journalism to train native peoples in journalism; to Ronald McDonald House in Toronto; to St. Michael's Hospital, Toronto, adult hearing clinic.
CLIFFORD E. LEE *Estd. 1969, Edmonton* CLIFFORD E. LEE, *founder of Nu-West Group of Edmonton (oil, gas, and real estate)*	$17,065 *(1980)*	$694 *(1982)*	Lila D. Lee (pres.), Lorraine Downey (sec.), Peter M. Owen (exec.dir.), Judith K. Padua (treas.), Dr. Sheila D. Campbell, Ann Dea, James M. Lee, Jeanie Maddison, Bruce Rawson, John Schlosser	Main area of interest is social services, arts, native people in northern Alberta, Yukon, and N.W.T. The foundation has purchased land near Edmonton for a nature sanctuary, has sponsored the concertmaster's chair of the Edmonton Symphony, and has provided a home for battered mothers and children.
LAIDLAW *Estd. 1949, Toronto* ROBERT A. LAIDLAW *(1886-1976), industrialist (mainly lumber), with further contributions directly or through estates of his brother* WALTER C. LAIDLAW *and his son* RODERICK W.L. LAIDLAW	$16,193 *(1980)*	$899 *(1980)*	Dr. R.G.N. Laidlaw (pres.), Frank I. Hayes, John M. Hodgson, Jeffery D. Laidlaw, Dr. Bruce J. Quarrington, Robert D. Smith, Ed Waitzer, Nathan H. Gilbert (exec. admin.). Advisory committee includes Harry Arthurs, Gerry Eldred, William Littler, David Silcox, Dr. Sheila Neysmith, Dr. Quentin Rae-Grant, Robin Ross, Dr. Brian Shaw	Supports a wide variety of projects and institutions in the arts, social services, conservation, heritage, and education. Recipients include Art Gallery of Ontario, Kids Can Press, National Ballet, Stratford Festival, Toronto Dance Theatre, Lester B. Pearson College, and Pond Inlet Community TV Society.
RHW *Estd. 1969, Montreal* R. HOWARD WEBSTER, *investor, president of Imperial Trust*	$14,159 *(1977)*	$445 *(1977)*	R. Howard Webster (pres.), William R. Ferguson (v-p/sec.), W. Ronald Shaw (treas.), Arthur J.E. Child, D. Altman Diehl, J. Stuart Herman, Mackenzie McMurray, Neill Phillips, Susan M. Riddell, Lorne C. Webster, James D. MacDonald, Don McDougall	Makes donations to hospitals, universities, and charitable institutions.
BEAVERBROOK CANADIAN *Estd. 1960, New Brunswick* LORD BEAVERBROOK *(1879-1964), investor, industrialist, press magnate*	$13,558 *(1979)*	$972 *(1979)*	Lady Violet Aitken (pres.), Douglas T. Waite (v-p), Alfred T. Madley (sec.-treas.)	Main beneficiaries are University of New Brunswick, Beaverbrook Auditorium, and Beaverbrook Art Gallery in Fredericton. Granting is limited to the founder's home province of New Brunswick.
DEVONIAN GROUP OF CHARITABLE FOUNDATIONS *Estd. 1973, Calgary* ERIC L. HARVIE *(1892-1975) and family (oil, gas, and real estate)*	$13,142 *(1982)*	$2,915 *(1982)*	Donald S. Harvie (chmn.), J.R. Fish (pres.), W.G.H. Robinson (sec.-treas.)	Innovative projects mainly in the areas of public parks (more than half the total disbursed), applied scientific research, and historic preservation. The foundation gave $1.5 million to the Halifax Maritime Museum. Unlike most foundations, which pay grants from income, the Devonian is committed to disbursing *all* its funds within 15-20 years.

Foundation and Source	Assets ($1000s)	Annual Grants ($1000s)	Officers and Directors	Areas of Interest
RICHARD IVEY *Estd. 1947, London, Ont.* RICHARD G. IVEY (*1891-1974*) *and* RICHARD M. IVEY *and corporations controlled by them*	$13,003 (1982)	$1,002 (1982)	Richard M. Ivey (pres.), Beryl M. Ivey (v-p), D.H. Gordon (sec.), Susan L. McLean (asst.sec.), D.A. Sharpe (treas.), Kathy Manuel (asst.treas.), R.W. Ivey	Main interests are health, education, social development, environment, and the arts, especially in London and southwestern Ontario. Recent major contributions have gone to U. of Western Ontario; University Hospital, London; Nature Conservancy of Canada; and Royal Ontario Museum.
WINDSOR *Estd. 1960, Montreal* SIDNEY A. WINDSOR, *investor, industrialist (incl. cannery in St. Jean, Que.)*	$11,978 (1982)	$960 (1982)	Robert B. Killam (pres.), Paul Britton Paine (v-p), J. Kevin Reynolds (sec.-treas.), Paul J. Dyer (asst.sec.treas.), Harold T. Martin, Robert L. Stanfield	Grants to charitable organizations, mainly in the Maritimes. Also education, particularly Maritime university buildings.
LAWSON *Estd. 1956, London, Ont.* THE LAWSON FAMILY (*printing, packaging, business forms*)	$11,366 (1980)	$697 (1980)	Col. Tom Lawson (pres.), A.M. MacIntosh (sec.), Ruth Kindersley	Supports charitable, religious, and educational activities.
J.-LOUIS LÉVESQUE *Estd. 1961, Montreal* J.-LOUIS LÉVESQUE, *investor, founder of Lévesque, Beaubien Inc.*	$11,000 (1981)	$500 (1981)	Suzanne Lévesque (pres./sec.), Jean Barrière (treas.), J.-Louis Lévesque, Jeanne B. Lévesque, Pierre-Louis Lévesque, André Charron	Supports various projects in health services, education, and culture, as well as the annual Prix au mérite de la Fondation J.-Louis Lévesque, instituted in 1980 and worth $100,000. (First two winners were Father Clément Cormier and Jean Drapeau.) The foundation has contributed greatly to the Montreal Heart Institute and the University of Moncton.
THE RICHARD AND JEAN IVEY FUND *Estd. 1965, London, Ont.* RICHARD G. IVEY (*1891-1974*) *and* JEAN IVEY (*1884-1974*) *of the London family of lawyers and financiers*	$10,500 (1982)	$698 (1982)	H. Lorraine Shuttleworth (pres.), K.L. Sumner (sec.-treas.), L.F. Stevens (asst.treas.), R.M. Ivey	Main interests are health, education, community development, the environment, arts, and culture; about two-thirds of the total goes to health and education.
THE BIRKS FAMILY *Estd. 1967, Montreal* *Certain members of the* BIRKS FAMILY *and* HENRY BIRKS & SONS LTD.	$10,300 (1982)	$550 (1982)	G. Drummond Birks (pres.), O.R. Macklem (sec.), D.E. Dunn (treas.), E.M. Ballon, G.R. Bourke	Supports a variety of activities, including universities, private schools, the arts, hospitals, mental health, fitness, YM-YWCA, Centraide-Montreal, human rights.
EATON *Estd. 1958, Toronto* JOHN DAVID EATON (*1909-73*), *department-store proprietor*	$9,097 (1982)	$1,001 (1982)	Frank F. McEachren (chmn.), C.M. Beattie (sec.), M.C. Payne (treas.), R.V.A. Jones (asst.sec.), D.E. Knechtel (asst.sec.), Signy Eaton, John C. Eaton, Fredrik S. Eaton, George R. Eaton, T.E. Eaton, G.D.deS. Wotherspoon	Supports activities mainly in the areas of the arts, education, health, social development, and social-welfare services. The foundation is a strong supporter of the United Way campaigns across the country.

Index

403